THE
ILLUSTRATED ENCYCLOPEDIA
OF
AIRCRAFT

THE
ILLUSTRATED ENCYCLOPEDIA
OF
AIRCRAFT

EDITED BY DAVID MONDEY F.R.Hist.S.

HAMLYN
London · New York · Sydney · Toronto

A QUARTO BOOK

Published by
The Hamlyn Publishing Group Limited
Astronaut House
Hounslow Road
Feltham
Middlesex, England

© Copyright 1978 Quarto Limited
ISBN 0 600 30378 0
First published March 1979
Reprinted August 1979

This book was designed and produced by Quarto Publishing Limited
13 New Burlington Street, London W1
Art editor: Martin Hendry
Designers: Marian Sanders, Mike Strickland
Editor: Donald Clarke
Jacket front illustration by Jim Bamber

Phototypeset in England by Vantage Photosetting Company Limited, Southampton
Colour origination by Welbeck Litho Plates, Bromley
Printed in Hong Kong by Leefung-Asco Printers Limited

The entries in the A–Z section of this encyclopedia were written by the contributing authors as follows:

A: H.F.King
B: David Mondey
C: Kenneth Munson and Pamela D. Matthews
D: John Blake
E: H.F.King
F: John Cook
G: Michael John Hooks
H: Michael Jerram
I: David Mondey
J: Kenneth Munson and Pamela D. Matthews
K: H.F.King
L: John Blake
M: John Cook
NO: Michael Jerram
PQR: Michael John Hooks
S: H.F.King
T: David Mondey
U: Michael Jerram
V: Kenneth Munson and Pamela D. Matthews
W: John Blake
XYZ: Michael Jerram

Frontispiece: **Boeing 747-124 wide-body commercial transport aircraft in the insignia of Wardair**

Opposite: **ANT-9 commercial transport, designed by one of the Soviet Union's most capable designers, the late A.N. Tupolev**

PHOTOGRAPHIC CREDITS
b=bottom, t=top, c=centre, l=left, r=right, u=upper
The Aeroplane: 138 b, 169 lower, 187 b, 190 b, 289 c. Aeroplane Photo Supply: 113 t. *Air et Cosmos*: 253 cr. Air Ministry: 39. Air Portraits: 69 tr. Jean Alexander: 80 tl, 233 tl. Hideya Ando: 204 br. R.D. Archer: 171 br. Archiv Schliephake: 190 t. Rudy Arnold: 133 b. Associated Press: 233 br. Gordon Bain: 22. Chris Barker: 36. M. Bayet: 160 br. Dr Alan Beaumont: 128 b. P.J. Bish: 155 t. John Blake: 256 tl. Peter M. Bowers: 97 b, 109 t, 220 lower, 282 cl. Austin J. Brown: 3, 62. Charles E. Brown: 159 t, 298 t. Bob Byrne: 245 b. Camuzzi: 220 tr. Ron Cole: 64 lower. J.B. Cynk: 147 t, 217 b, 255 t, 255 br. Joseph Demic: 80 bl. Deutsches Museum, Munich: 13, 21 b, 99 c, 111 b, 155 b. Downie and Associates: 232 b. Mary Evans Picture Library: 8. *Flight*: 19 b, 20, 80 br, 90 ul, 97 cr, 103 c, 160 t, 186 t, 230 t, 251 lower r, 264 bl, 301 c, 308 bl. Martin Fricke: 81 tr, 206 br, 229 bc, J.M.G. Gradidge: 69 tl, 163 br, 198 b, 217 t. P.L. Gray: 24 t. U. Haller: 161 bl, 294 bl. Historisches Museum am hohen Ufer, Hannover: 15 tr. Denis Hughes: 34 t. Imperial War Museum: 26 t, 178 tl, 188 c, 232 t, 251 t, 281 br. Michel Isaacs, *Air et Cosmos*: 58 b. Italian Air Ministry: 21. A.J. Jackson: 190 c. B.S.P. Keevill: 264 br. Nyle Leatham: 88 c. Howard Levy: 23 tl, tr, cl, cr, 90 br, 117 cl, 126 t, 149 br, 235 b, 245 u. Peter R. March: 123 b, 162 br, 229 br, 283 br. Martin and Keller: 241 c. T. Matsuzaki: 101 c. Douglas N. Maw: 74 t. Harry McDougall: 25, 30. Ministry of Defence: 52 b. Musée de l'Air: 11 tr, 15 tl, 18 b, 144 b, 160 c, 178 tr, 211 t. D. Noble: 112 ul. E. Percy Noel: 127 ul. Ronaldo S. Olive: 70 bl, 89 c, 128 c. Stephen P. Peltz: 109 c, 229 bl, 290 tl, 293 cr, 302 ul. Popperfoto: 60 t. Qantas: 9 cb, 11 tl, br. RAAF official photograph: 46. Radio Times Hulton Picture Library: 28 t. E. Riding: 143 br. Brian M. Service: 170 2nd to b. Smithsonian Institution: 12 b, 21 c. M.G. Sweet: 112 ur, 253 cl. TASS: 179 c, 286 t. U.S. Air Force: 14, 47 b, 48 t. U.S. Navy 19 t. L. Vallin: 237 b. Mick West: 268 br. Gordon S. Williams: 27, 38 b, 41 t, 50 tl, tr, 59 t, 136 t. Mano Ziegler: 189 b.
All other photographs from the collection of John W.R. and Michael Taylor.

The basic aim, from the beginning of this project, was to produce a single-volume encyclopedia of aviation for a general readership. It was, however, to be very different from any published previously, comprising a comparatively brief survey of aviation history, followed by an alphabetical listing of manufacturers of heavier-than-air, powered, production aircraft. The daunting feature, from the point of creating this alphabetical list, was that it had to extend from the Wright brothers to early 1978. It thus commemorates, by the time of its publication, the first three-quarters of a century of powered flight. So this, in effect, is the composition of this volume; it has, in addition, a brief glossary, and a detailed index of all the aircraft mentioned in the text.

How does one decide which companies merit inclusion: how many aircraft represent a production run? There are many gaps in company records: perhaps the intention was to build and market the XYZ Special, and a prototype was built and flown; but how many, if any, production aircraft followed? Such facts are not always recorded. So the list includes those companies which manufactured aircraft, and companies which it is believed built and sold at least some of their designs.

Inevitably, a major source of reference was *Jane's all the World's Aircraft*, which spans sixty-nine of those seventy-five years; but even this superb reference work has some strange entries and omissions in its earlier years. Unfortunately, there has not been the time available to research these oddities. Those who have worked to compile the volume have made it as accurate and complete as possible, but they are aware that there is scope for improving the detailed coverage. It has become abundantly clear, also, that in addition to its appeal to the general reader, this *Encyclopedia of Aircraft* could be extremely valuable to aviation historians, researchers and writers.

With this latter factor in mind, the Editor hopes that readers will communicate to him new facts and material for inclusion in a future edition that will, it is hoped, become a definitive and regularly updated book of reference.

I am grateful, indeed, for the hard and painstaking work of the aviation writers who contributed the words that you will read. The illustrations, in the main, have been provided by John W. R. and Michael Taylor, and a big thank you is due to them for making available some wonderful and rare pictures from their collection. An enthusiastic team at Quarto Publishing have given shape and 'eye-appeal' to this mass of raw material, and I am very appreciative of their patience and efforts in producing this potentially important volume.

David Mondey, 1978

CONTENTS

THE HISTORY OF FLIGHT	7
MAN BECOMES AIRBORNE	9
PIONEERS OF POWERED FLIGHT	15
THE FIRST WAR IN THE AIR	20
THE CONQUEST OF THE GLOBE	27
THE NEW AIRBORNE ARMIES	36
WORLD WAR IN THE AIR	41
KEEPING THE BALANCE OF POWER	46
UNIVERSAL TRANSPORT	53
THE A-Z OF THE WORLD'S AIRCRAFT	63
GLOSSARY	310
INDEX	314

THE HISTORY OF FLIGHT

MAN BECOMES AIRBORNE

IT IS UNLIKELY we shall ever know the name of the person to first comment that if God had intended men to fly he would have given them wings. It could, quite easily, have been the Chinese spectator of an unsuccessful launch of a man-lifting kite, perhaps one or more centuries before the birth of Christ. That is a realistic date for the first men to become airborne, and the desire to fly like the birds could well stretch back to prehistoric man, conscious of the ease with which winged creatures could elude land-bound predators.

Myth and fantasy fill the years that come between the wishes of those prehistoric ancestors and the first of the thinking men to consider seriously, but unsuccessfully, the mechanics of flight. Leonardo da Vinci (1452–1519), Italian artist-inventor, produced many designs for ornithopter (flapping-wing) aircraft but pru-

dently made no practical experiments. A hundred and fifty years after his death, in 1670, a Jesuit priest, Francesco de Lana-Terzi, had heard of the invention of the vacuum pump. This seemed to him to offer a possibility of flight, based upon the assumption that a thin metallic globe from which the air had been evacuated could be lighter than air and thus would float in the air. He failed to see the simple fact, about which most present-day school children could have advised him, that if his metallic spheres had been light enough to lift they would have been crushed by atmospheric pressure at the moment of evacuation.

The first lighter-than-air craft

Since schooldays most of us have believed that the brothers Etienne and Joseph Montgolfier were the first to launch a hot-air balloon. Recent research has

shown that another priest, the Brazilian Bartolomeu de Gusmão, demonstrated a practical model of a hot-air balloon at the court of King John V of Portugal, in 1709. On 8 August that year, before a distinguished gathering of reliable witnesses, de Gusmão showed the amazed audience that his small paper balloon, with burning material suspended below the open neck of the envelope, could rise in free flight within the confines of the Ambassador's drawing-room. Its brief journey was brought to an end when two servants, fearing it might set the curtains alight, dashed it to the ground. A lighter-than-air craft had thus been demonstrated 74 years before the first flight of a Montgolfier hot-air balloon took place.

This in no way detracts from the achievements of the Montgolfiers. Their first hot-air balloon was launched, prob-

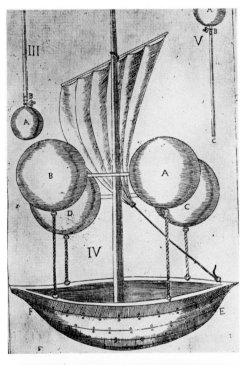

Bladud, (*above*), fabled ninth king of Britain, was an early 'jumper', who fixed artificial wings to his arms. De Lana Terzi's flying-machine (*centre*), was also a non-starter. The work of men like Leonardo da Vinci (*right*) gave a starting point to later thinkers. The first free flight in a *Montgolfière* (*left*) was undertaken by de Rozier and the Marquis d'Arlandes. The engraving (*far right*) records de Rozier's fatal cross-Channel attempt in a composite hot-air/hydrogen balloon. Both de Rozier and his companion Jules Romain were killed.

ably at Annonay, France, on 25 April 1783. Some 12 m (39 ft) in diameter, it climbed to a height of about 305 m (1,000 ft) before the hot air in the envelope cooled and it began its descent. The Montgolfier brothers are said to have been unaware that hot air alone was the lifting agent for their balloons, believing that a specially light gas was generated by the mixture of wool and straw which they burned below the open neck of the envelope.

A second demonstration, at Annonay, was given on 4 June 1783, but just prior to a third, command performance at the Court of Versailles on 19 September of that same year, when a sheep, a duck and a cock became the first living creatures to be artificially airborne, Professor J. A. C. Charles had demonstrated successfully a small hydrogen-filled balloon at Paris, on 27 August 1783.

Events were then to move quickly. On 15 October 1783 Francois Pilâtre de Rozier became the first man in the world to be carried aloft, sole passenger of a Montgolfier balloon tethered to the ground by a 26 m (84 ft) rope. Just over a month later, on 21 November 1783, de Rozier accompanied by the Marquis d'Arlandes, made the first free flight in a balloon, remaining airborne for 25 minutes, during which time they travelled about 8·5 km (5·5 miles) from their launch point. Free flight in a lighter-than-air craft had at last been realised. And although this was a beginning, it was also virtually the end of the Montgolfier balloon, superseded by the infinitely superior and practical hydrogen-filled balloon developed by J. A. C. Charles, in which he and one of the Robert brothers who had assisted in its construction made a free flight from the gardens of the Tuileries, Paris, on 1 December 1783. Their flight was one of 43 km (27 miles), their ascent witnessed by a crowd estimated at some 400,000, their balloon so well designed that it is essentially similar to the gas-filled balloon used to this day.

Making the balloon navigable

The expansion of ballooning as a sport was very rapid: at last man was free of the Earth which had been his habitat for so many centuries. There was no telling what achievements might now be possible. And within days of de Rozier's first flight in a

Montgolfière had come an appreciation of the potential which such a vehicle held for military pursuits, especially for reconnaissance. But there had to be some method of steering, for the balloon was possessed by the least zephyr. Grandiose ideas involving oars, sails and propellers were of no avail; it had to be understood that if an airborne vehicle was to be steerable it must be capable of independent movement, instead of being carried by the wind, so that movable aerofoil surfaces could impose a chosen direction of travel. From this realisation stemmed the initial airship designs, the envelope becoming elongated instead of spherical, with the provision of a power plant to provide forward motion independently of the breeze. This latter word is chosen advisedly: there was then no question of trying to fly in anything that might be classed as a wind.

The major problem, and the one which was to frustrate the pioneers of heavier-than-air craft, was the non-availability of a suitable lightweight and compact power plant. Thus, Frenchman Henri Giffard, who recorded the first flight of a manned, powered dirigible (Latin: 'able to be directed') on 24 September 1852, utilised a 2·2 kW (3 hp) steam-engine, driving a 3·35 m (11 ft) diameter propeller. The use of the word 'dirigible' in that record is rather open to question, for anything more than the merest suggestion of a breeze would have made it unsteerable. To Charles Renard and Arthur Krebs, officers of the French Corps of Engineers, goes the distinction of flying *La France*, the world's first fully controllable and powered dirigible. In this craft, on 9 August 1884, Renard and Krebs flew a circular course of about 8 km (5 miles), taking off from and returning to Chalais-Meudon, France. Powered by a 6·7 kW (9 hp) Gramme electric motor, driving a 7·01 m (23 ft) diameter propeller, *La France* achieved a maximum speed of 23·5 km/h (14·5 mph) during its 23 minute flight. Increased power had provided the speed necessary to make the vehicle controllable: but this seemingly small improvement had taken 101 years from the first flight of the Montgolfier balloon.

The first heavier-than-air craft

The beginning of heavier-than-air flight is the story of many men working towards a common goal. As in most combined and

international projects, there are men who stand out because of their advanced thoughts or brilliant innovations.

First must come the man now regarded as the 'Father of Aerial Navigation', the English Baronet Sir George Cayley (1773–1857). Back in 1804 he built what is generally regarded as the first successful model glider. This consisted of little more than a broomstick to which was mounted a kite-shape monoplane wing; at the aft end of the 'fuselage' were vertical and horizontal tail surfaces to provide control. With this device he was able to confirm that the principles of heavier-than-air flight were entirely feasible, and it was able to demonstrate stable flight over quite long distances.

From this first model he evolved gliders capable of carrying a small schoolboy in flight (1849), and his reluctant coachman during 1853. Both were passengers only, with no means of controlling their aircraft in flight. But in addition to his practical work, Cayley suggested the use of an internal combustion engine for powered flight, demonstrated how a curved aerofoil surface provides lift, and pointed out that biplane or triplane wings would provide maximum lift from a lightweight, robust structure. Cayley's 'Father' title was well-earned.

Cayley died in 1857, and in that same year a French naval officer, Félix du Temple, constructed and flew the world's first powered model aeroplane. This record was achieved with a clockwork motor, and subsequently du Temple's little monoplane was powered with a steam-engine. Seventeen years later this same inventor was flight testing a full-size man-carrying aeroplane, which was powered by either a hot-air engine or a steam-engine. Piloted by an unknown sailor, at Brest, this aircraft was the first in the world to achieve a short hop into the air, following launch down an inclined ramp.

Although men were beginning to learn how to construct a fixed-wing aircraft that could fly, their problem was now the same as that of the balloonist who wanted to steer his vessel: both needed a suitable power plant. A practical working layout for a suitable power plant was to be demonstrated by the German engineer Nicholas Otto, in 1876. The four-stroke cycle of operations for an internal combustion engine, which Otto evolved at that

THE EARLIEST DAYS

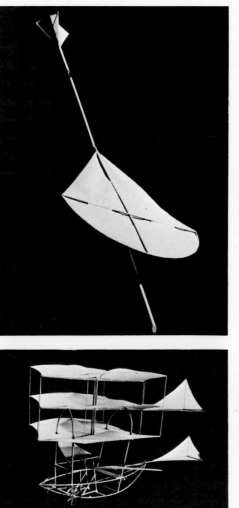

Cayley's model glider (*top, left*), with its adjustable aerofoil surfaces, enabled him to experiment with the problems of gliding flight, leading to the 'boy lifter' of 1849 (*left*). Clément Ader's *Éole* steam-powered

monoplane (*top*) was the first aircraft to lift itself from the ground, but failed to fly. Félix du Temple's monoplane (model *above*) made a short hop after launch down a ramp, powered by a hot-air or steam engine.

time, is still the basic principle upon which most piston-engines work, especially for motor cars and aircraft. But Otto's invention was in the future. The more practical among the pioneer aviators accepted the reality of the situation, and spent the period most profitably in improving airframe design, learning the best means of lightweight construction, and trying to discover practical means of controlling the aircraft when it became airborne.

The beginning of free flight

The most important of this group of pioneers was the German Otto Lilienthal (1848–1896), whose beautifully built lightweight gliders enabled him to make many thousands of flights. These were not just pleasure flights: Lilienthal was a prac-

tical researcher, building, modifying, improving, and at all times recording meticulously the results of his experiments for the benefit of other researchers.

Lilienthal's gliders were of the configuration which we would now call hanggliders, designed so that the mass of his body was disposed about the aircraft's centre of gravity when the machine was in a stable flying position. By body movements he could influence a degree of control on the craft's flight but, unfortunately, this did not allow rapid response to changing flight conditions. Despite his experience, Lilienthal was gravely injured in a flying accident on 9 August 1896, brought about by a control problem which could not be resolved quickly enough, and he died on the following day.

Lilienthal had been a source of inspiration to many, but influenced especially the work of the British pioneer builder/pilot Percy Pilcher (1866–1899), who flew his first glider in 1895. Pilcher travelled to Germany to meet and talk with Otto Lilienthal, from whom he obtained a great deal of practical advice. But Pilcher, too, was to die on 30 September 1899, when his *Hawk* glider crashed to the ground at Market Harborough.

There was a third important glider pioneer—a builder not a flyer—who collected information from every possible source, publishing this *pot-pourri* under the title *Progress in Flying Machines*. American railway engineer, Octave Chanute (1832–1910), the compiler of this book, was to develop the Lilienthal-

Hiram Maxim's giant steam-powered craft (*below*), spanning 31·7 m (104 ft) developed so much lift that it broke away from its safety rails. At the same time Germany's Otto Lilienthal (*right*) was flying well-built hang-gliders. Despite an advanced engine, Langley's *Aerodrome* (*bottom left*) failed to fly, both attempts at flight ending in the river.

type craft into a classic glider. More importantly for powered flight, his book, his advice and his friendship, were to inspire the brothers Orville and Wilbur Wright.

There are many links in the chain of progress towards the realisation of powered flight, some big and many small. All contribute to the end result, and it is unfortunate that space will not allow us to relate them all. One of the final links was undoubtedly Germany's Gottlieb Daimler, who in 1885 developed the world's first single-cylinder internal combustion engine. This utilised the four-stroke principle of operation devised by his fellow countryman, Nicholas Otto, and used petrol as its fuel. As it was developed to provide a power-to-weight ratio far superior to any other form of engine then available for aircraft propulsion, the would-be aviators realised that the necessary power-plant had arrived.

But this was to be of no avail to American Samuel Pierpont Langley, the man who so nearly made the Wright brothers just aviation pioneers. Langley was a scientist, Secretary of the Smithsonian Institution, and his collaboration with Charles Manley to build and fly his *Aero-drome* aircraft resulted in the creation by

Manley and his associate Stephen Balzer of a remarkably advanced five-cylinder radial petrol-engine. Despite this advantage, Langley's aircraft failed to become airborne on two occasions. Both times—7 October and 8 December 1903—the aircraft crashed into the Potomac River. Most observers believed the *Aerodrome* fouled its launching device on both dates, but it has been suggested that the aircraft's structure disintegrated. Either way, the stage was clear for the Wright brothers.

The historic picture (*below*) is of the first flight of the Wright *Flyer* on 17 December 1903. Orville Wright, who was at the controls, later wrote: *The course of the flight up and down was exceedingly erratic. The control of the front rudder* (elevator) *was difficult. As a result, the machine would rise suddenly to about ten feet, and then as suddenly dart for the ground. A sudden dart when a little over

Powered flight becomes reality

The achievement of that cold Thursday, 17 December 1903, has been told so many times that much of the excitement has gone. Except, perhaps, for those who have learned to fly: who understand that moment of magic when the aircraft loses contact with the ground and becomes a living creature, free in three-dimensional space: so very nearly a bird in flight.

The brothers Orville and Wilbur deserved their success, because of their de-

***120 feet from the point at which it rose into the air ended the flight.* Three others followed, the last and best of that day covering 260 m (852 ft), but ended with the elevator being damaged when the *Flyer* landed. When it was overturned by a gust of wind more damage followed. The ironical feature of these flights was that the world failed to learn that a man had been airborne and in control of a powered**

termination to overcome the very real difficulties that beset them. If they hadn't got it they made it; if it didn't work, they found out why and changed their design.

And when the *Flyer* was dismantled on that historic day it was an end to the first phase of powered flight. The world's first powered, sustained and controlled flight had been accomplished. It was also a beginning: the expansion of aviation to facilitate world travel and inaugurate a hoped-for era of peace.

heavier-than-air craft. It was not until three years later, in November 1906, that the little Brazilian Alberto Santos-Dumont electrified aviation progress in Europe by recording a first flight in his No. 14-*bis* of nearly 61 m (200 ft). Both aircraft were really dead-end designs, but their achievement and influence inspired new ideas and efforts. In the short-term, more powerful engines were the key to success.

PIONEERS OF POWERED FLIGHT

IT IS IRONICAL that the 'beginning' with which we closed the last chapter was then, so far as the world is concerned, no beginning at all. In fact, it was not until almost three years later, on 23 October 1906, when the Brazilian Alberto Santos-Dumont achieved a flight of nearly 60 m (200 ft), in Paris, that the world realised the first flight of a powered heavier-than-air craft had been accomplished. This was because the flight was observed by thousands, photographed and recorded in the world's newspapers. Almost three weeks later, on 12 November, he covered 220 m (722 ft) in the same aircraft, his so-called '14-*bis*'.

Santos-Dumont's aircraft was a strange-looking machine, with box-kite-like wings. It seemed even more odd when it was realised that it flew with the tail way out in front and the wings at the back. This configuration has earned the name 'canard', because such craft have some resemblance to a duck in flight. The box-kite wings stemmed from the original research of Lawrence Hargrave in Australia. Hargrave had perfected the design of the box-kite in 1893, and the lightweight and robust construction of this device, together with its good lifting characteristics, encouraged a number of European designers to adopt this form of structure for their early attempts to build the ideal aircraft.

By 1907, the Wright design was beginning to have an influence upon European constructors, leading to a combination of Wright features with the Hargrave box-kite. In reality, it was a dead-end design, with only a short road for its followers to travel. It is worth explaining at this point that the power plant of the above aircraft was mounted so that the propeller was not only behind the engine, but also aft of the main wing structure. The arrangement was called, somewhat inaccurately, a pusher propeller.

New designs emerging in Europe were quite different, comprising monoplane and biplane aircraft with the engine mounted at the forward end of the fuselage and the propeller at the front of the engine. This was known as a tractor configuration, the propeller pulling the entire machine through the air. A little thought will bring the realisation that the propeller in a pusher configuration is doing exactly the same thing, but it has proved convenient—even to this day—to call the forward-mounted propeller a tractor, and the aft-mounted version a pusher.

By the beginning of 1908 there was some progress in Europe, but control of

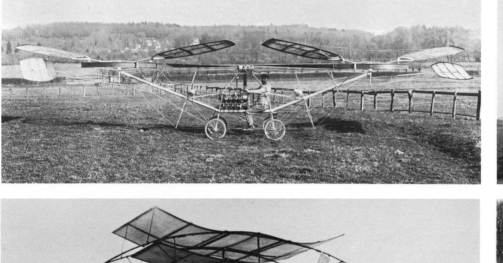

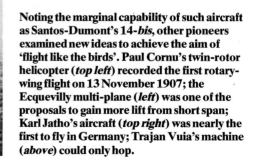

Noting the marginal capability of such aircraft as Santos-Dumont's 14-*bis*, other pioneers examined new ideas to achieve the aim of 'flight like the birds'. Paul Cornu's twin-rotor helicopter (*top left*) recorded the first rotary-wing flight on 13 November 1907; the Ecquevilly multi-plane (*left*) was one of the proposals to gain more lift from short span; Karl Jatho's aircraft (*top right*) was nearly the first to fly in Germany; Trajan Vuia's machine (*above*) could only hop.

By 1908, when Wilbur Wright demonstrated the *Flyer A* (*below*) in France, the two brothers had refined its design almost to the ultimate. In Europe the pioneers were still trying to evolve a really practical aeroplane. Aircraft such as the Koechlin Boxkite (*right*) and Blériot/Voisin with cellular wings (*below right*) owed much to the work of the Australian Lawrence Hargrave.

the aircraft in flight had not graduated beyond the elementary stage. Men were airborne in powered aircraft, but their flight was far from emulating that of a bird: they were more akin to tightrope walkers, certainly in the air, but very limited in their flight pattern. To illustrate the point, the first flight to exceed one minute's duration had been recorded by Henry Farman, flying his Voisin-Farman I biplane on 10 November 1907. On 13 January 1908 the same combination of aircraft and pilot recorded completion of the first 1 km (1·6 miles) circle flown in Europe, in a time of 1 min 28 sec. At the then current stage of aviation development on the East side of the Atlantic, this was no mean achievement, and won for Henry Farman the 50,000 francs Deutsch/Archdeacon Grand Prix d'Aviation. But changes were imminent.

The moment of truth
In the summer of 1908 Wilbur Wright visited France, bringing with him a Wright *Flyer A*, with which to give a series of demonstration flights. He based himself initially at Hunaudières, near Le Mans, and very soon had uncrated and assembled his aircraft.

On 8 August, in the cool, windless, near-twilight of that summer evening, he prepared to take off before a highly critical audience of European—mostly French—pilots. Collectively they considered themselves the hub of aviation development and achievement. After all, there was really no certainty that the Wrights had flown prior to the great

achievement of Santos-Dumont. And, with a nudge of the elbow: "You know how these Yankees exaggerate."

There was a sudden roar from the engine, focusing attention, but by then Wilbur and the *Flyer* were airborne. But look, here indeed is the legendary birdman, climbing, turning, banking with unbelievable perfection and grace. Man and machine are one, weaving dream patterns in a sunset sky. The audience is silent, breathless, eyes almost blinded by emotion. Too soon it is ended as, with engine throttled back, Wilbur sets the *Flyer* calmly and gracefully on the ground. The spectators are still silent, still breathless. Then suddenly the cheers ring out; of amazement, of appreciation, of congratulation. Wilbur has demonstrated, convincingly, the considerable lead which the Wrights then held in aviation capability and their

mastery of control. From that moment forward European aviation was spurred to progress in leaps and bounds.

New achievements: new power
The European pilots were soon to discover that Wilbur was indeed one of the brotherhood, prepared to talk about design and improvements, and his demonstrations and influence had a profound effect on the rapid development of European aviation. By the end of 1908, flying from Auvours, France, Wilbur had made more than 100 flights totalling in excess of 25 flying hours. His last flight of the year, on 31 December, occupied 2 hrs 20 min 23 sec, during which he covered a distance of 124 km (77 miles) to set a new world record and win the Michelin prize.

And while Wilbur was busy in Europe, Orville Wright was demonstrating at Fort

Three aircraft showing evolutionary changes in basic design. The Voisin (*top*) is typical of the structure evolved from the box-kite. Farman's biplane (*above*) shows a blend of Wright and Voisin ideas. A. V. Roe's Triplane (*left*) is typical of new tractor propeller layouts.

Myer, Virginia, the *Flyer* which had been acquired by the United States Army. These demonstrations began from 3 September 1908, and people came in their thousands to see an aeroplane in flight for the first time. They were as thrilled and excited as the European spectators but tragically, within a matter of two weeks, the flights came to an end when the aircraft crashed. Orville was seriously injured, his passenger—Lt. Thomas E. Selfridge—was killed, the first man in the world to die in a powered aircraft accident. Subsequent investigation showed that a disintegrating propeller blade severed a bracing wire, allowing the tail unit to collapse. It is not in the nature of things that progress in any area is a continuous story of success.

Lessons were being learned in the very active European area, too, with the first use of ailerons for lateral control, the first powered flight being recorded in Britain by American S. F. Cody, and the first tentative 'hops' being achieved by Britain's A. V. Roe. And one of the lessons, learned by hard experience, was that overloaded engines overheat, lose power, and quickly opt out of the task of keeping their aircraft in the air. One of the prime requirements of a good aviator was the ability to keep an eye constantly appraising suitable emergency fields so that, when the engine overheated and called it a day, a quick and safe landing could be made in the chosen area.

It was all part of the sport of aviation, and didn't matter a great deal at a time when there was even enjoyment to be had in stripping, repairing and rebuilding a troublesome engine. It was likely to prove disconcerting, however, if aircraft were to be developed for the carriage of passengers, and unless engines of increased power became available there would be little scope for enlarging or reinforcing the "stick and string" airframe of the day.

Introduction of the rotary engine

Louis and Laurent Seguin, in France, began to investigate the problems associated with existing engines so that they could develop a new power plant which would satisfy the requirement of the day, as well as meet the needs of the future. Engines in use at that period were of two main types: in-line, which stemmed directly from the motor-car industry; and radial (the cylinders disposed radially around a circular crankcase), which had been developed as an aircraft power plant. The former were penalised at the outset by their origin, tending to be excessively

heavy and with the added disadvantage of needing a water cooling system, plus drag-inducing radiator. The radial engine relied upon air cooling, then far from effective because of bad cylinder design, and had large frontal area which held down the forward speed of the entire aircraft—a vicious circle of inefficiency.

The Seguins adopted a new engine configuration which could utilise air cooling, and consequent weight-saving, with cylinders and crankcase rotating around a fixed crankshaft; the aircraft's propeller was virtually one with this rotating mass. The resulting power plant, its cylinders rotating through the air, was adequately cooled, permitting the development of far more powerful engines. In addition, the flywheel torque of this revolving engine produced smooth power, even at small throttle openings. Despite the rather awesome appearance which a rotary engine presented on the first confrontation, it proved to be a most important interim power source, presenting airframe designers—for the first time—with as much power as was needed at the state of the art then existing.

One disadvantage was that, because the cylinders were rotating, a conventional carburettor set-up could not be used to supply the combustible mixture. Instead, a fuel/air mixture was admitted to the crankcase, entering the cylinders via ports in the cylinder walls. This raised lubrica-

tion complications, making essential the use of an oil not miscible with petrol. The resulting need for castor oil meant that engines had a characteristic smell which is associated nostalgically with rotary engines to this day. And because centrifugal force ensured that large quantities of oil passed straight through the engine, out of the exhaust ports and into the slipstream, both airframe and pilot were coated liberally. The oil consumption of a rotary engine could be from 25 to 50 per cent of the total fuel consumption, which meant that, in the long term, engines of this type would have proved totally unsuitable for long-range flight. Apart from that, when larger and more powerful engines were needed, the gyroscopic effect of the rotary

engine would have made handling the aircraft very difficult.

In those early years these factors were unimportant, and Gnome engines—as the Seguins named their creations—were to power many significant aircraft during the seven or eight years following their entry into service in 1909.

Elimination of natural barriers

This year was to see another important event in early aviation, the attainment of a milestone of great future significance. On 25 July, at approximately 05.17 hours, a frail-looking monoplane landed on the Northfall Meadow, close alongside Dover Castle, Kent. Piloted by Frenchman Louis Blériot, this man/machine combination

The historic moment of Blériot's arrival at Dover (*opposite top*) gave some idea of the potential of the aeroplane. In early 1910, Henri Fabre (*opposite bottom*) recorded the first flight from water of a powered aircraft. Later that same year Eugene Ely flew a Curtiss biplane off the cruiser USS *Birmingham* (*above*); in May 1912 Commander Sampson took off from the deck of the battleship HMS *Hibernia* (*left*), while it was under way, the first aviator to perform this feat.

had just completed the first crossing of the English Channel by a heavier-than-air craft. Blériot's Type XI monoplane which had made the crossing, in a time of 37 minutes, was powered by a three-cylinder Anzani engine of only 18·6 kW (25 hp). Despite the efficiency of Blériot's airframe, the engine almost succumbed to the contemporary problem of overheating, prevented from failure by a fortuitous shower of rain which cooled it sufficiently to complete the Channel crossing. Subsequently, Blériot monoplanes were to complete many important pioneering flights, but few could have caused such military concern as this first Channel crossing. For the first time it was clear that an island's geographic insularity was no longer adequate protection, relying solely upon its 'moat' of surrounding sea, policed by a strong navy.

Blériot monoplanes were to achieve some important first flights, including the first over the Alps (23 September 1910), the first London-Paris non-stop (12 April 1911), first official carriage of airmail in Britain (9 September 1911) and the United States (23 September 1911) and, inevitably, the first use of an aeroplane in war, on 22 October 1911.

Moves toward military aircraft

But regardless of the growing capability of the aeroplane, few military leaders could appreciate its potential other than for re-

connaissance purposes. This, despite the fact that, as early as 30 June 1910, Glenn Curtiss in America had demonstrated it was possible to drop weapons from an aircraft in flight. Subsequently, the first rifle was fired from an aeroplane on 20 August 1910, the first live bomb dropped from one on 7 January 1911, and later that same year a torpedo was launched from an aircraft for the first time.

Meanwhile, the potential of the aeroplane for naval use had not gone unnoticed. On 14 November 1910, Eugene Ely had flown a Curtiss biplane off the American Cruiser USS *Birmingham*: on 18 January 1911, he landed a similar aircraft on the Cruiser USS *Pennsylvania*. In Britain, Lt. C. R. Samson had made the first official flight from the battleship HMS *Africa*, on 10 January 1912. Four months later, during the Naval Review off Portland in May 1912, the then-promoted Commander Sampson was the first to fly an aeroplane off a ship under way, taking-off from the forecastle of HMS *Hibernia*.

But the lack of military acceptance was of little concern to the pioneers. Their aim, from the outset, had been to give to man the wings of a dove of peace. Orville Wright was to comment: "... we thought (*my brother and I*) that we were introducing into the world an invention which would make future wars practically impossible." A British pioneer, Claude Grahame-White, in a book written in as-

sociation with British aviation journalist Harry Harper, was to state "... the globe will be linked by flight, and nations so knit together that they will grow to be next-door neighbours."

The aim, from the outset; the belief, throughout these early years of development; the hope, so frequently expressed by the pioneers of aviation, was that the aeroplane would prove an instrument of peace in the world.

While people of all nations gazed at the aeroplane in wonder, as daring young men created those first flights which are the delight of today's historians, one nation was quietly building the biggest military air force in the world. When the First World War began, on 4 August 1914, Germany had approximately 280 aircraft available for use by its Army and Navy. Britain and France combined had slightly more aircraft in military service; Belgium had only 24. Significantly, however, the military potential of the aircraft in German use was, at that time, superior to that of the machines available to the Allies. In any event, it was of little importance to which of the combatant nations an aircraft belonged at that time. None were very lethal, except to their occupants. But this was only at the war's beginning. The aeroplane was to demonstrate, very quickly indeed, that it could—when properly used—prove a military weapon of the greatest importance.

THE FIRST WAR IN THE AIR

HAVING STATED that Britain entered the First World War with a not insignificant number of aircraft, it is necessary to explain why it could hardly be considered a potent military force. For a start, only a very small number of officers of the army could believe that the aeroplane had the capability of being used for wartime operations. There was, at the outset, no question of it being used for offensive purposes as it was unarmed. Let us be fair, though: its pilot carried a revolver, if he could gain access to it beneath the voluminous clothing worn to keep him reasonably warm in his open cockpit. His orders, on the initial Channel crossing to join the BEF, were to ram any Zeppelin airship which he might encounter *en route*, since this was the only hope he had of destroying such an aircraft. In one respect, his safety equipment was first class. The inflated rubber inner-tube around his waist promised security if a forced-landing in the Channel was dictated by engine-failure. He had no problems with carrying a parachute; he didn't have one. High authority believed the provision of such a device might encourage the pilot to abandon a damaged aircraft prematurely, instead of using his skill to get it back to base.

It was believed, however, that—providing the weather was fairly calm—it should be possible to use the aircraft as a reconnaissance platform for a trained observer. Reduced to the simplest terms, few had faith in a military aeroplane; and the aeroplanes available to the military were hardly suitable for day-to-day, all-weather use.

There was a contradictory problem with stability. Because the only role envisaged for the aircraft was one of observation, it was assumed that the observation platform should be as stable as possible. Aircraft designers worked hard to provide their brain-children with this characteristic. Most successful was the young British designer Geoffrey de Havilland, whose B.E.2 biplane was a superb example of the inherently-stable aircraft. Flying a B.E.2B, Lt. Gilbert Mapplebeck, in company with Capt. (later Air Chief Marshal Sir) Philip Joubert de la Ferté in a Blériot XI monoplane, flew the first Royal Flying Corps (RFC) reconnaissance flight on 19 August 1914. The B.E.2 developed to its B.E.2C version was, perhaps, the most perfect observation aircraft of the First World War. Unfortunately, this very characteristic of stability was to prove a serious problem at a later stage.

Reconnaissance aircraft prove their value

At the war's beginning the German advance was breathtakingly fast. By the time it had been slowed to a halt on the banks of the River Marne, the new and untried appendages of the British and French armies had already demonstrated that aerial reconnaissance was of vital importance. Without its use in this initial stage of the First World War, the conflict might have ended in the first few weeks, with the German armies in Paris. This early use of the new air arm had shown that not only was an observation aircraft able to report on enemy positions, the movement of reinforcements and supplies, and the sites chosen for munition dumps; it proved also, very quickly, that by spotting for batteries of field guns, and directing their fire, this hit-and-miss weapon had gained new importance. Communications which relied initially upon message-dropping and visual signalling were soon superseded by wireless telegraphy. And to make sure that an observer missed no small detail which might be of significance, aircraft were soon provided with cameras so that photographs could be studied and examined minutely for any information they might reveal.

But it should not be imagined that such developments were confined to the Allied air forces. The German High Command realised just as quickly the potential of these new eyes in the sky, and it became clear to the combatant nations that serious efforts must be made to prevent enemy reconnaissance aircraft from overflying home territory. This was especially true in areas where important troop movements were in progress, or where poker tactics were being used to hold a weak point in the line with minimal strength.

Military aircraft for different roles

From this need stemmed the entire family of military aeroplanes: firstly, arms for the reconnaissance aircraft; then escort fighters to accompany them over enemy

Following trials with the Royal Aircraft Factory B.E.2a, the B.E.2c evolved as a prime example of an inherently stable aircraft, which meant it could be flown hands-off. When 'gusted' off an even keel it could usually right itself.

LIGHTER-THAN-AIR CRAFT

The airship represented the first true achievement of the pioneers towards the realisation of practical flight. The balloon was a great sporting vehicle, but if flight was to become commercial, the vehicle must have a means of being steered from point to point and be able to carry a worthwhile payload. Airships such as that demonstrated by Roy Knabenshue in America (*right*) represented the first minimal advancement towards this aim in the early 1900s. The military potential of the developing airship was soon appreciated, and vessels such as the Italian semi-rigid P-type (*top*) were used for reconnaissance and bombing attacks in 1912. It was Count Ferdinand von Zeppelin in Germany, however, who succeeded in designing and building large Zeppelin airships (*below*) which, initially, were formidable weapons in WW1, and the most practical post-war airships.

The Bristol Fighter (*foreground*), known to WW1 pilots as the Brisfit, first flew on operations in April 1917. Its debut was disastrous, but the machine developed to excellence, remaining in RAF service until 1932. The Sopwith Pup, which went into service in 1916, was considered a superior aircraft by von Richthofen.

territory; fighters to take on enemy fighters; bombers to attack the bases from which an enemy's reconnaissance or fighter aircraft were deployed; bombers to attack factories building such aircraft, their engines and weapons. On the ground, steadily improving anti-aircraft guns were developed, to ensure that their high-velocity shells would keep observation aircraft at an altitude where they would be less able to carry out their task effectively.

The reconnaissance task was not limited to heavier-than-air craft; large numbers of gas-filled observation balloons were used initially by most combatant nations, until such time as they became sitting targets for fast aircraft armed with incendiary bullets. Germany, in particular, had developed a fleet of large Zeppelin airships, the majority of which were intended originally for use as naval reconnaissance vessels. Only as the war developed were they used instead as long-range strategic bombers.

These latter vessels were awe-inspiring weapons which seemed able to roam at will over British targets. Their size alone was frightening, with a length of more than 195 m (640 ft). But as defending

fighter aircraft gained the ability to climb above their operational height, and to attack them with incendiary bullets, they became far too vulnerable. When, on 5 August 1918, the pride of the German Naval Airship Division, the 211 m (692 ft 3 in) long L.70 was shot down over the North Sea, the use of airships as offensive weapons came to an end.

Development of fighter aircraft

The need to prevent an enemy's reconnaissance aircraft from having the freedom of the sky above your territory or lines meant that some way had to be devised to destroy the unwanted aircraft. Anti-aircraft guns were one of the weapons chosen for the task, but the likelihood of hitting a moving target some thousands of feet in the air was then a question of luck rather than judgement. They served to keep enemy aircraft flying high and, if the barrage was heavy enough, to keep them away from a particular area.

In the air, initial combat involved opposing pilots taking pot-shots at each other with pistols: their observers soon joined in, often using rather more accurate rifles, but there was an element of

medieval combat about these early encounters, with rather more than a hint of knightly conduct on both sides. It was not to last, because the need to prevent an enemy from getting back to base with important photographs or information was vital: so was the task of eliminating an aircraft that was directing the fall of heavy shells against your defensive positions.

So machine-guns were taken into the air, fired initially by the observer. This was practical for two-seat escort fighters, but was of little use to the pilot of a single-seat aircraft, who needed a machine-gun that was fixed rigidly to the aircraft and fired forwards. It was difficult to aim such a weapon, and if it jammed it was useless, unless within the pilot's reach. One solution was to mount the gun centrally, so that the pilot aimed his aircraft at the enemy, but there was still the problem of access to the gun for clearing stoppages and, in the case of a Lewis gun, of reloading with new drums of ammunition. The ideal position was on the upper fuselage, directly forward of the pilot's windscreen, but this meant that the stream of bullets would have to pass through the disc of the rotating propeller.

French pilot Roland Garros and French aircraft designer Raymond Saulnier mounted a machine-gun in the ideal position on a Morane-Saulnier single-seat fighter, attaching steel deflector plates to the backs of the propeller blades to deflect any bullets which would otherwise splinter the wooden blades. Garros was able to demonstrate quickly the effectiveness of such a weapon, destroying at least three enemy aircraft before force-landing in enemy territory.

The significance of the machine-gun and deflector plates was appreciated quickly by the Germans who inspected the captured aircraft. Initially they wanted to copy this crude system, but designers Leinberger and Lübbe of the Fokker Company devised an interrupter gear which timed the discharge of bullets from a forward-mounted machine-gun so that they would pass between the propeller blades. The resulting combination of highly manoeuvrable Fokker monoplanes with forward-firing machine-guns proved a serious problem to the Allies.

The Royal Flying Corps, in particular, found itself at a grave disadvantage. The inherently stable B.E.2c was useless

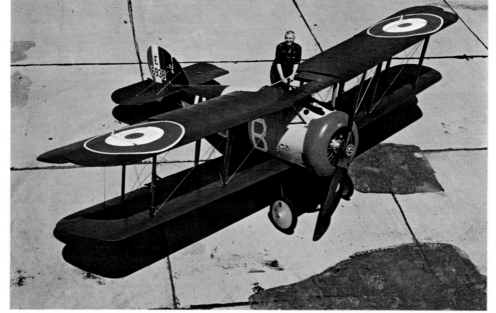

Britain's Sopwith Snipe (*above*) was one of the best fighter-scouts of WW1. When the United States became involved they had no significant combat aircraft, and had to rely on supplies from their Allies. They built, however, an excellent trainer in the JN series, and a JN-4 is shown (*top left*). Typical of fighter-scouts used by the Americans in France is the French Nieuport 28C-1 (*far left*). The Fokker Dr.1 triplane (*below*) is one of the best remembered German aircraft, flown by Manfred von Richthofen, but the Fokker D.VII (*left*) is regarded as one of the great warplanes of all time; armistice terms demanded that all were surrendered to the Allies.

The Zeppelin Staaken R.VI (*below*) was one of Germany's so-called Giant bombers, spanning 44·21 m (138 ft 5½ in), which had sufficient range to carry its load of eighteen 100 kg bombs to attack not only targets on the Eastern and Western Fronts, but to the heart of England's capital city. Maximum take-off weight of the R.VI was 11,460 kg (25,265 lb), equalling the take-off weight of about sixteen Avro 504Ks, (*bottom*). This superb training aircraft has a unique place in aviation history, because the foundation of modern flying training was evolved with this aircraft in the hands of instructors of the RFC's School of Special Flying, men who used the techniques of flying training developed by Major R. R. Smith-Barry. But even this diminutive trainer had started life as a reconnaissance aircraft, and had first won its spurs bombing Zeppelin sheds in Germany. When, on 21 November 1914, Royal Naval Air Service Avro 504s recorded the first ever strategic bombing attack by a formation of aircraft, each carried the diminutive load of four 20lb bombs.

when attacked, unable to out-manoeuvre the enemy and, because the observer who was armed with the machine-gun was restricted in his field of fire by the wings, their struts and bracing wires, unable to fight back effectively. Within no time at all, the observation aircraft of the Allies were being driven from the sky, unless accompanied by a mass of escorting fighters. This was the beginning of the period of dominance by the German air force known as the 'Fokker Scourge', lasting from October 1915 until May of the following year.

For the Allies it was essential to evolve rapidly a new family of very manoeuvrable and hard-hitting fighter aircraft and, in the main, the RFC's requirements were met by the Royal Aircraft Factory at Farn-borough, Hampshire. The British Admiralty followed a different line of procurement, relying upon private manufacturers, and some of their aircraft—such as the Sopwith Pup—were adopted also by the RFC. The French aircraft industry followed similar lines of development, as involvement in the same theatres of war brought identical experience. This nation's industry was to benefit from the fact that it had been well established prior to the war, enabling it not only to produce excellent aircraft for the needs of its own armed forces, but having also adequate productive capacity to build aircraft in quantity for its Allies. This was to be of considerable importance in April 1917 when the United States entered the war, for although that nation's armed forces possessed some 250 aircraft, none were more effective than the simplest training aircraft of the belligerent nations. At the end of the Second World War about seventy-five per cent of United States military aircraft operating at the Western Front had been supplied from French or British manufacturing sources.

The development of bomber aircraft

Germany's early reliance upon the Zeppelin airships to fulfil the long-range strategic bombing requirement had meant reduced priority for the development of heavier-than-air craft to carry out both tactical and strategic bombing attacks. The Allies, on the other hand, had never envisaged the deployment of airships in such a role, both Britain and France

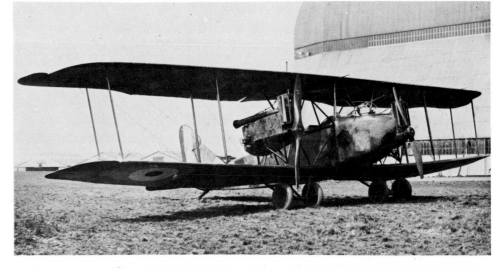

Germany's A.E.G. G.IV (*right*) was another of the significant bomber aircraft that evolved during WW1. Its range proved inadequate and the majority were used for short-range tactical missions. The Vickers Vimy (*below*) was intended as a strategic bomber to attack industrial targets in Germany. It was too late to see operational service in WW1, but made many important post-war flights, including the first heavier-than-air North Atlantic crossing.

confining the activities of such aircraft to maritime patrol, in the North Sea and Mediterranean respectively. Both nations found them to be valuable anti-submarine weapons, not by taking direct action themselves, but by calling upon other naval forces to deal with these vessels.

As a result, the Allies were rather quicker to become involved in the development of suitable aeroplanes to satisfy the tactical or strategic role. Early attacks against the Zeppelin sheds were made by fighter aircraft carrying small bombs, but gradually, as the importance of attacks against military targets and supply bases and factories became apparent, manufacturers in Britain and France began to embark on the development of bomber aircraft.

One of the most important early aircraft to enter service with the RFC in the bomber capacity was the D.H.4 day bomber, hitting the enemy hard under the operational guidance of the RAF's legendary father-figure, Hugh Trenchard. By

1917 both the RFC and the German air force were making use of specially-developed heavy bombers, Britain using the Handley Page 0/100 and F.E.2b.

Germany had evolved the Gotha heavy bomber and Zeppelin-Staaken series of giant bombers. When the former made daylight attacks on London in June and July 1917, appearing to range freely over the capital without any sign of opposition, the resulting public outcry ensured that the subject of this alarming gap in Britain's defences was debated in Parliament and, following enquiry and investigation, resulted in the creation of the independent Royal Air Force on 1 April 1918.

First Chief of the Air Staff was Major-General Sir Hugh (later Lord) Trenchard, and when he found difficulty in working with the Secretary of State for Air, he resigned as Chief of the Air Staff and returned to France to create the Independent Air Force in June 1918. As a firm believer in the capability of air power, Trenchard was the ideal man to establish

the Independent Force, comprising initially day bombers transferred from the RAF, plus Handley Page 0/400s borrowed from the former Royal Naval Air Service, then integrated into the RAF. In the closing stages of the war even bigger bombers were being developed by British manufacturers, including the Vickers Vimy and Handley Page V/1500. Both were completed too late to be used on wartime operations.

When the war ended, on 11 November 1918, all of the nations involved had gained an appreciation of the capability of air power. In particular, Hugh Trenchard in Britain, William ('Billy') Mitchell of the US Army Air Service and Giulio Douhet of the Italian Air Force had become dedicated protagonists of air power, convinced that a nation which possessed a potent air force could dominate the army and navy of an aggressor. We shall see how, in the inter-war years, these beliefs helped to shape the air forces which were to become involved in the Second World War.

THE CONQUEST OF THE GLOBE

THERE STILL EXISTS a widespread belief that wartime utilisation of aircraft in a combat or offensive role had brought about complete emancipation of the aeroplane. In fact, no such thing had happened. In the main, an airframe still relied upon a mass of struts and bracing wires to maintain its rigidity. The real change had come in the development of far more powerful engines: the 37·3–74·6 kW (50 to 100 hp) power plants with which the various nations had gone to war, had been replaced by engines that were no less reliable, and which had outputs ranging from 149–224 kW (200 to 300 hp).

Thus, the constant cry of the aircraft designer for more power had been met. But instead of developing 'clean' aircraft, free from drag-inducing struts and bracing wires, designers had tended to follow their noses, building bigger, better equipped, machines that relied upon the increased power of their engines to drag them through the air. The external appearance of a biplane of 1918 tended to differ little, except in size, from that produced by the same company in the early days of the war.

The growing capability of aircraft during the war was clearly recognised by those interested in the post-war development of civil air services. As early as 5 October 1916, George Holt Thomas in Britain had registered a company named Aircraft Transport and Travel Ltd.; shortly afterwards, in France, Pierre Latécoère was planning how he might link his native country with Morocco. His ultimate dream was an air service for passengers, cargo and mail, spanning the South Atlantic to South America.

They, and others like them, had failed to appreciate that considerable development of specialised aircraft was necessary before such air services became routine. They had also overlooked the fact that the potential air traveller was not yet ready to accept the aeroplane as the best means of getting from A to B. The majority of people who, in those early post-war years, would have the need to travel for business or pleasure, were still under the impression that flying was for heroes, certainly not for the mere man in the street.

The first post-war civil airline services
On 25 August 1919, Aircraft Transport and Travel inaugurated the first post-war scheduled civil air service between London and Paris. This was followed first by Handley Page Transport and then by S. Instone and Co., both operating services over the same route. France had also started civil operations, recording the first scheduled international passenger service between Paris and Brussels, on 22 March 1919. Compagnie des Messageries Aériennes and Compagnie des Grands Express Aériens also began services between London and Paris, with the result that too many aircraft were chasing a nonexistent queue of passengers. Within a few years the competing private companies operating these and other European services found themselves in grave financial difficulties, leading to the formation of national airlines such as Air France, Deutsche Lufthansa, Imperial Airways, KLM and Sabena.

With the aircraft that were available to the early airlines in the immediate postwar years, flying could be considered uncomfortable rather than unsafe. The only machines then obtainable were ex-military, with limited accommodation adapted for the carriage of passengers. What had been the gunner's position in a D.H.4 day-bomber, for example, could be provided with seats for two passengers, crammed face-to-face in the narrow fuselage, beneath a celluloid-windowed fuselage lid. Ventilation just happened; heating could be provided by heavy clothing, rugs and a hot-water bottle. A pair of household wooden steps was provided to make it easy to board the aircraft. And the single fare could cost you about £6 from London to Paris. For the current equivalent sterling value one could fly from London to New York today.

So, travel by air was expensive and unpopular. Only the wealthy or the brave took to the air. For them it was probably a good investment, for the passengers of an aircraft which had made one or more forced landings would have acquired a fund of exciting anecdotes which would ensure their selection as dinner guests for months ahead. Believe it or not, one of Aircraft Transport and Travel's 'airliners' made a record 22 forced landings on a single 'flight' between London and Paris.

The beginning of the great flights
Some catalyst was needed, powerful enough and widely reported, which would convince the 'man in the street' that he, too, could fly as a passenger. In Britain, the *Daily Mail* newspaper had, from the date of the first powered flight in Europe, done much to sponsor aviation progress

The Swallow (*above*) is typical of the open-cockpit biplanes with which such men as Charles Lindbergh first pioneered the airmail routes of North America.

The Vickers Vimy (*below*) was the type used by Alcock and Brown to record the first historic non-stop west–east crossing of the North Atlantic; the Ryan Monoplane *Spirit of St. Louis* (*bottom*) carried Charles Lindbergh on the first great New York–Paris flight, an epic solo achievement. The airship R.100 (*right*), designed by Barnes N. Wallis (later

Sir), also flew the North Atlantic, to and from Canada in the Summer of 1930. The Vimy's flight was made without the aid of any sophisticated navigational devices; yet inertial guidance systems of modern airliners provide pin-point landfall at transatlantic ranges. Lindbergh's achievement was one of indomitable courage and skilful navigation, his

primary problem to keep awake for almost 34 hours of flight. The R.100, with 44 people on board, made its double Atlantic crossing with such ease that it seemed the future of long-range transport could be satisfied by such aircraft. It was wishful thinking: a number of fatal accidents soon showed that airships were not the answer.

by the promise of substantial prizes for specific achievements. There had been, for example, £1,000 for the first cross-Channel flight, £10,000 for the first London–Manchester flight, and £10,000 for the winner of the first 'Round Britain' air race. All of these prizes had been won before the war and, so far as the public was concerned, long forgotten.

The *Daily Mail* had offered another £10,000 prize, for the first crossing of the North Atlantic, and this was won by Captain John Alcock and Lt. Arthur Whitten Brown who flew from St. John's, Newfoundland to Clifden, County Galway, Ireland (Eire) on 14–15 June 1919. Their mount was a specially-prepared Vickers Vimy, which it will be recalled had been developed as a long-range strategic bomber late in the war. This was the first of the great achievements that were, over a period of time, to convince the non-flying public that a new, safe method of fast travel was developing rapidly.

Less than six months after Alcock and Brown's North Atlantic crossing the Australian brothers Captain Ross and Lt. Keith Smith set off to make the first flight between England and Australia. They, too, used a specially prepared Vimy, completing the 18,175 km (11,294 miles) flight between 12 November and 10 December 1919, to win a £10,000 prize offered by the government of Australia.

From that moment on, the pace of progress got faster and faster. The first flight

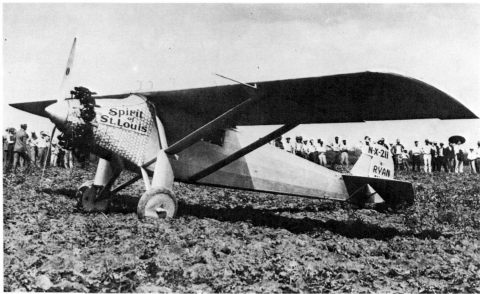

across Australia had been accomplished between 16 November to 12 December 1919; the first flight between Britain and South Africa from 4 February to 20 March 1920; the first non-stop crossing of the United States on 2–3 May 1923; the first round-the-world flight was completed between 6 April and 28 September 1924; and the first aeroplane flight over the North Pole on 9 May 1926.

All of these flights gained world headlines, and brought some measure of confidence in the aeroplane. But something was still needed to capture the hearts and imagination of ordinary people all over

the world. Then, at 07.52 hrs on 20 May 1927, a small (14 m; 46 ft span) single-engined monoplane literally staggered off a rain-soaked field at Long Island, New York. Heavily laden with fuel, it only just cleared obstructions at the end of the field and climbed slowly, almost reluctantly, into lowering skies. The pilot, little-known except to his colleagues involved in carrying the US Air Mail, headed his aircraft out over the Atlantic, aiming for the diminutive target of Le Bourget airport, Paris. Thirty-three hours 39 min later, in the glare of car headlights and before an almost unbelievable crowd of cheering

people, the little Ryan monoplane *Spirit of St. Louis* came in to land at Le Bourget. Never again could its pilot claim anonymity, for this was the legendary Charles Lindbergh. His flight, the first solo non-stop crossing of the North Atlantic, was that which more than any other enchanted the peoples of the world. If, they argued, one man in a small aeroplane with only one engine could fly safely from New York to Paris—a distance of 5,810 km (3,610 miles)—then air travel must be safe for anyone wanting to travel over domestic and short-range intercontinental services. This single achievement gave a tremendous fillip to air services everywhere, and especially to domestic services in the United States.

On the subject of achievements, during the two years which followed Charles Lindbergh's Atlantic crossing, Costes and Le Brix made the first flight across the South Atlantic; 'Bert' Hinkler flew solo from England to Australia; Kingsford Smith and Ulm with a two-man crew achieved the first trans-Pacific flight; Sqdn. Ldr. Jones Williams and Flt. Lt. Jenkins of the RAF flew non-stop from England to India. In August 1929, the German *Graf Zeppelin* made a round-the-world flight in just 3 weeks.

Developments in lighter-than-air craft

The post-war development of airships had seemed to offer an important means of travel on long-distance routes. When, between 2 and 6 July and 10 and 13 July 1919 the British airship R-34 flew to Canada and back to accomplish the first airship crossing and the first two-way crossing of the North Atlantic, the protagonists of lighter-than-air craft were convinced that there was immense potential for cruise-liner type services over long ranges.

Germany, forbidden to build aircraft by the terms of the Versailles Treaty, attempted to resuscitate the airship service between Berlin and Friedrichshafen which had operated so successfully pre-war, but this was soon stopped by the Allied Control Commission. Count von Zeppelin had died before the war's end and his associate from the early days, Dr. Hugo Eckner, had taken over control of the company. They were difficult times, but Dr. Eckner ensured the continuance of the company by building the LZ.126 by way of reparations to the US. This ship, named the USS *Los Angeles*, was an immense success in US Navy Service, accumulating well over 5,000 flight hours before being scrapped finally in 1939.

The Zeppelin company went on to build the highly successful *Graf Zeppelin*, first flown on 18 September 1928, and subsequently the world's largest airship, the LZ.129 *Hindenburg*, which was 245 m (803·81 ft) in length with a maximum diameter of 41 m (134·5 ft).

Britain also built two large airships for civil air services, the R.100, designed for

the Airship Guarantee Company by a team under the leadership of Barnes Wallis (later Sir), and the R.101, designed and built at the Air Ministry's Royal Airship Works at Cardington, Bedfordshire. Between 29 July and 16 August 1930, the R.100 flew to Canada and back on a proving flight which was highly successful. The R.101, on the contrary, crashed at Beauvais, France, on its proving flight to India, killing 48 of its 54 occupants. This event brought to an end the development of British airships, and the R.100 was scrapped.

In America both the Army and Navy operated a number of airships, the latter having a large quantity of non-rigid 'ships in service at various times. In addition, the US Navy operated the German-built USS *Los Angeles*, acquiring subsequently two more large rigid vessels, the USS *Akron* and USS *Macon*. When both these latter 'ships were lost at sea, in 1933 and 1935 respectively, the Navy's rigid airship programme was brought to an end.

In Germany, the *Graf Zeppelin* was going from success to success: it seemed that a vessel had been designed and built which could provide the long-range civil services which it was believed was within the capability of such aircraft. By the time this airship was scrapped, in 1940, it had accumulated 17,178 flying hours, made—among nearly 600 flights—140 Atlantic crossings, and had carried 13,100 passengers. The Zeppelin company had

The Ford Trimotor, or 'Tin Goose' as it was known popularly, had been produced originally in the 1920s. It utilised the corrugated metal skin which had been pioneered by Hugo Junkers in Germany, hence its nickname. Junkers later produced a tri-motor monoplane, but of cantilever low-wing configuration.

a cruising speed of only 160 km/h (100 mph)—so that Anthony Fokker described them as having built-in headwinds—these majestic aeroplanes gained such a reputation for safety and comfort that, in the 1930s, they carried more passengers between London and the Continent of Europe than all other airlines combined. E and W versions of the H.P.42 carried 24 and 38 passengers respectively, the latter serving on the short-haul European routes. They accommodated the flight crew within the fuselage on a flight deck for the first time: it was finally understood that the pilot and his crew would be able to work far more efficiently under such conditions than if they were frozen to the marrow and exposed in an open cockpit to the worst the weather could offer.

Even greater changes were coming, in America, where domestic air routes had expanded rapidly following the stimulus of Lindbergh's Atlantic flight. They had a good basis on which to develop, for the US Air Mail Service had linked major towns across the nation with navigational beacons, airfields and other facilities. All that was needed was a new generation of specially-designed transport aircraft.

On 8 February 1933 a very significant prototype aircraft made its first flight: the Boeing Model 247, which set entirely new standards. A low-wing monoplane of all-metal construction, powered by two 410 kW (550 hp) Pratt & Whitney air-cooled radial engines, it introduced several important new ideas that would add considerably to the performance of aircraft the world over. These included retractable landing gear, variable-pitch propellers, control surface trim tabs, de-icing equipment and an automatic pilot. It was the first twin-engined aircraft capable of climbing with a full load on the power of one engine, a fact which added considerably to safety in the critical areas of take-off and landing.

When the Model 247 was introduced into service by United Air Lines (UAL), a passenger could travel coast-to-coast across America in less than 20 hours, and this high-speed service sparked off a spate of development as a result of which the US manufacturers gained a lead in the production of civil transport aircraft which they have managed to retain to this day.

Other US airlines, losing revenue to

every reason to believe that, as a result of their experience with the *Graf Zeppelin*, the subsequent *Hindenburg* would recoup the company's fortunes, and that airline operators would want to acquire similar craft to inaugurate prestigious long-range services. It was not to be. Because supplies of non-inflammable helium could not be obtained to inflate the *Hindenburg*, her gas cells had been filled instead with hydrogen. When the giant airship approached the mooring mast at Lakehurst, New Jersey, on 6 May 1939, static electricity ignited venting gas and, within seconds, the Hindenburg collapsed in a blazing mass. By a miracle, 62 of the 97 people on board escaped with their lives, but this disaster was the last straw. Commercial airship development came to an end.

Start of the flying clubs

Just a couple of years before Lindbergh's North Atlantic flight, an important aircraft had been designed and built by Geoffrey de Havilland in the United Kingdom. This was the de Havilland Moth, the prototype of which flew for the first time on 22 February 1925. A lightweight biplane,

powered by a four-cylinder in-line engine, it was the aircraft chosen to start the government-sponsored British Flying Club Movement. It was built subsequently in America, Australia, Canada, Finland, France and Norway, and is regarded generally as being responsible for the start of the worldwide flying club movement.

The de Havilland Moth was one link in the chain which made people aware of the potential of air travel. Subsequent achievements by ordinary people flying Moths added new links to the chain, including the first solo flight from England to Australia by a woman, accomplished by Amy Johnson between 5–14 May 1930. (And such is the affection for the Moth that in early 1978, Flight Lieutenant David Cyster flew one from Darwin to London to commemorate the 50th anniversary of Hinkler's solo flight to Australia in 1928.)

New airliners enter service

Next came another link, in 1931, when Britain's Imperial Airways introduced a fleet of Handley Page H.P.42/45 four-engined biplane airliners. Despite having

DEVELOPMENTS IN PASSENGER COMFORT

The first post-war civil aircraft were somewhat casual conversions of machines which had been used by the air forces during WW1. The austere accommodation available in the immediate post-war years did little to enthuse travellers to take to the air, and it was not until purpose-built airliners began to enter service that the passenger was able to find a degree of comfort. The Argosy airliners of Imperial Airways in 1927 had a steward to serve a buffet lunch to the 18 passengers on its *Silver Wing* service (*right*). Very different is the interior of a modern wide-body jet airliner such as the McDonnell Douglas DC-10 (*below*), which has accommodation for a maximum of 380 passengers in air-conditioned luxury. The original 'Jumbo jet', Boeing's Model 747, can carry as many as 500 passengers.

The Handley Page W9 *Hampstead* (*below*) was developed from the earlier W8b 12-passenger airliner. It differed by having three engines, instead of two, providing a higher cruising speed, and could seat 14 passengers in wicker chairs.

In the early 1930s this scene at Croydon Airport gave immense pride to those who worked hard to put civil aviation on a sound footing in the UK. This Handley Page H.P.42W *Horatius* of Imperial Airways was one of four Croydon-based 42Ws which linked London with Europe. But the Boeing Model 247 (*right*), a contemporary, made these reliable biplanes look as if they had originated in another age.

G-AAXD

UAL, decided to approach the Douglas Company to produce a competing aircraft. The resulting DC-2 proved to be even more comfortable than the 247, carried four more passengers, was faster, and introduced wing trailing-edge flaps which improved take-off and landing performance. From the DC-2 Douglas evolved a wider-fuselage DST (Douglas Sleeper Transport), followed by one of the most famous aircraft in the history of civil aviation, the 21-seat DC-3. In the period 1939–1940, when some 80 per cent of civil transports used by America's domestic airlines were DC-3s, a 100 per cent safety record was maintained. As this is written, in 1978, large numbers of these remarkable aircraft remain in service with airlines around the world.

Development of intercontinental routes
With the establishment of domestic routes in Europe and North America, airlines began to investigate the possibility of inaugurating intercontinental services over long ranges. Not surprisingly, most countries decided to use for such services aircraft which could operate from water: after all, 70 per cent of the Earth's surface

The Douglas C-47 (*left*) is a military variant of the DC-3. Both earned a unique place in aviation history, primarily because of their reliability. The contemporary German Junkers Ju 52/3m (*bottom left*) gained equal respect; the name *Tante Ju* bestowed by Luftwaffe pilots showed their trust in this multi-purpose transport aircraft.

link Africa and South America, with landplanes providing the service over the remainder of the route. And to ensure that the flying-boats could take off with maximum fuel and full payload, a method of catapulting these aircraft off depot ships was adopted, enabling regular air mail services to begin on 7 February 1934. Subsequently, improved Dornier Do 26s were able to make a direct, unassisted crossing, and when the Second World War brought the service to an end, well over 300 crossings had been completed by various Dornier flying-boats.

Conquest of the North Atlantic

What about the North Atlantic? A good question, for it seems strange that this, the first ocean to be conquered by both airship and aeroplane, should not have been the first to have regular air services linking the Old and New World.

It was not for want of enthusiasm that the North Atlantic was the last of the oceans to be conquered by air, for the commercial potential was apparent to all. Distance, unreliable weather and strong prevailing westerly winds conspired to make such a service impossible until reliable aircraft of long-range capability were available for the task.

Not until the late 1930s was the time considered right, and the interested nations began experimental flights. France utilised a six-engined flying-boat, the Latécoère 521, which made its first crossing to New York, via Lisbon and the Azores, in August 1938. Germany experimented with the depot ship technique which had been used on the South Atlantic route, several crossings being made by this method in 1936 and 1937 by Dornier Do 18 flying-boats and Blohm und Voss Ha 139 seaplanes. And in 1938 a specially-prepared Focke-Wulf Fw 200 Condor landplane made a successful Berlin-New York and return flight, pointing the way to the future.

Interim British solutions included the Short-Mayo composite, the S.21 *Maia* flying-boat taking off with the S.20 *Mercury* seaplane carried pick-a-back. The *Mercury* could thus be air-launched with a maximum fuel load and payload, which made it impossible for it to get into the air without assistance. On 20–21 July 1938 *Mercury* made the first commercial crossing of the North Atlantic by a heavier-

is covered with water, and the development of flying-boats appeared to make good sense. Thus, when Britain decided to introduce the Empire Air Mail Scheme in late 1934, which meant that Imperial Airways would carry all mail for Commonwealth countries, the airline ordered a fleet of four-engined flying-boats from Short Brothers. Designated S.23, the first of these, named *Canopus*, made its first revenue flight on 30 October 1936: by mid-1938 S.23s were operating a through service from Southampton to Sydney.

America looked out across the vast reaches of the Pacific Ocean, planning a route via island stepping stones. Bases were therefore prepared on Wake Island and Guam—both US territory—to permit a route from San Francisco via Honolulu, Wake and Guam to Manila, with the first stage—to Honolulu—being the longest (3,853 km; 2,394 miles). The Martin Company built three four-engined flying-boats for this service, to the specification of Pan American Airways, and the first of these M-130 boats, the *China Clipper*, inaugurated the first trans-Pacific mail service on 22 November 1935. It was not until 21 October 1936 that fare-paying passengers were first carried.

France and Germany were both interested in developing a route across the South Atlantic. France began by establishing a service between Toulouse and Dakar, but it was 1928 before it was possible to open a route between Toulouse and Buenos Aires. This was not, however, a full air route, the ocean sector being operated by ships. It was not until 12 May 1930 that legendary French pilot Jean Mermoz took off from Senegal in the Latécoère seaplane *Comte de La Vaulx* to make the first direct crossing to Natal. More suitable aircraft were needed before a regular service could be established, and three-engined Couzinet 71 flying-boats began a regular South Atlantic mail service on 28 May 1934. But passengers were not carried over this route until after the Second World War.

Germany, initially, opted to use the *Graf Zeppelin* across the South Atlantic, the first trial flight from Friedrichshafen to Rio de Janeiro beginning on 18 May 1930. Proving successful, airship services between Germany and Recife, Brazil, were inaugurated on 20 March 1932 and continued at an average of one return trip per month into 1936. The alternative German plan was to use Dornier flying-boats to

Once upon a time flying-boats dominated the long-range air travel scene. This intentionally begins like a child's fairy story because there was a romantic and almost magical aura about these great vessels. Open waterways used for take-off meant there was no serious restriction to the length of run, so flying-boats were usually much bigger than landplanes of the same era. The Boeing 314 (*above*) provided the first regular transatlantic services. The Sikorsky S-42 (*left*) surveyed both Atlantic and Pacific; while the Grumman Goose (*below*) operates both from land and water, making it a true amphibian.

than-air craft, flying non-stop from Foynes to Montreal. It was, however, an impractical solution, and proved to be of no commercial use. Britain experimented also with the use of Short C-class flying-boats which were air refuelled to maximum capacity by Handley Page Harrow tankers after take-off, and completed successfully a series of trial flights which terminated on 30 September 1939, after Britain had become involved in the Second World War.

It remained for America's Pan American Airways — which had been making experimental flights simultaneously with those of Imperial Airways — to inaugurate the first regular transatlantic mail service on 20 May 1939. Finally, on 8 July 1939, Pan Am's Boeing 314 *Yankee Clipper* flying-boat carried 17 passengers and the mail on the inaugural northern route transatlantic service.

It had taken so long to achieve success on this, the most difficult ocean route in the world, it seems unjust that the achievement was overshadowed and overlooked as a result of the gathering war clouds in Europe. By the end of the Second World War, a complete new generation of civil airliners was in prospect.

THE NEW AIRBORNE ARMIES

WITH THE SIGNING of the Versailles Treaty the 'war to end wars' was over. The cost in human lives was almost unbelievable; the cost in monetary terms was to bring enormous problems to all the nations which had been involved. Germany was forbidden to build or operate military aircraft; the other nations, believing that the four years of madness would have taught an unforgettable lesson, reduced their armed forces to a minimum.

Apart from the reductions in manpower and the disposal of surplus equipment, it meant that for some years ahead air forces would have to make do with the types of aircraft that had equipped their squadrons at the war's end. For aircraft manufacturers it was a bleak prospect as contracts for thousands of machines were cancelled. To stay in business many had to move into different fields of manufacture, often turning to the production of furniture and other domestic goods of which their national home markets had been starved during the war. As we have seen, the world was not then ready for a large civil aviation industry and, in consequence, there was no demand for the development of new civil aircraft. Practically the only

aviation work available was the conversion of wartime aircraft for civil use, and even this requirement was very limited.

National developments
With the end of the war, Hugh Trenchard was reappointed Chief of the Air Staff in 1919. He took with him to the Air Ministry his profound belief in strategic air power and a determination to ensure that before he relinquished the reins he would build the foundation of an air force that could deal with any eventuality.

The United States Army Air Service had ended the war with a rapidly growing force. In immediate tactical command of its front line squadrons at the Western Front was Colonel William ('Billy') Mitchell, a disciple of Trenchard. After a period with the Army of Occupation, he returned to America to find that the Air Service had been reduced to a mere shadow of its wartime strength. Appointed Assistant Chief of the USAAS, Mitchell, too, was determined to bring about changes, convinced of the doctrine of strategic air power, as well as of the need to make the Air Service an independent force, free of Army control.

There was yet another prophet of air power, the Italian General Giulio Douhet, who in 1921 published a treatise *The Command of the Air*, expressing his convictions that stategic air power should be the dominant feature of military planning, since both armies and navies would eventually become subservient to air power.

France, which with Belgium had been the main board on which the battles of the First World War had been played, was thinking primarily in terms of defence. The immense and costly fortifications called the Maginot Line were constructed, in the firm belief that it would prove more than adequate to prevent another invasion from Germany.

Japan had no significant aircraft industry until the early 1920s, and prior to that time only small numbers of aeroplanes of European design had been built under licence. Realising that her small Army and Navy air forces needed practical instruction in military aviation, a service mission was invited from France in 1919 to provide essential education for the Army air force in aerial combat, gunnery, reconnaissance and bombing techniques. This was so successful that, in 1921, the Japan-

These between-wars military aircraft have a disparity in size, but both played a significant role in RAF training. The de Havilland Tiger Moth primary trainer (*bottom left*) remained in service for 15 years. The Vickers Virginia (*below*) was an important night bomber, teaching skills invaluable in WW2, when RAF Bomber Command was primarily a night force.

ese Navy invited a similar mission from Britain. This also proved of great importance, providing technical instruction which covered subjects from the basics of flight control to aerial photography and the use of torpedo-launching aircraft. The lessons were well learned and in just 20 years the Japanese had created formidable air forces.

In Russia, after the holocaust of the Communist Revolution, a new and powerful air force was created gradually. Much assistance in the later development of the Red Air Force came from German sources, in return for facilities at Lipezk, in Russia, where for eight years the new Luftwaffe was trained in secret.

Trenchard plans the future RAF

A most important event in British military aviation came in 1919, with the publication in December of an official document which has found its way into history as Trenchard's White Paper. In this, the Chief of Air Staff advocated the retention of an independent air force, with small units to be trained especially for co-operation with the Navy and Army. This led to the creation at a later date of the Fleet Air Arm and Army Air Corps. But the most important section of this document was that which detailed Trenchard's proposals for the training of a Royal Air Force which, though small, could be expanded as needed in a time of national crisis. Furthermore, this high quality and careful training, allied to the practical experience which the air force gained while helping to maintain law and order, or as a result of involvement in the small-scale wars and insurrections which persisted almost continuously between the First and Second World Wars, was to provide an elite corps of airmen, both in the air and on the ground. When the real challenge came, in 1939, they were ready for it.

The Importance of the Schneider Trophy

The surplus of aircraft which the RAF inherited at the end of the First World War meant that, in the main, they had to soldier on into the early 1930s before any significant new machines came their way. When they materialised, some bore the imprint of the influence on aircraft and engine design which had resulted from the Schneider Trophy Contests initiated by Jacques Schneider, in France, in late 1912. Schneider's original aim had been to speed the development of aircraft which could operate from water, believing that the future of air transport was linked closely with water-borne aircraft, or hyro-aeroplanes as they were then known. But these international contests evolved into air races between high speed seaplanes, most of which had just about sufficient room within their streamlined fuselage to accommodate a pilot.

In the development of these aircraft, designers learned a great deal about building sleek monoplane—and biplane—structures, the importance of streamlining and the significance of an aircraft's shape in keeping drag to a minimum. At the same time, specialist designers evolved far more powerful engines. These were, of course, short life racing engines, but the experience they gained in building, testing and operating such machines led to new power plants of

New generations of fighter aircraft were developed between the wars. The Boeing P-26 of the US (*left*) and the biplane built by Emile Dewoitine in Switzerland (*bottom left*) had similar bluff lines, being built around radial engines. R. J. Mitchell's Supermarine S 6B (*below*) had the streamlined form that later graced the Spitfire.

greater reliability and much improved power/weight ratio. The Curtiss D-12 engine and Curtiss/Reed propeller developed in America was one of these remarkable power plants of the early 1920s, a small-diameter propeller allowing the construction of an engine which needed no reduction-gear drive to ensure that the propeller tips did not exceed a certain critical speed. This simplification not only reduced the overall weight of the engine, but meant that power needed normally to drive the reduction gearing was available instead for propulsion. In the UK, the Rolls-Royce R (racing) engine of 1,752 kW (2,350 hp) which speeded the Supermarine S 6B seaplane to victory in 1931, finally winning the Schneider Trophy outright for Britain, was developed initially into a new 746 kW (1,000 hp) military power plant called the Merlin. The Supermarine S.4, S.5 and S.6 series of racing seaplanes designed by R. J. Mitchell led him to the creation of the famous monoplane eight-gun Spitfire fighter, which utilised the Merlin engine as its power plant. In aviation, as in the motor car industry, the spur of competition improved not only the capability of

the vehicle, but also its mechanical efficiency and reliability.

Development of air forces
In America, Billy Mitchell campaigned ceaselessly for an independent air force, demonstrated (though under unrealistic conditions) that aircraft had the capability of sinking capital ships, and following persistent campaigning and criticism of senior command was court martialled, and sentenced to five years suspension from duty. Instead, he resigned from the service so that he could continue to use every means at his disposal to influence the creation of the kind of air force which he was certain the United States needed.

Despite Mitchell's efforts, America retained Army and Navy air forces, the former service operating primarily for army co-operation until the provision of long-range bombers and defensive fighters in the 1930s brought a change of policy. In the inter-war period the US Navy built six aircraft carriers and procured a series of ship-board aircraft, mostly with dive-bombing capability. When, in 1926, a navy squadron of dive-bombers demonstrated dramatically the potential of such

aircraft, not only did the US Navy adopt such tactics as standard for anti-shipping operations, but both Germany and Japan made due note of this information.

Germany's Ernst Udet was so impressed by the potential of dive-bombing that he influenced the development of aircraft with such capability to serve with the Luftwaffe, the creation of which service was announced officially on 9 March 1935. The idea was taken up enthusiastically, to the extent that a special dive-bomber was created, the Junkers Ju 87 Stuka, but the Luftwaffe directed that new bombers being developed by the German industry must also have a dive-bombing capability. There was little support for a long-range strategic bomber, except from the Luftwaffe's first Chief of Staff, Lt.-Gen. Wever. After his death, in 1936, he was superseded by General Kesselring, an advocate of tactical support for the Army, with the result that Germany had no long-range strategic bombers for operations throughout the war. Instead, design and production was concentrated on short-range lightly-armed bombers intended for daylight use. The first standard single-seat fighter to be operated by the Luftwaffe

was the rugged-looking Heinkel He 51 biplane, but this was soon followed by Willy Messerschmitt's superb Bf 109 (later Me 109) single-seat fighter which, in progressively developed versions, was to serve the German air force throughout the Second World War.

Aircraft produced in Italy during this period were mostly of biplane configuration, their performance limited somewhat by the quality of the engines provided to power them. In retrospect, this seems ironic during a period when the Italian aircraft industry was producing some excellent aircraft and powerful engines to compete in the Schneider Trophy Contests. Even after the Macchi-Castoldi 72 had achieved a new world speed record, in 1934, the aircraft industry was instructed to continue the production of radial air-cooled engines for military use. Not until Italy was able to obtain higher-powered Daimler-Benz in-line engines from Germany during the war did production of high-performance fighter aircraft become a reality. Two exceptions to this were the Fiat C.R.32 biplane fighter and Savoia-

Marchetti S.M.79 bomber, both remarkable aircraft. The latter was classed among the best land-based bombers of the Second World War.

Japan had been busy building up the strength of her air forces from the time that the French and British missions had visited that country. The Navy's air arm expanded most dramatically, with new and effective aircraft equipping the six aircraft carriers that were built between the wars.

Germany's announcement of the creation of the Luftwaffe caused great concern in both Britain and France, especially as German propaganda was designed to exaggerate the size and capability of this new force. Immediately, both nations initiated massive re-armament programmes. In the case of Britain it led to the design and development of aircraft such as the Spitfire and Hurricane fighters, and Blenheim and Wellington bombers with which the war was begun, as well as the important four-engine strategic bombers that entered service as it progressed. France was not so successful; her aircraft industry was

Classic trainer of the USAAC and USN, the Stearman Kaydet earned fame for its rugged reliability; more than 8,000 were built.

newly-nationalised and in a state of disorder, with the result that the only significant new aircraft entered service too late to be of any use in the nation's defence.

Most of the nations which were to become involved in the Second World War had, during the inter-war years, had some opportunity of using their air forces operationally, thus gaining valuable experience. Britain had used her air force for policing and air control in the Middle East and on the North West Frontier. Germany, Italy, Russia and, on a much smaller scale, France and Britain, had been involved in the Spanish Civil War. Italy had been at war with Abyssinia and Albania, Japan with China and Russia. America's policy of neutrality had sufficed to keep the nation from war, but this meant that when war broke out in Europe, on 1 September 1939, the capability of her Army Air Corps was far behind that of the European nations.

WORLD WAR IN THE AIR

THE INVASION of Poland by German forces on 1 September 1939 was not such a shock as the speed and efficiency with which this brave nation, possessing only a small and outdated air force, was ruthlessly eliminated as a fighting unit. The German *Blitzkrieg* technique, with Stuka dive-bombers providing close support for massive Panzer divisions of tanks and armoured vehicles, swept all before it. Within seventeen days it was all over, and Germany and Russia were busy dividing the first spoils of their uneasy alliance.

When the first air raid sirens sounded in Britain, on 3 September 1939, soon after Prime Minister Neville Chamberlain had told the nation by radio that Britain and France were again at war with Germany, most civilians believed that bombs would soon come raining from the sky. This was not surprising, for they had been conditioned to expect it by a concentrated year of Air Raid Precautions, from newsreel pictures of air raids during the Spanish Civil War, and by early BBC reports of the invasion then in progress in Poland.

The Spitfire (*right*) and Hurricane (*below*), were both eight-gun fighters and both powered by Rolls-Royce engines.

Germany overruns Western Europe

But Hitler then had no intention of fighting simultaneously on two fronts, and it was not until 3 April 1940, when there had been time to prepare for the new campaign in the West, that his war machine was unleashed again; first against Denmark, then Norway, Belgium, Holland and France. By June 1940, the German army and air force could stand and look across the English Channel and see their next target—Britain. It was not to prove quite so easy to eliminate.

The year which Britain had gained, when Neville Chamberlain signed the 1938 Munich peace agreement with Adolf Hitler, was put to good use by the RAF and the nation's aviation industry. Worthwhile numbers of eight-gun Hurricane and Spitfire fighters could be deployed against the enemy, and Britain's development of radar, allied to the reporting network of the Observer Corps and RAF Control Centres, meant they could be used with maximum effect. It was not necessary to fly endless patrols in case the enemy attacked. Instead, the fighters could wait and be directed to attack the enemy aircraft as and when necessary.

Contrary to popular belief, Germany

The Spanish-built version of the Messerschmitt Me 109 (*below*) gives an authentic impression of the Luftwaffe's fighter which took part in the Battle of Britain. Opposing bombers are pictured (*opposite*): the Vickers Wellington (*right*) and Dornier Do 217 (*bottom right*) were both used extensively in a variety of roles.

had also developed a radar system, but had not provided the back-up which existed in Britain to direct defending fighters to meet hostile aircraft. In any event, such a comprehensive system proved unnecessary in the first stages of the war, because German defences proved more than adequate to deal with daylight attacks: so effective, indeed, that British bombers could only be sent over German targets by night.

Battle of Britain

Thus, when Germany launched her air force to knock out Britain's air defence, the RAF had some 700 front-line fighters and about 300 more aircraft in reserve, ready and spoiling for the fight which has since become known as the Battle of Britain. By the time it was over, in early September, the Germans had been driven from the daylight sky over Britain: henceforth her bombers had to operate by night. As well as providing a psychological and practical victory for the RAF and the nation it protected, the German Luftwaffe had lost its most experienced pilots.

Space does not permit a detailed coverage of the aircraft involved in the Second World War: instead we must look at the trends which developed as the war itself progressed.

Developments in Britain

Most of the nations which were involved in the war still had biplane aircraft in service at the time of their entry. Britain's air arms all had fairly large quantities of such aircraft, but only the Gloster Gladiator remained in first-line service as a fighter. It was soon to disappear; but one biplane remained in front-line service until after VE-Day, the Fleet Air Arm's famous 'Stringbag': the Fairey Swordfish torpedo-bomber. The Hurricane was gradually superseded by the Hawker Typhoon and Tempest but, in many differing variants, the Supermarine Spitfire remained in service until peace was restored. The Bristol Company, well known for the Blenheim I fighter and Blenheim IV medium-bomber, produced the Beaufighter which enjoyed considerable success as a night fighter and was developed subsequently for use in a wide variety of duties.

The de Havilland Company, long renowned for producing the sensational,

built the 'Wooden Wonder', better known as the Mosquito, which served as fighter, bomber and reconnaissance aircraft, flying high and fast enough so that for most of the war nothing could catch it. Britain had begun in 1936 the development of long-range strategic bombers, resulting in the four-engined Halifax, Stirling and Lancaster bombers which ranged over Germany by night as the war developed. In the initial stages it was the Blenheim, Vickers Wellington and Handley Page Hampden which were the mainstay of Bomber Command.

Regia Aeronautica and the Luftwaffe

Italy, under the dictatorship of Mussolini, had developed its *Regia Aeronautica* into a large air force, and experience gained during its operations in Ethiopia and in the Spanish Civil War should have ensured that it would prove a potent and valuable ally for the Luftwaffe. This did not prove to be the case, for despite the development of some excellent fighter and bomber aircraft, it lacked the *esprit de corps* which distinguished the achievements of the Luftwaffe, RAF, Commonwealth air forces, and the USAAF.

As mentioned previously, the Messerschmitt Me 109 was the Luftwaffe's primary fighter at the beginning of the war. It was to be joined by another superb fighter, designed by Kurt Tank, the Focke-Wulf Fw 190. This aircraft rather dumbfounded the 'experts', who had believed for so long that a fighter must have

an in-line engine if it was to be sleek and fast. Kurt Tank and BMW showed that a properly cowled bluff-fronted radial engine, with air ducted to a cooling fan, could provide sparkling performance, and was free from the weight and vulnerability of a liquid-cooling system. For bombing capability, Germany relied initially upon three medium bombers, the Dornier Do 17, Heinkel He 111 and Junkers Ju 88. The Ju 87 had its initial glory in the first *blitzkrieg* attacks, but was to prove also an important aircraft for deployment against the one-time ally—Russia—which Germany had invaded, with considerable early success, on 22 June 1941. The famous Stuka, however, was slow and vulnerable to enemy fighters, and therefore useless unless Germany was in complete control of the sky.

Russian aircraft production

But like Napoleon before him, Hitler had not appreciated sufficiently the vast areas of land into which the Russians could retreat strategically to blunt the enemy's attack. Neither had he been prepared for the ferocious severity of the Russian winter; and it is doubtful whether anyone could have believed that despite the disruption and chaos of a full-scale invasion, the Russians would be able to move their aircraft industry far behind the fighting areas and resume production surprisingly quickly. From such conditions came a series of Yakovlev fighter aircraft able to confront the Luftwaffe on equal terms.

Supplies of large numbers of fighter aircraft from Britain and the United States enabled the Russian industry to produce other types of aircraft and, in particular, the Ilyushin Il-2 *Sturmovik* ground-attack aircraft. Heavily armoured to protect it from ground fire, the Il-2 was armed with guns, rockets and bombs to provide a most effective tank-destroying capability, taking heavy toll of German armour.

Japan goes to war

Japan, in 1941, had come to the decision that despite the odds the nation's survival, as a result of sanctions imposed by the United States, made it essential for Japan to gain access to supplies of aviation fuel and/or crude petroleum. Indonesia was the nearest source of supply, but this would be available to the Japanese only as conquerors. Cut off from external fuel supplies, Japan's reserves were dwindling rapidly because of the continuing war against China. It was now or never.

At dawn on the morning of 7 December 1941, a Japanese naval task force was steaming close to Hawaii. At 07.40 hours 183 aircraft were over Oahu Island, and streaking to attack Pearl Harbor; as this first group finished its mission, a second wave of 167 aircraft came in to add to the devastation on the ground. Taken com-

pletely by surprise, and while Japanese diplomats were still negotiating peace terms in America, the US Pacific fleet had been virtually eliminated as a fighting unit for some time to come. Happily for the US Navy, its aircraft carriers were at sea, escaping the fate of Battleship Row, where four battleships, two destroyers, a target ship and a minelayer had been sunk; four battleships, two cruisers and a destroyer seriously damaged. When, three days later, the British battleships *Prince of Wales, Repulse* and an escorting destroyer were sunk at sea by Japanese naval aircraft, the beliefs expressed by Billy Mitchell were shown to be valid. No longer could surface vessels afford to ignore the danger in the sky.

Japan had learnt well from the teachings of the Western military missions, especially the Navy which had realised from an early date the potential of the aircraft carrier. And despite the reports which had come to the Western nations from China, none had appreciated that Japan had developed such a wide range of high performance aircraft. They were to discover, in due course, that in many cases this performance resulted from lightweight structures void of armour protection for the crew and without adequate precautions to make fuel and hydraulic systems safe from attack. American pilots soon learned that even if an enemy had superior performance, he needed only to be hit hard once to be turned into a torch.

Japanese innovation provided some

American bombers included the Douglas DB-7 (*Havoc* and *Boston*) light bomber (*right*), the most extensively-built and widely-used aircraft in this category. The Boeing B-17 Flying Fortress (*centre*) is known especially well in Britain for its vital contribution to round-the-clock bombing of European targets during WW2. The Boeing B-29 Superfortress (*bottom*), designed to meet the USAAF's requirement for a long-range strategic bomber, proved of vital importance in the closing stages of WW2, destroying Japanese cities with incendiary weapons, and is remembered for its two atom bomb attacks.

The Gloster-Whittle E.28/29 (*left*) was Britain's first aircraft to take to the air under the power of a gas turbine engine, the work of Sir Frank Whittle. The first turbojet-powered aircraft to fly, on 27 August 1939, was the German Heinkel He 178, powered by a gas turbine engine developed by Dr. Pabst von Ohain.

excellent aircraft as the war progressed, but none were more devastating than the *Kamikaze* ('Divine Wind') suicide flights which in the final ten months of the war accounted for no less than 48·1 per cent of all US warships damaged and 21·3 per cent of all ships sunk during the whole of the Pacific War.

America's European/Pacific involvement

American involvement in the war after the Japanese attack on Pearl Harbor meant that, in the long run, success for the Western Allies was inevitable. Even before America was precipitated into battle, the Japanese Navy had expressed the opinion that in a long drawn out war America must win, because of the enormous productive capacity at that nation's disposal.

Britain and the US came to an agreement on production of aircraft: in the main Britain would concentrate on short/medium-range aircraft for combat in the European theatre of operations, while America would build long-range bombers and transport, plus suitable fighter aircraft, with which to fight the long-range island-hopping war in the Pacific Ocean.

Thus, in Europe, British bombers were deployed against enemy targets by night, US bombers by day, to provide round-the-clock attacks. Escorting the bombers over enemy territory by day were such classic American aircraft as the Lockheed P-38 Lightning, North American P-51 Mustang (especially after it was fitted with the Merlin engine) and Republic P-47 Thunderbolt: the escorted aircraft were mainly Boeing B-17 Flying Fortresses and Consolidated B-24 Liberators.

RAF Bomber Command concentrated on large scale attacks by night, with targets pinpointed by Pathfinders which illumi-

nated the bombing area for the masses of Halifax, Lancaster and Stirling bombers following behind. The primary result of such concentrated strategic bombing was to reduce Germany's supplies of fuel to a point where it was impossible to prevent the relentless attacks from the air.

As the war neared its end, both Britain and Germany were to deploy aircraft using a completely new power plant — the gas turbine — which had been developed independently by Frank Whittle in Britain and Pabst von Ohain in Germany. This latter country was also to use operationally the world's first rocket-powered interceptor, the Messerschmitt Me 163B. None of these aircraft were built in sufficient quantity or appeared early enough to have significant influence on operations.

In their final attempts to avoid defeat, Germany launched pilotless V-1 flying bombs and V-2 ballistic rockets against Britain, the base from which British and American aircraft blasted their homeland, and from which the invasion of D-day was launched, but this came too late to have any effect on the final outcome of the war. Overrun, defeated, Adolf Hitler dead, Germany besieged by Britain, America and their Allies in the West, and with the Russians fighting in a devastated Berlin, war in Europe ended on 8 May 1945.

In the Pacific theatre, heroic and bitter fighting by the American Army and Marines had driven the Japanese back towards their home islands. The availability of the Boeing B-29 Superfortress meant that massive incendiary attacks could be launched against Japanese targets. One such raid on Tokyo, on 9 March 1945, destroyed a quarter of the capital, and nearly 84,000 people lost their lives. Five months later, on 6 August and 9 August, the world's first operational atomic bombs were dropped over the cities of Hiroshima and Nagasaki respectively. The prospect of continuing annihilation of Japanese citizens and property on such a scale was inconceivable. On 10 August Japan's leaders decided on immediate surrender, and on 2 September 1945 the documents were signed on board the battleship USS *Missouri*. Six years and one day after Germany's invasion of Poland, the Second World War was over. From first to last it was a conflict which had shown the impact of aviation as a primary military weapon.

KEEPING THE BALANCE OF POWER

AT THE BEGINNING of the Second World War the two main opposing fighters, the Messerschmitt Me 109 and the Supermarine Spitfire, were capable of approximately the same maximum speed at optimum altitude, that is about 571 km/h (355 mph). By the end of the war both had gained 30–40 per cent in weight, had engines with anything up to double the power, and speeds as much as 25 per cent faster, despite the increased weight. In the main, the increased weight came from extra equipment, more armament, and additional fuel capacity to increase range and to cope with the demand of the higher-powered engine.

The problem of compressibility

This was the trend for most aircraft which were in military use over a period of years and, with certain specific exceptions, the increased speed, as well as overall improvement in performance, came from engines of greater power, and more efficient propellers. But as the war progressed and new aircraft entered service, generally improved technology made it possible for level flight speeds in excess of 708 km/h (440 mph) to become fairly commonplace. In the latter stages of the war it was not uncommon for late versions of aircraft such as the British Hawker Typhoon and the American Lockheed P-38 Lightning to exceed these speeds in a dive, their pilots reporting violent shuddering of aerofoil surfaces. In some cases control surfaces, wings and tail units were torn away, and many pilots lost their lives as a result: for the first time they were encountering the effects of compressibility, a phenomenon then known primarily in advanced aerodynamic theory.

When an aerofoil surface approaches the speed of sound, the air ahead of the aerofoil is unable to move aside fast enough, and a shockwave forms both at the leading-edge and trailing-edge of the aerofoil. If it has not been specially designed, not only will the wing (or any other aerofoil surface) be buffeted by this shockwave, but additional drag will also be induced.

Considerable research on this problem was carried out in Germany during the war, especially in relation to the Messerschmitt Me 163 Komet, the world's first rocket-powered combat aircraft which, in the Me 163B-1a version, was

capable of a speed of 959 km/h (596 mph) at 3,000 m (9,840 ft). It was discovered that a swept wing, that is one in which the angle between the wing leading-edge and the centreline of the rear fuselage forms an angle of less than 90 degrees, was able to be flown at above-normal speeds without the onset of buffeting. This sort of research information became available to the world's aircraft manufacturers in the early post-war years.

At that time, Britain held a considerable lead in the development of turbine engines, and the RAF's Gloster Meteor F.3s, which were powered by 8·90 kN (2,000 lb st) Rolls-Royce Derwent I turbojets, were the equipment of the RAF's first jet-fighter wing in 1945. The maximum speed of this version was 668 km/h (415 mph); but the piston-engined de Havilland Hornet F.1, which entered RAF service in 1945, had a maximum speed of 780 km/h (485 mph). At that period of time the newly-developed turbine engine had not attained the propulsive efficiency which the engine/propeller combination was capable of at the peak of its development.

Supersonic flight

As the power output of gas turbines began to grow rapidly, it was soon clear that the time was fast approaching when it would be possible for aircraft to travel at more than the speed of sound. This represents a velocity of about 1,193 km/h (741 mph) in dry air at 0°C (32°F), such speed being expressed as Mach 1·0, after the 19th century Austrian Ernst Mach, who studied the propagation of sound waves. Thus, Mach 0·75 represents three-quarters of the speed of sound. Before

new generations of aircraft could travel in excess of Mach 1 as routine, it was necessary to build a research aircraft which would comprise a very strong structure to survive aerodynamic buffeting, and utilise all then-known aerodynamic improvements, together with a powerful engine, to provide the necessary thrust.

Under contract to the National Advisory Committee for Aeronautics (NACA), the Bell Aircraft Company in America designed and built such an aircraft, designated X-1, powered by a rocket engine. Air-launched at 9,145 m (30,000 ft) altitude from a B-29 Superfortress motherplane, this aircraft was flown progressively nearer to the speed of sound by a young USAF pilot, Charles 'Chuck' Yeager. At times the aircraft was buffeted so badly that it seemed an impossible task: then, on 14 October 1947, Yeager slipped through what the media had dubbed 'the sound barrier' to the smoothness of supersonic flight. Subsequently, he flew the Bell X-1A at a speed of 2,655 km/h (1,650 mph), and the knowledge gained from this research was to make possible a whole new range of combat aircraft which was developed all over the world.

The Berlin Airlift

It is unlikely that any serious-thinking person imagined that the Second World War was to prove the 'war to end wars'. It left behind it far too many new and potentially hazardous situations. One of these situations was the partition of Berlin, partly occupied by the Soviet Union, which also controlled the surface routes for transport into and out of West Berlin, which was occupied by British, French and US forces. Clearly, the Russians believed

that by closing the surface routes the Western Allies would leave Berlin and its population to fend for itself. Instead, the city was sustained from the air in an important operation known as the Berlin Airlift, and for almost a year military and civil pilots ferried essential materials and food into Tempelhof, Gatow and, in the latter months, Tegel. The Allies had effectively demonstrated that they were prepared to face any cost to ensure continuing peace. Furthermore, this warning of potential danger to peace in Europe speeded up the formation of the North Atlantic Treaty Organisation (NATO), which took place in April 1949.

The Korean War

The next major trial of strength was to come in Korea when, at 04.00 hours on 25 June 1950, the north Korean infantry, spearheaded by Soviet-built tanks, streamed in their thousands across the 38th Parallel to attack the Republic of Korea. The United Nations Security Council called immediately upon all member nations to assist in repelling the attackers, and troops from many countries were to be involved in bitter combat on Korean soil. In the air the battle was fought primarily by the USAF, USN and RAAF, and in this three-year struggle there came three developments important

for military aviation: a re-birth of aerial reconnaissance, the introduction of tactical air co-ordinators (known later as Forward Air Controllers), and the rapid evolution of the helicopter as a military weapon. There came also, in this conflict, the first air battles between jet fighters.

Large-scale reconnaissance was needed in this new type of war, resulting in the introduction of new techniques and new equipment, as well as the realisation that reconnaissance capability of the highest order would be permanently essential for the prevention of more general war. At the beginning of the evolution of these new techniques was the tactical air

The first operational turbojet-powered aircraft to enter service in the UK was the Gloster Meteor, and the picture (*opposite page*) shows Meteors of the RAAF's No. 77 Squadron operating in Korea. But at that time there was still a lot to be learned about gas turbines and the design of aircraft to reap the full potential of the immense power that such engines promised. In the meantime piston-engined aircraft such as the US Navy's Douglas AD-1 Skyraider (*above*) proved still valuable in post-WW2 conflicts. So, did the North American F-82 Twin Mustang (*left*), developed as a long-range escort fighter. The Fleet Air Arm's Hawker Sea Fury also fought with distinction in Korea, one from 802 Squadron destroying the unit's first MiG-15 on 9 August 1952.

New types of aircraft evolved soon after WW2. Helicopters such as the Bell H-13 Sioux (*left*) proved themselves vitally important in the Korean War. Flight refuelling techniques (*below*) make it possible to deploy aircraft over vast ranges. Spy-planes like the Lockheed U-2 (*bottom left*) can provide important information.

initiated by the US, after Fidel Castro had shown that close links existed between his regime and the Soviet Union. When surface-to-air missile (SAM) sites of Russian origin were discovered on the island, more intensive reconnaissance showed that Russian-built medium-range ballistic missiles were being installed and trained against the highly-industrial area of the north-east US.

American President John F. Kennedy advised his NATO allies of the situation, launched the massive US deterrent forces into an action alert state and called the Russian bluff. Within a short space of time the missile sites were being dismantled and the weapons shipped back to the Soviet Union.

Importance of reconnaissance

When this crisis was resolved, on 29 October 1962, there was no doubt of the importance of a first class reconnaissance capability, and this desirable aim was persued energetically by governments all over the world. Not only was the aeroplane involved heavily in such work, but gradually a whole family of pilotless drone aircraft have been developed to carry out such tasks. And as man learned to make his first journeys into space, and evolved the technique of placing satellites into Earth orbit, these too have been given reconnaissance capability, as a part of the delicately-balanced deterrent policy which has so far prevented a nuclear war between major powers, or the beginning of a vast conventionally-weaponed Third World War.

It has not proved adequate—and neither has the gradual development of advanced and potent combat, close-support and strategic aircraft—to prevent conflicts such as that called loosely the Vietnam War, and a host of smaller wars, fought for political, nationalistic and economic reasons, which have plagued mankind since 1964.

Space does not permit a detailed list of military aircraft which have evolved in the post-Second World War years. Instead, it is possible only to mention briefly the trends of development, which have been similar among the major powers. And because, with one or two notable exceptions, lesser powers are unable to face the astronomical research and development costs of a new significant military aircraft,

co-ordinator. A pilot and observer, flying in a lightweight aircraft, maintained visual reconnaissance over a battle area until relieved, relaying constantly by radio to an operations centre the state of the battle below. They could call in strike aircraft and direct them to a target, making a very valuable contribution to the battle on the ground. In this conflict rotary-winged aircraft—helicopters— which had seen just a taste of experimental use before the Second World War ended, were to prove invaluable in the kind of war being fought in Korea. Because of their go-anywhere capability, they were able to carry troops and supplies into forward areas inaccessible to any other form of transport. On their return journey to base they could operate as air ambulances, carrying men injured in battle for immediate treatment at field hospitals. By this action, the death rate from wounds in Korea was reduced to the lowest figure then recorded in military history. Helicopters were able to demonstrate also that if armed, even with comparatively simple weapons, they could be developed into an important close-support aircraft for tactical operations.

Cuban Crisis

The Cuban crisis of 1962 was another shock to all nations, threatening a Third World War, and highlighting the importance of reconnaissance in a world which, thanks to the development of a whole armoury of nuclear—or thermonuclear—armed intercontinental ballistic missiles, has achieved the ability to destroy itself. Routine reconnaissance of Cuba had been

In the early post-war years came the first of the supersonic fighters. Aircraft such as the US Navy's LTV F-8 Crusader (*opposite, top*) and USAF's Lockheed F-104 Starfighter (*opposite, bottom*) evolved from research programmes that investigated problems of supersonic flight and how to build airframes to fly at such speeds.

New-generation fighters entering service with the world's air forces include the McDonnell Douglas F-15A Eagle air-superiority fighter (*top left*) operational with the USAF; the Grumman F-14A Tomcat (*top right*) is a carrier-based multi-mission fighter of the US Navy, which has swing-wings to cater for carrier landings plus high-speed performance. The Panavia Tornado multi-role combat aircraft (*centre*) will be operational in the late 1970s. The Dassault Mirage F-1 multi-mission fighter (*bottom*) is now in French Air Force use; not only can it fly at Mach 2·2, but it can operate from sod runways.

they too have equipped their air forces with weapons developed by the major powers of the East or West.

Bomber aircraft have grown in capability to the extent that the Boeing B-52 Stratofortresses, still serving with the USAF's Strategic Air Command, have a range of 20,115 km (12,500 miles), to enable them to deliver nuclear weapons against any target in the world. The Soviet Union has nothing in exactly the same class, but has a formidable force of missile-armed strategic bombers capable of posing severe problems to the West if any major confrontation developed.

Most nations, East and West, have short/medium range bombers that would have been regarded as terrifying weapons if available in the Second World War. The French Dassault Mirage IV-A, for example, delivered to the French Air Force in the period 1964–1967, has a maximum speed of Mach 2·2 and can carry 7,257 kg (16,000 lb) of conventional bombs, or a nuclear weapon with a yield of 70KT.

One of the latest close-support aircraft is the US Fairchild Republic A-10A, now entering service with the USAF. Heavily armoured, to protect the pilot from ground weapons, it is armed with a 30 mm seven-barrel cannon which has alternative firing rates of 2,100 and 4,200 rounds per minute, and can carry a maximum external weapon load of 7,257 kg (16,000 lb). Even the 8·69 m (28 ft 6 in) span Anglo-French Jaguar A and S are armed with two 30 mm cannons and can carry up to 4,536 kg (10,000 lb) of external weapons.

It is this weapon-carrying capability, coupled with the speed and agility of these aircraft, which is so impressive. The Jaguar A or S is a single-seat tactical support aircraft, and yet is able to carry a variety of weapons practically equivalent in weight to the bomb load of early versions of the Boeing B-17 Flying Fortress.

The kind of turbine power which gives this kind of capability can also move a reconnaissance aircraft like the Soviet Union's Mikoyan MiG-25 (code-named 'Foxbat' in the West) at Mach 3·2, or enable an interceptor such as the McDonnell Douglas F-15 Eagle to climb to a height of 29·9 km (18·6 miles) in just under 3·5 minutes: which is climbing at a rate in excess of 8 km (5 miles) a minute.

To add to the mobility of such aircraft, most have in-flight refuelling capability, so that by planned rendezvous with airborne tankers, they can be given intercontinental range. This has made it possible for air forces to deploy a 'policing' force anywhere in the world at short notice, with long-range transports carrying men and equipment to maintain and operate hard-hitting aircraft that can be in action within hours instead of days.

The British Aerospace (BAe) HS Harrier (*below*) was the world's first VTOL combat aircraft, developed from the earlier P.1127 Kestrel, and in service with the air arms of Spain, UK and USA. The BAe HS Nimrod (*bottom*), developed from the de Havilland Comet, is an important maritime patrol and ASW aircraft.

Both Britain and the Soviet Union have developed jet-propelled fixed-wing vertical take-off and landing (VTOL) aircraft, the Hawker-Siddeley Harrier and Yakovlev Yak-36 respectively, which take-off and land by means of the jet efflux from turbine engines, a transition to forward flight then permitting the fixed wings to provide lift conventionally.

Aircraft of this kind are, obviously, valuable for ship-board operations, but the development of through-deck carriers and improved catapults and arrester gear make it possible for even high performance aircraft to operate from carriers.

The evolution of nuclear submarines, able to deploy ballistic missiles, has brought emphasis to the development of maritime reconnaissance aircraft that have also an anti-submarine warfare (ASW) capability. Thus, Britain's Hawker-Siddeley Nimrod has an endurance of some 12 hours, and is able to detect underwater submarines and launch against them a variety of torpedoes, depth charges, mines and bombs.

Rotary-winged aircraft have been developed to act as flying cranes, work as troop carriers, and act as armed attack aircraft. New generations of jet trainers ensure the training of competent pilots and, in many cases, can be used also as light strike aircraft.

All in all, military aircraft have been developed to a point where they are capable of an almost frightening kill capability. This, on the face of it, would have been abhorrent to the aviation pioneers, who hoped and believed that the aeroplane would be an instrument of peace. Nevertheless, this military potential of the aeroplane has done much to ensure the avoidance of a war between the world's major powers with its potentially catastrophic consequences.

UNIVERSAL TRANSPORT

THE READER will recall that the First World War had done little to improve the airframe structure of aircraft involved. Power plants, however, had been developed from reasonably dependable low-power units to engines of four or five times the power, as well as good reliability.

The Second World War brought about more wide-ranging changes, with extensive improvement in the aircraft's structure and systems. Radar, which had been almost in an embryo state at the war's beginning, developed as a navigational aid, providing an aircrew with a map of the terrain below, which was unaffected by clouds or darkness; radio was not only capable of providing reliable communications on a round-the-world basis, but had been harnessed also to create new and accurate navigational systems and bad-weather landing aids. And America's involvement in the war with Japan, away across the far reaches of the Pacific Ocean, had necessitated the development of transport and cargo aircraft with long-range capability as a priority requirement.

Once again, the persistent cry from airframe designers for more power had resulted in the evolution and production of engines of up to 2,610 kW (3,500 hp). Not only were they more powerful, but most were supremely reliable. In addition, the 'jet' or gas turbine engine had begun its development. Germany had flown the world's first aircraft to be powered by a turbojet—the Heinkel He 178—on 27 August 1939. Britain's Gloster/Whittle E.28/39 had not flown until 15 May 1941, but just over three years later, on 27 July 1944, the twin-engined Gloster Meteor, powered by two 7·6 kN (1,700 lb) thrust Rolls-Royce Welland I turbojet engines, was used in action for the first time. At this early date the gas turbine was already proving a practical engine and would, very quickly, be developed to produce almost unbelievable power.

There was one other contributory factor which had great significance in the enormous post-war expansion of civil aviation: during the war years thousands and thousands of people had travelled by air as routine. They had learned that no longer

The eight-engined Bristol Brabazon airliner, designed to carry 100 passengers, was too advanced to gain sales interest.

was flying fit only for heroes; if transport aircraft were able to carry people from one side of the world to the other for military purposes, then most certainly they would be capable of carrying them around the world on more peaceful business. If air fares were low enough, they would also prove a wonderful means of speeding holiday travel.

End of the flying-boat era
It will be recalled that America had established the first transatlantic passenger services with Boeing flying-boats, and these were maintained throughout the war. Other nations, too, attempted to keep their civil routes open, and even Britain ensured that some long-range links with Commonwealth countries were operated throughout the war. These were really the last years of the flying-boat, for with the return to peace the long-range landplane transport aircraft, which had spanned the

world in military service, were converted hastily for civil use. Suitable airfields, with all essential services, had been built all over the world for the operation of such aircraft, and it made good sense to continue to use these aeroplanes, with which air and ground crews were familiar, for the carriage of fare-paying passengers.

America, which had concentrated on producing long-range bombing and transport aircraft during the war, was in a strong position to supply the needs of civil airlines which would soon be clamouring for passenger and cargo transport aircraft. This factor, plus the pre-war lead they had gained in this field due to the excellence of civil airliners produced by the Boeing and Douglas companies, was to ensure for the United States a lead in this field of aviation which they have retained to this day.

Britain had been aware during the war years that a return to peace would mean a struggle for the British builders and

operators of civil aircraft, and had endeavoured to establish guidelines by means of the Brabazon Committee of 1942/43, which had the task of drawing up plans for the development and construction programmes that would be initiated with a return to peace. The speed of development and innovative progress was such that it was not possible for that Committee to forecast with complete accuracy the post-war needs of civil aviation. As a single example, the Saunders Roe Princess flying-boat, developed as a Brabazon recommendation, was born into a world which no longer needed such aircraft. Perhaps the most important work of this Committee was to encourage designers and manufacturers to take a brief look into the future. If it had done no more than recommend that designer/manufacturers should examine the possibilities of the gas turbine engine, the Brabazon Committee would have been well worthwhile.

In the immediate post-war years, the first generation of airliners were developed from wartime aircraft: the Boeing Stratocruiser (*left*) owed its origin to the B-29. De Havilland in Britain built a new airliner to utilise the newly-emerging and powerful gas turbine engine, the Comet 1. When this failed in service a new Comet 4 (*below*) emerged.

First post-war airliners

So, in the first post-war stage, quick conversions or derivations of wartime bombers served the airlines until the first generation of new aircraft appeared. Thus, in Britain, the Wellington led to the 21/27-seat Vickers Viking, and aircraft such as the Lancastrian, York and Tudor were all members of the Lancaster family. In America, an interim airliner, which evolved from the Boeing B-29 Superfortress, was to prove of great importance when put to work on the North Atlantic route in 1949. This was the Boeing Model 377 Stratocruiser, powered by four 2,610 kW (3,500 hp) Pratt & Whitney radial engines to provide a maximum speed of about 560 km/h (350 mph) and range of up to 6,400 km (4,000 miles). It was followed by aircraft such as the Douglas DC-6 and DC-7, Lockheed L.1049 Super Constellation and L.1649 Starliner. The DC-7C Seven Seas and L.1649A Starliner represented the piston-engined airliner at the peak of its evolution.

In Britain, new-generation airliners were being developed around the gas turbine engine, in the construction of which power plants this nation then held a considerable lead. First to appear was the Vickers Viscount, the Type 630 prototype of which flew for the first time on 16 July 1948. It had a pressurised cabin to accommodate 32 passengers, and its four 1,029 kW (1,380 hp) Rolls-Royce Dart gas turbine engines each had a reduction-gear drive to a four-blade constant-speed propeller. This type of engine, known as a turboprop, is beautifully smooth in operation, the power unit being devoid of reciprocating components. The expanding gases produced for combustion drive the turbine, and it in turn powers the compressor section of the engine and drives the reduction gear. For speeds up to about 560 km/h (350 mph), such a power plant is more fuel-efficient than a pure jet (turbojet) engine. The Viscount 700 which evolved from the 630 prototype was an immediate success, with accommodation for 47–60 passengers, and a total of 445 were built.

First turbojet airliners

Also in Britain, at about this same time, the de Havilland company were completing the construction of an aircraft to utilise turbojet power plants. This was the Comet 1, the prototype of this flying for the first time on 27 July 1949. The Comet inaugurated the world's first jet airliner service, operated by BOAC on 2 May 1952, on its London–Johannesburg route; soon these aircraft were speeding also between London–Singapore, London–Tokyo, and in all cases cutting previous scheduled flight-times in half. There was every reason to believe that British manufacturers were in a position to gain a substantial share of the world market for airliners.

Then came disaster, when three Comets disintegrated in flight. Subsequent investigation showed that metal fatigue was responsible for the structural failure, information which enabled aircraft manufacturers across the globe to initiate new fail-safe methods of construction. By the time that de Havilland had incorporated such features into a new Comet 4, Britain had lost its lead in these new-generation airliner types, and has never regained it.

In America, the Boeing company had been busy during this period with the design and construction of a turbojet airliner, and the prototype of this flew successfully for the first time on 15 July 1954. This was the Boeing 367–80, known as the Dash Eighty to all the Boeing family of workers, and known to the world as the superb Boeing 707, of which (together with the similar Model 720) well over 900 have been delivered to airlines all over the world.

From this basic design Boeing have since evolved the short/medium-range 727 with three engines, and short-range 737 with two engines, of which nearly 1,500 and over 500 have been ordered respectively. From McDonnell Douglas has come the DC-8, and Britain attempted, unsuccessfully, to join this big league with the introduction of the Vickers VC10 in April 1964, and larger (163-seat) Super VC10 which went into service a year later.

McDonnell Douglas in America and

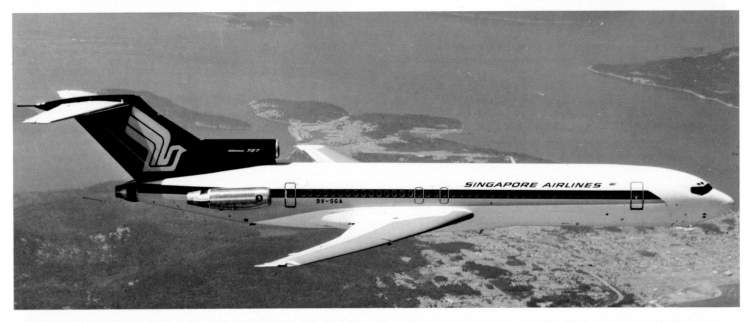

The failure of the Comet 1 was due to metal fatigue. From the investigation of this problem manufacturers learned to build new fail-safe structures. Boeing produced the superb Model 707 (*top left*) which serves with airlines all over the world, and evolved a relates series of airliners such as the Model 727 (*centre left*). The Model 747 (*bottom left*) was the world's first wide-body jet, since followed by such aircraft as the Lockheed TriStar, McDonnell Douglas DC-10 (*right*), and the slightly smaller A300B Airbus (*below*) developed by a consortium of European aerospace manufacturers. A long-range version of this last aircraft is now in service.

the British Aircraft Corporation have competed in fulfilling a requirement below that of the foregoing categories, with the introduction of the Douglas DC-9 in 1965 which had accommodation for 80 passengers. BAC's equivalent was the 89-seat One-Eleven, but this latter company has achieved sales of only about one quarter of the nearly 900 DC-9s sold by McDonnell Douglas. Fokker-VFW in the Netherlands has also produced a successful aircraft in a similar category, the 65–85 seat F.28 Fellowship, which entered service first with Braathens SAFE, in Norway, in March 1969.

Russia's national airline, Aeroflot, has followed a similar pattern of development of its civil routes in the post-war years. Ilyushin Il-12 and Il-14 aircraft carried the bulk of air traffic until 1956, when the nation's first jet airliner, the Tupolev Tu-104, entered service on 15 September of

that year. It revolutionised air travel in the Soviet Union, offering immense reductions in route times. As in the West, Russian designers have shown interest in the development of turboprop-powered aircraft, attracted by their economical operation, and large numbers of Ilyushin Il-18s have been built. And in the same way that manufacturers like Boeing have evolved a family of long-, medium/short- and short-range aircraft, the Tupolev design bureau have followed a similar pattern with the Tu-114, -124, -134 and -154; similarly, the Antonov bureau have produced a family of civil aircraft for use by Aeroflot.

One trend of more recent years has been brought into being as a result of the enormous cost of designing, developing and producing a completely new aircraft from scratch. This has prompted international collaboration to share the cost, and despite the difficulties caused by varia-

tions in language and temperament, it has proved a successful plan, fusing together the best thoughts, ideas and designs of a variety of minds, with different approaches to any specific problem. In the field of civil aircraft, international collaborations have produced such aeroplanes as the technically successful Anglo/French Concorde supersonic transport, and the superb Airbus Industrie wide-body Airbus.

Supersonic transport aircraft

The development of the supersonic civil transport began with agreement between the British and French governments, and between BAC and Sud-Aviation, in November 1962, to collaborate in the development of such an aeroplane. Construction of the first two prototypes began in 1965, the year in which a model of a Soviet supersonic transport, the Tupolev

The ultimate in civil transport at one time appeared to be an airliner that could carry passengers at supersonic speed. The Anglo/French Concorde (*below*) and Soviet Tupolev Tu-144 (*bottom*) are both in service, halving block times by comparison with subsonic turbine powered airliners but proving less economic in operation.

Tu-144, was shown at the Paris Salon. Subsequently, on 1 May 1967, the US Federal Aviation Administration signed a contract with The Boeing Company for the construction of two Boeing 2707 SST prototypes. The American project was cancelled by the US Senate in 1971, by which time the Tu-144 and first Concorde prototype had flown, on 31 December 1968 and 2 March 1969 respectively. On 21 January 1976 Concorde aircraft of Air France and British Airways inaugurated the world's first supersonic passenger services, but the Tupolev Tu-144 had been the first to fly commercially, on 26 December 1975, carrying airmail and freight.

The wide-body transport

Wide-body civil transport aircraft originated in the United States, and an announcement in April 1966 gave the news that Boeing had received a contract for 25 Model 747s for Pan American World Airways. Few then appreciated just what the 747 was all about, but as it became known that its wing spanned 59·64 m (195 ft 8 in), that its 57 m (187 ft) long cabin was 6·13 m (20 ft 1½ in) wide and 2·54 m (8 ft

Large airliners and stylish jet fighters capture our attention, but vast numbers of less exciting general aviation aircraft are important to our everyday life. The DHC Twin Otter (*below*) can provide air services in remote areas; the Taylorcraft Topper (*bottom*) does an equally important job of crop dusting, or spreading fertilizers to boost crop production.

4 in) high, and that it could accommodate up to 500 passengers, the media dubbed it immediately the 'Jumbo Jet'—a name which has stuck.

First entering service on Pan Am's New York–London route on 22 January 1970, well over 300 of these aircraft have since been delivered. They have been followed into service by the McDonnell Douglas DC-10 (5 August 1971), which can seat 380 passengers, the Lockheed TriStar (15 April 1972), which accommodates a maximum of 400 passengers, and the internationally-built Airbus A300 (23 May 1974) which has a seating capacity of 336 passengers.

This latter aircraft, Europe's first widebody jet transport, has been built and developed by Aérospatiale of France, Deutsche Airbus (MBB and VFW-Fokker) of Germany, Fokker-VFW of the Netherlands, CASA of Spain and Hawker-Siddeley Aviation (now British Aerospace) in the United Kingdom.

General aviation

But aviation is made up of so much more than civil transports, whatever the size of aircraft. General aviation can be regarded

as covering all other aspects of civil flying, and this field has expanded enormously since the war. The 'Big Three' in America, Beechcraft, Cessna and Piper, have collectively built more than a quarter of a million aircraft, the greater percentage of these since 1946, with a predominance of light planes. Beech, for example, has built more than 10,000 examples of its 4/5-seat Model 35 Bonanza; Cessna has produced more than 23,000 two-seat Model 150s; Piper has built more than 40,000 of the

two-seat PA-18 Cub and its predecessors.

In America, the Experimental Aircraft Association has fostered the development of home-built aircraft, helping its members to achieve for themselves the dream of flight. Thousands of these aircraft have been constructed all over the world, some of them of advanced design, some subsequently even becoming production aircraft, but most showing in their standards of construction a loving care that would have gladdened the hearts of the pioneers.

One of the 'impossible' dreams of flight became reality in 1977, when Dr. Paul McCready's Gossamer Condor man-powered aircraft (*left*) recorded a first flight. And it is equally satisfying, in this age of noise, to see an airship such as the Goodyear *Europa* (*bottom left*) making its way serenely through the summer sky.

Rotary-wing aircraft

Designers had attempted from the earliest days of powered flight to build aircraft which could take-off and land vertically. Thus have developed rotary-wing aircraft, important work on the rotating wing being carried out initially by the Spaniard Juan de la Cierva, who designed the first successful autogiro. But it was not until the immediate post-war years that really practical helicopters evolved, developing as rugged and reliable vehicles during the Korean War.

Since that time, such aircraft have, perhaps, come nearest to satisfying the aims of the pioneers, for they have demonstrated a remarkable capability to assist as search and rescue aircraft in both man-made and natural disasters. They carry sick and injured persons from places which are inaccessible for any other form of transport; they dust crops, spread insecticides and fertilisers, rescue the foolhardy, help in construction and logging, simplify the inspection of power lines and pipework, fight forest fires, and help the conservation of our habitat in many ways.

Back into history

More recently, yet harking backwards into aviation history, has come the new sport of hang-gliding, following development of the Rogallo flexible wing and even more efficient Jalbert Parafoil. All over the world young people have been building and flying hang-gliders as an exhilarating sport, perhaps unaware that they are emulating the pioneers who provided the final stimulus for the achievement of powered flight.

An even more exciting event, and one which would have been regarded as a miracle by the pioneers, was the achievement of Dr. Paul McCready in America during 1977. Taking off at Shafter, California, on 23 August, his Gossamer Condor aircraft, powered and controlled by racing cyclist Bryan Allen, was flown in a figure-of-eight around two pylons 0·8 km (0·5 mile) apart. This was the first significant man-powered flight, and won for Paul McCready the £50,000 Kremer Prize which had been so long in finding a home.

One step further back was achieved on 7 January 1973, when Cameron Balloons in Britain flew the world's first hot-air airship. Once again airships have begun to appear in the skies, with examples built in Australia, Britain, Germany, and Japan, as well as the excellent non-rigid helium-filled dirigibles (or 'blimps') built in the

No aviation history, however brief, could end without at least one glimpse into the future. We have not mentioned man's exploration into space. The Space Shuttle orbiter *Enterprise* (*above*) represents a culmination of aerospace technology, being designed to fly in space and the atmosphere.

USA by the Goodyear Tire and Rubber Company, which has produced more airships than any other company in the world—a total of 301.

Hydrogen-filled balloons can still be seen taking part in sporting events, but the summer skies of today are often dotted with the brightly coloured hot-air balloons which take this brief history back to the brothers Montgolfier and Father Bartolomeu de Gusmão.

The somewhat sophisticated controllable kites which have captured the enthusiasm of thousands of youngsters are, perhaps, too representative of modern technology to carry our thoughts back to the beginning of heavier-than-air flight in China many centuries ago. It is the plastic kite, printed with coloured birds and dragons, which links the ages; a modern version of an ancient invention reminding us of the 2,000 years of development which have made possible the brilliant achievements of modern aviation.

AAC/USA

American Aviation Corporation; formed in 1964 to develop and manufacture the AA-1 Yankee side-by-side two-seat monoplane (formerly called Bede BD-1) using aluminium honeycomb fuselage construction and metal-to-metal bonding throughout. Also produced a trainer version (American Trainer) and a four seater (American Traveler).

AACHENER SEGELFLUGZEUGBAU GmbH/Germany

In 1920 Aachen Flugzeugbau was successful with gliders built to the designs of Prof. Klemperer. In 1921 the name was changed and in 1923 the K. F. glider-related light aeroplane (also a Klemperer design) was in production. In 1924 a two-seat low-wing monoplane was also flown.

AAMSA/Mexico

Aeronáutica Agrícola Mexicana SA was formed in 1971, after agreement between Rockwell International (USA) and Industrias Unidas SA of Mexico to take over manufacture of Quail Commander and Sparrow Commander agricultural monoplanes. The Sparrow programme is finished, and the Quail Commander (a more powerful development with larger hopper) currently built as AAMSA Quail.

ABBOTTS-BAYNES AIRCRAFT LTD./UK

see Carden-Baynes Aircraft Ltd.

ABRAMS AIRCRAFT CORPORATION/USA

Formed in 1937 to build the Explorer twin-boom pusher monoplane to the design of Talbert Abrams, president of the Abrams Aerial Survey Corp.

ACAZ/Belgium

Ateliers de Constructions Aéronautiques Zeebrugge was formed after WW1. Built in 1924–1925 the T.2 light two-seat cabin monoplane, largely of duralumin, with cantilever wing and low-drag undercarriage. Began construction of a two-seat fighter in 1926.

ACME AIRCRAFT CORPORATION/USA

Established in 1928 to build light rigidly-braced sporting biplanes.

ACME/USA

Air Craft Marine Engineering Company, formed in Los Angeles, California, in September 1954 to build a prototype of the Anser four-seat twin-jet amphibian.

ADAM/France

Etablissements Aéronautiques R. Adam, specialists in light aircraft, which were built in small numbers during the early 1950s. R.A.14 and 15 were side-by-side two-seaters; R.A. 17 an agricultural derivative. R.A.14 intended for amateur construction, but also delivered complete.

ADC AIRCRAFT LTD./UK

Formed March 1920 to take over from His Majesty's Disposals Board surplus aircraft not required for use by the diminishing RAF. Value of stock about £100 million, stored in six depots, main one at Waddon Aerodrome, Croydon, Surrey. Specimen aircraft demonstrated in many parts of the world, and drawing office formed under J. Kenworthy, formerly with Austin and Westland. Many modifica-

AAMSA Quail (formerly Quail Commander) agricultural aircraft

Adam R.A. 14 two-seat lightweight sporting aircraft

tions (e.g. Lamblin radiators) made on standard military types, notably Martinsyde F.4, which was developed later as the ADC 1 with Armstrong Siddeley Jaguar radial engine. Eight of this type sold to Latvia in 1926, in which year Nimbus Martinsyde (with ADC Nimbus engine) appeared. Ceased trading 1930.

ADLERWERKE GmbH/*Germany*

Formed in 1934 at Frankfurt as Adlerwerke vorm. Heinrich Kleyer AG, to take over Frankfurter Flugzeugbau Max Gerner GmbH (*q.v.*). First product was the Adler G.IIR light two-seat biplane (formerly Gerner G.IIR).

ADVANCE AIRCRAFT COMPANY/*USA*
see Waco Aircraft Company

AEG/*Germany*

Allgemeine Elektrizität Gesellschaft; the Flugtechnische Abteilung of this great electrical company built its first aircraft in 1910, and soon established a flying school. Early designs included a Wright-type biplane, a monoplane, flying-boat and floatplane, but the Z 6 (B 1) biplane of 1914 was the first type built in quantity, and introduced the company's characteristic steel-tube construction. Also in

Aerial Distributors DW-1 Distributor Wing agricultural aircraft

1914 came the Z 9 (B II) which saw limited war service, though less than the later C II-C IV types. By far the most notable products were the twin-engined G I-G IV, relatively small three-seat multi-purpose aircraft, for tactical rather than strategic use. Best known was the G IV (in service late 1916); G V was a larger three-bay design, entering service 1918. Production of G series totalled 542, 50 G IVs being used for night bombing behind Allied lines in August 1918. Other wartime types (experimental) included single-seaters and 'Giants'. J II civil cabin biplane built 1918 had a two-seat cabin in place of the gunner's position, as well as a door and steps. The company made other contributions to the development of German airlines, and the G V was converted for service with Deutsche Luft-Reederei.

AERAUTO SA/*Italy*
Formed shortly before WW2 to build two-seat roadable monoplane.

AERIAL DISTRIBUTORS INC./*USA*
In the early 1970s was developing Distributor Wing monoplane, prototype of which had flown in 1965. Agricultural equipment was an integral part of the aircraft; power for spraying and dusting by a separate engine.

AERIAL SERVICE CORPORATION/*USA*
Formed 1920. Built Mercury night-mail biplane with Liberty engine, an unusual inverted sesquiplane configuration.

AERITALIA SpA/*Italy*
Formed 12 November 1969 by equal shareholding of Fiat and IRI-Finmeccanica to combine Fiat aerospace activities (except engines) and those of Aerfer and Salmoiraghi. Fully operational January 1972. In September 1976 IRI-Finmeccanica bought Aeritalia stock owned by Fiat. Has co-operation agreement with Boeing. Comprises Combat Aircraft, Transport Aircraft, and Diversified Activities Groups. Main products: Aeritalia G91Y twin-

Left: **Aeritalia F-104S, Italian-built version of the Lockheed Starfighter.** *Below:* **Aeritalia G222 twin-turboprop general-purpose military transport**

jet development of very successful single-jet Fiat G91; Aeritalia G222 twin-turboprop high-wing transport; Aeritalia (Lockheed) F-104S serving with Italian and Turkish Air Forces. As Panavia partner, designed and developed variable-geometry wing and other important features of Tornado multi-role aircraft.

Aero Boero 180 three-seat lightweight cabin monoplane

Aerocar Model I, Moulton Taylor's practical roadable aircraft

Aero Commander Model 500, typical high-wing executive transport

Aero Commander 200, developed from Meyers 200B light aircraft

AERMACCHI/*Italy*
see Macchi

AERO BOERO/*Argentina*
Aero Talleres Boero SRL is based at Córdoba. Aero Boero 95 (March 1959) was a development of the Piper Cub—a three-seater made in several versions over several years. The 180 was originally a four-seater, later a three-seater. Current range is 150 RV, 180 RV and RVR, 150 Ag, 180 Ag and 260 Ag. Last named is a low-wing agricultural aircraft, which was first flown in prototype form 23 December 1972, and which in 1977 was being developed for production.

AEROCAR INC./*USA*
From February 1948 had under development a flying automobile designed by M. B. Taylor. Prototype completed October 1949. Aerocar Model I, with Lycoming O-320 engine, used for tests which led to FAA Airworthiness Certification of the Aerocar on 13 December 1956. Extensive development undertaken to enhance flight and road performance. Accumulated road travel on six Aerocars exceeds 321,865 km (200,000 miles) and more than 5,000 flying hours. Other light aircraft made, including Coot and Sooper-Coot flying-boats. Kawasaki motor-cycle engine developed for aircraft.

AERO COMMANDER INC./*USA*
Formed in 1944 in Culver City, California, as Aero Design and Engineering Company (*q.v.*). Associated particularly with fast twin-engined monoplanes, mainly for executive use. Entered general aviation 1952 with Aero Commander 520, though produced other types (e.g. Snow and Call Air) under own company name. By summer 1962 production of all types totalled 1,200. After North American Rockwell Standard merger in 1967, single-engined and twin-engined types continued in development. Single-engined Model 112 delivered to customers from 1972. Low-wing twin-engined Rockwell Commander 700 being produced jointly with Fuji in Japan. Thrush Commander was very notable specially-designed agricultur-

al aircraft. The entire Thrush Commander range were sold to Ayres Corp and then became known by the Ayres name. The Shrike Commander 500S continues the 'high-wing twin' tradition.

AERO-CRAFT MANUFACTURING COMPANY/*USA*

The firm was established at Detroit, Michigan, in 1928, and exhibited its first product (the 3-seat Aero Coupe) at the 1928 Detroit Aero Show.

AERO DESIGN & ENGINEERING/*USA*

Formed in 1944 to build Aero Commander twin-engined high-wing light transport monoplane. Aero Commander 520 certificated 30 January 1952. Succeeded by Model 560 in 1954. Aero Commander 680 Super in production in late 1955. Various models supplied to US Army as L-26, and by 1957 more than 550 Aero Commanders of several models in worldwide service. The company merged in 1967 with North American Rockwell Standard and the new combine was known as Aero Commander Inc. (*q.v.*).

AERO-DIFUSIÓN SL/*Spain*

Registered as a company at Santander to manufacture, overhaul and repair aircraft. As an experiment in 1954 built a Jodel lightplane; under name Popuplane made licence-built versions of Jodel D.112 and D.119, and under new management made a refined version of the Aero-Difusión Jodel D.1190S, which was called the Compostela.

AERO-FLIGHT AIRCRAFT/*USA*

In late 1940s built Streak two-seat monoplane and derivatives. Metal construction and slotted flaps were features. Three models built were all fast, though low-powered.

AERO INDUSTRY DEVELOPMENT CENTRE/*Taiwan*
see AIDC

AEROMARINE KLEMM CORPORATION/*USA*

Formed 1928 as a component of Aeromarine Plane & Motor Co. Inc. to make German-designed Klemm low-wing monoplanes, under licence granted to the new company in New York City. US-built Le Blond engines fitted. Model AKL-26 had 60–153 km/h (37–95 mph) speed range. Sales inhibited by economic depression 1930–1931.

AEROMARINE PLANE & MOTOR CO. INC./*USA*

Established before WW1 at Keyport, NJ. In 1917 received from US Navy largest single order for aircraft then placed by that Service: 50 Model 39-A and 150 Model 39-B biplane trainers (wheel or float undercarriage). Model 700 served for early torpedo-dropping tests. Two 39-B used for deck-landing experiments.

Type also made first landing (1922) on US Navy's first carrier (USS *Langley*). AS-1 and 2 were fighters, but more important were company's flying-boats (200 Model 40F ordered 1918). After the war, converted D.H.4s, built 25 Martin bombers (completed winter 1923/24) and undertook flying-boat conversions for civil use, thus making significant contributions to commercial flying (e.g., New York–Atlantic City service 1919). Two F-5Ls (Aeromarine Model 75) with accommodation for twelve passengers used on Key West–Havana run until 1923, when air mail subsidies withdrawn. In 1923 built metal-hulled flying-boat and biplane mail-carrier. PG-1 low-level fighter completed by Boeing.

AEROMERE SpA/*USA*

Based at Trento in 1950s. Acquired from Aviamilano licence for Falco series (F.8 Falco, designed by Stelio Frati, was first flown in June 1955). Falco was noted internationally for high performance on low power, due to smooth wooden construction and aerodynamic refinement. Company became Laverda SpA.

Aero Difusión D.119 Popuplane, a licence-built Jodel design

Aeromarine flying-boat, typical of such aircraft in the 1920s

AERONASA/*Spain*

Constructora Aeronaval de Levante SA, established factory in Castellon de la Plana, near Valencia. Licence-builder in early/middle 1960s of Piel Emeraude French light aircraft.

**AERONÁUTICA AGRICOLA
MEXICANA SA**/*Mexico*
see AAMSA

AERONÀUTICA ANSALDO SA/*Italy*
see Ansaldo

AERONÀUTICA D'ITALIA/*Italy*

Aeronàutica d'Italia SA was the aeronautical branch of Fiat, occupying the factories of the old Ansaldo company which it had absorbed by the 1920s, although the Ansaldo name was still used. For this company and the Società Italiano Aviazione the name Fiat (or Fiat-Aviazione, or Fiat-Divisione Aviazione) was used after 1924. For an outline of development of Fiat types see under *Fiat*.

AERONÁUTICA INDUSTRIAL SA/*Spain*
see AISA

**AERONÁUTICA MILITAR
ESPAÑOLA**/*Spain*

Established at Cuatro Vientos, near Madrid, headquarters of the Spanish Military Air Service. Had its own workshops and laboratory and before 1931 was said to have produced several types of aircraft.

**AERONAUTICAL CORPORATION OF
AMERICA**/*USA*

Incorporated November 1928 at Cincinnati, Ohio. Famous for Aeronca series of high-wing wire-braced monoplanes. These had two-cylinder engines of Aeronca design, or those of other manufacturers, and despite low power these aircraft were sometimes fitted with Edo floats. Original landplane model had empty weight of only 180 kg (398 lb). C-2 and C-3 series well known in 1930s, and C-2 held many class records. Refinement of C-3 continued through early 1930s. Also built low-wing cantilever type Model L, or C-70 from 1935. Flight of 16,093 km (10,000 miles) in early-model Aeronca (Peterborough, England to Johannesburg, South Africa in 130 hr flying time) proved dependability of very light aircraft and supported company claim to have built and marketed first aeroplane of this class in USA. Name Aeronca also used for strut-braced Scout and Chief series of high-wing monoplanes built in late 1930s.

**AERONAUTICAL CORPORATION OF
GREAT BRITAIN LTD.**/*UK*

Registered in London to build Aeronca light monoplanes developed by Aeronautical Corporation of America (*q.v.*). Based at Peterborough in the mid-1930s, its output was small. Used Aeronca engines built in England as Aeronca JAP (J. A. Prestwich, also builders of motor-cycle engines). Chairman was H. V. Roe, who with his brother A. V. Roe had founded A. V. Roe & Co. Ltd. 1913. Pending production of British model called Aeronca 100, 16 American-built C-3 airframes assembled at Hanworth, London.

**AERONAUTICAL PRODUCTS
INC.**/*USA*

Formed in Detroit, Michigan, in 1935. In 1942 began development of cheap helicopter. First flown April 1944. Improved type (A-3) tested 1945. Both had nose-mounted engines.

**AERONAUTICAL RESEARCH &
DEVELOPMENT CORPORATION**/*USA*
see ARDC

**AERONAUTICAL SYNDICATE
LTD.**/*UK*

Formed June 1909 by pioneer Horatio Barber (1875–1964). After building an unsuccessful tractor monoplane the Syndicate became identified with the Valkyrie series of canard (pusher) monoplanes. From Salisbury Plain, Wilts., moved its scene of operations, in September 1910, to Hendon Aerodrome, London, leasing three of the eight hangars belonging to the Blériot Company. On 4 July 1911 the Valkyrie B was used to transport the first air-cargo in Britain (a box of Osram lamps). Several Valkyrie canard pushers built. Not easy to fly, but used successfully for training. Early in 1912 twin-propeller Viking biplane built. This was the last of Barber's designs, for in April 1912 he retired as an active designer, after making a very substantial contribution to the early development and promotion of Hendon as an aeronautical centre.

AERONAUTICS INDIA LTD./*India*
see Hindustan Aeronautics Ltd.

**AERONAUTIC SUPPLY
COMPANY**/*USA*
see Benoist Aircraft Company

**AERONCA AIRCRAFT
CORPORATION**/*USA*

Incorporated originally as Aeronautical Corporation of America (*q.v.*), but name changed in 1941. Quantity production of Fairchild trainers and liaison aircraft ceased 1944, and for post-war production company developed new types. Also had licence for Erco 'two control' system. Champion two-seat strut-braced high-wing monoplane was particularly successful, and between 1946 and 1951 company built over 10,000 Champions and over 600 Army liaison derivatives. Champion production ended 1950. Many variations, including Chief (1947), Super Chief (1948). Arrow marked low-wing departure. Since 1950 company has been a sub-contractor, but towards the end of the 1960s undertook, in conjunction with American Jet Industries Inc. (*q.v.*), de-

Model L3, one of many lightplanes built by Aeronca during the 1920–1930s

Aeronca 65, a typical example of the company's high-wing design

Aero Resources Super J-2 autogyro

velopment of a light strike version of the Super Pinto, built originally as a jet primary trainer. In January 1978 entered an agreement to build the Fox-jet twin-turbofan light transport aircraft designed by Tony Team Industries Inc.

AERONOVA COSTRUZIONI AERONÀUTICHE/*Italy*

Established in the 1940s to manufacture a roadable monoplane designed by Ing. Pellarini. Designated Aeronova A.E.R.1, it was powered by a Lycoming flat-four engine, and the prototype made its first flight on 9 May 1948.

AERO RESOURCES INC./*USA*

This company assumed responsibility in 1974 for continued production of the J-2 gyroplane, designed by Mr. D. K. Jovanovich, and manufactured previously by McCulloch Aircraft Corporation (*q.v.*). It developed also an improved version, with 149 kW (200 hp) engine, designated Aero Resources Super J-2.

AERO SPACELINES INC./*USA*

Formed at Van Nuys, California, in 1961 for Boeing Stratocruiser and C-97 conversions. Built Pregnant Guppy, Super Guppy and Mini Guppy, with extremely deep high-capacity fuselage, intended initially for transportation of large rockets and spaceflight equipment.

Aero Spacelines Super Guppy transport

Pregnant Guppy, like Super Guppy (above), intended for transport of outsize equipment

AEROSPATIALE/France

Société Nationale Industrielle Aérospatiale was formed 1 January 1970 by French government decision, as a result of merger of Sud-Aviation, Nord-Aviation and SEREB. Thus became biggest aerospace company in Common Market on European Continent. Concorde supersonic transport developed in co-operation with British Aircraft Corporation Ltd.; A300 European Airbus in co-operation with Deutsche Airbus GmbH, Hawker Siddeley Aviation, VFW-Fokker and CASA; Transall turboprop-powered transport with MBB and VFW-Fokker. Aérospatiale products are N262 and Frégate high-wing light transports; Corvette turbofan-powered light transport. Light piston-engined aircraft produced through subsidiary Socata. Helicopter activities cover design and production of several types, including 5/6-seat Ecureuil, 10-seat Dauphin and Super Frelon (up to 37 seats). Agreements with Westland in UK cover joint development and production of Puma and Gazelle helicopters and Westland-designed Lynx. Agricultural version of well-established Rallye is being developed; also floatplane version. Main Aérospatiale organisation is divided between Aircraft, Helicopter, Tactical Missiles and Space and Ballistic Systems Divisions.

Aérospatiale SA 360 Dauphin helicopter

Aérospatiale SA 330 Puma

Aérospatiale Corvette multi-purpose twin-turbofan transport

AEROSTAR AIRCRAFT CORPORATION/USA

Formed 1 July 1970, following an agreement the previous November between Butler Aviation International Inc. and American Electronic Laboratories Inc., to acquire Mooney Aircraft Corp., which was a subsidiary of the latter organisation. The Aerostar Ranger was, in prototype form, the former Mooney Mark 21; Aerostar Chaparral was an updated version of the Super 21.

AERO TALLERES BOERO SRL/Argentina

see Aero Boero

AEROTEC/Brazil

Sociedade Aerotec Ltda, Engenharia Aeronáutica formed 1968. Designed and built Uirapuru which, as T-23, was ordered by Brazilian, Bolivian and Paraguayan air forces and civil flying clubs. In the Brazilian Air Force the T-23 succeeded the locally-built Dutch Fokker types. Aerotec also makes wings for EMBRAER Ipanema agricultural aircraft, starter pods and components.

AEROTECHNIK ENTWICKLUNG UND APPARATEBAU GmbH/Germany

In early 1960s began development of cheap, easy-to-fly helicopter, a prototype of which

Aerotécnica AC-14 light helicopter

Aerotec T-23 Uirapuru two-seat primary trainer

Aerotechnik WGM21 helicopter prototype

Aero L-39 two-seat basic and advanced jet trainer

was completed in 1968. Other single-seat models followed, but development of WGM22 two-seater ended mid-1970s.

AEROTÉCNICA SA/*Spain*
Formed to develop and build helicopters of French (Jean Cantinieau) design. Also licensed for Matra-Cantinieau production. Two prototypes of AC-12 built in Madrid by mid-1950s (first one flown July 1956) and a few delivered to Spanish Air Force. Type was unorthodox in layout and featured transmission and reduction gear on automobile principles. AC-14 development flew July 1957, but Aerotécnica organisation dissolved in 1962.

AERO TOVARNA LETADEL Dr. KABES/*Czechoslovakia*
Founded at Prague 1919. Owned originally by a lawyer, this company made accessories as well as building aircraft. Built copies of Austrian Phönix (Brandenburg) biplanes, but later developed own designs. A-11 and A-30 —both international record-breakers—were two-seat reconnaissance biplanes of 1920s and 1930s; A-34 was a light two-seater; A-35 a four-passenger monoplane; A-38 a nine-seat cabin biplane. By early 1930s company was making A100 two-seat multi-purpose aircraft and A102 fighter. Aero M.B.200 was French Marcel Bloch bomber, licence-built, and partly sub-contracted to Avia; Aero 204 was 8-passenger civil monoplane; a military development of this aircraft was designated Aero 304.

A fast medium bomber was tested in 1938, but war prevented its production.

AERO VODOCHODY NARODNI PODNIK/*Czechoslovakia*
Established 1 July 1953, perpetuating the old Czech name Aero. Since then has seven times received Red Banner award of the Ministry of Engineering and UVOS. Achieved technical distinction and international success 1963–1974, when major product—for several countries—was Delfin jet trainer (first flown April 1959; more than 3,000 built). Type succeeded in production in late 1972 by L-39, following its selection as standard jet trainer of all Warsaw Pact countries except Poland. L-39 forms part of training system, which comprises also special simulator, ejection training simulator and mobile automatic test equipment.

AESL/*New Zealand*
Aero Engine Services Ltd. was established in 1954 and until 1966 did engine repair and overhaul. Early 1967 acquired rights for Victa Airtourer, thenceforth produced as AESL Airtourer. Also made AESL Airtrainer two/three-seater. Amalgamated 1 April 1973 with Air Parts (NZ) Ltd. (*q.v.*) to form New Zealand Aerospace Industries Ltd.

AFIC (PTY) Ltd./*South Africa*
Formed 1967 to build developed version of Italian Partenavia P.64B, designated RSA 200. Production was suspended pending new arrangements for manufacturing facilities.

AGO-FLUGZEUGWERKE GmbH/*Germany*
Initials of Ago were those of Aerowerke Gustav Otto (founded 1912) but the name was first applied in 1911 to products of Aeroplanbau G. Otto and Alberti. Modified biplane of Gustav Otto (German aviation pioneer, 1883–1926) and developments of Farman design were early products, but in 1912/13 came a seaplane of original design, followed by other types. During 1915/16 developed three pusher reconnaissance types: C I, C II and C III with twin tail-booms, but showing high efficiency despite layout. C I caused a stir on introduction at the Western Front by reason of twin-boom design, for which Swiss engineer A. Haefeli (earlier with Farman) was responsible. C IV was tractor biplane with sharply tapered wings; about 70 in service 1917/18. Experimental types included seaplanes. Ago name disappeared until late 1930s, but during WW2 was again current for Ao 192 Kurier light twin-engined monoplane (built 1938).

AGOSTINI/*Italy*
Società Aeroplani Livio Agostini was founded by Livio Agostini and Adriano Mantelli. Products were marketed as Alaparma (*q.v.*).

AESL CT/4A two/three-seat Airtrainer

AFIC RSA 200 four-seat light monoplane

AGUSTA/*Italy*

Costruzioni Aeronàutiche Giovanni Agusta SpA. Foundations of the company were laid in 1907, when Giovanni Agusta built his first aeroplane. Several more built before WW1. Firm revived 1923, specialising in light aircraft. Ag.2 of 1927 was a small parasol monoplane; AZ-10 twin-engined civil transport of 1954 was designed by Filippo Zappata (noted for his work with CANT and Breda). After WW2 built fixed-wing four-seater. In 1952 Agusta was granted a licence to build Bell Model 47 helicopters. First Agusta-built example flew May 1954, and by end of 1976 over 1,200 were built before production ended. The company produces Bell Iroquois models as Agusta-Bell 204B and 205, twin-engined Model 212 and Model 206 Jet Ranger helicopter series. In 1967, under Sikorsky licence, production of

Agusta AZ-8 Zappata-designed four-engined civil transport

SH-3D helicopters began, and in 1974 production of HH-3F (S-61R). Together with Meridionali, SIAI-Marchetti and other Italian companies, Agusta is involved in production of the Boeing Vertol Chinook. Agusta-designed

helicopters include the twin-turboshaft A 109A eight-seater (flown 1971) and A 129 development. Agusta have evolved special 'pop-out' floats, stowed inside fuselage, and missile installations.

Agusta-Bell 204AS anti-submarine helicopter

Agusta-designed A 109 eight-seat helicopter

AICHI TOKEI DENKI KABUSHIKI KAISHA/*Japan*

Established 1899, but first built aeroplanes in 1920 and aero-engines in 1927. From 1920s essentially a supplier to the Japanese Navy, but built civil types also, including a mailplane for the Japan Air Transport Company. Had technical agreement with Heinkel in Germany and imported specimen aircraft, which they developed for Japanese Navy requirements. Resulting aircraft (D1A type of 1934) sank US gunboat *Panay* in 1937. Later D3A monoplane was perhaps the most famous of the company's types, duplicating German interest in dive-bombers. Code-named 'Val' by the Allies, this type attacked Pearl Harbor 7 December 1941, and was also successful against British warships in the Indian Ocean. H9A1 twin-engined flying-boat was built in numbers; also notably E16A reconnaissance floatplane;

B7A attack bomber; and the M6A catapult-launched submarine-borne bomber, intended to attack such targets as the lock gates of the Panama Canal.

AIDC/*Taiwan*

Aero Industry Development Centre, established 1 March 1969 in succession to Bureau of Aircraft Industry (set up in Nanking in 1946,

Aichi M6A1-K Nanzan (Southern Mountain) conversion trainer

Aichi D1A1, Type 94, carrier-based dive bomber

moved to Taiwan 1948). In 1968 a branch of the Bureau built the first Chinese-constructed PL-1A, a version of the US Pazmany PL-1. This type used extensively. In 1969 AIDC began production of Bell helicopters for Chinese Nationalist Army. Later undertook production of US Northrop Tiger II tactical fighter. In 1970 began development of T-CH-1 two-seat turboprop-powered trainer, of AIDC design. In 1972 began work on AIDC XC-2 twin-turboprop high-wing transport.

AIDC XT-CH-1A secondary trainer

AIR & SPACE
MANUFACTURING INC./USA
Produced in 1960s at Muncie, Indiana, a slightly modified version of Umbaugh light two-seat autogyro (developed 1957–1962). Promoted this as Air & Space Model 18-A. Total of 110 built by the end of 1965, and several exported.

Air & Space Model 18-A autogyro

AIRCO/UK
The Aircraft Manufacturing Company Ltd. was established by George Holt Thomas (1869–1929), a great promoter of flying in Britain, engaging (for instance) Louis Paulhan for exhibition flights. In 1911 Holt Thomas acquired British rights for Farman aeroplanes, and early in 1912 formed the above-named company. Wishing to establish the firm's own design department he secured, in 1914, the services of Geoffrey (later Sir Geoffrey) de Havilland, who had already achieved success at the Royal Aircraft Factory, Farnborough, Hants. Centred at Hendon, London, the new company made several types of notable military aircraft, more generally known by the prefix D.H. than the strictly correct Airco. These were the D.H.1 and 1A two-seat pushers; D.H.3 and 3A twin-engined pushers; D.H.4 two-seat tractor (representing, as a fast day-bomber, one of the greatest aeronautical advances of WW1); D.H.5 single-seat tractor with backward stagger; D.H.6 tractor trainer; D.H.9, an extensively developed D.H.4; D.H.9A, an even greater advance; D.H.10 and 10A, built in pusher and tractor forms (notably tractor); D.H.11 twin-engined bomber; and D.H.14 and 15 single-engined bombers. Early civil transport types were D.H.16 and D.H.18. Other companies controlled by Airco built flying-boats, aero-engines and airships. After

the war Holt Thomas founded Air Transport and Travel Ltd., and The Aircraft Manufacturing Co. was shut down, making way for de Havilland Aircraft Co. Ltd (q.v.). Airco name was temporarily revived January 1958 for production of D.H.121 jet transport.

Airco D.H.2 single-seat scout

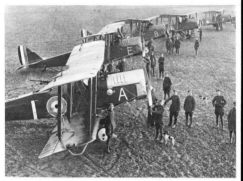

Airco D.H.4 two-seat day bomber

Airco D.H.9A, used extensively post-WW1 by RAF for air policing

AIRBUS INDUSTRIE/International
The company was established as a 'Groupement d'Intérêt Economique' to manage the development, manufacture and marketing of the A300 wide-bodied short/medium range twin-engined transport. A300B was first flown on 28 October 1972. Many developed versions were considered, and by February 1978 orders and options totalled 94. Six airframes were involved in the certification programme. Prime contractors are Aérospatiale (SNIAS) and Deutsche Airbus GmbH, while Hawker Siddeley has prime responsibility for wings (firm orders had been received for 100 sets by February 1978).

Airbus Industrie A300B2 (D-AIAB) in the insignia of Lufthansa

Air-Metal AM-C 111 STOL transport

AIRCRAFT DISPOSAL COMPANY LTD./*UK*
see ADC Aircraft Ltd.

AIRCRAFT INVESTMENT CORPORATION LTD./*UK*
Formed 1929 to deal in or build lighter- or heavier-than-air craft. Technical advisor Sir Henry Segrave, pilot and sportsman. This group had interests also in Saunders-Roe Ltd. and Blackburn Consolidated Ltd. (founded 1929). Segrave designed twin-engined Segrave Meteor 1, built by Saunders-Roe, known also as Saro Segrave Meteor 1, and flown in King's Cup Race 1930 by Major A. P. Holt. Segrave killed in Saro-built motor-boat during speed record attempt in 1930, but development of Meteor 1 continued by Blackburn.

AIRCRAFT MANUFACTURING COMPANY LTD./*UK*
see AIRCO

AIRCRAFT MANUFACTURING DEPOT/*Indian Air Force*
Took over hangars at Kanpur (Indian Air Force Station) when a decision was taken to build the Hawker Siddeley 748 as a Dakota replacement. First set of jigs set up at Depot by mid-1960 and first Indian-built 748 (delivered unassembled from England) flew 1 November 1961. Production of type continued, in addition to other work, including sailplanes. In June 1964 the Depot was incorporated in Aeronautics (India) Ltd., and later became Kanpur Division of Hindustan Aeronautics Ltd. (*q.v.*).

AIR CRAFT MARINE ENGINEERING COMPANY/*USA*
see ACME

AIRLIFTS INC./*USA*
see Cancargo Aircraft Manufacturing Co. Ltd.

AIRMARK LTD./*UK*
Formed early 1969. Acquired all rights to T.S.R.3 ultralight monoplane designed by Tom Storey in 1967. Also undertook development of US Cassutt Special racing monoplane, building three modified examples under the designation Airmark Cassutt 111M and offering construction kits.

AIR MECHANICS INC./*USA*
Revival of Alexander Aircraft Company (*q.v.*), partly by former employees. Conducted service department of Alexander products, and during the 1930s made D-1 and D-2 two-seater monoplanes of new design.

AIR-METAL FLUGZEUGBAU UND ENTWICKLUNGS GmbH & CO. KG/*Germany*
Formed early 1970s for production of STOL transport aircraft. Eight variants planned of this high-wing twin turboprop design, and prototype of AM-C111 version well advanced in 1976. Information available in early 1978 suggests company unable to proceed further with construction due to lack of finance.

AIR-MOD ENGINEERING COMPANY/*USA*
see Doyn Aircraft Inc.

AIR NAVIGATION & ENGINEERING CO. LTD./*UK*
see ANEC

AIR NOVA (Pty) LTD./*South Africa*
Formed to make Reed Falcon single-seat aerobatic biplane, developed from Rooivalk of the late 1960s. Also sales and service centres for Beechcraft and Piper aircraft and manufacture of special spraying equipment.

AIR PARTS (NZ) LTD./*New Zealand*
In 1957 acquired Australasian sales rights for Fletcher FU-24, and in 1964 acquired manufacturing rights. FU-24 had been designed initially for top-dressing work in New Zealand, to which country initial series of 100 was delivered. Several variants developed, including two turboprop versions. On 1 April 1973 the company was amalgamated with Aero Engine Services Ltd. (*see* AESL) to form New Zealand Aerospace Industries Ltd.

Airmark/Cassutt 111M US-designed racing monoplane

Air Parts Fletcher FU-24 agricultural aircraft

AIRPLANE DEVELOPMENT CORPORATION/USA

Subsidiary of the Cord Corporation. Founded in the early 1930s, its first product had the designation V-1 allocated by the designer, Gerald Vultee, who was for some years chief engineer of the Lockheed Aircraft Company. The V-1 was a clean-looking 8-seat commercial transport of low-wing monoplane configuration. Powered by a 522 kW (700 hp) Wright Cyclone, it had a maximum speed of 362 km/h (225 mph).

AIRSPEED LTD./UK

Founded February 1931 to build the Ferry 3-engined low-performance biplane, designed specifically for short-range pleasure flying ('joy riding'). Prototype Ferry, to Sir Alan Cobham's specification, went on tour with his National Aviation Day Displays 1932 and 1933; joined by second example 1932. In 1933 two more Ferries (four only built) acquired by John Sword of Midland and Scottish Air Ferries Ltd.

AIRSPEED (1934) LTD./UK

Established 1934 at The Airport, Portsmouth, Hants. in association with shipbuilding interests of Swan, Hunter and Wigham Richardson. Developed the single-engined Courier monoplane (first British aircraft with retractable undercarriage to go into production), sixteen built. The Envoy was an enlarged twin-engined development (50 built) and was developed into Oxford advanced trainer for RAF. By July 1945 8,751 Oxfords had been built by several makers. During 1946–1948 over 150 Oxfords converted to civil Consul, but most notable civil product (associated also with the Airspeed Division of the de Havilland Aircraft Co., of Christchurch Aerodrome, Hants.) was the Ambassador high-wing twin-engined airliner, mainly operated by British European Airways. Pre-war construction of Queen Wasp radio-controlled target aircraft and Fleet Shadower accentuated company's versatility. In 1950 the de Havilland D.H.115 Vampire Trainer was built by Airspeed.

Airspeed Ferry, in which many Britons experienced their first flight

Airspeed Ambassador, important post-WW2 transport of BEA

AIR TRACTOR INC./USA

Produces low-wing agricultural monoplane developed from Snow S-2B, designed in the 1950s. Founder Leland Snow is now Air Tractor president.

AIR TRANSPORT MANUFACTURING CO. LTD/USA

In 1938 built a three-engined high-wing six-seat aircraft, unusual in its class for the number of engines.

AISA's own-design GN autogyro

AISA Avion I-11B two-seat training or sporting monoplane

AISA/*Spain*

Aeronautica Industrial SA, engaged since 1923 on aircraft manufacture, repair and maintenance. In 1927 built some of earliest Cierva Autogiros, a type originated in Spain. H.M.1 and 5 trainers and H.M.9 glider tug built 1943; H.M.3 seaplane and H.M.7 cabin monoplane 1947; took over Aircraft Department of Iberavia SA (including helicopter designs); flew I-11 1953; built AVD-12 high-wing all-metal monoplane to designs of Emile Dewoitine mid-1950s. Tandem-seat trainer I-115 went into production for Spanish Air Force at same period; also I-11B tourer/trainer. Repair work has embraced several modern types of helicopter, while fixed-wing production continued with Italian-designed Siai-Marchetti four-seater. Rotary-wing work continues with AISA Autogyro GN, having jump take-off capability, which is scheduled to fly in 1979.

AJI Hustler Model 400 prototype

AJI/*USA*

American Jet Industries Inc., founded 1951; specialists in modification and repair of executive and transport aircraft, including large cargo types. Successful programme of Cessna turboprop conversions. In June 1968 first flew Super Pinto, a jet primary trainer or light strike aircraft developed from TT-1 Pinto built by Temco (*q.v.*). Co. Work also done on five-seat executive version. Under 1974 expansion programme, concentrated production facilities at Van Nuys Airport, California, building Hustler Model 400, a seven-seat business/utility monoplane with supercritical wing, conventional turboprop and 'standby' turbofan in rear fuselage. First flight 11 January 1978.

AJI Super Pinto jet

ALAPARMA SpA/*Italy*

Founded 1945 to develop A.M.6 twin-boom aircraft with engine of pusher configuration, first built 1942. To this formula made ultra-light A.M.8, also A.M.10 two-seater. A.M.75 Baldo was one of same series, all designed by Adriano Mantelli.

ALASKA INTERNATIONAL CORPORATION/*USA*

In 1962 acquired from Silvaire Aircraft Company (*q.v.*) all rights to the Luscombe Silvaire two-seat all-metal light aircraft.

ALBATROS FLUGZEUGWERKE GmbH/*Germany*

Established late 1909 at Berlin-Johannisthal by Dr. Walter Huth. Original name Pilot-Flugtechnische was only briefly retained. At first built biplanes and (under licence) French Antoinette monoplanes. From 1911 was building highly efficient biplanes and in 1912 turned attention also to marine aircraft. In 1912 and later, Hellmuth Hirth and others broke several records on Albatros landplanes. Development benefited from participation of Ernst Heinkel who, in 1913/14, designed large single-engined three-bay biplane, forerunner of numerous reconnaissance and multi-purpose types. C III of 1915 remained in service until early 1917, and was built by several other firms. Historic line of single-seat fighters began with D I and D II, in service 1916. D III (1917) was 'vee-strutter'; W 4 a single-seat fighter seaplane, less known than landplanes though 118 delivered to German Naval Air Service. Decline of Albatros land fighters was marked by company building Fokker D VII in 1918.

First civil aircraft was single-engined six-passenger L 58 high-wing cantilever monoplane of 1923; L 73 was twin-engined transport; L 75 was biplane trainer and L 79 a single-seat biplane with symmetrical wing-section specially developed for inverted flight. L 100 was low-wing monoplane; L 101 a parasol monoplane. One Albatros biplane was adapted for advanced research (water tanks for trim, cameras etc.). Aircraft manufacture ceased 1930. Company merged with Focke-Wulf 1930/31.

Left: Albatros C I two-seat general purpose biplane
Below: Albatros D III, one-time mount of Manfred von Richthofen

Allison Super Convair, turboprop conversion of Convair 580

ALBERT AÉRONAUTIQUE/*France*

Formed 1926 as Avions Albert to build Albert (licence Tellier-Duhamel) high-wing light monoplanes. Named as above, in early 1930s built A-61 and A-70 two-seat monoplanes and A-140 racer for 1933 Coupe Deutsch de la Meurthe, though this latter machine was not completed in time. Construction was of wood. A-20 of 1929 was a two-seat twin-engined aircraft.

ALCO/*USA*

Allison Airplane Company, established in 1920 to build a small single-seat high-wing monoplane known as the Alco Junior Coupe. Power plant was a single 30 kW (40 hp) Szekely 3-cylinder radial air-cooled engine.

ALEXANDER AIRCRAFT COMPANY/*USA*

Formed August 1925 at Colorado Springs, Colorado, as division of Alexander Industries Inc., then of Denver. Concentrated on Eaglerock three-seat civil biplane, with Curtiss OX-5 engine. When supplies of this cheap power plant exhausted (1928) redesigned aircraft for other engines. Eleven Eaglerock biplanes still registered in USA in 1960s. D-2 was two-seat strut-braced high-wing cabin monoplane. Low-wing Bullet series designated by firearm calibres (.22, .32, .45 etc.). Company succumbed to US financial depression, but continued manufacture as Air Mechanics Inc. (*q.v.*) and in 1934 designed a five-seat low-wing monoplane.

ALHAMBRA AIRPORT & AIR TRANSPORT COMPANY/*USA*

With Allan H. Lockheed as president built a new version of his Duo twin-engined monoplane. Type was called Alcor Duo-6 and was distinctive in having two Menasco engines placed horizontally. Though Alcor conformed

with Lockheed 'star names' system and development was pursued in 1930s no production resulted. Alcor was not a Lockheed Aircraft Corporation product.

ALLGEMEINE ELEKTRIZITÄT GESELLSCHAFT/*Germany*
see AEG

ALLIANCE AEROPLANE COMPANY LTD./*UK*

Founded in London During WW1 by Lord Waring, and built large assemblies for Handley Page bombers. Shortly after the war amalgamated with the British Aerial Transport Co. and British Nieuport & General Aircraft Co.; also with other smaller companies including Ruffey, Arnell & Baumann Aviation Co. With last-named company the Alliance P.1 biplane trainer originated. For trans-Atlantic attempt built (1919) a special biplane with 21-hour endurance, which was sometimes called

Alliance-Napier by reason of latter company's Lion engine; otherwise P.2 Seabird. A second example crashed attempting Australia flight.

ALLIANCE AIRCRAFT CORPORATION/*USA*

In late 1920s made Argo 3-seat biplane and Hess Warrior 7-cylinder radial engine of 86 kW (115 hp).

ALLIED AVIATION CORPORATION/*USA*

Organised January 1941 to make moulded-plywood aircraft structures. In 1943 built large amphibious glider for US Navy. Was developing in 1945 prototype of Allied Trimmer light twin-engined flying-boat amphibian. Manufacturing rights acquired by Commonwealth Aircraft Inc., Kansas City, Missouri.

ALLISON AIRPLANE COMPANY/*USA*
see Alco

ALLISON DIVISION OF GENERAL MOTORS/*USA*

Until May 1956, managed at Indianapolis, Indiana, Convair 580 conversion programme, then sub-contracted to Pacific Airmotive.

ALON INC./*USA*

Formed December 1963 by two former Beech officials. Acquired all assets of Aircoupe two-seater from former owners (city of Carlsbad, New Mexico) promoting improved version as Alon AirCoupe. Alon, of McPherson, Kansas, merged with Mooney Aircraft Corporation in October 1967.

Alon X-A4 prototype (foreground) and A-2 Aircoupe

ALPAVIA SA/*France*

Founded 1958 by Mm d'Assche and Noin. Made slightly modified Jodel D-117-A (two per month from January 1959). In 1962 partnership with René Fournier resulted in Avion-Planeur RF3 with Volkswagen engine.

ALPHA AVIATION COMPANY/*USA*

Established early 1970s to manufacture a re-engined and updated version of the Luscombe 11A Sedan under the designation Alpha 11D. Primary changes were the introduction of a fixed tricycle landing gear and provision of a 134 kW (180 hp) engine.

ALPHA JET/*International*

see Dassault-Breguet/Dornier

AMBROSINI/*Italy*

After incorporation of Società Aeronàutica Italiana with Ing. A. Ambrosini & Cie (Ambrosini was a pioneer pilot), specialised in fast tourers and sporting monoplanes, though SAI 1 was biplane. SAI 7 held speed record in its category. S.S.4 was experimental tail-first fighter. SAI 207 was light fighter, developed during war. Smooth wooden construction and very clean design gave high performance on low power (as in company's sporting types) and 2,000 were ordered, though only 13 completed, type being replaced for proposed production of SAI 403, work on which finished at war's end. Intended sub-contractors were Savoia-Marchetti and Caproni. In 1948 S 1001 Grifo broke more records. S 7 delivered in small numbers and developed into outstanding Super S 7 (1950s). F 7 Rondone was 3/4-seat cabin tourer.

AMERICAN AERONAUTICAL CORPORATION/*USA*

Formed at Long Island, New York, October 1928 to build two types of Savoia-Marchetti

Alpavia Avion-Planeur lightweight aircraft designed by M. Fournier

flying-boat. These comprised S-55, as mentioned under Società Idrovolanti Alta Italia (*q.v.*), and S-56 three-seat biplane amphibian, the latter having an American Kinner engine. In 1931 the Dayton Airplane Engine Co acquired a controlling interest in the company.

AMERICAN AIRCRAFT COMPANY/*USA*

Formed 1939 to take over Security Aircraft Corporation, including manufacturing rights for Security S1-B two-seat tourer/trainer, a number of which were in production in the summer of 1939.

AMERICAN AIRMOTIVE CORPORATION/*USA*

In the late 1950s built in quantity NA-75 agricultural aircraft, a development of Stearman

Model 75 (Boeing Kaydet). Alternatively offered new high-lift wings and special modification kits. In eight years more than 200 Stearmans were fitted with new wings, permitting loads of over 907 kg (2,000 lb).

AMERICAN AVIATION CORPORATION/*USA*

see AAC

AMERICAN EAGLE AIRCRAFT CORPORATION/*USA*

Established 1925 in Kansas City, with E. E. Porterfield as president. In 1926 built three-seat civil biplane with Curtiss OX-5 engine. Specially noted for American Eaglet light parasol monoplane—first two-seat light aeroplane to be granted Approval Type Certificate by US Department of Commerce. Several hundred Eaglets built before company sus-

Alpha Jet twin-turbofan close support aircraft

Ambrosini Super 7 lightplane, developed from earlier S 7

pended operations in 1930 economic depression. Later merged with Lincoln Aircraft Company Inc.

AMERICAN EAGLECRAFT COMPANY/*USA*

In 1942 revived American Eaglet light monoplane by building a new prototype. Tests postponed until after war. By end of February 1960 had built one Eaglet and was supplying plans for amateur builders. Company later sold to Mr. John Spach.

AMERICAN EAGLE-LINCOLN AIRCRAFT CORPORATION/*USA*

Established May 1931, in merger between American Eagle Aircraft Corp. and Lincoln Aircraft Co. In early 1930s built American Eaglet two-seat light parasol monoplane, which had particular success. Eagle-Lincoln P.T. biplane was a trainer and Eagle-Lincoln A.P. a three-seat cabin monoplane.

AMERICAN HELICOPTER COMPANY/*USA*

Incorporated July 1947 for research and development on XA-5 pulsejet-powered helicopter. Taken over April 1954 by Fairchild Engine & Airplane Corp. Work on the XH-26 pulsejet helicopter was terminated by US Government.

AMERICAN JET INDUSTRIES INC./*USA*
see AJI

AMIOT/*France*

Avions Amiot products were known formerly by SECM prefix, latterly as SECM-Amiot or, generally, Amiot, after founder Felix Amiot. Amalgamated 1929 with Avions Latham. Amiot 101 of late 1920s was monoplane fight-

er; Amiot 122 was three-seat single-engined bomber, of which about 20 built by 1934. Type served with French Air Force and in Brazil. Firm later concentrated on large all-metal multi-engined aircraft, using light-metal stampings, though well before 1940 introduced stressed-skin construction. In the 1930s works at Colombes and Caudebec were reconditioning several types of metal aircraft for French Government. Changes in structural techniques were matched by aerodynamic advances; thus Amiot 143, widely used by French Air Force in 1930s, attained less than 320 km/h (200 mph), whereas Amiot 350 series of 1940 were about 161 km/h (100 mph) faster. As Avions Amiot remained part of France's 'independent' industry.

AMPHIBIANS INC./*USA*

Based at Garden City, NY. Built Privateer light civil amphibian flying-boats, with braced monoplane wing and pusher engine, from 1932, with progressive improvements. Tail was carried on streamlined structure attached to hull.

ANAHUAC/*Mexico*

Fábrica de Aviones Anahuac SA established in the late 1960s to develop agricultural aircraft suited to national requirements. Prototype Tauro 300 first flew 3 December 1968. Improved Tauro 350 with more powerful radial engine (261 kW; 350 hp) was in production in 1977.

Amiot 354 mailplane, used by Vichy for North Africa service in WW2

Privateer amphibian flying-boat developed by Amphibians Inc

American Helicopter XH-26 had pulsejet-driven rotor

Anahuac Tauro 300 Mexican-developed agricultural aircraft

Anatra D two-seat reconnaissance biplane

Andreasson BA-4B lightweight single-seat biplane

ANATRA/*USSR*

Zavod A.A. (for Arturo Antonovich) Anatra founded Odessa 1913. Important during WW1, with factories at Odessa and Simferopol, Ukraine. By 1917 company was building own designs, plus Voisins and Nieuports, to a total monthly output of 80. Anatra VI (designed 1915) was essentially a developed Voisin; hence initial letters signifying 'Voisin Ivanov'. From March 1915 one year's output of VI type was intended to total about 150, though this quantity not completed until mid-1918. Anatra D was German Albatros derivative, with distinction of using rotary engine. Later DS had Salmson radial engine. Company activities ceased in early 1920s.

ANDERSON, GREENWOOD & COMPANY/*USA*

Originally incorporated 1941 for research into private-owner aircraft, but closed down and re-formed after war. Developed AG-14 light pusher monoplane of all-metal construction. First flight October 1947, but company completed only four production models before engaging in sub-contract work.

ANDREASSON, BJORN/*Sweden*

During 1950s designed several types of light aircraft, promoted under the designer's name in San Diego, California. Tiny BA-4B single-seat biplane was designed for amateur construction. Seventh design (BA-7) was better known as Bölkow Junior, and by April 1968 combined Swedish and German production was about 250. First of type had been flown in USA during 1958, then shipped to Sweden.

ANEC/*UK*

Air Navigation and Engineering Co. Ltd. formed at Addlestone, Surrey, as successor to the Blériot and Spad Aircraft Works, which had built Spads and had been awarded a contract for S.E.5a fighters, though name ANEC was associated with new civil aeroplanes. Three monoplanes (ANEC I, IA and II) designed by W. S. Shackleton, were among Britain's earliest ultra-light aircraft. ANEC IV Missel Thrush (designer J. Bewsher) was light biplane, but ANEC III was large single-engined transport biplane, to designs of G. H. Handasyde, who had no production facilities for his own Handasyde Aircraft Co. Ltd. First

ANEC III flown March 1926. Three of type contributed to development of aviation in Australia, two being converted to Larkin Lascowls, one of which was not retired until June 1932.

ANSALDO/*Italy*

Aeronàutica Ansaldo SA established late in WW1 by engineering and shipbuilding firm of Gio. Ansaldo (formed 1896). After the war a separate company was formed, named Società Anònima Aeronàutica, Turin, though title was variously rendered. Ansaldo achieved aeronautical eminence in 1917 by providing a single-seat fighter of original Italian design (Italy having previously used French types). Aircraft was A-1 Balilla. About 150 built; others, licence-built in Poland, served well into 1920s. S.V.A.5 was also a fighter, though more notable for fast reconnaissance flights and record-breaking, which had Warren-truss wing bracing, later characteristic of Fiat biplanes. Before Ansaldo merged completely with Fiat, in 1925, company built A.300 two/three-seat multi-purpose biplane, extensively produced and used. Hydrofoils fitted to a seaplane de-

Anderson Greenwood AG-14 all-metal twin-boom monoplane

ANEC I, one of the first ultra-light aircraft built in UK

Ansaldo A 400 utility biplane

Ansaldo S.V.A.5 Primo fighter

velopment of S.V.A.5 presaged later developments in UK and USA. Initials S.V. signified Savoia Verducci. Ansaldo/Fiat links were implicit in name Rosatelli. Pomilio name also linked by 1918 take-over.

ANT/*USSR*
Central Aero-Hydrodynamic Institute, Moscow. Founded by Bolshevik government 1 December 1918 under Professor N. E. Zhukovskii; based on Moscow Technical University's pre-Revolution research organisation. Departments for study of propellers, aero-engines, aeronautical construction materials, flight testing etc. Separate flight test centre for Soviet Air Force established 1920; alternative centres for aero-engines 1930 and materials 1932. Zhukovskii died 1921; succeeded by S. A. Chaplygin (1921–1941), N. I. Kharlamov, M. N. Shulzhenko and (since early 1960s) V. M. Myasischchev. New facility built 1931 at Stakhanov, Moscow; continued until 1939. Most aircraft designs prior to WW2 carried ANT designations (for details see under

Tupolev); other designers also employed, some eventually heading their own bureaux, e.g. Petlyakov and Sukhoi. Aircraft with TsAGI designations included Komta twin-engined 10-passenger triplane of 1922; 1-EA to 5-EA and A-4 to A-15 series of helicopters and autogyros from various designers between 1928–1940; and TsAGI-44 (MTB-2) four-engined flying-boat bomber, redesignated from ANT-44 after arrest of Tupolev in 1936.

After WW2 TsAGI became purely research centre and moved to new premises at Zhukovskaya, near Ramenskoye. New facilities since provided for new Hydrodynamic Institute at Novosibirsk.

ANTONI/*Italy*
Società Italiana Brevetti Antoni completed in 1923 an experimental aircraft with variable-camber wing to patents and designs of Ing. Guido Antoni. Firm was wound up shortly afterwards. Antoni, an inventor in several fields, was first associated with aviation in 1912.

ANTONOV/*USSR*
First aircraft designed by Oleg Konstantinovich Antonov (1924) was OKA-1 glider, followed 1926–1929 by OKA-3 to 7. Continued to build gliders during and after the war. In 1943 was working on Yakolev fighters, but fame rests on An-2 'workhorse' biplane of 1946. Type used for passenger, freight, exploration, ambulance and agricultural work; fitted with wheels, skis or floats and licence-built in several countries. Russian production of An-2 series ended in the mid-1960s after about 5,000 were built in USSR alone. An-3 is a turboprop development of same aircraft. An-12, a large four-turboprop high-wing transport, is essentially similar to the widely-used An-10, but with rear loading and refinements such as provision for special skis, with improved brakes, heating and air-conditioning. An-14 is a successful light twin-piston-engined transport. An-22 is an exceptionally large transport along general lines of An-12, but scaled up to have a span of 64·4 m (211 ft 4 in). The type set many payload-to-height records before production finished in 1974. An-24 is an extensively-used twin-turboprop transport; An-26 an An-24 development (both types in DC-3 replacement class). An-28 is a turboprop development in An-14 class; An-32 a development of An-26; An-40 may be a turbofan-powered replacement for An-22. An-72 STOL freighter was first flown in December 1977, and strongly resembles Boeing YC-14. Antonov is definitely in forefront of Soviet aircraft design, especially respecting STOL transports, one of his 'trademarks' being the anhedral angle on his big high-wing types.

Antonov An-22 ('Cock') long-range heavy transport

Antonov An-12 ('Cub') four-turboprop transport

AQUAFLIGHT INC./USA

Formed in 1946 to build Aqua twin-engined amphibian. Aqua I prototype tested in Philadelphia as a pure flying-boat; Aqua II tested as landplane also. As W-6 the type was developed for small-scale production.

ARADO FLUGZEUGWERKE

GmbH/Germany

In WW2 a manufacturer of great importance, largely in connection with production of aircraft for other companies, but also in the development and production of its own types. Originated in early 1917 with creation of Werfte Warnemünde der Flugzeugbaus Friedrichshafen as a subsidiary of Flugzeugbau Friedrichshafen GmbH. Aircraft work ceased in 1918, but the factory was acquired 1921 by Hugo Stinnes, and was briefly engaged in shipbuilding. In 1924 Walter Rethel (formerly with Kondor and Fokker) joined as designer, and Stinnes created a Yugoslav subsidiary named Ikarus (q.v.). Arado Handelsgesellschaft mbH established 1925. S I trainer biplane flown that year, followed by other trainers, SD II and III fighters and civil aircraft—notably VI of 1928 (high-wing transport) and L II light cabin monoplane. Walter Blume (formerly with Albatros) appointed chief engineer 1932; name Arado Flugzeugwerke adopted 4 March 1933. Ar 68 was Luftwaffe's first fighter; Ar 66 trainer also delivered in quantity. Notable designs thereafter were Ar 80 monoplane fighter; Ar 95 multi-purpose aircraft and torpedo-carrier; Ar 196 ship's catapult floatplane—extensively used in WW2; Ar 231 experimental submarine-borne monoplane; Ar 232 military transport, remarkable for unique multi-wheel landing gear, Ar 240 heavy fighter/light bomber; and—most significant of all—Ar 234 jet-propelled single-seater, built both with two and four turbojets and tested initially with jettisonable wheeled take-off trolley. Used for reconnaissance and bombing, the Ar 234 was the world's first jet bomber and the second jet-propelled aircraft to enter service.

ARCTIC AIRCRAFT COMPANY/USA

Established at Anchorage, Alaska to build and market as the S.1BE a strut-braced high-wing monoplane known as the Arctic Tern, a developed version of the Interstate S.1A, first flown in the 1950s.

ARDC/USA

Aeronautical Research & Development Corporation acquired all rights to Brantly helicopters from Lear Jet Industries in early 1969, then formed a Brantly Division. Promoted ARDC/Brantly Model B-2E. Five-seat Model 305 with engine of 227 kW (305 hp) first flew in 1964, but is also promoted as ARDC/Brantly type.

AREA DE MATERIAL

CÓRDOBA/Argentina

Established 10 October 1927 as Fábrica Militar de Aviones. In 1928 secured licence for Avro Gosport (British biplane trainer) and eventually made 33 for Argentine Air Force. In 1931 made to original designs the first of a number of light single-engined monoplanes (Ao.C.1). On 20 October 1943 name was changed to Instituto Aerotícnico. On 23 January 1957 became a State enterprise under the title of Dirección Nacional de Fabricaciones e Investigaciones Aeronáuticas (DINFIA). Reverted to its original name 1968.

ARGONAUT AIRCRAFT INC./USA

First product (1935) was Pirate three-seat monoplane amphibian, with Menasco Pirate engine. Main use of Menasco engines had previously been in racing aircraft.

ARIEL AIRCRAFT INC./USA

Formed in 1940 to produce a light two-seat cabin monoplane. This was of a semi-cantilever low-wing configuration, externally braced below the wing only.

Arado Ar 95 general-purpose torpedo-bomber-reconnaissance seaplane

Arado Ar 234B Blitz (Lightning) jet bomber

Arctic Aircraft/Interstate Arctic Tern

ARMSTRONG WHITWORTH, SIR W. G., AIRCRAFT LTD/UK

Established 1914 as Aeroplane Department of engineering company Sir W. G. Armstrong, Whitworth & Co. Ltd. In September 1914 built unsuccessful F.K.1 single-seater. Later (during the war) F.K.3 and F.K.8 two-seat observation aircraft delivered in quantity, as improvements on Government-designed B.E.2c. Experimental types of WW1 included quadruplanes and Armadillo and Ara biplane single-seat fighters. Aeroplane Department closed late 1919, but new company, named above, formed 1920. Outstanding products between the wars were Siskin single-seat fighter and Atlas army co-operation aircraft for RAF, both introducing some steel construction. Scimitar fighter (1934) was among the world's fastest with radial engine, partly due to company's associations with engine-builders Armstrong Siddeley. Notable airliners were the three-engined Argosy biplane (1926); four-engined Atalanta monoplane (1932); and the much larger Ensign (1938). Company's most famous product was Whitley twin-engined bomber (1936) in which year Hawker Siddeley

Armstrong Whitworth Whitley V long-range night bomber

Group was formed, with Armstrong Whitworth as a member company. In July 1943 the 1,824th Whitley left the assembly line at Baginton, Coventry, the type having achieved several historic 'firsts' in RAF service. Albemarle (600 built) used as glider-tug and transport, and Avro Lancaster bombers built in dispersed factories. After the war, from basic Gloster design, company developed and produced in quantity Meteor two-seat night

fighter. When this type was well advanced undertook development of Hawker Sea Hawk naval fighter. Avro Lincolns, Hawker Hunters and Gloster Javelins also produced. Experiments made with flying-wing aircraft and prone-pilot position. Apollo turboprop airliner (1949) had no commercial success, though Argosy twin-boom four-turboprop freighter (1959) gained limited civil and military orders.

Armstrong Whitworth Argosy 20-passenger civil transport

Armstrong Whitworth-built Hawker Sea Hawk carrier-based fighter

Arrow Active 2 single-seat sporting biplane

ARPIN, M. B. & COMPANY/UK

At West Drayton, Middlesex, built during 1937–1938 a two-seat pusher cabin monoplane, the A-1, with MacLaren crosswind tricycle undercarriage. Re-engined 1939 for Army evaluation, but not adopted.

ARROW AIRCRAFT & MOTOR CORPORATION/USA

In late 1920s made three models of two-seat sport or training biplane (the Arrow Sport and Arrow Sport Pursuit). Standard type of 1935 was Model F two-seat low-wing monoplane with Ford V-8 converted automobile engine, awarded contract by the Bureau of Air Commerce.

ARROW AIRCRAFT (LEEDS) LTD./UK

Largely designed by A. C. Thornton (responsible for Blackburn Bluebird of 1924), the

Arrow Active 1 of 1931 was a single-seat all-metal aerobatic biplane with military-training potential. Active 2 of 1932 was re-engined and had new centre-section; but though company made aircraft components it built no aeroplanes in quantity.

ARSENAL DE L'AÉRONAUTIQUE/*France*
Established in 1936 in old Breguet works at Villacoublay. Products generally designated by initials of Vernisse (director) and Galtier (designer). VG 30 was lightweight fighter; VG 33 a more powerful development (200 ordered and many being assembled by June 1940). Arsenal-Delanne 10 was unorthodox tandem-monoplane two-seater, flown 1941. Experimental work on fast and unorthodox aircraft resumed after war, when VB 10 fighter with tandem piston engines and contra-rotating propellers was flown. VG 70 had German Junkers Jumo 004 turbojet; VG 90 was naval jet fighter; 5.501 a pilotless aircraft; 0.101 a research monoplane for testing aerofoil sections, spoilers, etc. After 1954 became SFEC-MAS (Société Française de Construction de Matériaux Spéciaux).

ASTRA SOCIÉTÉ DE CONSTRUCTIONS AÉRONAUTIQUES/*France*
Obtained from the Wright Brothers in 1909 a licence to build their aircraft in France. Introduced own modifications, and one Astra-Wright was used for early bombing trials. Triplane also built. During WW1 made military aeroplanes and airships, having been famous for lighter-than-air craft before the war. Components also manufactured. In 1921 amalgamated with Nieuport as Nieuport-Astra, thenceforth abandoning airship work entirely.

Arsenal VB 10 tandem-engined experimental fighter

Arsenal VG 90 experimental jet fighter for naval use

ATELIERS DE CONSTRUCTIONS AÉRONAUTIQUES BELGES/*Belgium*
Established in Brussels 1933. In that year LACAB T.7 advanced trainer entered for Belgian Government competition, and in 1934 company began construction to official specifications of the LACAB GR.8 twin-engined multi-seat fighter sesquiplane.

ATELIERS DE CONSTRUCTIONS AÉRONAUTIQUES ZEEBRUGGE/*Belgium*
see ACAZ

ATELIERS ET CHANTIERS DE LA LOIRE/*France*
see Gourdeau et Leseurre

ATLANTIC AIRCRAFT CORPORATION/*USA*
Established at beginning of 1923 and started active operations in May, remodelling 100 D.H.4s. Held patent rights and licence to build Fokker aircraft in USA, and largely associated with Anthony Fokker, who went to USA in 1922 and played a part in founding the company at Hasbrouck Heights, NJ. Fokker was

Prototype of South African Atlas C4M STOL light transport

also design consultant to other US companies. AO-1 was two-seater of characteristic Fokker biplane form for artillery observation; XLB-2 —officially prefixed Atlantic-Fokker or Atlantic (Fokker)— of 1927/28 was first twin-engined US Air Corps monoplane bomber. Type not adopted despite Fokker's experience with large civil monoplanes. C-2 and C-2A of late 1920s also were typical Fokker-type high-wing cantilever monoplanes.

ATLAS AIRCRAFT COMPANY/*USA*
Formed in 1949 by J. B. Alexander and Max B. Harlow to build H-10 four-seat cabin monoplane of all-metal stressed-skin construction.

ATLAS AIRCRAFT CORPORATION OF SOUTH AFRICA (PTY) LTD./*SA*
Formed at Kempton Park, Transvaal, January 1965 to establish an aircraft industry in South Africa, jointly with the Industrial Development Corporation. Has completed manufac-

Atlas Impala of SAAF, licence-built Aermacchi M.B.326M

ture of Impala Mk 1 (M.B.326M) under Aermacchi licence. Mk 2 version being developed; also Atlas C4M utility STOL light transport, first flown February 1974. Company has held marketing rights for several foreign aircraft and has done extensive maintenance and overhaul work for SAAF.

AUBERT, PAUL, AVIONS/*France*
Aubert-Aviation was formed 1932, but in 1938 name was changed to above and PA-20 trainer was shown at Paris Salon. Sub-contract work on Morane-Saulnier trainers ceased June 1940. After war PA-20 was revived as PA-201 and PA-204 (high-wing cabin monoplanes with cantilever undercarriage; common name Cigale). As Cigale Major PA-204 was certificated in 1951.

AUSTER AIRCRAFT LTD./*UK*
Company was formerly called Taylorcraft Aeroplanes (England) but in March 1946 this was changed as above and the works were transferred from Thurmaston, Leicester to Rearsby, Leicester. Auster name was well established in WW1 by light observation (AOP) monoplanes known as Taylorcraft Austers. Many of these made an important contribution to the development of post-war light aviation. The type mainly concerned was the Auster 5, or Model J, three-seater with Lycoming engine. As war neared its end Taylorcraft designers were already looking to the civil market, and the outcome was the Autocrat, often British-powered and widely used not only for ordinary tasks but also, for instance, to test the Rover TP.90 gas turbine. In the 1950s came the Aiglet and the Autocar, one of the latter type being used to test the Saunders-Roe hydro-ski landing gear. Its name notwithstanding, the Aiglet Trainer differed greatly from the Aiglet, and the Agricola was an entirely new low-wing agricultural aircraft, first flown December 1955. To supersede the AOP6 the entirely new military AOP9 was tested in March 1954, by which time the British Army and RAF had received nearly 2,000 Austers.

Auster's first fully aerobatic aircraft, the Aiglet Trainer

Auster AOP6 two-seat Air Observation Platform

Auster lightweight ambulance or freight aircraft

AUSTIN MOTOR COMPANY (1914) LTD./*UK*

Centred at Northfield, Birmingham, Warks, this engineering company became a War Office contractor for aeroplanes during WW1, building over 2,000 of 'outside' design. In 1917 the Aircraft Department, managed by J. D. North (best known for his later Boulton Paul associations) contemplated aircraft of original design, though the Austin Ball Scout of 1917 was attributed largely to Capt Albert Ball VC, the great fighter pilot. The Osprey (1918) was a triplane single-seater designed by C. H. Brooks; the Greyhound two-seat fighter was flown after the Armistice; and civil types were · the Kestrel side-by-side two-seater (awarded 2nd prize in an Air Ministry competition) and the tiny Whippet single-seater, for which high hopes were entertained, though only five were built. Aircraft activities ceased 1920, but in 1936 the 'shadow factory' scheme ensured that the Austin name once again had aircraft connections. Production of Fairey Battles began October 1937; first aircraft tested July 1938.

Austin Whippet single-seat biplane (33·5 kW; 45 hp Anzani engine)

Austin Osprey single-seat triplane

AUSTRALIAN AIRCRAFT & ENGINEERING CO. LTD./*Australia*

Based at Sydney, New South Wales, in the early 1920s, with works and aerodrome at Mascot. Built six Avro 504Ks for the Royal Australian Air Force (as agents for A. V. Roe & Co, *q.v.*). Also built—to designs of H. E. Broadsmith—a six-seat commercial biplane, and this aircraft was taken over by the Commonwealth Government, but lack of further

support caused the firm to go into voluntary liquidation.

THE AUTOGIRO COMPANY OF AMERICA/*USA*

Licensed in 1930 by Cierva Autogiro Co. of UK, the US company itself arranged sub-licences to Pitcairn and Kellett. For three years experimented with own AC-35 Autogiro—a

roadable cabin type, delivered to Experimental Development Section of Bureau of Air Commerce in 1937. The folding rotor-blades had direct control. ('Autogiro' is spelled with an 'i' if it is an aircraft of Cierva origin.)

AVIA/*Italy*

Azionaria Vercellese Industrie Aeronàutiche: first flew F.L.3 two-seat cabin monoplane in 1939. 400 built of this type between 1939 and 1942. Production resumed after the war, until the end of 1947, when company was absorbed by Francis Lombardi. Types known as Lombardi (AVIA) included L.M.5 Aviastar, first produced 1945.

AVIAMILANO COSTRUZIONI AERONÀUTICHE/*Italy*

During 1950s, after production of Falco F8L was transferred, under licence, to Aeromere, the company continued to build P.19 two-seat trainer and F.14 four-seat cabin monoplane. The latter—named Nibbio—was four-seat cabin development of Falco. Aviamilano also built prototype of F.250 three-seat cabin monoplane, but sold rights to Siai-Marchetti. Aviamilano Construzioni Aeronàutiche went into liquidation 1968.

AVIAN AIRCRAFT LTD./*Canada*

Formed February 1959 to develop a special wingless autogyro type, the Avian 2/180. First flew 1960, but accident delayed development. In 1964 Canadian Government provided financial assistance for further research and development. Certification granted in 1968.

AVIA AKCIOVA SPOLECNOST PRO PRUMYSL LETECKY/*Czechoslovakia*
Original Avia company founded 1919. Taken over by Milos Bondy a Spol about 1923, but acquired 1926 by Skoda, who also made Hispano-Suiza aero-engines under licence. Early Avia designers were named Benes and Hajn; hence initials in aircraft designations. BH-1 was light sporting two-seater; BH-3 a low-wing strut-braced single-seat fighter for the Czechoslovak National Defence Ministry; BH-25 a five-seater; BH-26 a two-seat fighter; BH-33 a single-seat biplane fighter developed from the BH-21. Company made Fokker F.VII/3m under licence, and Avia F IV IX was a Fokker-designed bomber. Before the war the company built fast metal-skinned transports of original design—Avia 51, 56 and 57. B 534 biplane was outstanding single-seat biplane fighter (445 built) used by Czechoslovak Air Force and widely considered best of class in Continental Europe. B 71 was Soviet-designed monoplane bomber; S 199 was post-war improvised development of German Bf 109. In 1945 works were reconstituted under Government, but production of Avia 36 light monoplane was resumed and Douglas C-47s were converted for civil use. Soviet Il-14M built as Avia 14.

Above: Avia 14 Salon, Czech-built version of the Il-14M. *Below:* Avia BH-21 fighter with ski landing gear.

Above: Aviamilano P.19 Scricciolo lightplane
Right: Avian 2/180 Gyroplane two-seat autogyro

AVIATIK/Germany

Automobil und Aviatik AG was founded in 1910. An Aviatik biplane crashed as early as June that year; but company named as above in 1911. Made French Farman biplanes and Hanriot monoplanes, but developed original types also. On outbreak of war in 1914 transferred works from Mülhausen, Alsace, to Freiburg-im-Breisgau. Developed B I reconnaissance aircraft from earlier Pi 5. Although unarmed, B I was used operationally. C I–C III series (1915 onwards) were armed, and reversed earlier pilot-at-back arrangement. C III used for bombing also. Company also made a few twin-engined Gotha bombers before working on larger R types. Designed post-war civil aircraft, but activities ceased 1919, and a new company formed to take over the concern which went into liquidation.

AVIATION SPECIALTIES INC./USA

In January 1971 received certification for a turbine-powered conversion of Sikorsky S-55 helicopter, designated S-55-T.

AVIATION TRADERS (ENGINEERING) LTD./UK

Formed at Bovingdon, Herts 1947 to sell aircraft and spares. In 1949 acquired base at Southend, Essex to maintain aircraft on Berlin Airlift. During 1952–1955 built Bristol Freighter centre-sections. Sold about 20 civil Percival Prentices. Conversion of the 20-year-old Douglas DC-4 into a cheap car-ferry first considered January 1959. Type was called Carvair; first flight June 1961; 21 built. Less successful was company's own medium-range airliner, the Accountant, with two Rolls-Royce Dart turboprops, flown July 1957 and backed by managing director F. A. Laker.

Aviatik standard biplane, with unequal span (sesquiplane) wings

Aviation Specialties' S-55-T turbine conversion of Sikorsky S-55

Aviation Traders ATL98 Carvair car ferry, converted from the Douglas DC-4

AVIBRAS/*Brazil*
Sociedade Avibras Ltda in 1963 was testing prototype of A-80 Falcão side-by-side two-seat low-wing monoplane, of wooden construction with plastic skin. Brazilian government contracts received for several projects, including single-seater with Volkswagen engine; but in 1967 the company withdrew from the aviation industry.

AVIMETA/*France*
Société Avimeta was formed in 1926 as a separate aeronautical firm by Établissements Schneider, exploiting use of structural material 'Alférium'. The Avimeta AVM-88 of 1927 was a parasol monoplane two-seat fighter with corrugated skin.

Aviation Traders ATL90 Accountant 1 airliner

Avibras A-80 Falcão two-seat cabin monoplane

Avro CF-105 Arrow, in 1958 one of the most advanced fighter aircraft

AVIOLANDA MAATSCHAPPIJ VOOR VLIEGTUIGBOUW NV/*Netherlands*
Founded December 1926. Before WW2 built under licence Dornier Wal twin-engined flying-boats for Royal Netherlands Naval Air Service and Curtiss Hawk biplane fighters for East Indies Army Air Service. After war made assemblies for Gloster Meteor, Hawker Hunter and Lockheed Starfighter. Made N.H.I. Kolibrie helicopter. Developed AT-21 pilotless drone and aircraft components (e.g. passenger ramps). Extensive repair and overhaul work also undertaken.

AVION INC./*USA*
Formed 1942 to undertake research, engineering and production of military aircraft. Orders during war included sub-assemblies for Northrop and Lockheed. In January 1943 received Northrop sub-contract for three XP-79 jet fighters, one of which (MX-324) was the first US rocket-propelled aircraft to fly, on 5 July 1944.

AVIONS AMIOT/*France*
see Amiot

AVIS FLUGZEUGWERKE UND AUTOWERKE GmbH/*Austria*
After WW1 built two types of high-wing monoplane trainer and the B.G.VI three-engined transport biplane, the wings of which were cantilevered outboard of struts near fuselage.

AVI SOCIEDAD ANÓNIMA INDUSTRIAL COMERCIAL Y FINANCIERA/*Argentina*
In October 1958 began development of Avi 205 multi-purpose high-wing monoplane. First flight was in September 1960.

AVRO/*UK*
see Roe, A.V. & Co. Ltd.

AVRO AIRCRAFT LTD./*Canada*
Formed as part of Hawker Siddeley Group after acquiring Victory Aircraft Ltd. (Crown-owned) in July 1945. In 1946 Group took over Turbo-Research Ltd. Technical innovations brought company brief world fame. Built first jet transport on American continent (C-102 Jetliner) 1949, though no sales followed. CF-100 was world's first straight-wing combat aircraft to exceed Mach 1 (in a dive, 18 December 1952). Type first flown January 1950 and developed as two-seat all-weather interceptor through five marks. About 700 built, serving in Canada and Europe and supplied to Belgian Air Force. Was to have been followed in production by CF-105 Arrow, with delta wing. First Arrow completed October 1957 and flew 1958; but project cancelled February 1959 after expenditure of about 400 million dollars. The Arrow was a victim of the wide-spread belief that the interceptor role could best be performed by a missile. Three years later Canada had to buy McDonnell F-101 Voodoo fighters from the USA. Also experimented with three-engined lift-fan Avrocar.

AZIONARIA VERCELLESE INDUSTRIE AERONÀUTICHE/*Italy*
see AVIA

B

BA/*UK*

In the mid-1930s Major E. F. Stephen formed at Hanworth, Middlesex, a company originally titled British Klemm Aeroplane Company Ltd. to build under licence the German Klemm L.25 two-seat lightweight sporting aircraft under the name B. K. Swallow. Also built six B.K.1 Eagle 1 three-seat cabin monoplanes, similar to Klemm L.32 but redesigned by G. A. Handasyde. A total of 22 B.A. Eagle 2s were subsequently built.

BAC/*UK* (1935)

The British Aircraft Company (1935) Ltd. built a series of gliders in the early 1930s. In 1932 one was fitted with landing gear and a Douglas motorcycle engine driving a pusher propeller. A small number were produced before designer and owner of the company C. H. Lowe Wylde was killed while flying the initial conversion on 13 May 1933. Company taken over by Austrian pilot Robert Kronfeld, becoming Kronfeld Ltd. (*q.v.*).

BAC/*UK* (1960)

British Aircraft Corporation formed in February 1960 to unite the aircraft and guided weapon activities of Bristol Aeroplane Company Ltd, English Electric Company Ltd, and Vickers Ltd. It then had four wholly-owned subsidiaries: Bristol Aircraft Ltd, English Electric Aviation Ltd, Vickers Armstrongs (Aircraft) Ltd, and British Aircraft Corporation (Guided Weapons) Ltd, plus a controlling interest in Hunting Aircraft Ltd. On 1 January 1964 British Aircraft Corporation (Operating) Ltd. was formed to be responsible for the business conducted formerly by the subsidiaries. At the same time, BAC acquired the remaining shares of Hunting Aircraft Ltd.

BACC/*USA*

Business Air Craft Corporation, formed on 15 July 1963 to combine Howard Aero Inc. (*q.v.*), Alamo Air Service and Alamo Aviation Inc. in a single company. Continued production of the Howard 500 12/16-seat transport, the similar 350 and 250 under the respective designations BACC BA400, Models H-350 and H-250.

BACH AIRCRAFT COMPANY INC./*USA*

Founded in March 1927, the company produced a number of civil aircraft before introducing the Bach Air Yacht in 1928. This was a three-engined commercial transport with a maximum capacity of two crew and ten passengers. Had nose-mounted engine of 164 kW (220 hp) or 298 kW (400 hp), with one 75 kW (100 hp) or 93 kW (125 hp) engine mounted on the bracing strut beneath each wing.

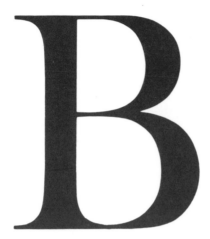

B.K. Swallow two-seat monoplane

BAe (BAC) One-Eleven airliner

BAe (BAC) Strikemaster two-seat trainer/light attack aircraft

Howard 250, a conversion of the 10/12-passenger Lodestar L-18

BACHEM-WERKE GmbH/*Germany*

From 1944 this company, with a design team led by Dipl. Ing. Erich Bachem (formerly technical director of Fieseler-Werke), began development of the Ba 349 Natter. This vertically-launched rocket-powered piloted missile was intended to attack Allied bomber concentrations. Following launch, the pilot would attack the enemy aircraft with unguided rockets, and complete his sortie after a parachute extraction from the expendable aircraft and descent to the ground. The rear-fuselage of the Natter and its Walter rocket motor was also recovered by parachute. So far as is known only one piloted launch was made, in February 1945, when test pilot Lothar Siebert was killed. The Allied advance prevented completion of the project, and none of these aircraft were used operationally.

BACINI E SCALI NAPOLETANI/*Italy*

This company established an aircraft department in 1923 to carry out repairs to seaplanes and flying-boats on behalf of the Italian Air Ministry. Began in the late 1930s to manufacture components for the Italian aircraft industry and to build aircraft under sub-contract for the *Regia Aeronàutica*.

BACON/*USA*

Erle L. Bacon Corporation established at Santa Monica, California, to build an extensively updated version of the North American T-6 tandem two-seat advanced trainer. Known as the Bacon Super T-6, the prototype first flew in April 1957.

BAe/*UK*

Nationalised enterprise, founded in April 1977, uniting British Aircraft Corporation, Hawker Siddeley Aviation, Hawker Siddeley Dynamics and Scottish Aviation. Companies retained their identities at first, but have become divisions of British Aerospace.

BAHNBEDARF AKTIEN-GESELLSCHAFT/*Germany*

Established in 1922, this company had formerly produced railway equipment. In 1924 began the production of lightweight sporting aircraft, including the BAG E.1, D.1 and D.11a. The latter was a two-seater with folding wings so that it could be stored in a garage.

BALDWIN AIRCRAFT CORPORATION/*USA*

Baldwin Aircraft Corporation acquired the plant and equipment of Ordnance Engineering Corporation to continue production of the Orenco (*q.v.*) designs.

BARCLAY, CURLE & CO. LTD./*UK*

Barclay, Curle & Company of Whiteinch, Glasgow, built 100 examples of the Royal Aircraft Factory B.E.2e under sub-contract. Order also received for the construction of 50 Fairey F.22 Campania two-seat patrol seaplanes in 1917.

BAe (HS) HS 748 twin-turboprop transport aircraft

BAe (HS) Hawk two-seat jet trainer

Bacon Super T-6 conversion of the North American T-6 trainer

91

BARKLEY-GROW AIRCRAFT CORPORATION/*USA*

Established in 1935 to manufacture an eight-seat twin-engined light transport aircraft designated Barkley-Grow T8P-1. Similar in appearance to the Lockheed Electra, the design incorporated a multi-spar stressed skin wing structure. Patented by A. S. Barkley, this latter feature eliminated the need for ribs or bulkheads in the wing.

BARTLETT AIRCRAFT CORPORATION/*USA*

Immediately after WW2 the Bartlett Aircraft Corporation, of Rosemead, California, began production of a lightweight two-seat cabin monoplane designated the Bartlett LC 13-A Zephyr 150. This aircraft was developed from the Babcock monoplane of the mid-30s.

BAT/*UK*

Founded in 1917 by Samuel (later Lord) Waring in premises previously occupied by Joucques Aviation Company. The British Aerial Transport Company's chief designer was Frederick Koolhoven, formerly with Sir W. G. Armstrong, Whitworth & Company Ltd. (*q.v.*). His first design for the new company was the BAT F.K. 22 Bat, a small single seat fighter. Failure of the ABC Mosquito engine for which it was created resulted in a new and smaller aircraft being designed, the F.K.23 Bantam, powered by the ABC Wasp. Only nine production aircraft were built and none saw service in WW1. Other BAT designs included the F.K.24 Baboon, F.K.25 Basilisk and, finally, the F.K.26, a civil transport aircraft with accommodation for four passengers, of which only four examples were built. The F.K.27 was a single side-by-side two-seat var-

iant of the Bantam. When the company was disbanded post-war, its assets were distributed between Alliance Aeroplane Company Ltd. and Nieuport & General Aircraft Company (both *q.v.*), also founded by Samuel Waring.

BATHIAT-SANCHEZ/*France*

Established at Issy-le-Moulineaux as successors to Roger Sommer, and with a flying school at Bouy, Marne, were producing in 1914 a single-seat high-wing monoplane with tractor propeller, and a two-seat biplane with pusher propeller.

BATWING AIRCRAFT CORPORATION/*USA*

This company built, in the mid-1930s, a two-seat tailless monoplane aircraft to the design of Mr. W. F. McGinty, a member of the instructional staff of the Boeing School of Aeronautics. Power plant comprised a 56 kW (75 hp) Pobjoy engine with pusher propeller.

Baumann Brigadier, with twin engines in a pusher configuration

BAUMANN AIRCRAFT CORPORATION/*USA*

Established in 1945 by J. B. Baumann, a former designer and engineer with the Lockheed Aircraft Corporation. Designed and built the Baumann Model 250 Brigadier prototype; production aircraft were designated Model 290.

BÄUMER AERO GmbH/*Germany*

This company was founded by Herr Bäumer, who was killed in July 1927 while flight-testing a high performance monoplane. In addition to operating a flying school at Hamburg, the company designed and manufactured a number of lightweight aircraft. Best known was the Bäumer Sausewind, a two-seat low-wing monoplane.

BAYERISCHE FLUGZEUGWERKE/*Germany*
see BFW

BAT F.K.26 four-passenger airliner, first exclusively civil transport built post WW1

Beagle Airedale four-seat touring aircraft

Beagle B.206 twin-engined light transport

BEAGLE AIRCRAFT LTD./UK
Beagle Aircraft Ltd. was, immediately before its dissolution, a state-owned company, acquired in August 1968, to continue the production and development of light aircraft in Britain. The company was founded in 1960, and became in 1962 a subsidiary of British Executive and General Aviation Ltd, prior to which it had absorbed Beagle-Auster Aircraft Ltd. and Beagle-Miles Aircraft Ltd. The Auster interests were disposed of to Hants & Sussex Aviation Ltd, which continued to provide spares and modification support to all Auster aircraft in service. The company went into voluntary liquidation on 27 February 1970. Beagle produced Auster-designed aircraft, conversions of ex-military Austers, the B.206 twin-engined light executive transport of which 20 served with the RAF as the Basset, and the B.121 Pup two/three-seat light aircraft. A military trainer

version of the latter aircraft, known as the Bulldog, was also produced; production of this was continued by Scottish Aviation (q.v) after Beagle went into liquidation.

BEARDMORE, WILLIAM & CO./UK
Well-known British engineering and ship-building company which turned to aircraft construction just before WW1, following receipt of licence to build German DFW biplane, to be powered by Beardmore-built Austro-Daimler engine. Built large numbers of aircraft under sub-contract during war. Under leadership of G. Tilghman Richards produced original aircraft, including W.B.III, a re-designed Sopwith Pup with folding wings, and folding or jettisonable landing gear. Designed and built a small number of civil aircraft in the years immediately following WW1.

BÉARN/France
Constructions Aéronautiques du Béarn was responsible for production of the Minicab two-seat lightweight cabin monoplane designed by Yves Gardan. Designated Béarn Minicab GY-201, it was powered as standard with a 48 kW (65 hp) Continental flat-four engine.

BEATTY AVIATION COMPANY/UK
Mr. G. W. Beatty, US pilot, visited Britain in 1912 to demonstrate Gyro aero-engine. Returned 1913 and founded flying-school at Hendon. Built biplane 1916, later powered by engine of own construction. Began construction of aircraft and components in 1918.

BEDEK AIRCRAFT COMPANY/Israel
see Israel Aircraft Industries (IAI)

Beardmore Inflexible, an advanced bomber design of 1928, powered by three Rolls-Royce engines

Beecraft Wee Bee

Beecraft Honey Bee V-tailed lightweight monoplane

BEE AVIATION ASSOCIATES
INC./*USA*

Known originally as Beecraft Associates Inc, this company built the diminutive Wee Bee in 1949, in which the pilot lay in a prone position. It was followed by the larger V-tailed Honey Bee, which first flew on 12 July 1952.

BEECH AIRCRAFT
CORPORATION/*USA*

Founded in 1932 by the late Walter Beech and Mrs Olive A. Beech, who in 1978 was still Chairman of the Board. Pioneer designer and constructor of lightplanes, had manufactured more than 40,000 aircraft by 1978. Delivered the 10,000th example of its Beechcraft Bonanza Model 35 in February 1977, at which time the Bonanza was entering its 31st year of production. Construction of twin-turboprop powered business/light passenger/freight aircraft gaining importance. Company also supplies military aircraft, and is concerned in the construction of aircraft and missile components and missile targets for the US Army. Designed, developed and manufactured the cryogenic gas storage system for NASA's Apollo and Skylab projects. Latest work includes provision of power reactant storage assembly for NASA's Space Shuttle orbiter.

Beech D.17 four-seat lightplane

Beech Bonanza four/five-seat monoplane

Beech Super King Air light transport

Beech B99 Airliner 17-seat transport

Beech Model 18 light transport. More than 4,000 built for military service in WW2

Bell P-39 Airacobra, which had nose-mounted cannon

Bell X-1 rocket-powered research aircraft

BELL/USA

Original company, Bell Aircraft Corporation, responsible for P-39 Airacobra and P-63 Kingcobra of WW2. Built first US turbojet, the P-59 Airacomet fighter trainer. Built the rocket-powered Bell X-1, in which USAF pilot Charles Yeager was the first to exceed the speed of sound, on 14 October 1947. Subsequent X-1A flown at 2,655 km/h (1,650 mph) in 1953. Company subsequently known as Bell Aerosystems, then became on 5 July 1960 Bell Aerospace Corporation, a wholly-owned subsidiary of Textron Inc, which had acquired the former Bell Aircraft Corporation. Responsible for the Bell Model D2127 tilting-duct research aircraft; two lunar Landing Research Vehicles (LLRV) for NASA, to train astronauts to land safely on the moon; Automatic Carrier Landing System (ACLS), used currently on US Navy aircraft carriers; and has been involved with an air cushion landing system which will enable military transports to land and take off from practically any surface.

Bell Helicopter, originally a division of Bell Aircraft, later became a wholly-owned subsidiary, and since 1 January 1976 is known as Bell Helicopter Textron. Responsible for design and construction of the Bell Model 47, the first helicopter to receive Approved Type Certificate from the US Civil Aviation Authority,

The 47G-5A variant of the Bell Model 47 light helicopter, in production more than 25 years

on 8 March 1946, and which remained in production for more than 25 years. Had produced well over 22,000 helicopters by early 1978; noted specially for Huey Cobra and Sea Cobra helicopter gunships. Involved currently in development of XV-15 tilt-rotor research aircraft, which made its first free hovering flight on 3 May 1977. Successful development promises forward level speeds of 615 km/h (382 mph).

Bell XV-3 tilt-rotor research aircraft

Bell VTOL research vehicle

Bell AH-1J Sea Cobra armed helicopter

Bellanca Super Viking four-seat light aircraft, powered by a flat-six engine

BELLANCA AIRCRAFT CORPORATION/USA

Known originally as International Aircraft Manufacturing Inc. (q.v.) became first Bellanca Sales Company (a subsidiary of Miller Flying Service) to manufacture and market two versions of the Bellanca Model 14 four-seat light business aircraft designed by G. M. Bellanca: three versions, known as Bellanca Viking series, available currently. Acquired assets of Champion Aircraft Corporation 1970, and changed name to Bellanca Aircraft Corporation. Currently building and marketing three aircraft produced formerly by Champion Aircraft.

Bellanca Model 19-25 Skyrocket II six-seat lightplane

BELLANCA AIRCRAFT ENGINEERING INC./USA

Formed in 1950s by G. M. Bellanca and his son, August T. Bellanca. Developed from 1963 a six-seat light aircraft, constructed of high strength glassfibre-epoxy laminates, which made its first flight in March 1975. Production of this model 19-25 Skyrocket is planned.

BELLANGER FRÈRES/France

Once-famous manufacturer of motor cars, built a flying-boat to the design of M. Denhaut, originator of the Donnet-Denhaut aircraft. Built subsequently a number of experimental aircraft designed to improve the lift characteristics of an aircraft's wing.

BENDIX HELICOPTER INC./USA

Designed and built in 1947 a single-seat experimental helicopter designated Bendix Model K. A four-seat development, the Model J, had completed over 100 hours of flight testing in early 1948 and was to be revised before the start of production.

Bellanca of Canada CH-300 Pacemaker

BENES & MRÁZ TOVARNA NA LETADLA/Czechoslovakia

Founded 1935 by P. Benes, well-known designer of light aircraft, in conjunction with the industrialist J. Mráz. Benes had been a founder of the Avia company, and subsequently chief designer of Ceskoslovenska-Kolben-Danek (CKD Praga, q.v.). Producers of several different types of one-and two-seat lightweight sporting aircraft.

BENNETT AVIATION LTD./NZ

This company built and developed a single-engine agricultural monoplane, designated

Rare picture of Benoist biplane flying-boat

Bennett P.L.11 Airtruck, designed by Luigi Pellarini. Somewhat similar to the P.L.7 agricultural aircraft, designed by Pellarini for the Kingsford Smith Company in Australia, it flew for the first time on 2 August 1960.

BENOIST AIRCRAFT COMPANY/USA

Known originally as the Aeronautic Supply Company, and established at St. Louis, Missouri, built in 1914 a small biplane flying-boat known as the Benoist XIV Air-Boat. Power plant comprised a 52 kW (70 hp) Sturtevant or 56 kw (75 hp) Roberts engine driving a pusher propeller.

BENSEN AIRCRAFT CORPORATION/USA

Founded by Dr. Igor B. Bensen, formerly chief research engineer of the Kaman Corporation (*q.v.*), to develop a series of lightweight autogyros. Examples built and supplied to USAF for research purposes, but marketed primarily in kit form for amateur construction.

BERGAMASCHI CANTIERI, AERONÀUTICI/Italy

Originally operators of a flying school, began in 1927 to build single-seat and two-seat training aircraft—the Bergamaschi C-1 and C-2 respectively—which incorporated improvements to facilitate flying training. These included a well-sprung landing gear and aerodynamic features to improve stability. Absorbed into Caproni group (*q.v.*) 1931 as Caproni Aeronàutica Bergamasca.

BERIEV/USSR

Starting seaplane design in 1928, G. M. Beriev became the leading designer of Russian water-based aircraft. Chief designer of the TsKB seaplane group in 1930; was responsible for the twin-engined MBR-2 flying-boat, Be-2 reconnaissance seaplane and Be-4 flying-boat. Beriev design bureau became centre of Soviet seaplane development in 1945, a major flying-boat project being the twin-jet Be-10. Be-12 twin-turboprop reconnaissance amphibian currently in service with Soviet Naval Air Force. Beriev Be-32 18-passenger twin-turboprop transport, similar to the Be-30, was in service with Aeroflot in 1978.

BERLINER AIRCRAFT COMPANY INC./USA

Established in 1926 by H. A. Berliner to build the Berliner Monoplane, intended initially to equip his own Potomac Flying Service. H. A. Berliner was the son of Emile Berliner, designer of an aero engine, a helicopter, and the gramophone.

BERLINER-JOYCE AIRCRAFT CORPORATION/USA

see B/J Aircraft Corporation

BERNARD/France

Known originally as A. Bernard, company was founded in the latter years of WW1. Its title was changed in 1924 to Société Industrielle des Métaux et du Bois (SIMB; *q.v.*). The latter company was wound up in 1926, but the Société des Avions Bernard was established in late 1927 to manufacture the Bernard 190T, a ten-seat transport aircraft designed by SIMB.

BERWICK, F. W., & COMPANY LTD./UK

This company, established at Park Royal, northwest London, built a number of D.H.4, D.H.9 and D.H.9A aircraft during WW1 under sub-contract to The Aircraft Manufacturing Company (AIRCO, *q.v.*). Was the recipient of a contract for 1,000 ABC Dragonfly engines which was cancelled when the unreliable behaviour of this new engine became apparent.

BESSON/France

Known originally as Marcel Besson et Cie, Société des Constructions Aéronautiques et Navales Marcel Besson was responsible for construction of some attractive triplane flying-boats, all powered by single engines in a pusher configuration. Built also in 1927 the M.B.35 monoplane seaplane and M.B.36 three-engined flying-boat.

BFW/Germany

Began aircraft construction during WW1 and produced a number of prototypes, the company being originally called Bayerische Flugzeug-Werke. Post-war, when aircraft construction was forbidden under the Treaty of Versailles, became the still-famous Bayerische Motoren-Werke (BMW), building motorcycles, motor car and aero-engines. Reformed at Augsberg in 1926, taking over the factory of the former Bayerische Rumpler Werke. Built a number of successful commercial aircraft, including BFW M-20 twelve-seat transport. Willy Messerschmitt joined the company as Chief Engineer in 1928, evolving the Bf 108 Taifun four-seat cabin monoplane, and the Bf 109—without doubt the most famous German aircraft of all time—before the company became Messerschmitt AG (*q.v*) in July 1938.

Bensen Super Bug light autogyro

Beriev MBR-2 flying-boat

Beriev M-12 (Be-12) amphibian flying-boat

Berliner-Joyce P-16/PB-1, first to be designated in the USAAC's 'Pursuit, Biplane' category

BINDER AVIATIK KG/*Germany*
In conjunction with Schempp-Hirth KG (*q.v.*)
began production in 1966 of the CP 301 S
Smaragd. Built under licence, this aircraft was
a de luxe version of the Piel Emeraude.

BIRD AIRCRAFT CORPORATION/*USA*
In 1928 the Brunner-Winkle Aircraft Corporation was founded to manufacture a three-
seat open cockpit commercial biplane known
as the Bird biplane. In March 1929 the Bird
Aircraft Corporation was incorporated, with
William E. Winkle as Vice-President, to continue production of the Bird biplane with a
variety of power plants ranging from
75–123 kW (100–165 hp). It was made available subsequently in four- and five-seat arrangements.

**BIRD WING COMMERCIAL
AIRCRAFT COMPANY**/*USA*
Founded at St. Joseph, Missouri, in 1928 to
build a three-seat commercial biplane. Powered by a 67 kW (90 hp) Curtiss engine, the
Imperial had a maximum speed of 145 km/h
(90 mph).

**THE BIRMINGHAM CARRIAGE
COMPANY**/*UK*
Built D.H.10 aircraft during WW1 under sub-
contract to The Aircraft Manufacturing Company Ltd. Received a contract also for the
construction of 70 Handley Page 0/400 heavy
bombers.

B/J AIRCRAFT CORPORATION/*USA*
B/J Aircraft Corporation was the name dele-
gated by North American Aviation Inc. to the
Berliner-Joyce Aircraft Corporation after it
had been acquired by North American. The
company continued production of one type
developed by Berliner-Joyce, namely the B/J
P-16, a two-seat biplane fighter for the US
Army Air Corps. The company ceased to operate in the year 1934.

**BLACKBURN & GENERAL AIRCRAFT
LTD**/*UK*
The Blackburn Aeroplane Company was
founded by Robert Blackburn, who had designed, built and flown his first aircraft in 1910.
Throughout the company's history the emphasis was on the design and production of

Blackburn Beverley military transport

Blackburn Buccaneer low-level strike aircraft

naval aircraft; its first for the Royal Navy was
the twin-engined GP seaplane of 1916. A similar landplane, the Kangaroo, was supplied to
the RAF in 1918. Aircraft to serve with the
Navy include the Baffin, Blackburn, Buccaneer, Dart, Firebrand, Ripon, Roc, Shark
and Skua. In 1930 acquired Cirrus Hermes
Engineering Company. Blackburn Aircraft
Company founded 1936. In 1949 merged with
General Aircraft Ltd. (*q.v.*) of Feltham, Middlesex. Latter company founded 1934 and pro-

duced such aircraft as Monospar twin-engined
lightplane, Cygnet and Owlet. Built pressurised version of Monospar, which was first pressurised aircraft built in UK. Built Hotspur and
Hamilcar gliders during WW2. New 1949
company known as Blackburn & General Aircraft Ltd. Company name reverted to Blackburn Aircraft Ltd. in 1959, when Blackburn &
General became the holding company. Became part of the Hawker-Siddeley Group in
1960, losing its individual identity in 1963.

Blackburn Kangaroo bomber, used for anti-submarine patrols in WW1

Blériot 127/2 twin-engined military aircraft; armament of 3 or 4 machine-guns and up to 1,000 kg (2,205 lb) of bombs

BLANCHARD, CONSTRUCTIONS AÉRONAUTIQUES/France

Founded in January 1923 by M. Blanchard, a designer who had worked for the Farman brothers and Georges Levy. Specialised in the construction of flying-boats. A single-seat racing monoplane was designed to take part in the 1924 Schneider Trophy Contest, which was cancelled because not enough aircraft were ready to compete.

BLÉRIOT, SOCIÉTÉ AÉRONAUTIQUE/France

The French aviation pioneer Louis Blériot achieved a unique place in aviation history by making the first crossing of the English Channel in a powered aircraft (his Type XI monoplane) on 25 July 1909. This success resulted in the formation of the above company to produce the Type XI monoplane, and many significant first flights were made with these aircraft. Aircraft of this type, and derivatives such as the Parasol, served with the French forces, the RFC and RNAS at the beginning of WW1, as well as with other air arms. In post-war years took over the SPAD (q.v.) interests and built many examples of these aircraft.

BLÉRIOT AND SPAD AIRCRAFT WORKS/UK

Established at Addlestone, Surrey, to provide support for Blériot and SPAD aircraft operated in the UK. Built Avro 504A trainers under sub-contract to A. V. Roe Ltd. during the course of WW1.

BLOCH, MARCEL, SOCIÉTÉ DES AVIONS/France

In 1933 Marcel Bloch established a small factory at Courbevoie, Paris, to build light aircraft. The company built its first fighter aircraft, the Bloch 130 in 1933–34, the first flight

Blériot Type XI monoplane, one of the most famous pioneering aircraft

of this prototype being made on 29 June 1934. Production Bloch 131s entered service in 1938. Subsequent production included the Bloch 151/152/155 monoplane fighter, Bloch 175 light bomber, and Bloch MB 200 and MB 210 bomber aircraft. Nationalisation of the French aircraft industry in 1937 combined the Blériot and Bloch companies as Société Nationale de Constructions Aéronautiques de Sud-Ouest (q.v.) with Marcel Bloch as its Managing Director.

BLOHM UND VOSS/Germany
see BV

BODIANSKY/France

In 1930 Avions Bodiansky produced an advanced two-seat light monoplane, the Bodiansky 20 monoplane, which featured a welded steel-tube fuselage structure, as well as manually and automatically operated leading-edge slots and trailing-edge flaps.

Bloch 131 four-seat reconnaissance bomber

Bloch MB 200 night bomber of the between-wars era

Boeing Model 314 Clipper, the type used by Pan American to inaugurate mail/passenger services across the North Atlantic

BOEING/USA

Founded 15 July 1916 by William E. Boeing as Pacific Aero Products Corporation. Name changed to Boeing Airplane Company 26 April 1917. Bid successfully for the San-Francisco-Chicago air mail route in 1927 and formed subsidiary Boeing Air Transport to operate the route; as other airlines were acquired, this became Boeing Air Transport System. Merged with Pratt & Whitney, Standard Steel Propeller Company, and two small aircraft manufacturers to form United Aircraft & Transport Corporation in 1929. All continued to operate under original identities; United Air Lines formed as holding company of airlines. In 1934 legislation prevented aircraft and engine manufacturers from operating airlines: those of the former Boeing Air Transport System reorganised into a new United Air Lines. Boeing, together with Stearman (q.v.), a wholly-owned subsidiary, adopted the name Boeing Aircraft Company. The name Boeing Airplane Company was readopted in 1948. In May 1961, following acquisition of Vertol (q.v.) in 1960, became known as The Boeing Company.

First product B & W Seaplane of 1916, designed by William Boeing in conjunction with Conrad Westervelt. First production order was for Model C seaplane. First post-WW1 design was the B-1 three-seat flying-boat. Built ten US Army-designed GA-1 armoured ground attack triplanes, followed by 200 Thomas-Morse MB-3A pursuit aircraft. First real success with own-design military aircraft came in 1923, with the PW-9/FB series, which had a fabric-covered welded steel tube fuselage. Boeing Model 40 designed for carriage of airmail plus two, and later four, passengers established Boeing Air Transport. Model 80 12-passenger transports with three Pratt & Whitney Wasp engines introduced by Boeing Air Transport in 1928. World's first airline stewardesses introduced on these aircraft 1930. Model 80A with more powerful

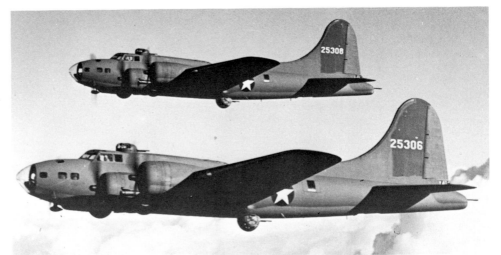

Boeing B-17 Flying Fortresses, used extensively in the European theatre of war

Boeing's famous Model 247, in 1933 a world-leading civil transport design

Boeing Model 707-320, a four-turbofan civil transport of which sales are approaching the 1,000 mark.

Hornet engines and seats for 18 passengers followed. Biggest military order to that date came in 1931 when US Army ordered 135 P-12E single-seat fighters and US Navy 113 of the similar F4B-3: total of 586 aircraft in this series built by 1933. Boeing Model 200 Monomail, mail/cargo aircraft, first flew May 1930; revolutionary aircraft with cantilever all-metal monoplane wing, retractable main landing gear, and a specially designed anti-drag cowling for its single Hornet engine. A second Monomail, Model 221, had six-seat passenger cabin. Military development of this aircraft resulted in B-9 bomber, forcing evolution of new fighter types. Boeing produced P-26 single-seat all-metal monoplane fighter, of which 136 bought by US Army. Biggest step forward came with the Model 247, most advanced conception of a transport aircraft anywhere in the world at that time. Introduced wing and tail unit leading-edge de-icing; control surface trim tabs and, in production aircraft, controllable-pitch propellers and autopilot. It was the first twin-engined monoplane transport that could climb with a full load on the power of one engine. Significant milit-

Boeing B-52D heavy bomber of the USAF's Strategic Air Command

ary aircraft since that period have included the B-17 Flying Fortress, of which 12,731 examples were built; B-29 Superfortress; B-47 Stratojet; and the B-52 Stratofortress. Aircraft which have made important contributions to global air transport include the Model 314 flying-boat; Model 377 Stratocruiser; Model 707 turbojet airliner; and ensuing Models 720/727/737. The Model 747 'Jumbo-Jet' was the world's first wide-body transport aircraft.

The easily-recognisable Boeing Model 747 four-turbofan heavy transport, which pioneered the wide-body concept

Boeing Vertol 107 tandem-rotor turbine-engined helicopter

Boeing Vertol CH-46 Sea Knight approaching a carrier

BOEING VERTOL COMPANY/*USA*

On 31 March 1960 Vertol (*q.v.*) became a Division of The Boeing Company with the title Boeing Vertol Company. Continued production of the Vertol-designed Model 107 23/25-seat twin-rotor transport aircraft, built subsequently in civil and military versions. A development of the Model 107, designated KV-107, is being built under licence by Kawasaki Kokuki Kogyo Kabushiki Kaisha (*q.v.*) in Japan. Developed enlarged version as Model 114 Chinook military helicopter which, in addition to the 700-plus supplied to the US Army, serves also in Alaska, Australia, Canada, Germany, Hawaii, Iran, Italy, Korea, Spain, and Thailand. Announced early 1978 that Britain was to acquire 30 of the most advanced Chinooks.

BOISAVIA/*France*

Designed and built in the late 1940s a four-seat cabin monoplane known as the Boisavia B-60 Mercurey, the prototype of which first flew on 3 April 1949. Variants included agricultural and glider-tug versions.

BÖLKOW GmbH/*Germany*

This company was founded on 1 May 1956, becoming established at Ottobrunn bei München in 1958. Until 1 January 1965 was known as Bölkow Entwicklungen KG, adopting above title following acquisition of a one-third interest in the business by Boeing. Bölkow held a 25% interest in Entwicklungsring Süd (EWR, *q.v.*). Aircraft produced include the BO 207 four-seat light aircraft, BO 208 C Junior (a licence-built version of the Malmö MFI-9) and the BO 105 five-seat light helicopter, which features a rigid main rotor of glassfibre reinforced plastics. This helicopter continues in production in 1978 under the designation MBB BO 105, signifying that it is now built by Messerschmitt-Bölkow-Blohm (*q.v.*).

Bölkow BO 208 C Junior two-seat lightweight aerobatic aircraft

Bölkow BO 46 helicopter built to test the Derschmidt high-speed rotor system

BONDY, MILOS, &
COMPANY/*Czechoslovakia*

see Avia Akciova Spolecnost pro Prumysl
Letecky

BONOMI/*Italy*

In 1929 Aeronàutica Vittorio Bonomi built a
two-seat cabin monoplane to the design of Ing.
Abate. This was developed subsequently by
Captain Bonomi and produced as the Bonomi
25 Monoplane.

BORDELAISE/*France*

Derived from the aircraft department of Dyle
et Bacalan, Société Aérienne Bordelaise was
controlled by the Nieuport-Delage company.
Production included the Bordelaise D.B.70, a
twin-fuselage design with accommodation for
20 passengers, which was powered by three
engines. A military version, designated
A.B.20, had four engines.

Borel floatplane, one of the first seaplanes used by the Royal Navy

BOREL/*France*

Formed in 1909 by Gabriel Borel, Établissements Borel was an early constructor of floatplanes. One of the first aircraft to serve with
the British Navy was a Borel monoplane, purchased in 1912, and at least eight were in
service with the Naval Wing before the beginning of WW1. A high performance two-seat
fighter was built to the design of M. Boccacion,
but too late for wartime service. Known subsequently as Société Générale des Constructions
Industrielles et Mécaniques (*q.v.*).

BOULTON PAUL AIRCRAFT LTD./*UK*

Established as building constructors in Norwich, Norfolk, turned to sub-contract construction of aircraft in WW1 which included
RAF F.E.2d, Sopwith 1½-Strutter and Sopwith
Camel. Known originally as Aircraft Department of Boulton & Paul Ltd. As WW1 neared
end, the company decided to continue in aircraft industry. First original design P.3 single-
seat biplane fighter which did not, however,
enter production. Designed and built P.6 research aircraft, which provided much data for
later P.9. P.7 Bourges twin-engined fighter-
bomber built at the end of 1918, followed later
by somewhat similar Bugle. Neither entered
RAF service. Continued to build small numbers of civil aircraft during between-war years.
Sidestrand 3/4-seat medium bomber entered
RAF service with one squadron in April 1928.
Replaced by improved Overstrands, with
power-operated gun turret, in 1934. When
production ended, in 1936, company re-
established at Wolverhampton, Staffs. Name
of Boulton Paul Aircraft Ltd. adopted 1934.
Designed and built P.82 Defiant for RAF,
prototype first flew 11 August 1937: two-seat
fighter with power-operated gun turret was
entirely new concept and enjoyed initial operational success. Production ended 1943 after
more than 1,000 built. Designed P.108 Balliol
three-seat advanced trainer for RAF, 162 built
subsequently as two-seat Balliol T.2, of which
30 built under sub-contract by Blackburn Aircraft Ltd. (*q.v.*). Built P.111 and P.120 for
research into behaviour of delta wing at tran-
sonic speeds.

***Right:* Boulton Paul P.111 delta wing
research aircraft**

Boulton Paul Overstrand medium-bomber with power-operated gun turret

Brantly B-1 co-axial rotor helicopter

Brantly B-2 two-seat light helicopter

BRANDENBURGISCHE
FLUGZEUGWERKE/*Germany*
see Hansa und Brandenburgische Flugzeug-Werke GmbH.

BRANTLY HELICOPTER
CORPORATION/*USA*
Founded by N. P. Brantly, who designed the Brantly B-1, with co-axial rotors, in 1943. From this design he developed the improved Model B-2, utilising the rotor evolved for the B-1, a two-seat helicopter which first flew on 14 August 1956. Subsequently entered production as Model B-2A, superseded by B-2B in 1963. Larger Model 305, a five-seat aircraft, first flew in January 1964. Company acquired by Lear Jet Industries Inc. (*q.v.*) in May 1966.

BRANTLY-HYNES HELICOPTER
INC./*USA*
The Brantly helicopter interests, which had been acquired by Lear Jet Industries in 1966, passed to Aeronautical Research and Development Corporation (*q.v.*) in 1969, and to Brantly Operations Inc. in late 1970. On 1 January 1975 Michael K. Hynes founded Brantley-Hynes Helicopter Inc., having gained ownership of the Brantly interests. Production of Model B-2B and Model 305 was continuing in 1977.

BRATUKHIN/*USSR*
Involved in helicopter development since the late 1930s, I. P. Bratukhin first designed a twin rotor helicopter, with an engine and related rotor mounted at each end of an outrigger. Designated 2MG Omega, this was completed in 1941. Vibration problems resulted in construction of Omega II in 1943. A series of similar twin-rotor helicopters were built up to the year 1948.

Brantly Model 305 five-seat light helicopter

Breda Ba 88 Lince (Lynx) twin-engined medium attack bomber

BREDA/*Italy*
A large industrial concern, based in Milan, Società Italiano Ernesto Breda began the construction of aircraft in 1917. In the immediate post-WW1 years, when no production aircraft were being built, concentrated on research and constructed a number of experimental aircraft. Began the construction of all-metal aircraft in 1922. Production aircraft have included Breda 15 two-seat lightweight sporting aircraft of 1930, Breda 25 and 28 training biplanes, and the Breda 33 two-seat sports monoplane of 1932, from which time production concentrated mainly on military aircraft. These included Breda Ba 27 single-seat monoplane fighters, which equipped a squadron of the

Formation of single-seat Breda Ba 65's

Chinese Air Force in 1937; Ba 65 one/two-seat fighter-bomber/reconnaissance monoplane, which saw service in the Spanish Civil War; Ba 88 Lince twin-engined medium attack bomber, produced also by Meridionali (*q.v.*) under sub-contract. Breda also built a number of Junkers Ju 87Bs under licence as the Breda 201 Picchiatelli before suspension of production soon after the Italian surrender.

BREDANARDI COSTRUZIONI
AERONÀUTICHE SpA/*Italy*
Established on 15 February 1971 by Nardi SA per Costruzioni Aeronàutiche (*q.v.*), and Breda, a member company of the EFIM state-

owned financial group, each with a 50% holding. Initiated manufacture of helicopters under a licence granted by Hughes Helicopters (*q.v.*), and is building the Hughes 300C, 500C, 500D, and 500M under the respective designations of BredaNardi NH-300C, NH-500C, NH-500D and NH-500M-D (TOW). The latter is a multi-role military helicopter armed with TOW missiles.

BREGUET AVIATION/*France*
Louis Breguet, founder of Société Anonyme des Ateliers d'Aviation Louis Breguet in 1911, was a French pioneer of rotary-wing flight. The aircraft built by the Breguet brothers lifted a man off the ground on 29 September 1907, but did not constitute a free flight. BU3 biplane bomber prototype of 1915 built under subcontract by Edouard and André Michelin as Breguet-Michelin BUM. Improved SN3 entered production with Michelin 1916 as BUC. Breguet 14 tractor biplane of 1917 was a significant French wartime bomber. Its successor, the Breguet 19 of 1921, remained in service until 1936. One specially-prepared Breguet 19 (*Question Mark*), flown by Costes and Bellonte, made first east-west aircraft crossing of North Atlantic September 1930. Built Short Calcutta flying-boats under licence during 1930s as Breguet Bizerte. Breguet elected not to be included in nationalised industry 1936; his factories were, however, incorporated. Regained some independence in 1939 through purchase of former Latécoère factories. Avions Marcel Dassault became major stockholder 28 June 1967. Anglo-French company Société Européenne de Production de l'Avion École de Combat et d'Appui Tactique (SEPECAT–*q.v.*) formed between British Aircraft Corporation and Breguet Aviation 1966 to design and develop tactical support/advanced trainer. Built four 941s unpressurised cargo/passenger transports, which utilise deflected slipstream technique to give STOL capability, for French Air Force. Breguet Type 1150 Atlantic maritime patrol aircraft selected by NATO, prototypes ordered 1959; production aircraft built internationally by Belgium, France, Germany, Netherlands and USA. For later production see Dassault-Breguet Aviation.

Breguet 693 attack bomber

BredaNardi NH-500, a licence-built version of the Hughes 500

Two-seat Breguet 19 A2, successor to the Breguet 14 night bomber

Breguet 765 Sahara 176-troop military transport developed from the Br 763 Deuxponts

Brewster SB2A Buccaneer

BREWSTER AERONAUTICAL CORPORATION/*USA*

Founded in the mid-1930s, the first product of this company was a two-seat scout/bomber for the US Navy designated SBA. When this aircraft entered production in 1937–1938, the company had inadequate productive capacity and 30 were built by the Naval Aircraft Factory as SBNs. The F2A Buffalo which followed was the first monoplane fighter to serve with the USN, and was also used by the armed forces of Belgium, Britain, Finland and Netherlands

East Indies. The later SB2A Buccaneer, though built in quantity, proved totally unsuitable for front-line service.

Bristol Fighter (F.2B), nicknamed 'Brisfit', one of the best general-purpose combat aircraft of WW1

BRISTOL AEROPLANE COMPANY LTD./*UK*

Founded at Bristol, Somerset, in February 1910 as British & Colonial Aeroplane Company Ltd. First began construction of a number of biplanes under licence from Société Zodiac (*q.v.*), but these were not completed because the sample aircraft received from France could not be induced to take to the air. First aircraft produced were Bristol biplanes, usually known as the Boxkite, which initially were little more than copies of the Henry Farman biplane. Flying schools established at Larkhill, on Salisbury Plain, and at Brooklands, Surrey, 1911. February 1911 Deutsche Bristol-Werke established at Halberstadt, Germany, to operate a flying school and build Bristol aeroplanes; arrangement cancelled 23 June 1914. First military aircraft were monoplanes designed by Henri Coanda; No. 105 shared third place with a Deperdussin in the Military Aeroplane Competition of 1912. Bristol Scout, or 'Baby Biplane', evolved by Frank Barnwell 1914. The Bristol Fighter, dubbed the 'Brisfit', entered service in 1917 to become regarded as the best general-purpose combat aircraft of WW1. Be-

Bristol Boxkite, more accurately the Bristol biplane of 1910

Brewster F2A Buffalo, first monoplane fighter of the US Navy

BRITISH AERIAL TRANSPORT COMPANY/*UK*
  see BAT

BRITISH AEROSPACE/*UK*
  see BAe

BRITISH AIRCRAFT COMPANY/*UK*
(1935)
  see BAC

Bristol's graceful turboprop Britannia

Bristol Type 170 Freighter cargo aircraft

tween wars, Bristol Bulldog biplanes equipped nine RAF Squadrons by 1932 and were most widely used fighter until 1936. Bristol Type 138A of 1936 captured World Altitude Record in September, 1936, regained it from Italy in June 1937 at altitude of 16,440 m (53,937 ft). Bristol Type 142, built as executive aircraft for Lord Rothermere, became the military Blenheim, an important light bomber in the early period of WW2. Beaufighter, first flown July 1939, became RAF's first night fighter, subsequently an important anti-shipping aircraft armed with rockets, torpedoes and bombs. Designed and built prototype of eight-engined 100-passenger Brabazon I, first flew 4 September 1949; scrapped 1953 for financial/political/technical reasons. Type 170 Freighter first flown 2 December 1945 and 213 built subsequently. Turboprop-powered Britannia first flew 16 August 1952, made the first non-stop airliner flight London–Vancouver (8,208 km; 5,100 miles) 29 June 1957, and first North Atlantic passenger service to be flown by a turbine-powered airliner on 19 December of the same year. Rotary-wing development resulted from formation of

a helicopter department in 1944; initial flight of Bristol Type 171 prototype made 27 July 1947. Subsequently produced as Sycamore, entering service with RAF as its first British-designed helicopter in 1952. Research and development of tandem-rotor helicopters resulted in Type 192 Belvedere, but by the time this entered service with the RAF, in 1961, Bristol's helicopter department had become the Bristol Helicopter Division of

Westland Aircraft Ltd. (*q.v.*) Company's aircraft activities reorganised as Bristol Aircraft Ltd. in January 1956, wholly owned by Bristol Aeroplane Company Ltd. This company was absorbed into the British Aircraft Corporation (BAC, *q.v.*) in June 1960. Following the acquisition of the Cosmos Engineering Company in 1920, the Bristol Company was also a major builder of aero-engines.

Bristol Beaufort reconnaissance-torpedo-bomber

BRITISH AIRCRAFT
CORPORATION/UK

see BAC

BRITISH AIRCRAFT
MANUFACTURING COMPANY
LTD./UK

see BA

BRITISH & COLONIAL AEROPLANE
COMPANY LTD./UK

see Bristol Aeroplane Company Ltd.

BRITISH CAUDRON COMPANY
LTD./UK

Established at Cricklewood, London just before WW1 to provide product support to
French Caudron aircraft being operated in Britain. Built nine Caudron G.3s under licence.
During WW1 built D.H.5s under sub-contract
to Aircraft Manufacturing Company Ltd; B.E.
2s under sub-contract to the Royal Aircraft
Factory; and F.1 Camels under sub-contract to
Sopwith Aviation Company Ltd. (all q.v.).

BRITISH KLEMM AEROPLANE
COMPANY LTD./UK

see British Aircraft Manufacturing Company Ltd.

BRITTEN-NORMAN (BEMBRIDGE)
LTD./UK

Britten-Norman Ltd. was founded in 1955 to
specialise in equipment for agricultural aircraft. Flew prototype of BN-2 Islander, a twin-
engined feeder-line transport, on 13 June
1965. BN-2A Trislander, with a third engine
mounted on vertical tail, first flown 11 September 1970. Military version of BN-2, named
Defender, first demonstrated 1971, able to
carry 522 kg (1,150 lb) of mixed weapons on
underwing pylons. Name changed to Britten-
Norman (Bembridge) Ltd. in November 1971,
when company ran into financial difficulties.
Assets acquired in August 1972 by Fairey
(q.v.). In late 1977 the company was again in
financial difficulties and an official receiver
appointed. Sales and full product support was
continuing in early 1978.

BROCHET/France

In the early 1950s Avions Maurice Brochet
designed and built lightweight sporting aircraft. In addition to production versions, some
were intended also for amateur construction.
Designations of these included the M.B.70,
M.B.71, M.B.80, M.B.100 and M.B.101.

**Britten-Norman BN-2A Trislander in the
insignia of Trans-Jamaican Airlines**

Brochet M.B.80 lightweight sporting aircraft

Britten-Norman BN-2 twin-engined Islander light transport

BRUNNER-WINKLE AIRCRAFT CORPORATION/*USA*

see Bird Aircraft Corporation

BRUSH ELECTRICAL ENGINEERING COMPANY LTD./*UK*

Built under sub-contract to A.V. Roe & Company Ltd. during WW1 Avro 504c, 504J/K and 504K trainers; and for Short Bros. seaplanes of the Admiralty Type 830 and Admiralty Type 184.

BÜCKER FLUGZEUGBAU GmbH/*Germany*

Founded at Johannishal in 1932, its first aircraft was the Bü 131 Jungmann trainer, designed by Swede Anders Andersson. The prototype first flew on 27 April 1934. It was followed by the Bü 133 Jungmeister in 1935 and by the extensively built Bü 181 Bestmann in 1936. Production of the latter continued after WW2 by Zlin in Czechoslovakia and, under Czech licence, by Egypt's Heliopolis Aircraft Works in the 1950s.

BUHL AIRCRAFT COMPANY/*USA*

Known originally as the Buhl-Verville Aircraft Company, based at Detroit. This company was founded in March 1925, with its head office and works at Marysville, Michigan. Builders of three- and five-seat transport biplanes known as the Airster and Airsedan series.

BUNYARD AIRCRAFT COMPANY/*USA*

In 1931 Mr. K. Bunyard designed and built a small biplane flying-boat, following this with a design for an unusual amphibian which failed to materialise in prototype form. At the end of WW2 he began production of a three-seat lightweight amphibian flying-boat known as the Bunyard BAX-3 Sportsman. A four-seat version was designated BAX-4.

Buhl LA-1 Bull-Pup ultralight monoplane

Bücker Bü 181 Bestmann cabin monoplane

Bücker Bü 133 Jungmeister single-seat aerobatic trainer

BURGESS COMPANY & CURTISS/USA

Established at Marblehead, Massachusetts, originally built Wright types under licence. By arrangement built three single-float seaplane variants of the British Dunne tailless biplane, two of which were sold to the US Navy which carried out with these aircraft its first experiments in aerial gunnery. Produced also in the period 1916–1918 a number of training and experimental seaplanes of original design.

BURGFALKE FLUGZEUGBAU/Germany

Building originally examples of the Scheibe and Vogt sailplanes, Burgfalke developed a two-seat lightweight semi-aerobatic training aircraft designated M-150 Schulmeister. It was based on the WN-16 which had been designed by the Wiener-Neustadt company.

BURNELLI AIRCRAFT CORPORATION/USA

Founded 1920, Remington-Burnelli Airliner produced in that year. Vincent Burnelli concentrated on the development of fuselage structures which would contribute some degree of lift, augmenting that of the wing. The Burnelli VB-14B transport of 1936 could accommodate a crew of two and 14 passengers in a fuselage which was virtually an integral part of the wing.

BURNS AIRCRAFT COMPANY/USA

Began development in 1964 of high-performance 6/8-seat business aircraft powered by two Continental flat-six engines. The prototype Burns BA-42 flew for the first time on 28 April 1966.

Burgess-Dunne seaplane, licence-built version of the Dunne tailless biplane

BUSCAYLET ET CIE/France

Built aircraft under sub-contract during WW1. In 1923 secured services of Louis de Monge as a designer, producing in 1924 a single-seat monoplane fighter with 224 kW (300 hp) Hispano-Suiza engine. It was notable for being of all-metal construction, except for fabric covering of wing and tail surfaces.

BUSHMASTER AIRCRAFT CORPORATION/USA

Formed in August 1970 to produce a modern version of the 1920s Ford Tri-Motor, under the designation Bushmaster 2000. This updated design of the aircraft first built by the Stout Metal Airplane Company (q.v.) was evolved by Aircraft Hydro-Forming Inc. This latter company was acquired by the Whittaker Corporation in February 1969, who wished to dispose of the Tri-Motor programme. Improvements, by comparison with the original design, included more powerful lighter-weight engines with constant-speed fully-feathering propellers, and new aircraft systems of more modern conception.

Bushmaster 2000, a modernised version of the Ford Tri-Motor designed by William B. Stout.

Blohm und Voss Ha 139 seaplane; type was used for North Atlantic service trials

BV/Germany

Blohm und Voss was a famous shipbuilding concern, based on the Elbe at Hamburg. Its aircraft division, Hamburger Flugzeugbau GmbH (*q.v.*), turned to construction of maritime aircraft in the early 1930s. In 1937 Hamburger Flugzeugbau adopted the title of the parent company. Successful designs of Dr. Ing. Richard Vogt initiated under the Ha designation continued in production becoming designated, for example, Bv 138 instead of Ha 138. True Blohm und Voss developments included the Bv 222 Viking, the largest flying boat to attain operational status in WW2, and the even larger Bv 238, evolved too late to enter production in WW2. The only prototype Bv 238 was destroyed by air attack four days before VJ-day.

Blohm und Voss Bv 238 six-engined prototype, largest flying-boat built during WW2

Blohm und Voss Bv 138 long-range patrol flying-boat

C

CAARP/*France*

Coopérative des Atéliers Aéronautiques de la Région Parisienne initially specialised in modification and repairs. Began manufacture of components for sailplanes under licence, and in 1965 contracted from Scintex-Aviation (*q.v.*) to produce Super Emeraude light aircraft. Prototype only of C.P. 100 two-seat version of Emeraude was built. CAARP became associated with Avions Mudry et Cie (*q.v.*) in manufacture of CAP 10 and 20 aerobatic aircraft in the early 1970s, being responsible for building of CAP 20 and fuselages for CAP 10. Final assembly of the latter was undertaken by Mudry at Berney—companies being merged in early 1978.

CAC/*UK*

Civilian Aircraft Company Ltd. formed at Burton-on-Trent by Harold D. Boultbee, formerly assistant chief designer of Handley Page Ltd. Sole product was C.A.C. Mk I Coupé, a two-seat high-wing cabin monoplane tourer built at Hedon, near Hull, and flown July 1929. A novel design for its time, there were initial difficulties and only five were built. Last four designated Mk II Coupé (uprated Armstrong-Siddeley Genet Major engine); company closed in 1933.

CAIN AIRCRAFT CORPORATION/*USA*

Established 1 January 1931, this company designed and produced a two-seat lightweight sporting aircraft known as the Cain Sport. It was powered by a 71 kW (95 hp) Cirrus engine, licence built by the US ACE (American Cirrus Engine) Corporation.

CAIRNS AIRCRAFT SYNDICATE/*USA*

Started in late 1928 as the Cairns Development Company; was taken over by Cairns Aircraft Corporation in August 1929. Began to develop advanced-design all-metal low-wing monoplane. First product was the Model A, first flown April 1930; second design evaluated by the US government but most of the 1930s dedicated to development work. Model A built for a new Cairns-designed engine, and in 1938 Models B and C.

CALLAIR/*USA*

Call Aircraft Company formed originally as Call-Air in 1940–1941 by Renel, Ivan and Spencer Call to design and develop the Call-Air Model A two-seat light Cabin monoplane with Continental flat-four engine. Updated version with Lycoming flat-four certificated in 1946. Other models were the A-2 (Lycoming) and A-3 (Continental). Named changed to Callair Incorporated around 1950, producing the Model 150 (Callair A4) in 1955. A-5 and A-6 (uprated) were agricultural adaptations. Callair were purchased by Intermountain Manufacturing Company (*q.v.*) in 1962, and this company continued the development of aircraft for agricultural use.

Callair B-1 agricultural aircraft

CAMAIR/*USA*

Camair Division of Cameron Ironworks Inc. took over the Twin Navion programme from Temco (*q.v.*) in mid-1950s. Continued under the name Camair 480, for which certification obtained by the re-titled Camair Aircraft Corporation in September 1966. The aircraft was a conversion of twin-engined North American/Ryan Navion four-seat cabin monoplane with two Continental flat-six engines.

CAMPBELL AIRCRAFT LTD./*UK*

Based at Hungerford, Berkshire, Campbell acquired UK rights for manufacture and sale of Bensen range of US Gyro-Gliders and Gyro-Copters in 1959. First licence-built example flew August 1960. Bensen range reduced to two models in 1969, when Campbell designed own two-seat light autogyro, the Curlew. Development abandoned in favour of the single-seat Cricket in July 1969; 47 were built by April 1972. Cougar single/two-seat prototype flew March 1973, but was not produced.

Campbell Cricket light autogyro

Camair Twin Navion four-seat cabin monoplane

CAMS/*France*

Chantiers Aéro-Maritimes de la Seine founded 1921, specialising in production of marine aircraft; technical director and chief designer from 1927 was Maurice Hurel. Best-known products were flying-boats CAMS 33, built 1923–1926 originally for the Schneider Trophy race; CAMS 37, for shipborne observation/patrol; and the CAMS 51, 53 and 55 family, of which the CAMS 55 was a patrol bomber. Company acquired in 1933 by Société des Avions et Moteurs Henry Potez (*q.v.*). Factories at Sartrouville and Vitrolles nationalised in 1937.

CAMS 55 twin-engined flying-boat patrol-bomber

CANADAIR LTD./*Canada*

Formed December 1944 at Cartierville, Montreal, from Aircraft Division of Canadian Vickers Ltd. (*q.v.*), as a 'Crown Company'. Purchased 1946 by Electric Boat Company of New York; later that year became a subsidiary of General Dynamics Corporation (*q.v.*). First contract (1944) to build the DC-4m (Merlin-engined version of the Douglas DC-4) for the RCAF. Eventually built 71, including commercial versions, and converted many wartime C-47s into post-war commercial DC-3s. Since 1949 has licence-built more than 1,900 North American F-86 Sabre jet fighters for the RCAF and the US Military Assistance Programme; more than 700 Lockheed T-33 Silver Star jet trainers; 200 Lockheed F-104 Starfighters for the RCAF; and 240 Northrop F-5s for the Canadian Armed Forces and Royal Netherlands Air Force. Products of its own design have included the CL-28 Argus maritime patrol aircraft (32 built); CL-41 jet trainer/ground attack aircraft (210 for Royal Canadian and Malaysian Air Forces); 39 CL-44 Yukon and Forty Four military/civil transports; and three prototypes of the CL-84 tilt-wing VTOL research aircraft. Company was repurchased by the Canadian government in December 1975. Programmes current in 1977–1978 include the CL-215 water bomber/utility amphibian (nearly 50 built) and the CL-89 battlefield reconnaissance RPV (over 500 built), plus major sub-contract work for the US Navy's P-3C Orion and its Canadian derivative, the CP-140 Aurora. Prototype due to fly in Spring 1978 of the CL-600 Challenger twin-turbofan executive/freight transport.

Engaged also in production of rear fuselages for the Boeing 747SP, as well as spares, and the modification/repair/overhaul of various other types of aircraft.

Canadair Argus maritime patrol aircraft of the RCAF

Canadair CL-215 water bomber, scooping water from the Pacific

Canadair CL-44 swing-tail cargo carrying aircraft

CANADIAN AEROPLANES
LTD./*Canada*

Government-sponsored company, formed late 1916 taking over works and staff of Curtiss Canada at Long Branch, Toronto, where over 1,200 Curtiss JN-4C two-seat biplanes were built. In 1918 licence production began of Avro 504K to replace JN-4s at Canadian training establishments. One hundred ordered, but only one or two delivered before the Armistice. Sub-contractor also for Felixstowe F.5 maritime patrol flying-boat.

CANADIAN ASSOCIATED AIRCRAFT
LTD./*Canada*

Founded in 1938; factories at St. Hubert, Quebec and Malton, Ontario. Contracted directly by the British government to speed up British re-armament programme for the RAF. Basically acted as parent company for six Canadian firms: Canadian Car & Foundry Co, Canadian Vickers, Fairchild Aircraft, Fleet Aircraft, National Steel Car Corporation and Ottawa Car & Aircraft (all *q.v.*). First contract in Autumn 1938 for 80 Handley Page bombers, later increased, but company wound up in 1942.

CANADIAN CAR & FOUNDRY
COMPANY LTD./*Canada*

Called CCF and later Can-Car, initially the largest company in Canada for the manufacture of railway equipment. In 1937 acquired licence to build Grumman GE-23 (FF-1) two-seat biplane fighters, in factory at Fort William, Ontario, including 40 for Republican Spain.

Built prototype of little-known FDB-1 fighter biplane in 1938. Orders for large numbers of Avro Ansons, Hawker Hurricanes, Avro Lancasters and Curtiss Helldivers. Seven new factories opened by mid-WW2.

Early post-war obtained Canadian licence for Burnelli 'lifting fuselage' designs; flew prototype CBY-3 (twin Wasp engines) August 1945. Accommodation was three crew plus 38 passengers or 22 passengers and freight. Development of CBY-3 by subsidiary Cancargo (*q.v.*). In 1947 acquired assets of Noorduyn Aviation Ltd. (*q.v.*); continued manufacture of Mk V Norseman and variants until early 1950s; re-sold it to its designer in 1953. In early 1950s designated products 'Can-Car' beginning with North American Harvard Mk 4s built under licence at Fort William for RCAF and NATO air forces. Gained contract to build 100 Beechcraft T-34A Mentor piston-engined trainers in 1952–53 for USAF and also for RCAF. Re-titled Canadian Car Company Ltd. in mid/late 1950s.

CANADIAN CURTISS AEROPLANE
COMPANY LTD./*Canada*

At Long Branch, Toronto, this company built 18 Curtiss JN-3 ('Jenny') two-seat biplane trainers in 1915–1916. RNAS order for 100 twin JNs cancelled in 1916; factory acquired in 1916 by Canadian Aeroplanes Ltd. (*q.v.*).

CANADIAN VERTOL AIRCRAFT
LTD./*Canada*

Wholly-owned subsidiary of Vertol Aircraft Corporation (*q.v.*); formed February 1954 at

former RCAF air base Arnprior, west of Ottawa, to repair and overhaul RCAF/RCN Vertol helicopters. Also produced in 1957 small number of Vertol Model 42A—exclusively Canadian civil conversion of RCAF H-21B helicopters used to supply stations of the mid-Canada radar chain.

CANADIAN VICKERS LTD./*Canada*

Established 1911 at St. Hubert, Montreal, as subsidiary of Vickers Ltd. (*q.v.*). Aircraft division formed 1922; first Canadian company to build aircraft commercially. First contract was for six UK-designed Viking IV amphibians for Canadian Air Force. These followed from 1924 by 61 Vedette single-engined flying-boats and amphibians, its most successful product, designed in Canada by W. T. Reid. During the 1920s six other designs appeared: the Varuna, Vista, Vanessa, Velos, Vigil and Vancouver. Of these, only the Veruna (eight) and Vancouver (six) flying-boats went into production. In the 1930s the company licence-built Fairchild and Fokker designs and Northrop Deltas. During WW2 40 Supermarine Stranraer flying-boats (for the RCAF), 230 Consolidated OA-10 Catalinas for the USAAF and 149 Canso amphibians for the RCAF were built, plus hulls for 600 more Catalinas and fuselages for 40 Handley Page Hampden bombers. Took over Canadian Associated Aircraft (*q.v.*) in 1941, and in following year moved to government factory at Cartierville, near Montreal. In December 1944 became a separate autonomous company under new name of Canadair Ltd. (*q.v.*), which was later to become a subsidiary of General Dynamics.

Canadian Vickers Vancouver II flying-boat

CANARY, AERO TECHNIK/*Germany*

Jack Canary began in 1967 licence production of pre-war Bücker Bü 133D-1 Jungmeister single-seat aerobatic biplane, powered by rebuilt Siemens-Halske Sh 14A radial or modern alternative. Three built in works of Josef Bitz Flugzeugbau at Augsburg/Haunstetten; production then transferred to Wolf Hirth GmbH at Nabern/Teck. Total of eight ordered (first one flown Summer 1968), but activities suspended after death of Mr. Canary in August 1968. Four were completed by Bitz and Hirth; the programme was abandoned as uneconomic in January 1972.

CAN-CAR/*Canada*

see Canadian Car & Foundry Company Ltd.

CANCARGO AIRCRAFT MANUFACTURING COMPANY LTD./*Canada*

This wholly-owned subsidiary of the Canadian Car & Foundry Company (*q.v.*) was formed about 1950 to build the Burnelli Loadmaster transport. Only the CBY-3 prototype was built, by CCF; the rights in this aircraft were acquired in 1952 by Airlifts Inc. of Miami, and reverted eventually to Ballard Aircraft Corporation.

CANSA/*Italy*

Name of Costruzioni Aeronàutiche Novaresi SA assumed 1 May 1936 by former Aeronautica Gabardini SA (*q.v.*). Head office and factory at Cameri; began with repair and maintenance work on aircraft and engines. First product was C.5 single-engined one/two-seat training biplane (Fiat or Alfa Romeo engine), built in some numbers in late 1930s for civil market. The C.6 was a less successful development. CANSA then became subsidiary of Fiat (*q.v.*), producing small numbers of F.C.12 fighter/trainer monoplane (first flown 1940) and also the F.C.20 twin-engined ground attack aircraft.

CANT/*Italy*

Company originally called Cantieri Navale Triestino created 1923 as subsidiary of Cantieri Navali di Monfalcone to manufacture civil/military marine aircraft. Most designs produced between 1923–1930 were work of R. Conflenti, including such flying-boats as Cant 6 three-engined biplane bomber; Cant 6 *ter*, commercial transport version; Cant 7, 7 *bis* and 7 *ter* single-engined trainer biplanes; Cant 10 and 10 *ter* five/six-seat single-engined light transport biplanes; Cant 18 trainer; Cant 22 three-engined eight/ten-seat commercial transport; Cant 25 single-seat fighter. Land-

CRDA Cant Z.506 Airone (Heron) seaplane

planes included Cant 23 transport and Cant 36 trainer.

Company changed its name in 1931 to Cantiere Riuniti dell'Adriatico. Chief designer Filippo Zappata (formerly of Blériot) completely reorganized the company 1933–1936. From 1934 most aircraft had Z prefixes, marine aircraft being numbered in 500 series, beginning with Z.501 Gabbiano biplane reconnaissance/bomber, first flown 1934. Followed by Z.504 two-seat fighter biplane flying-boat and Z.505 twin-float three-engined monoplane, both 1935. Latter developed into Z.506 (1936), built as reconnaissance/bomber/ASR for Regia Aeronàutica (Z.506B Airone) and as commercial transport for Italian airlines (Z.506A and C). Landplane version built by Piaggio (*q.v.*). Built Z.508 and Z.509, monoplane flying-boat bombers, and world's largest floatplane: Z.511 four-engined trans-Atlantic mail/freight variant, first flown 1943. The Z.515 twin-engined twin-float monoplane (coastal reconnaissance), built 1938–1939.

Landplanes (designated in 1000 series) included Z.1007 and 1007 *bis* Alcione three-engined bomber; Z.1011 twin-engined medium bomber/transport; Z.1012 three-engined transport; Z.1015 three-engined derivative of Z1017 *bis*, first flown January 1939 and used in torpedo trials early in WW2. Final type was Z.1018 Leone, twin-engined medium bomber intended to replace Alcione, probably Italy's best wartime design but too late to see service. Did not continue aircraft manufacture in the post-war period.

CAP/*Brazil*

Companhia Aeronáutica Paulista formed at São Paulo shortly after WW2 to produce CAP 1 Planalto low-wing advanced trainer; CAP 4 Paulistinha high-wing cabin monoplane, and similar CAP 5 Carioca. The second was the most successful; improved version later built by Nieva (*q.v.*). Company came under control of IPT (*q.v.*) in late 1940s.

CAPITAL AIRCRAFT CORPORATION/*USA*

Founded at Detroit, Michigan, in 1928, this company produced a lightweight two-seat sporting and training monoplane known as the Capital Air Trainer.

CAPITAL HELICOPTER CORPORATION/*USA*

Established January 1954 for continued development of C-1 Hoppi-Copter, built previously by Hoppi-Copters Inc. (*q.v.*). C-1L, first flown 1954, was a redesigned and simplified version of original 1945 prototype.

CAPRONI/*Italy*

Italy's oldest and, at one time, largest aircraft manufacturer, the Caproni group comprised more than twenty companies, of which the principal aircraft building members were Aeroplani Caproni Trento, Caproni Aeronàutica Bergamasca, Caproni Vizzola SpA, Compagnia Nazionale Aeronàutica,

Aeronàutica Predappio SpA and Officine Meccaniche Reggiane SpA. Isotta-Fraschini aero-engine company was also part of the group.

Company's founder, Count Gianni Caproni di Taliedo, built and flew his first aircraft in May 1910, thereafter associating with various partners until WW1. Achieved an international reputation with the Ca 1-Ca 5 series of large tri-motor biplane and triplane bombers, built by a company called Società per lo Sviluppo dell'Aviazione in Italia, with factories at Taliedo and Vizzola. Early post-war publicity gained by Ca 60, an enormous eight-engined 'triple-triplane' of 1921, intended to carry 100 passengers. After formation of Regia Aeronàutica in 1923, Caproni achieved success with such military aircraft as the Ca 36, Ca 73 and Ca 74. The following decade produced the Ca 101, Ca 111 and Ca 133 range of 'Colonial' aircraft. and a series of multi-purpose reconnaissance/light bomber/transport types, production of which was shared with the Bergamasca subsidiary.

Cantieri Aeronàutici Bergamaschi (q.v.) had been absorbed by Caproni in 1931. Initially built Ca 100 and Ca 101, then built the new aircraft to the designs of Ing. Cesare Pallavicino. Major production types during 1934–1944 were A.P.1 single-seat fighter, followed by the family of multi-purpose twin-engined aircraft: Ca 309 Ghibli; Ca310/310 bis Libeccio; Ca 311 Libeccio; Ca 312 bis Libeccio; Ca 314 and 316.

More than 2,500 examples of the Ca 100 training/touring biplane were built during the 1930s; the Ca 161 bis, a single-seat single-engined biplane, set an international altitude record of 17,083 m (56,046 ft) that remains unbeaten today in its class. The Caproni-Campini CC-1 of 1940 was Italy's first and the world's second aircraft to fly by jet propulsion, though it was not powered by a turbine. During WW2 the company was chiefly concerned with the production and development of the Ca 310-Ca 314 multi-purpose twin-engined aircraft and with the Reggiane Re. 2000-Re. 2005 series of single-seat fighters. During the lifetime of the group some 180 different types were built, as well as licenced construction of almost as many by other designers.

The parent company went bankrupt in 1950. Aeroplani Caproni Trento survived the bankruptcy and in May 1952 flew Italy's first post-war jet light aircraft, the F.5, designed by Dott. Ing. Stelio Frati.

Caproni Vizzola Costruzioni Aeronàutiche SpA was formerly the Scuola Aviazione Caproni, the oldest flying school in Italy, and is the only part of the company which survives today, currently producing the Calif series of sailplanes. Earlier it remodelled the Ca 133 for ambulance and military transport duties and assisted in production of the Breda Ba 65. Its

Caproni Ca 97 high-wing monoplane

Caproni Ca 33 (Ca 3) three-engined bomber

Caproni Ca 73 of unusual inverted-sesquiplane configuration

first original design was the F.4 single-seat fighter designed by Ing. F. Fabrizi, flown in 1940. Prototype F.6 had more powerful engine.

CARDEN-BAYNES AIRCRAFT LTD./UK

Sir John Carden was associated with British light aviation after designing the 750 cc ultra-light engine for the Gloucestershire Gannet in the early 1920s. Went into partnership with L. E. Baynes in 1930 to produce a one-off single-seat powered glider. In 1936 built a single Bee,

a small two-seat high-wing monoplane with two Carden Ford S.P.1 modified car engines, flown in 1937. Development of B-3 three-seat halted by WW2.

CARIBE DOMAN HELICOPTERS INC./Puerto Rico

Acquired assets of Doman Helicopters Inc. (q.v.) in August 1965. Tooling began January 1966 to produce Doman D-10B helicopter; however, rights repurchased by parent company in late 1967, emerging as Berlin Doman Helicopters Inc.

CARMA MANUFACTURING COMPANY/USA

Established 1948 to manufacture electrical, mechanical, and aircraft control equipment. Aircraft manufacturing division formed in 1954 at Tucson, Arizona to build a turbojet-powered two-seat trainer, the Carma VT-1 Weejet. Prototype first flew 30 March 1956.

CARSON HELICOPTERS INC./USA

Formed in 1963 at Perkasie, Pennsylvania, to develop conversion schemes to improve payload and performance of standard US light helicopters i.e., Bell 47 and Hiller UH-12. A four-seat conversion of three-seat Bell 47G called the Carson Super C-4 was also produced. Company later became a helicopter overhaul organisation and charter operator.

CARSTEDT INC./USA

In December 1966 produced a 'stretched' version of the de Havilland D. H. 104 Dove with AiResearch turboprop engines. It was called the Carstedt Jet Liner 600 and had 18 seats; a small number were built for commuter airline use. Company acquired by Texas Airplane Manufacturing Co. Inc. (q.v.) in mid-1970s.

CASA/Spain

Construcciones Aeronáuticas SA formed 3 March 1923, with factory at Getafe, to produce all-metal aircraft for Spanish Air Force. Began by licence-building Breguet XIX reconnaissance-bomber biplanes followed by other aircraft of foreign design including Dornier Wal flying-boats (at Cadiz), Vickers Vildebeest torpedo-bombers, Gotha Go 145C biplane trainers, Junkers Ju 52/3m transports, Bücker Bü 131 and 133 aerobatic trainers and Heinkel He 111 medium bombers. After WW2 opened design department; first series product was Dornier Do 27 general-purpose lightplane, followed by CASA-201 Alcotan, CASA-202 Halcon and CASA-207 Alcotan twin-engined transports of own design. In late 1960s/early 1970s completed 70 Northrop F-5 fighters under licence for Spanish Air Force, and in 1978 was producing C-212 Aviocar twin-turboprop transport and developing new C-101 jet trainer. In 1972 took over Hispano Aviación as well as the ENMASA aero-engine concern in June 1973. CASA currently has six factories, and other work includes major repair and overhaul of aircraft for Spanish and US Air Forces, and component manufacture for Dassault Falcon 10 and Airbus A300.

CASPAR-WERKE AG/Germany

Established in 1921 in ex-Fokker factory at Travemünde to continue business of Hanseatische Flugzeugwerke Karl Caspar AG of Hamburg. Started with manufacture of seaplanes including S.1 twin-float monoplane and Heinkel-designed U.1 and U.2—1922 prototypes for detachable wing biplanes to be carried by submarines. A four-seat open-cockpit light transport was followed by the

CASA C.212 Aviocar twin-turboprop STOL transport

Carson conversion of the Bell 47

CASA-207 Azor military transport

Carstedt Jet Liner 600, a conversion of the de Havilland Dove

CLE.11 in 1923, a two-seat high-wing cabin monoplane. In 1925 came the CT-1-5 series of light aircraft designed by Karl Theiss; and CLE.12 eight-seat single-engined transport. Lightplane designs C.17, 23, 24 and 26 followed; then in 1926 the C.27 seaplane training biplane; C.30 reconnaissance aircraft; C.32 agricultural biplane—one of the world's first— with payload of 900 kg (1,984 lb); the C.35 Priwall eight-passenger biplane of 1927 (also used by Deutsche Luft Hansa as freighter); and the C.36 reconnaissance aircraft. Lack of orders for these types caused the factory to close in 1928.

Caudron G.III biplane trainer of WW1

CAUDRON/France
Gaston and René Caudron established aeroplane factory as Caudron Frères at Romiotte (Seine) in 1910. Initial flight of the first of a series of highly successful biplanes (G.I, II and III) February 1911. G.III considered extremely reliable and used widely as a trainer in WW1. Single-seat monoplane trainer produced in 1912. G.IIIAs were built for military use in 1914; used extensively by France, UK, Belgium, Russia and Italy as two-seat reconnaissance/artillery observation aircraft. Several hundred built, mostly in France, but also by British Caudron (*q.v.*) and in Italy. Series continued with G.IV (1915)—several military variants; also in that year the prototype R.4 appeared—three-seat bomber, very solid and well armed. The R.11 with five Lewis machine-guns was produced a few months before the Armistice was declared.

The company had moved to Issy-les-Moulineaux (Seine) by 1919 and post-war products included C 23 (and/or C 232) two-seat biplane, which inaugurated French commercial air services on 10 February 1919 with flight from Paris to Brussels; C 61 three-engined six/eight passenger biplane; three-engined seven-seat development of C 61; C 183, a further modernisation of two previous aircraft of which one only was built, in 1925.

The company, known as Société Anonyme des Avions Caudron, ran into financial difficulties and was reorganized as Société Caudron-Renault. Next became notable for distinctive streamlined aircraft from its designer Marcel Riffard, who joined in 1932. His C363 took second place in 1933 Coupe Deutsch race; developed versions took first three places in 1934 and 1935, first two places in 1936. Derivatives of these included the Rafale series of single- and two-seat sporting/racing aircraft of the late 1930s. Fifteen C 690Ms built as ad-

vanced trainers for the Armée de l'Air; series ended with the C 720. Followed by the single-seat C 580 and C 680; C 600 Aiglon series; C 620/C 630 Simoun four-seat cabin monoplane; C 640 Typhon series; the little-known C 670 ground-attack prototype; and the single-seat C 860, built in 1938 for an attempt (never made) on 1936 Paris-Tokyo flight record established by a Simoun. About 1700 examples built in about ten years of C 440 (later AA.1) Göeland, twin-engined six-passenger transport. Two series of light fighters developed from Coupe Deutsch racers: following C 710 and C 713 prototypes, four-gun C 714 entered service. Improved variants CR 760 and 770 under development when France collapsed. The factories built aircraft for Germany during the Occupation. Later nationalised as Ateliers Aéronautiques d'Issy-les-Moulineaux; incorporated into SNCAN (*q.v.*) in late 1945.

Caudron Simoun four-seat cabin monoplane

Caudron C 23, built originally as a night bomber

Cavalier Aircraft versions of the North American F-51D Mustang

CAVALIER AIRCRAFT CORPORATION/*USA*

Successor to Trans-Florida Aviation (*q.v.*) acquired during 1960s type certificate for North American F-51 Mustang, producing two-seat (tandem) business/sport conversions of F-51D as Cavalier 2000 series and building new single-seat F-51Ds for the USAF counter-insurgency Military Assistance Programme.

Prototype of Mustang II—two-seat COIN patrol/attack version equipped with heavier armament—flew December 1967; prototype Turbo Mustang III (with Rolls-Royce Dart) in 1969. Second prototype flew in April 1971, equipped with Lycoming T55 engine, by which time the programme had been sold to the Piper Aircraft Corporation (*q.v.*) but then the company was dissolved.

CCF/*Canada*
see Canadian Car & Foundry

CEA/*France*
Centre Est Aéronautique formed at Dijon October 1957 by Pierre Robin and Jean Delemontez (ex-Jodel, *q.v.*); began production with the DR 100 Ambassadeur, a three-seat

Centre Est Sicile Record lightweight cabin monoplane

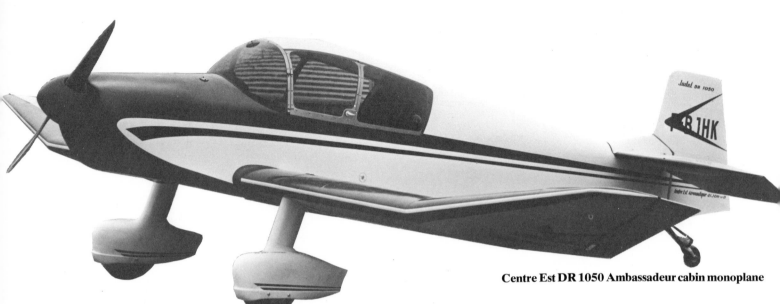

Centre Est DR 1050 Ambassadeur cabin monoplane

version of the Jodel D.11, designed by Robin and first flown July 1958. Built also by Société Aéronautique Normande. Delivered 500th aircraft in June 1967. Subsequent products also mainly two- to four-seat private owner models. Name of company subsequently altered to Avions Pierre Robin (Centre Est Aéronautique); the latter part dropped from marketing name about 1974.

CENTRAL AERO-HYDRODYNAMIC INSTITUTE/*USSR*
see ANT

CENTRALA FLYGVERKSTÅDERNA/*Sweden*
Royal Swedish Air Force maintenance depots at Malinslätt (CFM, later CVM) and Västerås (CFV, later CVV). Established 1926/27, and from 1928 until mid-1930s built foreign aircraft under licence for RSWAF, including Focke-Wulf Fw 44 Stieglitz; Fokker C.V-D and -E and Hawker Hart.

CENTRALA INDUSTRIALA AERONAUTICA ROMANA/*Romania*
Authority responsible since 1968 for all Romanian aircraft production. Major factories are IRMA at Bucharest and ICA at Brasov; also produces, in collaboration with Yugoslavia, the Orao twin-jet fighter/ground attack aircraft (*see* VTI/CIAR).

CENTRAL AIRCRAFT COMPANY LTD./*UK*
Founded in London, late 1916, subsidiary of established joinery company, R. Cattle Ltd.

Aircraft and components built during 1918 under licence. Produced in 1919, at Northolt, Middlesex, small biplane trainers designed by J. S. Fletcher, the company manager. Original designations were C. F., later changed to Centaur. The Centaur IV (C.F.4) was a three-seat Renault-engined tourer. The next model was the Centaur IIa (C.F.2A) a twin-engined commercial transport biplane with Beardmore engines. Two were built, equipped with seats for six/seven passengers or to carry half a ton of mail or freight.

CENTRO TÉCNICO DE AERONÁUTICA/*Brazil*
see CTA

CENTRO VOLA A VELA/*Italy*
see CVV

CENTRAL STATES AERO COMPANY LTD./*USA*
Established at Bettendorf, Iowa, this company produced a small two-seat sporting monoplane known as the Central States Monocoupe. Powered by a 52 kW (70 hp) engine, this aircraft was reputedly able to become airborne within the short space of five seconds from starting its take-off run.

CENTURY AIRCRAFT CORPORATION/*USA*
Amarillo, Texas, based company which in 1977 certificated a re-engined (TPE 331) version of Handley Page Jetstream Mk 1 twin-turboprop transport; conversion carried out by Volpar Inc. (*q.v.*)

CERVA/*France*
Consortium Européen de Réalisation de Ventes d'Avions is a joint venture started 1971 by Siren SA and Wassmer Aviation (*q.v.*) to build and market CE.43 Guépard four-seat light aircraft, an all-metal development of the Wassmer Super 4/21, first flown May 1971. Prototype of generally similar CE.44 Cougar flown October 1974, and CE.45 Léopard late 1975. Partnership ended Autumn 1977 due to bankruptcy of Wassmer.

CESKOMORAVSKA-KOLBEN-DANEK/*Czechoslovakia*
see CKD-Praga

CESKOSLOVENSKÉ ZÁVODY AUTOMOBILOVÉ A LETECKÉ, NARODNÍ PODNIK/*Czechoslovakia*
Blanket title: Czech Automobile and Aircraft Works, National Corporation, covering all national manufacture from 1945 until mid-1950s. The Zavody Letecke (aircraft works) incorporated the former Aero, CKD-Praga and Letov factories, plus Walter (engines) while Avia, Mraz and Zlin plus the Skoda car works came under Závody Automobilové. Built under licence several Soviet types (Ilyushin Il-14 and 28, MiG-15). Czech designations for MiG-15 were CS-102, S-103; Il-14 built as Avia 14. Early indigenous products included the Tom-8 (or L-208) two-seat trainer; L-40 Meta-Sokol four-seat light trainer/tourer; L-60 Brigadyr three/four-seat light STOL monoplane; Zlin 226 Trener and 326 Trener-Master; Aero 145 and Super Aero; L-200 Morava four/five-seat twin-engined air taxi/business aircraft; and HC-2 Heli-Baby and HC-3 light helicopters.

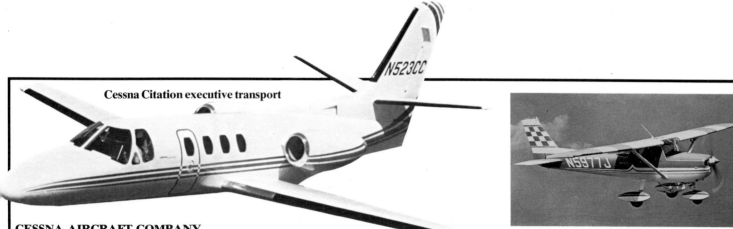

Cessna Citation executive transport

Cessna 150 Aerobat lightplane

CESSNA AIRCRAFT COMPANY
INC./USA

Clyde V. Cessna, originally a motor mechanic, built his first aircraft at Enid, Oklahoma, in Spring 1911. Built and flew several more before moving to Wichita, Kansas, in 1917. Founded Travel Air Manufacturing Company (*q.v.*) with Walter Beech and Lloyd Stearman on 5 February 1925. Disagreed with company policy on aircraft design and in 1927 built self-financed monoplane which developed into Airmaster and Model 195 series of four-seat cantilever high-wing cabin monoplanes. Cessna-Roos Aircraft Company established with Victor Roos on 8 September 1927; Roos backed out and on 31 December the present Cessna company was incorporated.

Production of 'A' series (again with cantilever wings) began 1928, as did BW three-seater. Built DC-6 prototype 1929, followed by four-seat DC-6A and 6B. Cessna tried to keep factory functioning during the depression, producing 300 CG-2 primary gliders, but finally had to close in 1931. Company continued to exist and build several highly successful custom-built racers. Factory re-opened 1934, but Clyde sold his interests and company continued to be run by his son, a nephew and T. Salter. Went on to develop highly successful Airmaster series and in 1939 the first Cessna twin, the T-50 five-seat cabin monoplane. Latter built in large numbers including nearly 1,200 Crane trainer versions for the RCAF. Adopted also by USAAF, US Army and Navy, and over 5,000 produced during WW2, serving in all theatres.

After the war, Cessna began building light aircraft for private and business use. The most successful early models were Models 140 and 170, plus later Models 172, 305, 180 and others which became world-renowned. Model 305 used widely for liaison duties during Korean War and later as L-19/OE-1 Bird Dog (over 3,500 built). In March 1952 acquired Seibel Helicopter Company (*q.v.*) and the CH-1 four-seat helicopter was developed and built in small numbers. In 1972 Cessna became the world's first company to have produced 100,000 aircraft. Production has included nearly 2,000 twin-engined jet trainers and A-37 strike aircraft for the USAF and US Military Assistance Programme.

Cessna Model 402 Businessliner light transport

Cessna A-37B (Model 318E) light strike aircraft

Cessna AGwagon duster/sprayer agricultural aircraft

CFA/*France*
Compagnie Française d'Aviation established at Billancourt in late 1930s to build a version of pre-war Salmson Cri-Cri. Developed also a post-war variant, the D-7 Cri-Cri Major two-seat high-wing cabin monoplane. Only a few built; superseded by prototypes of D57 Phryganet (first flight 7 November 1950) of similar general layout and D21T-4 Super Phryganet (first flown 30 July 1951). All three designed by Paul J. Deville of Salmson.

CHAMPION AIRCRAFT CORPORATION/*USA*
This company was formed by Robert Brown

after acquiring rights in the Aeronca Model 7 Champion two-seat training/touring monoplane in June 1954. Aeronca Aircraft Corporation (*q.v.*) ceased manufacture of the Champion in 1951. Production began at Osceola, Wisconsin, in late 1954; subsequent models included the 7EC Traveler, 7FC Tri-Traveler, Sky-Trac, Challenger and Citabria. By mid-1960s the Citabria had become the main production version. In 1961 Champion Aircraft Corporation produced the single-seat parasol-wing Model 8 Citabria Pro for professional aerobatic pilots. Bellanca Aircraft Corporation (*q.v.*) acquired the company's assets on 30 September 1970, by which time some 1,500 Citabrias had been built.

Champion Citabria aerobatic lightplane

Champion Olympia high-wing monoplane

Champion Scout light utility aircraft

Chance Vought & Sikorsky VS-44A Excalibur flying-boat

CHANCE VOUGHT/*USA*
Lewis & Vought Corporation (*q.v.*) renamed Chance Vought Corporation after WW1. From 1922–1926 produced UO-1 observation float biplanes (developed from VE-7/9) and FU-1 catapult fighter seaplanes for US Navy, followed in 1927 by 02U observation landplanes for same customer, first of several Vought designs to bear the name Corsair. Moved to East Hartford, Connecticut, in about 1930, where until 1935 it continued the Corsair series with 03U observation biplanes and similar SU scouts, again for US Navy. Became Chance Vought Division of United Aircraft Corporation (*q.v.*) in 1934, initially continuing production at East Hartford of 03U/SU Corsairs. These were followed by Vought SBU two-seat scout-bomber, designed in 1932 and produced for US Navy between 1935–1937. Joined with Sikorsky Division of UAC in April 1939 to form Chance Vought and Sikorsky Aircraft Division of United Aircraft Corporation (*q.v.*). Became Chance Vought Aircraft Inc. after becoming separate and independent from UAC on 1 July 1954. Main product during this stage of its history was the unorthodox F7U Cutlass, which was in production 1952–1955 for the US Navy. Deliveries began also in 1957 of the F-8 (originally F8U) Crusader, development and production of

Chance Vought F7U Cutlass carrier-based fighter

122

which continued as the LTV F-8 after further company metamorphoses into Chance Vought Corporation (from 31 December 1960), and a merger on 31 August 1961 with Ling-Temco Electronics Inc. to form Ling-Temco-Vought Inc. (*q.v.*). Within the latter structure, Vought became, successively, the Aerospace Division of LTV, then Vought Aeronautics Company (Division of LTV Aerospace Corporation); since 1 January 1976 it has continued its activities as Vought Corporation (*q.v.*), a subsidiary of the LTV Corporation.

CHANTIERS AÉRO-MARITIMES DE LA SEINE/*France*
see CAMS

CHANTIERS AÉRONAUTIQUES DE NORMANDIE/*France*
Name from 1940 of the former Amiot factory at Cherbourg, which contributed to production of the Junkers Ju 52/3m during the occupation of France.

CHASE AIRCRAFT COMPANY INC./*USA*
Established New York 1943 by Michael Stroukoff to develop experimental assault/cargo gliders. Produced XCG-14, XCG-14A and CG-18A. Moved to Trenton, New Jersey, late 1946, developing a powered version, 30-troop YC-122 Avitruc, first flown 18 November 1948. Twelve built for USAF trials but no further production. Followed by larger C-123 Avitruc, first flown 14 October 1949, derived from XG-20 cargo glider; this project later taken over by Fairchild (*q.v.*) as C-123B and re-named Provider. An XC-123A prototype (four General Electric turbojets) flew on 21 April 1951: first flight of a US transport powered by jet engines. Chase became wholly-owned subsidiary of Willys Motors Inc. of Toledo, Ohio, in 1953, itself owned by Kaiser-Fraser (*q.v.*). In June 1953 a USAF contract for 300 C-123Bs was cancelled, a smaller contract going to Fairchild that Autumn. *See also* Stroukoff Aircraft Corporation.

CHEETAH LIGHT AIRCRAFT COMPANY LTD./*Canada*
Clairco formed 14 January 1964 at St. Jean, Quebec, by David Saunders (an RCAF pilot 1957–1963). Built and flew, in 1962, an all-wood two-seat light aircraft named Cheetah. Founded company to build a four-seat all-metal improved version, the Super Cheetah; prototype built by Aircraft Industries of Canada. This flew September 1964, but no production took place.

Chase YC-122 Avitruc light assault transport

CHETVERIKOV/*USSR*
A 1928 graduate of Leningrad Institute of Transport Engineering, I. V. Chetverikov worked briefly with D. P. Grigorovich (*q.v.*) before joining the TsKB (Tsentralnoe Konstruktorskoe Byuro—Central Design Bureau). From 1931–1933 was in charge of seaplane development section; responsible for designing MDR-3 reconnaissance flying-boat; OSGA-101 light amphibian; and related SPL submarine-borne small floatplane. His ARK-3 flying-boat was a failure, but the three-seat MDR-6 (or Che-2) of 1937 was produced for Soviet Naval Aviation—50 built at Taganrog between 1939 and German invasion of Crimea in 1941. Development, but no further production, of MDR-6 continued during WW2; after

Chetverikov MDR-6 flying-boat

completion in 1947 of three prototypes of the eight-passenger TA-1 flying-boat, this bureau was closed down in 1948 and Chetverikov became a lecturer.

CHILTON AIRCRAFT/*UK*
Operated from Chilton, near Hungerford, Berkshire, in 1936 to build D.W.1 single-seat light aircraft designed by Hon Andrew W. H. Dalrymple and A. R. Ward; an attractive low-wing open-cockpit wooden monoplane with fixed 'trousered' landing gear and Carden-Ford engine, first flown April 1937. Three D.W.1s built, followed by one faster D.W.1A, first flown July 1939. Design of D.W.2 only half finished when WW2 began and it was never completed.

During the war company did sub-contract work for MAP and aircraft industry generally. Dalrymple died in a flying accident in December 1945 and company re-registered on 5 June 1946 as Chilton Aircraft Company Ltd. Prototype Olympia single-seat sailplane built 1947; rights in this sold to Elliotts of Newbury Ltd. (*q.v.*) in 1952—company began work in electrical industry.

Chilton D.W.1A single-seat lightplane

Chincul-built Piper PA-28-140 Cherokee cabin monoplane

CHINCUL SAC/*Argentina*
Wholly-owned subsidiary of La Macarena SA, distributor of Piper Aircraft Corporation (*q.v.*) products in Argentina. Chincul has manufactured Piper aircraft since 1972 including Aztec, Turbo Aztec, Pawnee, Cherokee, Navajo and Seneca. Cheyenne production was to begin in 1977.

CHRISLEA AIRCRAFT COMPANY LTD./*UK*
Based originally at Heston, Middlesex, in 1936, building joint designs of R. C. Christophorides and B. V. Leak. In 1938 one L.C.1 Airguard was built: a two-seat, low-wing cabin monoplane for Civil Air Guard. Company transferred to Kentish Town shortly before WW2, undertaking sub-contract work for aircraft industry. Moved again in 1947 to Exeter Airport, where during 1948–1950 a series of four-seat lightplanes were constructed: Series 1 CH.3 Ace; Series 2 CH.3 Super Ace and Series 4 CH.3 Skyjeep. The first of these high-wing cabin monoplanes was flown in August 1946, but high operating costs and unacceptable control system affected sales of the Ace and Super Ace: more conventional system used on 1949 Skyjeep. Total production (all three types) about 26 aircraft. In 1952 assets acquired by C. E. Harper Aircraft Ltd. and all surviving models were scrapped.

Chrislea CH.3 (series 2) Super Ace lightplane

CICARÉ AERONÁUTICA/*Argentina*
From late 1960s, designed and built Cicaré I and II experimental light helicopters. Followed September 1976 by C.K.1 (originally CH-III) two/three-seat light helicopter for training and agricultural use, aimed mostly at the South American market. Pre-series batch of five under construction in 1977.

Cicaré II three-seat light helicopter

Cierva C.30A Autogiro

CIERVA AUTOGIRO COMPANY
LTD./*UK*

Company founded 24 March 1926 by Air Commodore J. G. Weir, specialising in construction of Autogiros designed by famous Spanish pioneer aviator Juan de la Cierva (1886–1936). Two best-known craft were C.8L, first rotorcraft to fly the English Channel, and C.30A, built by A. V. Roe (*q.v.*) as Rota for RAF. Production of other Autogiros licenced by Cierva to Airwork (C. 30, C. 30P); Avro (C.6, C.8, C.9, C.12, C.17, C.19, C.30A, C.30P); British Aircraft Manufacturing Co. (C.40); Comper (C.25); de Havilland (C.24, C.26); George Parnall & Co. (C.10, C.11); and Westland (CL.20) (all *q.v.*). Weir formed a separate company (G. & J. Weir Ltd, which see) in 1933, and re-established Cierva Company in 1944. After WW2 evolved (jointly with above company), the W.9, a two-seat helicopter using jet thrust to counteract torque. The W.11 Air Horse three-rotor design was built for Cierva by Cunliffe-Owen (*q.v.*); designed specifically for crop-spraying, it was first flown 8 December 1948. The W.14 Skeeter, small two-seat helicopter, first flown 8 October 1948. Both designs taken over in 1951 by Saunders-Roe (*q.v.*), together with other Cierva projects. Company then concentrated on research—eventually re-emerged as Cierva Rotorcraft Ltd, and bought up Rotorcraft Ltd. (*q.v.*) in April 1966 and Servotec Ltd. in 1968. The prototype CR.LTH-1 flew 18 October 1969 but was not produced due to lack of funds.

CIVILIAN AIRCRAFT COMPANY
LTD./*UK*
see CAC

CKD-PRAGA/*Czechoslovakia*

Ceskomoravska-Kolben-Danek, maker of aero-engines from 1915, including several marketed under the name Praga. Began aircraft construction in 1931, subsequent products including the Praga E.40 two-seat training biplane and E.45 single-seat fighter biplane, and a family of two/four-seat light cabin monoplanes designated E.114 Air Baby, E.115, E.210 and E.214. Factory overrun by German invasion during WW2, but operated by Germany as Böhmisch-Mährische Maschinenfabriken AG (Bohemian-Moravian En-

Cierva three-rotor W.11 Air Horse helicopter

gineering Works). Re-established post-war under new title of Závody Letecké Praga, producing, inter alia, updated models of the E.114 and E.210/211.

CLARK AIRCRAFT
CORPORATION/*USA*

Subsidiary of Fairchild (*q.v.*) formed 10 February 1938 under presidency of Harold Clark. He developed Duramold process of constructing fuselages in moulded halves of a plastic compound material, joined along top and bottom centrelines. Production of prototype Clark F-46A three/four-seat monoplane followed, using this technique, at Fairchild's Hagerstown, Maryland factory.

CLARK AIRCRAFT INC./*USA*

Clark 1000 single-seat agricultural biplane, produced at Marshall, Texas, was first flown March 1956 and put into production the following spring.

CLAYTON & SHUTTLEWORTH
LTD./*UK*

This company were sub-contractors during WW1 for the construction of Handley Page 0/100, Sopwith Triplane, Sopwith Camel and Vickers Vimy, all built at Lincoln.

CLÉMENT-BAYARD/*France*

Adolphe Clément-Bayard, former bicycle and car manufacturer, became interested in aeronautics in 1908 and was known primarily as a producer of airships and, in more minor capacity, of aero-engines and aircraft. Was pioneer of welded steel tube airframe construction. Built and engined small number of Santos-Dumont Demoiselles 1909–1910. Gnome-engined Clément-Bayard two-seat monoplane set world distance record of 410 km (255 miles) February 1913. Same year other Gnome-engined civil/military monoplanes appeared; also three-seat monoplane. At Olympia Aero Show (London, March 1914) exhibited an all-steel armoured monoplane. In 1928 sold his factory to Citröen.

CLYDE ENGINEERING COMPANY
LTD./*Australia*

Contracted in 1939–1940 to build wing units for Avro Anson twin-engined trainers and assemble Ansons in Australia for Commonwealth Air Training Plan. Merged early 1948 with Fairey Aviation Company Ltd. of UK (*q.v.*), becoming Fairey Clyde Aviation Company Pty. Ltd, carrying out repair/overhaul of Fairey Firefly and Hawker Sea Fury aircraft for Royal Australian Navy. Renamed Fairey Aviation Company of Australia Pty. Ltd. (*q.v.*) in November 1951.

CKD-Praga E.114 Air Baby lightplane

Colonial Skimmer amphibian flying-boat

CMASA/*Italy*
Costruzioni Meccaniche Aeronàutiche SA; previously SA Industrie Aeromarittime Gallinari (*q.v.*); established 1922 at Marina di Pisa as Società di Costruzioni di Pisa (*q.v.*) to licence-build Dornier Wal flying-boats. Title CMASA adopted in 1930; became subsidiary of Fiat (*q.v.*) same year. Production included G.8 two-seat aerobatic training/touring biplane (1934); M.F.4 radial-engined flying-boat (1933); M.F.5 (development of Wal); M.F.6 two-seat fighter/reconnaissance floatplane; M.F.10 two-seat fighter/reconnaissance shipborne flying-boat (1935); BGA twin-engined floatplane/bomber (1936); and twin-engined, twin-float R.S.14 reconnaissance seaplane. The latter was the most successful, serving throughout WW2. Assisted also in production of Fiat fighters in late 1930s/early 1940s. Activities suspended on Italian Armistice (September 1943). The C.S. high-speed monoplane and J.S.54 six-engined civil flying-boat were then under development, but never produced.

CNA/*Italy*
Compagnia Nazionale Aeronàutica, founded in 1920 at Cerveteri Aerodrome, Rome, moving to CNA-owned Littorio civil airport (Rome), eventually becoming a member of Caproni group (*q.v.*). Mainly a licence builder of others' designs, but in mid/late 1930s own products included C.N.A.15 low-wing and C.N.A.25 high-wing four-seat cabin monoplanes (both CNA-engined). During 1939–1940 said to have produced PM1 two-seat high-wing monoplane with flat-four engine.

CNNA/*Brazil*
Companhia Nacional de Navegação Aérea, took over manufacture of Muniz-designed aircraft from Companhia Nacional de Navegação Costiera (CNNC, *q.v.*) around 1941. Produced Muniz M-11 two-seat primary trainer, designated HL-1, with strong resemblance to Piper Cub; batch of 50 HL-6 tandem two-seat low-wing monoplane trainers was begun 1943. Other designs included HL-2 and HL-4. In

1947, improved Series B versions of the HL-1 and HL-6 appeared; the company's activities had ceased by about 1950.

CNNC/*Brazil*
Companhia Nacional de Navegação Costiera, founded at Ilha do Viana, Rio de Janeiro, in late 1930s to manufacture Muniz-designed M-7 and M-9 biplane trainers; basically an Army aircraft workshop. In early 1940s, re-named Fábrica Brasileira de Aviões (*q.v.*); see also Muniz.

CNT/*Italy*
see Cantiere Navale Triestino

COBELAVIA/*Belgium*
Compagnie Belge d'Aviation in the mid-1960s built Nipper single-seat ultra-light aircraft at Kortessem. Nipper Aircraft (*q.v.*) took over sole manufacturing rights of this aircraft in June 1966.

COCKSHUTT MOULDED AIRCRAFT LTD./*Canada*
Subsidiary of Cockshutt Plow Company, which produced parts for Canadian Ansons in 1940, was formed Summer 1942 to manufacture moulded plywood fuselage components for Anson Mks V and VI built in Canada by Federal Aircraft Ltd. (*q.v.*). Work began late 1942, aircraft delivered between March 1943 and December 1944. Later built fuselages of D. H. Mosquito B. Mk.25 for de Havilland Canada (*q.v.*).

CODOCK/*Australia*
Cockatoo Dockyard & Engineering Co. Ltd. opened an experimental aviation department in the early 1930s, under the guidance of Wing Cdr L. J. Wackett, formerly in the RAAF. In 1933 designed and built a twin-engined monoplane, the Codock, for Sir Charles Kingsford-Smith, who had made the first Pacific air crossing in 1928. A six-seat monoplane of the

cantilever-wing Fokker type, it was powered by two 123 kW (165 hp) Napier Javelin engines.

COLGATE AIRCRAFT/*USA*
Colgate-Larsen Aircraft Corporation succeeded Spencer-Larsen Aircraft Corporation (*q.v.*) around 1940, continuing its work at Amityville, Long Island, NY on novel-design small four-seat amphibian flying-boat, the CL-15 (formerly SL-15). From 1941 engaged on sub-contract work for other military aircraft building programmes, especially after US entry into WW2.

COLLIER AIRCRAFT CORPORATION/*USA*
Formed by W. S. Collier in 1939 to build CA-1 Ambassador two-seat light trainer biplane.

COLOMBES, ATELIERS AÉRONAUTIQUES/*France*
Amiot (SECM) company after nationalisation; AAC came under control of Junkers (*q.v.*) during the occupation of France in WW2 and began producing Junkers Ju 52/3m transports for the Luftwaffe. After the war continued building these aircraft under French government contract, designated AAC-1 Toucan. More than 400 produced; when order was completed, factory taken over by Aérocentre-SNCA du Centre (*q.v.*).

COLONIAL AIRCRAFT CORPORATION/*USA*
David B. Thurston and four other designers founded this company in 1946 to produce the C-1 Skimmer two/three-seat single-engined amphibian. First flown 17 July 1948; certificated 1955, but first major model produced in 1957 (four-seat C-2 Skimmer IV). Manufacturing rights sold October 1959 to Lake Aircraft Corporation (since 1962 the Lake Aircraft Division of Consolidated Aeronautics Inc. (*q.v.*). Still being produced in 1978 as four-seat LA-4-200 Buccaneer.

COLUMBIA AIRCRAFT CORPORATION/USA
During 1928–1929 produced the Triad high-wing wheel/float amphibian at Valley Stream, Long Island, NY, at which time the company was known as Columbia Air liners Inc. Name changed to above and later built 330 Grumman J2F-6 Ducks for the USN. Two Grumman-designed XJL-1 (Duck replacement) prototypes were built. The company was taken over in early 1946 as part of the Commonwealth Aircraft Corporation (q.v.); it went into liquidation in 1948.

COMMONWEALTH AIRCRAFT CORPORATION PTY. LTD./Australia
Established Port Melbourne, 1936, as basis of an independent Australian industry. Took over Tugan Aircraft (q.v.) that year and chief designer Wing Cdr. L. J. Wackett. First product was North American NA-33, built under licence as CA-1 to CA-16 Wirraway for RAAF, starting in July 1939. Followed by Wackett-designed prototype CA-2 Wackett two-seat trainer, production version designated CA-6. Company also produced the only Australian-designed fighter to serve in WW2,

the CA-12, 13, 14, 19 Boomerang. Post-war products included the prototype CA-22 and production CA-25 Winjeel trainer for the RAAF; the CA-28 Ceres agricultural aircraft; and over 200 North American Mustangs built as CA-17 and 18. First jet aircraft were North American F-86F Sabres, licence-built and modified to use the Rolls-Royce Avon turbojet, thought by many to be the best Sabre variant. Recently CAC has participated with Government Aircraft Factories (q.v.) in licence-production of Dassault Mirage III-0 (CA-29) and III-D, as well as Aermacchi

Columbia single-engined flying-boat

Commonwealth Wackett two-seat trainer

Australia's nationally-designed Boomerang fighter

M.B. 326H jet trainers. Became a public company in 1975 and contracted to build 56 Bell 206B JetRanger II helicopters for Australian Army, all delivered by early January 1978. Other contracts include work for Boeing, Sikorsky, Pratt & Whitney and Hawker Siddeley (*q.v.*). Commonwealth Aircraft Corporation were specialising in 1978 in the manufacture and repair of gas turbine engines.

COMMONWEALTH AIRCRAFT INC./*USA*

This company was formed in Kansas City October 1942, after the acquisition of Rearwin Aircraft & Engines Inc. (*q.v.*) by New York interests. In 1943 it received substantial orders for Waco CG-3A and 4A troop-carrying gliders for the USAAF. It obtained manufacturing rights in 1945 for the Trimmer three-seat twin-engined light amphibian (prototype only), formerly built by Allied Aviation (*q.v.*) In 1946 Commonwealth Aircraft Inc. began producing Model 185, a development of the pre-war Rearwin Model 175. Early that year the company took over the Columbia Aircraft Corporation (*q.v.*), all manufacturing being transferred to the latter's Valley Stream factory. In March 1946 it acquired a non-aircraft company at Port Washington as a manufacturing base for the Trimmer, which did not go into series production. The Skyranger model was built in small numbers in 1946–1948.

COMPAGNIE BELGE D'AVIATION/*Belgium*
see COBELAVIA

COMPANHIA NACIONAL DE AVIÕES LTDA/*Brazil*
see CONAL

COMPER AIRCRAFT CO. LTD./*UK*

The company was formed at Hooton Park, Cheshire, on 14 March 1929 by Flt. Lt. Nicholas Comper and others. Formerly with Airco (*q.v.*), Comper had also been responsible for the Cranwell Light Aeroplane Club series of amateur-built lightplanes, the C.L.A. 2, 3 and 4A. The company's first product was the C.L.A. 7 Swift, a single-seat high-wing sporting aircraft, which was first flown in Spring 1930 and built between 1930 and 1934 (one was owned by the Prince of Wales, later Edward VIII). The company moved to Heston, Middlesex, in 1933; the one-off three-seat Mouse and single-seat Streak monoplanes were built in that year, followed by a single Kite two-seat tourer developed from the Streak. In 1934 the company closed, to re-register as Heston Aircraft Company (*q.v.*).

Licence-built Commonwealth Wirraway trainer

COMTE/*Switzerland*

Flugzeugbau A. Comte built in early/middle 1920s a few German types (e.g. Sablatnig) under licence at Hargen, near Zürich. First own-design was AC-1 fighter prototype of 1927; followed by AC-3 twin-engined bomber. Best known for series of small high-wing cabin monoplanes such as three-seat AC-4 Gentleman (built 1928–1930).

CONAL/*Brazil*

The name stands for Companhia Nacional de Aviões Ltda; a prototype five-seat high-wing cabin monoplane Conal W-151 Sopocaba was designed and flown in August 1964, but none were produced. The company was licensed for conversions of the Dumod I and Dumod Liner made by the American Dumod Corporation (*q.v.*) but none were apparently built.

Prototype of the Conal W-151 cabin monoplane

Comper C.L.A.7 Swift single-seat sports aircraft

The eighth production Anglo-French Concorde

CONCORDE/*International*
Anglo-French supersonic transport developed following 29 November 1962 agreements between French and British governments and aircraft/aero-engine companies. Airframe manufacturers BAC and Aérospatiale (both *q.v.*); engine contractors are Rolls-Royce and SNECMA. Production authorised of two prototype, two pre-series and 16 production aircraft. An interesting feature is that fuel is pumped from one part of the aircraft to another to counteract trim changes between subsonic and supersonic flight.

CONROY AIRCRAFT CORPORATION/*USA*
Formed 1968–1969 by Jack M. Conroy at Santa Barbara airport, California, offering aircraft and services for the petroleum and other 'bulk' cargo industries. First ventures included turboprop conversions of Douglas DC-3 (Conroy Turbo Three) and Fairchild C-119 Flying Boxcar. Conroy developed original Guppy series of giant transports (see Aero Spacelines); also converted Canadair CL-44D-4 swing-tailed, long-range freighter as Conroy CL-44-0, with enlarged-diameter fuselage

(flown November 1969); and Stolifter (flown 1969) single-turboprop conversion of Cessna Super Skymaster, with upward-opening aft fuselage. Turboprop conversion of Grumman Albatross amphibian flown February 1970; company ceased trading shortly afterwards.

CONSOLIDATED AERONAUTICS INC./*USA*
Parent company since 1962 of Lake Aircraft (*q.v.*), producer of LA-4-200 Buccaneer four-seat amphibian.

Conroy Airlift, an outsize Canadair CL-44

Conroy Turbo Albatross, a conversion of Grumman's amphibian

129

CONSOLIDATED AIRCRAFT CORPORATION/*USA*

Original factory was quickly outgrown by the company formed 29 May 1923 and moved to Buffalo, NY, leasing part of a wartime Curtiss factory, in 1924. In the 1920s and 1930s produced small numbers of civil types but main output was military and between 1924–32 included more than 770 PT-1/311 and NY primary training biplanes for the USAAC and Navy, plus a small batch of similar 0-17s for observation duties. Thomas Morse Aircraft (*q.v.*) acquired 1929. In the 1930s Consolidated specialised in marine aircraft, P2Y twin-engined patrol flying-boats being built 1931–1933; followed by P-30 single-seat fighter monoplanes for the Army in 1933–1935. In Autumn 1935 company moved to San Diego, California, gaining a harbour for testing its maritime designs, which continued with the P3Y/PBY Catalina family. During a ten-year production life, 2,400 Catalinas were built by Consolidated and hundreds more by other companies. Production of PB2Y Coronados began in 1939. In 1940 Hall Aluminium Company acquired. Company began a five-year programme of building more than 11,000 B-24/C-87/PB4Y/RY Liberator and Privateer bombers, transports and patrol aircraft for the US services and the RAF. Liberator production was also undertaken by Ford, Douglas and North American (*q.v.*). Final wartime product was the TBY Sea Wolf. A 34% controlling interest in Consolidated acquired December 1941 by Vultee Aircraft Inc. (*q.v.*), and management links from then led to merger of the two companies on 17 March 1943 as Consolidated Vultee Aircraft Corporation (see next entry).

Consolidated PBY Catalina patrol flying-boat

Consolidated PB2Y-3 Coronado flying-boat

Consolidated B-24 Liberator bomber/reconnaissance aircraft

CONSOLIDATED VULTEE AIRCRAFT CORPORATION/*USA*

Amalgamation from 17 March 1943 of Consolidated Aircraft Corporation and Vultee Aircraft Inc. (both *q.v.*), whose wartime production programmes are listed under these separate headings. By the end of WW2 Consolidated Vultee was largest aircraft manufacturing organisation in the USA, with factories at San Diego and Vultee Field, California; Fort Worth, Texas; Nashville, Tennessee; Wayne, Michigan; New Orleans, Louisiana; Miami, Florida; and Allentown, Pennsylvania; plus modification centres at Tucson, Arizona; Elizabeth City, North Carolina; and Louisville, Kentucky. Late-war/early post-war programmes included B-32 Dominator long-range bomber; L-13 liaison/observation aircraft; and multi-engined B-36 intercontinental bomber. The company entered the commercial field with first flight, in summer 1946, of twin-engined Model 110, from which later stemmed well-known 240/340/440 Metropolitan series of medium-sized short-haul airliners. Various noteworthy military prototypes included the XB-46 jet bomber, XP-81 single-seat mixed-power escort fighter, XF-92 rocket-powered interceptor, XA-41 close-support aircraft and XF2Y Sea Dart hydro-ski fighter; and a small number of R3Y Tradewind four-engined transport flying-boats were built for the US Navy. In the early 1950s Consolidated Vultee began calling its products 'Convair' types, and on 30 April 1954 it became the Convair Division of General Dynamics Corporation (*q.v.*), who were then the major shareholder.

CONTINENTAL AIRCRAFT CORPORATION/*USA*

Based at Amityville, Long Island, NY, in 1919: was then building KB-3T two-seat trainer bi-plane, designed by Vincent Buranelli, and powered by Curtiss OX engine.

CONTINENTAL COPTERS INC./*USA*

Since 1959 has produced assorted versions of the El Tomcat—specialised single-seat agricultural conversions of Bell Model 47 helicopter. Successive variants have included Mks IIIA, IIIB, IIIC, V, V-A, V-B, VI, VI-A and VI-B, of which approximately 70 (all versions) completed by end of 1977; also markets kits for operator conversion. Since late 1960s/early 70s has assembled Bell 47G series helicopters to order.

CONTINENTAL INC./*USA*

With Robert E. Fulton Jr. as President, company was formed 1945 at Danbury, Connecticut. Prototype Airphibian flew 7 November 1946, a two-seat 'roadable' aircraft, with tricycle landing gear, detachable wings/tail/rear fuselage. Certificated December 1950 as Fulton Model FA-2 Airphibian; production model, designated FA-3, appeared 1954.

Continental Copters El Tomcat Mk VI-B

Convair CV twin-engined short-range airliner

CONVAIR/*USA*

Convair Division of General Dynamics Corporation; title adopted from 30 April 1954 by Consolidated Vultee (*q.v.*) following acquisition in 1953 of major shareholdings by General Dynamics. Major products have been the Convair F-102 Delta Dagger and F-106 Delta Dart interceptors; B-58 Hustler supersonic bomber; and Convair 880 and 990 four-jet commercial transports. Developed subsequently F-111/FB-111 variable-geometry combat aircraft, now the responsibility of GD's

Convair RB-36 heavy bomber retrieving RF-84F parasite fighter

131

Convair XFY-1 VTOL tail-sitter research aircraft

Convair B-58 Hustler supersonic bomber

Convair F-102A Delta Dagger fighter-interceptor

Fort Worth Division (q.v.). Convair was grouped with GD's Fort Worth and Pomona Divisions in September 1970 to form single Convair Aerospace Division, but Fort Worth was again made a separate division in June 1974. Convair Division is currently responsible for commercial aircraft and space exploration systems, product support for Convair 240/340/440 and derivatives and the Convair 880/990. It also builds major components for the McDonnell Douglas DC-10, Space Shuttle Orbiter vehicle and Tomahawk cruise missile.

COOK AIRCRAFT
CORPORATION/USA
Founded by John A. Cook in 1968 at Torrance, California, to market JC-1 Challenger four-seat cabin monoplane. Two prototypes built (first flight May 1969). Third prototype flew November 1971, but crashed January

1972, killing Cook. Company continued, hoping for certification with a fourth (modified) aircraft, first flown 1972; but activities ceased in mid-1970s.

CORNELIUS AIRCRAFT
CORPORATION/USA
Based at Dayton, Ohio; received order for one XBG-3 glider bomb in 1942, but project was cancelled. In 1944, two prototypes of XFG-1 were built; this was a fuel-carrying piloted glider to be towed behind long-range bombers and cut adrift when empty. Again, idea not adopted operationally by USAAF.

COSMIC AIRCRAFT
CORPORATION/USA
In May 1970 acquired all rights in manufacture of F-23 single-seat agricultural monoplane,

produced previously by D. D. Funk Aviation Company Inc. (q.v.) two models: F-23A (Continental radial) and F-23B (Jabobs radial). Production apparently ceased in early 1970s.

COSTRUÇÕES AERONÁUTICAS
SA/Brazil
Originated May 1940 as government-backed private company under French designer René Couzinet (q.v.), at Lagão Santa, Minas Gerais, to build civil and military aircraft. First licence was for North American NA-16 (AT-6 Texan) advanced trainer, but none were produced.

COURIER MONOPLANE
COMPANY/USA
Formed 20 December 1928, produced a braced high-wing monoplane powered by a 75 kW (100 hp) Kinner radial engine.

COUZINET/France

Distinguished French engineer, René Couzinet, began manufacturing aeroplanes in 1928 with the stylish tri-motor monoplane Couzinet 10 Arc-en-Ciel prototype, designed for trans-Atlantic flight. It was destroyed by fire, but the Couzinet 70, developed from the Couzinet 30, was also called Arc-en-Ciel and intended for Aéropostale's trans-Atlantic mail service to South America. After route-proving flight by Jean Mermoz in January 1933 it was extensively modified as Couzinet 71 and entered regular service in May 1934. Air Couzinet 10 of 1937 was totally unrelated twin-engined monoplane. Couzinet himself went to Brazil in the late 1930s, assisting with the development of their aviation industry.

COVENTRY ORDNANCE WORKS LTD./UK

Established at Coventry 1911, absorbing former Warwick Wright company (q.v.) and inheriting two excellent designers—Howard T. Wright and W. O. Manning—who designed the model 10 (Gnome engine) and Model 11 (Chenu engine) biplanes. Built at Battersea and test-flown at Brooklands as possible entries for RFC Military trials, August 1912; neither did very well. No. 10 was modified extensively later in the year and flew successfully at Brooklands. No further original designs prior to WW1. During the conflict C.O.W. acted mainly as sub-contractor on Royal Aircraft Factory (q.v.) aircraft, including B.E.2 and B.E.8 series; B.E. 12/12a; R.E.7 and R.E.8. Also built Sopwith Snipe single-seat fighters. Basically acknowledged, however, as armaments firm (e.g. warship gun installations) and developed rapid-firing aircraft gun (1½ lb shell) intended for Royal Aircraft Factory F.E.4 fighter/bomber and projected Airco (de Havilland) D.H.8., and a 37 mm development was later mounted in Vickers and Westland F.9/27 fighter prototypes, but its weight prohibited its acceptance for fighters.

COX-KLEMEN AIRCRAFT CORPORATION/USA

Based at College Point, Long Island, NY; supplied three TW-2 tandem two-seat biplane trainers for USAAS in 1922. Followed 1923–25 by six examples for USN of XN-1/XS-2 experimental twin-float scout Seaplanes intended for carriage aboard submarines. Also produced two XA-1 prototype ambulance aircraft for US Army.

CRAWFORD ALL-METAL AIRPLANE COMPANY/USA

Established in 1928 at Los Angeles, California, built all-metal aircraft to special order.

Production included a six-seat cabin monoplane, designated Crawford 65, which had corrugated alclad sheet covering for the fuselage, wing and tail surfaces, pioneered by Hugo Junkers in Germany.

CROPMASTER AIRCRAFT PTY. LTD./Australia

Amalgamation of Yeoman Aircraft Pty Ltd. (q.v.) and Yeoman Aviation Pty Ltd. which, in 1959, began building prototype Yeoman YA1, which first flew in January 1960. This one/two-seat agricultural low-wing monoplane started production in 1964 as YA1 Cropmaster; the projected tricycle landing gear YA5 Fieldmaster was not built, and in 1967 production rights in the YA1 were sold to the Cameron-Gray Aircraft Company of the United States.

CROSBY AVIATION CORPORATION LTD./UK

At Knutsford, Cheshire, Crosby began producing (around 1974) factory-built versions of the Andreasson (q.v.) BA-4B single-seat homebuilt biplane. Five built or under construction by 1978.

CROSLEY AIRCRAFT CO./USA

Established in 1929 at Cincinnati, Ohio, this company was a subsidiary of the Crosley Radio Corporation. It produced two- and three-seat open cockpit high-wing monoplanes known respectively as the Crosley C-1 and C-2. These two models pioneered the advantages of interchangeability, with the complete wing, tail surfaces, landing gear, engines and engine mountings being common to both.

CROWN AIRCRAFT CORPORATION/USA

Originally the Aircraft Division of Crown Motor Carriage Company. Produced to direct order in 1930 the B-3 Custombuilt two-seat sporting/training biplane.

CRUSADER AIRCRAFT CORPORATION/USA

Between 1933–1934 built Crusader AF-4 four-seat cabin monoplane with two Menasco in-line engines, twin-boom and twin tail.

CTA/Brazil

Centro Técnico de Aeronáutica, established at São José dos Campos as aeronautical research centre in late 1950s by Brazilian Air Ministry; CTA originally had two divisions. A group within the IPD (Research and Development Division)—Departamento de Aeronaves (q.v.) or PAR was responsible for the BF-1 Beija-Flôr (Humming Bird) two-seat helicopter, first to be designed, built and flown in Brazil.

CUB AIRCRAFT COMPANY LTD./Denmark

Created late 1930s at Lundtofte as Scandinavian assembly factory for US Piper Cub light aircraft; doubtful if any were in fact built.

CUB AIRCRAFT CORPORATION LTD./Canada

Established 1937 at Hamilton, Ontario, to build American Piper Cubs. Early 1931 obtained licence to build Harlow PJC-2 all-metal monoplane. New factory at Hamilton was completed 1940. Production resumed in 1945 of Canadian variant known as Cub Prospector; company does not appear to have survived for more than a year or so after this.

CUBITT LTD./UK

Sub-contractor during WW1 for production at Croydon, Surrey, of de Havilland D.H.9 day bomber.

CULVER AIRCRAFT CORPORATION/USA

Formed at Columbus, Ohio, in 1939 by K. K. Culver. Took over manufacturing and sales rights of Dart Model G two-seat low-wing

Culver Cadet two-seat cabin monoplane

cabin monoplane from Dart Manufacturing Corporation (*q.v.*) same year. First own product, the Cadet, was a two-seat light cabin monoplane (Continental flat-four engine). In 1940–1941 developed two-seat Models LFA and LCA tourer, based on the Cadet, but with retractable landing-gear. Production ceased when America entered WW2, company then carrying out sub-contract work for US aircraft industry. Moved to Wichita, Kansas, 1941, and concentrated entirely on producing radio-controlled pilotless aircraft based on LFA (nearly 2,400 produced) for use as PQ-8/TDC and PQ-14/TD2C gunnery target drones with USAAF and USN. When this ended in 1946, Culver began developing the Model V civil lightplane, first flown September 1945. Four built as drones designated XPQ-15. Company went bankrupt in late 1946—remaining assets acquired mid-1956 by Superior Aircraft Company (*q.v.*).

CUNARD STEAMSHIP COMPANY/*UK*
Cunard built factory at Aintree late 1917/early 1918 after receiving contract on 22 November 1917 to build 500 Bristol Fighters. Production began March 1918, although in the previous month factory had been taken over by Ministry of Munitions and renamed National Aircraft Factory No. 3 (*q.v.*). Production ended after only 126 aircraft completed.

CUNLIFFE-OWEN AIRCRAFT LTD./*UK*
Company founded at Southampton Municipal Airport, Eastleigh, Hampshire, to build 'flying wing' (lifting-fuselage) aircraft based on Burnelli (*q.v.*) concept. First product was improved version of Burnelli UB-14 known as O.A.1 (two crew, 15 passengers). Second version (three crew, 20 passengers) designed as O.A.2, but not produced owing to outbreak of WW2. France acquired O.A.1 and used it in Africa during the war. Extensive sub-contract work for Air Ministry undertaken—mostly on 'anglicising' US Consolidated Vultee, Lockheed and Martin Lend-Lease aircraft for RAF. Late 1945 converted a number of Lancaster B.III bombers for air/sea rescue. In 1946 began design of airliner, the Concordia 10-seat passenger transport, first flown May 1947. Prototype and one other built, but work suspended November 1947 due to insufficient orders. Also built that year the prototype W.10 helicopter for Cierva (*q.v.*); this project shelved too, and shortly afterwards company changed its interests away from aviation.

CUNNINGHAM-HALL AIRCRAFT CORPORATION/*USA*
Randolph F. Hall, with other ex-employees of Thomas-Morse Aircraft Corporation (*q.v.*),

Cunliffe-Owen Concordia medium-range transport

formed this company at Rochester, NY, in 1928, in collaboration with the US automobile company James Cunningham, Son & Company. First aircraft was a six-seat passenger transport (twin-engined PT-6), but only two built. Followed by Model X-90(N) tandem two-seat biplane with special high-lift wings, entered for Guggenheim Safe Airplane Competition 1929. A developed version (also high-lift wings) led to GA-21M all-metal monoplane in 1934, which re-appeared after a year or so as GA-36 with Super Scarab engine. In 1937 built PT-6F biplane light freighter, a two-seat development of PT-6 with 512 kg (1,128 lb) payload and Wright Whirlwind engine. Company ceased building complete aircraft and produced sub-contract aircraft components for other firms during WW2. It was dissolved in 1948.

CURTISS AEROPLANE AND MOTOR COMPANY/*USA*
Created January 1916 from former (though separate) Curtiss Aeroplane Company (Hammondsport, NY) and Curtiss Motor Company, opening new aircraft factory at Buffalo, NY. A third factory (Garden City, Long Island, NY) became Boat Hull Department for flying-boat production. Burgess Company of Marblehead, Massachusetts, became a subsidiary in February 1916. Aircraft built during WW1 included A and AH biplanes for USN; Models D and E for US Army; Model F flying-boats for USN; H-4 Small Americas; H-12 Large Americas; and H-16 Large Americas (plus 150 by Naval Aircraft Factory, *q.v.*).

Best-known were JN-4/JN-6 'Jenny' trainers—5,000 built, plus 1,200 by Canadian Curtiss (*q.v.*); HS flying-boats; MF flying-

Curtiss JN-4 'Jenny', historic and well-loved US trainer

boats; N-9 floatplanes; British S.E.5a fighters; Orenco D fighters and F-5L flying-boats. Total production during WW1 was 4,014 aircraft and 750 aero-engines.

Post-war production, mostly 1920s, included NC-1/2/3/4 trans-Atlantic flying-boats (four only); Oriole, Eagle and Seagull civil types (little success achieved with the few built). Followed by a series of Army (R-6/R-8 etc.) and Navy (CR/R2C/R3C etc.) racers. Twelve B-2 Condor biplane bombers were followed by PW-8 biplane fighters; P-1/P-6 US Army Hawks; F6C US Navy Hawks; 0-1/11/39 and A-3 Falcons for US Army. The few Carrier Pigeons and Larks were followed by one Tanager biplane, which won 1929 Guggenheim Safe Airplane Competition. Subsequently produced N2C Fledgling; F8C/0C

Falcon and F8C/02C Helldivers for USN. Foundation of Curtiss-Robertson division (*q.v.*) in 1928 was followed by a merger with Wright Aeronautical Corporation (*q.v.*) on 9 August 1929 to become Curtiss-Wright Corporation (*q.v.*).

CURTISS-REID AIRCRAFT COMPANY/*Canada*

Founded in Montreal in January 1929 by a merger of the Reid Aircraft Company (founded 1928) and the Curtiss Aeroplane & Motor Company of New York. W. T. Reid, formerly chief designer of Bristol Aeroplane Company (*q.v.*), had founded Reid Aircraft to build a light biplane of his own design. This was produced by the new company as the Curtiss-Reid

Rambler, powered by a licence-built Cirrus engine, and at least six of these aircraft were supplied to the RCAF. Opened flying school in 1930. Built also the Courier, a single-seat lightweight mail-carrying monoplane.

CURTISS-ROBERTSON AIRPLANE MANUFACTURING CORPORATION/*USA*

Founded at St. Louis, Missouri, in 1928 as division of Curtiss-Wright Corporation (*q.v.*) with William B. Robertson as President. Main products were Robin three-seat high-wing cabin monoplane (noted for its endurance records) and Kingbird seven-passenger development with twin engines. Neither was produced on a large scale.

Curtiss NC-4, the first aircraft to make a North Atlantic crossing (in stages)

Curtiss SB2C Helldivers, carrier-based scout-bombers

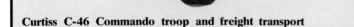

Curtiss C-46 Commando troop and freight transport

CURTISS-WRIGHT CORPORATION, AIRPLANE DIVISION/*USA*

Formed from merger on 9 August 1929 between Curtiss Aeroplane and Motor Company Inc. and Wright Aeronautical Corporation (both *q.v.*). Subsequent production mainly by Curtiss Airplane Division of Curtiss-Wright (aircraft still being 'Curtiss' types rather than 'Curtiss-Wright', except for those with 'CW' designations. Travel Air (*q.v.*) became another subsidiary in 1930. In 1936, complete reorganisation dissolved all main subsidiaries except Wright Aeronautical Division. From 1930 onwards, main products included F9C Sparrowhawk fighter, carried on board USN airships; F11C/BFC Goshawk for USN and export versions Hawk I/II/III/IV; SBC Helldivers for USN; SOC Seagull for USN; BT-32/CT-32/T-32 Condor bomber and civil/military transport; A-8/10/12 Shrike for USAAC; P-36 for USAAC and export Hawk 75s; one CW-20 prototype (later used by BOAC); C-46 Commando (USAAF) and R5C (USN) transport developments of CW-20; CW-21 Demon fighters; SNC trainers for USN, developed from CW-21; P-40 Warhawk/Tomahawk/Kittyhawk fighters for USAAF and other Allied services, of which 13,738 built during WW2; C-76 Caravan transports for USAAF; 0-52 Owl observation biplanes for USAAF/USN; S03C Seamew for USN and Fleet Air Arm; SB2C Helldiver; AT-9 Jeep twin-engined trainers for USAAF; SC Seahawk scout seaplanes for USN; Republic P-47 Thunderbolt fighters for USAAF. Total WW2 production (1940–1945) was 26,755 aircraft and 223,036 aero-engines.

After the war many Curtiss factories closed and most aircraft construction as such discontinued. Some Boeing B-29 modification undertaken until end of 1945, but Curtiss-Wright basically then undertook overhaul and repair of aircraft; manufacture of components, subassemblies and spare parts. By 1952 was concerned exclusively with production of aero-engines and propellers. At the end of the 1950s Curtiss-Wright made a brief return to aircraft production with Skydart rocket-propelled target drone and prototype VZ-7AP VTOL 'flying Jeep' for Army trials. The X-19A was last type produced by the company—a six-seat convertiplane with twin engines driving tandem pairs of tilting propeller/rotors; first flight 26 June 1964; development discontinued 1966. By 1978 main activities of the Corporation included nuclear research, data transmission and research into new advanced engine designs for USAF and NASA—although it still makes components for Boeing 747 'jumbo' jets.

Curtiss-Wright X-19A VTOL research aircraft

Curtiss-Wright VZ-7AP 'flying Jeep' research aircraft

Curtiss P-40 Warhawk, the last of the Curtiss Hawk series

CUSTER CHANNEL WING CORPORATION/*USA*

Set up during early 1950s to develop 'channel-wing' concept devised by its President, Willard R. Custer. (Wing contours formed semi-circular channel/duct in which two pusher engines were suspended). Small-scale experimental aircraft with this configuration flown December 1951; another test aircraft flew shortly afterwards. Followed by Custer CCW-5 (flown July 1953) a modified Baumann Brigadier (built by that company—*q.v.*) with a channel wing and two Continental engines, and

Custer CCW-5 research aircraft

expected to take off in a few feet, rise vertically, hover and land vertically. First production model flew June 1964. Custer retired early 1968, but remained as consultant throughout prolonged certification programme by DeVore Aviation Service Corporation. Despite its founder's efforts to keep the company solvent, Custer Channel Wing Corporation eventually closed through lack of funds.

CVV/*Italy*

Centro Volo a Vela, Politecnico di Milano, fundamentally a research and development centre attached to Milan Polytechnic after WW2 to study soaring flight. Production included gliders and sailplanes, but in the late 1940s/ early 1950s the Centro Volo a Vela also produced prototypes of the P.110 three/four-seat cabin monoplane and P.M. 280 Tartuca single-seat low-wing monoplane.

C. W. AIRCRAFT/*UK*

Established 1936 by C. R. Chronander and J. I. Waddington to design and develop Cygnet two-seat all-metal cabin monoplane, which first flew in 1937. Rights in Cygnet acquired by General Aircraft Ltd. (*q.v.*) in 1938; C. W. was then re-formed as Chronander Waddington Aircraft Ltd, a company which was not concerned with the building of aircraft.

D

DAIMLER COMPANY LTD./UK

A motor car company founded 1897 in Coventry. Built under sub-contract during WW1 the Royal Aircraft Factory B.E.2c, B.E.12/12a, R.E.8 and Airco D.H.10. Proposed production of cannon-armed F.E.4 ground attack aircraft cancelled.

DAIMLER MOTORENGESELLSCHAFT WERKE/Germany

Built Mercedes aero engines from 1910. Constructed Friedrichshafen FF, G III, G IV and other aircraft under licence during WW1. Designed and built G I/R four-engined Giant, 1916; L.8 single-seat fighter, 1918. L.9, L.11, L.14 parasol fighters followed. Ceased production at main works 1919.

DAIMLER-WERKE ATKIEN-GESELLSCHAFT/Germany

Continued operations when main Daimler works closed. Experimental motor glider developed into L.15 (1923) and L.20 (1924) under chief designer Dr. Ing. Hans Klemm. Odd parasol-wing twin-engined two-seater for 1925 Rundflug won class prize. In 1927 became Leichtflugzeugbau Klemm.

DARJAVNA AEROPLANNA RABOTILNITZA/Bulgaria

State Aircraft Works, Bojouristhe, Sofia. Aero department of Ministry of Railways, Posts and Telegraphs. Subject to Versailles limitations, but by 1932 had produced DAR-4, three engined transport for state airline. Of several subsequent designs, only the DAR-10F of 1941 reached production.

DARMSTADT AKADEMISCHE FLIEGERGRUPPE/Germany

Established in 1921 by students at the Technical High School, Darmstadt, for building and testing aircraft. Produced a number of sail-planes, and from 1924 a series of advanced light aircraft that held several class records. Work on powered aircraft ended 1939.

DARRACQ MOTOR ENGINEERING COMPANY/UK

Branch of French motor car company of Alexandre Darracq, based at Fulham, London. In WW1 built under sub-contract Airco D.H.5, RAF F.E.8 and Sopwith Dolphin.

DART AIRCRAFT LTD./UK

Formed at Dunstable, Bedfordshire, in 1936 to build ultralight single-seat aircraft to designs of A. R. Weyl. First were Dunstable Dart, later named Dart Pup, and Flittermouse, both with parasol wing and pusher propellers. Three Dart Kittens were built in UK, as well as one in Australia from plans. Ceased operations 1939.

DART MANUFACTURING COMPANY/USA

Formed 1937 at Columbus, Ohio, to manufacture Dart G two-seat light aircraft. This was a version of the aircraft known originally as the Monosport, designed and built by the Mono Aircraft Corporation (q.v.). Taken over by Culver Aircraft Company (q.v.) of Columbus in 1939.

DAR-10F two-seat bomber, only Bulgarian combat aircraft in WW2

Dart Kitten II ultra-light single-seat sportsplane

DASSAULT BELGIQUE AVIATION
SA/*Belgium*
   see SABCA

DASSAULT-BREGUET/*France*
The result of the 1969 merger, Avions Marcel Dassault-Breguet Aviation has developed the Mirage and Breguet 1150 Atlantique and the Breguet 941S STOL transport. Engaged currently on the SEPECAT Jaguar with British Aerospace.

DASSAULT-BREGUET/DORNIER/*International*
Following agreement between the French and German governments in 1969 to procure a new subsonic basic and advanced training aircraft, suitable for deployment also in a close-support or battlefield reconnaissance role, Dassault-Breguet and Dornier (both *q.v.*) are developing such an aircraft. Known as the Alpha Jet, it is being built primarily by these two companies, but SABCA (*q.v.*) in Belgium and other French and German companies are also involved. The Alpha Jet is powered by twin turbofan engines, and for weapon training or in a close-support role it can carry up to 2,250 kg (4,960 lb) of mixed weapons. Currently enter-

Dassault Super Etendard carrier-based fighter

ing operational service in 1978, it was expected that procurement for the Armée de l'Air and Luftwaffe will be about 200 aircraft each.

DASSAULT, MARCEL, GÉNÉRAL AÉRONAUTIQUE/*France*
Marcel Dassault designed under his original name Marcel Bloch (*q.v.*) before WW2. As Avions Marcel Dassault built the MD 315 Flamant light transport for the Armée de l'Air in 1945. A highly successful and continuing line of fighters for France and export began with the Ouragan (1949); followed by swept-wing Mystère (1952); after-burning Super-

Dassault Super Mystère single-seat fighter

Mystère (1959) was first European supersonic production aircraft. Etendard naval fighter appeared 1958. Large family of aircraft have included Mirage I (1955); delta Mirage III (1960); Mirage V; Milan; Mirage IV; Mirage III/V VTOL strike fighter; F2 interceptor and G8 variable-geometry aircraft. Also produced successful executive Falcon 10, 20, 30, 40 twin jets (originally called Mystère; US production called fan Jet Falcon), and three-jet Falcon 50. In 1969, Dassault acquired majority holding in Breguet Aviation (*q.v.*). Current production: Mirage F1, III, 5; Mercure 200; Falcon 10, 20, 50; and Super Etendard. Involved in formation of Air-Fouga (Etablissements Fouga), 1956.

Dassault-Breguet Mirage III-R reconnaissance aircraft

Dassault Mystère-Falcon twin-turbofan executive transport

Dassault-Breguet developed
Br. 1150 Atlantique long-range
maritime reconnaissance aircraft

Davis-Douglas Cloudster, the first Douglas design, of 1921, with 313 kW (420 hp) Liberty engine

DÄTWYLER/*Switzerland*

Max Dätwyler & Co, based at Bleinbach-Leupenthal, produced in 1960 a glider-tug based on the Piper Super Cub, which it designated MDC-Trailer. Produced subsequently a modernised version of the Bücher 131 Jungmann, known as the Lerche. In 1971 began development of a two-seat trainer.

DAVIS AIRCRAFT CORPORATION/*USA*

Founded at Richmond, Indiana, by Walter C. Davis to take over Vulcan Aircraft Company (*q.v.*). Production of American Moth continued as Davis V-3 and the D-1 series of fast parasol-wing two-seaters began in 1929.

DAVIS AIRCRAFT CORPORATION/*USA*

Between 1958 and 1961, Leon D. Davis began development and production of the five-seater

DA-1 light aircraft. Designed subsequently a number of light aircraft for construction by amateur enthusiasts.

DAVIS-DOUGLAS CORPORATION/*USA*

Formed in 1920 at Santa Monica, California, by Donald W. Douglas, with finance from Davis, to produce the first Douglas design, the 1921 Cloudster. Formerly chief engineer of the Glenn L. Martin Company (*q.v.*), Donald W. Douglas was to found the Douglas Aircraft Company (*q.v.*) in the year 1928.

DAYTON-WRIGHT AIRPLANE COMPANY/*USA*

Formed during WW1 at Dayton, Ohio, for quantity aircraft production, with Orville Wright as consulting engineer. Built Liberty-engined D.H.4 (the 'Liberty plane') and Standard J-1. In 1919 built a limousine version of

D.H.4, single-seat Messenger, and also a three-seater. In 1920 Milton C. Baumann designed their revolutionary RB Racer, with solid all-wood wing, totally enclosed cockpit, and retractable landing gear linked to rod-operated leading- and trailing-edge camber-changing flaps. Built the USB-1, an Engineering Division redesign of the Bristol fighter; 1921 twin-engined seaplane; side-by-side two-seat TR-3 (last rotary-engined design for US Army) and single-wheel landing-gear TR-5. In 1922 built Douglas DF-2. In 1923 the parent company, General Motors, abandoned aviation and dissolved Dayton-Wright; aeronautical work of the company taken over by Consolidated Aeronautics Inc. (*q.v.*).

DEEKAY AIRCRAFT CORPORATION LTD./*UK*

Built the side-by-side two-seat Knight, designed by S. C. Hart-Still at Broxbourne in 1937. One completed; scrapped during WW2.

Dayton-Wright FP-2, designed for Canadian forest patrols

Dayton-Wright K-T Cabin Cruiser three-seat tourer

P.R.34 long-range reconnaissance version of the superb de Havilland Mosquito

DE HAVILLAND AIRCRAFT COMPANY LTD./*UK*

Geoffrey de Havilland built his first successful aircraft in 1909, selling it to the War Office. Taken on as designer at the Balloon Factory (later Royal Aircraft Factory), between 1911 and 1914 he designed the F.E.2, S.E.1, S.E.2, B.E.1 and B.E.2. In 1914 he joined the Aircraft Manufacturing Company (*q.v.*) at Hendon, designing the D.H.2 pusher fighter, D.H.3 and D.H.10 twin-engined bombers, D.H.5 fighter and D.H.4 day bomber. The latter was extensively built in the USA. The D.H.9 and 9a were variations; the 9a equipped post-war RAF bomber squadrons and it, too, was built in the USA. Nearly 3,000 were constructed in Russia as the R-1.

The D.H.51 Hummingbird ultralight was the best entrant in the 1923 Air Ministry competition, but de Havilland realised that their passion for lightness was an error and in 1925 produced the first Moth to more sensible proportions. It was perhaps the most famous light aircraft ever built and was sold all over the world. A number of cabin monoplanes and a military version, the Tiger Moth, followed; over 8,000 Tigers were built for various air forces.

The three-engined D.H.66 Hercules was flown by Imperial Airways from 1926, replacing D.H.10s, and in the 1930s many domestic and foreign airlines used the twin-engined D.H.84/89 Dragon/Dragon Rapide and D.H.86 four-engined Express.

In 1934 de Havilland offered a special twin-engined racer, of wood, for entrants in the England-Australia race. At a fixed price of £5,000 this gamble paid off; three D.H.88 Comets were entered and one of these three won. By 1939 the firm was producing the D.H.91 Albatross, a fast airliner with four engines; the twin-engined D.H.95 Flamingo feeder-liner and the diminutive D.H. 94 Moth Minor. All production of these ceased at the outbreak of WW2, which also cut short a promising bomber-trainer, the D.H.93 Don. In 1938 work started on a fast unarmed wooden bomber, the Mosquito, based on a scaled-down twin-engined version of the

de Havilland Tiger Moth two-seat elementary trainer

de Havilland D.H.10 three-seat bomber

de Havilland Comet 1 jet airliner

D.H.91. It became one of the most versatile aircraft of its time, and by the end of the war a single-seat fighter version attained a speed of 760 km/h (472 mph). The Vampire, de Havilland's first turbojet fighter, Venom, Sea Venom and later Sea Vixen, served for a decade after the war.

Back in civil work, they produced the twin-engined Dove, four-engined Heron and in 1949 the first jet airliner in the world, the D.H.106 Comet. The Comet 1 ran into constructional problems, but the mark IV achieved considerable success. The D.H. 121 Trident, a three-engined airliner for BEA, and the D.H.125 executive jet, both of which sold well, are still in production in 1978. They were the last DH designs, the firm merging into the Hawker-Siddeley Group (*q.v.*).

de Havilland Canada DHC-6 Twin Otter twin-
turboprop STOL transport aircraft

DE HAVILLAND AIRCRAFT OF
CANADA LTD./*Canada*

Formed in 1928 at Downsview, Toronto, as a
constructional and service facility. Built 1,553
Tiger Moths (1938–1945), erected about 40
D.H.60M Moths, a Giant Moth, some 25 Puss
Moths and 200 Tigers (from UK-built parts).
Developed ski and float installations for DH
products. Built 1,134 Mosquitos (1942–1945)
and 54 Fox Moths (post-war). Undertook design and construction of the Tiger Moth replacement, the DHC-1 Chipmunk, built in
Canada, Britain and Portugal. Further Canadian designs have concentrated on STOL capability: the DHC-2 Beaver, DHC-3 Otter,
DHC-4 Caribou (their first twin), DHC-5 Buffalo, DHC-6 Twin Otter, DHC-7 QSTOL
(Quiet STOL) four engined airliner. In 1978
work was in progress on the jet-STOL research
augmentor-wing Buffalo. The company became part of the Hawker-Siddeley Group in
1960, but retain the name de Havilland.

DE HAVILLAND AIRCRAFT OF NEW
ZEALAND LTD./*New Zealand*

Formed 1939 at Rongotai, Wellington. Produced a small number of Tiger Moths from
1940. After the war reverted to overhaul and
servicing, and assembled Devons, Fox Moths
and Chipmunks.

DE HAVILLAND AIRCRAFT PTY.
LTD./*Australia*

Formed 1927 at Melbourne, the first overseas
holding by DH, as service agent, assembling
imported Moths. Moved to Sydney 1929. Between 1939 and 1942 built 1,085 Tiger
Moths and 87 Dragons; 212 Mosquitos
(1942–1947); 120 Vampires (1948–1961).
Local designs were the DHA G2 troop-
carrying glider and the post-war DHA 3
Drover three-engined transport. Acquired
CAC Lidcombe (1959); Bristol Aeroplane
Company (Australia) Pty. Ltd. (1962); Fairey
Aviation Company of Australia Pty. Ltd.
(1963). In 1960 became Australian Hawker
Siddeley Company, the name changing in 1963
to Hawker de Havilland Australia Pty. Ltd.

DELANNE/*France*

Maurice Delanne produced his first design, a
light aircraft, the D.II 'L'Ibis Bleu' at
Chateauroux in 1929. Proposed a tandem wing
arrangement (the 'Nevadovich biplane') in
1936. Virtues claimed for this arrangement
included an exceptional c.g. travel and very low
stalling speed. The Delanne 20 research aircraft was built on this principle by the Société
Anonyme Française de Recherches
Aéronautiques in 1938. A full-scale fighter
design, the Arsenal-Delanne A-D 10, was

built by Arsenal de l'Aéronautique (*q.v.*) at
Villacoublay in 1939. Completed during the
German occupation, it was taken to Germany
for further testing.

DELHAMENDE/*Belgium*

Took over production of the D-158 Tipsy Nipper from Avions Fairey Belge, designed originally by M. Tips to be sold as a kit. Del-
hamende marketed it under the name
Cobelavia from the early 1960s, and sold all
Nipper rights to Nipper Aircraft in the UK in
1966.

DEL MAR ENGINEERING
LABORATORIES/*USA*

A weapons systems support and training systems designer/manufacturer of Los Angeles,
California, produced a series of very original
experimental ultra-light helicopters from
1940, as well as a helicopter training system.
Production ended by 1974.

DE MONGE, LOUIS/*France*

A propeller designer from the Société
Anonyme des Etablissements Lumière, who
designed and built a single-seat racer in 1921.
In 1924 built a 'scale model' of a Burnelli-type

de Havilland Canada DHC-5D Buffalo
utility transport

Del Mar DH-1A Whirlymite

One of the earliest successful racing aircraft, a Deperdussin monoplane

flying wing, with two 40 hp engines. Also built the Koolhoven F.K. 31 under licence. In 1924 he joined Buscaylet et Cie (*q.v.*) and gave up independent design.

DENNY/*UK*
William Denny and Brothers, a Dumbarton engineering firm, built 150 R.A.F. B.E.2c/2e aircraft under sub-contract in WW1.

DEPARTEMEN AGKATAN UDARA REPUBLIK INDONESIA, LEMBAGA INDUSTRI PENERBANGAN NURTANIO/*Indonesia*
Formed at Bandang in 1966 from the Institute for Aero Industry Establishment. LIPNUR built a prototype series of light aircraft and from 1963 began production under licence of the Polish PZL 104 utility aircraft under the name of Gelatik (Rice Bird). Also manufactures the LT-200, a modified Pazmany PL-2 light aircraft for military and civil training.

DEPARTAMENTO DE AERONAVES (PAR)/*Brazil*
The aircraft department of the Instituto de Pesquisas e Desenvolvimento (IPD). From 1970 concentrated entirely on research, all design and development being handed over to Embraer. Between 1959 and 1964 developed prototypes of the Beija-Flôr two-seat light helicopter, designed especially for Brazilian conditions by Prof. Heinrich Focke, formerly of Focke-Achgelis.

DEPARTMENT OF AIRCRAFT PRODUCTION (AUSTRALIAN GOVERNMENT)/*Australia*
Built the Bristol Beaufort under licence, with a great deal of local redesign of parts and detail. Some 700 were built, 1939–1943, as well as 364 Beaufighters (1943–1945) and some Lancasters. After the war, was renamed Division of Aircraft Production, Department of Supply and Development. From 1946 production switched to Lincoln B Mk 30 (73 built). Canberras were produced at the Department's plant at Fisherman's Bend.

DEPERDUSSIN/*France*
Société Provisoire des Aeroplanes Deperdussin established in 1910, and built during 1912–1913 a series of very advanced monoplane racers with tulip wood monocoque fuselages. A 'Dep' was the first aircraft to exceed 160 km/h (100 mph), in 1912, and Prévost flew one to win the 1913 Schneider Trophy

race at Monaco. In 1913 Deperdussin was arrested for embezzlement and the company was taken over by Louis Blériot. The same initials were retained, but now stood for Société Pour Aviation et ses Dérivées (SPAD) (*q.v.*).

DESCAMPS/*France*
Elysée Alfred Descamps designed a machine-gun-armed fighter in 1913, but this was not put into production. For a time he worked with Aviatik at Mulhouse, then went to Russia in 1914 to become chief engineer to Anatra. After the revolution he returned to France and built several fighter and bomber prototypes. In 1923–1924 he was carrying out experimental work for the French government.

DE SCHELDTE/*Netherlands*
This Dordrecht company, N.V. Koninklijke Maatschappij De Scheldte, the aircraft division of a shipping organisation, was formed in 1935. It took over the designs of Pander and Zonen (*q.v.*) when that company went out of business in 1934. Occupied up to 1940 in design and construction of lightweight biplanes. The Scheldemusch was the first production light aircraft with a steerable nosewheel. After 1945 began glider construction and Dakota conversion. In 1951 acquired licence for production of Saab Safir.

DESOUTTER AIRCRAFT COMPANY LTD./*UK*
Pioneer pilot Marcel Desoutter re-entered aviation by establishing this company at Croydon in 1929, building 41 examples of a modified version of the Koolhoven F.K. 41 three-seater.

DETROIT AIRCRAFT CORPORATION/*USA*
Formed in 1929 as a parent corporation to take control of several firms hit by the depression: Lockheed Aircraft Company, Ryan Aircraft

LIPNUR Model 90 Belalang lightweight aircraft

Desoutter Mk. 1, a modified Koolhoven FK 41

Corporation, Eastman Aircraft Corporation, Blackburn Aircraft Corporation, Aircraft Development Corporation, Marine Aircraft Corporation, Parks Airlines Ltd. and the Winton Engine Corporation. The consortium itself failed shortly afterwards.

DEUTSCHE AIRBUS GmbH/*Germany*

The Munich-based German partner in Airbus Industrie (*q.v.*). It consists of Messerschmitt-Bölkow-Blohm (MBB) and VFW-Fokker, and is responsible for manufacturing the forward fuselage, between the flight deck and wing box, upper centre and rear fuselage and vertical tail surfaces of the A300 Airbus. Construction began in 1969 and the Airbus first flew in 1972.

DEUTSCHE BRISTOL-WERKE/*Germany*

Founded at Halberstädt in 1912, to manufacture products of the British & Colonial Aeroplane Company (*q.v.*), but severed connection with the parent company in 1914. Subsequently it developed and built its own designs under the name of Halberstädter Flugzeugwerke (*q.v.*).

DEUTSCHE FLUGZEUG-WERKE GmbH/*Germany*

Formed by Bernard Meyer at Lindenthal, Leipzig, in 1910, it built Maurice Farman biplanes under licence and produced its own Mars biplane and a copy of the Jeannin Taube and Etrich Stahl-taube in 1914. During the war the DFW B series (unarmed) and C (armed) two-seaters were well-known, the C V in particular being licence-built also by Aviatik and Halberstadt. In 1916 DFW produced the R.I. and R.II giant bombers, very clean designs with engines in the fuselage. Planned civil development of these after the war had to be abandoned and they were scrapped, but civil conversions of C types were built. The company built no aircraft after 1920, amalgamating with Allegemeine Transportanlagen Gesellschaft Maschinenbau (ATG).

Dewoitine D.500 four-gun fighter, one of a series of combat monoplanes

DEUTSCHE FORSCHUNGSINSTITUT FÜR SEGELFLUG/*Germany*

Established as the Rhön-Rossiten-Gesellschaft at Wasserkuppe in 1925. It became DFS on moving to Darmstadt in 1933 and undertook glider research. Designed and built the successful DFS 230 assault glider in WW2, and the DFS 228, an air-launched rocket aircraft used as a research vehicle for the DFS 346, a swept-wing reconnaissance project expected to reach 2,655 km/h (1,650 mph) at 20,120m (66,000 ft). Also undertook development of Me 163 and Mistel composite bomber. Experimented with delta designs by Dr. Alexander Lippisch and evolved piloted V-1. In 1946 the DFS 346 project and its engineering design staff were taken by the Soviets to Podberczhye, where the project was said to have been completed.

DEWOITINE/*France*

Founded at Toulouse in 1922 by Emile Dewoitine to build all-metal aircraft. His first fighter, the D.1, appeared that year and his ultra-light D.7 of 1923 was demonstrated in

the USA. Designed and built a number of fighters, of which the D.21 of 1927 was built in Switzerland and France and in 1929 in the Argentine. Dewoitine went to Switzerland in 1927 as no French orders were forthcoming, and formed the Société Aéronautique Dewoitine. Returned to France 1930, establishing a manufacturing agreement with Lioré et Olivier (*q.v.*), who were entrusted with the redesign of his D.531 to become the D.37 for the Armée de l'Air. He produced two long-range aircraft, both lost on record attempts, and airliners for Air France, but in the main developed a successful family of fighters, the last of which, the D.520 of 1938–1940, was known as the 'French Spitfire'. Merged into SNCAM (*q.v.*) in 1936. During the war the Group formed the Société Industrielle pour l'Aviation, with the organisation that represented General Motors in France, building the Arado 196, 199 and developing the Ar 296.

DFS/*Germany*

see Deutsche Forschungsinstitut für Segelflug

Dewoitine D.21 prototype, a successful fighter

DINFIA IA 46 Ranquel lightplane

DFW/*Germany*
see Deutsche Flugzeug-Werke GmbH

DHC/*Canada*
see de Havilland Aircraft of Canada Ltd.

DICK, KERR AND COMPANY/*UK*
Built 110 Felixstowe F.3 twin-engined flying-boats at their Preston works under sub-contract in WW1.

DIETRICH/*Germany*
Richard Dietrich first built a monoplane at his Hanuske works, in 1912, and learned to fly a year later. In 1922 produced the DP.1, one of the first light aircraft in Germany. About that time the name was changed to Dietrich-Gobiet, of Kassel. In 1924 built a cantilever biplane resembling a Fokker D.VII, as well as other designs, but by 1925 (when company reverted to original name) was in serious financial trouble, becoming bankrupt in 1927.

DINFIA/*Argentina*
Dirección Nacional de Fabricaciones e Investigaciones Aeronáuticas originally founded in 1927 as the Fábrica Militar de Aviones (FMA) (*q.v.*) for aeronautical research and production. Became Instituto Aerotécnico in 1943, Industrias Aeronauticas y Mecánicas in 1953. Nationalised 1957, with aircraft works at the Fábrica Militar de Aviones at Córdoba, under DINFIA name. Began with design and construction of IA 46 light aircraft, twin-engined transports IA 35, IA 45, the IA 38 four-engined tailless transport designed by Dr Reimar Horten, and the IA 37, a small delta wing aircraft. In 1966 began licence construction of Cessna 182 and indigenous light turboprop and piston-engined transports. Reverted to name FMA in 1968, becoming part of Area de Materiel Córdoba division of the Argentine Air Force.

DITS/*France*
Les Etablissements Henri Dits founded in 1922 to build the designs of pioneer Breguet pilot, Réné Moineau, starting with a small metal aircraft for tropical service. During

DINFIA IA 50 Gurani II prototype, twin-engined light transport

WW1 produced an aircraft with twin propellers driven by engine mounted transversely in the fuselage.

DITTMAR/*Germany*
A designer of high performance sailplanes, Heine Dittmar produced a motorised version of his Segelmöwe in 1953–1954 as the HD 153 Möwe two-seat light aircraft. Wing and tail detached for road transport. A small number of these aircraft, and of the later HD 156 three-seat aircraft, were built.

DOAK AIRCRAFT CO. INC./*USA*
Incorporated in 1940 in Los Angeles, California, developing the Model 16 VZ-4Da under contract to the US Army Transportation Research and Engineering Command, 1958. This featured ducted propellers rotating at wingtips, and was transferred to NASA for further evaluation. Doak sold out to Douglas Aircraft Company (*q.v.*) in early 1960s.

DOBLHOFF/*Germany*
Friedrich Doblhoff began work on a jet helicopter in 1942, with a piston engine delivering ram air via a compressor to tip orifices. Development was taken up by Wiener-Neustädter Flugzeugwerke (*q.v.*) and resulted in four models of the WNF 342.

DOCKYARD CONSTRUCTIONAL UNIT/*Malta*
Between November 1917 and December 1918 built 18 F.3 flying-boats under sub-contract to the British government.

DOMAN/*USA*
Founded in 1945 by Glidden J. Doman at Danbury, New York, to construct rotorcraft with hingeless rotorblades and totally enclosed self-lubricating hub. Produced LZ-la, LZ-2a Pelican, LZ-4, LZ-5 and a developed version, DB-10B, in 1953. At one time known as Doman-Frasier Helicopters Inc. Doman H-31 of 1952 was licence-built by Hiller Aircraft Company Inc. (*q.v.*). Operations transferred to Puerto Rico, with continued production of DB-10B and name changed in 1967 to Berlin-Doman Helicopters, recognising interests of Chairman Dr Don R. Berlin.

Doak Model 16 VTOL research aircraft

Doman LZ-5 light helicopter

DOMINION AIRCRAFT CORPORATION/*USA*

Established originally at Vancouver, Canada, but production and development is being carried out at Renton, Washington. First aircraft produced was the Skytrader 800 STOL twin-engined transport, which flew for the first time on 21 April 1975.

DONNET/*France*

Operated under the name Hydravions J. Donnet at Neuilly-sur-Seine, after Percheron replaced Denhaut as designer in 1918. Did not long survive WW1, but some flying-boats used on the Antibes-Ajaccio service, 1921–1928.

DONNET-DENHAUT AND DONNET-LEVEQUE/*France*

Based at Ile de la Jatte from 1912, designing and building light, fast, single-engined flying-boats for the French Navy, RNAS and others. Total of 58 2/3-seat flying-boats acquired by US Navy for coastal patrol in European waters in 1918, and two sent to USA.

DORAND/*France*

In 1916 Colonel Dorand, then head of the Section Technique d'Aviation, designed a two-seat reconnaissance biplane which was produced at the government aircraft factory at Chalais-Meudon and also by Farman.

DORNIER/*Italy*

SMCA Dornier founded at Marina di Pisa in 1922 to produce the Dornier Wal flying-boat. A great commercial success, it was built also by Japan, Spain and the Netherlands and was used on both European and international routes during the 1930s.

DORNIER/*Spain*

Oficinas Técnicas Dornier was set up after WW2 by Dr. Claude Dornier. First designed the Do 25, from which the very successful Do 27 STOL aircraft was built. Spanish Company Construcciones Aeronáuticas SA (*q.v.*) produced 50 of these aircraft.

DORNIER-WERKE GmbH/*Germany*

Dr. Claude Dornier was employed by Count Zeppelin in 1910, and in 1914 was in charge of the design and construction of large all-metal marine aircraft at Zeppelin-Werke Lindau. Here he produced the Rs I in 1915, then the largest aircraft in the world, with a span of 43·5 m (145 ft 9 in). By 1918, three more giant flying-boats had been built, Rs II, III and IV, as well as prototypes of single-seat and two-seat fighters. All were based on Dornier's views on advanced metal construction. After the war the works transferred to Manzel, near Friedrichshafen, where some two-seaters for the Swiss Air Force were completed. At Manzel, between 1920 and 1925, appeared the Libelle, Delphin, Komet and Merkur, small civil aircraft, and the Falke, an unsuccessful fighter. In 1922 the company became Dornier Metallbauten GmbH and in 1926, as the Manzel works were too small, it transferred to Altenrhein in Switzerland (see Aktien Gesellschaft für Dornier Fluzeuge). In 1932 production was re-established in Germany, this time as Dornier-Werke GmbH, beginning with the military Wal (later the Do 18) and Do 11 bomber supplanted later by the Do 23. In 1934

Dornier Do 24 maritime patrol flying-boat

appeared their first modern warplane, the Do 17, evolved from a fast, six-passenger mailplane designed for Deutsche Luft Hansa. The Do 17 and its successor, the Do 217 which served as a night fighter, were the only Dornier designs to see large scale production during 1935–1943. Towards the end of the war they produced the remarkable push-pull twin-engined heavy fighter, the Do 335, which with a top speed of 763 km/h (474 mph) was probably the fastest piston-engined fighter to be developed in WW2.

After the war, Dornier became established in Spain (see above). The first post-war aircraft developed completely in Germany was the twin-engined STOL Do 28. An experimental STOL jet transport followed, the Do 31, and the Do 29 research aircraft. From 1966 the company has been developing the Skyservant and has been involved in international programmes. Collaboration with Dassault-Breguet (*q.v.*) on the Alpha Jet included research into a supercritical wing, but pressure of work caused Dornier to withdraw from the consortium of Airbus Industrie (*q.v.*) formed to develop the A300 transport.

One of the most important flying-boats produced by Dornier, the Wal had influence on later designs

DORNIER/*Switzerland*
By 1926 the German Dornier works at Manzel had become too small, and the main factory was transferred to Altenrhein, in Switzerland. Here, for the next three years, Aktien Gesellschaft für Dornier Flugzeug were occupied in building three Do X flying-boats, the largest aircraft of their time, and powered by 12 engines. Two were sold to Italy. Bomber designs followed, the Do N, P and Y being built 1929–1931. These led to the Do F which, like the Do 11, began in 1933 to re-equip the German Air Force. However, in 1932 production was resumed in Germany. The Swiss factory subsequently became the Eidgenössisches Flugzeugwerk (*q.v.*).

RWD 5 *bis* ultra light sportplane

DOSWIADCZALNE WARSZTATY LOTNICZE /*Poland*
Founded in Warsaw in 1933 to take over assets and liabilities of RWD, the aeronautical section of Warsaw Technical High School, which

had been building to the designs of Rogalski, Wigura and Drzwiecki, initially in the school workshops, later those of the government. Production continued under the RWD name until 1939.

Dornier's Do X was one of the first attempts to provide a large-capacity long-range flying-boat

Dornier Do 13 medium-bomber of the 1930s

Dornier Do 28 D-2 Skyservant STOL transport

Below: The superb, ubiquitous Douglas DC-3, in the insignia of British European Airways

Douglas SBD Dauntless carrier-based scout/dive-bomber

DOUGLAS AIRCRAFT COMPANY/*USA*

The Davis-Douglas Cloudster of 1920 was Donald W. Douglas's first design. It was followed in 1921 by the DT torpedo-bomber for the US Navy, the largest single-engined aircraft in the USA at the time. Four modified DTs, known as Douglas World Cruisers, made the first round-the-world flight in 1924 with Army crews. The Douglas Aircraft Company was formed in 1928 and in 1932 a former Douglas engineer, Jack Northrop, set up the Northrop Aircraft Company and produced an

Douglas DC-2 of Swissair

all-metal low wing dive-bomber, the XBT-1/A-17. Northrop and Douglas merged in 1937 (Douglas with a majority stock holding in the company) and in 1938 it became Douglas-El Segundo. The dive-bomber design progressed, via the Douglas TDB Devastator of 1934, to become the US Navy's first monoplane, and was followed by the Dauntless SBD. Ultimate Douglas development of the single-engined bomber was the 1945 Skyraider, which served in many roles until 1968, both in Korea and Vietnam. Last single-engined military design by Douglas was the very successful small delta-wing fighter, the A4D Skyray.

The first twin-engined Douglas design appeared in 1925—the T2D for the US Navy. The B7 of 1930 was the first of a series for the US Army, and was followed by the B-18 in 1935. The most famous twin, however, was the DB-7/A-20 Boston (and night fighter Havoc), which first saw action in June 1940. A total of 7,385 were built, of which 3,125 went to Russia. The A-26/B-26 Invader of 1945, developed from the A-20, served in Korea and Vietnam, and the Boston/Havoc concept was

taken into the jet age by the Skywarrior and Skynight. A version of the former became the B-66 Destroyer, Douglas's—and the USAF's—last conventional light attack bomber.

In 1933, under pressure from United Airlines' Boeing 247, Transcontinental & Western Air turned to Douglas to provide a competing aircraft. The first DC-1 (Douglas Commercial) appeared in prototype only, but 131 DC-2s followed in 1932–1936. A wide-bodied sleeper version, the DST, led to the DC-3 in 1936, which was to be the most famous airliner of all time. In 1940 the USAAC ordered it as the C-47 transport. Douglas built 9,255 of the 10,125 produced, and in 1961 1,000 were still in military use, and 600 civil DC-3s remained in operation in the US in 1974. Douglas, consulting five airlines, developed a four-engined version, the DC-4, in 1941. The Army commandeered all civil DC-4s on US entry into the war, and 1,162 military C-54s were built. After the war, many reverted to DC-4 status, to be

Douglas C-133A Cargomaster strategic heavy freighter

DC-10 three-turbofan wide-body transport built by Douglas Aircraft division of McDonnell Douglas Corporation

succeeded by the DC-6 and DC-7. Douglas temporarily lost their lead in transport when Boeing produced their Model 707, but are building currently the very effective DC-9 and DC-10 airliners.

Military transport design continued with the big C-124 Globemaster in 1950, and C-133 Cargomaster 1957, a heavy strategic freighter capable of carrying all the then current IRBMs or ICBMs. In 1947 Douglas went supersonic with the jet D-558-1 Skystreak and D-558-2 rocket Skyrocket built for NASA. The latter held the world's speed record in 1953 at 1,981 km/h (1,231 mph) and achieved Mach 2·01 at 19,810 m (65,000 ft) in 1953. The later X-3 research aircraft was intended for flight at up to Mach 3. There was a brief involvement in executive jets with the PD-808 Vespa-jet, production being transferred from El Segundo to Rinaldo Piaggio before, in 1967, the company merged with McDonnell Aircraft to become McDonnell Douglas (both *q.v.*).

DOWNER AIRCRAFT INDUSTRIES INC./*USA*
Formed at Alexandria, Minnesota, in 1959, from the former Northern Aircraft Inc. (*q.v.*), to continue production of the Bellanca Model 14 (see Bellanca Aircraft Corporation). Built the Model 14-19-2 Cruisemaster and the Downer Bellanca 260 Model 14-19-3. Further development was undertaken by Inter-Air Inc. (*q.v.*). Following merger with American Aviation Corp. of Freeland, Michigan, supplied parts and conversion kits for Seabee.

DOYLE AERO CORPORATION/*USA*
Harvey Doyle, of Baltimore, Maryland, produced his first light aircraft, the Oriole, in 1929. Prior to this he had been designer for the Vulcan 'American Moth'.

DOYN AIRCRAFT INC./*USA*
This Wichita, Kansas, company, offering conversions to provide more power and performance to Cessna models 150, 170, 172, 175 and Cardinal, was taken over by Air-Mod Engineering Company of Oklahoma City. The Cessna 170 conversions were known as the Doyn Dart I; the Dart II of the mid-1960s was a refined version of the Piper Apache. Beech Travelair conversions were also completed.

DRIGGS AIRCRAFT CORPORATION/*USA*
Founded in 1927 by Ivan H. Driggs at Lansing, Michigan, who designed and built his first aircraft in 1915. Later worked as engineer for Dayton-Wright. In 1924, in conjunction with Johnson Airplane and Supply Company, built two Driggs-Johnson DJ-1 Bumblebee racers, followed by a second version in 1925. Developed Dart Model 1 for Air Corps research on high-lift wings in 1926. Driggs products included Dart II and Skylark III. Driggs left to work for Luscombe (*q.v.*) on the 1934 Phantom I and Driggs design rights went to Phillips Aviation in 1938.

DRUINE/*France*
Roger Druine built his first aircraft in 1938 at the age of 17. Built a single-seat cabin monoplane, the Aigle, in 1948. His 1950 single-seat

Dumod Liner conversion of the Beech 18

Turbulent has been produced in small numbers by Rollason Aircraft & Engines Ltd. and Stark Flugzeugbau (both *q.v.*). Rollason also built the 1955 two-seat Druine Condor.

DUMOD CORPORATION/*USA*
Based at Opa Locka, this company produced a modified Beech 18, increasing performance considerably, under the designation Dumod I. A further development, known originally as the Infinite, later as Dumod II, was produced from 1964. Rights to both acquired by Broome County Aviation in 1972.

DURAMOLD AIRCRAFT CORPORATION/*USA*
The Duramold F.46A, designed by Colonel V. E. Clarke and financed by Fairchild, was built in 1938 to test plastic-bonded plywood processes. It was also used by Fairchild as a test bed for their 313 kW (420 hp) Ranger engine. Research based on this aircraft was employed in the design of the Fairchild AT-21 Gunner.

DURANT AIRCRAFT CORPORATION/*USA*
Established at Oakland, California, to manufacture a two-seat biplane called the Durant-Standard J.1. This was a re-engined version of the two-seat trainer built originally by the Standard Aircraft Corporation (*q.v.*) and powered as the J.1 by a Hall-Scott engine of 149 kW (200 hp).

DURBAN AIRCRAFT CORPORATION/*South Africa*
Formed in 1962 to continue production of the Aeriel Mk II light aircraft, developed and built originally by Genair (*q.v.*) and subsequently by Southern Aircraft Construction Co. and Robertson Aircraft Sales and Service.

DYLE ET BACALAN/*France.*
The large naval dockyard Société Anonyme de Travaux Dyle et Bacalan formed an aeronautical company in Paris in 1925 to develop an all-metal civil and military aircraft. Built armoured fighter and bomber. Renamed Société Aérienne Bordelaise (*q.v.*) in 1930.

E

EAC/*France*
Etudes Aéronautiques et Commerciales SARL was formed in 1960 to build modified versions of Jodel lightweight monoplanes. Also offered kits for amateur construction.

EAC/*USA*
Engineers Aircraft Corporation was founded at Stamford, Connecticut, to manufacture a lightweight two-seat monoplane designated EAC-1. Powered by a Wright-built version of the British Gipsy four-cylinder in-line air-cooled engine, an example was exhibited at the New York show in 1930.

EARL AVIATION CORPORATION/*USA*
Based at Los Angeles about 1930. Built Earl 95 two-seat lightplane with American Cirrus engine; also two-seat biplane called Earl Popular, with tandem open cockpits.

EASTBOURNE AVIATION COMPANY LTD./*UK*
Founded at Eastbourne, Sussex by F. B. Fowler. Built in 1913 a single-seat tractor monoplane; in 1914 two types of tractor bi-plane, one single-seat and one two-seat, the latter for military use. Seaplane built for 1914 Circuit of Britain had 'buried' engine driving two propellers through shafts. During war 'Circuit' seaplane was modified, but then abandoned. Company built Avro 504s and B.E.2cs under contract. Firm's aerodrome near Eastbourne taken over by Royal Navy.

EAST COAST AERONAUTICS INC./*USA*
Subsidiary of Barium Steel Corporation. In late 1950s made two Lockheed Shooting Stars almost entirely of magnesium. Also built Australian Jindivik pilotless target under licence for US armed services.

EASTERN AIRCRAFT DIVISION, GENERAL MOTORS/*USA*
Five car factories converted for WW2 production of Grumman Wildcats and Avengers. Completed 1,000th Avenger on 5 December 1943 and 2,500th Wildcat 11 April 1944. Production of new Grumman fighters planned, but Japanese surrender intervened, and the plants were re-converted to car production.

See also under Ford on wartime conversion of American car factories.

EASTMAN AIRCRAFT CORPORATION/*USA*
Division of Detroit Aircraft Corporation. Made Eastman Flying Yacht four-seat flying boat or three-seat amphibian of sesquiplane configuration. Also built Eastman Sea Rover and Sea Pirate biplane flying-boats.

EBERHART AEROPLANE & MOTOR COMPANY INC./*USA*
Parent company was Eberhart Steel Products Co. (established 1918), making not only aircraft, but bomb-carriers, bombsight synchronising gears etc. In 1922 assembled fifty British-designed S.E.5E fighters from spare parts, 'E' suffix denoting company name and plywood-covered fuselage. Aircraft division, named as above, formed in 1925. Developed steel-construction techniques and supplied components to US aircraft industry. Experimental XFG-1 Navy fighter tested 1926/27.

ECTOR AIRCRAFT COMPANY/*USA*
This company was formed in order to produce the Cessna L-19 Bird Dog, dating from 1950s, under the names of Ector Mountaineer and Super Mountaineer.

Ector Super Mountaineer, developed from the Cessna L-19 Bird Dog

Edo XSOE-1 single-seat observation floatplane

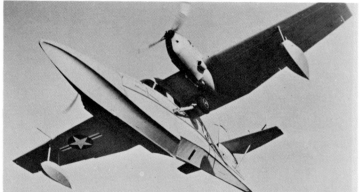

Experimental Edo hull on Grumman Widgeon amphibian

EDO AIRCRAFT CORPORATION/USA

Incorporated 1925. Carried out three years of research and development in connection with seaplanes and flying-boats. From 1928 was famous for standardised float installations, and by 1947 over 300 types of aircraft had been equipped with Edo floats. During WW2 made sub-assemblies for Grumman Hellcat. First Edo-designed aircraft was the unsuccessful XSOE-1 single-seat observation floatplane. Company name changed in November 1947 to Edo Corporation. In 1962 fitted a Grumman amphibian flying-boat with experimental Gruenberg hydrofoils.

EIDGENÖSSICHES FLUGZEUGWERK
EMMEN/*Switzerland*

This is the Swiss government's aircraft establishment for research and development, as well as for production, modification and maintenance of military aircraft. In an official specification of 1934 (see next entry) the company had designed the C-36 monoplane. Newly named as above, it revived the design in 1938, and built 160 as C-3603. Of C-3604 development only 13 were built. Later made French Aérospatiale Alouette III helicopters and Dassault Mirage fighters, and under Hawker Siddeley contract assembled and modified Hunters, the last in 1976. Now participating in assembly programme for 72 Northrop F-5E/F Tiger II tactical fighters.

EIDGENÖSSICHE KONSTRUKTIONS
WERKSTÄTTE/*Switzerland*

Formed at Thun early in WW1. Made aircraft to designs of A. Haefeli, who was earlier with Farman and Ago. First was DH-1 pusher (six built in 1916) showing Ago influence; DH-2 was tractor which went into production as developed DH-3 (110 of these two-seaters built). DH-4 was fighter prototype of 1918; DH-5 (1919; 60 built) a DH-3 replacement; DH-5A a higher-powered version of 1928, with steel-tube fuselage (22 built). To a government

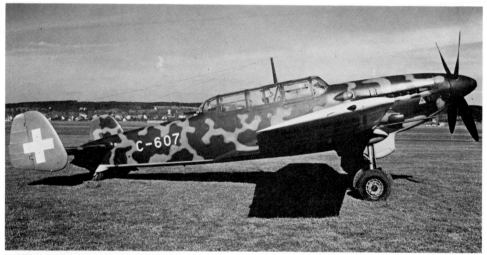

EFW C-3604 ground-attack aircraft

EKW MA-7 single-seat fighter prototype

EKW C-35 biplane fighter

specification of 1934 it built the C-35 multi-purpose two-seat biplane as a replacement for the Fokker C.V-E, which it resembled, and which it had produced jointly with Dornier since 1932. C-35 first flown in 1935; 80 delivered from 1937. (See also previous entry.)

EKIN/UK

W. H. Ekin (Engineering) Company Ltd. formed at Crumlin, Co. Antrim, Northern Ireland March 1969 to undertake production of six McCandless gyroplanes. First one flew Feb-

ruary 1972. Extensive re-design then undertaken and new prototype flew February 1973. Modified type called WHE Airbuggy.

ELIAS, G. & BROTHERS INC./USA

Formed in 1881, but made aircraft only after WW1, at Buffalo, NY. By 1929 had made nine experimental types for US air services and Post Office, as well as armament types for the Air Corps. In 1922 made first of seven EM/EO 'Marine Expeditionary' two-seat biplanes (wheels or floats). XNBS-3, tested August

1924, was large twin-engined bomber with steel-tube fuselage and wooden wings. Elias-Stupar was twin-engined cantilever civil biplane. EC-1 of 1927–1928 was 'convertible' light parasol monoplane—that is, the cockpit could be open or closed.

ELLIOTS OF NEWBURY LTD./*UK*
Formed 1895 to make furniture. Turned attention to aircraft components in 1939. During WW2 sub-contracted for many types, including Airspeed Oxford, Supermarine Spitfire and de Havilland Mosquito. In August 1947 flew Eon light four-seat low-wing monoplane, later altered to re-engined Eon 2. Also made gliders (Eon, Olympia etc.). Eon T.16/48 was side-by-side trainer project by Elliotts and Aviation & Engineering Projects Ltd.

EMAIR/*USA*
In 1970 this division of Emroth Company began production at Harlingen, Texas of Emair MA-1 agricultural biplane (Boeing-Stearman Model 75 derivative). Type had received FAA certification in Hawaii, though built by Air New Zealand and first flown in that country July 1969. Emair's production of 25 ended January 1976. Of more powerful MA-1B, ten were delivered by April 1977. Special features include new wings and hopper forming integral part of fuselage.

EMBRAER/*Brazil*
Empresa Brasiliera de Aeronáutica SA began operations in January 1970 to promote the Brazilian industry. In August 1974 signed cooperative agreement with Piper Aircraft Corporation, and in 1975 with Northrop. Work on Tiger II components started 1976. Present production: the notably successful Bandeirante twin-turboprop light transport (first flown October 1968) and the pressurised

Xingu series: Xavante (licence-built Italian Aermacchi jet trainer and attack aircraft); EMB-201A Ipanema agricultural aircraft; also versions of several Piper types. Work in hand on maritime reconnaissance version of Bandeirante.

EMIGH TROJAN AIRCRAFT COMPANY/*USA*
Successor to the Emigh Aircraft Corp, continuing development during 1950 of Emigh Trojan A-2 light all-metal cabin monoplane, which was built in small numbers 1948–1950. Metal fuselage was in two halves, joined on centre line. Interchangeability of components was a special feature.

EMPRESA BRASILIERA DE AERONÁUTICA SA/*Brazil*
see EMBRAER

EMPRESA INDUSTRIAS AERONÁUTICAS DEL ESTADO/*Argentina*
As Industrias Aeronáuticas y Mecánicas del Estado (IAME) formed 28 March 1952 to take over State activities concerning military and civil aircraft, and incorporating the Instituto Aerotécnico (formerly Fábrica Militar de Aviones). I.A.35 was twin-engined multi-purpose monoplane; I.A.33 Pulqui II (first flown February 1951) a swept-wing jet fighter designed by Kurt Tank. Six Pulqui built 1955/56.

EMBRAER EMB-201A Ipanema single-seat agricultural aircraft

EMBRAER EMB-110 Bandeirante (Pioneer) general-purpose aircraft

Emair MA-1B heavy-duty agricultural aircraft

EMBRAER EMB-121 Xingu, Brazil's first pressurised transport

Engineering & Research Ercoupe, in 1937 an advanced lightplane

EMSCO AIRCRAFT CORPORATION/*USA*

A subsidiary of the large Emsco industrial chain. First products were Emsco Challenger monoplane, with US-built Curtiss Challenger radial engine, and Emsco Cirrus with American Cirrus (British designed) in-line engine. B.3A of early 1930s was eight-seat low-wing monoplane; B.7 was two-seat sports monoplane.

ENGINEERING & RESEARCH CORPORATION/*USA*

Established 1930. After making important components for other aircraft, designed and built the novel Ercoupe monoplane, developed from the original Weick 'easy-to-fly' type and first flown in October 1937. Fred E. Weick was the company's chief engineer. The type was

notable for its control system, which eliminated rudder pedals, and was first marketed in 1940. Production ceased on US entry into WW2, during which company was fully engaged in defence contracts. Difficulty of obtaining duralumin led to re-designed Ercoupe in 1941 of composite construction. In August 1941 one aircraft was used to demonstrate benefits of JATO (jet-assisted take-off) compared with conventionally-powered aircraft. Two examples were bought by US Army as experimental radio-controlled targets. After the war civil Ercoupe production was resumed.

ENGINEERING DIVISION, BUREAU OF AIRCRAFT PRODUCTION/*USA*

A division of the US War Department, created in 1918. Responsible for US developments of de Havilland designs, and 14,000 were ordered, though not delivered. Division also experimented with other types of original design. In 1920 it completed its most remarkable product: GAX (GA-1) very large heavily armoured pusher triplane (armament one 37mm cannon and eight Lewis guns) of which type Boeing built ten. Also made TP-1 two-seat fighter and TW-1 trainer, but a special racer was cancelled. The Bureau was later called Engineering Division, Air Service; subsequently Material Division Air Corps (1926). Moved from McCook Field (where the GAX was built) to Wright Field October 1927. Numerous types and variants had associations with the Engineering Division, including Pomilio, Bristol Fighter and Packard-LePere developments. Also VCP-1 single-seat fighter, which won first Pulitzer Race (1920).

ENGINEERS AIRCRAFT CORPORATION/*USA*
see EAC/*USA*

Engineering Division VCP-R racing version of VCP-1 fighter

Sperry-built Engineering Division R-3 racer, designed by Alfred Verville

English Electric Canberra T.17 for electronic countermeasures training

ENGLISH ELECTRIC COMPANY LTD./*UK*

Though this company became part of British Aircraft Corporation in 1960, its origins date back to 1911 at its Coventry Works (Coventry Ordnance Works Ltd.) where quantity production of aircraft not of company's own design was undertaken during WW1. After the Armistice, development centred on the Kingston flying-boats, following the lines of the Cork, a product of the Phoenix Dynamo Manufacturing Company Ltd. which concern was then also part of English Electric. Original features manifest in Ayr flying-boat and Wren ultra-light monoplane (1923), but aircraft work ceased in the mid-1920s. In 1938 it was resumed, with contracts for the Handley Page Hampden (followed by the Halifax). In May 1944 an order was placed for de Havilland Vampire jet fighters. Over 1,000 Vampires built before production got under way on company's own Canberra—the first British jet bomber and the first to serve with the RAF. Canberra production continued for ten years, totalling over 1,300 examples, including 403 licence-built Martin B-57s for the USAF. Numerous variants developed, notably for reconnais-

English Electric (later BAC) Lightning; the RAF's first Mach 2 fighter

sance, and other countries using the type included Ecuador, France, Peru, Rhodesia, Sweden and Venezuela. Many records broken (e.g. London-Cape Town December 1953). Lightning twin-jet single-seat fighter of 1952 was RAF's first supersonic fighter (in level flight); entered service December 1959. Much development of this type was undertaken by British Aircraft Corporation, but two-seat version emanated from English Electric.

English Electric single-seat ultra light Wren, with 398 cc ABC engine

ENSTROM HELICOPTER CORPORATION/*USA*

As R. J. Enstrom Corporation, was formed in 1959 to develop experimental helicopter, first flown November 1960. Developed type (F-28) flown May 1962; and deliveries of further-improved F-28A began in 1968. First year's production was 43 aircraft. In 1968 first tests were made with turboshaft installation. After intervening acquisition, and operation as part of Pacific Airmotive Aerospace Group, resumed manufacture as present company. By 29 June 1977 the 500th Enstrom helicopter had been delivered. One notable feature of three-seat F-28A was manufacture of entire cabin shell of laminated glassfibre reinforced plastics. Late turboshaft development called the Spitfire offered by Spitfire Helicopter Company.

ENTLER-WERKE/*Germany*

Based at Wilhelmshaven. Built in 1922 a small two-seater cantilever biplane, in conjunction with Prof. Junkers, which had corrugated sheet-metal covering. Development was intended, and in summer 1922 an English selling price of £222 was mentioned. By 1925 the firm had ceased to exist.

ENTWICKLUNGSRING SÜD GmbH/*Germany*
see EWR

ERLA-MASCHINENWERK GmbH/*Germany*

Though established in 1934, the real beginnings were in 1933 as Nestler und Breitfeld of Erla. Type Erla 5 was a single-seat monoplane with an engine of 14·9 kW (20 hp). From 1934 undertook quantity production of Arado Ar 65 and 68, He 51 and Bf 109 (including early 'C' sub-type from 1937, as well as numerous later variants); also produced assemblies for other military types.

ESHELMAN, CHESTON L., COMPANY/*USA*

Formed 1942. Made several experimental types, notably FW-5 ('The Wing'), having centre section built integrally with the fuselage (not to be confused with the more famous Northrop 'flying wing' of 1947), and a low-wing monoplane in which a tubular steel spar formed the fuel tank. Latter type revived after the war as E.F.100 Winglet.

ESNAULT-PELTERIE, ROBERT/*France*

Robert Esnault-Pelterie (1881–1957) was a pioneer in aircraft design and development,

Enstrom F-28A three-seat utility helicopter

One of the early classic monoplanes, the Etrich Taube

rocketry and aero-engine construction. Especially noted for tractor monoplanes and metal-tube construction. Following construction of Wright-type gliders (1904), he tested REP 1 (1907) and REP 2 (1908) powered by his own engines. Founded in 1908 Association des Industriels de la Locomotion Aérienne and merged with Chambre Syndicale des Industries Aéronautiques. Developed central-float seaplane. Vickers in England acquired licence for REP monoplanes in 1911. A few French-built REP monoplanes (including parasol type) used in WW1. After the Armistice Esnault-Pelterie, who was something of a visionary, increasingly concerned himself with the problems of spaceflight.

ESPENLAUB FLUGZEUGBAU/*Germany*

Gottlieb Espenlaub achieved an international reputation in the 1920s building and flying gliders. Company formed at Düsseldorf early in the 1930s to build light aeroplanes as well as gliders. Types included a tailless monoplane, a two-seat high-wing monoplane and a five-seat high-wing cabin monoplane with engine of about 93·2 kW (125 hp). During WW2 a Riga subsidiary made stress calculations for Bf 109G wooden tailplane.

ESSEX AERO LTD./*UK*

Following wide experience in aircraft-component applications of magnesium alloys,

built in the late 1940s two-seat (side-by-side) Sprite low-wing monoplane of all-magnesium construction. Made ultra-light components for many aircraft, including Bristol Brabazon. Also carried out repairs, modifications, furnishings etc.

ETRICH/*Austria/Germany*

Austrian Igo Etrich (1879–1967) experimented in aeronautics from 1899. After working with engineer Franz Wels he made a tailless glider with backswept wings in 1907. This was intended to be powered, and led to the Etrich Taube monoplane (bird-like, with backswept warping outer wings and fan-like tail) in 1909–1910. Object was inherent stability, with first flight at Wiener-Neustadt in November 1909. Small-scale production (Etrich Flieger Werke) and competitive success followed, in UK and other countries and the type was imitated frequently. Early Etrich pilots included Hellmuth Hirth. Jointly with his businessman father, Etrich had a private experimental establishment at Josefstadt. Etrich A-1 and A-2 monoplanes served with Austro-Hungarian Army before WW1. Etrich Flieger-werke GmbH established at Liebau, Silesia, in 1912, independent of Motorluftfahrzeug Gesellschaft of Vienna and Rumpler of Berlin, each of whom held a licence for the Taube. Rumpler built the type from 1911–1914, and other German makers built similar machines, as used by the German Army before and

Evangel 4500-300 cargo/passenger transport, designed for easy repair in the field

during WW1. First product from Liebau was a remarkable three-seat cabin monoplane having variable incidence and camber, and nose-wheel landing gear. In 1914 the company was absorbed by Brandenburgische Flugzeugwerke (*q.v.*).

ÉTUDES AÉRONAUTIQUES ET COMMERCIALES SARL/*France*
see EAC

EULER-WERKE/*Germany*
August Euler (1868–1957) was a pioneer pilot/builder, active in 1909–1910. In 1910 he patented a machine-gun installation for aircraft, and at the wish of the German War Department, some sort of presentation of it was withdrawn from the Berlin Aeronautical Exhibition of 1912. Euler acquired a licence for Voisin aircraft, and Prince Heinrich of Prussia took his pilot's certificate on an extensively modified example of the type. At least 30 other Germans learned to fly on this aircraft. An early wartime reconnaissance type was the B II tractor biplane (built at Frankfurt in late 1914), an early version of which had tricycle landing gear; B III was a licence-built LVG; Type C a pusher of 1916; Dr 1-Dr 4 were triplanes. A quadruplane was also built (though top surfaces were really full-span ailerons) but Euler types achieved little distinction after 1916.

EUROPEAN AIRBUS/*International*
The name European Airbus was used throughout the late 1960s, pre-dating the Airbus Industrie entry in this book. In June 1965, the first discussions were held between British and French industrial representatives concerning a collaborative project for a large-capacity

EWR VJ101 vertical take-off research aircraft

short-medium range transport; almost simultaneously a study group was formed in Germany. There were talks and proposals every year until Airbus Industrie was founded in 1969.

EVANGEL AIRCRAFT CORPORATION/*USA*
Designed twin-engined STOL light passenger/cargo aircraft in 1962. Prototype Evangel 4500-300 first flew in June 1964, having rugged structure and intended for bush operations. Manufacture ceased in 1974 after seven production aircraft were built.

EWR/*Germany*
Entwicklungsring Süd GmbH was formed of a Bölkow, Heinkel and Messerschmitt design consortium on 23 February 1959 at the sugges-

tion of the Federal German Defence Ministry, to develop a Mach 2 VTOL intercepter. By May 1963 70 flights had been made with VJ101C research aircraft, which had tilting jet-pods at wingtips. Studies were made for an entirely different VJ101D fighter. Heinkel withdrew in late 1964, and in July 1965 EWR changed from a consortium into a limited company. There was later an unsuccessful partnership with Fairchild Hiller.

EXCALIBUR AVIATION COMPANY/*USA*
In October 1960 acquired all rights for conversion programme (for which it already had responsibility) of Beechcraft Queen Air and Twin-Bonanza marketed by Swearingen Aircraft. Continues production at San Antonio, Texas. New company has adopted the name Queenaire 800 for former Swearingen 800.

F

FÁBRICA DE AVIONES ANAHUAC
SA/*Mexico*
see Anahuac

FABRICA DE AVIONE S.E.T./*Romania*
Founded Bucharest 1923 to develop aircraft designed by Grigore C. Zamfirescu for Divisia I-a Aeriana. Designs included S.E.T. 7 biplane trainer, S.E.T. 7K reconnaissance variant, S.E.T. 10 biplane advanced trainer, S.E.T. XV biplane fighter; also made Fleet 10G trainers.

FÁBRICA BRASILIERA DE
AVIÕES/*Brazil*
Assumed responsibility from CNNA for continued production of M-7 Gipsy Major-powered primary trainer and M-9 advanced trainer with Gipsy Six engine, designed by Lt. Col. A. M. Muniz. Acquired licence to build Fairchild PT-19 in 1942.

FÁBRICA MILITAR DE
AVIONES/*Argentina*
see FMA

FÁBRICA NACIONAL DE
AERONAVES/*Chile*
The company was founded in June 1953 with temporary facilities at Los Cerrillos Airport,

Santiago, and later moved to new premises at Rancagua. It was dissolved in 1960. It converted PBY-6A flying-boats into 28-passenger airliners and built 50 Chincol primary trainers for the Chilean Air Force (the prototype was first flown in December 1955).

FÁBRICA NACIONAL DE
AVIONES/*Peru*
State factory established at Las Palmas Airport, Lima, in May 1937 with Società Italiana Caproni (*q.v.*) as partner supplying plant and tooling. 12 of contracted 25 Caproni Ca 100 trainers completed up to 1939; facilities used for general overhaul from June 1941.

FABRIQUE FÉDÉRALE D'AVIONS,
EMMEN/*Switzerland*
See Eidgenössisches Flugzeugwerk

FAIRCHILD/*USA*
Sherman Fairchild founded Fairchild Airplane Manufacturing Corporation in 1925. Changed to Fairchild Aviation Corporation in 1929 when The Aviation Corporation acquired controlling interest. Sherman Fairchild withdrew in 1931, retaining a subsidiary, Kreider-Reisner Corporation, Hagerstown, Maryland, which was renamed Fairchild Aircraft Corporation in 1935; became Fairchild Aircraft Divi-

sion, Fairchild Engine and Airplane Corporation in 1939; Fairchild Stratos Corporation in 1961; Fairchild Hiller Corporation in 1964 on acquisition of Hiller Aircraft Company; Fairchild Industries Inc. in 1971. Acquired Republic Aviation Corporation in September 1965 and 90% interest in Swearingen Aviation Corporation in November 1971.

Built FC-1, FC-2 and Model 71 lightplanes 1925–1931. Continued production of Kreider-Reisner Model 24C8, later supplied in four-seat version as USAAF UC-61 Forwarder and as RAF Argus. M-62 Cornell trainer introduced 1940 with variety of engines. AT-21 gunnery trainer entered production in 1942. C-82 Packet twin-boom cargo/troop transport flown September 1944; superseded by developed C-119, first flown November 1947. Manufactured 326 C-123 Providers 1954–1958, designed by Chase Aircraft. Licence-production of Fokker F-27/FH-227 airliner began 1957; 205 built.

Hiller UH-12 and H-1100 helicopters continued in production after acquiring that company. 100 Pilatus Turbo-Porters begun June 1966; 15 of COIN version delivered to USAF as AU-23A Peacemaker, transferred to Royal Thai Air Force. In 1967 work initiated on 52 USAF AC-119 gunships. Contracts awarded after acquisition of Republic for weapons delivery enhancement of F-105 Thunderchief, sub-contract assemblies for McDonnell Douglas F-4, Boeing 747. Won USAF A-X compet-

Fairchild Hiller Turbo-Porter floatplane

Fairchild Model 71, equally at home on wheels or floats

ition for close-support aircraft, prototype YA-10A flown 10 May 1972; currently in production for USAF Tactical Air Command and USAFE. Feature is nose-mounted GAU-8A Avenger 30 mm seven-barrel cannon. Also currently manufacturing wings for Swearingen's Merlin and Metro twin-turboprop aircraft and continuing licence-production of Turbo-Porter. Subsidiary Fairchild Aircraft Service Division in Florida provides overhaul, maintenance and conversion facilities.

FAIRCHILD AIRCRAFT LTD./*Canada*

Formed 1929 with premises at Lonqueil, Quebec, parent company having withdrawn manufacturing licence from Canadian Vickers. Built 21 Model 71 seven-seaters 1930–1935, Super 71 with metal monocoque fuselage in 1934; two Super 71P photographic aircraft for RCAF in 1936. 24 Model 82s produced 1935–1938. One Model 34-42 Niska and two Model 45-80 Sikanis, first flown 1937. Wartime production of Bristol Bolingbroke for RCAF; 300 Curtiss Helldivers for US Navy 1943–1945. All-metal F-11 Husky built 1946–1948. Aircraft production stopped 1948; Husky design sold to Husky Aircraft Ltd. in 1955.

Fairchild-built C-123 Provider, evolved from the Chase XG-20 cargo glider

Fairchild AC-119 heavily armed gunship

Fairchild Republic A-10A, USAF's latest close-support aircraft

Fairchild XC-120 Packplane, which could fly with or without cargo pod

FAIREY AVIATION LTD./UK

Founded by C. R. (later Sir Richard) Fairey, initially to build 12 Short 827 seaplanes. Leased premises at Hayes, replaced by new factory 1917–1918. Became a public company 5 March 1929 and the following year opened new airfield at Harmondsworth, later requisition and incorporated as site for London's Heathrow Airport. Reorganised as holding company The Fairey Company Ltd. 31 March 1959, aircraft manufacturing subsidiary becoming Fairey Aviation Ltd., and the Stockport plant Fairey Engineering Ltd. Fairey Aviation Ltd. merged with Westland Aircraft Ltd. 1960. Britten-Norman (Bembridge) Ltd. acquired 1972. Fairey group into liquidation 1977; engineering activities acquired by National Enterprise Board; Britten-Norman (q.v.) operated by liquidator pending sale.

Company designs include F.2 twin-engined biplane fighter; camber-changing trailing-edge flaps introduced on Hamble Baby. Fairey III series introduced 1917; final model IIIF entered production 1926 and declared obsolete 1940. Fairey Hendon (1930) was the first British cantilever monoplane heavy bomber; Long-range Monoplane captured absolute distance record for Britain 1933. The famous Fairey Swordfish ('Stringbag') torpedo bomber entered production in 1936; 2,392 were built by Fairey and Blackburn; this was the only biplane to remain in service throughout WW2. Other famous aircraft included Battle light bomber; Fulmar fleet fighter; Barracuda dive-bomber. Firefly name revived for Rolls-Royce Griffon-powered monoplane

Belgian-built Fairey Fox II day bombers

which entered FAA service in 1943, serving in Korea in 1950. First FAA aircraft to combine search and strike roles was the Gannet with Double Mamba coupled turbines; developed Gyrodyne convertible helicopter 1946; Jet Gyrodyne 1953; Rotodyne compound helicopter airliner 1957. Fairey Delta 2 research aircraft set world airspeed record of 1,822 km/h (1,132 mph) on 10 March 1956.

FAIREY AVIATION COMPANY OF AUSTRALASIA PTY. LTD./Australia

Formed in 1948 as Fairey-Clyde Aviation Co. Pty. Ltd., named changed to above November 1951. Bankstown, Sydney, facility overhauled

aircraft for Royal Australian Air Force and Royal Australian Navy, converted RAN Firefly AS.5s to T.5 standard. Special Projects Division concerned with Jindivik, Meteor and Canberra drones at Woomera missile test range.

FAIREY AVIATION COMPANY OF CANADA LTD./Canada

Incorporated November 1948 to provide overhaul and repair of aircraft for Royal Canadian Navy. Ceased operations March 1970. Converted ex RCN Avengers for agricultural and fire-fighting duties Martin Mars flying-boats converted into water-bombers 1960.

Fairey IIID, most of which served with Fleet Air Arm　　　　**Fairey Rotodyne, advanced compound helicopter airliner**

FAIREY SA/Belgium

Société Anonyme Belge Avions Fairey registered 12 September 1931. Plant bombed 10 May 1940, re-opened October 1946. Reorganised as Fairey SA 1964. Established originally to build Fairey Firefly II biplane fighters and Fairey Fox three-seat day bombers. Licence-production of 80 Hawker Hurricanes curtailed by bombing 1940, only two com-

pleted. Factory extended 1950–1951 when work began on Gloster Meteor F.8s for Belgian Air Force, also conversion of Meteor F.4s to T.7 standard. 240 Hawker Hunter F.4s and F.6s built 1955–1960; other activities included collaboration in multi-national F-104G and Atlantic programmes. Supplied rear fuselages and nose cones for single-seat variants of Mirage V for Belgian Air Force in joint prog-

ramme with SABCA. Following UK Fairey's acquisition of Britten-Norman (Bembridge) Ltd. in 1972 Islander and Trislander production was transferred to Gosselies until affected by liquidation in October 1977. Sub-contract work for Aérospatiale and VFW-Fokker has been undertaken and the plant was scheduled to be a final assembly facility for European General Dynamics F-16s.

FAIRTRAVEL LTD./*UK*

Formed in 1962 to build Piel CP.301 Emeraude, modified to comply with British certification requirements and known originally as the Garland-Bianchi Linnet.

FALCON AIRCRAFT MANUFACTURING COMPANY/*USA*

Established 1958 to acquire engineering and production rights to Baumann Brigadier, re- engined with two 130 kW (175 hp) Continental engines to become B-350 or B-360 Falcon De Luxe Brigadier.

FARM AVIATION LTD./*UK*

Revived programme initiated by de Havilland Aircraft in 1958 to convert Chipmunk primary trainers for agricultural use. Three machines converted for the company's own use, followed by others for agricultural aircraft operators.

FARNER AG, FLUGZEUGBAU/*Switzerland*

Farner AG was an overhaul and repair organization which produced a two-seat biplane in 1934, and in 1935 a four-seat WF.21/C4 monoplane based on the Compte AC-4, which was a three-seat aircraft called the Gentleman. Prototype WF.12 two-seater built 1943, powered by Cirrus Minor located behind cabin and driving via shafts a tractor propeller mounted at wing level.

FARMAN/*France*

On 9 November 1907 Henri Farman, in a Voisin biplane, became the second man to sustain level powered flight for more than a minute. At a 1909 Reims meeting he flew his own Farman III, the first aircraft with effective ailerons. Brother Maurice was also a designer; the two formed Avions Henri et Maurice Farman at Billancourt, eventually nationalised in 1937, becoming part of SNCAC (*q.v.*).

Maurice Farman designed the MF-7 Longhorn (1913) and MF-11 Shorthorn (1914) both used as trainer and observation aircraft by the Allied forces. Farman F.20 and F.40 developed, the latter with streamlined two-seat nacelle and powered by 100 kW (135 hp) Renault engine. Farman F.50 night bomber followed; four-engined F.140 night bomber introduced 1925, replaced by F.221 and F.222 in 1937, the latter used subsequently by Vichy air force after June 1940 as a transport. Civil airliners included the F.60 Goliath. Twin-engined F.180 biplane, F.190 single-engined monoplane introduced 1928, three-engined F.300 in 1930.

After nationalisation, in 1939 the Farman brothers acquired the licence to manufacture the Stampe SV.4 trainer biplane. Although SNCAC was assigned manufacturing rights post-war, Farman retained licence and with Jean Stampe the Société Anonyme des Usines Farman developed Monitor I monoplane powered by 104 kW (140 hp) Renault engine. Variants included the II, III and IV, the latter being taken over by Stampe et Renard, Brussels. Farman retains aviation facility at Paris.

Farman MF-7 Longhorn trainer/observation aircraft of WW1

Farman F.222 36·0 m (118 ft) span monoplane bomber

The Farman biplane which made first flight in Japan (1910)

Farman F.40 reconnaissance, and occasionally bomber aircraft

FAUCETT SA, CIA. DE AVIACIÓN/*Peru*
Aircraft operator, founded by Elmer Faucett, owning airport at Santa Cruz, Lima. Developed aircraft in 1930s for its own airline use and for Huff-Daland Dusters Inc. which it managed. Designs, based on Stinson, included F.19 eight-passenger cabin monoplane. Production discontinued 1947.

FBA/*France*
    see Schreck FBA

FEDERAL AIRCRAFT CORPORATION/*USA*
Incorporated 1928 by some workers who had helped build the Ryan monoplane for Charles Lindbergh. Known originally as Ryan Mechanics Monoplane Company. CM-1 Lone Eagle was a four-passenger cabin monoplane powered by Wright Whirlwind radial engine.

FEDERAL AIRCRAFT FACTORY/*Switzerland*
    see Eidgenössisches Flugzeugwerk

FEDERAL AIRCRAFT LTD/*Canada*
Set up as Canadian Crown Company to coordinate production of Avro Anson navigation trainers for use under British Commonwealth Air Training Plan. Developed Anson II with revised hydraulically-operated undercarriage and flaps, Anson V with moulded plywood fuselage. Later assumed coordination responsibility for Canadian Lancaster, Mosquito and other programmes. Disbanded 30 June 1946.

FEIGL & ROTTER/*Hungary*
Louis Rotter designed light aircraft in the 1920s, the 82 kW (110 hp) Le Rhone-engined Feiro I all-wood four-seater being the first post-WW1 civil aircraft to be built in Hungary. Produced subsequently the improved Feiro Daru and the lightweight Feiro Dongo side-by-side two-seater.

Faucett F.19 eight-seat cabin monoplane

FFA C-3605, a turboprop conversion of the EKW C-3603

FFA/*Switzerland*
The re-organised Swiss Dornier-Werke Altenrhein, Flug- und Fahrzeugwerke AG discontinued development of Morane-Saulnier piston-engined fighters after completing prototype D-3803. Awarded development contract July 1952 for P-16.04 interceptor/ground attack aircraft with Armstrong-Siddeley Sapphire, first flown 28 April 1955. Programme cancelled by Swiss Government but continued as private venture until June 1960; five aircraft built. Participated in licence-production programmes for de Havilland Vampire and Venom, Pilatus P-3, Mirage IIIRS and IIIS. Designed and manufactured Diamant glassfibre sailplane. Currently producing, under agreement with SIAI-Marchetti signed in 1967, AS-202 Bravo two-seat trainer/aerobatic aircraft.

FFA P-16 interceptor/ground attack aircraft

FFA AS-202 Bravo two-seat training aircraft

FFVS/*Sweden*

On 1 January 1941 the Air Board of the Royal Swedish Air force instituted Flygförvaltningens Verkstad and its own design, which became the FFVS J-22 fighter, first flown September 1942. Sub-contracted programme with final assembly at Air Board Workshops, Ulvsunda; the first of more than 200 was delivered 1 September 1943.

FIAT, SOCIETÀ PER AZIONE/*Italy*

Renamed 1949 to succeed Aeronàutica d'Italia (*q.v.*), inheriting its plant and programme. (Fiat's Divisione Aviazione merged subsequently with Aerfer as Aeritalia (*q.v.*) formed 12 November 1969, fully operational 1 January 1972.) Fiat G49 advanced trainer flown September 1952. G80 jet trainer with de Havilland Goblin 35 engine, first flown 9 December 1951, was first post-war Italian jet aircraft. In conjunction with Macchi built 80 de Havilland Vampire FB.52As; built 221 F-86K all-weather fighters for Italy, France and West Germany, first example completed June 1955. G91 adopted as NATO light tactical fighter; prototype flown 9 August 1956 and several hundred built subsequently. Prototype of G91Y variant first flew 27 December 1966; 65 built for Italian Air Force. Licence-built 205 F-104S Starfighters for Italian Air Force. G222 twin-turboprop military transport project initiated prior to establishment of Aeritalia.

FIESELER, GERHARD/*Germany*

Gerhard Fieseler Werke GmbH established by the aerobatic pilot in 1930. Fi 2 Tiger produced for Fieseler's own use. Fi 5R two-seat light-plane and Fi 97 four-seat cabin monoplane preceded Fi 156 Storch liaison and communications aircraft with high-lift slots and flaps. Also built Fi 167 torpedo bomber/reconnaissance biplane, designed for carrier operation. Manufactured Messerschmitt Me 109 fighters.

Fiat C.R.42 highly manoeuvrable biplane fighter

Fiat G91Y single-seat tactical reconnaissance-fighter

Fiat G55 Centauro, a fast single-seat fighter

Fieseler Fi 156 Storch multi-purpose STOL aircraft

FIRESTONE AIRCRAFT COMPANY/*USA*

Formed in 1946 by name change from G&A Aircraft Inc., a subsidiary of Firestone Tire and Rubber Company. G&A's XR-9 single-seat helicopter developed as XR-9B tandem two-seater. Also built two-seat CA-45D. Development discontinued 1947.

FISHER BODY DIVISION, GENERAL MOTORS/*USA*

Entered aircraft production in the 1940s with design team headed by Don Berlin, formerly of Curtiss. Developed Eagle fighter with Allison engine, prototype first flown 30 September 1943. Eight XP-75s and five P-75As were built before the programme ended.

FLAIR AVIATION COMPANY/*USA*
see Fletcher Aviation Company

FLANDERS, L. HOWARD LTD./*UK*

Built two-seat Flanders B.2 biplane, powered by 52 kW (70 hp) Gnome Rhone rotary engine, first flown 1912 and acquired by Admiralty 1914. Flown at RNAS Great Yarmouth.

FLÉCHAIR SA/*France*

Company building experimental aircraft designed by Ing. Roland Payen, who had been involved in research and development of delta-winged aircraft since 1933. Payen's Pa. 49, flown 22 January 1954, was the first French jet-powered delta-wing aircraft.

FLEET AIRCRAFT INC./*USA*

Established in Buffalo, NY, Fleet produced the Fleet Model 2 with Kinner engine, and built a military two-seat primary trainer for the US Army Air Service. Designated PT-6, it was an improved version of the PT series initiated by Consolidated Aircraft Corporation, of which Fleet was a subsidiary.

FLEET AIRCRAFT LTD./*Canada*

Formed 1929, a subsidiary of the US company, to assemble and market the Fleet trainer. Wartime production included the Fairchild Cornell PT-19. Fleet Model 80 Canuck two-seat lightplane also built in quantity 1946–1947, after which aircraft production ceased. In 1952 Fleet acquired type certificate for Super-V twin-engined Beech Bonanza conversion from Bay Aviation Services Co., Oakland, California.

FLEETWINGS DIVISION OF KAISER CARGO INC./*USA*

Formed 1929 and acquired Keystone Aircraft Corporation factory in 1934. Specialist in stainless steel structure, including wings for the Douglas Dolphin and company's own Sea Bird amphibian, which was the first stainless steel aircraft to receive US Approved Type Certificate. Wartime production included subcontract parts manufacture. Acquired by shipbuilder Henry J. Kaiser in March 1943 and developed Model 23 Tandem and Model 33 trainers. Designed XBTK-1 torpedo bomber in 1943; only three completed.

FLETCHER AVIATION COMPANY/*USA*

Began in 1941 as Fletcher Aviation Corporation, developing FBT-2 trainer and CQ-1A two-seat target-control aircraft. FL-23 two-seat observation/liaison aircraft built for 1950 USAF competition, followed in 1953 by FD-25 Defender light ground support aircraft. FU-24 utility agricultural aircraft introduced

Firestone lightweight helicopter, an early post-war design

Flanders B.2 biplane, served with RNAS in 1914

Fleet Model 80 Canuck two-seat lightplane

1954, developed for New Zealand where 100 were assembled by James Aviation Ltd. Acquired by AJ Industries in 1960 and was briefly renamed Flair Aviation before assuming name as above. Introduced FU-24A six-seat passenger/cargo version. Manufacturing and sales rights for FU-24 series sold to Air Parts (NZ) Ltd. (*q.v.*) in 1964.

FLETTNER GmbH/*Germany*
Innovative aerodynamic researcher who became interested in rotary-winged flight in 1920s; Anton Flettner's first helicopter made tethered flight in 1932, blades rotated by tip-mounted engines. BMW Bramo Sh14A-powered Fl 184 two-seat gyroplane flown 1935 and, in following year, single-seat experimental Fl 185 helicopter prototype. Flettner Fl 265 with twin inter-meshing rotors appeared in 1939 and six were built before production was halted in favour of the Fl 282 Kolibri, first flown in 1941. 24 were built.

Fletcher FU-24 Utility agricultural aircraft

FLIGHT DYNAMICS INC./*USA*
Developed Flightsail VII two-seat amphibian powered by a 67 kW (90 hp) Continental C90. Design commenced 1966; first flown October 1970.

FLIGHT ENGINEERS LTD./*New Zealand*
Joint company formed by agricultural operator Barr Brothers and Marine Helicopters Ltd. to maintain own fleets, but also undertook licence-assembly of Transavia PL-12 Airtruk agricultural aircraft, programme commencing 1973. T320 version powered by Continental Tiara engine introduced 1977.

FLUGZEUG-UNION-SÜD GmbH/*Germany*
Joint company formed in 1956 by Ernst Heinkel GmbH and Messerschmitt AG to manufacture Potez Air Fouga Magister jet trainers for Luftwaffe. 194 aircraft built, components being constructed by Heinkel's Speyer factory and by Messerschmitt at Augsburg with final assembly and flight-test at München-Riem.

FLUGZEUGWERFT LÜBECK-TRAVEMÜNDE GmbH/*Germany*
Founded in May 1914 at Travemünde Privall to specialise in seaplane design and construction. Aircraft included F.1, a two-seat reconnaissance aircraft, powered by a Mercedes D III engine, three of which were built. The F.2 biplane (11 built) was slightly larger, with a Mercedes D IV engine, and armed with a Parabellum machine-gun. A total of 34 armed reconnaissance patrol biplanes with Benz IV engines were built 1917–1918.

FLYGFÖRVALTNINGENS VERKSTAD/*Sweden*
see FFVS

FLYGINDUSTRI, AB/*Sweden*
Subsidiary of Junkers Flugzeug Werke AG, established at Linhamm, Malmö, effectively escaping restrictions on aircraft construction in Germany. Civil production included the A 20 two/three-seat mail/freight aircraft introduced in 1923, G 23/G 24 three-engined nine-passenger airliners in 1924/25 and the single-engined, six-passenger W 34 built up to 1935. Three-engined K-30C bomber built 1924 and supplied to Russia as R 42; K-37 twin-engined light bomber flown 1927; 174 built in Japan by Kawasaki and Mitsubishi. K-47 monoplane appeared 1928, used as research aircraft for dive-bombing techniques, benefiting later Ju 87 programme.

Fletcher FD-25 Defender lightweight ground support aircraft

FMA Aé.M-01 two-seat military trainer

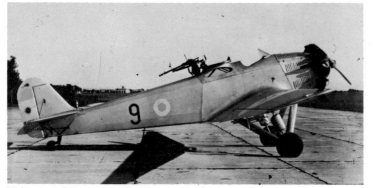

FMA Aé.M.B.1 bomber aircraft prototype

FMA/*Argentina*

Fábrica Militar de Aviones established at Córdoba 1927; redesignated Instituto Aerotécnico 20 October 1943, incorporated into Industrias Aeronáuticas y Mecánicas del Estado 1952, became Dirección Nacional de Fabricaciones e Investigaciones Aeronáuticas 1957, reverted to FMA in 1968. Licence-production 1927–1943 included Avro 504R, Dewoitine D.21C, Bristol F.2B, Focke-Wulf Fw44J, Curtiss Hawk 75. Indigenous designs included Aé.C-l three-seat monoplane, Aé.C-2 trainer in 1932; Aé.T-l five-seater in 1933; Aé.C-3 light aircraft in 1934, with Aé.M-01 built for Argentine Army. El Boyero two-seater built 1939–1940. Currently delivering IA.58 Pucará COIN aircraft to Argentine Air Force, developing IA-62 primary trainer.

FOCKE-ACHGELIS UND CO
GmbH/*Germany*

Formed in 1933 by Heinrich Focke, formerly of Focke-Wulf, and aerobatic pilot Gerd Ach-

FMA IA.58 Pucará twin-turboprop COIN aircraft

gelis. Developed world's first completely successful helicopter, Fw 61, flown as a prototype on 26 June 1936. Also designed Fw 186 Argus As10C-engined autogyro to similar requirement that had produced the Fieseler Storch. Twin-rotor Fa 223 Drache, first flown August 1940, ordered into production 1942 at Hoyenkamp factory, later at Laupheim; in 1945 a captured Drache became first helicopter to cross English Channel. Fa 330 Bachstelze rotor kite deployed operationally aboard U-boats from 1942.

FMA Aé.C-2 two-seat postal and training monoplane

Focke-Achgelis Fw 61 twin-rotor helicopter

FOCKE-WULF FLUGZEUGBAU
GmbH/*Germany*

Association between Heinrich Focke and Georg Wulf formalised 1 January 1924 with formation of Focke-Wulf Flugzeugbau AG at Bremen. Financial support followed success of A 7 Storch two-seater, flown November 1921. Wulf killed 29 September 1927 test-flying F-19 Ente canard. In 1931 acquired licence to build Cierva C.19 Mk. IV autogiro. Focke concentrated on rotary-wing activities, fixed-wing design was entrusted to Kurt Tank, formerly of BFW and of Rohrbach Metallflugzeug GmbH. Albatros Flugzeugwerke GmbH, Berlin, amalgamated with Focke-Wulf. On Focke's resignation to form Focke-Achgelis, Tank appointed Technical Director. Reorganised June 1936 as GmbH under control of AEG. Ceased operations 1945, reformed 1951 and combined with Weser Flugzeugbau to form Vereinigte Flugzeugtechnische Werke. First company design was A 16 three/four-seat commercial transport, followed by the eight/nine-seat A 17, the more powerful 650 hp BMW VI-powered A 29 and the three-crew/ten-passenger A 38 airliners. S 24 Kiebitz two-seat trainer won 1931 German Aerobatic Championship flown by Gerd Achgelis who conducted maiden flight of Fw 44 Stieglitz trainer late summer 1932, widely used by embryo

Luftwaffe and in European and South American countries. First Tank design produced in any numbers (approximately 1,000) Fw 56 Stosser fighter/dive-bomber advanced trainer, followed in 1935 by Fw 58 Weihe communications aircraft/crew trainer and in 1938 by Fw 189 reconnaissance aircraft. Fw 200 Condor airliner flown July 1937, developed into Fw 200C long-range reconnaissance aircraft. With production total of more than 19,000, Fw 190 fighter was the most notable of Focke-Wulf's designs; after first flight on 1 June 1939, entered squadron service August 1941. High altitude version, with revised high aspect ratio wing, designated Ta 152.

Germany's superb Focke-Wulf Fw 190 fighter

Focke-Wulf Ta 152, Ta designation honouring designer Kurt Tank

Focke-Wulf Fw 200 Condor, civil airliner which became a potent anti-shipping aircraft

FOKKER AEROPLANBAU
GmbH/Germany
Registered originally Fokker Aviatik GmbH, on 22 February 1912, Antony Fokker's first company operated under the above name at Berlin-Johannisthal and moved to Schwerin, Mecklenberg in 1913. Name changed later to Fokker Flugzeugwerke. Company liquidated following Fokker's return to Holland after WW1. Fokker E series monoplanes flown successfully by Boelcke, Immelmann and others 1915–1916. Introduced interrupter gear, allowing bullets from a forward-firing machine-gun to pass between the propeller blades, virtually inventing the fighter plane. Fokker Dr.I triplanes built 1917–18, exponents including von Richthofen and Voss. Followed into production by D VII biplane entering service April 1918. Ensuing D VIII parasol monoplane introduced Fokker cantilever wing. Also built 400 AEG C.IV trainers. F II developed at Schwerin 1919, first of Fokker high-wing passenger aircraft.

FOKKER AIRCRAFT CORPORATION OF AMERICA/USA
Antony Fokker's Atlantic Aircraft Corporation was reorganised on 16 September 1925, inheriting premises at Hasbrouck Heights, Teterboro, and the order book for the Noorduyn-designed Universal. Factory at Passaic, New Jersey opened 1927. Glendale, West Virginia factory opened August 1928. General Motors Corporation acquired a 40% holding May 1929; Fokker resigned July 1931.

Improved Super Universal six-seater introduced 1927; 123 built. Three-engined 12-passenger F.10 flown April 1927; 65 built, first three for Western Air Express, forerunner of TWA. Followed by 59 14-seat F.10As. Fokker 32, first US four-engined airliner, flown 1929, having 32 seats and powered by two pairs of Pratt & Whitney Hornet engines in tandem with tractor and pusher propellers; ten built. Military designs included 1929 0-27 observation aircraft, of which 14 built.

FOKKER INDUSTRIA AERONÁUTICA
SA/Brazil
Initial production of 100 Fokker S-11 two-seat primary trainers, followed by 50 examples of S-12 tricycle landing gear version. Five S-14 Mach trainers assembled from Dutch-made components, prior to construction of 45 locally manufactured aircraft.

Fokker Eindecker (monoplane) fighter of WW1

Fokker F.14 Mailplane, product of Fokker in America

Fokker D VII, one of the most potent fighters of WW1

Fokker Dr.I Dreidecker (triplane) of WW1

Fokker F.VII trimotor, one of the early pioneering airliners

FOKKER/*Netherlands*
Full company name NV Koninklijke Neder-
landse Vliegtuigenfabriek Fokker. Originally
founded 21 July 1919 with factory at Veere,
Zeeland, assembly at Amsterdam. New factory
at Schiphol opened 1951. Later acquired Aviolanda (*q.v.*) and formed joint company with
Vereinigte Flugzeugtechnische Werke in
1969. Pre-war civil airliners included eight-
passenger F.VII, flown from Amsterdam to
Batavia in 1924, and the F.VII-3m three-
engined variant which, from 1928, was the
most extensively built (116). Enlarged into
14–16-seat F.XII in 1930. F.XX tri-motor
with retractable landing gear built 1933, and
four-engined F.XXXVI 32-seat and F.XXII
22-seat airliners built 1934 and 1935 respectively. Principal military aircraft built
1919–1925 included C.I, C.III and C.V biplanes, used widely in Europe, China, Japan,
Russia and South America. D.XXI monoplane
fighter introduced 1936, flown in combat in
WW2 by Dutch and Finnish units. G.1 twin-
boom twin-engined attack aircraft of 1936 also

saw limited service, as did T.VIII twin-engined
reconnaissance floatplanes flown to England in
May 1940. Production during Occupation included Arado Ar 196 floatplanes, Bücker Bü
181 Bestmann trainers and Dornier Do 24
flying-boats. Post-war activity included conversion of military Dakotas and Skymasters for
civil use, production of S.11 and S.12 piston-
engined and S.14 jet trainers between 1947
and 1955. Licence-production included 24
Hawker Sea Furies, 460 Hunter F.4 and F.6
fighters, final assembly and parts manufacture
of 350 Lockheed F.104Gs.

**Fokker F.27 Friendship medium-range
airliner**

Fokker C.X reconnaissance/ground attack biplane

Fokker D.XXI single-seat monoplane fighter

Folland Gnat lightweight fighter

Ford TriMotor, known affectionately as the 'Tin Goose'

Fornaire F-1A Aircoupe, evolved from the Ercoupe 415

FOLLAND AIRCRAFT LTD./*UK*

Formed in 1937 as reorganised British Marine Aircraft Co., Hamble; became Hamble Division, Hawker Siddeley Aviation 1959. Undertook subcontract work on Bristol Blenheim and Beaufort, de Havilland Mosquito and Hornet, Short Sunderland and Supermarine Spitfire, among others. First original design was Fo 108 testbed aircraft, 12 built to Specification 43/37. Further subcontract participation in Comet, Sea Vixen, Britannia, Hunter and HS 748 programmes. Lightweight fighter designed by W. E. W. Petter flown initially as Fo 139 Midge, then as Fo 141 Gnat with Bristol Orpheus engine. Sold to Finnish and Indian Air Forces as fighter aircraft and developed as Fo 144 Gnat T.1 trainer for the RAF.

FORD MOTOR COMPANY/*USA*

Henry Ford provided backing for William Stout's Stout Metal Airplane Company, maker of the 2-AT single-engined eight-passenger airliner. Ford purchased Stout in 1925 and provided premises at Dearborne where Stout designed the first Ford 3-AT Tri-Motor, a modified 2-AT with three Wright J-4 engines. Howard Hicks replaced Stout and developed the 4-AT, 78 of which were built. The larger 5-AT, with three 313 kW (420 hp) Pratt & Whitney Wasps, was introduced in 1928, the last 'tin goose' being built in June 1933.

In 1941 Ford built a new factory and airfield at Willow Run, Michigan, where 5,107 Consolidated B-24E/H/J/L heavy bombers were built. A production run of 5,168 B-24Ns was cancelled at the end of the war. XC-109 bulk fuel tanker prototype converted from B-24E. A Ford factory at Iron Mountain, Michigan made 4,190 Waco CG-4A gliders.

See also Eastern Aircraft Division, General Motors on wartime aircraft production by car manufacturers.

FORNAIRE AIRCRAFT COMPANY/*USA*

Forney Manufacturing Company acquired production rights for Engineering and Research Corporation's Ercoupe 415 two-seat light aircraft in April 1955. First production F-1 Aircoupe flew on September 1956. Offered later as Fornaire Execta, Explorer and Expediter. Rights sold in 1960 to the city of Carlsbad, New Mexico.

FOSTER WICKNER AIRCRAFT COMPANY LTD./*UK*

Established in 1934 by G. N. Wickner, V. Foster and J. F. Lusty, initially at the latter's furniture factory at Bromley-by-Bow, London. Mr. Wickner's earlier designs, built in Australia, included Wicko Sports Monoplane and Wicko Lion, both high-wing monoplanes on which the prototype Wicko F.W.1 was based. Of wooden construction, the F.W.1 was powered by a Ford V-8 engine, and became F.W.2 with Cirrus Minor and F.W.3 with Cirrus Major. Nine production aircraft built 1938–1939 at Southampton were designated G.M.1 with Gipsy Major engine.

FOUGA/*France*

Fouga's aircraft department formed 1936, subsequently building designs of M.Pierre Mauboussin who, with M.Castello, developed Castel-Mauboussin gliders and sailplanes. Operated postwar as Etablissements Fouga et Cie, becoming Air Fouga September 1956 when company was taken over, in equal shares, by Breguet, Dassault, Morane-Saulnier, Sud Est

Fouga Gemeaux two-seat twin-fuselage research aircraft

and Ouest Aviation. Acquired by Henry Potez May 1958, renamed Potez Air Fouga. Early activities included production of Mauboussin 123 trainer, Castel C.25S, C.30S and C.300S gliders. Castel-Mauboussin CM.10 transport glider built for French military forces, also CM.100 powered version with two Renault engines. In the later CM-101R Renault engines augmented by two Turbomeca Piméné turbojets. Experience with CM.8-R.9 Cyclôpe and with the Gemeaux led to development of the CM.170R Magister jet trainer, first flown 23 July 1952 and subsequently built in quantity for French Air Force and overseas customers. Company operated as Potez Air Fouga until 23 September 1961, when it was completely absorbed into Etablissements Henry Potez SARL. Continued development of CM.170 Magister and CM.175 Zephyr naval version, which were first flown as production aircraft on 30 May 1959.

Fouga CM.170 Magister, world's first jet trainer

FOUND BROTHERS AVIATION
LTD./*Canada*
Established at Malton, Ontario, in 1948 to build four-seat cabin monoplane designed by Captain S. R. Found. FBA-1A prototype first flown 13 July 1949. Developed version designated FBA-2A flown 11 August 1960 and FBA-2C five-seater on 9 May 1962. Six-seat Model 100 Centennial, with 216 kW (290 hp) Lycoming engine flown 7 April 1967 and superseded earlier models.

FOURNIER/*France*
René Fournier built RF.01 single-seat light aircraft/powered sailplane with modified Volkswagen engine, first flown 6 July 1960. Government assistance for development of improved RF-2, with 25 kW (34 hp) Rectimo-VW engine, subsequently produced by Alpavia (*q.v.*) as RF-3, with slightly uprated engine, first flown March 1963. M. Fournier designed a series of light aircraft of similar configuration for Sportavia-Putzer and Indraero. Established subsequently Avions Fournier to develop revised version of his RF-6 Sportsman, designated RF-6B; first flown 12 March 1974. About 40 have been built.

Found FBA-2A five-seat utility transport

FRAKES AVIATION INC./*USA*
Specialists in turbine conversions of piston-engined aircraft, including Grumman Mallard with two Pratt & Whitney turboprop engines, and Grumman Ag-Cat which with a similar engine becomes Turbo-cat. Under contract to Mohawk Air Services, Frakes modified and obtained certification for the Mohawk 298, an updated Nord 262, with two 875 kW (1174 shp) turboprop engines for use by Allegheny Commuter airlines system.

Fournier RF-8 two-seat trainer built by Indraéro SA

Frake's turboprop conversion of Grumman Mallard

FRIEDRICHSCHAFEN GmbH/*Germany*

Flugzeugbau Friedrichschafen established with factory at Mansell, later at Warnemünde, producing many seaplane designs for German Navy. FF 29 twin-float reconnaissance seaplane introduced November 1914 for coastal patrol and fighter versions. Replaced by FF 49, with more powerful Benz Bz IV engine, introduced in May 1917. Also built land-based aircraft, including G III long-range bomber with two Mercedes D IV engines, used on Western Front in 1917.

FUJI JUKOGYO KABUSHIKI KAISHA/*Japan*

Successor to Nakajima Aircraft Company, established 15 July 1953 with factory at Utsunomiya City. Built Cessna L-19E Bird Dog observation aircraft under licence. Concluded agreement with Beech in November 1953 to manufacture Beech B45 Mentor trainers; total of 124 built, deliveries commencing August 1954. From Mentor Fuji developed LM-1 Nikko four-seat liaison aircraft, first flown June 1955. Similar two-seat KM-2 developed. KM-2B with widened fuselage and tandem seating for two selected as JASDF primary trainer in August 1975. Fuji has assembled or built more than 120 Bell 204B/B2 helicopters since 1962. Fuji T-1 two-seat jet trainer was first post-war Japanese jet aircraft. Forty T-1As built with Bristol Orpheus engines, and

Friedrichshafen G IIIa twin-engined long-range bomber

20 T-1Bs with Japanese engines. FA-200 Aero Subaru four-seat light aircraft first flown 12 August 1965; more than 300 built to date. Work on FA-300 twin-engined light transport began 1971, continued as joint venture with Rockwell International, USA, following agreement signed 28 June 1974, as Rockwell Commander 700; prototype first flown in Japan, 13 November 1974.

FUNK AIRCRAFT COMPANY/*USA*

Formed 1941 at Coffeyville, Kansas, successor to Akron Aircraft Inc., to market Funk Bros.

Model B two-seat monoplane. Production resumed after WW2, aircraft re-designated B-85-C Bee, with Continental C-85 engine. Manufacturing rights acquired in 1962 by Thomas H. McLish of Sharon, Pennsylvania.

FUNK, D.D., AVIATION COMPANY/*USA*

Founded in 1950 at Salina, Kansas, by Don D. Funk and produced F-23 agricultural aircraft in two versions, F-23A with 179 kW (240 hp) Continental W-670 engine and F-23B with 205 kW (275 hp) Jacobs R-755.

Fuji FA-200 Aero Sabaru four-seat lightplane

Fuji KM-2B tandem, two-seat primary trainer

Fuji T-1F2, Japan's first post-war jet aircraft

Funk B.2 lightweight two-seat monoplane

G

GABARDINI SA/*Italy*
Manufactured a 60 kW (80 hp) rotary-engine two-seat monoplane at Novara in 1913, used for a non-stop flight between Milan and Venice. Company subsequently opened factory at Cameri in 1914 to build a military version of this monoplane, powered by a smaller engine. Also built biplane trainers. Nothing more heard of company until it produced a two-seat light cabin monoplane, the Lictor 90, in 1935.

GABRIEL BROTHERS/*Poland*
A small company which produced the P.5 single-seat parasol monoplane in the 1920s.

GAC/*USA*
General Airplanes Corporation founded in June 1928 at Buffalo; by 1930 had produced GAC 101 Surveyor three-seat twin-engine high-wing cabin monoplane; GAC 102A Aristocrat three-seat high-wing cabin monoplane; and the GAC Mailplane sesquiplane.

GAC/*USA*
Situated on Long Island, New York, General Aircraft Corporation produced the Skyfarer

two-seat cabin monoplane with simplified controls in 1941, but sold manufacturing rights to Grand Rapids Industries Inc. (*q.v.*) in 1943. GAC built Waco CG-4A gliders for the USAAF in WW2. A company with the same name, but based at El Segundo, California, announced plans in 1969 for a 36-seat STOL transport, the GAC-100, powered by four Pratt & Whitney PT6A-40 turboprop engines.

GAF/*Australia*
　　see Government Aircraft Factories

GAIL AIRCRAFT ENGINEERING COMPANY/*USA*
Based at Sacramento, California. Built agricultural aircraft, including the Model 202 Mantis, first flown May 1956 with 142 kW (190 hp) Lycoming engine.

GALLAUDET ENGINEERING COMPANY/*USA*
Built seaplanes during WW1 at New York factory. A twin-engine biplane seaplane built for US Navy featured a four-bladed pusher

Gail Model 202A Goldduster agricultural aircraft

GAC 102A Aristocrat, used by Richard Byrd's expedition to the Antarctic

propeller which revolved around the fuselage behind the wings. Later built 5-seat biplane tourer, the Liberty Tourist, and rebuilt 25 DH-4s for US Army. Company dissolved 1923 and factory acquired by Consolidated Aircraft Corporation (*q.v.*).

GALLEÃO/*Brazil*

Former naval workshops which built aircraft for Brazilian Air Force, including Focke-Wulf Fw 44 primary trainers and Fw 58 twin-engined advanced trainers. In 1946 a batch of Fairchild PT-19 trainers was built under a licence agreement.

GALLINARI/*Italy*

This was a shipbuilding company which built seaplanes during WW1, and tested them at the Marina di Pisa.

G AND A AIRCRAFT INC./*USA*

Formerly the AGA Aviation Corporation (*q.v.*), G and A Aircraft succeeded the Pitcairn-Larsen Autogiro Co Inc (*q.v.*), which itself took over the Pitcairn Autogiro Company (*q.v.*) in 1940. In 1943, G and A was acquired by the Firestone Aircraft Company (*q.v.*) of Akron, Ohio, together with almost 200 patents concerned with rotary-wing aircraft. G and A built gliders and experimental autogiros in WW2, and carried out subcontract manufacture.

GANNET AIRCRAFT/*USA*

Formed at Sun Valley, California, in late 1950s to produce modified version of Grumman Widgeon amphibian known as Super Widgeon and powered by two 224 kW (300 hp) Lycoming engines. Company used SCAN 30 airframes (licence-built in France) for initial conversions.

GARDAN/*France*

Light aircraft designer responsible for the CAB Minicab, Supercab and Sipa 200 and 300. Designed four-seat, all-metal lightplane, the GY-80 Horizon, which flew in July 1960 with 112 kW (150 hp) Lycoming engine. Horizon subsequently entered quantity production with Sud Aviation (*q.v.*) under an agreement signed in 1962.

GARLAND-BIANCHI AIRCRAFT COMPANY/*UK*

Formed in 1955 by P. A. T. Garland and D. E. Bianchi to licence-build the Piel CP.301 Emeraude two-seat light aircraft, subsequently renamed Linnet. Built two aircraft before a

Gallaudet Chummy Flyabout two-seat monoplane

Gallaudet D-4 seaplane with mid-fuselage mounted pusher propeller

Gardan GY-80 Horizon four-seat lightplane

Gates Learjet 25 ten-seat twin-jet executive transport

new company, Fairtravel Ltd. (*q.v.*) was formed by AVM Don Bennett to take over production. Fairtravel Ltd. built three more Linnet aircraft, the last of which was delivered in 1965

GARRETT, RICHARD, & SONS/*UK*
Built 60 R.A.F. F.E. 2bs under sub-contract in 1918. Received contract for a further 100 but this was cancelled at end of WW1.

GASHULYAK, YAROSLAV /*USSR*
Designed the G-1, a single-seat helicopter powered by Irbit two-cylinder motor-cycle engine in the spring of 1961. The aircraft is said to have gone into production for flying clubs following successful tests at Kirovograd in the Ukraine.

GATARD/*France*
M. Albert Gatard designed and built several light monoplanes in mid-1950s with a new control system using a variable incidence large-area tailplane. AG 01 Alouette was a two-seater, AG 02 Poussin a single-seater and AG 03 Hirondelle two-seat side-by-side. Development of all three of these aircraft continued into the 1970s.

GATES AIRCRAFT CORPORATION/*USA*
Established 1929 by Ivan R. Gates. Acquired manufacturing rights for Belgian Stampe and Vertongen RSV.18-100 and 26-100 aircraft. No details found of numbers built, if any.

GATES LEARJET CORPORATION/*USA*
William P. Lear founded the Swiss American Aviation Corporation (*q.v.*) in 1960 to build a twin-jet executive aircraft, originally designated SAAC-23 and later named Learjet. Tooling was completed in Europe but moved to Wichita, Kansas, in 1962, when the company became known as Lear Jet Corporation. In 1967 Bill Lear sold his 60% interest in the company to Gates Rubber Corporation, and in 1970 the name was changed to Gates Learjet Corporation. A number of models of Learjet have been built; by mid-1977 the company had produced more than 700 aircraft of this type.

GAZUIT-VALLADEAU/*France*
Known mainly as light aircraft maintenance company. Gazuit was formerly a designer with Morane-Saulnier and Valladeau had been a sub-contractor for some Wassmer aircraft. The company produced a 2/3-seat light aircraft, the GV 103L, which first flew on 1 May 1969.

Subsequently built a second example with the intention of finding a sponsor for production of the type, but this did not materialise.

GEE-BEE/*USA*
see Granville Brothers Aircraft Co.

GEEST FLUGZEUGBAU
GmbH/*Germany*
Formed in 1915 at Berlin-Oberschöneweide with capital of 80,000 marks. Built number of allegedly inherently stable monoplanes during WW1.

GENAIR/*South Africa*
Durban-based (General Aircraft (Pty) Ltd.) built the Piel Emeraude two-seat light aircraft under the name Aeriel Mk.II. First prototype flown in October 1959, with first production aircraft in February 1960. Aeriel was subsequently built by Southern Aircraft Construction and Robertson Aircraft Sales but in September 1962 Durban Aircraft Corporation (*q.v.*) was formed to continue its construction.

GENAIRCO/*Australia*
General Aircraft Company Ltd. formed in 1929 at Sydney/Mascot Aerodrome. Built large factory, initially carried out overhauls, but by 1930 had designed a three-seat biplane, the Genairco, powered by Cirrus Hermes engine. Produced subsequently a four-seat version. Company thought to be inactive by about the year 1934.

GENERAL AEROPLANE
COMPANY/*USA*
Based at Detroit, Michigan; built three types of aircraft during WW1 and operated a flying school. The aircraft were Gamma S biplane with floats; Gamma L, similar but with wheels; and the Beta flying-boat. All were powered by engine installations having pusher propellers.

GENERAL AIRCRAFT COMPANY
LTD./*Australia*
see GENAIRCO

GENERAL AIRCRAFT
CORPORATION/*USA*
see GAC

GENERAL AIRCRAFT LTD./*UK*
Established 1931 at Croydon Airport. Chief designer was Swiss H. J. Stieger. Acquired world rights from Mono-Spar Company for

Gates Learjet 24D eight-seat twin-jet light executive transport

General Aircraft GAL 58 Hamilcar X powered assault glider, intended for operation in the Pacific theatre of war

their system of construction for aircraft up to 1,360 kg (3,000 lb) laden weight. First type was ST-3 three-seat enclosed cabin monoplane with two 33·5 kW (45 hp) Salmson engines. Later built series of light twins, plus single engine pre-WW2 Cygnet monoplane, first light all-metal stressed-skin civil aircraft in UK, and an experimental open-cockpit version, the Owlet. Took over premises of British Aircraft Manufacturing Company in 1938. Built Hotspur training gliders and later Hamilcar assault gliders during WW2. Post-war work included conversion of Mosquitos as target tugs and design of GAL-60 Universal Freighter, built as the Beverley after General Aircraft merged with Blackburn in January 1949.

GENERAL AIRCRAFT (PTY) LTD./South Africa
see Genair

GENERAL AIRPLANES CORPORATION/USA
see GAC

GENERAL AIRPLANE SERVICE/USA
Fixed-base operator at Sheridan, Wyoming, in early 1950s. Converted Piper J-3s, PA-11s and PA-12s for agricultural work by installation of bigger engines. Company's Model II ag-plane was a mixture of Piper parts with a 149 kW (200 hp) Ranger engine from Fairchild PT-19. A new lower wing was added to make it a biplane; first flight 12 October 1953.

GENERAL AVIA/Italy
Established in 1970 by Dott. Ing. Stelio Frati, designer of a series of light aircraft from the Ambrosini F.4 to F.250 (subsequently developed as the SIAI SF.260), to build aircraft of Frati design. First was the F.20 Pegaso light twin. Two prototypes were built and an agreement was reached for production aircraft to be manufactured by Italair (*q.v.*).

GENERAL AVIATION MANUFACTURING CORPORATION/USA
Incorporated in May 1930, with W. H. Miller as Chief Engineer. The Fokker Aircraft Corporation, in which General Motors Corporation held 41% interest, was taken over by General Aviation Manufacturing Corporation in summer 1931. In 1933, merger concluded between GAC and North American Aviation Inc. (*q.v.*). GA built F-15 twin-engine pusher monoplane flying-boat for USCG and GA.43 ten-passenger single-engine cabin monoplane, which later became known as Clark GA.43.

GÉNÉRAL AÉRONAUTIQUE/France
Formed in February 1930 by a number of the most important French aircraft manufacturers, and one engine manufacturer, as a result of a concentration and rationalisation of policy proposed by the French Air Minister. Companies were Lorraine-Hanriot, Chantiers Aéro-Maritimes de la Seine, Nieuport-Delage, Société Aérienne Bordelaise, Société d'Emboutissage et de Constructions Aéronautiques, Latham, and Société Lorraine (all *q.v.*).

GENERAL DYNAMICS CORPORATION/USA
A major reorganisation in 1961 resulted in General Dynamics' 12 operating divisions being divided into two major groups. On the aerospace side, the Western Group contained components of the Convair division, which itself had its origin in 1923 as the Consolidated Aircraft Corporation (*q.v.*), merging in 1943 with Vultee Aircraft Inc. to form Consolidated Vultee Aircraft Corporation (both *q.v.*). Before this, Consolidated had taken over two other aircraft companies, Thomas Morse and

General Dynamics F-16 single-seat advanced combat fighter

General Dynamics F-111E two-seat tactical fighter

General Dynamics F-111A two-seat tactical fighter-bomber of the USAF

Hall Aluminium (*q.v.*). In 1954, Consolidated Vultee merged with the General Dynamics Corporation to become the Convair Division, at which time the CV-880 and 990 jet transports were in production, together with F-102 and F-106 fighters, and the B-58 Hustler was at an advanced stage. In 1978 General Dynamics was building the F-16 fighter, and licence-production of this aircraft is also taking place in several European countries. Support was continuing also for the F-111.

GENERAL DYNAMICS CORPORATION, FORT WORTH DIVISION/*USA*

Separate division of General Dynamics since June 1974, before which it was a part of Convair division. Currently responsible for F-111/FB-111 variable-geometry combat aircraft and General Dynamics F-16 air superiority fighter, in large-scale production for USAF and several NATO air forces.

GENERAL MOTORS (EASTERN AIRCRAFT DIVISION)/*USA*

A division of the General Motors Corporation, formed in January 1942 for aircraft production in five of the Corporation's US eastern seaboard factories. Built Grumman Wildcats under designation FM-1 (first flew 1 September 1942), and Avengers as TBM-1.

GENERAL WESTERN AERO CORPORATION/*USA*

Built Meteor two-seat light monoplane in early 1930s, powered by 75 kW (100 hp) Kinner engine.

GÉRIN/*France*

Jacques Gérin developed a biplane with variable wing area, the Varivol. Wings could be wound in and out by electric motor. Full size tests in wind tunnel at Chalais Meudon followed by flying tests in March 1936. Pilot M. Demimuid killed in Varivol crash on 29 November 1936, but this was not attributable to variable-wing mechanism, which was intact.

GERMAN BIANCO SA/*Argentina*

Large industrial company which formed division in 1944 for glider production and aircraft repair. Began licence-production of Italian Macchi M.B.308, flying the first in February 1959. Production was completed in the late 1960s.

GERMANIA FLUGZEUGWERKE GmbH/*Germany*

Formed at Leipzig during WW1 to produce aircraft under sub-contract. Also operated a flying school. Closed at time of Versailles Peace Treaty.

GERNER GmbH/*Germany*

Foundation date not known, but by 1931 had built a two-seat all-steel light aircraft, the G.II.R, powered by BMW or Salmson engine. Later version was G.II.R6 with Hirth H.M.60 engine. Completely taken over in 1934 by specially formed new company, Adlerwerke GmbH of Frankfurt (*q.v.*).

GERONIMO CONVERSIONS CORPORATION/*USA*

Successor to Vecto Instrument Corp. and Vecto Aircraft Engineering Division (*q.v.*), having acquired the assets of both companies on their owner's death in 1965. Geronimo was based at San Antonio, Texas, and carried out Vecto-designed conversions on the Piper Apache, fitting bigger engines and improving the aircraft's internal and external appearance. Company name changed to Seguin Aviation (*q.v.*) in late 1960s.

GILLIS AIRCRAFT CORPORATION/*USA*

Incorporated in 1927 at Battle Creek, Michigan, Gillis made its debut at the 1928 Detroit Air Show with the Crusader four-seat commercial cabin biplane, powered by a 93 kW (125 hp) Ryan Siemens engine.

GLENNY & HENDERSON/*UK*

Company at Byfleet, Surrey, which built two Henderson-Glenny HSF.II Gadfly single-seat light aircraft in 1929, one with an ABC Scorpion II engine, the other with a Salmson AD.9 radial.

GLOBE AIRCRAFT CORPORATION/*USA*

Formed originally as the Bennett Aircraft Corporation to manufacture aircraft with Duraloid, a new type of bonded plywood. Produced twin-engine eight-seat monoplane, the BTC-1, about 1940. Company reorganised and renamed Globe Aircraft Corporation in 1941. First design under new name was the GC-1 Swift, a two-seat light monoplane with retractable landing gear and Continental engine. Development stopped by war, but produced post-war from 1945. Company built also Beech 18s for US Government during WW2.

Globe GC-1 Swift two-seat lightweight cabin monoplane

GLOSTER AIRCRAFT COMPANY LTD./UK

Formed in 1917 as the Gloucestershire Aircraft Company Ltd. to take over sub-contract work from the Aircraft Manufacturing Company and H. H. Martyn & Co Ltd. of Cheltenham. D.H.4 and D.H.6 fuselages had been built by Martyn, and by the end of the war the company had supplied 461 Bristol Fighters and 165 RAF F.E.2bs, as well as Nieuport Nighthawks and other fuselages.

Fifty Nighthawks, renamed Sparrowhawks, were built for Japan to a 1920 order and soon after the first true Gloucester aircraft, the Bamel single-seat racing biplane, was designed and built in less than four weeks. Its designer, H. P. Folland, joined the company soon after the Bamel's completion. A line of biplane fighters followed—the Grebe and Gamecock being notable successes, and in 1926 the company was renamed Gloster Aircraft Company Ltd, moving its main factory to Hucclecote, Gloucester. Joining the Hawker Siddeley Group (*q.v.*) in 1934, Gloster continued fighter production with the Gauntlet and Gladiator—the latter being the RAF's last biplane fighter. During WW2 Gloster built 2,750 Hurricanes and 3,330 Typhoons, and produced Britain's first jet aircraft to specification E28/39, flying the first of two single-jet prototypes in 1941 and leading eventually to the twin-jet Meteor in 1944. A total of 3,545 Meteors were produced by Gloster and Armstrong Whitworth and Gloster's final production aircraft was the twin-jet delta-wing Javelin all-weather fighter, flown in 1951, of which 435 were produced for the RAF. Gloster ceased aircraft production in 1956.

Gloster Meteors, the first RAF jet fighters

Gloster Javelin twin-jet delta-winged fighter

Gloster Gauntlet, last open cockpit biplane in RAF service

GOEDECKER FLUGZEUGBAU/Germany

Small company at Niederwalluf-on-Rhine, said to have built copy of captured Avro biplane around 1915, plus several Taubes. Also ran flying school. Closed at time of Versailles Peace Treaty.

GOETZE/Germany

Commandit Gesellschaft Richard Goetze founded in WW1 with four factories in the Berlin area. Reputed to have built Otto biplanes.

Goodyear GA-2 Duck three-seat amphibian

GOLDEN EAGLE AIRCRAFT CORPORATION/USA

Incorporated in 1929 at Inglewood, California, with F. M. Smith as Chief Engineer. Built Golden Eagle Chief high-wing two-seat training monoplane at that time. Three versions built with engines from 45–47 kW (60–100 hp).

GOODYEAR AIRCRAFT CORPORATION/USA

Formed 1940 to take over the Goodyear Zeppelin Corporation. Served as aircraft manufacturer and sub-contractor to numerous companies during WW2, including complete construction of the FG-1 Corsair, a Chance Vought design. Reverted to lighter-than-air craft post-war, but built a few GA-2 Duck three-seat experimental amphibians in 1947–8. GA-400R light single-seat helicopter flown in May 1954. Produced the Goodyear Inflatable Aircraft with an inflatable wing in mid-1950s.

GOSPORT AIRCRAFT CO.LTD./UK

Formed in early part of WW1 at Gosport, Hants. Built flying-boats, mainly Norman Thompson FBAs plus some Porte F.5s.

GOTAVERKEN/Sweden

Shipbuilding company, opened an aircraft department for licence-construction of Hawker aircraft for Swedish government. Received order for Hart biplanes powered by Swedish-built Pegasus engines in 1935. This company subsequently built a few light aircraft of its own design, most notable amongst which was the GV.38 high-wing monoplane.

Gotha G.III twin-engined heavy bomber of WW1

Gourdou et Leseurre Type A parasol-wing monoplane fighter

Goupy experimental triplane

GOTHAER WAGGONFABRIK
AG/Germany
Operated aircraft works and flying school at Gotha and seaplane school at Warnemünde in WW1. Manufactured large quantities of aircraft during the war; including seaplanes and twin-engine bombers. Closed by Versailles Peace Treaty. Reopened in mid-1930s with two-seat training biplane, Go 145. In WW2 built Bf 109 fighter and Do 17Z bomber, also Go 242 glider and a powered version designated Go 244.

GOUPY/France
Company engaged largely in experimental work but built a few biplanes of its own design from around 1913.

GOURDOU ET LESEURRE/France
Joint designers of a parasol-wing monoplane in 1918. Few built. Developed into C.1 fighter of 1922 with retractable landing-gear and Gnome-Bristol Jupiter engine. In 1925 became associated with the French dockyard Ateliers et Chantiers de la Loire, with change of name to Loire-Gourdou-Leseurre. In 1929 disassociated with LGL and returned to original title.

GOVERNMENT AIRCRAFT
FACTORIES/Australia
Aircraft production at Australian Government-owned factories began during WW2 with Bristol Beauforts and Beaufighters, and later included Lancasters and Lincolns (see Department of Aircraft production). Designed and produced Jindivik target aircraft, flown in 1952, after a piloted version, Pika, had flown in 1950. Built Mirage fighters and trainers for the RAAF in 1960s–1970s. Latest design is Nomad twin-engine STOL transport, first flown in 1971 and currently in production.

HANS GRADE FLIEGER
WERKE/Germany
Hans Grade was the first German to fly in a triplane of his own design and with his own engine. Prior to WW1, Grade had a civil flying school at Bork. His aircraft were not adopted by the military. First German looping flights made in a Grade monoplane, with complete landing gear provided above and below wing! Sold factory to Aviatik (q.v.) during WW1.

GAF Nomad Search Master, a maritime version of this STOL utility aircraft

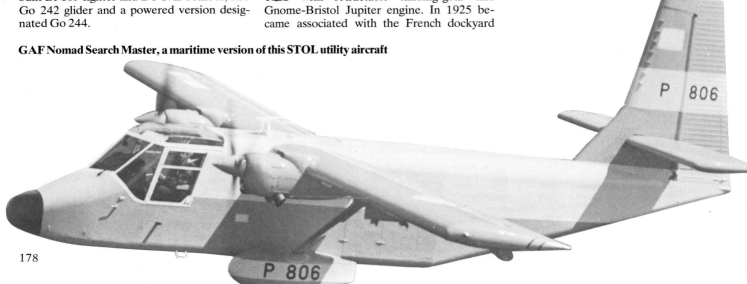

Grahame-White Type 10 *Charabanc* five-seat biplane

Grahame-White Type 11 *Warplane*, with pusher engine, built in 1914

GRAHAME-WHITE AVIATION COMPANY LTD./UK
Founded by Claude Grahame-White in 1909, company began operations with flying school at Pau, France. Moved to England, and acquired Hendon Aerodrome in 1911 and built factory. Acquired agency in 1913 for Morane-Saulnier monoplanes and built these for War Office. Also built own design biplane in 1914, adopted by Admiralty as standard school machine. Three-engine Ganymede bomber of 1918 had two tractor and one pusher propeller with twin fuselages. Company stopped producing aircraft in 1919.

GRAND RAPIDS INDUSTRIES INC./USA
Furniture manufacturer which built wooden parts for aircraft and gliders in WW2. Acquired manufacturing rights of Skyfarer two-seat light cabin monoplane from General Aircraft Corporation (*q.v.*) in 1943. Aircraft had simplified control system and was the second aircraft to be certificated by the US Civil Aeronautics Board as characteristically incapable of spinning. Design was shelved because of war; licence transferred to Le Mars Manufacturing Company in 1944.

GRANVILLE BROTHERS AIRCRAFT INC./USA
Based at Springfield, Massachusetts, Granville became known for the 1930–1933 series of Gee-Bee racers, first of which achieved second place in the 1930 All-America Air Derby round the US. Company succeeded by Granville, Miller and de Lackner in 1934. Built Granville R6H Cyclone-engined monoplane for England–Australia race, but aircraft only reached Bucharest.

GREAT LAKES AIRCRAFT CORPORATION/USA
Established in 1929 at Cleveland, Ohio. Built aircraft for US Army and Navy, plus a series of single and two-seat biplanes, beginning with the 2T-1A single-seater and including also the

Gee-Bee Sportster, one of the highly successful Granville Brothers racers

Great Lakes Sport Trainer, a two-seat sporting biplane

TG-1 Torpedo bomber. Company re-appeared in mid-1960s to build scaled-down kit version of Great Lakes Sport Trainer known as Baby Great Lakes.

GREEK NATIONAL AIRCRAFT FACTORY/*Greece*

British company Blackburn Aeroplane & Motor Company developed aircraft factory at Phaleron, Athens, following a 1925 agreement with Greek Government. Subsequently built there Blackburn Velos torpedo-bombers, Avro 504 variants and Breguet 19s.

GRENCHEN, FLUGZEUGBAU/*Switzerland*

A small-scale builder of the WF.21/C4 four-seat monoplane designed and also built by Farner AG (*q.v.*).

GRIGOROVICH, D. P./*USSR*

Russian designer of the P.L.1 four-seat high-wing commercial monoplane, built by a State factory at Leningrad in mid-1920s, powered by 75 kW (100 hp) Bristol Lucifer engine.

GROPPIUS/*USSR*

Two-seat commercial biplane designed by E. E. Groppius and built in late 1924 by a State factory in Moscow. Powered by 224 kW (300 hp) Hispano-Suiza engine.

GRULICH/*Germany*

Deutscher Aero-Lloyd, the air transport company, built a high-wing training monoplane, designed by Dr. Ing. K. Grulich in 1925. Designated S.1, it could have either 56 kW (75 hp) or 75 kW (100 hp) Siemens engine.

GUERCHAIS/*France*

Located at St. Cloud, company formed in mid-1920s and built several light monoplanes of its own design, first being Guerchais-Hanriot. Built T-9 light cabin monoplane with 89 kW (120 hp) Renault engine in 1930. See also Roche Aviation.

GUILLEMIN/*France*

M. J. Guillemin designed a high-wing single-engine light postal or ambulance monoplane, the J. G. 40, shown at the 1930 Paris Air Show on the Blériot Aéronautique stand. The latter company acquired the licence to build aircraft designed by M. Guillemin. A two-seat light aircraft, the J.G.10, competed in the French Air Ministry Light Aeroplane Competition of 1931, but retired with engine trouble.

Grumman UF-1 Albatross general-purpose amphibian

Grumman FF-1 two-seat carrier-based US Navy fighter

GRUMMAN AIRCRAFT ENGINEERING CORPORATION/*USA*

Incorporated 1929, at Farmingdale, New York. Contractor to US Navy and Coast Guard. Built FF-1 and SF-1 two-seat biplane fighters with retractable landing gear, plus all-metal amphibian, the JF-1, later known as the Duck. Production included Wildcat/Hellcat/Bearcat/Tigercat series and TBM Avenger during WW2, plus Widgeon and Goose amphibians. Present production includes the F-14 Tomcat, E-2 Hawkeye and A-6 Intruder, while the company's subsidiary, Grumman American Aviation Corporation, produces the Gulfstream 2 executive transport and the Lynx, Cheetah, Tiger, Cougar and T-cat family of light aircraft. It also markets the Super AgCat cropduster, built for Grumman by Schweizer Aircraft.

Grumman A-6E Intruder, an advanced two-seat carrier-based attack bomber

Grumman TBF/TBM Avengers, US Navy standard torpedo-bomber in WW2

Grumman F-14A Tomcat carrier-based multi-mission fighter

GULDENTOPS/*Belgium*

Operators of the Belgian National Aviation Schools founded in 1936 at Brussels, Kiewit and Gosselies. M. Guldentops designed and built several light aircraft, and after he took over the Société Bulte a training biplane known as the Bulte-Guldentops appeared in 1938, powered by a Cirrus Hermes engine.

GV/*Sweden*
see Gotaverken

GWINN AIRCAR COMPANY INC./*USA*

Formed at Buffalo in 1935 by Joseph M. Gwinn Jnr, a former chief engineer with Consolidated Aircraft Corporation (*q.v.*). First product, in 1937, was Gwinn Aircar, a two-seat cabin biplane with tricycle landing gear which was claimed to be stall- and spin-proof.

GYRODYNE COMPANY OF AMERICA INC./*USA*

Known originally as P. C. Helicopter Corporation, the Gyrodyne Company was incorporated in New York in August 1946 for the development of advanced rotary-wing aircraft. Bought a five-seat co-axial design from defunct Helicopters Inc, and developed it into the G.C.A.2 Projected G.C.A.7 Helidyne with stub wings and two engines with pusher propellers mounted above wings. One-man portable helicopter, XRON-1 Rotocycle, developed for US Navy Bureau of Aeronautics in mid-1950s, plus some ground-cushion vehicles.

GYROFLIGHT LTD./*UK*

Formed in 1969 to develop gyroplanes designed by Ernest Brooks, who was killed when his ultra-light Mosquito gyroplane crashed. Gyroflight produced a small number of Hornet single-seat gyroplanes and gyrogliders in the early 1970s.

GYROPLANE/*France*

Produced the G-20 two-seat light observation and liaison helicopter immediately following WW2.

Gyrodyne G.C.A.2C with co-axial rotors

HAL/*India*
see Hindustan Aeronautics Ltd.

HALBERSTÄDTER FLUGZEUGWERKE
GmbH/*Germany*
Halberstädt's first aircraft, the C.I reconnaissance biplane, first flew in May 1916, and together with more powerful C.III and C.V developments, was produced in large numbers in WW1. The CL class two-seat escort fighters were particularly successful in ground-strafing roles during the campaigns of Autumn 1917. Halberstädt's D-class single-seater scouts were strong and manoeuvrable, but inferior to Allied fighters in speed. A number of D.II and D.III scouts were built by Hannoversche Waggonfabrik AG (*q.v.*). The Halberstadt D.V, which was the company's final scout design, appeared in early 1917.

HALL ALUMINUM COMPANY/*USA*
Founded 1927 to develop a prototype naval flying-boat based on the hull-design of Britain's Felixstowe F.5 for the US Naval Aircraft Factory (*q.v.*). The twin-engined Hall PH-1 was superseded by PH-2 and PH-3 variants which served in small numbers with the US

Coast Guard during WW2. In 1936 Hall flew the XP2H-1 four-engined patrol bomber, largest American-built flying-boat at that time.

HAMBURGER FLUGZEUGBAU
GmbH/*Germany*
Formed originally by Blohm und Voss in 1933 (*see* Bv.). Aircraft production resumed 1956 with licence manufacture of Nord Noratlas for Luftwaffe. Co-operated in licence-production of Luftwaffe Lockheed F-104Gs and assisted with design work of Fokker F28 and Dornier

Do 31E V/STOL project. HFB 320 Hansa Jet 6/11-seat business jet first flew 1964. Not engaged in aircraft construction in early 1978.

HAMILTON AIRCRAFT COMPANY
INC./*USA*
Overhaulers of surplus military aircraft for overseas disposal. Reworked ex-USAF North

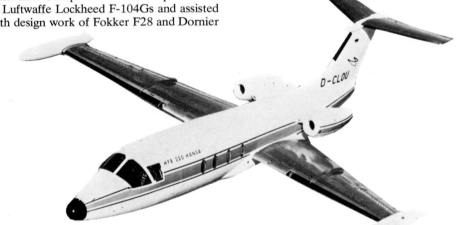

HFB 320 Hansa 9/13-seat twin-jet executive transport

Halberstadt CL.II two-seat fighter-escort

Hall XFH-1 *Fighter*, single-seat naval aircraft

Hamilton Westwind, a turbrop-powered conversion of the Beech 18

American T-28 trainers as Hamilton Nomair for civil and military customers. A Beech 18 conversion—the Hamilton Little Liner—has now been superseded by turboprop Hamilton Westwind II and III, with a lengthened fuselage Westwind IV under development.

HAMILTON METALPLANE DIVISION OF BOEING/USA

Manufactured propellers and metal flying-boat hulls under sub-contract in 1920s, before developing the all-metal, cantilever-winged Hamilton Metalplane in 1926. An airliner version followed in 1928 and served chiefly with Northwest Airways. Hamilton steel propellers were the company's major innovation before merging with Boeing and United Aircraft Corporation in late 1928.

HAMMOND AIRCRAFT CORPORATION/USA

Formed 1931 to take over production of Ryan Speedster biplane from Detroit Aircraft Corporation (q.v.). A prototype twin-boom two-seat lightplane was built 1934 and designated Hammond Model Y. Redesignated subsequently Stearman-Hammond Y-1S, and produced in small numbers until abandoned in 1938.

HANDASYDE AIRCRAFT COMPANY LTD./UK

A former partner in Martin & Handasyde Ltd. (q.v.), George Handasyde set up his own company at war's end and constructed a glider for the Daily Mail's 1922 Itford Meeting. For the Lympne Motor Glider Competition in 1923 he produced a small powered monoplane which was built by the Air Navigation & Engineering Company. In 1929 Handasyde joined the Desoutter Aircraft Company as general manager.

Hamilton Nomair T-28-R1 two-seat military trainer

Handley Page E (H.P.5) the first really successful design by Frederick Handley Page

HANDLEY PAGE LTD./UK

In June 1909 Frederick Handley Page (later Sir) established this company, building a series of monoplanes with crescent-shaped wings inspired by the Austrian designer Jose Weiss. In

WW1 the company became well-known through its 0/400 and V/1500 heavy bombers, the former of which led to the W8 airliner of 1920 which entered service with Handley-Page Air Transport. The Handley-Page HP.42

Handley Page V/1500 long-range bomber, Britain's biggest aeroplane of WW1

airliner, which served with Imperial Airways from 1931, set new standards on routes throughout the British Empire. Military bombers were also produced, including Hinaidis, Hyderabads, Heyfords and, early in WW2, the twin-engined Hampden. Best known was the Halifax bomber, which shared with the Lancaster Bomber Command's offensive against Germany. After WW2 the Hastings military transport and its civilian Hermes counterpart went into · production, and Handley-Page created the crescent-winged Victor 'V' bomber, which remains in service with the RAF in a tanker role. Handley Page's last project, before liquidation in 1970, was the Jetstream twin-turboprop executive transport/feeder liner, which was taken over by Scottish Aviation and will eventually serve with the RN and the RAF.

HANDLEY-PAGE (READING) LTD./UK
In June 1948 Handley Page took over the former Miles Aircraft Ltd. (q.v.) of Woodley, Reading and with it the Miles Marathon four-engined feeder-liner. Handley-Page (Reading) produced the aircraft as a navigational trainer for the RAF and also as a short-haul airliner. The Reading-based company was responsible also for development of the HPR.3 Herald airliner, which flew initially with four piston-engines in 1955, and was manufactured subsequently with two Rolls-Royce turbines as the Dart Herald.

HANNAFORD AIRCRAFT COMPANY/USA
After acquiring in 1948 manufacturing and marketing rights to the pre-war Rose Parakeet single-seat sports biplane from Rose Aeroplane & Motor Company (q.v.), Hannaford offered production versions of the aeroplane with 30–63 kw (40–85 hp) engines. No current production.

Handley Page Victors, the last of the British 'V' bombers to enter service

HANNOVERSCHE WAGGONFABRIK AG/Germany
Hannover, a manufacturer of railway rolling stock, began licence production of Aviatik C.1, Rumpler C.1A and Halberstädt scouts in 1915 before proposing a compact two-seat escort fighter to German High Command. This biplane-tailed CL. II aircraft entered service in late 1917, and was succeeded by the CL. III and CL. IIIa, built also under licence by Luftfahrzeug Gesellschaft (q.v.) as CL. IIa. Small numbers of the enlarged C. IV and CL. V were constructed also, together with experimental CL. III with various engine and airframe changes. The company's fighters were known popularly as 'Hannoveranas'.

HANRIOT/*France*

Aeroplanes Hanriot et Cie was founded during WW1. Hanriot's first design was the Le Rhone-engined HD1 sesquiplane fighter, rejected by the French services but subsequently proved very successful with Italian and Belgian pilots. An HD2 floatplane version, and more-powerful HD3 two-seat reconnaissance/escort fighter were also built. After WW1 Hanriot licence-manufactured British Sopwith aircraft designs and produced the H43 advanced bi-plane trainer; H46 Styx liaison and ambulance monoplane, and the H131 low-wing racing monoplane, which won the 1931 Coupé Michelin. In 1930 the company became a division of Société Général Aéronautique (SNCAC), manufacturing aircraft under the Lorraine-Hanriot name (both *q.v.*).

Hanriot HD1 fighter, used by the Belgian and Italian air forces

Hansa Brandenburg D1, licence-built by Phönix and Ufag

Hanriot H182 braced high-wing monoplane

HANSA UND BRANDENBURGISCHE FLEGZEUGWERKE GmbH/*Germany*

With Ernst Heinkel as chief designer, this company produced the most important German seaplanes of WW1, commencing with the KDW single-seater developed from the D1 landplane, followed by the W.12 with characteristic Hansa upswept fuselage and 'upside down' tail arrangement. The W.29 monoplane set the pattern for Heinkel's later designs, outperforming Allied aircraft in combat from introduction in April 1918. A larger W.33 model was delivered before the Armistice, but continued in production in Finland and Norway as the A-22 until the mid-1920s, as did the W.29 in Denmark.

HANSEATISCHE FLUGZEUGWERKE KARL CASPAR AG/*Germany*

Founded as the Zentrale für Aviatik at Hamburg-Fuhlsbüttel in late 1911; began by building Etrich/Rumpler Taube monoplanes. In 1913 re-named Hansa-Flugzeugwerke, merging shortly before WW1 with Brandenburgische Flugzeugwerke of Igo Etrich, becoming the Hansa and Brandenburgische Flugzeugwerke (*q.v.*). This partnership dissolved in 1916, the Hamburg factory being re-named Hanseatische Flugzeugwerke Karl Caspar AG. Next two years spent mainly in licence-building other companies' aircraft, although an interesting cannon-armed twin-engined fighter prototype by Caspar appeared in late 1918. Before end of WW1 company acquired the ex-Fokker factory at Travemünde, eventually closing the Hamburg works and transferring its activities there. It was here, in 1921, that Caspar Werke AG (*q.v.*) was formed.

HARLOW ENGINEERING CORPORATION/*USA*

Formed 1938 to develop the Harlow PJC-2 four-seat all-metal cabin monoplane which remained in production until December 1941. Four PJC-2s were delivered to the United States Army Air Force as UC-80s. A PC-5A two-seat trainer version was developed in 1939 and assembled under licence 1941–1942 by Hindustan Aeronautics Ltd. (*q.v.*). After America's entry into WW2, Harlow Engineering was engaged in military contract work.

HARRIS & SHELDON LTD./*UK*

Birmingham-based company which, in 1918, sub-contracted to build a batch of 100 Bristol F.2Bs powered by Sunbeam Arab engines.

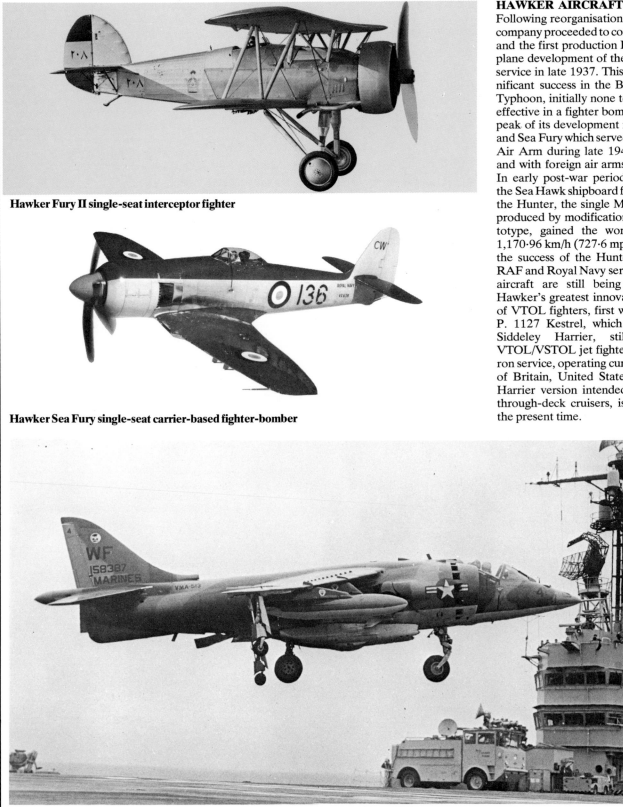

Hawker Fury II single-seat interceptor fighter

Hawker Sea Fury single-seat carrier-based fighter-bomber

HAWKER AIRCRAFT LTD./*UK*

Following reorganisation in 1933, the Hawker company proceeded to concentrate on fighters, and the first production Hurricane—a monoplane development of the Fury—first entered service in late 1937. This fighter achieved significant success in the Battle of Britain. The Typhoon, initially none too successful, proved effective in a fighter bomber role, and saw the peak of its development in the Tempest, Fury and Sea Fury which served with RAF and Fleet Air Arm during late 1940s and early 1950s, and with foreign air arms well into the 1960s. In early post-war period Hawker developed the Sea Hawk shipboard fighter, progressing to the Hunter, the single Mk3 version of which, produced by modification of the original prototype, gained the world speed record at 1,170·96 km/h (727·6 mph) in 1953. Such was the success of the Hunter, which remains in RAF and Royal Navy service, that refurbished aircraft are still being exported in 1978. Hawker's greatest innovation was in the field of VTOL fighters, first with the experimental P. 1127 Kestrel, which led to the Hawker Siddeley Harrier, still the only true VTOL/VSTOL jet fighter in front-line squadron service, operating currently with the forces of Britain, United States and Spain. A Sea Harrier version intended for operation from through-deck cruisers, is being developed at the present time.

Hawker Siddeley Harrier VTOL/VSTOL jet fighter, developed from the P. 1127 Kestrel

Hawker Hunter interceptor fighters

Hawker Osprey taking-off from an aircraft carrier

Hawker Siddeley HS 748 of Austrian Airlines

HAWKER ENGINEERING CO. LTD./UK

In 1921 Harry Hawker, former Sopwith test-pilot, took over the premises of the former Sopwith Aviation Company (*q.v.*), and although he died that same year in a crash the re-established company began building a series of military aircraft, beginning with the single Duiker monoplane, and followed by the Woodcock. Under the design leadership of Sydney Camm (later Sir), produced such aircraft as the Danecock biplane and the Horsley bomber/torpedo-bomber, Mk1 versions of which were the last all-wooden aircraft built by the company. Best known of all H. G. Hawker products were the Hart/Demon/Audax/Osprey two-seaters and the beautiful Fury single-seat fighter; all had entered production before the company name was changed to Hawker Aircraft Ltd. (*q.v.*) in 1933.

HAWKER SIDDELEY AVIATION LTD./UK

In mid-1963 the Hawker Siddeley Group incorporated the Hawker, de Havilland, Avro, Armstrong-Whitworth, Folland and Blackburn companies into Hawker Siddeley Aviation, the aircraft products of each company to be known as Hawker Siddeley aircraft.

Hawker Hurricanes, the RAF's first eight-gun fighter

HAYDEN AIRCRAFT CORPORATION/*USA*

Formed 1955 to build the Stout Bushmaster 15-AT, a modern development of the Ford Tri-motor transport. Initial pre-production series of three aircraft planned with financial support from Air-Craft & Hydro Forming Inc.

HAYES AIRCRAFT CORPORATION/*USA*

Specialist military conversion company, which adapted 137 North American TB-25L/N Mitchell bombers for pilot training and from 1958 developed and manufactured jet-boosted tanker conversion of the Boeing B-50 Superfortress for USAF. This last aircraft was designated the KB-50J/K.

HEATH AIRCRAFT COMPANY/*USA*

Formed in 1926 by Ed Heath, whose 1928 Baby Bullet mid-wing monoplane racer exceeded 160 km/h (100 mph) on only 24 kW (32 hp). Heath Super Soarer biplane glider, built 1930, was first unpowered aircraft to loop-the-loop. 1931 Heath Parasol, designed to be powered by a converted motor cycle engine, sold in large numbers to amateur builders.

HELICOM INC./*USA*

Founded in 1954 as Helicopter Engineering Research Corporation by Harold E. Emigh, designer of the Emigh Trojan lightplane, to develop and market a single-seat personal helicopter. Known as the Helicom Commuter

Heath Parasol ultra light monoplane

Jr Model H-1A, the prototype first flew in 1960, and was sold both in ready to fly form and as a kit for assembly by amateur constructors. A ground trainer version was developed also, mounted via a gimbal to a castoring base which was too heavy for the helicopter to lift from the ground. There was sufficient movement built into the mounting to permit a lift of 0·46 m (1 ft 6 in), tilt of 7° and 360° rotation.

Heinkel He 111, an extensively-used multi-purpose bomber of the Luftwaffe

HEINKEL/*Germany*

Ernst Heinkel established his own company shortly after the liquidation of Hansa Brandenburg (*q.v.*) building a series of single-engined seaplanes (He 1 to He 8), in Sweden to circumvent the Treaty of Versailles' ban on the construction of military aircraft in Germany. The He 51 biplane fighter went into production for the Luftwaffe in the 1930s and served with the Condor Legion in Spain. When the Heinkel He 70 passenger/mailplane appeared in 1932, ostensibly for Deutsche Lufthansa, it was the most advanced aerodynamic design then seen in Europe. A natural outgrowth of this design was the Heinkel He 111 twin-engined bomber which served with the Luftwaffe throughout WW2. A Rolls-Royce Merlin-engined version of the He 111 was built by CASA in Spain, and served with the Spanish Air Force until the late 1960s. Heinkel also produced late in the war the He 162 Volksjäger (People's Fighter), a lightweight turbojet fighter constructed almost entirely of wood. Heinkel had designed and built the world's first jet aircraft, the He 178, in 1939 and other significant Heinkel projects included the He 177 Greiff heavy bomber and the He 219 Uhu night fighter.

Heinkel He 112 single-seat fighter

Heinkel He 162 Salamander jet fighter

Helio Model H-550A Stallion ten-seat utility aircraft

Helio Super Courier light STOL monoplane

HELICOPTER TECHNIK MÜNCHEN
GmbH/*Germany*
Founded to produce the Skytrac two-seat lightweight multi-purpose helicopter, designed originally by Wagner Helicopter Technik (*q.v.*). The HTM FJ-Skytrac received both German and FAA certification, and the company developed a kit to convert the Skytrac into a four-seat light helicopter known as the HTM Skyrider. Production terminated due to lack of capital.

HELIO/*USA*
Founded 1948 as Helio Aircraft Corporation to develop the two-seat Koppen-Bollinger lightplane. Four-seat STOL derivative Helio Courier entered production 1954. Superseded by the H-391B, H-395 and H-395A Super Couriers introduced from 1958. Helio H-250 and H-295 six-seat utility aircraft flew in 1964 and 1965 respectively, and were produced for both civil and military use. Super Couriers in USAF service had the designation U-10. The H-550A Stallion with turboprop engine followed but is now out of production. Helio was acquired by General Aircraft Corporation (*q.v.*) in 1969, but the assets have since been acquired by Helio Courier Ltd. which produces H-295 Super and HT-295 Trigear Couriers.

HELIOPOLIS AIR WORKS/*Egypt*
Formed 1950 to manufacture a local version of the German Bücker Bü 181D Bestmann as the Gomhouria trainer for Egypt, Jordan, Libya, Saudi Arabia, Somalia and the Sudan.

HELITEC CORPORATION/*USA*
Aviation Specialties Inc. (*q.v.*) developed a turbine-engined conversion of surplus military Sikorsky S-55 helicopters, first certificated in the USA in 1971. Helitec Corporation was founded subsequently to continue the conversion and marketing of the S-55 for sale in the USA, Canada, Europe and South America.

HELWAN AIR WORKS/*Egypt*
Inaugurated by President Nasser in 1962, Helwan's first project was the licence-manufacture of the Spanish Hispano HA-200 Saeta jet trainer, known in Egypt as Al Kahira. German designer Willy Messerschmitt headed a Helwan team to develop the HA-300 supersonic fighter which first flew in prototype form in March 1964.

HENDERSON SCOTTISH AVIATION
FACTORY/*UK*
Sub-contractors in WW1, built a batch of 100 Avro 504K training aircraft.

HENDY AIRCRAFT COMPANY/*UK*
This company's first design was the Hendy 281 Hobo, a small single-seater utilising Basil Henderson's patented wing construction. A tandem two-seat derivative, the Hendy 302, was built by George Parnall and Company (with whom Hendy amalgamated in 1935) and was entered in the 1930 King Cup Air Race. The 1934 Hendy 3308 Heck was an advanced three-seater constructed by Westland Aircraft for Whitney Straight.

HENSCHEL FLUGZEUGWERKE
AG/*Germany*
Henschel's Hs 123 dive-bombing biplane was tested during the Spanish Civil War, and though obsolescent, served with the Luftwaffe until 1942 in close-support roles, particularly on the Russian Front. The Henschel Hs 126 was a parasol wing, two-seat observation/liaison aircraft, which first entered Luftwaffe service in 1938. A twin-engined, single-seat close support and ground attack aircraft—the

Helwan Al Kahira, licence-built version of the Hispano HA-200

Helwan HA-300 single-seat delta-wing lightweight fighter

Henschel Hs 123A, the Luftwaffe's last biplane aircraft

Heston Phoenix five-seat cabin monoplane

Hs 129—was produced in some numbers, and was used to effect on the Eastern Front, particularly as a tank-buster. The final Hs 129B-2/R-4 version was armed with a 75 mm cannon. Completed a prototype jet dive-bomber—the Hs 132—but this did not fly before the end of the war. The company experimented also with a number of wire-, radio- and even television-guided missiles.

HESTON AIRCRAFT CO. LTD./UK
Founded 1934 to take over the assets of Comper Aircraft Company Ltd. (q.v.). Developed the Heston Type 1 Phoenix in 1935, a five-seat cabin monoplane with retractable landing gear—the first to be fitted to a British high-wing aircraft. Heston built also the 1,715 kW (2,300 hp) Napier Sabre-powered Heston Type 5 racer. Sponsored by Lord Nuffield for a British attempt on the World Speed Record, it crashed during flight testing. A second example was never completed.

HIGGINS AIRCRAFT INC./USA
This New Orleans-based company was subcontracted by Curtiss-Wright in 1942 to manufacture the Curtiss C-46 Commando military transport aircraft. Only two aircraft had been built by Higgins when the contract for 500 was cancelled.

HIGGINS INDUSTRIES INC. HELICOPTER DIVISION/USA
Under the direction of Enea Bossi, this subsidiary of the Andrew Higgins shipbuilding concern was developing a twin-engined, four-passenger helicopter and a two-seat experimental helicopter when the parent company's military contracts terminated and all aircraft work was suspended.

Heston Aircraft twin-boom Air Observation Post

HILLER AVIATION/*USA*

Formed in 1973 after acquiring the design rights, tooling and spares for Hiller 12E light helicopters from Fairchild Industries (*q.v.*). The company provides support currently for operators of Hiller helicopters and produces three-seat UH-12E and four-seat UH-12E-4 turbine conversions of the UH-12E, which have been developed in conjunction with Soloy Conversions.

HILLER HELICOPTERS/*USA*

This company produced in 1948 the Hiller UH-12 and subsequently supplied the aircraft to civilian operators, and as H-23B and OH-23C/D Ravens to the US Army and to foreign air arms under the MDAP programme. Three-seat UH-12E and four-seat UH-12E4 variants were developed also, and the Hiller HOE-1 Hornet ramjet ultra-light helicopter and 'Flying Platform' were two military experimental types devised by the company. After amalgamation with Fairchild Industries (*q.v.*) the Hiller FH-1100 turbine transport helicopter was produced for the expanding executive transport market, but is no longer in production.

HILLS & SONS/*UK*

Manchester-based woodworking firm which acquired a licence to produce the Czechoslovakian Praga E.114 Air Baby two-seat lightplane. Thirty examples manufactured from 1936, known as Hillson Pragas. A single Hillson Helvellyn two-seat, mid-wing lightplane was built and flown in 1939 and one Hillson Pennine was produced, but not flown prior to the outbreak of war. During WW2 the company was involved in contract work for the Air Ministry and developed an experimental 'slip-wing' conversion of the Hawker Hurricane which enabled the aircraft to take off at greater than normal gross weight, releasing the upper wing in flight.

HINDUSTAN AERONAUTICS LTD./*India*

Hindustan Aircraft Ltd. (formed in 1940) was amalgamated with Aeronautics India Ltd. (formed 1963) to establish Hindustan Aeronautics Ltd. in October 1964. Hindustan Aircraft designed and built the first indigenous Indian aircraft, the Hindustan HT-2 two-seat trainer which first flew in 1951 and was produced for the Indian Air Force and civil flying clubs. The HUL-26 Pushpak high-wing lightplane, based on the American Aeronca Chief, entered production in 1959 and the HAOP-27 Krishak derivation was manufactured as a liaison aircraft for the Indian Air Force and Army. Deliveries of the HAL HJT-16 Kiran two-seat jet trainer began in 1966. The HF-24

Hiller Model 12E-4 four-seat helicopter

Hiller X-18 tilt-wing VTOL research aircraft

Hillson Bi-Mono lightweight sportsplane

HAL HAOP-27 Krishak liaison aircraft

HAL HF-24 Marut single-seat fighter

Marut single-seat fighter was designed by a team led by Kurt Tank, and the HAL Ajeet lightweight jet fighter, developed from the Folland/Hawker Siddeley Gnat which HAL licence-produced, began series production for the Indian Air Force in 1978. HAL builds also the HA-31 Basant agricultural aircraft and licence-manufactures SA-315B Lama and SA-316B Alouette III helicopters. Overhaul of all Indian Air Force aircraft is undertaken, together with component manufacture in connection with India's space research programme.

HIRO NAVAL AIR ARSENAL/Japan
Hiro's Navy Type 90-1 three-engined flying-boat, built in the early 1930s, had Japanese-built Hispano-Suiza engines and bore a close resemblance to the German Rohrbach flying-boats. In 1932 the company started work on a twin-engined land-based attack bomber, Hiro G2H1, which went into production in 1935 as Navy Type 95. Only eight were built, two by the Mitsubishi company, who subsequently developed a long-range reconnaissance version which directly influenced the design of the successful Mitsubishi G3M bomber.

HIRTENBERGER/Austria
Hirtenberger Patronen Zündhutchen und Metallwarenfabrik AG began aircraft manufacture in 1935 after taking over Flugzeugbau Hopfner (q.v.). Only the Hirtenberger HS-9 parasol-wing training/touring monoplane was

produced. An open-cockpit tandem two-seater, it was built with either a 93 kW (125 hp) Siemens or 89 kW (120 hp) de Havilland Gipsy Major engine, the latter variant designated HS-9A.

HIRTH/Germany
Wolf Hirth GmbH, a pre-war manufacturer of sailplanes, made wooden sub-assemblies for Messerschmitt projects during WW2, including a high-speed glider-trainer for Me 163 Komet pilots, and components for the Me 321 and Me 323 Gigants. The re-established company, owned largely by Messerschmitt-Bölkow-Blohm (q.v.), is building Arnold Wagner's Acrostar competition aerobatic aircraft in small numbers, and supporting the Bölkow BO 107, 207, 208 and 209 lightplanes.

HISPANO AVIACIÓN/Spain
La Hispano Aviación SA manufactured the Fiat CR.32 biplane fighter as the HA-132-1 Chirri between 1938–1942. In 1943 the company received a contract to build under licence Messerschmitt Me 109Gs for the Spanish Air Force. Designated as the Hispano HA-1109, it was powered initially by a Hispano-Suiza HS-12Z engine and later, in HA-1109/1110 Buchon variants, by the Rolls-Royce Merlin. An indigenous HA-43D-1 advanced two-seat military trainer went into production for the Spanish Air Force in 1947, followed in 1953 by the HA-100EI replacement, with tricycle landing gear, designed by Willy Messerschmitt.

HAL licence-built HS 748 transport

Messerschmitt supervised also design of the HA-200 Saeta jet trainer which first flew in 1955, and which was later developed as the HA-220 Super Saeta single-seat light ground attack aircraft. Hispano merged with Construcciones Aeronáuticas SA (q.v.) in 1972.

HITACHI KOKUKI KABUSHIKI KAISHA/Japan
Founded in 1939, this company produced the Hitachi T-2 two-seat sesquiplane trainer of mixed wood and metal construction.

HOCKADAY AIRCRAFT CORPORATION/USA
Formed in 1937. Design work began on the CV-139 Comet two-seat high-wing cabin monoplane but was suspended in 1940 to undertake military contract work for other aircraft companies. The project was resumed in 1944 when the sole prototype was test flown.

Hispano licence-built Airco D.H.6

Hispano HS-42 advanced trainer

Hispano HA-220 Super Saeta

Holste Broussard transport and liaison aircraft

Holste MH.250 Super Broussard transport

HOLLANDAIR TB/*Netherlands*
Formed as an aeronautical trading concern in 1956 specialising in the overhaul of aircraft and engines. One example only of the Hollandair HA-001 Libel (Dragonfly) single-seat agricultural aircraft was built in 1957.

HOLSTE/*France*
Max Holste's first designs were the MH.52 two-seat lightweight sporting aircraft with tricycle landing gear and the MH.53 Cadet trainer variant, characterised by twin-fin tail surfaces, which appeared subsequently on the MH.1521M Broussard utility transport and liaison aircraft, produced in quantity for the French Air Force and Army. A twin-engined development, the MH.260 Super Broussard, was redesignated Nord 262 when Max Holste became incorporated with Nord Aviation (*q.v.*) in 1961. A small remaining private sector of the company is now part of Reims Aviation (*q.v.*), which builds Cessna aircraft under licence for European distribution.

HÖNNINGSTAD/*Norway*
Established 1936, Hönningstad designed and built the Norge Model A light transport aircraft in 1938. Designed a twin-engined, 12-passenger amphibian built by Norsk Flyindustri AS (*q.v.*), as the Finnmark 5A, which was intended specifically for operation in the Northern and Arctic regions, but only one prototype was completed. The Hönningstad Polar C5 bush-plane was built in 1948 by Widerøes Flyveselskap OG Polarfly (*q.v.*).

HOOPER & COMPANY/*UK*
This Chelsea-based company of coachbuilders was a sub-contractor during WW1, building Sopwith 1½ Strutters, Camels, Ship's Camels and Dolphins.

HOPFNER/*Austria*
Hopfner was the first Austrian company to manufacture an aeroplane after WW1, a three-seat monoplane known as the Hopfner S.1. A developed version with Gypsy Major engine was designated HS-1033. Hopfner produced also the HA-1133 four-seat twin-engined amphibian before being taken over in 1935 by Hirtenberger Patronen, Zundhutchen und Metallwarenfabrik AG (*q.v.*).

HOPPI-COPTERS/*USA*
The Pentecost Hoppi-Copter was a 41 kg (90 lb) personal helicopter pack designed to be strapped to an infantryman's back to make it possible for him to surmount terrain obstacles. It first flew in 1945, but landing shock problems proved insurmountable. A second version was tested later, with seat and landing gear, and two examples were acquired in 1948 for evaluation by the British Ministry of Supply. Capital Helicopter Corporation (*q.v.*) took over the patents in 1954 and flew a Hoppi-Copter with rotor blade-mounted pulse jets.

HORTEN GEBRÜDER/*Germany*
The Horten brothers conducted flying-wing experiments pre-war, building a series of tail-less high-performance gliders. The Horten Ho V and Ho VI were both powered aircraft, leading to the turbojet-powered Ho IX flown in the Summer of 1944. Before being destroyed in a landing accident after only a few hours flight, had been flown at a speed of 800 km/h (497 mph). This was developed by Gothaer Waggonfabrik (*q.v.*) as the Gotha Go 229 V3 single-seat fighter, but the Gothaer works were captured by advancing US forces before this prototype was completed.

HOWARD AERO INC./*USA*
Formed in 1947 as a modification, repair and maintenance organisation. In 1963 Howard combined with Alamo Aero Service, specialising in the conversion of ex-military Lockheed PV-1 Venturas and civilian Lockheed Lodestars as high-speed executive transports known as Howard 250s, 350s and 500s according to configuration and power plant. A three-engined version of the Beech Travel Air twin was also flown experimentally.

HOWARD AIRCRAFT CORPORATION/*USA*
Benjamin Howard built his first aeroplane—the DGA-1 ('*D*amn *G*ood *A*irplane')—in 1923 while working for the Curtiss Company. His DGA-3 *Pete* was a racer built for the 1930 US National Air Races and was succeeded by DGA-4 *Ike* and DGS-5 *Mike*. With DGA-6 *Mister Mulligan* Howard won all three major American racing titles in 1935 and it was this design which was de-

Howard Aero Model 500, a conversion of the Lockheed Lodestar

Howard DGA-15 five-seat floatplane

Hughes YAH-64 advanced attack helicopter prototype

veloped through several models into the Howard DGA-15 five-seat cabin monoplane which served with the US Navy in transport, instrument trainer and ambulance roles during WW2. The Howard DGA-18K two-seat primary trainer was produced in quantity during 1940–1942 for the US Government's Civilian Pilot Training Programme.

HTM/*Germany*
see Helicopter Technik München GmbH

HUFF-DALAND AIRPLANES INC./*USA*
Produced a number of single-engined military biplanes in the early 1920s, when James McDonnell (later of the McDonnell Douglas Company) was chief engineer. The XLB-1 three-seat, single-engine light bomber was tested in 1923 and was developed as the twin-engined XLB-3, with a crew of five. In 1924 Huff-Daland was reorganised as Keystone Aircraft Corporation (*q.v.*) and the production bomber aircraft was known by this latter company name.

HUFFER/*Germany*
Flugzeugbau Dr. Georg Huffer produced a civilian version of the WW1 Fokker D. VII fighter, known as the Huffer H.9. The aircraft was an open-cockpit two-seat training/ sporting aircraft powered by a Mercedes engine. A parasol-wing monoplane, designated HB.28, was also designed and built by the company in the late 1920s.

HUGHES AIRCRAFT COMPANY/*USA*
Founded in 1935 by the businessman/film magnate Howard Hughes to produce the Hughes H-1 racing aeroplane. In this, Hughes established an international landplane speed record of 567·23 km/h (352·46 mph). The Hughes XF-11 experimental, twin-engined, twin-boom photo-reconnaissance aircraft, which had contra-rotating airscrews, crashed on its first test flight seriously injuring Hughes, who subsequently sponsored the massive Hughes Hercules ('Spruce Goose') flying-boat. Made entirely of wood, this eight-engined aircraft had the greatest wing span (97·54 m; 320 ft) of any aircraft built to date

Hughes Model 300 three-seat light helicopter

and made its one and only flight on 2 November, 1947 with Howard Hughes at the controls. Between 1949–1952 the Hughes Aircraft Company built and tested the XH-17 heavy-lift helicopter designed as a 'flying crane' for the USAF.

HUGHES HELICOPTERS/*USA*
Known formerly as the Hughes Tool Company, became a Division of the Summa Corporation in the early 1970s. Hughes first two-seat light helicopter, the Model 269, first flew in

Hughes Hercules flying-boat, the world's largest flying-boat, and the largest aeroplane ever to have flown

1955. It remains in production, though much-modified, as the Hughes 300. Production of the OH-6A Cayuse turbine helicopter for the US Army and other military forces led to the commercial Model 500 one/seven-seat light helicopter, currently produced as the Model 500D, with a military 500M-D variant in production. Hughes won the US Army's competition for an Advanced Attack Helicopter (AAH) with its Model 77, a twin-turbine design which first flew in 1975, and which has the Army designation YAH-64.

HUMBER/UK

The Humber Motor Company Ltd. manufactured a British version of the Blériot XI in 1910 known as the Humber-Blériot Monoplane. At the 1910 Olympia Aero Show Humber exhibited a single-seat monoplane to the design of Hubert Le Blon. Powered by a three-cylinder Humber engine, it had variable-camber wings and a small diameter tapering wooden boom serving as the structural link between wing and tail unit. Two further Blériot modifications were built to the design of Captain T. T. Lovelace, and two Roger Sommer biplanes were completed towards the end of 1910. One of the latter carried the first official air mail in India.

HUNTING AIRCRAFT LTD./UK

In 1957 the Hunting-Percival Company (q.v.) was renamed Hunting Aircraft and continued with production of the Provost, Jet Provost, Prince, Pembroke and Sea Prince aircraft before being absorbed by the British Aircraft Corporation (q.v.). BAC had a controlling interest in the company on its formation in 1960, and acquired the remaining shares in 1964.

HUNTING-PERCIVAL AIRCRAFT LTD./UK

The Percival light aircraft manufacturing company became part of the Canadian-owned Hunting Group in 1954. Production was undertaken of the Percival P.56 Provost trainer for the Royal Air Force and several overseas forces. A turbine-powered derivative, the P.84 Jet Provost, flew shortly after the merger and was delivered to the RAF subsequently as their standard basic jet trainer. This remains in production in much-modified form as the BAC Strikemaster. The Percival P.50 Prince twin-engined light transport was manufactured for civilian operators, and as the Pembroke C.1 for the RAF, Swedish Air Force, Luftwaffe, and several other air arms, and as the Sea Prince for the Fleet Air Arm. An executive President variant was manufactured in small numbers after the company became Hunting Aircraft Limited (q.v.) in 1957.

Hunting Percival Pembroke

Hunting Percival Provost two-seat trainer

HUNTINGDON AIRCRAFT CORPORATION/USA

Incorporated in 1928 at Bridgeport, Connecticut, this company developed two aeroplanes—the Huntingdon II two-seat landplane, powered by a Wright-built Gypsy, and the Huntingdon 12, a four/six-seat amphibian with Pratt & Whitney Wasp engine.

HUREL-DUBOIS/France

Formed to develop Maurice Hurel's theories on high-aspect ratio wings. His first design, the Hurel-Dubois HD-10 single-engined research aircraft, flew in 1948 and led to a twin-engined

derivative, the HD-31. Production versions included the HD-32 transport, HD-33 freighter and HD-34 photo survey aircraft for the Institut Géographique National. While still active in the French aviation industry, the company is no longer an aircraft constructor.

HUSKY AIRCRAFT LTD./Canada

Formed 1955 to re-establish a production line for the Fairchild F-11 Husky bush-plane which first flew in 1946. Production models were offered in land or float-plane versions and designated F-11-2 Leonides Husky and F-11-3/4 Super Husky.

Hurel-Dubois HD-32 transport aircraft

Hurel-Dubois HD-10 research aircraft

IJ

IA/*Argentina*
   see Fábrica Militar de Aviones

IABSA/*Brazil*
Indústria Aeronáutica Brasileira SA produced in the late 1960s a two-seat lightweight primary trainer/sporting aircraft under the designation IABSA Premier 64-01. Had under development a single-seat aerobatic biplane, the IABSA Aerobatic 65-02.

IAI/*Israel*
   see Israel Aircraft Industries

IAME/*Argentina*
   see Empresa Industrias Aeronáuticas y Meccánicas del Estado

IAR/*Romania*
   see Regia Autonoma Industria Aeronautica Romana

IBERAVIA/*Spain*
This company, which was established in 1946, began the development of aircraft in 1948. A two-seat training glider, designated IP-2, was designed but construction was undertaken by AISA (*q.v.*). Designed and built in 1950 a two-seat lightweight training/sporting aircraft known as the I-11, followed by the I-115 basic trainer. Was involved in helicopter design when the company was taken over by AISA.

ICA/*Romania*
Intreprinderea de Constructii Aeronàutice is the Brasov unit of the Centrala Industriala Aeronautica Romana (*q.v.*), formed by reorganisation of the national aircraft industry in 1968. Undertakes repair and overhaul of light aircraft; builds aircraft of its own design, such as the IAR-824 six-seat general-purpose light aircraft, and IS-28/IS-29 sailplanes; manufactures Aérospatiale SA 316B Alouette III helicopters under licence; participates in licence-construction of the Britten-Norman BN-2A Islander; and carries out series production of nationally-designed aircraft.

IKARUS AD/*Yugoslavia*
Formed at Novi Sad in 1923, Ikarus was one of the country's largest aircraft manufacturers. Initial production centred on a number of S.M. training flying-boats, followed by a military type I.O. In 1926 the company acquired a licence to build the Potez 25 biplane, and established a new factory at Zemun for its production.

ILYUSHIN/*USSR*
During the early 1920s Sergei Vladimirovich Ilyushin was a student at the Zhukovskii Military Air Academy, and began glider design. From 1935 one of the most successful Soviet aircraft designers, beginning with Il-4 (DB-3) bomber developed from TsKB-26 design, of which nearly 7,000 built. Most famous was the Il-2 Shturmovik armoured ground-attack aircraft, a vital weapon in the defeat of the German invasion of Russia, and of which more than 36,000 were built. Post-WW2 developed Il-12 and Il-14 transports which established Aeroflot's civil airline network. Il-28 bomber of 1948 (in class of British Canberra) was first Soviet jet-bomber, remaining in large-scale use for many years. Il-18 civil transport, which entered service with Aeroflot in 1959, was nation's first turboprop airliner. Il-38 anti-submarine/maritime patrol aircraft developed from Il-18. Il-62 114/186-seat turbofan-powered transport, which inaugurated Aeroflot's Moscow–New York service in July 1968, was Soviet Union's first long-range jet-

Ilyushin Il-62 four-turbofan long-range commercial transport

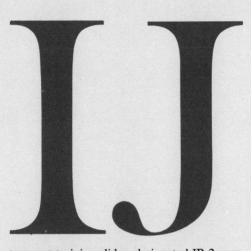

Ilyushin Il-38 maritime reconnaissance version of the Il-18 transport

powered airliner. Il-76T four-turbofan medium/long-range freight transport entered service early 1970s. Il-86 wide-body transport first flew 22 December 1976 and development was continuing in early 1978.

IMAM/*Italy*
see Meridionali

IMCO/*USA*
Intermountain Manufacturing Company acquired at public auction the former Callair Inc. (*q.v.*), developing from the well-known Callair series of agricultural aircraft an improved model designated IMCO Callair A-9. A scaled-up version, the B-1, first flew on 15 January 1966. IMCO sold the Callair assets to Rockwell Standard Corporation (*q.v.*) in December 1966, which continued production of these aircraft at Afton, Wyoming, under the banner of Aero Commander (*q.v.*).

IMPA/*Argentina*
Industria Metalúrgica e Plástica SA was a munitions factory which opened an aircraft department in September 1941. A new factory opened at Quilmes Airport, Buenos Aires, in December 1944. Products included prototypes of RR-11 two-seat low-wing cabin monoplane (1942) and Chorlito light single-seat trainer (1943). Only production aircraft was the Tu-Sa (or LF-1), of which 25 were built 1943/1944.

INDÚSTRIA AERONÁUTICA BRASILEIRA SA/*Brazil*
see IABSA

INDUSTRIA METALÚRGICA E PLÁSTICA SA/*Argentina*
see IMPA

INDUSTRIA VALTION LENTOKONETEHDAS/*Finland*
see IVL

INDUSTRIE MECCANICHE E AERONÀUTICHE MERIDIONALI/*Italy*
see Meridionali *entries*

INLAND AVIATION COMPANY/*USA*
Founded in the late 1920s, this company built a

two-seat monoplane of braced parasol-wing configuration, known as the Inland Sport. The more powerful Super Sport, with an 82 kW (110 hp) Warner Scarab engine, established an American Height Record on 25 October 1929, and a World Speed Record for light aircraft on 12 February 1930.

INSTITUTO AEROTÉCNICO/*Argentina*
see Fábrica Militar de Aviones

INSTITUTO DE PESIQUAS TECHNOLÓGICAS/*Brazil*
see IPT

INTER-AIR/*USA*
International Aircraft Manufacturing Inc. established at Alexandria, Minnesota, to build a new version of the Bellanca Model 14-19-3A four-seat light aircraft designed originally by G. M. Bellanca (*see* Bellanca Aircraft Corp.).

INTERCEPTOR COMPANY/*USA*
Original company, Interceptor Corporation, established 18 November 1968. First aircraft produced was Interceptor 400, a turbine-

IMCO Call Air A-9, a trend-setting agricultural aircraft

IPT FG-8 Guanabara executive transport

IAI Kfir-C2 multi-purpose combat aircraft

engined development of the Myers 200C built as the Model 200D by Aero Commander Inc. (*q.v.*), from whom Interceptor Corporation acquired all rights and tooling. Prototype Interceptor 400 first flew 27 June 1969. Was sold and subsequently repurchased by current Interceptor Company, who acquired Type Certificate at end of 1974. The current interceptor 400 is an advanced 4-seat cabin monoplane with what is an unusual feature for this class of aircraft, namely a pressurised cabin, and is powered by a 496 kW (665 shp) Garrett-Air Research turboprop engine.

INTERCITY AIRLINES COMPANY/*Canada*
Formed in 1947 to construct and develop a three-seat helicopter, designed by American engineers Bernard Sznycer and Selina Gottlieb, designated SG VI-D. This was a conventional single rotor/anti-torque tail rotor type, with a 125 kW (165 hp) Franklin engine.

INTERMOUNTAIN MANUFACTURING COMPANY/*USA*
see IMCO

INTERNATIONAL AIRCRAFT CORPORATION/*USA*
Founded at Cincinnati, Ohio, the company was incorporated in 1928. Production included the International F-17 Sportsman, a three-seat open cockpit biplane, and the F-18 Air Coach, a six-seat enclosed cabin biplane.

INTERNATIONAL AIRCRAFT MANUFACTURING INC./*USA*
see Inter-Air

INTERSTATE AIRCRAFT & ENGINEERING CORPORATION/*USA*
Founded in April 1937, this company was originally a manufacturer of hydraulic and other

precision components for the US aircraft industry. Produced in 1940 the Cadet two-seat light cabin monoplane which, after US entry into WW2, was developed as a light liaison and observation aircraft for the US Army. Designed and built a number of drone aircraft prototypes for both US Army and Navy. All were pilotless radio-controlled weapon carriers.

INTREPRINDEREA DE CONSTRUCTII AERONAUTICE/*Romania*
see ICA

INTREPRINDEREA DE REPARAT MATERIAL AERONAUTICE/*Romania*
see IRMA

INVINCIBLE AIRCRAFT CORPORATION/*USA*
In the late 1920s the Invincible Metal Furniture Company of Manitowoc, Wisconsin, formed an aircraft division to build a four-seat cabin monoplane. The fuselage and tail unit were welded steel-tube structures, the wing of wooden construction. Access to the cabin was by a completely circular door on the starboard side of the fuselage.

IPT/*Brazil*
Instituto de Pesiquas Technólogicas (National Institute of Technical Research) was concerned primarily with research into materials suitable for use by the national aircraft industry. Was also responsible for the construction of a small number of lightweight cabin monoplanes.

IRELAND AIRCRAFT INC./*USA*
One-time sales representative of the Curtiss Aeroplane and Motor Company, G.S. Ireland founded his company to manufacture an aircraft known as the Ireland Comet, which com-

bined surplus Curtiss Oriole fuselages with new wings and tail unit. Incorporated in 1926, the company began production of the Ireland Neptune, a five-seat amphibian flying-boat.

IRMA/*Romania*
Intreprinderea de Reparat Material Aeronautice is the Bucharest unit of the Centrala Industriala Aeronautica Romana (*q.v.*), formed by reorganisation of the national aircraft industry in 1968. Specialises in the repair and overhaul of aircraft and engines for Tarom and other airlines, and is manufacturing under licence the Britten-Norman BN-2A Islander.

IRWIN AIRCRAFT COMPANY/*USA*
In 1916 J. F. Irwin designed a small single-seat monoplane, designated M-T, which was powered by a motor-cycle engine. Post WW1 the company built an improved version, the M-T-2, powered by a 15 kW (20 hp) Meteor engine.

ISRAEL AIRCRAFT INDUSTRIES/*Israel*
Established 1953, originally as Bedek Aircraft Company, as a repair and maintenance organisation. Manufactured Slingsby sailplanes under licence from 1957, and also initiated licence production of the French Fouga Magister. Changed company title to Israel Aircraft Industries in April 1967, and now composed of several divisions and subsidiaries. Built Nesher

IAI Arava twin-turboprop utility transport

fighter 1969; an Israeli-designed interim version of the French Mirage III. Developed an improved version as the Kfir which was in service in the early 1970s. Designed light STOL transport known as Arava, prototype of which first flew 27 November 1969, and produced in IAI 101/102 civil and IAI 201 military versions. Acquired in 1967 all rights of Rockwell-Standard Corporation's Jet Commander twin-turbojet business transport: developed this into the improved twin-turbofan IAI 1124 Westwind, which entered production in 1976.

ITOH CHU KOKU SEIBI KABUSHIKI KAISHA/*Japan*
see Shin Nihon Koku Seibi Kabushiki Kaisha

ISSOIRE AVIATION/*France*
Company formed following bankruptcy of Wassmer Aviation (*q.v.*) by President/General Director of Siren SA (*q.v.*). Was to undertake production at Issoire from Spring 1978 of Silene and Iris sailplanes, and of ex-Wassmer light aircraft, plus sub-contract work for major French aerospace companies.

IVL/*Finland*
Founded in 1921 at Sveaborg, near Helsinki, to manufacture aircraft for the Finnish Air Force. First production was the A-22 seaplane, a licence-built version of the Hansa-Brandenburg W.33. A neat biplane reconnaissance/bombing aircraft, the Korka, was in production in the mid-1920s. Only one nationally-designed combat aircraft saw service in WW2, the Myrsky single-seat monoplane fighter.

JACKAROO AIRCRAFT LTD./*UK*
Formed late 1950s at Thruxton, Hampshire, to produce the Thruxton Jackaroo widened-fuselage four-seat version of the de Havilland Tiger Moth. First 'production' conversion flew on 15 April 1957, and quite a number of Tiger Moths were converted subsequently to Jack-

Jackaroo 'wide-body' version of the Tiger Moth

aroos. Company designed also a four-seat low-wing lightplane called the Paragon, being re-formed in early 1960s as Paragon Aircraft Ltd. (*q.v.*) to produce it under new name of Paladin.

JAMIESON CORPORATION/*USA*
Formed late 1940s as Jamieson Aircraft Company Inc. to develop and produce the J-2-L1 Jupiter, a small, three-seat low-wing monoplane with retractable landing gear and a Vee tail. Name changed in middle/late 1950s, and in December 1958 flew prototype of a four-seat, single-tailed development of Jupiter known as the Take 1. This was certificated in mid-1963 and limited production of an improved model, the Jamieson 'J', soon began.

JANOX/*USA*
Manufacturer of reflector landing systems which, in about 1970, acquired Navion Aircraft Corporation (*q.v.*). Intended to continue production of Navion Model H in new factory at Coshocton, Ohio; instead, Navion Aircraft Corporation was purchased in late 1972 by Mr. Cedric Kotowicz, who moved all assets to a new plant at Wharton, Texas, subsequently setting up the Navion Rangemaster Aircraft Company (*q.v.*).

JDM/*France*
Founded late 1940s by Jean Dabos to market Roitelet (Wren) single-seat ultra-light monoplane. Poinsard-engined prototype flew successfully but lack of suitable production engine prevented manufacture and by 1951 company had been dissolved.

JETSTREAM/*UK*
Company formed September 1970 to continue development/construction and production of H.P.137 Jetstream twin-turboprop transport after closure that year of Handley Page Aircraft Ltd. (*q.v.*). Initial production line laid down at Northampton late 1970 for Jetstream Series 200, but manufacture taken over late 1971/early 1972 by Scottish Aviation (*q.v.*) before any aircraft had been built.

JODEL/*France*
Established at Beaune in March 1946, by Jean Delemontez and Edouard Joly—former as business and technical manager; latter as test pilot. Initial activities concerned with repair of gliders and light aircraft of Service d'Aviation Légère et Sportive on behalf of French government. In parallel, Jodel designed and built C.9 Bébé single-seat light monoplane, first flown

Jamieson 'J' four-seat cabin monoplane

Jodel D.117 two-seat cabin monoplane

Jodel D.9 Bébé single-seat lightplane

January 1948. After official tests with D.9, French government ordered two prototypes of two-seat D.11 (Salmson engine) and D.111 (Minie engine). Followed by D.112, and D.140 Mousquetaire. All built for private use in France and other countries. Licence-built by other French companies including Alpavia, Société Aéronautique Normande and Wassmer (all *q.v.*). Licences for building in Germany, Italy, Spain and other continental countries also granted. Delemontez left to join Pierre Robin at Centre Est Aéronautique (CEA, *q.v.*) in 1957. Company continued and by 1978 was engaged primarily in design and development of Jodel aircraft and consultancy to builders of its products.

JOHNSON AIRCRAFT INC./*USA*

In 1945 developed at Fort Worth, Texas, the Rocket 140 and 185 retractable-gear low-wing cabin monoplanes. Reorganised 1947 as John-son Aircraft Corporation, developing from the Rocket the four-seat Bullet 125. This was built under licence by Texas Aircraft Manufacturing Company (*q.v.*), later being acquired by that company and re-named Texas Bullet.

JOHNSON AIRPLANE & SUPPLY COMPANY INC./*USA*

Dayton, Ohio, firm supplying aeronautical equipment and rebuilding surplus military aircraft. Expanded in 1926, rebuilding DH-4s and also producing the Canary, a single-engined three-seat biplane. Last product (first flown December 1936) was the Twin-60, a twin-pusher-engined two-seat open-cockpit biplane with 22 kW (30 hp) Cherub engines.

JONES AIRCRAFT CORPORATION/*USA*

Formed 1935 by Ben Jones after acquiring rights in D-25 biplane previously built by the New Standard Aircraft Company (*q.v.*). Jones built 10 of these in 1938, in factory at Schenec-

tady, New York. In 1937 it introduced the S-125 and S-150 two-seat light cabin mono-planes, powered by Menasco engines.

JOUCQUES AIRCRAFT COMPANY/*UK*

During WW1 sub-contractor for Royal Aircraft Factory (*q.v.*) B.E.2b at Willesden, London. Taken over 1917 by British Aerial Transport Company (BAT, *q.v.*).

JOVAIR/*USA*

New name from middle/late 1950s of D. K. Jovanovitch's Helicopter Engineering and Research Corporation (*q.v.*), continuing development of the little JOV-3 tandem-rotor helicopter. From 1949 this had been entrusted to Aircraft Division of McCulloch Motors Corporation, which developed a slightly larger model, the MC-4C. In February 1953 this became the first US tandem-rotor helicopter to receive commercial certification. Jovair Corporation was formed some years later and took the design a stage further, resulting in the Sedan 4E (certificated 1963) of which limited production began in 1965. In June 1962 Jovair flew the prototype J-2 two-seat light autogyro; both programmes were taken over 1969–1970 by McCulloch Aircraft Corporation (*q.v.*).

Jovair J-2 two-seat light autogyro

Jovair Sedan 4E tandem-rotor helicopter

Junkers Ju 87 *Stuka* dive-bomber

Junkers Ju 88 used in a variety of roles

JUNKERS FLUGZEUG UND MOTORENWERKE AG/*Germany*

Professor Hugo Junkers (1859–1935) became enthusiastically interested in aircraft development and worked for several aero-engine manufacturers. Convinced that all-metal structure was the ultimate answer to successful aircraft design, he produced the experimental J1 'Blechesel' ('tin donkey') cantilever monoplane which flew on 12 December 1915—giving unexpectedly stable performance. Then teamed briefly with Anthony Fokker (*see* Junkers-Fokker-Werke). Junkers Flugzeug Werke AG formed at Dessau 24 April 1919, first concentrating on all-metal civilian transports such as F 13 four-passenger monoplane (more than 350 built). In 1923 received concession from Soviet government to build aircraft in old Russo-Baltic factory at Fili, near Moscow; established Swedish subsidiary, AB Flygindustri (*q.v.*), near Malmö, and formed Junkers Motorenbau GmbH for production of aero-engines. After death of Hugo Junkers the company became state-owned and, amalgamating with the aero-engine firm, became Junkers Flugzeug und Motorenwerke AG in 1936—then the largest aviation company in the world. For German rearmament programme, Junkers built factories in many other parts of Germany, and in Czechoslovakia and France. Major types produced included G24 and G31 airliners of 1925/1926: W33 and W34 cargo transports, used also as trainers by Luftwaffe; the G38 'flying wing' aircraft of 1928—prototype flew

6 November 1929—production models carried 34 passengers plus seven crew. Some used as military transports in early stages of WW2. On 13 October 1930 came first flight of famous Ju 52 cargo transport. Three-engined Ju 52/3m based on latter used in wide variety of roles up to and including WW2, with production totalling more than 4,850. Pre-war production continued with Ju 60 and Ju 160 airliners, Ju 86 bomber, transport and trainer, and Ju 87 dive-bomber in many versions. Followed by Ju 88/188/388 family of twin-engined bombers. The Ju 90/290/390 family began as four-engined 38/40-seat airliners, converted as heavy transport/reconnaissance types in WW2. Junkers was among first companies to produce military jet aircraft; two prototypes of their Ju 287 with swept wings were captured by Russians in 1945. After WW2 aircraft production ended, and with absorption of small aero-engine plant by Messerschmitt group (*q.v.*) in 1975, the Junkers name disappeared entirely.

JUNKERS-FOKKER-WERKE AG/*Germany*

Prof. Hugo Junkers built his J 1 aircraft in 1915 to exemplify his 1910 patent for a cantilever all-metal wing. Six J 2s were then built, but when J 4 ground-attack biplane was ordered for German Army he was not geared for mass production. Thus, Junkers-Fokker-Werke was formed at Dessau on 20 October 1917, with equal shares held by Junkers and Anthony Fokker. Conflicts of personality caused Fokker and Junkers to separate in 1918, and the following April Junkers re-formed as Junkers Flugzeugwerke AG (see above).

JUNKERS/*Spain*

Avions Metalicos Junkers was founded at Madrid in 1923 to provide facilities for the construction of Junkers aircraft in Spain. A two-seat all-metal monoplane was in production in 1924.

Junkers G38 between-wars civil transport

Junkers Ju 52/3m, numbered among the most famous civil/military transports

K

KABES, Dr., AERO TOVARNA
LETADEL/*Czechoslovakia*
see Aero Tovarna

KAISER-HUGHES INC./*USA*
Henry J. Kaiser was a world leader in ship-building, associated primarily with the prefabricated Liberty Ship of WW2. In 1942 Kaiser proposed construction of 5,000 transport flying-boats for troop carrying. Lacking aviation experience, he formed a joint company with Hughes Aircraft (*q.v*), Hughes to do the design and Kaiser the construction of the Hughes-Kaiser HK-1, the world's largest aircraft. In November 1942 a contract was signed for three aircraft, one for static test and two for flight. By 1944 construction of the first was still at the preliminary stage; the US Army and Navy withdrew technical assistance; the contract was reduced to one aircraft; Kaiser withdrew, and thereafter the design was called the Hughes H-4 Hercules.

KALININ/*USSR*
Konstantin Alexievich Kalinin patented a wing of elliptical form in 1923, and in 1925 built the K-1 (RBZ-6), a small high-wing monoplane. Most notable developments were the K-4 (22 built) and the scaled-up K-5 (260 built, 1930–1934). K-5, typically an eight-seater, made a significant contribution to Russian civil aviation. K-7 was an exceptionally large experimental bomber of 1933, having two faired underslung tandem-wheel landing-gear units and six engines. K-12 and K-13 were also bombers. In all, Kalinin designed sixteen types before his bureau was disbanded in 1938.

KAMAN AIRCRAFT
CORPORATION/*USA*
Formed in 1945 by Charles H. Kaman to develop a special servo-flap control system for helicopter rotors and 'synchropter' intermeshing twin rotor system. The aim was elimination

of anti-torque tail rotor. K-125A built in 1947; K-190 in 1948; K-225 built in small numbers as YH-22 from 1949. HOK-1 delivered in quantity to US Navy and Marines during 1950s; HTK-1 to Navy as trainer/ambulance, and also adopted as remote-controlled drone. By late 1960s, well over 200 HH-43 turbine-powered rescue helicopters were serving with the USAF. Seasprite was flown in 1959, retaining servo-flap system, though on a conventional main rotor. This was developed in many versions; experiments included stub wings

serving as sponsons, also single- or twin-engined power plant. In the late 1960s much subcontracting undertaken, together with development of Rotorchute and allied devices. Kaman Aerospace Corporation (a subsidiary) has done much conversion work.

KAMAN AIRCRAFT OF CANADA
LTD./*Canada*
Formed in the mid-1950s to study possible Canadian market for Kaman helicopters.

Kaiser-Fleetwings XBTK-1 bomber-torpedo prototype

Kaman Huskie helicopter

Kaman Seasprite utility helicopter

KAMOV/*USSR*

Nikolai Ilych Kamov studied design of autogyros and helicopters from 1929. He gained distinction for lightweight single-seat helicopters after WW1. More important were Ka-15 and Ka-18, built in quantity and exported. Turbine-powered Ka-25 (continuing well-established Kamov formula of two three-blade co-axial contra-rotating rotors) first shown in 1961; used for ship-board anti-submarine work. Piston-engined civil type Ka-26 first flew in 1965; this multi-purpose type also serves with the air forces of Hungary and Sri Lanka.

KARHUMÄKI/*Finland*

Veljekset Karhumäki OY founded in 1924. In the 1930s the Viri single-seat light monoplane was built, design by Finnish Club of Aeronautical Engineers. In 1939/1941 a new factory was built, near Halli airfield, where trainers for Finnish air force were built; also the Karhu 48-seat strut-braced high-wing cabin monoplane with skis, wheels or floats.

KARI-KEEN AIRCRAFT INC./*USA*

Formed in June 1928 as a subsidiary of Kari-Keen Manufacturing Company Inc., which made automobile accessories. Built Kari-Keen 90 high-wing side-by-side two-seat light cabin monoplane.

KARO AVIACIJOS TIEKIMO SKYRIUS/*Lithuania*

The Lithuanian Army's aircraft factory, responsible for the construction of the Anbo 41, a two-seat day/night observation aircraft, and the Anbo 51 two-seat trainer, both monoplanes.

KAWANISHI KOKUKI KOGYO KABUSHIKI KAISHA/*Japan*

A Kawanishi biplane seaplane in July 1924 made a round-Japan flight in nine days. Company formed as above in November 1928, taking over works and wind tunnel (at Kobe) of Kawanishi Machine Works. Held Short Bros. licence and were Rolls-Royce agents. At the time of formation were supplying aircraft, components and accessories to the Japanese Navy. Early types included a single-seat biplane fighter and a two-seat long-range high-wing monoplane. At the end of 1930 moved to new works at Narao. In February 1933 flew new three-seat reconnaissance floatplane (E7K) adopted by Japanese Naval Service. Short and Rolls-Royce connections manifested in Navy type 90-2 (K.F.1) flying-boat, built in England, assembled in Japan. Built from 1936 a highly successful long-range maritime reconnaissance/bomber/transport flying-boat, the strut-braced H6K. Subsequent H8K had deep hull and cantilever wing. N1K single-seat fighter monoplane (1942) originated as floatplane but was developed into outstanding landplane. Projects included suicide aircraft based on German V-1. In 1949 the company re-emerged as Shin Meiwa (*q.v.*).

Kamov Ka-25 'flying crane'

Kawanishi K-6 biplane

Kawanishi H8K flying-boat

Kamov Ka-26 twin-engined helicopter

Kawanishi H6K4 ('Mavis') maritime patrol flying-boat

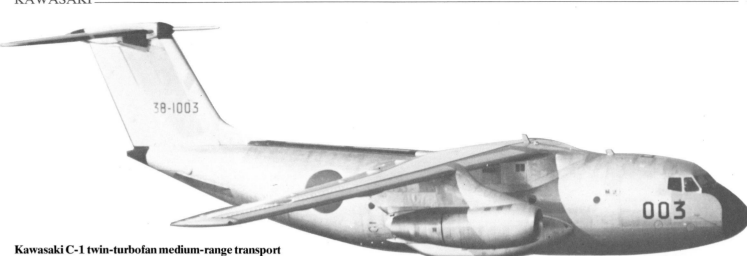

Kawasaki C-1 twin-turbofan medium-range transport

KAWASAKI KOKUKI KOGYO KABUSHIKI KAISHA/*Japan*

Formed in 1918 as subsidiary of heavy-industrial complex Kawasaki Jukogyo to build aircraft and aero-engines. Based at Kobe, in the early 1930s built Salmson biplanes and engines as well as own designs. Had Dornier licence for all-metal construction, and in December 1924 the first Kawasaki-Dornier Wal flying-boat made a notable flight with a German pilot. Thereafter made aircraft mainly for the Japanese Army. A designer of Kawasaki landplanes was German Dr. Richard Vogt, with the company 1923–1933. Vogt designs were Type 88 reconnaissance biplane (1927); Type 92 single-seat biplane fighter (1930), and Ki-3 single-engined biplane bomber. Japanese-designed were Ki-10 single-seat fighter biplane (1935), Ki-32 single-engined monoplane bomber (1937), Ki-45 fast and widely used twin-engined fighter (1939), Ki-48 twin-engined light bomber (1939), Ki-61 single-seat fighter (liquid-cooled engine and showing German influence (1941), Ki-100 radial-engined development (1944) and Ki-102 twin-engined fighter (1944). Kawasaki KAL-1 (July 1953) was the first post-war all-metal aircraft of Japanese design. In 1960 built development of Lockheed Neptune, following licence-production of 210 Lockheed T-33 jet trainers. Also made major components of NAMC YS-11 turboprop transport.

Company reorganised in April 1969 as Kawasaki Jukogyo Kabushiki Kaisha. In November 1970 flew C-1 twin-turbofan military transport; by mid-1975 had delivered 211 four-seat helicopters (KH-4, dating from 1962); by March 1977 had delivered 70 P-2J (Neptune development) patrol aircraft.

KAYABA/*Japan*

In 1939 a US-built Kellett KD-1A autogiro was exported to Japan. K. K. Kayaba Seisakusho developed Ka-1 along similar lines for Japanese Navy; used for observation, anti-submarine patrol (incl. shipborne), and for testing rocket-augmented rotors. Ka-2 was re-engined.

KELLETT AUTOGIRO CORPORATION/*USA*

Under Pitcairn-Cierva licence developed and built autogiros at Philadelphia from 1929. A K-3 was taken to the Antarctic by Admiral Byrd on his second expedition in 1933, piloted by William S. McCormick. K-4 had two side-by-side seats with demountable enclosure but retained wings. Kd-1 of 1934 had tandem seats but was wingless and had direct-control rotor. In 1938 US Army Air Corps bought seven Kellett autogiros for experimental use. From 6 July 1939 a Kellett KD-1B of Eastern Airlines operated the first scheduled mail service by a rotary-wing aircraft, from the roof of the

Philadelphia Post Office and the Camden airport. In 1939 Kellett exported an autogiro to Japan (*see* Kayaba). YG-1 was developed into XR-2 and XR-3 for the US Army. XR-8 and XR-8A of 1943/1945 had twin side-by-side rotors. As Kellett Aircraft Corporation the company later undertook research and development contracts and sub-contracting. Built its own KH-15 single-seat research helicopter (1954), the world's first rocket-driven helicopter. In late 1950s attempted unsuccessfully to resume production of pre-war KD-1A direct-control autogiro.

KELLNER-BÉCHEREAU/*France*

Avions Kellner-Béchereau was founded at Billancourt in 1933. Kellner had built car bodies; also SPAD fighters under contract from 1916. Béchereau was experienced in aircraft design (Deperdussin and SPAD types) and had patented new kinds of wooden construction, using moulds. During the 1930s the company made sixty fuselages for recently-ordered SPAD 510 fighter biplanes, using Béchereau

Kawasaki P-2J anti-submarine patrol aircraft

Kawasaki Ki-61 single-seat fighter

Kawasaki KH-4 light helicopter

Kayaba Heliplane autogyro

system. Built monoplane with Delage inverted engine for Coupe Deutsch de la Meurthe. In 1936 built a single-seat lightplane using Béchereau-patented 'double wing' (divided laterally, with rear parts hinged differentially to act as slotted flaps or ailerons), and in 1937 two side-by-side seater developments were built, one of metal and one of wood. With low-powered Train engine, aircraft of this type (E-1 single-seater) established class records. Company's aeronautical activities ceased in 1941.

KENNEDY AEROPLANES LTD./UK
Founded early in WW1 by Chessborough J. H. Mackenzie-Kennedy, with offices in South Kensington, London, following establishment of the Kennedy Aeronautic Company in Russia in 1909. In 1911 the founder met Igor Sikorsky and shared enthusiasm for large aircraft. Was associated in the English company with T. W. K. Clarke, well known in British aeronautics. Having gained War Office permission, construction started on the Kennedy Giant by the Gramophone Company Ltd. Late in 1916 components were sent to Northolt aerodrome for erection in the open. In 1917 attempts to fly the underpowered machine resulted in a 'hop'. Building of a bomber was started at Newcastle-on-Tyne, but financial failure came in 1920.

KENTUCKY AIRCRAFT CORPORATION/USA
Founded in 1926 to manufacture a three-seat biplane named the Kentucky Cardinal. The two aircraft completed were of welded steel tube construction and powered by Curtiss OX-5 engines. Company went into liquidation in 1927 following death of the principal.

KERR, DICK, & COMPANY LTD./UK
Based at Lytham St. Annes, near Preston, Lancs., where late in WW1 Felixstowe F.3 twin-engined flying-boats were built to Government contract. Fairey sub-contracted the first of three N.4 four-engined flying-boats to

the company. Dick Kerr built the superstructure, though the hull was made by May, Harden & May Ltd. and transported by road in 1919. In 1921 the flying-boat was dismantled and taken by road to the Isle of Grain, where it first flew 4 July 1923.

KEYSTONE AIRCRAFT CORPORATION/USA
Originally Huff-Daland; became Keystone March 1927, still centred at Bristol, Pennsylvania. Later absorbed Loening, becoming Keystone-Loening, and then became part of Curtiss-Wright. Keystone was main supplier of twin-engined bombers to US Army from 1927 to 1932. LB-5A (25 delivered in 1928) was first true Keystone bomber. Largest USAAF bomber order in a decade was for 63 LB-10A (all converted to B-3A and B-5A on change of Army categories). Last production contracts for bombers placed 1931 (for 25 B-4A and 39 B-6A). Pathfinder was three-engined civil transport; NK a biplane trainer for a 1928 competition (19 built); PK a twin-engined flying-boat based on NAF design (18 delivered in 1931). Patrician was three-engined 20-passenger low-wing monoplane. Other types were characteristically Loening, including the OL-8 biplane amphibian; the Air Yacht civil amphibian; and the Commuter four-seat cabin amphibian.

KINGSBURY AVIATION COMPANY/UK
To designs of The Aircraft Manufacturing Company Ltd. built D.H.6 trainer biplanes from 1917. Late in 1917 began construction of three triplane seaplanes, to carry Davis recoilless gun, but contract cancelled January 1918.

KINGSFORD SMITH AVIATION SERVICE PTY. LTD./Australia
Formed in 1946 from Kingsford Smith Air Service. Undertook sales, servicing and overhaul of light and medium aircraft, and in 1955 began design of special agricultural type which materialised as PL-7 Tanker biplane. Fuselage

was mild-steel tank; tail carried on tubular booms; tricycle landing gear. Flew September 1956. Later Cropmaster was entirely different low-wing monoplane, and special Auster conversions were offered. To these were added (1959/1960) E.P.9 conversion, details of which were supplied to Lancashire Aircraft. Company sold out in 1963 to Victa Ltd. of Milperra, Sydney.

KINNER AIRPLANE & MOTOR CORPORATION/USA
Formed in 1919. Known chiefly for its air-cooled radial engines. Aircraft designed by the company round its own engines included Courier two-seat parasol monoplane of late 1920s. In 1930s had in production Sportster strut-braced low-wing monoplane with open side-by-side seats. Sportwing was refined version; Playboy was wire-braced and enclosed; and Envoy was scaled-up Playboy seating four. Three Envoys acquired by US Navy as XRK-1 were not experimental, but staff transports. During 1937 company still offered six types of engine and was working on twin-engined Invader, but in 1938 was in receiver's hands, though continuing operations under control of a trustee.

KIRKHAM, CHAS. B./USA
Kirkham (1882–1969) was a friend and collaborator of Glenn Curtiss. He made motorcycle engines since about 1900, and in 1910 an aero-engine. In 1915 he joined Curtiss in engine work and is chiefly known in connection with the famous D-12. Wanting a fighter worthy of his K-12 engine, with its small frontal area, Kirkham planned a two-seat triplane with excellent streamlining, first flown 5 July 1918. To this record-breaker the name Kirkham Fighter, 18-T or Curtiss-Kirkham was applied, though the Curtiss name alone was later used for land and sea versions. US Army had 18-B biplane equivalent, also sometimes called Curtiss-Kirkham. Navy's two 18-Ts were later adapted for racing. In 1920s Kirkham's company Kirkham Products designed aircraft to special order.

Keystone Y1B-4 bomber prototype

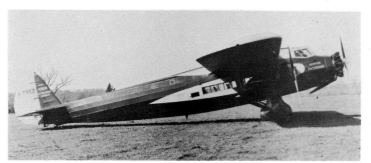

Keystone Patrician civil transport

KITZ KOPTERS INC./USA

In mid-1960s developed conversion scheme for increasing payload of Bell Model 47 helicopter, primarily for agricultural work. Also repaired, modified and operated Bell helicopters.

KJELLER FLYFABRIKK/Norway

The Norwegian Army Aircraft Factory, located at Kjeller. Built under licence during the 1930s Fokker C.V and de Havilland Gipsy Moth and Tiger Moth. Also did repair and overhaul of military-aircraft equipment, and experimental work.

KLEMM, HANNS/Germany

Hanns Klemm (1885–1961) was an eminent pioneer in the development of light aircraft. During WW1 he worked with Zeppelin, Dornier and Hansa und Brandenburgische Flugzeugwerke, and later with Daimler, for whom he designed biplanes and monoplanes, including fighters. After the war he concentrated on light and economical aircraft, sometimes called Daimler-Klemm. L 15 of 1919 was originally a glider, though later powered, but had high wing. True precursor of the classic Klemm low-powered two-seat line of low-wing monoplanes was L 20 of 1924. In December 1926 Leichtflugzeugbau Klemm GmbH was formed (notably associated with Böblingen) and L 25 was produced from 1927 with many types of engine, consolidating Klemm's now-established reputation. K 131 and K 132 of early 1930s were cabin types. Company renamed was formed August 1938, and was then making K 135 cranked-wing tourer/trainer series for Luftwaffe and export. In new type-number series built Kl 105-107. During WW2 contributed to military-aircraft production; after Klemm revived Kl 107 three-seat cabin model. Production ended November 1957.

KLEYER/Germany

Adlerwerke vorm Heinrich Kleyer AG was formed at Frankfurt am Main in 1934 to take over Frankfurter Flugzeugbau Max Gerner GmbH. Made low-cost low-powered all-metal light aircraft with Gerner engines.

KNOLL AIRCRAFT CORPORATION/USA

Formed to build aircraft to designs of Felix Knoll, formerly with Rohrbach and Heinkel in Germany. KN-1 of 1928 was a four-seat cabin biplane with forward stagger.

KOCHERGIN/USSR

A design team under the general supervision of V. P. Yatsenko designed in the early 1930s an unusually compact two-seat fighter biplane, called DI-6 or TsKB-11. Production began at the end of 1935.

KONDOR FLUGZEUG-WERKE GmbH/Germany

Designed and built military aircraft in WW1. D-1 single-seat fighter (1917) had elliptical wings; D-7 of the same year had unusual bracing.

KONINKLIJKE MAATSCHAPPIJ 'DE SCHELDE'/Netherlands

The aircraft department of a dockyard; opened in 1935 employing technicians from Pander. Built S.12 four-seat cabin monoplane, Scheldmusche light single-seat pusher biplane; best known for Scheldmeeuw single-seat flying-boat, which was built in all-metal as well as composite versions. From 1939 made wings for Dornier Do 24 flying-boats, Aviolanda building the hulls.

KOOLHOVEN, FREDERICK/Netherlands

Koolhoven (1886–1945) built and flew his first aircraft in 1910, but was later well known in the UK for his Deperdussin, Armstrong Whitworth and BAT associations. After the Armistice he returned to the Netherlands, and for the NV Nationale Vliegtuigindustrie designed the F.K.31 two-seat fighter-reconnaissance monoplane (1922). In 1926 he became a consultant engineer at The Hague; then designed several aircraft, including the F.K.41 three-seat cabin monoplane. In 1934 the NV Koolhoven Vlietuigen was formed, by which time it was claimed that 51 F.K. types had been produced. More followed, including the F.K.52, an out-

standing two-seat fighter biplane with cantilever undercarriage, and the F.K.58 single-seat fighter monoplane, which was ordered in quantity by France.

KREIDER-REISNER AIRCRAFT COMPANY INC./USA

Built the Midget in 1926, which did well in the National Air Races of that year. In 1927 built the Challenger three-seat open-cockpit biplane using the cheap Curtiss OX-5 (or other) engine. Smaller two-seater also made. In April 1929 company was bought by the Fairchild Airplane Manufacturing Corp. and the Kreider-Reisner types were added to the Fairchild series, the Challengers then being known as Fairchild KR biplanes (Challenger C-6 was KR-21; C-4 was KR-34). As a division of Fairchild Aviation Corporation in the mid-1930s, Kreider-Reisner built the Fairchild 22 two-seat open-cockpit monoplane and the Fairchild 24 cabin type, also producing the Fairchild 71 amphibian.

KREUTZER, JOSEPH, CORPORATION/USA

In 1928 made the Air Coach six-seat high-wing monoplane with 67 kW (90 hp) nose engine and two 48·5 kW (65 hp) units outboard.

KRONFELD LTD./UK

Formerly The British Aircraft Co. (1935) Ltd. of London Air Park, Feltham, Middlesex. Renamed as above in 1936, in which year 20 Drone ultra-light monoplanes were built, one model becoming known as Kronfeld Super Drone. The Kronfeld Monoplane of 1937 (likewise a pusher) was intended as a Drone successor, but only one was ever built.

KYLE-SMITH AIRCRAFT COMPANY/USA

Founded at Wheeling, West Virginia, to manufacture a two-seat biplane intended for sport and training, and powered by a radial engine. It was reported in 1919 that the company was also building to official specification, presumably under sub-contract.

Koolhoven F.K.43 four-seat cabin monoplane

Klemm L 35 lightplane

L

LAGG/USSR
see Lavochkin

LAIRD AIRPLANE COMPANY/USA
Emil Matthew 'Mattie' Laird built his first Model S aircraft in 1919. Commercial activity at Chicago began in 1920 with the Swallow, a redesigned Curtiss JN-4, claimed as first US commercial aircraft. Design sold to Lloyd Stearman's Swallow Aeroplane Manufacturing Company as the New Swallow. Built the first LC (Laird Commercial) 1924. Also designed Super Swallow, an improved New Swallow. Laird concentrated subsequently on custom-built sporting and racing aircraft, such as LC-DW Solution, the only biplane to win the Thomson Trophy. In 1931 Super Solution Jimmy Doolittle set US coast-to-coast records.

With same aircraft set record of 471·8 km/h (293·193 mph) at 1932 National Air Races. Production continued of three-seat Speedwing biplane. Last project was in 1936, redesigning and completing ex-Lawrence Brown racer for Col. Roscoe Turner, as LTR 14 Meteor.

LAIRD, CHARLES/USA
Charles Laird of Wichita, Kansas, built the Whippoorwill cabin biplane and changed company name in 1927 to avoid confusion with his brother 'Mattie' of E. M. Laird Airplane Company (above).

LAKE AIRCRAFT DIVISION, CONSOLIDATED AERONAUTICS/USA
Formed at Sandford, Maine and purchased manufacturing rights to Colonial Skimmer in 1959, marketed initially as Lake Skimmer. Merged with Consolidated Aeronautics (q.v.) 1962, continuing production as Lake LA 4A amphibian, the first under the Lake name appearing in 1960. Current (1978) production model is LA-4 200 Buccaneer. One LA-4 used by Bell Aerospace (q.v.) to test Air Cushion Landing System (ACLS) 1963–1968.

LAKES FLYING COMPANY/UK
Formed in 1911 by Captain E. W. Wakefield. Built the first successful British seaplane (designed by A. V. Roe) at Cockshott, Windermere. In 1912 built very interesting seaplane with central float, designed by Oscar T. Gnosspelius. Renamed Northern Aircraft Company (q.v.).

LAMBERT AIRCRAFT CORPORATION/USA
A Robertson, Missouri, company founded in 1934 by J. P. Wooster Lambert, of the Lambert Engine and Machine Company, to take over and continue production of aircraft designed by Mono Aircraft Corporation (q.v.) of Moline, Illinois, part of Allied Aviation Corporation (q.v.).

LAMSON AIRCRAFT COMPANY INC./USA
Manufacturers of the Model L.101 Air Tractor at Seattle, Washington, a 1953 agricultural aircraft designed by Central-Lamson. Production ceased in 1955.

LANCASHIRE AIRCRAFT COMPANY LTD./UK
Formed from Samlesbury Engineering, Ltd., 1960, who had bought Edgar Percival Aircraft Ltd. in 1959. Continued production of E.P.9 general purpose aircraft as the Lancashire Aircraft Prospector at Squire's Gate, Lancashire.

Lancashire Aircraft Prospector utility aircraft

Latécoère L.290 torpedo-bomber floatplane

Latham 42 flying-boat patrol bomber

LANDGRAF HELICOPTER COMPANY/*USA*

Incorporated 1943 at Los Angeles by Fred Landgraf, after several years development of H-2 two-rotor light helicopter, which first flew in 1944. US Army development contract 1945. Retractable tricycle landing gear, and overlapping synchronised rotors. UK licence held by Firth Helicopters of London, but parent company inactive by 1949.

LANIER AIRCRAFT CORPORATION/*USA*

E. H. Lanier formed company at Newark, New Jersey, in 1943, to continue research work on semi-flying wing STOL aircraft. Six research models were followed by single-seat Paraplane I, II and Commuter 110. Capable of sustained level flight at speed as low as 31 km/h (19 mph). The two-seat Commuter 120 was planned in 1961.

LANZIUS AIRCRAFT COMPANY/*USA*

A New York company, formed to design and build biplanes with variable incidence wings. Built aircraft to government contract 1917–1918.

LARKIN/LASCO/*Australia*

Formed as the Larkin-Sopwith Aviation Company of Australasia, which began operation in 1919 and became Lasco, at Melbourne, in 1921. Built 32 de Havilland Gipsy Moths under licence for the government. In 1930 built one- and three-engined transports, known as the Lascoter, Lascowl and Lasconder. At least one de Havilland D.H.50 constructed. Withdrawal of government subsidy and economic depression caused close-down.

LARKIN-SOPWITH AVIATION COMPANY OF AUSTRALASIA

see Larkin/Lasco

LARSON AERO DEVELOPMENT/*USA*

Based at Concord, California, and produced the D.1. agricultural aircraft in 1959 and the F-2 Baby ultra-light single-seat biplane in 1960.

LAS/*USA*

see Lockheed Aircraft Service Company

Latécoère L.521 six-engined commercial flying-boat

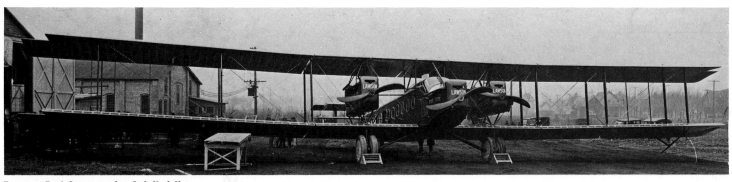

Lawson L-4 three-engined civil airliner

LATÉCOÈRE/*France*
The Forges et Ateliers de Construction Latécoère began their interest in aviation in 1917, showed an aircraft at the 1919 Paris Salon and another two, the LAT 4 airliner and LAT 6 bomber, in 1921. The Société Industrielle d'Aviation was formed in 1922. From 1925, Latécoère developed an airline to South America and built a series of commercial aircraft for this route. Part of the Toulouse factory went to SNCAM (*q.v.*) in 1936. Developed a series of bomber aircraft (L.28, L.29) and torpedo-carrying floatplanes, the L.290 and L.298—the latter in service in 1939–1940.

LATHAM/*France*
Jean Latham built flying-boats during WW1. After the war became Latham et Cie Société Industrielle de Caudebec, later Hydravions Latham, continuing the design and construction of single- and multi-engined flying-boats. In 1920 built the Gastambide-Levasseur variable-incidence biplane. Explorer Raoul Amundsen was lost on the Latham 47-2 searching for the crew of the airship *Italia* in 1925. In 1929 company amalgamated with Société d'Emboutissage et de Constructions Méchaniques, later Amiot, (both *q.v.*).

Some LeO flying-boats also built. In the 1930s developed a number of two- and four-engined commercial flying-boats, culminating in the six-engined L.521 *Lieutenant de Vaisseau Paris* of 1938 and L.631 of 1939. Construction of the latter was interrupted by the war, but four were eventually completed by Breguet (*q.v.*) and used on commercial routes in the Mediterranean until 1948. The firm was sequestered in 1945 under the name of Ateliers Aéronautiques de Toulouse, but returned to the original owners and name in 1947.

LAVERDA SpA/*Italy*
Formerly Aeromere SpA (*q.v.*), taken over by Dr. Laverda in 1964 to continue manufacture of the Super Falco under licence from Aviamilano Costruzioni Aeronàutiche (*q.v.*).

LAVOCHKIN/*USSR*
Semyon Alexse'evich Lavochkin headed a design bureau formed for fighter production under the 1938 programme. The first aircraft, the I-22, flew in 1939; also called LAGG-1 (Lavochkin, Gorbunov, Gudkov). Alterations on the production line 1940–1941 resulted in LAGG-3. Wood construction, with phenoformaldehyde impregnated fuselage. Superseded by La-5 with radial engines in 1942. Followed by 1943 La-7, 1945 La-9, 1946 La-11. This latter all-metal aircraft was the last piston-engined fighter in Soviet Air Force. Bureau later produced La-17, the first Soviet turbojet fighter with reheat. Bureau disbanded on Lavochkin's death in 1960.

LAWSON AIRCRAFT CORPORATION/*USA*
A. W. Lawson of Wisconsin designed a pursuit aircraft in 1918; not built. Followed by two-seat training biplane, and the twin-engined L-2 of 1920, built for the Lawson Airline Company. The L-4 three-engined airliner of 1922–1923 had sleeper berths and a shower.

Lebedef Lebed' 12 reconnaissance aircraft

Leduc 0.22 experimental ramjet-powered interceptor

LAZAROW, CWIETAN/*Bulgaria*
Worked for DAR before WW2. From 1946 built the LAZ-7M; LAZ-8 four-seat taxi; LAZ-11 ambulance version of -8; and LAZ-12 single-seat aerobatic aircraft. All except the LAZ-7 sporting monoplane were built in prototype form only. The LAZ-10H light helicopter was abandoned before completion. All powered aircraft production in Bulgaria ceased in 1961.

LEAR INC./*USA*
Founded as an electrical company at Santa Monica, California, in 1930. An aircraft engineering division produced the Learstar, a high-speed, long-range transport based on the Lockheed Lodestar, in 1953. First delivered in 1955; production taken over by PacAero Engineering Corporation (*q.v.*) in 1957.

LEAR JET INDUSTRIES INC./*USA*
Originally the Swiss-American Aviation Corporation (*q.v.*), founded by William Lear in 1960 to build a fast twin-jet executive aircraft. Various versions built in some numbers. Acquired Brantley Helicopters and themselves acquired by Gates Rubber Company of Denver, Colorado, becoming Gates Learjet (*q.v.*) in 1967.

LEAVEN BROTHERS/*Canada*
Limited re-production of 1945 Fleet Model 80 Canuck, 1965–1966.

LEBEDEF/*USSR*
Established at Petrograd in 1912, and during WW1 built numbers of aircraft of British and French origin. The original two-seat reconaissance Lebed' 12, was built until early 1919.

LEDUC FILS/*France*
Leduc began designing athodyds (ramjets) in 1929 at Argenteuil, as well as experimental aircraft in which to test them. The L.010-1, started 1937 and completed 1945, was first purely athodyd-powered manned aircraft to fly. Followed by L.010-2 and similar L.016-1 in 1951. All air-launched from Languedoc mother plane. In 1953–1954 appeared the L.021-01 and -02 and plans existed for a swept-wing aircraft with Atar 101 turbojet engine for independent take-off and an 0.22 supersonic fighter.

LEGERS BOURGOIS/*France*
Exhibited their first aircraft at the 1928 Paris Salon, a two-seat parasol-wing monoplane powered by an Anzani 3-cylinder engine, and

designated A.T.-35. Produced subsequently the B.T. three-seat low-wing monoplane with Michel 75 kW (100 hp) engine.

LENART AIRCRAFT COMPANY/*USA*
Founded by W. Lenart of Dowagiac, Michigan who built his first biplane aircraft in 1919. Produced a two-seat all-metal biplane in 1930.

LeO/*France*
see Lioré et Olivier

LETECKY NARODNI PODNIK/*Czechoslovakia*
Produced a large number of successful aircraft before WW2 under the name of Aero (*q.v.*). Established as Let in 1960 at Kumovice for licence production of the Soviet Yak-11 and the Z-37 Cmelák, Aero 45 and L-200D. In 1978 was producing the L-410 Turbolet.

LETALSKI INSTITUT "BRANKO IVANUS" SLOVENIJA/*Yugoslavia*
The former Letalski Konstrukcijski Biro (*q.v.*) and Institut LZS "Branko Ivanus" which combined in about 1968. In 1978 was building L-200D under licence.

LET L-410 Turbolet twin-turboprop transport

LIBIS 160 three-seat light sporting monoplane

Letord 7 twin-engined night bomber

LETALSKI KONSTRUKCIJSKI
BIRO/*Yugoslavia*
Lubljana aircraft design office founded in 1947 on an amateur basis by students of the Higher Technical School. Designed KB-6 Matajur, two-seat trainer and tourer, in production in the 1950s.

LETORD/*France*
This company built bombers to designs of the Section Technique de l'Aéronautique, 1916–1918, as the Etablissements Letord, at Chalais-Meudon. The last of these aircraft to be developed was intended as a night bomber. It was in the same class as the Handley Page bombers, with a wingspan of 25·91 m (85 ft). In 1923 Letord built an experimental aircraft for the government, which was evolved by Becherau, designer of the pre-war Deperdussins. In 1925, part of the works was let to Villiers (*q.v.*), who built racing aircraft and the small Albert biplane produced under licence of Tellier-Duhamel.

LEVASSEUR, PIERRE/*France*
Levasseur completed his first aircraft in 1911. Specialised subsequently in marine aircraft, largely for the French Navy. The Levasseur PL-8 was built specially for a transatlantic

Levasseur PL-7 carrier-based torpedo-bomber

flight from Paris to New York, in 1927, but was lost at sea. Company had ceased operations by mid-1930s.

LEVY/*France*
In 1915 Marcel Besson designed his first flying-boat, the development work and later production being carried out in the aircraft factory of Georges Levallois, a financier (Hyd-

ravions Georges Levallois et Levy). During WW1 flying-boats and bombers were produced for the French Navy by Levy-Besson, the latter setting up in his own name after the war. Twelve Levy-Lepen HB-2 reconnaissance flying-boats were operated in France by the US Navy and three were taken to USA. Levy-Biche marine aircraft were built for French Navy to 1927, when production was taken over by Levasseur.

Levasseur PL-14 seaplane torpedo-bomber

Levy GL 40 flying-boat patrol bomber

LTV Aerospace A-7E Corsair II carrier-based attack bomber

LEWIS AND VOUGHT CORPORATION/*USA*

This Long Island, New York, company built training aircraft in 1918 to designs of Chance M. Vought, for US Army. Later designs appeared under name of Vought.

LFG/*Germany*
see Luftfahrzeug GmbH

LIBIS/*Yugoslavia*
see Letalski Institut 'Branko Ivanus' Slovenija

LINCOLN AIRCRAFT COMPANY INC./*USA*

Official name of Lincoln-Page (see next entry) from 1929, but both names used indiscriminately.

LINCOLN-PAGE AIRCRAFT COMPANY/*USA*

Ray A. Page began construction at Lincoln, Nebraska in 1922 as the Nebraska Aircraft Corporation (*q.v.*) with the five-seat Air Coach. Between 1923 and 1925 offered the Lincoln-Standard Tourabout, a three-seat rework of the Standard J.1 of 1916. Also produced the Sport Lightweight biplane. Page acquired the rights to the New Swallow and redesigned this as the three-seater Lincoln-Page LP-3 in 1928, an attempt to catch up with developments in light aircraft design. In 1929 produced a two-seat trainer known as the Lincoln-Page Trainer. Last design was the parasol-wing Lincoln Playboy of 1931. Firm was now the Lincoln Airplane and Flying School.

LING-TEMCO-VOUGHT INC./*USA*

Formed from the 1917 Chance Vought Aircraft Company Inc. by merging with Ling-Temco Electronics in 1961, with a new Chance Vought Corporation as its aerospace division. First aircraft was a continuation and development of the F-8 Crusader supersonic carrier-borne air-superiority fighter of 1955. Developed into the LTV A-7A in 1966. Rationalisation in 1963 produced LTV Incorporated, which includes LTV Aerospace Corporation of which Vought Aeronautics Division is a part. Current LTV-7A Corsair II production is under the name of the Vought Corporation (*q.v.*). In 1964 in combination with Hiller-Ryan developed the XC-142A VTOL transport with swivelling wings. LTV Electro-systems developed the L450F quiet reconnaissance aircraft in 1970.

LINKE-HOFMANN WERKE/*Germany*

Railway engineers of Hundsfeld, Breslau, who entered aviation in 1916 by repairing and

LTV Aerospace F-8 Crusader carrier-based fighters

LTV-Hiller-Ryan XC-142A tilt-wing VTOL transport

LeO 20 twin-engined three-seat night bomber

building under licence Roland and Albatros aircraft. In 1917 completed their first R-plane (R = Riesenflugzeug = giant aircraft) contract. The R.I. rebuild later crashed on test. The R.II was the largest single-propeller aircraft ever built.

LIORÉ ET OLIVIER/France

Etablissments LeO of Levallois-Perret was founded by Henri Olivier and Fernand Lioré. Established as agricultural and industrial engineers in 1906, entered aviation 1908. Lioré worked with Witzig-Lioré-Dutheuil in 1912. Firm built Morane-Saulnier types before and during WW1, producing over 2,000. From 1916 built Sopwith 1½ strutter. In 1921 started up airline Aeronavale (Société Maritime de Transport Aériens) and in 1922 began design and construction of civil and military flying-boats and bombers. An airliner derived from the 1924 bomber served Air Union. Four engined flying-boats developed up to WW2. Cierva autogiros built under licence. LeO 45, built 1939–1940, was best French bomber of period and used for research after war. The Argenteuil factory became part of SNCASE and the Rochefort plant part of SNCASO (both *q.v.*) in 1936.

LIPNUR/Indonesia

see Departemen Angkaten Udara Republik Indonesia, Lembaga Industri Penerbangan Nurtanio

LISUNOV/USSR

Boris Lisunov was sent to the USA to study the Douglas DC-3 and prepare for production in the Soviet Union. Production under designation PS-84 began in 1939, entering service in the same year. In 1942 the PS-84 became known as the Li-2. The only Soviet wartime transport, it was used post-war by Aeroflot.

LITHUANIAN ARMY AIRCRAFT FACTORY/Lithuania

Based at Kaunas, Kovno and building its own design light aircraft from 1922. After the death of the designer Lt. Dobkevicius, the company built training and reconnaissance aircraft for the army.

LKB/Yugoslavia
see Letalski Konstrukcijski Biro

LLOYD FLUGZEUGWERKE GmbH/Hungary

Built 400–500 bomber, reconnaissance and fighter aircraft for the Austro-Hungarian Air Service. Called originally Ungarische Lloyd Flugzeug unde Motoren Fabrik, built DFW types under licence at Budapest.

LMSC/USA
see Lockheed Missiles and Space Company

LeO 451, only modern bomber in French service at beginning of WW2

Lloyd reconnaissance biplane of WW1

Lockheed Constellation four-engined transport

LOCKHEED AIRCRAFT CORPORATION/*USA*

Allan and Malcolm Loughead built their first aircraft, the Model G seaplane, in 1913. Formed the Loughead Aircraft Manufacturing Company at Santa Barbara, California in 1916. Built F-1 twin-engined flying-boat 1918, S-1 monocoque-fuselage biplane 1919. Company liquidated 1921. The Lockheed Aircraft Company of Hollywood was formed in 1926. Built the Northrop-designed high-wing Vega from 1925, a fast two-seater intended for airline work; 141 were built between 1925 and 1932. Company moved to Burbank 1928. Vega gave rise to low-wing series of transports, the Altair/Orion/Sirius, differing in seating arrangements. Many records and notable flights performed on these aircraft.

In 1929 Lockheed became part of the Detroit Aircraft Corporation, a multi-company body that went bankrupt in 1931. Lockheed brothers left the company, formed Lockheed Brothers Aircraft Corporation (*q.v.*) Company purchased by Robert E. Cross and Lloyd

Stearman for a consortium, resumed trading under old name. Launched a new series of twin-engined transports, starting with the Lockheed 10A Electra. In 1937 the L-14 Super-Electra appeared, a smaller executive version of the L-10A. RAF bought 250 bomber variants of 14, called Hudson, in 1938. L-18 Lodestar flew 1939, a lengthened and more powerful Model 14. Ventura of 1941 was a bomber variant of Model 18. Naval PV-1 came in 1942 and the torpedo-carrying PV-2 Harpoon in 1943. Success of the Harpoon led to long-range Neptune, main equipment of patrol squadrons 1947–1962.

In 1939 TWA formulated a requirement for a long-range transport and C. L. Johnson designed the 558 km/h (347 mph) Constellation, which first flew in 1943. First 22 requisitioned as military transports. Built up to 1958 in increasingly powerful, larger-capacity and

longer-range versions. In 1961 the C-130 Hercules turboprop military transport was introduced, followed by a greatly enlarged C-141 Starlifter in 1965, and the C-5A Galaxy, at 348,810 kg (769,000 lb.) gross weight and span of 67·88 m (222 ft 8½ in) the world's largest operational aircraft in 1978. Company also produced the four-turboprop Electra airliner and derived Orion long-range maritime reconnaissance aircraft.

The Lockheed P-38 Lightning of 1939, introduced as a high altitude interceptor, had world-wide use, mainly as ground-attack and fighter-bomber aircraft. First US jet fighter was Lockheed P-80 Shooting Star of 1945, which saw service in Korea. F-104 of 1954 was smallest ever American service aircraft

Lockheed P-38 Lightning twin-boom fighter

spanning 6·7 m (21 ft 11 in) and first fighter capable of sustained Mach 2·0. Saw wide service as part of US off-shore arms and aid deals.

Company now organised in several divisions. Current activities and recent history are: Lockheed Aircraft Company, Burbank, California, CP-140 Aurora, developed from Orion; S-3A Viking carrier-borne anti-submarine aircraft; L-1011 TriStar wide-bodied airliner. Also at Burbank is the Advanced Development Office, responsible for the SR-71A/YF-12 Mach 3·0 reconnaissance aircraft and U-2 spy-plane. SR-71A holds current world speed record at 3,529·56 km/h (2,193·17 mph) and sustained altitude record at 25,926 m (85,059 ft). Current project 1978 is the Stealth Fighter. Lockheed's Marietta, Georgia plant, second main division, is engaged on C-130 updates, C-141, YC-141B, C-5A, Jetstar II and L-100-50 stretched Hercules and Twin Hercules projects.

Lockheed SR-71A Mach 3 reconnaissance aircraft

Lockheed C-5A Galaxy military heavy transport

Lockheed L-1011 TriStar wide-body civil transport

Loening M-8 high-wing monoplane fighter

Loening amphibian, first to serve with USCG

LOCKHEED AIRCRAFT SERVICE COMPANY/*USA*

Division of Lockheed Aircraft Corporation. Designed and fitted major modifications to Boeing KC-135 including ALOTS (Airborne Light Optical Tracking System), C-133, C-130, C-121 Airborne TV and radio transmitting station/studio for Vietnam, and cargo Electra. Current work in 1978 on A-4S Skyhawk and Q-Star and C-130 conversions.

LOCKHEED AND INDUSTRIAS KAISER/*Argentina*

Formed in 1960 for production of the AL-60 (*see* Lockheed-Azcarate SA)

LOCKHEED-AZCARATE SA/*Mexico*

Formed by Juan F. Azcarate in 1957 with Lockheed, to design an aircraft specifically to suit Central American conditions. Built the LASA-60 4/6-seat utility aircraft in 1959. Construction undertaken by Lockheed-Azcarate, Macchi (*q.v.*) and Aviones Lockheed-Kaiser. Lockheed acquired a substantial holding in Aermacchi 1959.

LOCKHEED BROTHERS AIRCRAFT CORPORATION/*USA*

The Lockheed Brothers left the Company after the Detroit merger and set up the Airover Company, later called Alcor, to build the Unitwin, featuring two Menasco engines side-by-side in the nose, driving two propellers. The name of the company was changed to Lockheed Vega when it became a subsidiary of the revived parent organisation. The Lockheed Vega Twin then named Olympic Duo-4, crashed 1938. Firm also built low-wing Starliner and NA-35 trainer. During WW2 with Boeing and Douglas as the BVD pool, built B-17s. Allan Lockheed, during Alcor period, was associated with Alhambra Airport and Air Transport Company.

LOCKHEED MISSILES AND SPACE COMPANY INC./*USA*

Entered the aviation field with Q-Star, de-veloped from the QT-2 (Quiet Thrust) two-seater. Q-Star designed for night sensory missions in Vietnam. The 1967 X-26/QT-2PC quiet reconnaissance aircraft was based on a strengthened Schweizer SGS-2-32 glider, with silenced 134 kW (180 hp) Wankel engine. Saw limited service after the 1968 Tet offensive. Claimed to have operated undetected at 30 m (100 ft). A much modified version of this silent reconnaissance aircraft was developed in 1968 as the YO-3A.

LOENING AERONAUTICAL ENGINEERING COMPANY/*USA*

Grover C. Loening built a monoplane flying-boat in 1911. Formed company in 1918, and built his first Air Yacht (based on pre-war design). A two-seat monoplane fighter with very advanced features was ordered by the Government but contract for 2,000 cancelled at war's end. Produced very popular line of single-float, biplane flying-boats based on Air Yacht for civil and naval use. Merged with Keystone Aircraft Corporation (*q.v.*) in 1928. Built monoplane and biplane pursuits for the Army. After the take-over by Keystone, Loening set up the Grover-Loening Aircraft Company at Garden City, New York, as consultant and built small amphibian flying-boat XS2L for US Navy in 1931. Delivered XSL-2 experimental submarine-borne version in 1933.

LOHNER-DAIMLER/*Germany*

Formed 1911, producing Arrow biplanes. One sold to Austro-Hungarian army, 1911. Amalgamated with Etrich (*q.v.*) in 1912.

LOHNER/*Austria-Hungary*

Built one-, two-, and three-seat reconnaissance flying-boats during WW1, which were very successful. Early Macchi (*q.v.*) designs were copies of Lohner flying-boats.

LOIRE/*France*

Shipbuilders of St. Nazaire and la Baule who entered aviation on acquiring Gourdou and Leseurre (*q.v.*) in 1925 to become Loire-Gourdou-Leseurre. The latter left in 1929 and

Loire 46-C1 four-gun monoplane fighter

Lombardi Avia CM-3 lightweight monoplane

Loire started their own aviation department. The first original design appeared in 1931. In 1933, Nieuport-Delage (*see* Nieuport) merged with Loire to become the Groupe Loire-Nieuport. They built single and multi-engined flying-boats, both civil and military, and fighters for the navy. Also constructed Bloch 200 and Dewoitine 500 for the Armée de l'Air. In 1936 became part of SNCAO (*q.v.*).

LOMBARDA (AERONAUTICA) SA/*Italy*
Succeeded Aeronàutica Vittorio Bonomi (*q.v.*) in 1931, building light aeroplanes and gliders. After the Abyssinian War turned to military aircraft production. During WW2 built Heinkel He 111 and Loire 130.

LOMBARDI & CIE/*Italy*
This Vercelli company took over in 1947 from the 1939 Avia (Azionaria Vercellesi Industrie Aeronautiche) (*q.v.*) continuing production of the light FL-3 and building an experimental attack glider. Also sub-contract work on Fiat G-50. Post-war resumed production of FL-3 and small number of the LM-5 Aviastar, and 1949 LM-7. This latter was a prototype only; company then ceased aeronautical work and production taken over in 1953 by Meteor SpA (*q.v.*).

LONDON AND PROVINCIAL AVIATION COMPANY LTD./*UK*
Based in Edgware and opened a flying school at Hendon in 1914. Built some Caudron trainers for the school and two trainers designed in 1916 by A. A. Fletcher, formerly with Martinside (*q.v.*). Moved to aerodrome at Edgware. Small numbers of the Fletcher design were used, some in civil use after the war.

LONGREN AIRCRAFT INC./*USA*
A Topeka, Kansas, company which in 1921 pioneered vulcanised moulded fibre fuselages on small folding-wing light aircraft. Built an experimental aircraft for the US Navy in 1922. Liquidated in 1924, reformed about 1933 to build experimental metal monocoque fuselage.

LORING, DR. JORGE/*Spain*
Founded in Madrid by Dr. Loring of the Compañía Española de Tráfico Aereo. Received order for 20 Fokker C.IV for Spanish Army Air Corps in 1924. First indigenous design was the R.1 for the army. Further reconnaissance types followed, and light aircraft. Built Cierva Autogiro under licence.

LORRAINE-HANRIOT/*France*
Operated at Argenteuil as Aeroplanes Hanriot et Cie (*q.v.*) to 1930, when it became Lorraine-Hanriot, a division of Société Générale Aéronautique. When this organisation broke up in 1933 the company became known as Compagnie des Avions Hanriot.

LOUGHEAD BROS./*USA*
see Lockheed Aircraft Corporation

LOUIS-CLÉMENT/*France*
Based in Boulogne-sur-Mer. Produced a gull-wing monoplane racer at the 1919–1920 Paris Salon and an ultra-light single seat triplane.

LTV/*USA*
see Ling-Temco-Vought Inc.

LUALDI & CIE SpA/*Italy*
Established at Rome in 1953, and built an experimental helicopter, the ES53, incor-

porating the Hiller Rotormatic system. Became Hiller agents. Designed the L.55, L.57, L.59, each larger and developed from original. L.59 built at the Aermacchi works in 1961, was delivered to the Army Department of the Ministry of Defence.

LÜBECK-TRAVEMÜNDE/*Germany*
A subsidiary of DFW (*q.v.*) founded at Travemünde in 1914. Designed and built a small number of large, single-engined seaplanes for the German Navy 1917–1918.

LUBELSKA WYTWORNIA SAMOLOTOW/*Poland*
Formed at Lublin in 1936 to take over operations of the bankrupt company of E. Plage and T. Laskiewicz (*q.v.*). Took over some designs and began work on their own twin-engined bomber and a single-engined air ambulance.

Lualdi L.59 light helicopter

L.W.S.4 Zubr twin-engined monoplane bomber

LUFT TORPEDO GmbH/*Germany*

Based at Johannisberg and engaged in experimental seaplane fighter design in 1918. A small number were built for test purposes.

LUFTFARHZEUG GmbH/*Germany*

Founded by Krupp from the Flugmaschine Wright GmbH (originally Motorluftschiff Studiengesellschaft, 1906). Adopted Roland as trade name. Built Albatros B and C types under licence at Charlottenberg until their own Roland C.II of 1915. Built a series of 12 fighter designs, of which only the D.11 was built in quantity. Produced the V-19 Stralsund, the first aircraft designed for carriage by submarines. After the war converted and built civil aircraft until 1925, including single-engined landplanes and seaplanes for civil airlines. Operated a number of short-haul routes around the Baltic. Went into liquidation 1928.

LUFTVERKEHRS GmbH/*Germany*

Based at Johannisthal, Berlin; one of the largest German aircraft companies during WW1. Built Farmans under licence, their own first design being the B.1 of 1913. An efficient aircraft remaining in service for observation and training for some years, it was the forerunner of all German two-seat observation aircraft of 1914–1918. Developed lengthy series, including very popular C.V and C.VI as well as prototype fighters and bombers. Converted several post-war for service with civil airlines.

LUSCOMBE AIRPLANE CORPORATION/*USA*

Don A. Luscombe's first aircraft, the Monocoupe, was built by the Central States Aero Company (*q.v.*) of Davenport, Ohio. Became in 1928 the Mono Aircraft Corporation (*q.v.*) of Moline, Illinois, with Luscombe as President and chief engineer. He left in 1933 and next year set up the Luscombe Aircraft Engineering Company of Kansas City, producing the Phantom I, a very successful design developed by Ivan Driggs from the Monocoupe D-145. The first US metal light aircraft, 125 were built. Fabrication of parts was farmed out, reducing overhead costs on the production line. Production ceased during WW2 because of metal shortage, but was resumed in 1949. Following the L-4 Model 90 four-seater of 1934 came the 1937–1938 Model 8a of which 1,100 were built, and the 1940 Silvaire, of which production had reached 6,000 by 1961. The Skybaby and two other low-powered versions were built. The post-war company, based at Dallas, Texas, went bankrupt in 1949, but was revived with finance from Texas Engineering and Manufacturing Company Inc. (*q.v.*) under the old name.

LWF Butterfly ultra light monoplane

LWF Model H Owl triplane bomber prototype

LVG C.II reconnaissance/bomber aircraft

The emergency of the 1950s caused suspension of production and the company was bought by Temco Aircraft Corporation (*q.v.*), who sold manufacturing rights of the Silvaire Model 8 in 1955 to the Silvaire Aircraft Company (*q.v.*).

LVG/*Germany*
see Luftverkehrs GmbH

LWF ENGINEERING CORPORATION INC./*USA*

Formed 1915 at College Point, Long Island, by Joseph Lowe, Charles F. Willard and Robert G. Fowler. Patented Willard's laminated wooden monocoque fuselage, but all three left in 1916, after which name assumed to mean Laminated Wooden Fuselage. Converted twelve D.H.4s to single-seaters for US Post Office, and built experimental twin-engined version. Built series of their own designs, including trainers V-1, -2 and -3 of 1918–1919 for the Army. Constructed also Curtiss HS-2L and Douglas DT-2 for Navy, Martin NBS-1 for Army. In 1919 built ultra-light Butterfly and a three-engined triplane, Model H Owl, based on Caproni design. This was offered to the Army but was not accepted. Built Model T-3 for Army, 1923–1924, designed but did not build experimental XNBS-2. Company ceased production in 1924.

LWS/*Poland*
see Lubelska Wytornia Samolotow

M

MACCHI/*Italy*

Founded in 1912 at Varese, specialising in marine aircraft. During WW1 built L-1 licence-manufactured Lohner L-40 flying-boats, M-3 fighter and M-5 biplane flying-boat, developed into M-7 which won 1921 Schneider Trophy, an achievement repeated by M-39 in 1926. MC.72 float-plane set world airspeed record of 709·19 km/h (440·67 mph) on 23 October 1933. Pre-WW2 commercial flying-boats included twelve-seat MC.94 and 26-seat MC.100. MC.200 Saetta fighters produced from 1937, developed into MC.202 Falgore, and MC.205 Veltro. Post-war developments included MB.308 two/three-seat cabin monoplane, also built in Argentina by German Bianco SA (*q.v.*), MB.320 six-seat light twin and 150 M.416 licence-built Fokker S.11 trainers. Joint programme with Fiat to build Vampire FB.52As, followed by MB.326 jet trainer, first flown 10 December 1957 and currently in production in two-seat and single-seat armed strike trainer forms. At present developing MB.339 jet trainer to replace Fiat G-91 and earlier MB-326s. Lockheed 60 utility transport built under licence, wing used for AM.3C being developed jointly with Aerfer.

MACDONALD BROS. AIRCRAFT LTD./*Canada*

Formed maintenance organisation 1930, opened factory at Stevenson's Airport, Winnipeg, after outbreak of war, manufacturing components for Anson trainers, also a final assembly centre for Anson Vs built under scheme supervised by Federal Aircraft.

MAESTRANZA CENTRAL DE AVIACIÓN/*Chile*

Chilean Air Force Central Workshops; in 1947 built Tricolo-Experimental two-seat cabin monoplane, designed by Alfredo Ferrer and first indigenous Chilean aircraft. In early 1950s Captain H. Fuentes designed H.F. XX-02 trainer, built at El Bosque Air Base.

Macchi C.205N-1 Orione (Orion) interceptor prototype

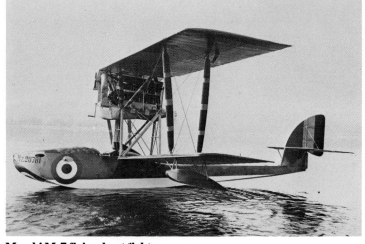

Macchi M-7 flying-boat fighter

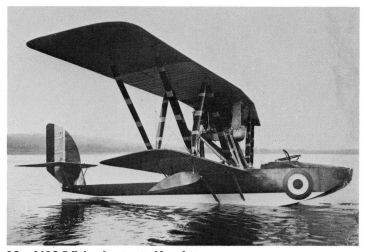

Macchi M-8 flying-boat patrol bomber

Magni Vittoile high-speed sporting monoplane

Manzolini Libellula III light helicopter

MAGNI-AVIAZIONE/*Italy*

Founded by Piero Magni in 1919, primarily research and development organisation but manufactured aircraft for other designers, including Jona J-6 tilting-wing sesquiplane and the conventional-winged J-6S military trainer. Magni's own aircraft included PM-3-4 Vale 1937 single-seat aerobatic aircraft and the derived PM-4-1 Supervale.

MAHONEY-RYAN AIRCRAFT CORPORATION/*USA*

Incorporated 1922 at St. Louis, Missouri, known originally as Ryan Airlines. Developed Ryan M-1 mailplane from which, in 1927, was derived *Spirit of St. Louis*, built for Charles Lindbergh's New York-Paris flight; commercial development produced as Ryan Brougham. Company merged with Detroit Aircraft Corporation 24 May 1929.

MAINTENANCE COMMAND DEVELOPMENT CENTRE/*India*
see MMPL

MAKINA VE KIMYA ENDUSTRISI KURUMU/*Turkey*
see MKEK

MALMÖ FLYGINDUSTRI/*Sweden*
see MFI

MANN AND GRIMMER/*UK*

Seventeen-year old R. Mann designed M.1 two-seat fighter-reconnaissance biplane, built with assistance of R. P. Grimmer and test-flown at Hendon 19 February 1915. Conventional radial engine, nose-mounted, but facing aft so that propeller shaft extending through fuselage drove interplane strut-mounted twin pusher propellers via chain drives. Wrecked 16 November 1915, development discontinued.

MANN, EGERTON & COMPANY LTD./*UK*

At its Norwich factory built 12 Short 184 or Mann, Egerton Type A seaplanes, and from this developed own Type B seaplane powered by Sunbeam engine. Built own design H.1 and H.2 shipboard fighter 1917. Sub-contract production of de Havilland D.H.9/9A, D.H.10/10A, Sopwith 1½ Strutters, Short Bombers and SPAD 7s.

Maranda Super Loisir two-seat cabin monoplane

MANSU HIKOKI SEIZO KABUSHIKI KAISHA/*Manchuria*

Established by Imperial Ordnance issued June 1938, incorporating aircraft manufacturing facilities of Manchuria Aviation Company which developed Hayabusa six-passenger cabin monoplane airliner, powered by Nakajima Kotobuki radial. Acquired Tachikawa Hikoki Kabushiki Kaisha (*q.v.*) in 1940.

MANZOLINI DI CAMPOLEONE/*Italy*

Designed Libellula co-axial single-seat light helicopter, first flown 7 January 1952, later developed as Libellula II with Walter Minor engine and certificated on 15 October 1962; Libellula III two-seater followed with Walter M332 engine.

MARANDA AIRCRAFT COMPANY LTD./*Canada*

Formed in Montreal by Bernard C. Maranda to develop and manufacture ultra-light aircraft, acquiring world-wide licence for Adam RA-14 and RA-17 high-wing monoplanes from French designer Roger Adam in 1957. These marketed as RA 14BM1 and BM3. Also developed Hawk BM4, based on Bearn Minicab, and Lark BM6 single-seat aerobatic biplane.

MARENDAZ AIRCRAFT LTD./*UK*

D. M. K. Marendaz designed the four-seat Mk.III cabin monoplane, two built by International Aircraft & Engineering Ltd. at Maidenhead 1937/1938. Marendaz company, at Barton-in-the-Clay, Bedfordshire, built prototype Marendaz Trainer two-seat monoplane which first flew December 1939.

MARINAVIA FARINA SRL/*Italy*

Founded in 1946 by industrial designer Domenico Farina with headquarters in Milan. Designed and built several gliders and sailplanes, and prototype QR.14 Levriero four-seat touring aircraft, powered by two de Havilland Gipsy Major 10 engines, first flown 1947, in which year it won Coppa dell'Aria at Milan.

Marshall (Lockheed) Hercules W.Mk.2 conversion for the RAF's Meteorological Research Flight

MARINENS FLYVEBATFABRIKK/*Norway*

Naval Flying-Boat Factory, established at Horten in 1915, to build aircraft for Royal Norwegian Navy, including early Farman designs, Hansa Brandenburg W.33 twin-float fighter reconnaissance aircraft and, during 1920s, a small number of Douglas DT-2B and DT-2C torpedo carriers. Breda Ba 28 trainer seaplane also built under licence. Indigenous seaplanes included M.F.8 biplane trainer, M.F.9 single-seat fighter, M.F.10 advanced trainer and M.F.11 three-seat reconnaissance aircraft.

MARK ABTEILUNG FLUGZEUGBAU/*Germany*

Engineering company, based at Breslau, which built 3- and 5-cylinder Baer radial engines and Reiseler sports monoplanes.

MARSH AVIATION COMPANY/*USA*

Based at Mesa, Arizona, developed conversion of Rockwell S2R Thrush Commander with AiResearch TPE 331 turboprop engine. First S2R-T Turbo Thrush delivered late 1976.

MARSHALL & SONS/*UK*

Based at Gainsborough, Lincolnshire, during WW1; manufactured under sub-contract Bristol F.2B with Sunbeam Arab engines.

MARSHALL OF CAMBRIDGE (ENGINEERING) LTD./*UK*

Formed originally as Marshall's Flying Schools Ltd., developed major engineering, overhaul and conversion organisation at Cambridge. During 1958–1960 produced much-modified

Auster T.7 designated Marshall MA.4, a boundary layer research aircraft built under Ministry of Aviation contract for Cambridge University.

MARTIN/*USA*

After withdrawal from Wright Martin Aircraft Corporation (*q.v.*), Glenn L. Martin formed his own company at Cleveland, Ohio, in 1917, occupying a new factory at Baltimore, Maryland, in 1929. During WW2 operated US gov-

Martin Baltimore light bomber for the RAF

Martin MB-2 short-range night bomber

Martin PBM-5A Mariner anti-submarine amphibian

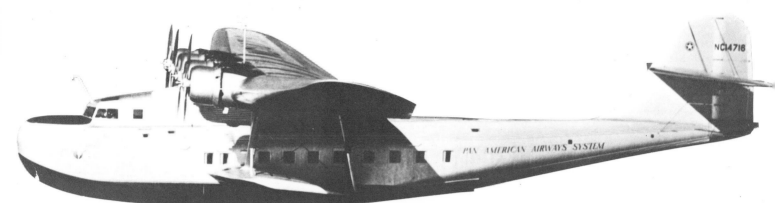

Martin 130 Clipper 26-seat flying-boat transport

Martin Marietta X-24A lifting-body research aircraft

Martin Marietta X-24B lifting-body research aircraft

ernment plant at Omaha, Nebraska. Aircraft production ceased 20 December 1960 when the last P5M-2 Marlin was handed over to US Navy. MB-1 twin-engined biplane bomber first flown 17 August 1918, followed by improved MB-2. Other inter-war military aircraft included MO-1 three-seat observation aircraft, PM-1 and PM-2 flying-boats for the US Navy and the B-10 and B-12 bombers. Latter developed into Model 167, supplied to RAF from 1940 as Maryland, and Model 187 which RAF used as Baltimore. B-26 Marauder, first flown 25 November 1940, ordered from drawing board, of which total production exceeded 4,700. US Navy flying-boats included five Mars transports, Mariner and Marlin patrol flying-boats, and XP6M-1 Seamaster four-jet flying-boat flown 14 July 1955. US Navy acquired AM-1 Mauler carrier attack and P4M Mercator patrol aircraft, USAF ordered English Electric Canberras licence-built as Martin B-57 from 1953. Civil production comprised Martin 130 26-seat flying-boats for Pan American 1934–1935, and Model 2-0-2 and 103 Model 4-0-4 airliners from 1947.

In the form of the Martin Marietta Corporation, Martin returned to piloted aircraft production in 1965 with SV-5 piloted lifting body research vehicle, built as SV-5J with J-85 or J-60 jet engine and as SV-5P or X-24A with XLR-11 rocket engine. Vehicle was launched from Boeing B-52 mother-plane.

MARTIN & HANDASYDE LTD./UK

Formed at Woking with premises at Brooklands, undertook sub-contract production of RAF Be.2c and S.E.5A. First original design was S.1 single-seat fighter, built 1914-October 1915. G.100, a large single-seat fighter with Beardmore engine, appeared in late 1915. Later examples with more powerful Beard-

more engine designated G.102; both known colloquially as Elephant, derived from their size. Six prototypes of F.3 fighter ordered 1917, developed into F.4 Buzzard which was ordered in quantity although only 52 had been delivered by Armistice in 1918. Some civil use in developed forms, some sold to overseas air forces. Company went into liquidation 1921.

MARTIN-BAKER AIRCRAFT COMPANY LTD./UK

Formed in 1934 by James Martin who had evolved a method of steel tube construction. Currently leading manufacturer of ejector seats, having made first live firing on 11 May 1945. Built experimental MB.1 two-seat light aircraft to demonstrate construction system,

Martinsyde F.4 Buzzard single-seat fighter

Martin-Baker F18/39 (MB.3) six-cannon fighter prototype

flown March 1935. Private venture MB.2 eight-gun fighter with Napier Dagger engine flown 3 August 1938. MB.3 experimental fighter with Napier Sabre first flown 31 August 1942, followed by MB.5 with Rolls-Royce Griffon 83 driving contra-rotating propellers, which made maiden flight 23 May 1944.

MARYLAND PRESSED STEEL COMPANY/*USA*
Aircraft department at Hagerstown, Maryland, built designs of Joseph Bellanca, who in 1919 developed single-seat biplane powered by 26 kW (35 hp) Anzani engine; also CE two-seat biplane. Activity ceased and Bellanca joined Omaha Aircraft Corporation in Autumn 1921.

MASARYKOVA LETECKÁ LIGA/*Czechoslovakia*
see Zlin

MATTLEY AIRPLANE & MOTOR COMPANY INC./*USA*
Established at St. Bruno, California, built a single-seat cabin monoplane known as the Fliver Plane. In 1933 had in production a lightweight one/two-seat parasol wing monoplane named the Mattley Fliver, powered by a 30 kW (40 hp) Continental engine.

MAUBOUSSIN/*France*
Pierre Mauboussin established design office and factory at Puteaux, Seine, developing Corsair light aircraft which was built as Corsair 120 and Corsair Minor. Production licence for all Mauboussin aircraft acquired by Société des Etablissements Fouga (*q.v.*) in 1936. Mauboussin 123, development of Corsair, built 1937–1938, and as M.129 1947–1948.

MAULE AIRCRAFT CORPORATION/*USA*
Formed by B. D. Maule at Jackson, Michigan, to manufacture M-4 four-seat light aircraft; production transferred to Moultrie, Georgia, September 1968. Prototype flown 8 September 1961, produced as M-4 with 108 kW (145 hp) Continental engine, as M-4 Rocket with 157 kW (210 hp) Continental. M-4 Strata-Rocket with Franklin engine led to M-5-220C Lunar Rocket, flown 1 November 1971, while M-4 Rocket became M-5-210C; M-5-235 with 175 kW (235 hp) Lycoming 0-540 engine also built.

MAY, HARDEN & MAY LTD./*UK*
Southampton-based subsidiary of Aircraft Manufacturing Company (*q.v.*) which built hulls for a number of flying-boats designed by other companies. These included 12 Porte Babies, two Phoenix P.5 Cork I/II, and 80 Felixstowe F.2A/F.5.

MAYO COMPOSITE AIRCRAFT COMPANY LTD./*UK*
Formed 1935 to develop Major R. H. Mayo's concept of composite aircraft. A heavily-loaded, long-range upper component, too heavy to become airborne under its own power, was carried aloft on the back of a short-range aircraft whose function was simply to effect take-off. Ordered by Air Ministry for experimental operation by Imperial Airways, the two components of the Short-Mayo Composite were built by Short Bros. at Rochester and comprised S.20 Mercury floatplane upper component and S.21 Maia as the lower. Components completed 1937, first separation in flight 6 February 1938. On 21 July 1938 The Mercury carried a 454 kg (1,000 lb) payload non-stop 4,667 km (2,900 miles) from Foynes, Eire, to Montreal and on to New York, a total distance of 5,214 km (3,240 miles) in 22 hrs 31 mins flying time.

Martin-Baker F5/34 (MB.2) single-seat fighter prototype

Short/Mayo Mercury/Maia composite aircraft

Maule M-4 four-seat light aircraft

MBB/*Germany*
see Messerschmitt-Bölkow-Blohm GmbH

MBB/KAWASAKI/*International*
Formed to jointly develop BK 117 8–12 seat multi-purpose helicopter under agreement signed 25 February 1977, MBB to design main and tail rotors, tail unit and hydraulic systems and Kawasaki responsible for fuselage, landing gear and transmission. Prototype scheduled to fly mid-1979.

McCANDLESS (AVIATION) LTD./*UK*
Founded by Rex McCandless at Newtownards, County Down, to develop single-seat gyro-plane built originally as M-2 in 1962. Developed later as M-4 with original Triumph motorcycle engine replaced by 1500 cc Volkswagen engine. Production M-4 built by W. H. Ekin (Engineering) Ltd. (*q.v.*).

McCARTHY AIRCRAFT COMPANY/*USA*
Established May 1925 at Grand Rapids, Michigan, as McCarthy Aeronautical Engineering Company, building Air Scout two-seat cabin monoplane with Anzani radial engine.

McCulloch MC-4 tandem-rotor helicopter

McCULLOCH AIRCRAFT CORPORATION/*USA*
In 1949 Helicopter Division of McCulloch Motors Corporation appointed as chief designer D. K. Jovanovich, formerly of Helicopter Engineering and Research Corporation (*q.v.*), who developed his JOV-3 as McCulloch MC-4 tandem rotor two-seat helicopter, first flown Los Angeles 20 March 1951. Four-seat version developed as MC-4E. Later initiated quantity production of Jovanovich's J-2 two-seat gyroplane, first flown June 1962.

McDonnell XV-1 experimental convertiplane

McDONNELL AIRCRAFT CORPORATION/*USA*
Incorporated 6 July 1939 at St. Louis, Missouri, merged with Douglas Aircraft Corporation Inc. (*q.v.*) 28 April 1967. Built Fairchild AT-21 gunnery trainers at Memphis, Tennessee, plant and designed XP-67 experimental twin-engined fighter in 1942. Developed first US Navy twin-jet fighter, FH-1 Phantom I, which was first flown 26 January 1945. Enlarged version was F2H Banshee, flown 11 January 1947. F3H Demon single-engined jet fighter, maiden flight 7 August 1951. XF-88 jet fighter for USAF cancelled 1950 but developed later as F-101 Voodoo, flown 29 September 1954, F-4 Phantom II twin-engined missile-armed attack fighter flown 27 May 1958, subsequently standard USAF, USN and

McDonnell Goblin parasite jet interceptor

USMC fighter, built also as reconnaissance variant and widely exported; 5,000th production F-4 scheduled 1978.

McDonnell F3H-2N Demon all-weather fighters

McDonnell Douglas A-4E Skyhawk attack-bomber

McDONNELL DOUGLAS CORPORATION/*USA*

Created 28 April 1967 as merger of Douglas and McDonnell (both *q.v.*). Continued development of F-4 at St. Louis and on 23 December 1969 received contract for F-15 Eagle air-superiority fighter, flown 27 July 1972. Evolving currently F-18 Hornet fighter and AV-8B Advanced Harrier for US Navy and US Marine Corps. Long Beach and Palmdale facilities continued production of A-4 Skyhawk attack aircraft, DC-8 and DC-9 jet airliners, and developed DC-10 maximum 380-seat airliner, first flown 29 August 1970. Two YC-15 prototypes built 1975 for USAF AMST programme, first machine made maiden flight 26 August 1975.

McDonnell Douglas F-15 Eagle fighter

McDonnell F-101 Voodoo interceptor fighter and tactical fighter-bomber

McDonnell FD/FH Phantom carrier-based fighter

McDonnell Douglas F-4 Phantom II fighter

McKinnon Turbo-Goose amphibian conversion

Meridionali-built Chinook transport helicopter

McKINNIE AIRCRAFT COMPANY INC./USA

Transocean Air Lines subsidiary, formed in 1947 at Fargo, North Dakota, developed all-metal two-seat McKinnie 165 with Franklin engine, first flown 10 August 1952.

McKINNON ENTERPRISES INC./USA

Conversion specialists at Sandy, Oregon, having entered field in 1953 with Grumman Widgeon with wingtip floats and Lycoming engines replacing the original Rangers. Grumman Goose also converted, as McKinnon G-21C with four Lycoming engines, and as Turbo Goose with two UACL turboprops.

Meridionali EMA 124 three-seat light helicopter

MERCKLE FLUGZEUGWERKE GmbH/Germany

Established at Oedheim, acquired from Dr. Winter of Brunswick Technical College licence to build Kiebitz two-seat STOL monoplane. In 1956 commenced development of SM-67 Turboméca Artouste-powered five-seat helicopter, initially as private venture and later to government contract.

MERCURY AIRCRAFT INC./USA

Formed at Menominee, Michigan, and developed B-100 four-seat cabin monoplane with Allied Monsoon (licence-built Regnier) engine, and BT-120 two-seat trainer biplane suitable for engines of 71–112 kW (95–150 hp).

MERIDIONALI-AERFER SpA/Italy

Succeeded Società Anònima Industrie Aeronautiche Romeo (q.v.) which had been formed in 1934 to absorb Officine Ferroviarie Meridionali's aviation activities; became part of Società Italiana Ernesto Breda (q.v.) group. Developed Ro.37 two-seat reconnaissance biplane which served October 1936 with Italian Aviacion Legionaria during Spanish Civil War and equipped Italian Air Force reconnaissance units during WW2. Also used operationally were Ro.43 two-seat, single-float catapult seaplane and single-seat fighter version Ro.44.

MERIDIONALI, ELICOTTERI/Italy

Formed by Augusta in 1963 as part of industrialisation programme in south Italy, operating Frosinone factory, which opened in October 1967, overhauling helicopters for Italian services. In April 1968 concluded agreement for licence-production of Boeing-Vertol CH-47C Chinook for Italian Army and for Iran. Also developed Agusta-designed EMA 124 three-seat helicopter based on Agusta-Bell 47.

MERVILLE/France

Propeller manufacturer established in 1919, began aircraft production 1959 with SM.30 single-seat sailplane; improved SM.31 prototype flown 11 January 1960. Also developed D.63 two-seat light aircraft based on Druine Condor, first flown 23 March 1962, with tricycle landing gear and Potez 4 E-20 engine.

Meridionali (IMAM) Ro.37 reconnaissance biplane

Meridionali (IMAM) Ro.57 single-seat fighter

Messerschmitt Me 109G (Bf 109G), the famous single-seat fighter of WW2

Messerschmitt Me 163, the world's first manned rocket-powered interceptor

MESSERSCHMITT GmbH/*Germany*

Founded by Willi Messerschmitt at Bamberg in 1923 as Messerschmitt Flugzeugbau; became GmbH 28 April 1926. Merged with Bayerische Flugzeugwerke (*q.v.*) 8 September 1927, but reconstituted June 1931 when BFW collapsed. BFW reformed 1933 and renamed Messerschmitt AG 11 July 1938. Amalgamated with Bölkow (*q.v.*) as Messerschmitt Bölkow GmbH 1968 and then with Hamburger Flugzeugbau (*q.v.*) to form Messerschmitt-Bölkow-Blohm (*q.v.*) 14 May 1969. S-16 powered glider flown 1924; M-18 three-passenger, single-engined airliners built for Nordbayerische Verkehrsflug AG and others 1925. Developed into M-20 and M-20b built for Lufthansa 1928. Highly successful M-23 two-seat sporting monoplane introduced 1929. After being renamed in 1938 continued production of BFW's Bf 108 and of Bf 109 fighter, Bf 110 twin-engined long-range fighter. Rocket-powered Me 163 fighter first flown August 1941, and first of Me 262 twin-jet fighters on 18 July 1942. Bf 110 developed into Me 210 fighter bomber first flown 2 Sep-

tember 1939, built up to 1944, and re-engined Me 410, which made maiden flight in late 1942. Me 321 Gigant troop carrier/cargo glider (54·68 m; 180 ft wing span) introduced 1941; 175 built together with 201 of Me 323 powered version with six Gnome Rhone radial

engines. Reconstituted post-war company formed Flugzeug-Union Süd (*q.v.*) with Heinkel in August 1956, building Fouga Magister under licence and later taking part in programmes for Fiat G-91, Lockheed F-104G, Transall C-160 and Bell UH-1D.

Messerschmitt Me 110 twin-engined fighter

Messerschmitt Me 410 fighter-bomber

MBB BO 105C five-seat light helicopter

MBB BO 209 Monsun two-seat lightplane

MESSERSCHMITT-BÖLKOW-BLOHM GmbH/*Germany*

Formed 14 May 1969 as merger of Messerschmitt-Bölkow GmbH and Hamburger Flugzeugbau GmbH (*q.v.*), headquarters at Ottobrun, Munich. Inherited its forebears' production programmes, including Bölkow's 208C Junior, 209 Monsun and 223 Flamingo light aircraft and BO 105 helicopter, also HFB's Hansa executive jet. Producing currently BO 105 and Tornado, latter by virtue of its 42·5% holding in Panavia, and is participant in Airbus, Transall, and Fokker-VFW F-28 programmes.

METALAIR CORPORATION/*USA*

see Pittsburgh Metal Airplane Co.

METEOR SpA COSTRUZIONI AERONÀUTICHE/*Italy*

Established in 1947, initially manufactured series of gliders and sailplanes, turning to powered aircraft in 1953 when company acquired assets of Francis Lombardi & Cie (*q.v.*), further developing FL.3 light aircraft, FL.53 two-seater, three-seat FL.54, and FL.55 four-seater. Own 82 kW (110 hp) Alfa 2 and 164 kW (220 hp) Alfa 4 engines powered two-seat Meteor Bis and four-seat Meteor Super.

METROPOLITAN WAGGON COMPANY/*UK*

Sub-contractor for Handley Page 0/400 bomber, of which 100 manufactured at Birmingham factory with Rolls-Royce Eagle VIII engines.

MEYERS AIRCRAFT COMPANY/*USA*

Formed 1936 at Tecumseh, Michigan. Developed OTW-160 biplane trainer and MEW-165W monoplane trainer for US schools within CAA War Training scheme. Post-war production included MAC 125 and MAC 145 two-seat cabin monoplanes with Continental engines. Meyers 200 four-seat cabin monoplane flown 8 September 1953, deliveries began 1959. Acquired by Rockwell-Standard Corporation (*q.v.*) 12 July 1965, marketed Model 200 as Aero Commander 200. Manufacturing rights in this model were acquired in 1977 by Meyers Aircraft Manufacturing Company of Broomfield, Colorado, who are currently building the Meyers 200D.

MFI/*Sweden*

AB Malmö Flygindustri is a subsidiary of Trellborgs Gummifabric AB, with Björn Andreasson as designer. His independently-designed BA-7 developed as MFI-9 two-seat light aircraft, production prototype flown 17 May 1961, licence production by Bölkow (*q.v.*) as 208C Junior. MFI-10 Vipan short-field four-seater flown 25 February 1961. Company acquired by Saab-Scandia (*q.v.*) in 1961 and evolved MFI-15 multi-purpose two/three-seat military aircraft, flown 11 July 1969, later renamed Safari and then further developed into MFI-17 Supporter armed ground-support version, first flown 6 July 1972.

MIAMI AIRCRAFT CORPORATION/*USA*

Established at Hieleah, Florida, in February 1929; designed and built Miami Maid five-seat amphibian monoplane with Menasco-Salmson radial, production aircraft powered by 224 kW (300 hp) Wright J-6 engine.

MiG/*USSR*

see Mikoyan & Gurevich

MIGNET DO BRASIL/*Brazil*

Formed early 1950s to build Mignet H.M.310 Estafette two-seat modernised version of the designer's earlier Pou-du-Ciel light aircraft; new development flown 1951 with Continental A90 engine.

Meteor FL.55 four-seat lightplane

MFI-15 (Saab) three-seat military aircraft

MFI-10 four-seat cabin monoplane

Mikoyan MiG-21 single-seat multi-role fighter

MIKOYAN & GUREVICH/*USSR*
A. Mikoyan and G. Gurevich design bureau
established 1938; still operating, although
Gurevich retired in early 1960s and Mikoyan
died 9 December 1970. MiG-1 fighters with
AM-35 engine produced 1940–1941; developed MiG-3 produced until 1942. First jet
aircraft built in quantity was MiG-9 with twin

RD-20 (BMW 003A) engines, flown 24 April
1946. Swept-wing MiG-15 with Russian copy
of Rolls-Royce Nene introduced 1947, built
under licence in Czechoslovakia and Poland.
Followed by approximately 9,000 of derived
MiG-17, with redesigned wing, manufactured
1950–1957. Twin Mikulin AM-5-powered
MiG-19 flown September 1953, built under

licence in Czechoslovakia, Poland and China.
Superseded by delta-winged MiG-21, in service in Russia from 1959 and, when built in
India, was first Russian aircraft manufactured
in non-communist country. Producing currently MiG-23 and MiG-27 variable-geometry
fighter and ground attack aircraft and MiG-25
twin-finned interceptor.

Mikoyan MiG-1 single-seat fighter of WW2   **Mikoyan MiG-15, Russia's first swept-wing jet-fighter**

MIL, MIKHAIL/*USSR*
Mil helicopter design bureau established 1947;
on Mil's death 31 January 1970 bureau headed
by Marat Tishchenko. Mi-1 first flown 1948,
also manufactured by WSK Swidnik in Poland

1956–1965. Enlarged Mi-4 introduced 1952,
also built in China. Mi-6 prototype flown 1957,
then world's largest helicopter, basis for Mi-8
and Mi-10 flying crane, both announced 1961.
Two Mi-6 rotor/power packages used on Mi-

12 with an overall rotors span of 67 m (219 ft
10 in), currently largest helicopter in world.
Mi-2, turbine-powered Mi-1 development,
flown 1962, production by WSK Swidnik in
Poland. Mil also building Mi-24 gunship.

Mil Mi-10K flying-crane helicopter   **Mil Mi-12 (V-12) world's largest helicopter**   **Mil Mi-1 general-purpose helicopter**

MILES AIRCRAFT LTD./UK

Formed in October 1943, successor to Phillips & Powis Aircraft Ltd. (q.v.) at Woodley, Reading. Into liquidation November 1947, aircraft interests acquired by Handley Page (Reading) Ltd. (q.v.). Developed M.33 Monitor target tug. Manufacture included M.38 Messengers, some at Newtownards, Northern Ireland; M.57 Aerovan light freighters, M.65 Gemini light twins. Also developed M.68 Boxcar, with detachable freight container; M.71 Merchantman, which was enlarged four-engined Aerovan, and M.60 Marathon feeder-liner, later produced by Handley Page.

F. G. MILES LTD./UK

Formed 1951 at Redhill, Surrey; transferred to Shoreham, Sussex, in 1952. Acquired by British Executive and General Aviation (q.v.) February 1961. Developed M.75 derivative of Gemini with Cirrus Major engines; M.77 Sparrowjet conversion of M.5 Sparrowhawk prototype; M.100 Student jet trainer, first flown 15 May 1957; H.D.M.105 aerodynamic test vehicle, which had Aerovan fuselage with Hurel-Dubois high-aspect ratio wing, flown 31 March 1957.

MILLER AIRCRAFT CORPORATION/USA

Formed 1937 at Springfield, Massachusetts, to market Zeta series of two-seat light aircraft; Z-1 with 71 kW (95 hp) Menasco B-4; Z-2 with 93 kW (125 hp) Menasco C-4; and Z-3 with 112 kW (150 hp) Menasco C-4S.

MILLET-LAGARDE/France

Formed by Mm. Millet and Lagarde to exploit latter's ML-10 twin-boom, heavily-staggered biplane four-seater, powered by 134 kW (180 hp) Regnier engine, and first flown 1949.

MITSUBISHI JUKOGYO KABUSHIKI KAISHA/Japan

Mitsubishi Heavy Industries Ltd. formed 11 April 1934, merger of Mitsubishi Shipbuilding

Miles M.3 Falcon three-seat cabin monoplane

Miles Master two-seat advanced trainer

Miles Aerovan transport

Mitsubishi A5M2 fighter

and Engineering Co. Ltd. and Mitsubishi Aircraft Co. Ltd. Long association with Japanese Navy, commencing with Type 10 operational 1922. Most notable aircraft were 1937 A5M4 'Claude'; 1942 J2M3 'Jack'; 1939 A6M3 'Zeke', which were all fighters; 1941 Ki-46 'Dinah' reconnaissance aircraft; 1940 G3M1 'Nell' and 1941 G4M1 'Betty' medium bombers; 1940 Ki-21 'Sally' heavy bomber; and its replacement, 1944 Ki-67 'Peggy'. Post-war

has built North American F-86F Sabres, Sikorsky S-55s, S-62As, and S-61s, and Lockheed F-104J Starfighters with Kawasaki, with which company it has also been manufacturing McDonnell Douglas F-4EJ Phantoms. Currently fulfilling orders for 59 T-2 supersonic jet trainers and 26 F-1 single-seat close air support derivatives. Developed MU-2 turboprop executive aircraft, built in Japan and assembled and marketed in USA.

Mitsubishi Ki-21, Type 97 heavy bomber

Mitsubishi A6M Zero-Sen, Japan's most famous fighter

Mitsubishi MU-2L twin-turboprop light transport

Mitsubishi T-2 two-seat jet-trainer

MKEK/*Turkey*
Full name Makina ve Kimya Endustrisi Kurumu. In 1952 MKEK took over THK factory at Ankara, together with existing designs. THK-15 became the MKEK Model 1, THK-16 the Model 2, THK-5 and 5A the Models 5 and 5A, THK-14 the Model 6 and THK-2 the Model 7. Developed Model 4 Ugur tandem two-seat primary trainer for Turkish Air Force, three presented to Royal Jordanian Air Force.

MMPL/*India*
For the Maintenance Command Development Centre, Air-Vice Marshall Harjinder Singh of the Indian Air Force designed Kanpur I four-seat light aircraft, prototype built at MCDC in 132 days. Kanpur II with 186 kW (250 hp) Lycoming engine, first flown October 1961.

MOHAWK AIRCRAFT CORPORATION/*USA*
Formed at Minneapolis in 1927, developing Spurwing two-seat monoplane with Warner Scarab engine and similar three-seater Redskin.

MOHAWK AIR SERVICES/*USA*
Subsidiary of Allegheny Airlines Inc.,

Washington D.C., formed to control conversion programme for Mohawk 298, UACL PT-6A-45-powered Nord 262 airliner, being undertaken by Frakes Aviation Inc. (*q.v.*). First example flew 7 January 1975.

MÖLLER FLUGZEUGBAU/*Germany*
Founded at Bremen late 1930s, built Stomo 3 single-seat cabin monoplane powered by 13 kW (18 hp) Kroeber M.4 engine. Similar Möller Sturmer had a 40 kW (53 hp) Zundapp engine.

MONO AIRCRAFT CORPORATION/*USA*
Formed at Moline, Illinois, manufacturing a series of two-seat, high-wing cabin monoplanes during 1920s and 1930s, including Monocoupe 70 with Velie radial engine and Monocoupe 110 powered by Warner Scarab. Company acquired by Lambert Aircraft Corporation (*q.v.*) July 1934. In a succession of acquisitions and amalgamations the Mono identity disappeared, but the Monocoupe configuration influenced many later designs.

MONOCOUPE AIRCRAFT OF FLORIDA/*USA*
Successor to Monocoupe Airplane and Engine

Corporation of Melbourne, Florida, developed Meteor four/five-seat cabin monoplane with two Lycoming 0-320 engines.

MONTEE AIRCRAFT COMPANY/*USA*
Formed by Kenneth W. Montee at Santa Monica, California, in early 1920s. Montee designed four-seat open cockpit monoplane, with Hall-Scott L-4 engine, in which he won second prize in 'On to New York' race at 1925 National Air Races; he died in December 1926 while engaged on a mapping operation.

MOONEY AIRCRAFT INC./*USA*
Formed June 1948 at Wichita, Kansas, 1953 and merged with Alon Inc. (*q.v.*) October 1967. Became Aerostar Aircraft Corporation (*q.v.*) on 1 July 1970, renamed Mooney Aircraft Corporation October 1973. Developed M-18 Mite single-seat light aircraft with Crosley engine; became M-18 Wee Scotsman with Lycoming engine. M-20 four-seat version first flown 10 August 1953 with Lycoming 0-320 engine, superseded by 0-360-A-powered M-20A and by all-metal M-20C Mark 21 in 1961. Square windows introduced 1967, in current production versions, which are 0-360-A1D-powered Ranger and Executive, and M20J or Model 201, both of which have Lycoming I0-360-A1B6D engines.

Mooney Mk.22 Mustang four-seat light aircraft

Mooney M-10 Cadet two-seat lightplane

MORANE-SAULNIER/France

Formed 1911 at Puteaux, Seine, by brothers Robert and Léon Morane with Raymond Saulnier, as Aéroplanes Morane-Saulnier. Acquired by Potez Group in 1963 and became Société d'Exploitation Etablissements Morane-Saulnier, reorganised as Gérance des Etablissements Morane-Saulnier 20 May 1965, subsidiary of Sud Aviation (q.v.). Developed series of parasol-winged fighters and training aircraft, beginning with 1913 Type L or MS.3; principal production aircraft throughout 1920s and 1930s included MS.130, MS.230 and MS.315 two-seat trainers. Series of single-seat monoplane fighters introduced from 1935, including MS.406s built for French Air Force up to Occupation; development of basic design continued by Morane-Saulnier design bureau and derived MS.450 built by Dornier Werke AG in Switzerland as D-3802A. Also built Fieseler Storch for Germans as MS.500 Criquet. After liberation developed MS.470 series of advanced trainers, several light aircraft and then MS.733 Alcyon basic trainer. MS.760 Paris introduced into French Air Force service in 1958. MS.880 Rallye touring aircraft first flown 10 June 1959 still being produced by SOCATA (q.v.).

MORAVAN NÁRODNI PODNIK/Czechoslovakia
see Zlin

MORAVKO-SLEZKÁ VAZOVKÁ TATRA/Czechoslovakia

Founded in 1935 as part of the Ringhoff-Tatra combine. Obtained licences to build the Avro 626 as T.126, and the Bücker Bü 131 Jungmann as the T.131. Produced also an own-design two-seat trainer under the designation T.1. Ceased production at the outbreak of WW2.

MORELAND AIRCRAFT INC./USA

Founded by G. E. Moreland in the late 1920s at Inglewood, California, to produce the Moreland M-1 three-seat biplane powered by a 168 kW (225 hp) Wright engine.

MORGAN & COMPANY/UK

Factory at Leighton Buzzard and manufactured during WW1 Sopwith 1½ Strutters, Airco D.H.6s, Avro 504Ks and Vickers Vimy bombers.

MORRISEY AVIATION INC./USA

Founded in 1949 by William J. Morrisey, at Long Beach, California, as Morrisey Aircraft Company to build Nifty tandem two-seater.

Initially flown with Continental A65 and later with Continental C90. Reorganised as Morrisey Aviation Inc. at Santa Ana, California, and in 1958 began delivery of series production aircraft as Morrisey 2150 with 112 kW (150 hp) Lycoming engine.

MORROW AIRCRAFT CORPORATION/USA

Formed at San Bernardino County Airport, California, by Howard Morrow, factory completed 1 April 1941. Developed Model 1-L

tandem two-seat trainer for Civil Pilot Training Program. Utilised plastic-bonded plywood construction and was powered by a Lycoming 0-435A engine.

MORSE AIRCRAFT CORPORATION/USA

Established at Ithaca, New York, in January 1917. Thomas brothers, backed by Morse Chain Company, built 100 S-4B single-seat biplane advanced trainers developed from Thomas S-4 prototype fighter, followed by 497

Morane-Saulnier 'Bullet' scout of WW1

Morane-Saulnier MS.406 single-seat fighter

Morane-Saulnier MS.225 fighter

Morrisey Nifty two-seat lightplane

Mosca MB *bis*, Russian fighter of WW1

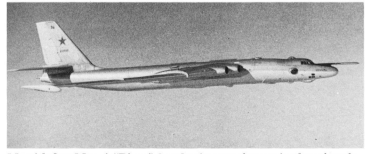

Mureaux 113 fighter/reconnaissance aircraft

improved S-4Cs. 200 Morse MB-3A fighters built by Boeing (*q.v.*) 1921–1922, in addition to 50 built by Thomas-Morse. 0-19 two-seat observation aircraft built 1928–1931.

MOSKOVSKIY AVIATSIONNI ZAVOD MOSCA/*USSR*
The Mosca Moscow Aviation Works was first established in Russia by F. E. Mosca, Savoia's designer, and by late 1916 this factory was building about five aircraft per month, these being Nieuport and Morane types built under licence. First original design was the Mosca MB, first flown in July 1915, a single-seat high-wing monoplane fighter which evolved from the Morane J. Followed by MB*bis* with forward-firing synchronised machine-gun.

MOSS BROTHERS AIRCRAFT LTD./*UK*
Formed in 1936 at Chorley, Lancashire, where prototype M.A.1 two-seat cabin monoplane was built 1937. Powered by Pobjoy Niagara III engine, it was converted to open cockpit configuration 1938. Following year open cockpit M.A.2 completed, powered by Cirrus Minor, and later converted to cabin version.

MOTH AIRCRAFT CORPORATION/*USA*
Formed at Lowell, Mass., in 1926 to manufacture de Havilland Moths under licence. Built 18 DH.60G and 161 DH.60M biplanes.

MOTORLUFTFAHRZEUG GESELLSCHAFT/*Austria*
Established in Vienna, was one of the early builders of heavier-than-air craft. Produced both the Etrich Dove and the Loehner Arrow.

MUDRY ET COMPAGNIE/*France*
Established by M. Auguste Mudry in former SAN factory at Bernay, Normandy. Currently building CAARP-developed CAP 10 two-seat and CAP 20 single-seat aerobatic aircraft. Merged in early 1978 with CAARP (*q.v.*).

MUEYETEMI SPORTREPULO EGYESULET/*Hungary*
Sport Flying Association of Technical University, Budapest. Designed and built light aircraft throughout 1920s and 1930s, including Gerle 13 with Armstrong-Siddeley Genet Major engine, M.19 tandem two-seat cabin monoplane powered by Gipsy Major and M.21 single-seat aerobatic biplane.

MULLER/*Germany*
Brothers Jacob and Philipp Muller formed Boots und Flugzeugbau Gebr. Muller at Darmstadt in 1908, manufacturing parts for Voisin aircraft being built under licence by August Euler. After WW1 they developed several light aircraft, including GMG V two-seat cabin monoplane with Argus As.16 or BMW Xa engine.

MUNIZ, CASSIO/*Brazil*
Established at São Paulo; developed Casmuniz 52 which was first all-metal twin built in Brazil. Designed for short-field, limited maintenance operations, with two Continental E185 engines. The four/five-seat Casmuniz 52 was first flown in April 1952 and subsequently taken over for flight test and production by Oficina de Mantencão e Recuperacão de Aviões Ltda.

MUREAUX/*France*
Les Ateliers de Construction du Nord de la France et des Mureaux, headquartered at Mureaux, Seine-et-Oise, absorbed into SNCAN 1 March 1937. Prior to this had developed a number of military prototypes including Mureaux 115.R2 two-seat fighter and Mureaux 200.A3 two/three-seat reconnaissance derivative, both with Hispano-Suiza 12Y engine; also Mureaux 190 single-seat fighter.

MYASISHCHEV, VLADIMIR/*USSR*
Myasishchev's design career included association with the ANT-16 and ANT-29 before work began, in 1940, on prototype DVB-102 twin-engined bomber. Bureau re-established in 1949 to develop four-jet long-range heavy bomber, which became Mya-4 Molot (NATO code-name: *Bison*) announced in 1953; also served as maritime research aircraft. Designed M-52 four-jet delta-winged strategic bomber seen at 1961 Soviet Aviation Day display, but not put into production.

Myasishchev Mya-4 ('Bison') bomber/reconnaissance/tanker aircraft

Myasishchev 'Bounder' strategic bomber

NO

NAGLER HELICOPTER COMPANY INC./*USA*

Nagler's Model NH-160 single-seat helicopter first flew in 1955. The VG-1 Vertigyro developed later comprised a Piper Colt aircraft fuselage with conventional engine. Its rotor system was driven by a turbine engine, enabling the craft to be flown either as a gyroplane, helicopter, or combination of both.

NAKAJIMA HIKOKI KABUSHIKI KAISHA/*Japan*

Nakajima's Ki-27 ('Nate') was the Imperial Japanese Army's first monoplane low-wing fighter, entering service in 1936 and outnumbering all other Japanese fighters at the time of Pearl Harbor. The B5N ('Kate') carrier-based torpedo bomber played a major role in that attack and was largely responsible for the sinkings of the US aircraft carriers during the Battle of Midway. Nakajima's Ki-43 Hyabusa ('Oscar') interceptor fighter, though deficient in firepower, was the mount of most Japanese fighter aces. The much less manoeuvrable Ki-44 Shoki ('Tojo') was used primarily as a home-defence fighter. Other significant Nakajima aircraft included the B6N Tenzan ('Jill') torpedo-bomber, the J1N1 Gekko ('Irving') three-seat reconnaissance/night fighter; the Ki-49 Donryu ('Helen') heavy bomber; and the Ki-84 Hayate ('Frank'), a good all-round Japanese fighter, though relatively unproven in battle. Nakajima developed also a floatplane version of the Zero fighter as the A6M-2 ('Rufe').

Nakajima Ki-4, Type 94 reconnaissance

Nakajima P-1 night mailplane

Nakajima B5N1, Type 97 bomber

NAMC/*Japan*
see Nihon Kokuki Seizo Kabushiki Kaisha

NAPIER AND MILLER LTD./*UK*
Built RAF B.E.2C and B.E.2E aircraft under sub-contract during WW1.

NAPIER & SONS LTD./*UK*
This well-known manufacturer of motor car and aero-engines built large numbers of RAF RE.8s and Sopwith Snipes under WW1 sub-contracts at its Acton, London works.

NARDI SA PER COSTRUZIONI AERONÀUTICHE/*Italy*
Established in Milan in 1933 by three brothers, Nardi's first aircraft was the F.N.305 two-seat tandem lightplane which flew in 1935 and was intended as a fighter trainer. A 1938 successor, the F.N.315 was exported to six countries and a light-attack version was flown experimentally. The first post-war product was the F.N.333 amphibian, a three/four seat, twin-boom design later acquired by SIAI-Marchetti (*q.v.*) and marketed from 1962 as the Riviera and in America as the North Star amphibian.

NATIONAL AERO MANUFACTURING CORPORATION/*Philippines*
A subsidiary of the Philippines Aerospace Development Corporation (*q.v.*) which began assembly and licence-manufacture of MBB (*q.v.*) BO 105 helicopters in 1974. Later that year a contract was signed with Britten-Norman (*q.v.*) for the assembly and eventual manufacture of the BN-2A Islander, and for the development and marketing of an amphibious version of the aircraft. Assembly of Islanders began in 1976 from sets of parts from the United Kingdom, and continues. In 1978 a four-seat utility aircraft was being developed in conjunction with the Philippine Government's National Sciences Development Board.

NATIONAL AIRCRAFT DIVISION OF AMERICAN AIRMOTIVE CORPORATION/*USA*
Established in 1956 to re-manufacture Boeing-Stearman PT-13/17 Kaydet trainers as the NA-75 agricultural aircraft. Modifications included new high-lift wings of all metal construction. The NA-75 was offered either in completed form or as a conversion.

NATIONAL AIRCRAFT FACTORIES/*UK*
Three factories established by the Ministry of Munitions in WW1 to increase the productive

National Dynamics built Explorer/Observer

capacity of Britain's aircraft industry. No. 1 at Waddon, Surrey, built Airco D.H.9s; No. 2 at Heaton Chapel, near Stockport, Airco D.H.9s and de Havilland D.H.10s; and No. 3 at Aintree, Lancs., built about 125 Bristol Fighters.

NATIONAL AIRWAYS SYSTEM/*USA*
In 1926 this company designed and produced the three/four-seat open-cockpit Air King commercial/touring biplane. Alternative engines offered included the OX-5, Hispano-Suiza and Wright Whirlwind.

NATIONAL DYNAMICS (PTY) LTD./*South Africa*
Formed 1975 after acquiring the prototype and all production rights of the Patchen Explorer/Observer four-seat cabin lightplane conceived originally by Thurston Aviation Corporation (*q.v.*) in the United States, as a landplane development of the Teal amphibian. Certification testing of the prototype is proceeding in South Africa, where National Dynamics also sells Schweizer Aircraft Corporation products and the Air Nova Falcon aerobatic sailplane.

NATIONALE VLIEGTUIGINDUSTRIE/*Netherlands*
Established after WW1 at 's-Gravenhage, this new company acquired as designer the well-known Frederick Koolhoven (*q.v.*). His designs for the company included the F.K.23A, a single-seat biplane fighter; F.K.29 three-seat commercial biplane; and F.K.31 two-seat high-wing monoplane which served in the pursuit, interception and army observation roles.

NATIONAL STEEL CAR CORPORATION LTD./*Canada*
In 1938 this company entered into an agreement with Westland Aircraft of Great Britain

(*q.v.*) to manufacture Westland Lysanders for the Canadian Government and later for the Royal Air Force. Under a similar arrangement National Steel Car also made North American Harvards, and contracted to build Yale trainers for Canada after the fall of France.

NAVAL AIRCRAFT FACTORY/*USA*
The US Naval Aircraft Factory at Philadelphia, Pennsylvania, was authorised in 1917 and established in early 1918. Its first, and major, task was the construction of 150 Curtiss H-16 patrol flying-boats. Built improved H-16s as F-5L, as well as Hanriot seaplanes and Loening two-seat monoplanes. Original designs of NAF include the PT-1/2 torpedo seaplanes of 1922; TS-1/3 carrier-based biplane fighters of 1922; and extensively-built N3N-1/3 primary trainer biplanes, which originated in 1934 and remained in service for 27 years. Production in WW2 included 300 Vought-designed OS2 N-1 observation/scout monoplanes, and 156 examples of the Consolidated PBN Nomad (perhaps better known as the PBY Catalina).

NAVAL AIR ESTABLISHMENT/*China*
First established in 1918, this organisation was re-located to Shanghai in 1931. Two principal aircraft types were built: the Chiang Hung two/three-seat touring seaplane, which first flew in July 1931, and the Chiang Gae'n two-seat reconnaissance biplane or advanced military trainer.

NAF N3N-3 primary training aircraft

Navion Rangemaster five-seat cabin monoplane

NHI-H3 Kolibrie helicopter

NAVION AIRCRAFT COMPANY/*USA*

Founded in 1965 by the American Navion Society to provide spares and support for owners of Ryan/North American Navion lightplanes. All rights to the aircraft were acquired and a developed version, the five-seat Navion Rangemaster H, was produced before the company was liquidated and taken over by the Navion Rangemaster Aircraft Company (*q.v.*).

NAVION RANGEMASTER AIRCRAFT COMPANY/*USA*

In 1972 Navion Rangemaster purchased the assets of the bankrupt Navion Aircraft Company (*q.v.*), including jigs, machine tools and spare parts to support Ryan/North American Navion lightplanes. In 1973 production of the Navion Rangemaster re-started, with the first aircraft flying late the following year. Consolidated Holding Incorporated acquired control of the company in 1975 and announced plans to manufacture the Rangemaster H at the rate of one per week.

NDN AIRCRAFT LTD./*UK*

Established early in 1977 by Desmond Norman (formerly of Fairey Britten-Norman) to develop the NDN-1 Firecracker two-seat trainer/sport aircraft. The first prototype flew in May 1977 and it was intended to obtain both British and US certification.

NEBRASKA AIRCRAFT CORPORATION/*USA*

Established at Lincoln, Nebraska, during WW1, was a builder of the Lincoln Standard biplane, and was also building aircraft under sub-contract to the US government.

NEDERLANDSE HELICOPTER INDUSTRIE NV/*Netherlands*

This company designed and built the NHI-H3 Kolibrie light helicopter which first flew in May 1956. For propulsion the Kolibrie employed ram-jets mounted at the tips of its rotor blades. Ten helicopters were built before production rights were handed over to Aviolanda Maatschappij voor Vliegtuigbouw (*q.v.*) who subsequently abandoned it.

NEIVA LTD./*Brazil*

Neiva produced 150 Model N621/T-25 Universal trainers for the Brazilian Air Force by 1975 and currently participates in the general aviation programme of EMBRAER (*q.v.*). EMB-710C Cariocas (Piper Cherokee Pathfinder), EMB-711C Coriscos (Arrow III), EMB-720C Minuanos (Cherokee 6) and EMB-721C Sertanejos (Cherokee Lance) are manufactured under licence from Piper.

Neiva N621 Universal (Brazilian AF T-25) trainers

Neiva Regente 360C four-seat utility aircraft

NESTLER LTD./UK
Became established in the British aircraft industry prior to WW1 by obtaining an agency for Sanchez-Besa aircraft. Sub-contractor for components in WW1. Built a single example of the Monosoupape Gnome-powered Nestler Scout to the design of Monsieur Boudot. It was destroyed at Hendon in 1917 and no further aircraft were constructed.

NESTLER UND BREITFELD/Germany
see Erma Maschinenwerk GmbH

NEW STANDARD AIRCRAFT CORPORATION/USA
In 1928 the Gates-Day Aircraft Corporation (q.v.) became New Standard Aircraft Corporation and the following year produced the White New Standard D-25 tandem, open-cockpit four-seat biplane, developed from the Gates-Day GD-24. The two-seat D-26, D-27 mailplanes and D-28 floatplane followed.

NEW ZEALAND AEROSPACE INDUSTRIES LTD./New Zealand
Aero Engine Services Ltd. and Air Parts (NZ) Ltd. amalgamated in 1973 to form New Zealand Aerospace Industries. Production of the Fletcher FU-24 agricultural aircraft and the AESL Airtrainer CT4 was integrated and examples have been delivered to Australia, Bangladesh, Iraq, Pakistan, Thailand and Uruguay. The Airtrainer CT4 was delivered to the air forces of Thailand, Australia and New Zealand and is now out of production. A turbine-powered version of the Fletcher FU-24 is under development.

NICHII KOKU KABUSHIKI KAISHA/Japan
Established at Kyoto in October 1939, by Kanegafuchi Cotton Mill and the Italian Fiat Company (q.v.), to produce Fiat aircraft and engines under licence.

NICHOLAS-BEAZLEY AIRPLANE COMPANY INC./USA
This company was established in Missouri in 1921 to supply aircraft materials and accessories. Two aircraft designs were built: the NB-4 three-seat open-cockpit low-wing monoplane which was offered with Lambert, Warner or Armstrong-Siddeley engines; and the NB-8 two-seat parasol-wing lightplane which was powered by a Szekely engine.

NIELSEN AND WINTHER AS/Denmark
During WW1 built Nieuport types under licence, and put into small scale production a biplane of their own design.

NIEUPORT/France
Designer Gustave Delage made the Nieuport company famous with his series of fighters. The sesquiplane Nieuport XI and XVIIs served with British, French, Belgian, Russian, Italian, Dutch, Finnish and American services during WW1. The improved Nieuport 28 biplane which appeared in 1917 was less successful, but best known for its exploits with the American 94th Aero Squadron ('Hat-in-Ring') in the hands of Eddie Rickenbacker and Raoul Lufbery. Nieuport aircraft were manufactured under licence in Britain and Italy.

Société Anonyme des Établissements Nieuport amalgamated with the Astra airship

Nieuport IIG light monoplane of 1912

Nieuport XVII biplane fighter of WW1

Nipper Mk.III single-seat lightplane

Nieuport-Delage 629 monoplane fighter

Nihon NAMC YS-11 twin-turboprop airliner

company, but all construction of airships was abandoned and the company name changed again to SA Nieuport-Delage. This new company's next project was the design and construction of two racing seaplanes for the 1929 Schneider Trophy races, but these aircraft were not finished in time to compete. The Nieuport-Delage 62-C1 was a single-seat sesquiplane fighter of partial wood construction, with monocoque fuselage, powered by a Lorraine or Hispano-Suiza engine. The 82-C1 was an all-metal version. Other projects included the N-D 481 single-seat, high-wing aerobatic or sporting monoplane; the N-D 641 mailplane; and the N-D 540 all-metal long-range passenger aircraft which had jettisonable long-range fuel tanks.

NIEUPORT & GENERAL AIRCRAFT/*UK*

Formed to licence-manufacture Nieuport fighter designs for the Royal Flying Corps and Royal Naval Air Service. Sopwith Camels and Snipes were also built under sub-contract. In 1917 H. P. Folland joined the firm's Cricklewood-based design team and produced the BN.1 fighter, followed by the Nieuport Nighthawk in 1919, which was produced by the Gloster Company (*q.v.*) when Nieuport & General closed down in 1920.

NIEUPORT-MACCHI/*Italy*

First became established in the aircraft industry in 1912, building Nieuport designs under licence. During WW1 built Nieuport XIs under the designation Nieuport 110 or 11000, as well as Nieuport XVII, Nieuport 27 and 29. Also undertook the manufacture of the French Hanriot HD1 sesquiplane fighter at its Varese plant during 1915.

NIEUSCHLOSS-SICHTIG AEROPLANE WORKS/*Hungary*

Established at Albertfalva, was building aircraft in 1923 to the design of Bela Oravecz and George Szebeny. These included a side-by-side two-seat monoplane, evolved by both designers, and a tandem two-seat monoplane.

NIHON KOKUKI SEIZO KABUSHIKI KAISHA/*Japan*

Following the decision made in 1956 to develop a medium-sized passenger airliner in Japan, a Transport Aircraft Development Association was established in May 1957, and succeeded in June 1959 by Nihon, responsible

for the development and manufacture of the NAMC YS-11 twin-turboprop airliner which was delivered to airlines in the United States, Europe and the Far East, and to the Japanese Air Self Defence Force. For the latter Nihon have converted one aircraft as YS-11E ECM (electronic countermeasures) with two more scheduled for conversion in 1979–1980.

NIPPER AIRCRAFT LIMITED/*UK*

In 1966 Nipper Aircraft acquired world marketing rights for the Fairey/Tipsy Nipper ultralight aeroplane, which it supplied in completed or kit form. After liquidation in May 1971 Nipper Kits and Components Limited was formed to support existing aircraft.

NIPPON KOKUSAI KOKUKI KOGYU KABUSHIKI KAISHA/*Japan*

Formed in June 1941 by the amalgamation of Nippon Koku Kogyu KK and Kokusai Kokuki KK, this small manufacturer produced subcomponents and built the Kokusai Ki 86 biplane trainer—a version of the German Bücker Bü 131 Jungmann.

Nord 262 twin-engine pressurised light transport

NORD-AVIATION/*France*

Nord-Aviation produced a version of the Messerschmitt Bf 108 Taifun, known as the Nord 1002 Pingouin, for the French military service immediately after WW2. A tricycle landing gear variant, the Nord 1101 Noralpha, and a re-designed civilian four-seat derivative, the Nord 1203 Norécrin, were also produced in quantity, together with Nord NC-853/856 Norvigie liaison/trainer aircraft delivered to the French army and to aero clubs in the mid-1950s. A batch of N.1402 Noroit twin-engined amphibians were built for the French navy; and the N.2501 Noratlas twin-boom, twin-engined transport, first flown 1952, was subsequently produced in France and Germany. Nord took over the Max Holste Super Broussard twin-engined transport design and developed it as the Nord 262 airliner, delivered to European and United States airlines and to the French navy by Aérospatiale (*q.v.*).

Nord N.2501 Noratlas twin-engined transport

Nord 3202 trainer of the French Army

NORD GmbH/*Germany*

Three German aircraft manufacturers —Hamburger Flugzeugbau, Siebel-Werke ATG GmbH and Weser Flugzeugbau GmbH (all *q.v.*)—formed this company to licence-manufacture Nord N.2501 Noratlas transports for the Luftwaffe, the first flying in August 1958.

NORDUYN AVIATION LTD./*Canada*

Designed and manufactured the Norseman eight/ten-seat cargo/transport aircraft which first flew in 1935 and was delivered to the Royal Canadian Air Force and the United States Air Force; with the latter service it was designated C-64A. Norsemans were especially popular as bushplanes in the northern regions of Canada and with civilian operators in northern Europe. The Canadian Car & Foundry Company (*q.v.*) acquired Norduyn's assets in 1946 and produced an improved Norseman Mark V until 1950. Norduyn licence-manufactured North American Harvard trainers during WW2 for both the RCAF and RAF.

NORSK FLYINDUSTRI AS/*Norway*

Formed in 1947 to produce the Finnmark 5A amphibian designed by Birger Honningstad (*q.v.*), and which failed to go beyond the prototype stage. Norsk also manufactured metal floats for a variety of aircraft.

Norduyn Norseman eight/ten-seat cargo/transport floatplane

NORTH AMERICAN AVIATION INC./*USA*

Formed originally as a holding company in 1928, North American's first product was the O–47 Army observation aircraft of 1937. The NA-16 Yale two-seat military trainer followed, being developed through fixed and retractable landing gear variants into the T-6 Texan/Harvard trainer which continued in production in Canada until 1954 and has served (and is still serving, in some cases) with virtually every non-Communist air arm in the world. North American's best known aircraft was the P-51 Mustang fighter, one of the best fighter aircraft of WW2. Most Mustangs served in Europe, flying escort duties for US Eighth Air Force bombers. Significant aircraft evolved by North American include the B-25 Mitchell twin-engined medium bomber; the B-45 Tornado, the first American four-jet bomber; and the F-86 Sabre, the USAF's first swept-wing fighter; the F-100 Super Sabre, the world's first operational fighter capable of supersonic speed in level flight, the T-28 Trojan/Fennec trainer and light ground attack aircraft which succeeded the T-6; the A-5 Vigilante carrier-based jet bomber/reconnaissance aircraft; the XB-70 Valkyrie supersonic bomber with Mach 3 speed capability; and the X-15 rocket research craft, which attained an altitude of 107,960 m (354,200 ft) in 1963 and was flown at a speed of 7,298 km/h (4,534 mph) in 1967. In the same year North American merged with the Rockwell Standard Corporation to form North American Rockwell (both *q.v.*).

North American F-86 Sabre

North American Harvard (AT-6 Texan) trainers

North American X-15 hypersonic research aircraft

North American B-25 Mitchell light bomber

North American P-51 Mustang long-range escort/fighter

NORTHROP/*USA*

Company had its foundations in California in 1929 when John K. Northrop built the Alpha, first all-metal stressed-skin aeroplane; the Beta 224 kW (300 hp) aircraft, first to exceed 322 km/h (200 mph) and the Gamma high-speed mailplane. After a brief spell as part of United Aircraft Corporation (*q.v.*), Northrop Aircraft Inc. was established 1939 to concentrate on military projects, including the A-17 attack-bomber and P-61 Black Widow three-seat, twin-boom night fighter, first aircraft in this category to be ordered by USAAF. Northrop experiments with the tailless XP-56 interceptor led to a number of post-war flying wing projects, culminating in eight jet-engined YB-49 flying-wing bomber of 1947. The F-89 Scorpion all-weather fighter entered production two years later, serving USAF and Air National Guard Units until 1963. Extending its activities into other fields, the Company changed its name to Northrop Corporation in the year 1959.

Northrop's current production is concentrated on the F-5 single-seat jet fighter, derived from the 1959 N-156 Freedom Fighter. The T-38 Talon two-seat trainer version was supplied to the USAF and the F-5 has been widely exported. The improved F-5E Tiger II is in production for the USAF, Chile, Switzerland and Middle East nations, and Northrop is co-operating with the McDonnell Douglas Corporation in the development of the F-18 Hornet shipboard fighter which is based on its YF-17 Cobra design. The Hornet is due to enter service in the early 1980s.

Northrop F-89 Scorpion two-seat fighter

Northrop P-61 Black Widow night fighter, with Curtis P-40K Warhawk behind

Northrop Delta 8-passenger high-speed transport

Northrop T-38 Talon fighters

NORTH AMERICAN ROCKWELL CORPORATION/*USA*

Following company re-organisation, the former Aero Commander division of Rockwell became part of NAR and its Shrike, Commander 685 and Turbo Hawk Commander twin-engined business aircraft were marketed under the new company name, together with Quail, Sparrow, Snipe and Thrush Commander agricultural aircraft and the Darter and Lark Commander single-engined lightplanes. The Model 112 Commander light plane and B-1 swing-wing supersonic bomber projects were started before the company name was changed to Rockwell International in 1973.

NORTHERN AIRCRAFT COMPANY/*UK*

Known formerly as the Lakes Flying Company (*q.v.*), operated a seaplane training school at Cockshott, Lake Windermere, and built the Lakes Waterhen and Seabird aircraft.

NORTHERN AIRCRAFT INC./*USA*

Purchased from Bellanca all rights, jigs and tooling for the Bellanca 14-19 Cruisemaster four-seat lightplane. The Bellanca Model 14 was one of the classic lightplane designs, since built by several manufacturers. First production of the Northern Cruisemaster started in October 1956. Northern also supplied spares, support and modification kits for Republic Seabee amphibians after a merger with the American Aviation Corporation (*see* AAC).

NUD/*Turkey*

Established in 1937 at Istanbul, NUD built gliders under licence and produced the two-seat NU D.36 training biplane and a prototype NU D.38 high-wing, twin-engined airliner which was designed to accommodate six persons.

NURI DEMIRAG TAYYARE FABRIKASI/*Turkey*
see NUD

NV NEDERLANDSCHE VLIEGTUIGENFABRIEK
see NV Koninklijke Nederlanse Vliegtuigenfabriek Fokker

OAKLAND AIRMOTIVE/*USA*

California-based company specialised in civilian executive transport conversions of surplus US Navy Lockheed PV-2 Harpoon patrol bombers. The resultant Oakland Centaurus seated 8/14 passengers and was offered as a high-speed corporate transport in the late 1950s and early 1960s. A twin-engined conversion of the Beechcraft Bonanza was also completed to order, and renamed Oakland Super V.

OAKLEY LTD./*UK*

Oakley controlled the Ilford Aeroplane Works, which undertook the installation of Curtiss engines in 1916. In 1917 the company was awarded a contract to build a batch of 25 Sopwith Triplanes, but only three had been completed before the aircraft had become obsolescent. Oakley also undertook component manufacture and aircraft repair work during WW1.

OBERLERCHNER, JOSEPH/*Austria*

A former manufacturer of sailplanes, Oberlerchner flew a prototype, all-wood two-seat JOB 5 lightplane in 1958. The developed JOB 15 four-seater, which had mixed metal/wood/glassfibre construction, entered production in 1961, powered by a Lycoming engine. It remains in service with Austrian and other European aero clubs, and is especially used as a glider-tug.

OEFFAG/*Austria*

Oesterreichische Flugzeug-Fabrik AG was a sub-contractor in WW1 to the German Albatros-Werke (*q.v.*) producing its Albatros D.II, D.III and D.V series scouts, together with licence-manufactured Austro-Daimler engines.

Oakland Airmotive conversion of the Beechcraft Bonanza

OERTZ-WERKE GmbH/*Germany*

Max Oertz, an established builder of yachts, entered the aircraft business in 1911. The company produced three examples of the mid-wing M1911–12 monoplane and a single developed M1912–13 model.

OESTERREICHISCHE-UNGARISCHE FLUGZEUGFABRIK/*Austria*

A subsidiary of the German Aviatik company (*q.v.*), this manufacturer built Aviatik B.I and B.II two-seat reconnaissance aircraft for the Austro-Hungarian Flying Service and worked on a single-seat scout version of the Aviatik C.I. This aeroplane, the D.I. Berg-Scout, was at first prone to wing failures under load, but eventually ran to 11 production batches.

OGDEN/*USA*

Established in 1929, Ogden's only product was the tri-motor Osprey cabin monoplane which was offered in three versions—the Model C, which carried two crew and four passengers, or seven passengers if the lavatory was removed;

the Model PB with Menasco B4 engines; and the Model PC with Menasco Pirate engines.

OGMA/*Portugal*

Founded in 1918 as a department of the Portuguese Air Force, Oficinas Gerais de Material Aeronáutico has been responsible for the licence-production or assembly of many military aircraft types, including the Vickers Valparaiso, Avro 626 Cadet, de Havilland Tiger Moth, Morane-Saulnier MS-233, de Havilland Chipmunk, Auster D-4 and D-6 and Dornier Do 27. Currently OGMA manufactures components for Aérospatiale SA-315B Lama and SA-318 Puma helicopters, and maintains and repairs all Portugese military aircraft and those of the Luftwaffe and European-based USAF and US Navy units.

OKAMURA/*Japan*

This branch of Nihon aircraft works built the N52 two-seat lightplane in 1952 and collaborated with Tokyo University students in the design and construction of a two-seat sailplane.

Oberlerchner JOB 15-150 four-seat lightplane

Omega BS-12D four-seat twin-engined helicopter

On Mark Marksman pressurised light transport

OMAREAL/*Brazil*

Oficina de Manutenco e Recuperaceo de Aviões Ltda, the Brazilian maintenance and overhaul facility based at São Paulo, acquired manufacturing rights to the Casmuniz 52 twin-engined five-seat lightplane in 1955. The Casmuniz 52 was designed and built by Cassio Muniz SA (*q.v.*) and was intended for easy construction from single-curvature metal to facilitate field repair in bush operations. OMAREAL took over the flight testing of the only prototype to be made, but no production of the aircraft ensued.

OMEGA AIRCRAFT CORPORATION/*USA*

Founded 1953 as a subsidiary of Allied Aero Industries to further develop the Sznycer-Gottlieb SG VI helicopter. The Omega BS-12 four-seat, twin-engined helicopter flew in 1956 and was succeeded by the BS-12D with

more powerful engines and the 1963 BS-12D3S supercharged version. Production was to have started in 1964 when all development was suspended after completion of four prototypes.

O'NEILL AIRPLANE COMPANY INC./*USA*

Formed 1962 to develop the Waco Model W Aristocrat design for which all rights were acquired. Two versions were evolved, the Model W Winner, which was to have been a series production machine; and the Aristocrat II for amateur construction. The O'Neill Pea Pod canard design was proposed also, but all activity on the Aristocrat terminated in 1974.

ONG AIRCRAFT CORPORATION/*USA*

This Kansas City-based company manufactured the Ong Model M-32W high-wing

monoplane, powered by a Warner Super Scarab engine, before America's entry into WW2.

ON MARK ENGINEERING COMPANY/*USA*

Formed 1954 as a specialist maintenance and modification contractor for Douglas B-26 Invader bombers, developing high-speed executive transport and heavily-armed counter-insurgency versions. The On Mark Marketeer was a six/eight-seat corporate transport based on the B-26 airframe. The externally similar Marksman featured a pressurised cabin. A B-26K Counter Invader was developed for the USAF's Tactical Air Command. In 1962 On Mark was responsible for the first Pregnant Guppy conversions of the Boeing Stratocruiser, on behalf of Aero Spacelines Inc. (*q.v.*), for the transportation of space rockets and other bulky cargo.

ORENCO/*USA*
Ordnance Engineering Corporation's Model 'D' single-seat biplane fighter was the first such aircraft of all-American design. Four wooden prototypes powered by 224 kW (300 hp) Wright-Hispano engines were built, followed by 50 production aircraft manufactured under licence by the Curtiss company.

ORLOGSVAERFTET/*Denmark*
The Royal Danish Naval Dockyard (Orlogsvaerftet) constructed 12 Hawker Danecocks under licence in 1927/1928. The aircraft was a single-seat biplane fighter derived from the Hawker Woodcock and was equipped with two 7·7 mm Madsen machine-guns. It remained in service until 1937 with the Royal Danish Air Force, which designated it the L.B.II Dankok.

OSRODEK KONSTRUCKCJI LOTNICZYCH/*Poland*
Formed 1957 by the Polish Minister of Heavy Industry to take over all design activities formerly conducted by the Polish Aviation Insti-tute. First design was the MD-12 four-engined feeder liner/photo-survey aircraft which flew in 1962. A developed version of Russian Yak-12 known as the PZL-101 Gawron (Rook) has been produced in quantity for agricultural and air-ambulance duties. Now superseded by the PZL-104 Wilga (Thrush) which is offered in agricultural, air-ambulance, transport, glider-tug and parachute aircraft roles and has been widely exported. Licence production is under way in Indonesia. Deliveries of the TS-11 Iskra (Spark) two-seat aerobatic jet trainer to the Polish Air Force began in 1963 and continues. (*See also* Panstwowe Zaklady Lotnicze).

OTTAWA CAR AND AIRCRAFT LTD./*Canada*
This pre-war manufacturer of street-cars entered the aircraft industry as Canadian agents for Armstrong-Whitworth, Avro and Armstrong-Siddeley, building Avro Tutor and Prefect trainers and Armstrong-Whitworth Atlas and Siskin fighters for the Royal Canadian Air Force. During WW2 parts for Hamp-den bombers, Hawker Hurricanes and Avro Ansons were manufactured, and Anson airframes shipped from England were assembled.

OTTO WERKE/*Germany*
Gustav Otto Flugmaschinenwerke built six M1912 two-seat biplane observation aircraft for the German Army in 1912. The aircraft was broadly similar to the French Caudron G series.

OUEST AVIATION/*France*
Formed in 1936, incorporating factories of Marcel Bloch, Blériot and Loiré et Olivier, subsequently merging with SNCASO (all *q.v.*) and changing name to Ouest Aviation in 1956. Original designs included S.O. 94R twin-engined trainer; S.O. 95 Corse and S.O. 30 Bretagne military transports; S.O. 4050 Vautour twin-jet bomber; and the S.O. 9000 Trident. The S.O. 1221 Djinn two-seat helicopter was produced, and Vertol H-21 helicopters manufactured under licence for the French Army. Ouest is now part of Aérospatiale (*q.v.*).

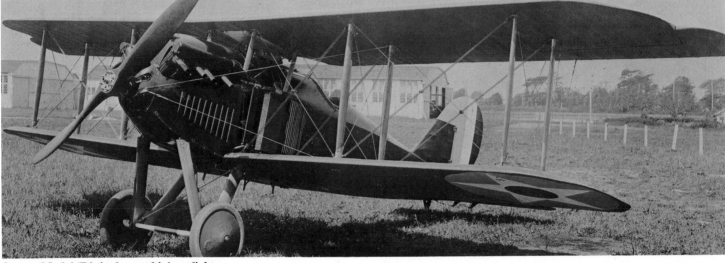
Orenco Model 'D' single-seat biplane fighter

Orenco F-4 four-seat tourer or mailplane

Ouest Aviation S.O. 4050 Vautour

PQ

PAC/*USA*

see Pacific Airmotive Corporation

PACAERO/*USA*

Formed in 1957 at Santa Monica, California, as a subsidiary of Pacific Airmotive Corporation (*q.v.*) to continue manufacture of the Learstar Executive transport, with two Wright Cyclone engines. PacAero also carried out modifications to other types, including conversion of North American T-28 trainers to Nomad standard with a bigger engine. Dissolved and merged with Pacific Airmotive Corporation's Aircraft Division in early 1960s.

PACIFIC AIRMOTIVE CORPORATION/*USA*

This company continued the work of PacAero (*q.v.*). It also produced a conversion of the Beech 18 known as the Tradewind, with single fin and rudder, tricycle landing gear and improved avionics. PAC also has considerable agency agreements and is heavily involved in modification, repair and maintenance contracts, and in 1968 took over the R.J. Enstrom Corporation (*q.v.*), manufacturers of light helicopters. Helicopter production was stopped in 1970 when the Purex Corporation, owner of Pacific Airmotive Corporation, began to reduce its aviation commitments.

PACIFIC AIRPLANE & SUPPLY CO./*USA*

Company founded in early 1920s at Los Angeles, California. First product was the Hawk six-seat twin-engined commercial biplane. Built Model C-1 single-seat racing monoplane in 1921, with 67 kW (90 hp) Curtiss OX-5 engine.

PACKARD-LE PÈRE/*USA*

Captain Le Père, of the French Aviation mission to the USA, designed a two-seat fighter, the LUSAC-11 (Le Père United States Army Combat) which was built by the Packard Motor Car Company in 1918. Thirty LUSAC-11s powered by Liberty engines and three LUSAC-21s with Bugatti engines were built, but contracts for quantity production were cancelled when WW1 ended.

Packard-Le Père LUSAC-11 fighter

Pacific Airmotive Tradewind, a conversion of the Beech 18

Panavia Tornado swing-wing multi-role combat aircraft

PANAVIA/*International*

Europe's most important military aircraft programme, the Tornado swing-wing multi-role combat aircraft, is a joint venture by British Aerospace (UK), MBB (West Germany) and Aeritalia (Italy) (all *q.v.*), with the project being managed by the specially formed Panavia Aircraft GmbH, based in Munich. The programme also involves many sub-contractors in the three countries concerned. Initial orders cover 809 Tornados: 385 for the RAF, 211 for the Luftwaffe, 113 for the German Navy and 100 for the Italian Air Force. Twelve prototypes have been built, the first flying at MBB's Manching factory on 14 August 1974, and the first service deliveries were scheduled for 1978.

PANDER & ZONEN/*Netherlands*

Woodworking company which took up aircraft construction in early 1920s, with Model D single-seat monoplane and Model E two-seat sesquiplane. Concentrated on special designs rather than mass production, but Pander aircraft were adopted by Dutch flying clubs. Built Postjager tri-motor low-wing mailplane in 1934.

PANSTWOWE ZAKLADY LOTNICZE/*Poland*

Poland's National Aircraft Establishment; built the P.1 single-seat fighter monoplane with Hispano-Suiza engine in 1929–1930, and subsequently the famous P.11 single-seat fighter and P.19 cabin monoplane. The PZL Loś medium bomber of 1937 was followed by the Wolk twin-engined fighter, Sum light bomber and Mewa reconnaissance monoplane by the beginning of WW2. The Polish industry ceased production at that time, but after political reorganisation in 1956 the aircraft industry was revived with production of Soviet aircraft and some indigenous types. In foreign markets all Polish aircraft subsequently appeared under the PZL title, such as the PZL-101 Gawron and PZL-104 Wilga utility aircraft of 1960 and 1962 respectively, the first being a development of the Yak-12. The Gawron was used extensively as an agricultural aircraft, along with the PZL-built An-2 biplane, but later purpose-built dusters and sprayers have in-

Pander & Zonen EH-120 Luxe two-seat sesquiplane

PZL P.37 Loś monoplane bomber prototype

PZL P.11 fighter, which fought a grim defensive action in WW2

cluded the PZL-106 Kruk, M-18 Dromader and the M-15 biplane, all currently in production. Recent licence agreements cover production in Poland of the Socata Ralle (as the PZL-110) and the Piper Seneca. PZL is also responsible for the TS-11 Iskra jet trainer and the Mi-2 helicopter.

PARAGON/*UK*
Formed early 1960s at Thruxton Aerodrome near Andover, Hampshire, from the earlier Jackaroo Aircraft Ltd. (*q.v.*), for conversion of

standard two-seat Tiger Moth biplanes to four-seat configuration by inserting a new wider centre fuselage and extending the top wing centre-section. 18 Jackaroo conversions were carried out by the company, which also designed a light monoplane, the Paragon (subsequently Paladin), but is was not built. Assets acquired 1964 by Hampshire School of Flying.

PARAMOUNT AIRCRAFT CORPORATION/*USA*
Founded in 1928 at Saginaw, Michigan. Built

Cabinaire four-seat cabin biplane with 123 kW (165 hp) Wright Whirlwind engine.

PARKS AIRCRAFT INC./*USA*
A division of the Detroit Aircraft Corporation (*q.v.*) by 1930, Parks had built training aircraft for its own companies, Parks Air College and Parks Air Lines. Subsequent to the Detroit take-over, Parks aircraft were built by Ryan (*q.v.*). Following Ryan's demise the Parks name was revived for the P-1H biplane built by Hammond (*q.v.*).

PARNALL & SONS/UK

Woodworking firm in Bristol who built seaplanes in WW1 to War Office specifications. Subsequently taken over by W. T. Avery and abandoned aircraft production (but see next entry).

PARNALL, GEORGE, & CO./UK

After the take-over of Parnall & Sons (*q.v.*) by W. T. Avery, George Parnall founded his own company with personnel from the former aircraft division of Parnall & Sons to continue aircraft manufacture under government contract. First product was the Puffin, a military central float amphibian with a single Napier engine. It was followed by a series of varying types from the Possum twin-engine triplane to the Plover fighter and Pixie ultra-light aircraft, Pete submarine-borne and Elf light biplanes. Built Hendy 302 monoplane for Henderson Aircraft Company (*q.v.*) in 1930. Parnall Aircraft Ltd. formed in 1935 to take over aircraft business and acquire patents, rights, etc. of aircraft armament of Nash & Thompson Ltd. and similar patents and rights of Hendy. Concerned with turrets and aircraft armament in WW2, and no longer produced aircraft.

PARQUE DE AERONÁUTICA/Brazil

The works at Rio de Janeiro's military air base built Waco biplanes for Brazilian Air Force mail services in late 1930s, also Muniz two-seat training monoplane.

PARTENAVIA/Italy

A Naples company formed in early 1950s to build series of light aircraft. First to enter production was the P-57 Fachiro of 1957, a four-seat high-wing monoplane with Lycoming engine. This was followed by various developments including the P.64 Oscar, also produced in South Africa under licence as the RSA.200 by AFIC (Pty.) Ltd. (*q.v.*), and the P.66C. Partenavia's first twin was the P.68 six-seat light transport, flown in 1968 and subsequently placed in production. Recent variants include the P.68R with retractable landing gear.

PASOTTI SpA/Italy

In early 1950s built four-seat F.6 Airone cabin monoplane with two Lycoming engines, followed by a single-engine version, the F-9 Sparviero, with Hirth engine.

PASPED AIRCRAFT COMPANY/USA

Based at Glendale, California. Built Skylark two-seat light cabin monoplane in mid-1930s, with 93 kW (125 hp) Warner Scarab engine; but there was no further development.

Parnall P.1, a Parnall-built version of the Fairey Hamble Baby

Parnall Prawn experimental flying-boat

Partenavia Observer, modified from the standard P.68

Partenavia P.68 Victor six-seat light transport

Parnall Plover single-seat carrier-based fighter

Pazmany PL-1 sportsplane, built subsequently as military trainer

Partenavia P.59 Jolly high-wing monoplane

Pemberton-Billing P.B.9 single-seat scout biplane

PAYEN/*France*

Engineer engaged in delta-wing aircraft research; built two deltas before WW2, and in 1954 flew PA-49 all-wood delta research aircraft powered by one Turboméca Pallas gas-turbine. Built several more experimental aircraft in early 1970s.

PAZMANY AIRCRAFT CORPORATION/*USA*

Founded as L. Pazmany & Associates at San Diego, California; produced the PL-1 two-seat light aircraft with Continental engine in 1962. A production version, the PL-2, had a higher powered engine. A number of PL-1s were built by the Chinese Nationalist Air Force as basic trainers, and examples of the PL-2 by the air forces of Indonesia, Korea, Thailand and Vietnam.

P.C. HELICOPTER CORPORATION/*USA*

see Gyrodyne

PEGLER & COMPANY LTD./*UK*

Doncaster, Yorkshire, company which built Sopwith Cuckoo torpedo-bombers under subcontract in 1918.

PEGNA & BONMARTINI/*Italy*

Formed in early 1920s in Rome to take over aeronautical work of Pegna-Rossi-Bastianelli, comprising the P.R.B. flying-boat and a small sporting monoplane. Company taken over by Piaggio (*q.v.*).

PEMBERTON-BILLING LTD./*UK*

Noel Pemberton-Billing began aeronautical experiments in 1903 continuing until 1909 with various engine designs and some monoplanes. Acquiring a factory at Woolston, Southampton, in 1913, he began to design and build marine aircraft, his P.B.1 biplane flying-boat being exhibited at the 1914 Olympia Show. An exception was the P.B.9 single-seat scout biplane, designed in one day and built in seven, flown in 1914. The P.B.29 night patrol quadraplane of 1915 was built in seven weeks from beginning of design, and paved the way for the improved version known as the Nighthawk. By the time this had flown, the company had been renamed Supermarine Aviation Works (*q.v.*).

PENNSYLVANIA AIRCRAFT SYNDICATE/*USA*

Formed in early 1930s to develop a rotary-wing aircraft, designed in Germany in 1926 by

Walter Rieseler and Walter Kreiser, and further developed in the USA by E. Burke Wilford. The Wilford Gyroplane accumulated a considerable amount of test flying, and was powered by a Kinner R-5 engine.

PERCIVAL AIRCRAFT LTD./UK

Formed in 1932 by E. W. Percival and E. W. B. Leake at Gravesend, moving to Luton in 1937. Built series of successful light aircraft beginning with the single-engine Gull and later twin-engine Q-6 six/seven-seat cabin monoplane. Percival Gulls were used for a number of record-breaking flights, and the type was developed subsequently into the Proctor light communications aircraft. Several Mew Gull racers were built in the late 1930s. After WW2, production of the Proctor continued for civilian customers, while a new three-seat trainer, the Prentice, appeared in 1946 and was built in quantity for the RAF and several overseas air forces. This was followed by the Provost trainer, which was ordered for the RAF in 1951. Following the experimental Merganser light transport of 1946, a larger version, the Prince, flew in 1948 and was produced in civil and military versions. The company's name was changed in 1954 to Hunting Percival Aircraft (q.v.).

Percival Mew Gull single-seat racing monoplane

Percival Proctor I communications aircraft

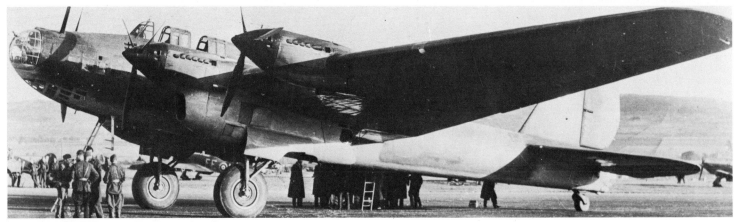

Petlyakov PE-8 four-engined heavy bomber

PETLYAKOV, V. M./USSR

Russian designer who headed a bureau before and during WW2. Notable designs were the PE-2 light bomber and PE-8 four-engined heavy bomber, the latter being a development of the 1936 ANT-42 with more powerful engines. The PE-8 entered service in 1941.

PETROLINI/Argentine

Took over production of El Boyero two-seat light monoplane from the Instituto Aerotécnico in late 1940s, and built 160 to government contracts for flying clubs and schools.

PETTERS LTD./UK

Yeovil engineering company which started producing Short seaplanes to Admiralty contract in 1915 at its new factory, known as the Westland Aircraft Works. The company was subsequently renamed Westland Aircraft (q.v.) in 1935.

PEYRET, LOUSE/France

Louis Peyret began aircraft construction with a glider, winning a Daily Mail £1,000 prize in 1922. Following year he produced a light aeroplane, which subsequently crashed, and later a light seaplane for M. Le Prieur, the Albessard

monoplane and the Mauboussin P.M.4 single-seat monoplane. Peyret became technical manager of Avions Mauboussin (q.v.).

PFALZ FLUGZEUGWERKE GmbH/Germany

Founded at Speyer-am-Rhein in 1913, company built the Otto biplane with Rapp engine in WW1, and subsequently obtained a licence to build Morane parasol monoplanes. Later built a series of single-seat biplane fighters, from the C.III and D.XII. Pfalz aircraft manufacture came to an end when the Armistice was signed.

Pfalz D.III, this company's first single-seat fighter

Phillips & Powis/Miles Mohawk built for Charles Lindbergh

Phillips & Powis/Miles Master trainer prototype

PHEASANT AIRCRAFT COMPANY/*USA*

Founded 1927 at Fond du Lac, Wisconsin, company's first product in mid-1920s was Pheasant three-seat commercial biplane with 67 kW (90 hp) Curtiss OX-5 engine, followed by Traveler single-seat cabin monoplane.

PHILIPPINE AEROSPACE DEVELOPMENT CORPORATION/*Philippines*

Government Corporation established in 1973 to promote development of a Philippines aerospace industry. Aircraft manufacture is undertaken by a subsidiary company, National Aero Manufacturing Corporation (*q.v.*), which is assembling 38 MBB Bö 105 helicopters and a large batch of Britten-Norman Islanders. A prototype four-seat utility high-wing monoplane powered by a 224 kW (300 hp) Lycoming engine is being built as a joint venture between PADC and the National Science Development Board; first flight was scheduled for mid-1978.

PHILIPPINE AIR FORCE/*Philippines*

Self Reliance Development Wing built prototype of three-seat primary trainer known as the XT-001, powered by a Lycoming engine. Very similar to Italian SIAI SF.260, of which 32 were bought for the PAF. The SRDW has also acquired prototype of American Jet Industries Super Pinto COIN aircraft.

PHILLIPS & POWIS AIRCRAFT LTD./*UK*

Formed in 1935 to take over aircraft manufacturing business operated by Phillips & Powis Aircraft (Reading) Ltd, which had produced the initial Miles Hawk series of light aircraft. Name changed 1943 to Miles Aircraft (*q.v.*).

PHILLIPS AVIATION CO./*USA*

Founded at end of 1930s in Los Angeles, California, to continue development of light two-seat monoplane, the Phillips I-B, designed originally by Aero Engineering Corporation. Also built CT-1 two-seat biplane.

PHOENIX DYNAMO/*UK*

Bradford company which became Admiralty contractors in WW1 for construction of Short 184 seaplanes, Short landplane bombers, Maurice Farman Longhorns and a pair of Armstrong Whitworth F.K.10 quadraplanes. Later built Felixstowe F.3 and F.5 flying-boats, and two Phoenix P.5 Cork flying-boats. Phoenix became part of the English Electric Co. Ltd. (*q.v.*) in 1918 and continued development of flying-boats, initially the P.5 Kingston.

PHÖNIX FLUGZEUGWERFT GmbH/*Austria*

This company manufactured a series of Phönix single-seat fighter aircraft powered by Austro-Daimler engines. The DI and DII were flown during WW1 by the Austro-Hungarian Flying Service, a few being fitted with cameras for pioneering high-speed aerial photo-reconnaissance work. Seventeen of the final batch of 122 Phönix DIIs were completed as improved DIII variants and transferred to the Swedish Army Air Service after the war.

PIAGGIO, RINALDO/*Italy*

SA Piaggio & Co., engineers and shipbuilders, produced some Caproni aircraft and parts during WW1, but subsequently abandoned aircraft manufacture until it took over Pegna & Bonmartini (*q.v.*) in 1923. First product was the Piaggio-Pegna pursuit monoplane with Hispano-Suiza engine. Later was associated with Società di Costruzioni Meccaniche Aeronàutiche in licence-construction of Dornier Wal flying-boats. Built P.32 twin-engined heavy bomber at end of 1930s and several four-engined P.108 heavy bombers during WW2. Resumed aeronautical work in late 1946 with conversion of Dakotas for airline service. Built P.136 five-seat twin-engined amphibian, prototype flying in 1948, followed by a series of trainers for the Italian Air Force; the P.149 was also licence-built by Focke-Wulf in Germany. Produced the P.166 executive transport in 1957, with two Lycoming engines and pusher propellers behind the wing, as with the P.136. Signed agreement with US Douglas company (*q.v.*) in 1961 for joint development of light utility aircraft, first flown in 1964. Powered by two Bristol Siddeley Viper turbojets, the aircraft was designated PD.808 and a small number were built. The present company was formed in 1964 as a separate concern, and is building components for Aeritalia and Panavia in addition to continuing development of the basic P.166 design, the latest DL3 variant having Lycoming turboprop engines.

PIASECKI AIRCRAFT CORPORATION/*USA*

Formed in 1955 by Frank Piasecki, who was concerned in development of vertical lift aircraft and flew the Model 59K Sky-Car flying jeep with an Artouste turboshaft engine in 1958 under a US Army contract. Technical interchange agreements were signed with Breguet Aviation (*q.v.*) in 1957, which included sales rights for that company's STOL transports in the USA and Canada, but these were dropped in 1962. Also provided engineering assistance to Agusta from 1960 for the AZ-101G and AZ-105 helicopters. Built prototype of PiAC 16H-1C Pathfinder compound helicopter in 1962, continuing development under a US Navy contract, but no production followed. Company has recently been researching the possibility of linking helicopter and aerostat principles.

PIASECKI HELICOPTER CORPORATION/*USA*

Formed in 1946 from the P-V Engineering Forum which had completed several rotary-wing contracts for NACA and the US Navy. The latter ordered an XHRP-1 helicopter which flew in 1945 and following successful

Piaggio P.108B, Italy's only heavy bomber of WW2

Piaggio P.166C 13-seat light transport

Piasecki VZ-8P VTOL test rig

Piasecki PiAC 16H-1 Pathfinder compound helicopter

Piasecki PV-3/US Navy HRP-1

tests it was placed in production. Further orders followed for XHJP-1 tandem rotor helicopters for USN shipboard operations and the large XH-16, which had a fuselage of DC-4 size. In 1956 the company became Vertol Aircraft Corporation (*q.v.*).

PIDEK INDUSTRIES/*Canada*
Former Polish Air Force pilot Joseph Pidek designed and built J.P.2B two-seat ultra-light helicopter at Vancouver in 1962. The aircraft was not developed beyond prototype stage.

PIEL AVIATION SA/*France*
Claude Piel produced a series of light aircraft from the early 1950s, most famous of which was the Emeraude two-seater with, in its origi-

nal CP.30 form, a 48·5 kW (65 hp) Continental engine. More than 200 Emeraudes of varying types were built under licence by companies in a number of countries, and many are still under construction by home builders. Piel also designed several other light aircraft, including the CP.80 Zef single-seat racer, and his most recent design was the CP.500 tandem-wing twin-engine light aircraft of 1974.

PIK/*Finland*
    see Polyteknikkojen Ilmailukerho

PILATUS FLUGZEUGWERKE AG/*Switzerland*
Formed in 1939, and became a subsidiary of the Oerlikon armaments company. First air-

craft was SB-2 Pelican six-seat light transport of 1944, prototype only built. Followed by P-2 advanced trainer, built in quantity for the Swiss Air Force in late 1940s, and the P-3 advanced trainer from 1953. Series production of the P-3 followed for the Swiss Air Force, and six went to the Brazilian Navy. In 1959 Pilatus flew the first PC-6 Porter STOL monoplane with a Lycoming engine, and this type has been in continuous production ever since, later developments using Astazou, Garrett and PT6 turboprop engines. Pilatus signed a licence agreement for production of Turbo Porters by Fairchild-Hiller (*q.v.*) in USA. Pilatus was also engaged in Mirage production and maintenance work for the Swiss Air Force. The company's latest production is the PC-7 Turbo Trainer, a PT6-powered version of the P-3, and first flown in 1966; there was little interest shown then but the project was revived in 1975 and is now going ahead with first orders in hand. Dornier is collaborating in marketing of the Turbo Trainer.

PINTSCH, JULIUS AG/*Austria*
This was an engineering company which started an aircraft department in mid-1930s to manufacture Raab Schwalbe II and Tigerschwalbe II general purpose biplanes for the Austrian Air Force.

Piel Emeraude two-seat lightplane

Piel C.P.70 Beryl two/three-seat lightplane

Pilatus PC-6 Turbo Porter STOL transport

Pilatus PC-7 two-seat Turbo Trainer

Piper Cherokee Six 6/7-seat cabin monoplane

Piper Aztec E six-seat cabin monoplane

Piper Navajo, company's first corporate/commuter transport

PIPER/*USA*

Formed originally as Taylor Aircraft Company (*q.v.*), reorganised as Piper Aircraft Corporation in 1937 at Lock Haven, Pennsylvania, with W. T. Piper as President. Initial production type was the Cub two-seat high-wing monoplane, of which 10,000 had been completed before the end of 1941. In 1948 Piper took over the Stinson Division of Consolidated Vultee Aircraft Corporation (*q.v.*) and acquired the Stinson Voyager production rights, but production of this type was soon halted. Piper's first twin was the four-seat Apache which entered production in 1954. The later four-seat single-engine Comanche, first flew in 1956. A whole line of light aircraft have followed the original Cub, from the Pacer/Tri-Pacer/Colt series of high-wing monoplanes to their successors, the Cherokee low-wing series, first of which flew in 1960. Piper produced the specialised Pawnee agricultural monoplane in 1959, and variants of this too are still being produced. Series of twins developed from the Apache to Aztec, Twin Comanche, Seneca, Navajo; the PA-38 Tomahawk is the latest in the line of Piper single-engine aircraft.

Piper Tri-Pacer high-wing lightplane

Piper's famous Cub, of which more than 40,000 have been built

PIPPART-NOLL
FLUGZEUGBAU/*Germany*
Based in Mannheim, built several Taube monoplanes in 1914 using steel cables below the wings in place of the normal bracing structure.

PITCAIRN/*USA*
Established in mid-1920s in Philadelphia, Pennsylvania, Pitcairn Aviation Inc. built series of biplanes including PA-5 Mailwing high performance single-seat mailplane used on US Air Mail routes. Turned to autogiro construction with PAA-1 of 1931. Name changed to Pitcairn Autogiro Company in early 1930s. Sold number of PA-18 and -19 autogiros, including a military version of the PA-34 two-seater to the USAAC. Plant and contracts taken over in 1940 by Pitcairn-Larsen Autogiro Company, in turn succeeded very shortly afterwards by Aga Aviation Corporation (*q.v.*).

PITTS AEROBATICS/*USA*
New company formed in 1977 at Afton, Wyoming, to continue sales and engineering of the Pitts aerobatic biplane at the same location by Aerotek Inc., which formerly built the Pitts S-2 for Pitts Aviation Enterprises. Aerotek continues to produce the S-2 for Pitts Aerobatics and the single-seat Pitts S-15 for pilots who do not wish to build their own.

PITTSBURGH METAL AIRPLANE CO./*USA*
Formed in 1929 to take over the San Francisco-based Thaden Metal Aircraft Company which had built the Thaden T-4 four-seat all-metal monoplane, powered by a Wright Whirlwind engine. Company name changed in 1931 to the Metalair Corporation (*q.v.*) when it became a Division of the General Aviation Corporation.

Plage I Laskiewicz-built Hanriot biplane

PLAGE I LASKIEWICZ/*Poland*
Engineering firm which formed an aviation department in 1920. Poland's first aircraft manufacturer, it was based at Lublin and built the Ansaldo Ballila, A-300 and Potez 25 under licence. Subsequently built series of indigenous designs such as the Lublin R-VIII reconnaissance biplane, R-XI five-passenger monoplane. Ceased production following German occupation in 1940.

PLANET AIRCRAFT LTD./*UK*
Built Satellite three-seat light aircraft with V-tail and pusher propeller in 1949. First aeroplane constructed entirely of magnesium sheet, it was powered by a Gipsy Queen engine. Aircraft did not fly and was subsequently broken up, fuselage of the second prototype being used in the Firth helicopter.

PLATT LE PAGE AIRCRAFT CO./*USA*
The Platt Le Page Aircraft Company was formed about 1940 for development and production of rotary-wing aircraft to US Government contract. Various types were under development by 1946, but little was subsequently heard of the company.

POBJOY/*UK*
Founded 1930 as Pobjoy Airmotors Ltd., engine manufacturer. In 1935 became public company and enlarged scope to include aircraft manufacture. Chairman was Oswald Short and managing director Arthur Gouge. Acquired licence to build Short Scion and Scion Senior light transports. Short Bros took over all Pobjoy's issued shares in 1938. Company was subcontractor for aircraft parts in WW2.

PODLASKA WYTWORNIA SAMOLOTOW/*Poland*
Established in 1923; produced own civil and military designs in quantity, and also engaged in licence production. Built wide variety of civil types in early 1930s, mainly for military, but included PWS 24T four-passenger cabin monoplane. Ceased production following German occupation in 1940.

Pitts S-2A aerobatic biplane

PWS 10 single-seat fighter

Polikarpov Po-2 utility biplane, built for more than 25 years

Portsmouth Aerocar Major

POLIKARPOV, N. N./USSR

Designer of fighter aircraft in early 1930s, such as the I-16, first monoplane fighter with enclosed cockpit and retractable landing gear, but most famous design was the 1927 Po-2 biplane, built in thousands.

POLYTEKNIKKOJEN ILMAILUKERHO/Finland

The Flying Club of the Finnish Institute of Technology was founded in 1932 and built a series of gliders; the PIK-20 high performance sailplane is still in production. PIK has also built several low-wing single-engine monoplanes, the PIK-11 in 1953, the PIK-15 glider tug in 1964, and the PIK-19 glider tug and two-seat trainer in 1972.

POMILIO/Italy

Company founded during WW1 which built biplanes powered by Fiat engines.

PONNIER/France

Former Director of the Hanriot factory at Rheims, Ponnier founded his own company around 1912 and built a monoplane which Emile Vedrines flew into second place in the 1913 Coupé Internationale d'Aviation at Rheims, achieving 198 km/h (123 mph).

PORTERFIELD AIRCRAFT CORPORATION/USA

Formed in 1934 by E. E. Porterfield, former President of American Eagle Aircraft Corp-

oration. Built two-seat light cabin monoplane which entered production in 1935. Suspended civil production when America entered WW2.

PORTHOLME AERODROME LTD./UK

Huntingdon company which built aircraft under sub-contract during WW1, including Sopwith Camels and Snipes, and Wight Seaplane Type 840s.

PORTSMOUTH AVIATION LTD./UK

Founded in 1932 as Wight Aviation Ltd. (q.v.) to operate air services to the Isle of Wight. Repaired military aircraft during WW2. Built prototype of Aerocar twin-boom high-wing six-seat aircraft, flown in 1947, but not put into production.

PÖSCHEL AIRCRAFT GmbH/Germany

Small company which built P-300 Equator six-seat STOL amphibian between 1968–1970. Its single Lycoming engine drove a pusher propeller at the end of the fuselage, behind the T-tail. A turboprop version, the P.400 Turbo Equator, crashed during tests in 1977.

POTEZ, HENRY/France

Founded during WW1 as Société d'Etudes Aéronautiques (q.v.) at Aubevillers, and built a two-seat tractor biplane, the Type 4C.2. Post-war the company became known as Henry Potez, and established itself as one of the major French aircraft manufacturers with a long series of civil and military aircraft. In 1937 Potez became part of the nationalised French aircraft industry in the SNCAN group. At that time it was producing the 56 twin-engine light transport, the 63 fighter-bomber and the Potez-CAMS 141 four-engine reconnaissance flying-boat, together with prototypes of the 661 twelve-passenger four-engine monoplane and the Potez-CAMS 160 six-engine flying-boat, a scale model of the proposed Type 161 transatlantic flying-boat. For sixteen years the company was not involved in aviation, but in 1953 produced the Potez 75 single-engine twin-boom ground attack aircraft, which was built by SNCAN. A contract for 500 for the French Army was awarded in 1956 but was cancelled later because of Military cutbacks. Took over Air-Fouga (see Fouga) in 1958, and continued production of that com-

pany's Magister jet trainer. Built two prototype turboprop transports, Potez 840, flying first in 1961. Proposed versions were 841 with PT6A engines and 842 with Astazou Xs, but production did not proceed beyond six aircraft.

Potez 25 two-seat reconnaissance aircraft

Potez 63-II three-seat reconnaissance aircraft

Also built Paris III twin-jet executive aircraft developed by Morane Saulnier. Potez was absorbed by Sud Aviation (q.v.) in 1967, which in turn became part of Aérospatiale (q.v.) in 1970.

PREDAPPIO SA/*Italy*
Division of the Caproni Group (*q.v.*) which produced two trainers in the late 1930s, the Ca.602 two-seat biplane and a single-seat aerobatic version, the Ca.603. Both were powered by Alfa-Romeo in-line engines.

PROCAER/*Italy*
see Progetti

PROGETTI COSTRUZIONI AERONAUTICHE SpA/*Italy*
Based in Milan, Procaer built several aircraft to the design of Stelio Frati, the first being the F15 Picchio, three-seat aerobatic monoplane, which flew in 1959 powered by a Lycoming engine. Cobra 400 two-seat light jet aircraft with Marbore engine was flown in 1960 but not developed. Recent developments have concerned the F15, and the latest F15F version was built for Procaer by General Avia (*q.v.*).

PROVENCE-AVIATION/*France*
The aircraft branch of Chantiers de Provence, a large naval dockyard in the mid-1920s. Produced the C.P.A.1 twin-engine military monoplane with two Lorraine-Dietrich engines.

PRUDDEN-SAN DIEGO AIRPLANE COMPANY/*USA*
Incorporated at San Diego, California, in 1927, to manufacture the TM-1 tri-motor high-wing monoplane seating six passengers and powered by Siemens-Halske engines. Super TM-1 had Ryan-Siemens wing engines and a Wright J-5c in the nose position.

PRVA SRPSKA FABRIKA AEROPLANA/*Yugoslavia*
First aircraft factory in Yugoslavia, established in 1925 for construction of military types under licence. PSFA produced indigenous Rogozarski two-seat reconnaissance biplane in early 1930s, powered by Walter Castor engine. Series of aircraft for Yugoslav Air Force followed, but the Rogozarski factory was destroyed in WW2. In 1946, the remnants of the Rogozarski, Ikarus and Zmaj companies were brought together into the government aircraft factories and resumed production.

PSFA/*Yugoslavia*
see Prva Srpska

PUGET PACIFIC PLANES INC./*USA*
Formed after WW2 at Tacoma, Washington, to build Wheelair IIIA four-seat twin-boom

Procaer Picchio lightplane

Pützer Elster B lightplane

light aircraft, powered by Lycoming engine. Believed not to have entered production.

PÜTZER/*Germany*
Alfons Pützer KG known primarily as sailplane manufacturer; produced an improved motorised version of the Doppelraab sailplane, known as the Elster in 1957. Small batch produced for German club use. Alfons Pützer and Comte Antoine d'Assche, director of the French company Alpavia SA (*q.v.*), formed a new company in 1966, Sportavia-Pützer (*q.v.*), to produce the Fournier series of light aircraft.

P-V ENGINEERING FORUM INC./*USA*
see Piasecki Helicopter Corporation

PWS/*Poland*
see Podlaska Wytwornia Samolotow SA

PZL/*Poland*
see Panstwowe Zaklady Lotnicze

PZL/*Poland*
New title (Light Aircraft Science and Production Centre, PZL-Warsaw) from 1 July 1976 of the former Wytwornia Sprzetu Komunikacyjnego—PZL Okecie (*q.v.*). In 1978 was continuing to build the PZL-104 Wilga and PZL-106A Kruk and was about to commence licence-production of the Socata Rallye 100 ST light aircraft as the PZL-110.

QANTAS/*Australia*
The well-known airline Queensland and Northern Territory Aerial Services Ltd, founded in 1922 to operate airline route Charleville-Cloncurry-Camooweal. Secured manufacturing rights of de Havilland D.H.50 biplane in 1926 and built several.

R

RAAB FLUGZEUGBAU GmbH/*Germany*
Formed in 1959; took over the Italian plant of
Col. Mario de Bernardi with plans to build his
Aeroscooter ultra-light aircraft in Germany.
Raab Flugzeugbau also acquired rights to
licence-produce Ambrosini Rondone four-
seat monoplane.

RAAB FLEUGZEUGBAU GmbH/*Greece*
Formed at Riga in 1934, but moved to Athens
in 1935 as Société Anonyme pour la Fabrication et l'Exploitation des Avions Raab.

**RAAB-KATZENSTEIN
FLUGZEUGWERKE**/*Germany*
Formed in 1925 by Raab & Katzenstein, formerly with Dietrich Flugzeugwerke (*q.v.*).
First product was Schwalbe two-seat training
biplane with Siemens engine. Built several
other light aircraft before company name
changed to Rheinische Luftfahrt Industrie
(Rheinland), continuing manufacture of an improved Schwalbe, the FR-2.

RACA/*Argentina*
  see Representaciones Aero Comerciales
Argentinas SA

RAE/*UK*
  see Royal Aircraft Establishment

RAMOR FLUGZEUGWERKE/*Austria*
Built KE-14 four-seat light cabin monoplane
of own design in early 1930s; powered by de
Havilland Gipsy 1 engine.

RANSOMES, SIMS & JEFFERIES/*UK*
Ipswich company building aircraft under sub-
contract in WW1, including Airco D.H.6s and
RAF F.E.2bs.

**RAWDON BROTHERS AIRCRAFT
INC.**/*USA*
Flying school operator which designed and
built a two-seat monoplane, the T-1, in 1949,
with Lycoming engine.

REARWIN AIRPLANES INC./*USA*
Based at Kansas City, produced Junior two-
seat light monoplane in 1931, followed by
Speedster with American Cirrus engine. Taken
over in 1935 by partnership called Rearwin
Airplanes. In 1937 bought assets of Le Blond
Aircraft Corporation.

REDWING AIRCRAFT LTD./*UK*
Founded 1929 by P. G. Robinson as Robinson
Aircraft Company and produced Redwing
two-seat light biplane with Armstrong Siddeley Genet engine. Works at Croydon, Surrey, was transferred to Colchester, Essex, in
December 1930 and in April 1931 name was
changed to Redwing Aircraft Ltd. In June
1932 Redwing bought Gatwick Aerodrome
and formed a school of flying and aeronautical
engineering, and in 1934 company moved back
to Croydon. A total of 12 Redwings was built,
last being delivered in 1933.

REGENT CARRIAGE CO. LTD./*UK*
London (Fulham) company which built Avro
504Bs under sub-contract during WW1.

REGGIANE SA/*Italy*
Built Caproni aircraft during WW1, but closed
its aircraft department after the war. Resumed
aircraft manufacture in mid-1930s, producing
the Ca.405 Procellaria high-performance
twin-engine bomber in 1937. Re 2000 Falco I
fighter appeared in 1940 with Fiat radial engine, and other versions followed. By 1946 the
company had ceased aircraft manufacture and
was building railway coaches.

Redwing II side-by-side two-seat biplane

Reggiane Re 2000 Falco I single-seat fighter

REGIA/*Romania*
Formed in 1925 as the state-owned Societate Anonima Industria Aeronautica Romania to build aircraft and aero-engines. Aircraft built under licence included the Potez 25, Morane-Saulnier 35, Fleet 10-G, PZL XIC and XXIV single-seat fighters. Indigenous designs included the IAR.15 single-seat fighter monoplane.

REID AIRCRAFT CO./*Canada*
Formed 1928 by W. T. Reid to build biplane of his own design; merged with Curtiss Aeroplane & Motor Company of New York.

REID & SIGRIST LTD./*UK*
Instrument manufacturer which opened an aircraft department in 1939 and built a twin-engined advanced trainer popularly known as the Snargasher, of which a prototype only was built. Sub-contract work during WW2 included production of Boulton-Paul Defiant two-seat fighters and modification of B-25 Mitchells for the RAF. Another trainer prototype, the R.S.3 Desford, was built in 1945.

REIMS AVIATION SA/*France*
Known as Société Nouvelle des Avions Max Holste (*q.v.*) until 1960, when the US Cessna company took over a 49% holding and company was renamed. Reims has licence-manufacturing rights for several Cessna types such as the Model 150, 172, 177, 182 and 337, and in its first 17 years produced nearly 4,200 aircraft. It is also a sub-contractor for Dassault-Breguet (*q.v.*).

REMINGTON-BURNELLI/*USA*
Was producing in 1924 the BR-2 Freighter, an all-metal biplane freighter designed specifically for cargo carrying. Typical of Junkers-inspired design, it combined the Burnelli lifting fuselage with corrugated light alloy skins.

Regia IAR.821 agricultural aircraft

RENARD/*Belgium*
Société Anonyme Avions et Moteurs Renard established 1927 as aero-engine manufacturer; produced the Epervier all-metal single-seat fighter in 1928–1929 with Sabca Jupiter engine designed by Alfred Renard. Constructions Aéronautiques G. Renard founded about 1929 to build commercial aircraft designed by Renard. First two types were R.17-100 four-seat single-engine cabin monoplane and R-30-300 tri-motor five-passenger cabin monoplane. R-31 reconnaissance and R-33 training monoplanes appeared in 1932–1933; advanced low-wing single-seat fighter R-36 with Hispano-Suiza engine exhibited at 1937 Brussels Aero Show. Company was inactive during WW2, but began to reorganise in 1945.

Reims Rocket, a licence-built Cessna 172

REP/*France*
see Esnault-Pelterie, Robert.

REPRESENTACIONES AERO COMERCIALES ARGENTINAS SA/*Argentina*
RACA began assembly of Hughes 500C helicopters in 1975 under licence. A minimum of 120 helicopters are to be built.

REPUBLIC AVIATION CORPORATION/*USA*
Founded as Seversky Aircraft Corporation (*q.v.*) at Long Island, New York, in 1931; name changed to Republic Aviation Corporation in

Republic Seabee four-seat light amphibian

Republic P-47 Thunderbolt, single-seat fighter/fighter-bomber

Republic F-105 Thunderchief supersonic tactical fighter-bomber

Rey 01 experimental monoplane

RFB RF1 six-seat STOL transport

1939. Secured $56.5 million contract for fighter from the USAAC in 1940, largest single fighter order ever placed until then by US Government. Built P-35, P-44 and P-43 Lancers for USAAC plus some EP-1s, based on P-35, for Swedish Government. Lancer design developed further into P-47 Thunderbolt for USAAF, of which 15,329 were built during WW2. Immediate post-war designs included the Seabee single-engine amphibian, the XF-12 high-altitude long-range four-engine photo-reconnaissance aircraft prototype, and the F-84 Thunderjet/Thunderstreak/Thunderflash series of jet fighters. The larger and heavier F-105 Thunderchief followed in 1955, and in 1965 the company became the Republic Aviation Division of Fairchild Hiller Corporation (q.v.).

REX FLUGMASCHINE GmbH/*Germany*
An aircraft works and flying school formed early in WW1 by Dr. Friedrich Hansen for construction of aircraft, chiefly Bristol and Morane monoplanes.

REY, FRANÇOIS/*France*
Built experimental R-1 twin-engine monoplane with variable-incidence wings, first flown

with normal wings in 1949, and with articulated wings in 1951. Original patents taken out in 1938 and an aircraft built in 1940, but was destroyed during the war.

RHEIN-FLUGZEUGBAU GmbH/*Germany*
RFB obtained licence from Rhein-West Flug (q.v.) to build the RW-3 Multoplane in 1957, flying first production aircraft in 1958 and following with a small batch. Built and flew RF1 six-seat STOL transport in 1960; with two Lycoming engines geared to drive single pusher propeller in a wide-chord duct. In 1968, VFW-Fokker (q.v.) acquired 65% of shares in RFB, and in 1969 RFB acquired a percentage holding in Sportavia company (q.v.). Company busy with military contracts for overhaul, and target towing for some years, but has recently built, in collaboration with Grumman-American (q.v.) the Fanliner two-seat light aircraft with Wankel rotary engine, first flown in 1973. It was re-engined in 1976 with a Dowty Rotol ducted propulsor. A second prototype has flown. Based on the Fanliner's promise, the Federal German Government awarded a contract for two AW1-2 Fantrainers with ducted fan engines, and the first flew in 1977. It will be evaluated for the Luftwaffe.

RHEINISCHE LUFTFAHRT INDUSTRIE GmbH/*Germany*
see Raab-Katzenstein

RHEIN-WEST FLUG/*Germany*
RWF formed at Porz-Westhoven, near Cologne, in early 1950s to develop a new light aircraft, the RW-3 Multoplane, basically a powered sailplane with Porsche engine driving a propeller mounted between the fin and rudder, and under the tailplane. The production licence was subsequently transferred to Rhein-Flugzeugbau GmbH (q.v.).

RICCI BROTHERS/*Italy*
Shipbuilding company which began aircraft manufacture in WW1. Post-war, the R.6 single-seat and R.9 two-seat sports-triplanes were built around 1920, plus the large three-engine twin-hull R.I.B. flying-boat. Company closed down in about 1925.

RICHMOND AIRWAYS INC./*USA*
Based at Staten Island, New York, for private hire and pleasure flights. This company built a Sea Hawk five-seat flying-boat in 1928, with Curtiss C-6 engine driving pusher propeller.

RIDDLE AIRLINES INC./*USA*
Operators of a large fleet of Curtiss C-46 twin-engine transports, Riddle produced a modification kit in the mid-1950s which added 64 km/h (40 mph) to cruising speed and 1,000 kg (2,204 lb) to the payload. The improved model was designated C-46R, and Riddle subsequently converted its own fleet of 32 to have Pratt & Whitney engines of 1,566 kW (2,100 hp).

RIESELER, SPORTFLUGZEUGBAU/*Germany*
Established at Berlin/Johannisthal Aero-

RFB AW1-2 Fantrainer with ducted-fan propulsion

Riley turboprop conversion of the Handley-Page Jetstream

RNAS Experimental Eastchurch Kitten, intended as ship-based fighter

Robin (Centre Est) DR 253 Régent lightplane

Robin HR.100/200 Royale four-seat lightplane

drome after WW1, Sportflugzeugbau Rieseler built a single-engine single-seat light sporting parasol monoplane with a two-cylinder Haacke engine which was put into production by Stahlwerk Mark (q.v.) at Breslau. A two-seat version, the R.IV/23, was subsequently developed.

RILEY AIRCRAFT CO./USA
Based at Fort Lauderdale, Texas, company specialised in conversions of existing types to improve performance. In 1953 converted Ryan Navion to twin-engine configuration as the Twin Navion with Lycoming engines, and by 1961 was producing a conversion of the Cessna 310 known as the Riley 65 Rocket. Later aircraft which received Riley conversions included the DH Dove and Heron, the Cessna 340 and 414, and, in 1975, the Handley-Page built Jetstream. Became Riley Turbo Sales Corporation about 1970, and Riley Turbostream Corporation shortly after.

RINGHOFFER-TATRA
AS/Czechoslovakia
Aviation department of the Ringhoffer-Tatra combine was formed in 1935. Built the Bücker Jungmann trainer under licence as the Tatra T.131, the T.1 two-seat cabin monoplane and the T.126 biplane trainer. Production was stopped by WW2.

RNAS EXPERIMENTAL
CONSTRUCTION DEPOT, PORT
VICTORIA/UK
Commissioned early in 1915 on the Isle of Grain as the R.N. Aeroplane Repair Depot and named Port Victoria to distinguish it from the original air station. Experimental Armament Section set up alongside, followed in 1916 by the Seaplane Test Flight. Began construction in 1916 with the P.V.1, a Sopwith Baby fuselage with modified wings and enlarged floats. There followed a series of seaplane prototypes, the Grain Kitten and Eastchurch Kitten landplanes and the final type to be built by the ECD, the Grain Griffin, a converted Sopwith B.1 single-seat bomber. The Depot was subsequently renamed the Marine Experimental Aircraft Depot.

ROBEY & CO. LTD./UK
Engineering company in Lincoln, Lincolnshire, which built Short 184 seaplanes to Admiralty orders in WW1.

ROBIN/France
Formed in 1957 as Centre Est Aéronautique to produce light aircraft; name changed to Avions

Rockwell B-1

Pierre Robin in 1969. Robin founded company in collaboration with Jean Delemontez, the engineer responsible for the Jodel series of light aircraft. First Centre Est type was the DR.100 three-seater and the basic design has constantly been refined through a number of variants. In 1978 the company was producing a whole series of light monoplanes, from the two/four-seat DR.400 with Lycoming engine to the HR.100 six-seater with Teledyne Continental Tiara engine.

ROBINSON HELICOPTER CO. INC./*USA*

Formed in 1973 to design and build a two-seat lightweight helicopter, the R22, which flew in 1975 with Lycoming engine. Production began in mid-1977.

ROCHE AVIATION/*France*

Company formed after WW2, with M. Guerchais as chief engineer—connection with prewar Avions Guerchais not known. Guerchais Roche produced several two-seat light aircraft from about 1946, the Types 35 with Renault engine, the 39 with Mathis radial engine, and the 30 with Ford V-8 engine, as well as the type 107 single-seat glider.

ROCK SEGELFLUGZEUGBAU/*Germany*

Mainly sailplane manufacturer, but built Krähe single-seat powered sailplane in 1957, with 13 kW (18 hp) Zink-Brändl engine.

ROCKET AIRCRAFT CORPORATION/*USA*

Formed in 1946 by take-over of Johnson Aircraft Inc. (*q.v.*) of Fort Worth, Texas. Johnson had designed the Rocket cabin monoplane in 1941, with moulded plastic plywood construction and Lycoming engine. The Rocket 185 received its Approved Type Certificate in April 1946.

ROCKWELL INTERNATIONAL/*USA*

Formed by merger of North American Aviation (*q.v.*) and Rockwell Standard Corporation in 1967. In 1973 North American Rockwell and Rockwell Manufacturing Company merged to become Rockwell International Corporation. Aircraft production since the 1967 merger has included the Aero Commander line of single and twin-engine aircraft, the turboprop OV-10 Bronco armed reconnaissance aircraft, T-2 Buckeye jet trainer, prototypes of the B-1 supersonic swing-wing bomber, and the Sabreliner executive and light jet transport.

ROE, A.V./*UK*

In 1906, A. V. Roe began aircraft design, and on 13 July 1909 was the first Briton to fly an all-British aircraft, namely his Roe I triplane. Two years later, in 1911, the renowned Avro Company was established. First aircraft to enter quantity production was the 504 trainer, built in large numbers and several versions. Then followed a long line of Avro biplanes including the Tutor, Cadet and Avian. In 1928 Avro acquired a licence to build the Fokker F.VIIB/3M as the Avro 618 Ten: it carried eight passengers and two crew, and construction included five for Australian National Airways. Rivalling the success of the 504 was the twin-engined Anson trainer and coastal patrol monoplane, flown as the Avro 652 civil transport for Imperial Airways in 1935. More than 10,000 Ansons were built in Britain and Canada between 1935 and 1952. The twin-engined

Robinson R22 two-seat lightweight helicopter

Avro 504s, one of the most famous trainers to ente

ROE

Avro Anson, the RAF's 'Faithful Annie' trainer/transport

Avro Canada CF-100 Canadian-designed jet fighter

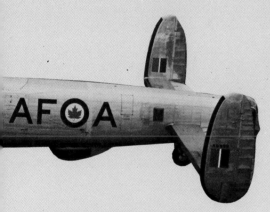
Avro Lancaster, the RAF's most successful heavy bomber of WW2

Manchester bomber of 1939, with the unproven Rolls-Royce Vulture engines, was not a success, but led to the superb four-engined Lancaster, of which 7,374 production examples were built during WW2. The York was a transport derivative using the same wings and tail plus a central fin, but with an entirely new fuselage seating 12 passengers. The Lincoln bomber was built as a replacement for the Lancaster, entering RAF service soon after VJ-day. Avro's post-war Tudor transport was not a success, and the company's last piston-engined aircraft was the Shackleton four-engined maritime reconnaissance aircraft. Following production of four Avro 707 delta research aircraft, the company produced the four-jet delta-wing Vulcan bomber which began to enter RAF service in 1956 and in later marks is still in use. Avro's last design before being restyled the Avro Whitworth Division of Hawker Siddeley Aviation, in 1963, was the Avro 748 twin-turboprop transport first flown in 1960 and remaining in production in 1978 as the British Aerospace HS 748.

ROE, A.V./Canada
In 1945 UK company A. V. Roe acquired Victory Aircraft Ltd. (q.v.) factory at Toronto/Malton Airport, where Lancasters, Lincolns, Ansons and a York were built during WW2. Avro Canada was the name applied to the new company, and it produced the first Canadian-designed jet fighter, the twin-engined CF-100. Prototype flew in 1950 and 639 were built for the RCAF and 53 for the Belgian Air Force. Flew prototype C-102 Jetliner in 1949, but no production order was received. Avro Canada became a member of the Hawker Siddeley Group in 1955, and in 1962 became Hawker Siddeley Canada Ltd. (q.v.). CF-105 Arrow delta twin-jet all-weather fighter prototype flew in 1958. Only five CF-105s were built before the project was cancelled in favour of Bomarc surface-to-air missiles. An interesting project was the Avrocar VTOL aircraft developed under a US Department of Defence contract and flown in 1959 in California. In its prototype form it was circular—in fact a flying saucer!

...vice

Avro Vulcan long-range bomber, world's first large bomber of delta-wing planform

263

ROHR AIRCRAFT CORPORATION/*USA*

Based at Chula Vista, California, was aircraft component sub-contractor in WW2. Built M.O.1 two-seat tail-first (canard) monoplane in 1946. No further aircraft production known.

ROHRBACH METALL FLUGZEUGBAU GmbH/*Germany*

Founded 1922 by Dr. Ing. Rohrbach to continue construction and development of all-metal aircraft designed by him when working previously with the Zeppelin company. Associated company, Rohrbach-Metall-Aeroplane Co. A/S formed in Copenhagen to avoid limitations imposed on construction in Germany. Built ten Ro-II seaplanes for Japanese Navy and Ro-IIIA for Turkey, followed by Rodra twin-engine flying-boat and Rofix single-seat fighter. Copenhagen plant closed in late 1920s when restrictions on German manufacture were lifted. German factory continued flying-boat and landplane construction, including Roland three-engined 10-passenger monoplane. In April 1934 Weser Flugzeugbau GmbH (*q.v.*) took over the company, and Dr. Rohrbach became technical director of Weser.

ROLAND LUFT FAHRZEUG GmbH/*Germany*

Pre-WW1 manufacturer of Parseval airships at Adlershof, subsequently built two-seat fighter and the Roland D.II single-seat fighter biplane during WW1. Production ceased at end of war.

ROLLASON AIRCRAFT AND ENGINES LTD./*UK*

Initially an aircraft sales and service organisation. Began aircraft construction in 1957 with Druine Turbulent single-seat light monoplane powered by a Rollason-converted Ardem motor car engine. In 1961 built two-seat Druine Condor with 56 kW (75 hp) Continental engine. Later versions used more powerful Continental engines. Rollason also rebuilt a number of Tiger Moths and other aircraft, and carried out float conversions of the Tiger Moth and Turbulent.

Rohrbach Rocco 10-passenger commercial flying-boat

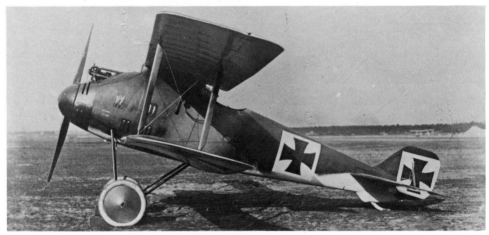

Roland D.II single-seat fighter, built also by Pfalz

ROMANO, E./*France*

Built R-3 seaplane with Hispano-Suiza engine in early 1920s to carry out research on seaplane floats. Subsequently produced series of aircraft from the R-5 all-metal flying-boat to R-16 general purpose tri-motor monoplane. Taken over to form part of the nationalised French aircraft industry in 1937, becoming part of the SNCASE group (*q.v.*).

ROMEO/*Italy*

As Officine Ferroviarie Meridionali in 1925, obtained rights to build Fokker aircraft under licence including the C.V., which was fitted with an Italian-built Jupiter engine and known as the Ro.1. Also built Fiat biplanes. In 1934 Società Anònima Industrie Aeronàutiche Romeo was formed to take over the aeronautical activities of Meridionali (*q.v.*), but within two years there was another change of name to Società Anònima Industrie Meccàniche e Aeronàutiche Meridionali (SAIMAM), and indigenous types of aircraft were produced including the Ro.37 and 45 reconniassance biplanes, the Ro.41 single-seat fighter, and the Ro.43 two-seat fighter seaplane. By 1936 SIAMAM had become part of Breda.

Rollason (Druine) Turbulent ultra-light monoplane

Rollason (Druine) D62 Condor lightplane

RRA J-1 Martin Fierro

RONCHETTI, RAZZETTI AVIACION SA/*Argentina*
Builders of J-1 Martin Fierro single-seat agricultural monoplane with 224 kW (300 hp) Lycoming engine. Prototype first flew in 1975 and a small batch is being produced.

ROOS, VICTOR H. AIRCRAFT CO./*USA*
Succeeded American Eagle-Lincoln Aircraft Corporation (*q.v.*) in mid-1930s, and continued to produce American Eaglet light monoplane with 33·5 kW (45 hp) Szekely engine.

ROOS-BELLANCA AIRPLANE CO./*USA*
Established 1922 at Omaha, Nebraska, to produce aeroplanes designed by Professor G. Bellanca, first being the Bellanca C.F. high-wing monoplane of about 1924, powered by an Anzani engine. Prof. Bellanca left the partnership in 1923 and joined the Wright Aeronautical Corporation (*q.v.*) the following year. Wright built several Bellanca monoplanes, the last of which established a World Endurance record, remaining in the air for more than 51 hours (see also Bellanca).

ROOTES SECURITIES LTD./*UK*
Managed the factory at Speke, Liverpool, established under the British Government's 1936 scheme to create "shadow" factories to augment the productive capacity of the aviation industry. This scheme brought the British motor car industry, which had some experience of quantity production, to aid the aircraft builders. Rootes' factory at Speke built Bristol Blenheim I and IV aircraft, and Beaufighter VIF and X came from their Blythe Bridge, Staffordshire, factory.

ROSE AEROPLANE & MOTOR/*USA*
Founded in Chicago by J. W. Rose in mid-1930s as Rose Airplane Corporation. Produced Parakeet light single-seat biplane with 30 kW (40 hp) Continental engine.

ROSS AIRCRAFT CORPORATION/*USA*
Company established in New York which built RS-1 light monoplane in 1940; war stopped production plans. A new model, the RS-2L two-seater, powered by a Lycoming engine, was built in 1942.

ROTOCRAFT LTD./*UK*
Formed jointly by Mitchell Engineering Group and Servotec Ltd. to develop the Grasshopper twin-engined light helicopter designed by Jacob Shapiro. Powered by two Walter Minor engines, this aircraft was first flown in 1962. A second example was built but the type did not enter production.

ROTOCRAFT SA (PTY.) LTD./*South Africa*
Founded in 1953 to develop the Minicopter single-seat light autogyro, prototype of which was designed and built by Mr. L. L. Strydom and flown in 1962. Several aircraft were built for South African customers.

ROTOR-CRAFT CORPORATION/*USA*
Company engaged in helicopter development immediately after WW2. Built two-seat helicopter for US Army under designation XR-11. Little more heard until the mid-1950s, when the RH-1 Pinwheel "strap-on" personal helicopter appeared in 1954.

ROYAL AIRCRAFT ESTABLISHMENT/*UK*
Known originally as the Royal Aircraft Factory, Farnborough, and was involved in dirigible construction and repair prior to WW1. It was renamed Royal Aircraft Establishment during the war and initiated biplane designs for the Royal Flying Corps, including the B.E.2 and F.E.2 series, F.E.8, R.E.8 and finally the S.E.5 fighter.

ROYAL ARMY AIRCRAFT FACTORY/*Denmark*
Formed in 1914 to undertake aircraft construction and repair work for the Royal Army Flying Corps. Built foreign aircraft under licence before WW2, including the Fokker C.VE reconnaissance biplane, and Gloster Gauntlet and Fokker D.XXI fighters.

ROYAL ARMY AIRCRAFT FACTORY/*Sweden*
Built series of indigenous designs for the Swedish Air Force from the mid-1920s. Early biplane types were the Tumeliten single-seat trainer and J.24B single-seat fighter, followed by S.21H.L reconnaissance biplane.

ROYAL NAVAL DOCKYARD/*Denmark*
Built seaplanes and flying-boats for the Danish Navy from 1914, comprising both original designs and licence-built types such as Hawker Danecock (Dankok).

RUFFY, ARNELL & BAUMANN AVIATION/*UK*
Italian Felix Ruffy and Swiss Edouard Baumann founded flying school at Hendon in 1915 and built subsequently several training aircraft of their own design. Company became part of the Alliance Aeroplane Company Ltd. (*q.v.*) when the latter expanded in 1918.

RUMPLER GmbH/*Germany*
Founded prior to WW1 as E. Rumpler Luftfahrzeugbau, with the company's works and flying school based at Berlin/Johannisthal aerodrome, and with a military flying school at Monchelberg. Began production with licence construction of Etrich Taube monoplane, but

Royal Aircraft Factory S.E.5a

Rumpler Taube 'Airliner'

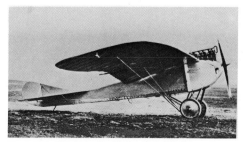
Rumpler (Etrich) Taube monoplane

Rumpler C.I reconnaissance aircraft

Russo-Baltic *Il'ya Muromets*

subsequently became famous for a series of armed biplane reconnaissance aircraft in WW1, including the C.I, C.IV and C.VII. Went into liquidation about 1919 due to lack of work.

RUSSO-BALTIC WAGGON WORKS/*Russia*
This large Russian engineering company, based at St. Petersburg, was only partly concerned with aircraft production. It was respon-

sible, however, for the construction of the *Il'ya Muromets* series of four-engined bombers, designed by Igor Sikorsky, which equipped Russia's Eskadra Vozduchnykh Korablei (Squadron of Flying Ships) in WW1. Largest of the series was the Type IM-Ye2, with a wing span of 34·50 m (113 ft 2¼ in), and gross weight of 7,000 kg (15,432 lb). The Sikorsky S-16 reconnaissance biplane was also built.

RUSTON PROCTOR & COMPANY/*UK*
Engineering company based at Lincoln, Lincolnshire, which constructed RAF B.E.2s, Sopwith Camels and Snipes under subcontract during WW1.

RYAN/*USA*
Founded 1928 at St. Louis, Missouri, as Mahoney-Ryan Aircraft Corporation (*q.v.*), deriving from Ryan Airlines, which began operations on US West Coast in 1922, and in 1926 began manufacture of Ryan M-1 mailplane from which Charles Lindbergh's transatlantic Ryan NYP *Spirit of St. Louis* was developed in 1928. Commercial version of the latter was Ryan Brougham, which was built in quantity. Ryan merged with Detroit Aircraft Corporation (*q.v.*) in 1929, but DAC did not

survive the slump in 1930–1931. T. Claude Ryan formed Ryan Aeronautical Company in 1933–1934, and produced the S-T training monoplane, forerunner of a series of successful Ryan trainers. The YO-51 Dragonfly of 1940 was observation monoplane built for the USAAC. A new fighter for the US Navy in 1943 reflected a 'braces and belt' outlook on the new gas turbine engine, resulting in a mixed power plant comprising a conventional piston engine and rear fuselage jet. Known as the FR-1 Fireball, it was too late to see operational

services in WW2. Acquired design and manufacturing rights of Navion four-seat all-metal monoplane from North American Aviation (*q.v.*) in 1947 and put it into quantity production. Ryan developed to a mid-1950s USAF contract the X-13 Vertijet, a delta-wing vertical take-off jet with Rolls-Royce Avon engine. A flex-wing research aircraft was built in 1961, and the XV-5A lift-fan research aircraft followed in 1964. Development of the 'fan-in-wing' VTOL principle has continued with two prototype aircraft, later restyled XV-5B.

Ryan PT-22 two-seat primary trainers

Ryan X-13 Vertijet tail-sitting fighter

S

SAAB/*Sweden*

Svenska Aeroplane AB founded at Trollhätan 1937 to develop and build military aircraft. In 1939 amalgamated with Aircraft Division of Svenska Järnvägsverkstäderna (*q.v.*) and moved main establishment to Linköping. From 1950 acquired other important facilities, including underground factory at Linköping. Name changed to Saab Aktiebolag May 1965; Malmö Flygindustri (*q.v.*) became a subsidiary in 1967; in 1968 merged with Scania-Vabis group, and is now called Saab-Scania. First aeroplanes were licence-built Junkers Ju 86K twin-engined bombers, Northrop-Douglas dive-bombers and North American trainers. First own-design production aircraft was SAAB-17 dive-bomber of 1940, used widely and of which 60 delivered to Ethiopia from 1947. SAAB-18 was twin-engined bomber, of 1942, some late examples of which had ejection seats. SAAB-21A of 1943 was piston-engined single-seat fighter; and the 21-R was jet development of the same aircraft; SAAB-29 was the so-called 'flying barrel' swept-wing jet fighter, in production until 1956; SAAB-32 Lansen of 1952 was fighter/attack two-seater. SAAB-35 Draken 'double Delta' fighter appeared in 1955; SAAB-105 was twin-jet light two-seater multi-purpose aircraft of 1963; SAAB-37 Viggen of 1967 with foreplane, delta wing and STOL capability remains a very potent weapon system. Civil types include SAAB-90 Scandia twin-engined 32-passenger transport; SAAB-91 Safir all-metal 3/4-seater, series-built from 1945. Latest aircraft are high-wing Safari, first flown in 1969, and military Supporter development.

SAAC/*Switzerland*

see Swiss-American Aviation Corporation

SÄÄSKI, OSAKEYHTIÖ/*Finland*

Founded 1928. Built two-seat biplane for wheels, skis or floats which was convertible for ambulance work and was developed into cabin type.

SABCA/*Belgium*

see Société Anonyme Belge de Constructions Aéronautiques

SABLATNIG FLUGZEUGBAU GmbH/*Germany*

Austrian Josef Sablatnig experimented and flew before WW1. Moved to Germany and in 1913 became a director of Union Flugzeugwerke GmbH (*q.v.*) where he did technical work and flying. When Union company went into liquidation (1915) founded above-named company in Berlin, famous for seaplanes used by German Navy, but built other types also. SF1 floatplane (1915) developed into very successful SF2 (licence-built by LFG and LVG; *q.v.*); SF4 was single-seat fighter floatplane, built both as biplane and triplane; SF5 was widely used SF2 replacement; SF8 was last Sablatnig floatplane built in numbers (trainer of 1918). Landplanes included trainers, single-engined night bombers and a monoplane. N1 was two-seat land fighter used at Kiel. After war developed civil types, including P1 four-passenger biplane, and P3 six-passenger high-wing monoplane. One light sports type built, but aircraft work ceased 1921.

SAFA/*France*

see Société Anonyme Française Aéronautique

SAGE, FREDERICK & COMPANY LTD./*UK*

Company engaged originally in fine wood-

SAAB-37 Viggen single-seat combat aircraft

SAAB-35 Draken all-weather fighter

SAAB Supporter light support aircraft

Die neueste Sablatnig-Luftdroschke.
Ein Eindecker von 200 P.S. mit geschlossener Passagier-Kabine.

Sablatnig Luftdroschke monoplane

work. In early 1915 was asked by Admiralty to build aircraft, and was first concerned with airships. In June 1915 received order for Short 184 floatplanes, and carried out modifications to, and built, Avro 504K trainers. Built own-design Sage Type II, two-seat biplane fighter, with enclosed crew and gunnery arrangements (flown 1916); Type III was trainer for Admiralty (flew 1917); Types 4a, b and c were patrol and trainer floatplanes which did not enter production.

SAIMAN/*Italy*
   see Società Anònima Industrie Meccàniche Aeronàutiche Navali.

ST. LOUIS AIRCRAFT CORPORATION/*USA*
Formed at St. Louis, Missouri, as a subsidiary (later a division) of the St. Louis Car Company. At 1929 Detroit Aircraft Show exhibited the Cardinal high-wing monoplane, the company's first aeroplane. Cardinal Senior which followed had more power. In mid/late 1930s made components but in 1940 delivered small batch of PT-15 biplane trainers to US Army. During WW2 made Fairchild PT-23 under sub-contract.

SALMSON/*France*
Founded 1912 at Billancourt, Seine, by Emile Salmson (1859–1917) to develop radial type water-cooled engines jointly designed by Canton and Unné as installed in French, British and Russian aircraft. In late 1915 turned to aeroplane construction. First was unorthodox Salmson-Moineau SM-1 of 1916, designed by René Moineau, with 'buried' power plant and twin tractor propellers. The Type 2 conventional two-seat reconnaissance tractor biplane was tested early 1917, with Salmson (Canton-Unné) engine. As the 2A2 it served with French and US squadrons and 2,300 were built. At Armistice 2A2 converted to Limousine, used by several European airlines. In mid-1930s turned to light aircraft, producing D6 Cricri parasol monoplane with small Salmson air-cooled radial engine (*see* Société Française d'Aviation Nouvelle).

SAN/*France*
   see Société Aéronautique Normande

SANDERSON, ANGUS & COMPANY/*UK*
Engineering company of Newcastle-upon-Tyne, Northumberland, which built aircraft under sub-contract during WW1, including Armstrong Whitworth F.K.8, Armstrong Whitworth Quadruplanes and Bristol Fighters.

SARGENT-FLETCHER COMPANY/*USA*
   see Fletcher Aviation Company

SASEBO NAVAL AIR ARSENAL/*Japan*
During WW2 built in quantity the Mitsubishi-designed F1M2 shipboard spotter/reconnaissance central-float seaplane—last operational biplane to serve with Japanese Navy.

SASO/*France*
   see Société Aéronautique du Sud-Ouest

SAUNDERS AIRCRAFT CORPORATION LTD./*Canada*
Formed 1968 to design and manufacture ST-27 conversion of British de Havilland Heron light transport. Major changes included turboprop power. Was working on successor (ST-28) when financial support ended 1976.

SAUNDERS, S.E. LTD./*UK*
Based at Cowes, Isle of Wight. Originally built boats, and later, hulls for fast motor boats and some of earliest flying-boats (e.g. Sopwith Bat Boat). Especially famous for 'Consuta' copper-sewn plywood construction. In 1913

Saunders-Roe Princess flying-boat

received order for B.E. biplanes. During WW1 built under sub-contract Avro 504 landplanes, Short 184 floatplanes and Norman Thompson and Felixstowe F.2A and F.5 flying-boats. Began own design, first of which was T.1 two-seater (1917) with detachable wings for shipboard stowage. Aircraft built post-war included the Kittiwake seven-passenger twin-engined wooden amphibian of' 1920 with camber-changing gear at both leading and trailing edges; Medina ten-passenger twin-engined wooden flying-boat of 1926; and Valkyrie three-engined military flying-boat of 1927 with developed form of Linton-Hope hull.

SAUNDERS-ROE LTD./*UK*
In 1928 pioneer pilot/constructor A. V. Roe (later Sir) acquired an interest in S.E. Saunders Ltd. (*q.v.*) and firm was reconstructed as above. First new product was Cutty Sark flying-boat, with Fokker-type wing, built in small numbers; also larger Cloud (1931) of which RAF had 16. Most successful product was twin-engined London biplane flying-boat of 1934 which served with RAF until 1941. Shrimp two-seat four-engined aircraft was built to serve as research vehicle for larger types. Company built the Supermarine Walrus and Sea Otter in quantity. SR/A1 of 1947 was world's first jet-propelled flying-boat fighter, but this was not ordered into service. Princess ten-turboprop commercial flying-boat of 1952

Saro Skeeter light helicopter

Salmson 2A2 two-seat reconnaissance biplane

Saunders ST-27, a de Havilland Heron conversion

Savary pre-WW1 biplane

Scheutzow Model B helicopter

Schweizer-built Grumman Ag-Cat

was a great technical achievment, but never entered service. SR.53, first flown in 1957, was experimental turbojet/rocket interceptor which demonstrated climb of about 15,240 m (50,000 ft)/min. Promising SR.177 development was abandoned despite international interest. Company entered helicopter field in early 1950s with small Skeeter (originally Cierva) though in 1928 S.E. Saunders had made Isaaco Helicogyre (which never flew) for the Air Ministry. Five-seat P.531 built 1958, but in 1959 company was acquired by Westland Aircraft (*q.v.*), which developed the P.531 as the Wasp/Scout.

SAVAGES LTD./*UK*
An old-established engineering and woodworking company of Kings Lynn, Norfolk, which built under sub-contract during WW1 Airco 1/1A; D.H.6. and Avro 504K aircraft.

SAVARY/*France*
Founded at Chartres by Robert Savary. Was building biplanes in 1910. Won order for three aircraft after military trials in 1911. In February 1913 Joseph Frantz established time-to-height record on Savary biplane with Salmson engine, carrying five passengers, but pre-war output was ten machines only. In 1915 Robert Savary was associated with Henri de la Fresnaye in forming a joint company to build Nieuport fighters. No aircraft built after WW1.

SCAN/*France*
see Société de Constructions Aéro Navales de Port-Neuf

SCENIC AIR LINES/*USA*
In early 1977 acquired from American Jet Industries (*q.v.*) engineering and manufacturing rights for turboprop conversions of Cessna Models 402 and 414, now known as Turbo Star 402 and Turbo Star Pressurised 414.

SCHEIBE-FLUGZEUGBAU
GmbH/*Germany*
Formed at Dachau, near Munich, in 1951 by Egon Scheibe, who at first built gliders designed by Scheibe in Austria. His Sperling two-seat light high-wing monoplane first flew August 1955, and was developed with new wing and tail as SF-23A and built in numbers until 1963. SF-24A Motorspatz built from 1959. SF-25 Motorfalke licence-built from 1970 by Slingsby Sailplanes Ltd. (*q.v.*) in UK as Type 61 Falke.

SCHELLER, BERNHARD/*Germany*
In early 1930s built cantilever low-wing two-seat monoplane with continuous head-fairing. Steel-tube construction.

SCHEMPP-HIRTH OHG/*Germany*
In 1935 at Göppingen, near Stuttgart, Wolf Hirth (*q.v.*) founded company named Sportflugzeugbau Schempp-Hirth to build sailplanes. In 1960s company named as above built the Milan G56 light tourer, also French Piel Emeraude under licence. During early 1960s production of powered aircraft ceased, licence rights for Emeraude being transferred to Binder Aviatik AG (*q.v.*).

SCHEUTZOW HELICOPTER
CORPORATION/*USA*
Formed early 1960s by Webb Scheutzow to build light helicopter with special rotor-head (blades carried on rubber bushings). Bee side-by-side two-seater flew 1966. Flight Certification programme resumed 1975.

SCHRECK, HYDRAVIONS FBA/*France*
Louis Schreck, South American representative for Delaunay-Belleville automobiles, returned to France in 1909. Joined Hanriot at Juvissey and in 1911, jointly with engineer named Gaudard, designed D'Artois flying-boat.

Formed Hydravions Schreck FBA, and aided by British capital acquired Donnet-Lévêque/Denhaut flying-boat patents, and was associated with that company until it was acquired by Bernard (*q.v.*) in 1934. FBA 16 was side-by-side two-seat flying-boat; FBA 17 a utility type which established a seaplane height record in December 1923. A development was brought by US Coast Guard in 1931. In the later 1930s Schreck was carrying out flying-boat repairs and sub-contract work.

SCHÜTTE-LANZ,
LUFTFAHRZEUGBAU/*Germany*
In 1909 the well-known company Luftschifflan Schütte-Lanz was established to build airships. This company's Luftfahrzeugbau was founded in 1915 at Zeesen, near Königswusterhausen, Brandenburg, in recognition of the fact that airships must be supplemented by aeroplanes. The C-1 of 1915 had an unconventional engine-installation; D-III built in 1916 was a single-seat fighter. Company built the Ago-Flugzeugwerke (*q.v.*) two-seat C-IV in quantity. Had studied 'giant' aircraft and was included in 1916 R-plane 'giant' programme. Contract awarded for six Staaken bombers. R.27-29 delivered late 1917 and became operational; three other Staaken machines (R.84-86) unfinished at Armistice. Company also made special equipment (e.g. bomb gear and engine-room telegraphs) for other builders of giants, but own ambitious twin-boom project of 1917 remained unrealised. After aircraft work ended company remained as plywood manufacturer.

SCHWEIZER AIRCRAFT
CORPORATION/*USA*
Primarily designers and makers of sailplanes, one of which (SGS 2-32) fitted with piston-engine was tested by Lockheed Aircraft Corporation (*q.v.*) as Q-Star for 'quiet reconnaissance' in Vietnam. On Q-Star was based the Lockheed YO-3A, using Schweizer wings and

Scheibe Motorfalke powered glider

tail, new fuselage and muffled engine. Company also builds for Grumman Aerospace Corporation (q.v.) the Ag-Cat agricultural biplane. In 1972 acquired rights for Teal light amphibian but in 1976 sold them to Teal Aircraft Corporation (q.v.). Makes fuselage assemblies for Piper Aircraft Corporation and structures for Bell Helicopters (both q.v.).

SCHWEIZERISCHE
FLUGZEUGFABRIK/Germany
see Flugzeugbau A. Comte

SCIM/France
see Société Générale des Constructions Industrielles et Mécaniques

SCINTEX-AVIATION SA/France
A division of Scintex SA, a mechanical and electrical equipment manufacturer, held an exclusive licence to build improved versions of the Piel Emeraude. Built the CP301C, also in C1, C2 and C3 versions; the two-seat Super Emeraude with fixed landing gear as the CP1310/CP1315; and the 4/5-seat ML 250 Rubis, with retractable landing gear, which first flew on June 1962.

SCOTTISH AVIATION LTD./UK
Formed 1935, but for several years was concerned mainly with aircraft repair work and management of flying school and airport (Prestwick, Scotland). First aircraft produced was Prestwick Pioneer single-engined five-seat STOL monoplane, first flown 1950. Twin Pioneer of 1957 first appeared as 16-passenger civil type, but was used also by RAF. Company re-engaged in important repair, maintenance and modification work, involving Lockheed aircraft, and made freighter conversion of Vickers Viscount. Has made large components for Lockheed Hercules over long period. Current aircraft are Bulldog (flown originally in 1968 as military trainer version of Beagle Pup); Bullfinch with retractable landing gear, first flown August 1976; and twin-turboprop Jetstream, developed 1966–1970 by Handley Page (q.v.). As a British Aerospace company offers support facilities for Beagle Pup, B.206 and Basset.

SEA/France
see Société d'Etudes Aéronautiques

SEAPLANE EXPERIMENTAL
STATION/UK
Located at Felixstowe, Suffolk, its products being identified by initial F. Particularly as-

Scottish Aviation Bulldog military trainer

sociated with J. C. Porte who, as a Squadron Commander in the RNAS, assumed command of the Felixstowe station in September 1915. Porte had started aeronautical work in 1909; his interest in flying-boats led him to join Curtiss, in USA, during 1914. Before taking command at Felixstowe had flown Curtiss flying-boats on operations, and set out to improve them. Felixstowe F.1 had wings and tail of Curtiss H.4 but Porte hull. F.2 was comparable development of H.12, and further improved as F.2A and used extensively from late 1917. Porte Baby was early 3-engined type, from one of which a Bristol Scout was air-launched in May 1916. F.3 was larger than F.2A, but though built in quantity was less highly regarded. Some were built in Malta Dockyard, others by British contractors. Some completed as further developed F.5, a type also used by US Navy and Japan. Felixstowe Fury was very large 5-engined type, flown (and wrecked) after Armistice.

SECAN/France
see Société d'Études et de Constructions Aéro-Navales

SECAT/France
see Société d'Études et de Construction d'Avions de Tourisme

SECM/France
see Société d'Emboutissage et de Constructions Mécaniques

Scottish Aviation Twin Pioneer STOL monoplane

SECURITY AIRCRAFT
CORPORATION/USA
As Security National Aircraft Corporation was established by W. B. Kinner, founder of Kinner Airplane & Motor Corporation (q.v.). Type SI-A was almost identical to Kinner Sportster. Taken over February 1937 by company named as above. New factory then built at Long Beach, California, to make Airster 2-seat monoplane and Security 5-cylinder radial.

SEEMS/France
see Société d'Exploitation des Etablissements Morane-Saulnier

SEGUIN AVIATION/USA
Company established in mid-1960s to produce a conversion of the Piper (q.v.) twin-engined Apache. Known as the Seguin/Piper Geronimo, it had more powerful engines, and many refinements to the original structure and equipment.

SEIBEL HELICOPTER COMPANY/USA
Established early 1948. Seibel had worked with Bell Helicopters, but joined the Boeing company (both q.v.) in 1946. With two collaborators built in 1947 S-3 light helicopter (lateral and longitudinal control effected by changing centre of gravity). S-4A of 1948 had special blade-attachment system patented for S-3. Followed by S-4B with more powerful engine and side-by-side seats. In March 1952 company taken over by Cessna (q.v.).

Seversky P-35 single-seat fighter

SEPECAT/*France*
see Société Européenne de Production de L'Avion d'Ecole de Combat d'Appui Tactique

SERV-AERO ENGINEERING INC./*USA*
At Municipal Airport, Salina, California, is converting to turbine power standard types of agricultural aircraft powered formerly by Pratt & Whitney radial piston-engines. In early 1977 was engaged in certification programme for Rockwell Thrush Commander. Other conversions, including those of Grumman Ag-Cat biplanes, have involved fitting the British Alvis Leonides engine.

SERVICE AVIATION COMPANY/*USA*
Was based at Wabash, Indiana, trading as Sattco. In summer of 1922 built Liberty-engined transport largely from D.H.4 parts. Pilot sat behind cabin in ply-covered fuselage.

SERVICIOS AEREAS DE AMERICA
SA/*Mexico*
In 1960s serviced and repaired aircraft and engines, but undertook licence-manufacture of higher-powered Maule M-4, developed specially for Mexican conditions and called Cuauhtemoc M-1.

SET/*Romania*
Established at Bucharest 1923. SET X was single-seat fighter/trainer biplane; SET XV single-seat fighter-biplane with enclosed cockpit, built in small numbers for Romanian Air Force during early 1930s; SET 7 was a specially equipped trainer; SET 7K a re-engined observation derivative ordered in series by Romanian Government. Later SET 31 also adopted officially.

SEVERSKY AIRCRAFT
CORPORATION/*USA*
Incorporated February 1931 by Russian-born Alexander P. Seversky (or De Seversky), WW1 military pilot who became US citizen 1927. A test pilot and consulting engineer, he established the Seversky Aero Corporation in 1922. Developed novel amphibious landing gear, promoted by Seversky Aircraft Corporation for fast all-metal fighter-type aircraft. Aircraft design owed much to Alexander Kartveli, who developed landplane fighters with retractable landing gear. In 1935 Seversky established new speed record for amphibious aircraft, and land-fighter development culminated in order for 77 single-seaters for USAAC, designated P-35. In 1939–1940, following orders for amphibians from USSR and landplanes from Japan, Sweden contracted for 120 export versions of P-35. Several fighter, multi-purpose and trainer variants developed, and BT-8 (first purpose-built machine of its class) adopted in USA. Seversky Executive (2 passengers in cabin behind pilot) won 1937 Bendix Trophy race. In 1939 company offered USAAC XP-41 single-seat fighter, but in October 1939 company was reorganised as Republic Aviation Corporation (*q.v.*). Special supercharger evolution for late Seversky fighters led to the famous Republic P-47 Thunderbolt long-range escort fighter/bomber.

SFAN/*France*
see Société Française d'Aviation Nouvelle

SFCA/*France*
see Société Française de Constructions Aéronautiques

SGP/*Austria*
see Simmering-Graz-Pauker AG

SHCHERBAKOV, A. Y./*USSR*
Leader of a design group which developed the twin-engined high-wing monoplane Shch-2 light transport, used for such duties as liaison, transport and supply of partisan forces late in WW2. After war adopted by Aeroflot. Robust structure, with fixed landing gear, and large double freight doors, to make the Shch-2 adaptable for a wide variety of transport duties.

SHCHETININ/*USSR*
In 1909 the first Russian aeronautical company, named Pervoe Rossikoe Tovarishchestvo Vozdukhoplana Vaniya S.S. Shchetinin after its principal founder, was established in St. Petersburg. A collaborator in the enterprise was another pioneer, the designer Y. M. Hakkel, and about 1912–1913 the company was joined by the later-renowned D. P. Grigorovich. First built Farman and Bleriot-type aircraft, but after Grigorovich joined, began to specialise in marine aircraft. First was the M-1 flying-boat of 1913, generally of Donnet-Lévêque type. M-5 of 1915 was a trainer and reconnaissance type built for the Imperial Navy. About 500 examples of the larger and higher-powered M-9 of 1915–1916 were built. Later construction included the M-11 single-seat fighter flying-boat; and the larger M-15 and M-20 reconnaissance aircraft.

SHIN MEIWA INDUSTRY COMPANY
LTD./*Japan*
Title of the Kawanishi company after re-establishment in 1949 as overhaul centre for Japanese and US aircraft. Also made components for other constructors, developed re-engined de Havilland Heron, but after contract in January 1966 directed attention especially to new marine aircraft. Rebuilt a Grumman Albatross as a dynamically similar flying model for projected STOL ASW flying-boat for Japanese Maritime Self Defence Force. This type developed as four-turboprop PS-1, but later also as US-1 amphibious search-and-rescue aircraft. PS-1 flew October 1967; US-1 (from land and water) late 1974. First pro-

Seversky BT-8 basic trainer

Shchetinin M-5 flying-boat trainer

Shin Meiwa search-and-rescue aircraft

Short Stirling, the RAF's first four-engined bomber

Short Belfast long-range strategic freighter

totype PS-1 converted later as water-bombing test vehicle. Basic type remarkable for low take-off and landing speeds, achieved by boundary-layer control system and large flaps for slipstream deflection. Company also carries out major sub-contract work for advanced Mitsubishi and Kawasaki aircraft (both *q.v.*).

SHINN ENGINEERING INC./*USA*
During early 1960s produced, as Shinn Model 2150-A, about 50 Morrisey (*q.v.*) 2150 utility two-seat lightplanes.

SHIN NIHON KOKU SEIBI KABUSHIKI KAISHA/*Japan*
Established December 1952 as Itoh Chu Koku Seibi Kabushiki Kaisha to maintain and repair light aircraft. In 1960 produced the N-58 Cyg-

net light cabin monoplane designed by students at Nihon University. Aided in development of, and produced, N-62 Eaglet four-seater also designed at Nihon University. Late in 1968 converted a number of North American T-6 Texan trainers to represent Nakajima B5N torpedo-bombers for film *Tora! Tora! Tora!* Adopted above company name on 29 May 1970, since when has concentrated on manufacture of aircraft equipment.

SHORT & HARLAND LTD./*UK*
In June 1936 Short Bros. Ltd. (see following entry) collaborated with shipbuilders Harland & Wolff to form above-named company. In WW2 built and had built under sub-contract Short Stirling four-engined bombers and Sunderland flying-boats; also Handley Page Herefords. In 1947 Short & Harland acquired

Short Brothers (Rochester & Bedford) Ltd, and altered name to Short Brothers and Harland Ltd, concentrating activities at Belfast, Northern Ireland. Sealand twin-engined amphibian flying-boat of 1948 was produced in small numbers. Sandringham and Solent flying-boats used by BOAC stemmed from the Sunderland. Of great technical significance was the SC.1 VTOL (jet-lift) research programme, which followed exploratory research by Rolls-Royce. First free vertical take-off made 25 October 1958. Company became heavily involved in production of English Electric Canberra and Bristol Britannia. From 1963 built Belfast heavy transports (four turboprops) and many Skyvan light piston-engined transports. Much important manufacture and modification work carried out for leading international constructors and operators under sub-contract.

SHORT BROS. LTD/*UK*
Founded by brothers Horace, Eustace and Oswald Short in 1909, though Eustace and Oswald had made balloons since 1898. At Leysdown, Isle of Sheppey, completed first biplane, construction of which had begun at Battersea, London, in 1909. Received order for six Wright biplanes in one of which Hon. C. S. Rolls made first double crossing of English Channel. Company pioneered in multi-engine and multi-propeller types and in tractor biplanes with folding wings for Naval use. Did more to aid development of early Naval flying

than any other British firm. New works at Rochester, Kent, started 1914. Most famous type was 184 torpedo-bomber, which was used at Battle of Jutland and was also the first to sink a ship at sea. During WW1 established airship works at Cardington, Bedfordshire. After WW1 developed Cromarty flying-boat but diversified in other fields. Gave special attention to all-metal aircraft (Silver Streak of 1920 and derivatives) and concentrated later on large civil and military flying-boats (Singapore biplane series for RAF from 1926; Calcutta and Kent for Imperial Airways). Six-engined

Sarafand of 1936 was then largest British flying-boat. Wing form developed for Scion and Scion Senior monoplanes used for famous fleet of Empire flying-boats in 1936, for equally-famous Sunderland military development; also on Short-Mayo composite aircraft and Stirling four-engined monoplane bomber. British Government now owns, directly or indirectly, 98 per cent of issued shareholding. Current aircraft are Skyvan developments and SD3-30 thirty-passenger turboprop type which first flew August 1974. Name Short Brothers Ltd. re-adopted June 1977.

Short G-Class long-range flying-boat

Short Skyvan light utility transport

SIAI-Marchetti SF.260W light strike aircraft

SHOWA HIKOKI KOGYO KABUSHIKI KAISHA/*Japan*

Before and during WW2 built the Douglas DC-3 under licence. After war was first Japanese aircraft manufacturing company to resume operations, under US Government contracts. Aided in manufacture of NAMC YS-11 Japanese-designed transport.

SIAI/*Italy*

see Società Idrovolanti Alta Italia

SIAI-MARCHETTI SOCIETÀ PER AZIONI/*Italy*

The former Savoia-Marchetti company (*see* Società Idrovolanti Alta Italia), the history of which it shares. Since 1946 has engaged in overhaul and repair work and developed new aircraft. Types have included SA.202 Bravo trainer produced jointly with FFA (*q.v.*) in Switzerland: S.205 four-seater and S.208 development. Initials in SF.260 denoted design by Stelio Frati, now offered in many variants. In 1968 company formed a Vertical Flight Division but increasing helicopter work is now in association with Agusta and Elicotteri Meridionale. SM.1019 light multi-purpose high-wing monoplane is currently in production. Other work in early 1978 includes overhaul of large aircraft serving with the Italian Air Force and involvement in national and multi-national aircraft programmes.

SIAT/*Germany*

see Siebelwerke-ATG GmbH

SIDDELEY-DEASY MOTOR CAR COMPANY LTD./*UK*

Based at Coventry, Warwickshire; was concerned in production of following aircraft during WW1: RAF R.E.7 and R.E.8; and Airco D.H.10. Own experimental types included R.T.1 of 1917–1918; a redesigned R.E.8; S.R.2 Siskin, developed from ideas of Maj. F. M. Green and precursor of famous Armstrong Whitworth line of fighters; and Sinaia twin-engined bomber, completed 1921, also associated with Armstrong Whitworth. In 1919 Armstrong Whitworth and Siddeley-Deasy combined to form in 1920 Sir W. G. Armstrong Whitworth Aircraft Ltd. (*q.v.*).

SIEBELWERKE-ATG GmbH/*Germany*

Name was that of F. W. Siebel (1891–1954) associated with early sport-flying in Germany and who helped form the Klemm company (*q.v.*) for which he took charge of new works at Halle (Saale). In 1937 Siebel established own company as Flugzeugwerke Halle GmbH (*q.v.*) later renamed as above. First aircraft was Fh 104 5-passenger monoplane of 1937. Si 201 was experimental military reconnaissance aircraft; Si 202 Hummel of 1938, a side by side 2-seater. In WW2 Siebel contributed to production of standard German military types;

also built own Si 204 communications aircraft, though this was mainly built by SNCAC (*q.v.*) in France. After war produced Si 222 Super-Hummel, and 3-seat Si 308. As member of Nordflug group helped with Noratlas.

SIEMENS-SCHUCKERT WERKE GmbH/*Germany*

Began airship construction in 1907. In 1909 manufactured aeroplanes, but poor results stopped work in 1911. Aeroplane department reopened 1914. In October started design of four-engined aircraft similar to that of Sikorsky in Russia. As entirely new venture company sponsored designs by two Steffen brothers leading to Giants R.I–VII of 1915–1917. R.VIII, which did not fly, was then world's largest aeroplane with span of 48·16 m (158 ft), and had experimental rotating gun-turret. Other advanced projects included steam-turbine monoplane and wire-guided flying bombs. Company also made E-I monoplane single-seat fighter and D-I copy of Nieuport. D-III and D-IV also built in quantity. Fighters were technically very advanced.

SIEMETZKI, ALFONS/*Germany*

Known also as Asro, and from Asro T–3 prototype single-seat turbine-powered helicopter (first flown December 1961) Siemetzki developed Asro 4 turbine-powered two-seater, ground tests of which began May 1964.

SIAI-Marchetti SM.1019 two-seat STOL lightplane

SIAT Flamingo two/four-seat light aircraft

Sikorsky S-58 in US Navy service

Sikorsky S-64 flying-crane helicopter

SIKORSKY AIRCRAFT DIVISION OF UAC/*USA*

Igor Sikorsky (1889–1972) founded company as Sikorsky Aero Engineering Corporation 5 March 1923. As young Russian built first helicopter in 1909, but no flight achieved. In 1912 was appointed to technical post with Russo-Baltic Waggon Works. Pioneered very large four-engined aircraft and continued development during WW1. After forming US company built large twin-engined S-29-A. Numerous experimental and production aeroplanes in late 1920s and 1930s, and in 1929 company became a division of United Aircraft Corporation (United Technologies). Name Sikorsky truly re-established by flying-boats and amphibians. S-38 twin-engined amphibian preceded S-40 four-engined flying-boat of 1931. S-42 had full-length hull, set new records and pioneered trans-ocean commercial flying. Sikorsky still lured by helicopter idea, and on 14 September 1939 flew his VS-300 in controlled flight. VS-300 much modified in

Sikorsky S-69 two-seat research helicopter

development. XR-4 of 1942 was first practical US military helicopter. Later types immensely varied: S-51, S-55 and S-58 established world fame. Today Sikorsky helicopters are operated by air forces of some 30 nations and by civil operators worldwide. Amphibious capabilities have further extended usefulness. Current production types: twin-turbine amphibious S-61, S-65 military transport, S-64 Skycrane. Under development: 3-engined CH-53E, S-69, and high-speed research types.

Sikorsky CH-53E heavy-lift helicopter

Sikorsky S-70 assault helicopter prototype

SILVAIRE AIRCRAFT COMPANY/*USA*

At end of WW2 production tooling for Model 8 Silvaire was moved by Luscombe Airplane Corporation (*q.v.*) to Dallas, Texas. In 1949 Luscombe company was brought by Temco Aircraft Corporation (*q.v.*) which built about 50 Silvaires. In 1955 the above-named company acquired rights and equipment for Model 8 Silvaire, inaugurated production at Fort Collins, Colorado, and flew first aircraft off line September 1956.

SILVERCRAFT SpA/*Italy*

Formed early 1962. In October 1963 flew XY prototype light helicopter, further developed with financial and technical assistance of shareholder Siai-Marchetti. SH-4 (flown March 1965) was first helicopter of all-Italian design and construction to receive both Italian and US certification. By late 1960s serious production had begun as Siai-Marchetti/Silvercraft SH-4, but under name Silvercraft alone 20 had been completed by

end of 1969 and deliveries began early 1970. Production had ceased by late 1970s but type was being developed during 1978 as SH-200.

SIMB/*France*

see Société Industrielle des Métaux et du Bois

SIMMERING-GRAZ PAUKER AG/*Austria*

A well-known engineering company which, in

Silvercraft SH-4 light helicopter

early 1960s, planned production of its four-seat twin-engined SGP-222, which had first flown May 1959. Plans abandoned by mid-1960s, though several prototypes built.

SIMMONDS AIRCRAFT LTD./*UK*

Formed September 1928, in which year O.E. (later Sir Oliver) Simmonds designed and built the Spartan two-seat biplane. Outwardly conventional, but planned for 'Spartan' economy (e.g. interchangeable wings and ailerons, and rudder interchangeable with elevator). At

SGP-222 lightplane prototype

Slingsby Hengist I 15-seat transport glider

Southampton, Hampshire, produced 49 examples, mostly for export, but some for National Flying Services Ltd. One made many Arctic flights. (*See* Spartan Aircraft Ltd.)

SIMPLEX/*France*

In early 1920s built tailless monoplanes to design of M. Arnoux, one of which was entered for 1922 Coupe Deutsch race. Wing was built in one piece.

SIMPLEX AIRCRAFT CORPORATION/*USA*

Founded 1928 at Defiance, Ohio. Built Red Arrow two-seat mid-wing monoplane, with optional cockpit enclosure. It was of wooden construction. A monoplane called the Kite was developed in 1931.

SIOUX AIRCRAFT CORPORATION/*USA*

Known earlier as Simplex Aircraft Corporation (*q.v.*); was incorporated at Defiance, Ohio, in 1928. Built aircraft under the name Sioux Red Arrow and Sioux Kite.

SIPA/*France*

see Société Industrielle Pour l'Aéronautique

SITAR/*France*

see Société Industrielle de Tolerie pour l'Aéronautique et Matériel

SKANDINAVISK AERO INDUSTRI AS/*Denmark*

Founded 1937 to build light aircraft. Financed by a large Danish industrial concern; took over aircraft business formerly conducted by Kramme & Zeuthen, builders of KZI light single-seat monoplane. Prefix KZ retained for KZII two-seat trainer, supplied to Danish Air Force; KZIII and VII four-seat cabin monoplanes; KZVIII aerobatic monoplane, and KZX artillery observation type. In mid-1950s turned increasingly to repair and maintenance of military aircraft, and aircraft production had ended by late 1950s.

SKODA-KAUBA FLUGZEUGBAU/*Czechoslovakia*

Founded spring 1942 at Cakowitz, near Prague. Worked for Germans. Experimental types included Sk-V4 light fighter-trainer with German Argus engine. SK257 development received German production order and five completed before Russians captured factory.

SLINGSBY SAILPLANES LTD./*UK*

In 1938, at Kirbymoorside, Yorkshire, built Kirby Kitten single-seat monoplane, designed by F. N. Slingsby. Chiefly famous for gliders. Motor Tutor of 1948 was Slingsby Tutor glider with engine and landing gear. Slingsby/Osbourne Twin Cadet of 1969 had two small engines outboard. Other conversions made, but Type 61 Falke was basically German Scheibe. Also built replicas, of Sopwith Camel, Rumpler etc. Name changed, and in 1969 Slingsby Aircraft Company Ltd. was acquired by Vickers Ltd. (*q.v.*), resuming construction of gliders.

SLOANE AIRCRAFT COMPANY INC./*USA*

Established in New York shortly before the US became involved in WW1. Built a military biplane with unusual back-swept wings. Believed to have built aircraft under sub-contract for the US government.

L. B. SMITH AIRCRAFT CORPORATION/*USA*

Established at Miami 1947. Operated manufacturing, conversion and servicing facilities for numerous types of aircraft, but also built its own Tempo II pressurised executive transport based on Douglas B-26 bomber, which first flew in 1959.

SMITH, TED, AIRCRAFT COMPANY INC./*USA*

In 1967 began production of Aerostar series of twin-engined business aircraft. Occupied new factory at Van Nuys, California 1968. Airframe concerned claimed to have only about 50% of components used in comparable types, with loads carried by unstiffened sections of metal skin. Some vertical and horizontal surfaces interchangeable. In 1972 became Ted R. Smith and Associates Inc, further developing Aerostar range, with distinctive mid-set wing.

SNCAC/*France*

see Société Nationale de Constructions Aéronautiques du Centre

SNCAM/*France*

see Société Nationale de Constructions Aéronautiques du Midi

SNCAN/*France*

see Société Nationale de Constructions Aéronautiques du Nord

SNCAO/*France*

see Société Nationale de Constructions Aéronautiques de l'Ouest

SNCASE/*France*

see Société Nationale de Constructions Aéronautiques du Sud-Est

SNCASO/*France*

see Société Nationale de Constructions Aéronautiques du Sud-Ouest

Smith Tempo II executive transport

Ted Smith Aerostar business aircraft

Smith Super 46C conversion of the Curtiss C-46 Commando

Snow S-2C agricultural monoplane

SNOW AERONAUTICAL CORPORATION/*USA*

Founded 1955 by Leland Snow to make agricultural aircraft of own design. Incorporated 1961; expanded 1963. Original Snow S-2B, a low-wing single-seat monoplane of metal construction, with fixed landing gear, received FAA Type Approval July 1958. By end of February 1965 260 aircraft of basic S-2 series

delivered to 19 American States and 11 foreign countries. Corporation acquired by Rockwell-Standard 1965 and known as Aero Commander (*q.v.*), Olney Division.

SOCATA/*France*

see Société de Constructions d'Avions de Tourisme et d'Affaires

SOCIETÀ ANÒNIMA INDUSTRIE MECCANICHE AERONAUTICHE NAVALI/*Italy*

Founded 1929, SAIMAN specialised in repair and maintenance of marine aircraft and boats. In 1932 built experimental C.10 monoplane with variable-incidence wing. During 1934–1938 made SAIMAN 200 two-seat trainer biplane and 201 and 202 two-seat touring monoplanes. SAIMAN 204 of 1939 was an experimental derivative, but LB.4 made by the company in 1938 was a very different twin-boom airframe with tricycle landing gear.

SOCIETÀ DI COSTRUZIONI MECCÀNICHE DI PISA/*Italy*

Established 1922 to build Dornier types under licence. In that tyear built six Wal and two Delphin. Wal developed as special military type for Spanish Navy, with Rolls-Royce Eagle engines. In 1926 a machine of this type flew South Atlantic.

SIAI S.M.72 three-engined bomber

SOCIETÀ IDROVOLANTI ALTA ITALIA/*Italy*

Forerunner of present Siai-Marchetti organisation (*see* Siai-Marchetti Società Per Azioni). Founded 1915 by Luigi Cape at Sesto Calende, with a seaplane base on Lake Maggiore. As Idrovolanti Savoia built FBA flying-boats under licence. Name 'Savoia' had a geographical and historical connotation (House of Savoy) and after the war new flying-boats were known by the name Idrovolanti Savoia, or Savoia. These achieved early distinction, notably in the 1920 Schneider Trophy contest. Names Savoia and Marchetti were linked in 1922, when Alessandro Marchetti became technical director of company renamed Società Idrovolanti Alta Italia—Savoia-Marchetti. In 1925 the company gained publicity when an S.16 *ter* was flown to Australia and Tokyo and back to Italy by Francesco De Pinedo. Famous types included the twin-hulled S-55 which, though first flown in 1924, is remembered chiefly for General Balbo's mass-formation flights of 1930 and 1933. Special long-range landplane S-64 broke world's duration and distance records in June 1930. Initials S. M. for type-numbers were not commonly applied until later, and then particularly in association with fast 3-engined civil and military types. Most famous was S.M. 79 bomber and torpedo bomber of WW2. Civil types included the record-breaking S.M. 75 of 1939. Last WW2 aircraft was S.M. 91 twin-boom fighter-bomber, but S.M. 84 bomber served as transport until 1948.

SIAI S-55X twin-hulled flying-boat

SIAI S.M.79 transport/bomber

SIAI S.8, a classic flying-boat

SCAN 30 version of Grumman Widgeon

S.I.A.-9B reconnaissance/bomber aircraft

SABCA-built Dassault Mirage 5

SOCIETÀ ITALIANO AVIAZIONE/*Italy*

Had close Fiat links (like Ansaldo and several other Italian companies) and its S.I.A. 7 and 9 series of two-seat reconnaissance-bomber biplanes, dating from 1917, were designed by Umberto Savoia and Rodolfo Verduzio. Structural weakness attributed to both and Type 9 was rejected by Italian Army on this account, though accepted by Navy.

SOCIÉTÉ AÉRONAUTIQUE DU SUD-OUEST/*France*

Formed 1935 at Bordeaux-Merignac by the Potez group (*q.v.*) when it took over the Société Aérienne Bordelaise (*q.v.*). Was intended as a decentralised production source for Potez and Bloch aircraft. Incorporated in SNCASO (*q.v.*) 1936.

SOCIÉTÉ AÉRONAUTIQUE FRANÇAISE/*France*

New name of Société des Avions Dewoitine (*q.v.*), conferred after Dewoitine's return to France from Switzerland. Dewoitine fighters were eventually responsibility of SNCAM. Meanwhile, D37 series of parasol-wing monoplane fighters was developed by Lioré et Olivier (*q.v.*), though name Dewoitine was sustained in fighter field primarily by the low-wing D500 series, many of which were built by Lioré et Olivier. Société Aeronautique Française gained greatest publicity with record-breaking D.332 *Emeraude*, first flown 1933, and with D.338 as used extensively by Air France in late 1930s. This latter aircraft was, perhaps, the finest 3-engined airliner in service before WW2, and continued in use after fall of France.

SOCIÉTÉ AÉRONAUTIQUE NORMANDE/*France*

Formed 1948. First prototype of the SAN-101 two-seat high-wing monoplane flew 1949. Built other light aircraft, notably Jodel D.150 Mascaret; 4/5-seat Jodel D.140 Mousquetaire; and D.140R, for use as glider tug and in mountainous areas. The products were known as SAN Jodel and attained considerable success, but company went into liquidation early in 1969.

SOCIÉTÉ ANONYME BELGE DE CONSTRUCTIONS AÉRONAUTIQUES/*France*

Formed December 1920. Had close SABENA associations and that airline used SABCA's only S.2 single-engined monoplane transport. Built Handley Page 3-engined airliners for SABENA Belgian Congo service; also Poncelet ultra-light monoplane and other private-owner prototypes. Held Breguet and Avia licences and from 1927 directed attention to metal construction. Outcome was S-XI 20-passenger monoplane with three 373 kW (500 hp) engines, as well as similar S-XII 4-passenger monoplane with three 89·5 kW (120 hp) engines. Built under licence Renard R.31 reconnaissance monoplane and Savoia-Marchetti S.73 transport. Built S.47 2-seat low-wing monoplane fighter of 1937 in collaboration with Caproni (*q.v.*). Company revived in 1950s. In 1960s assembled, maintained and repaired Republic F-84; also collaborated with Avions Fairey on Hawker Hunter and made Vautour components for Sud-Aviation. Much work of various kinds on Lockheed Starfighter, Dassault Mirage and Breguet Atlantic; also missile and space activities.

SOCIÉTÉ ANONYME DES ATELIERS D'AVIATION LOUIS BREGUET/*France*
see Breguet Aviation

SOCIÉTÉ ANONYME FRANÇAISE AÉRONAUTIQUE/*France*

In early 1930s licenced to build Netherlands-designed Koolhoven F.K.43 four-seat high-wing monoplane as SAFA F.K.43.

SOCIÉTÉ ANONYME POUR LA FABRICATION ET L'EXPLOITATION DES AVIONS RAAB/*Greece*

Formed at Athens in 1935, when Herr Raab transferred his aircraft manufacture from Riga. (*see* Raab Flugzeugbau)

SOCIÉTÉ ANONYME POUR LA RÉALISATION D'AVIONS PROTOTYPES/*France*

Established at Billancourt in 1926 to build

aircraft to the design of Louis Bécherau, formerly with Deperdussin and SPAD (*q.v.*). First production design was the C.2, a two-seat monoplane powered by a 373 kW (500 hp) Salmson engine.

SOCIÉTÉ ANONYME POUR L'AVIATION ET SES DÉRIVES/*France*
see SPAD

SOCIÉTÉ ANONYME POUR LES APPAREILS DEPERDUSSIN/*France*
see SPAD

SOCIÉTÉ BULTE/*France*
see Guldentops

SOCIÉTÉ DE CONSTRUCTIONS AÉRO NAVALES DE PORT-NEUF/*France*

Light monoplane flying-boat designated SCAN 20, built secretly 1941. Tested October 1945. Delivery of 23 to French Navy under way 1951. Also built Grumman Widgeon for French Navy as SCAN 30.

SOCIÉTÉ DE CONSTRUCTION D'AVIONS DE TOURISME ET D'AFFAIRES/*France*

Formed 1966 as subsidiary of Sud-Aviation (*q.v.*). Based at Tarbes to develop and produce group's light sporting and business aircraft. In 1968 sales exceeded 300 aircraft; main types then Horizon, Rallye, Diplomate and 7-seat Rallye 7. As subsidiary of Aérospatiale (*q.v.*), SOCATA still offers many versions of Rallye

SOCATA Rallye lightplanes

SRCM-153 Joigny lightplane

SECAT S.4 high-wing monoplane

SECAN Courlis twin-boom monoplane

SEEMS MS760 Paris light jet plane

(originated by Morane-Saulnier in 1958) but is developing as wholly new type the TB 10, for later production. Has made components for wide variety of aircraft, including Magister, Concorde and Airbus.

SOCIÉTÉ D'EMBOUTISSAGE ET DE CONSTRUCTIONS MÉCANIQUES/France

Founded 1916 by Félix Amiot. During WW1 built Morane, Breguet and Sopwith types. After war repaired Breguets and from 1921 helped in construction of early Dewoitine monoplane fighters. Specialised in metal stamping and press-work. Lutèce of 1921 was side-by-side two-seater biplane, using special form of steel-tube construction of SECM design. SECM 12 was two-seat single-engined night bomber (developed as SECM-Amiot 120B.N.2); 22 was trainer for French competition of 1923; 23 was 3-seat tourer; 24 an elementary trainer. Firm also made Lorraine-Dietrich aero-engines, as fitted in Amiot-SECM (or Amiot) 122 series of late 1920s.

SOCIÉTÉ DE RECHERCHES ET DE CONSTRUCTIONS MÉCANIQUES/France

Originally a specialist in aircraft hydraulic systems, began small scale construction of aircraft for other small manufacturers. After failing to obtain a licence to build the CAB Supercab, designed a new light plane known as the SRCM-153 Joigny, which first flew in March 1960. This was a three/four-seat monoplane with rectractable landing gear, powered by a Lycoming engine.

SOCIÉTÉ D'ÉTUDES AÉRONAUTIQUES/France

Formed 1916. Forerunner of Potez (q.v.) concerns. Made series of two-seat biplanes, notably SEA 4 reconnaissance aircraft and SEA 7, the latter a 'limousine' first flown December 1919.

SOCIÉTÉ D'ÉTUDES ET DE CONSTRUCTIONS AÉRO NAVALES/France

Subsidiary of Usines Chausson of automotive industry. After WW2 undertook to produce all-metal light aircraft. Resulted in Courlis twin-boom monoplane of 1946, with tricycle landing gear and special loading arrangements. After 1950 concentrated on components, including Speedpak freight-container for Lockheed Constellation, and external tanks for fast aircraft.

SOCIÉTÉ D'ÉTUDES ET DE CONSTRUCTIONS D'AVIONS DE TOURISME/France

Established in 1938, produced the RG-60 single-seat biplane, RG-75 two-seat cabin monoplane, and S.5 two-seat high-wing cantilever monoplane. Production ended at outbreak of WW2.

SOCIÉTÉ D'EXPLOITATION DES ÉTABLISSEMENTS MORANE-SAULNIER/France

Provisional name for the Morane-Saulnier company (q.v.) after it had been acquired in 1963 by the Potez Group (q.v.). MS760 Paris jet-propelled communications aircraft was developed further into 6-seat Paris III of 1964. Production also included Rallye-Club, Super-Rallye and Rallye Commodore, the latter first flown in February 1964 after formation of SEEMS.

SOCIÉTÉ EUROPÉENE DE PRODUCTION DE L'AVION D'ÉCOLE DE COMBAT D'APPUI TACTIQUE/France

An Anglo-French company formed May 1966 by Breguet Aviation and British Aircraft Corporation to design and produce the Jaguar light twin-jet strike fighter/trainer. Versions current: Jaguar A, French single-seat tactical support; Jaguar B, British 2-seat operational trainer (RAF designation Jaguar T. Mk2); Jaguar E, French trainer; Jaguar S, British single-seat tactical support; Jaguar International, export version, much as Jaguar S but more power. SEPECAT has further developments in prospect for attack and reconnaissance versions.

SOCIÉTÉ FRANÇAISE D'AVIATION NOUVELLE/France

Formed 1935 by M. Chasseris, a director of Nieuport (q.v.) for 25 years. Made light aeroplanes and gliders. Licenced for British BAC Drone 1935; modified to suit French requirements as SFAN 2. Larger two-seat model to same formula was SFAN 4.

SOCIÉTÉ FRANÇAISE DE CONSTRUCTIONS AÉRONAUTIQUES/France

Formed July 1934 to build light aircraft. First production model was SFCA Maillet 20, an unusual 3-seat cabin monoplane of very clean design, though with raised pilot's cockpit. SFCA Lignel 20 was 1/2 seat light monoplane with retractable landing gear. Company also had licence for Peyret 'tandem monoplane'—renamed and developed as Taupin.

SEPECAT Anglo-French Jaguar

SIPA S.12/121 two-seat advanced trainer

SOCIÉTÉ GÉNÉRALE DES CONSTRUCTIONS INDUSTRIELLES ET MÉCANIQUES/*France*

Known originally as Etablissements Borel (*see* Borel) denoting origin in 1909 by pioneer constructor Gabriel Borel. To designs of Paul Bocaccio built two-seat fighter after WW1.

SOCIÉTÉ INDUSTRIELLE DES MÉTAUX ET DU BOIS/*France*

Formed 1922, and best known by name Bernard, Adolphe Bernard built SPADs from 1917, original designs materialising only after Armistice. In December 1924 SIMB V2 (or Bernard) racing monoplane raised world speed record to 448·17 km/h (278·48 mph). Type 12C.1 was a low-wing all-metal monoplane fighter; 14C.1 was wooden sesquiplane fighter. In June 1929 special Type 190 (191GR) carried Assolant and Lefèvre on west-east North Atlantic crossing. A number of experimental aircraft built before closure in 1935.

SOCIÉTÉ INDUSTRIELLE DE TOLERIE POUR L'AÉRONAUTIQUE ET MATÉRIEL ROULANT/*France*

Produced, like a number of French contemporaries, designs by Yves Gardan. In late 1960s this included the GY90, 100 and 110. GY100 was four-seat tourer or aerobatic two-seater, production of which began September 1968.

SOCIÉTÉ INDUSTRIELLE POUR L'AÉRONAUTIQUE/*France*

Formed 1938 and until 1940 was manufacturing parts under sub-contract for Lioré et Olivier, Amiot and Morane types and overhauling Mureaux aircraft. First post-war production aircraft was S.10 (French version of Arado 396, for which the company had wartime responsibility). Developed versions were built in quantity. SIPA 901 (derived from S90 of 1947) flew 1948 and ordered by Government for Service de l'Aviation Légère et Sportive. Minijet, flown in 1952, was world's first all-metal 2-seat light jet; SIPA 300 was more conventional jet trainer. Later trainers and light aircraft included Coccinelle 2-seater, and 5-seat turboprop Antilope. Company has been associated with production of Caravelle, Mirage, Alouette and Concorde, and specialised in furnishing and equipping airliners. Taken over by subsidiary of Aérospatiale (*q.v.*).

SOCIÉTÉ NATIONALE DE CONSTRUCTIONS AÉRONAUTIQUES DE L'OUEST/*France*

Formed January 1937, incorporating Breguet and Loire-Nieuport establishments. Made series of Loire 46 gull-wing single-seat fighters, some of which went to Spain and fought in Civil War; also Loire-Nieuport LN 41 single-seat cranked-wing dive-bombers, a few of which saw action against advancing Germans in 1940. New company had associations also with Loire 210 central-float fighter seaplane of 1939; Loire 130 flying-boat for shipboard catapult launch; and Loire 70 three-engined reconnaissance flying-boat.

SOCIÉTÉ NATIONALE DE CONSTRUCTIONS AÉRONAUTIQUES DU CENTRE/*France*

Formed February 1937. Incorporated Farman and Hanriot establishments. Played part in final development of Farman line of four-engined heavy bombers which had engines in tandem underslung pairs, derived from F.211 of 1931. One converted Atlantic mailplane of this form was first Allied aircraft to bomb Berlin. Of Hanriot origin was the NC600 (derived from H.220) twin-engined fighter prototype flown in 1939, though abandoned when the SNCAC former Hanriot factory at Bourges was chosen to build Breguet 696. After German withdrawal SNAC built 64 Focke-Wulf Fw 190 as NC900. Company dissolved 1949.

SOCIÉTÉ NATIONALE DE CONSTRUCTIONS AÉRONAUTIQUES DU MIDI/*France*

Formed February 1937, Occupied Dewoitine (*q.v.*) factory at Toulouse. Designed and produced D.520 monoplane fighter, first flown 1938, of which about 400 delivered and 180 more ordered later under Franco-German Armistice authorisation. The second mentioned batch was built by SNCASE (*q.v.*) which by 1941 had absorbed SNCAM. D.750, first flown 1940, was unusual twin-engined multipurpose folding wing monoplane for operation from planned aircraft-carriers.

SOCIÉTÉ NATIONALE DE CONSTRUCTIONS AÉRONAUTIQUES DU NORD/*France*

Formed early 1937. Incorporated elements of Potez, Amiot, Breguet, CAMS and Mureaux (all *q.v.*). Dominant concern was production of Potez 630 series of twin-engined multipurpose aircraft. Peak output reached in May 1940. Development of basic type (e.g. Potez 671 specialised fighter with elliptical wingplan) was also SNCAN concern. In 1949 took over part of liquidated SNCAC. In 1954, when company flew prototypes of trainers later built in quantity, amalgamated with Société Française d'Études et de Constructions de Matériels Aéronautiques Spéciaux (SFECMAS, formerly Arsenal de l'Aéronautique) (both *q.v.*). From January 1958 called Nord-

SNCAC NC853 two-seat lightplane

SNCAN 1101 Noralpha cabin monoplane

SFECMAS 1402 Gerfault delta-wing research aircraft

SNCAN 1500 Griffon turbo-ramjet research aircraft

SNCASE SE.200 six-engined commercial flying-boat

Aviation. Under new name continued development of Nord/SFECMAS Gerfaut delta-wing fighter; also Griffon, with fuselage forming outer casing of very large ramjet with turbojet in centre for take-off and to ignite ramjet. Noratlas twin-boom transport, though first flown September 1949, continued in production and development under new name, achieving wide success. Nord name was emphasised in Noroit flying-boat and Noréclair shipboard aircraft.

SOCIÉTÉ NATIONALE DE CONSTRUCTIONS AÉRONAUTIQUES DU SUD EST/*France*

Formed December 1936. Incorporated elements of Lioré et Olivier, Potez, Romano and SPCA (all *q.v.*). Company thus became responsible for development and production of Le045 twin-engined bomber, first flown January 1937, outstanding in many points of design and much used and adapted during and after WW2. Built also Romano trainers and Le043 catapult floatplane, of type first flown December 1934. In 1941 the company absorbed SNCAM (*q.v.*). Early post-WW2 products included Languedoc four-engined airliner, developed from Bloch 161 of 1939, which entered service between Paris and Algiers in 1946, and was ordered additionally for military use. Military types in development included Grognard twin-jet attack aircraft of 1950; the unique trolley-launched skid-landing Baroudeur strike aircraft of 1953; and Mistral and Aquilon developments of the British de Havilland Vampire and Sea Venom. Especially notable original developments were the Alouette helicopter series first flown in 1951, and the rear-engined twin-jet Caravelle in 1955. Became part of Sud-Aviation (*q.v.*).

SOCIÉTÉ NATIONALE DE CONSTRUCTIONS AÉRONAUTIQUES DU SUD OUEST/*France*

Formed November 1936. Incorporated elements of Marcel Bloch, Lioré et Olivier, Blériot and SASO. A prime responsibility was development and production of Bloch types, especially single-seat fighters derived from MB150 of 1936. Redesign facilitated production and improved performance, resulting in MB151 and 152. By June 1940 production totalled about 600, involving five plants. MB175 twin-engined bomber was in production and was revived after WW2 as torpedo aircraft. Several other prototypes built, including four-engined bomber. In 1941 company was merged into SNCAO (*q.v.*). In 1942 completed forerunner of Bretagne twin-engined transport, though not flown until 1945; then used commercially and experimentally.

Numerous and varied post-WW2 types included distinctly unusual forms of rotary wing aircraft, Aeriel (1948) and Djinn (1953) with tip jets, and Farfadet convertiplane (1953). The eminently successful Vautour multi-purpose twin-jet flew 1952, and was much developed thereafter. High speed research types were swept-wing Espadon and—of special technical interest—straight-wing mixed-power Trident, first flown 1953 (well before formation of Ouest-Aviation in 1957).

SOCIÉTÉ PROVENÇALE DE CONSTRUCTIONS AÉRONAUTIQUES/*France*

The aircraft branch of the Société Provençale de Constructions Navales and the Messageries Maritimes. In March 1925 acquired sole rights for construction of Météore aircraft from

SNCASE Grognard twin-jet attack aircraft

SNCASE Baroudeur skid-landing strike aircraft

SNCASO Bretagne transport

SNCASO SO.1221 Djinn helicopter

SNCASO SO.1310 Farfadet convertiplane

Soko G2 Galeb basic trainer

Solar XRON-1 experimental helicopter

Compagnie Générale de Constructions Aéronautiques. Built Météore 63 three-engined flying-boat. Under Paulhan-Pillard licence built E.5 three-engined monoplane flying-boat and T3-BN.4 twin-engined twin-float coast-defence floatplane. SPCA 30-M.4 was big multi-seat landplane fighter with two fuselages and central nacelle. Type 40T was three-engined all-metal airliner which gave

good service in early 1930s. In 1936 company's Marseilles works were leased by Government for SNCASE (*q.v.*).

SOKO/*Yugoslavia*
Founded in 1951, and produced licence-built Westland Whirlwind helicopters. Designed the G2 Galeb two-seat armed jet basic trainer,

produced for the Yugoslav Air Force and for export; the J-1/RJ-1 Jastreb attack and reconnaissance versions of the G2-A Galeb; a TJ-1 Jastreb trainer; is building the Aérospatiale/Westland (*q.v.*) Gazelle helicopter under licence; and is developing with Romania the Orao strike aircraft.

SOLAR AIRCRAFT COMPANY/*USA*
In 1931–1932 at Lindbergh Field, San Diego, California, built Solar MS-2 sesquiplane all-metal ten-passenger transport aircraft. Was also a manufacturer of aircraft components.

SOMMER, ROGER/*France*
First began aeronautical work in 1904. Special Sommer biplane of 1911 lifted 13 persons. After a dormant period the company resumed aircraft construction 1915, and at the Armistice the Sommer works was claimed to have been producing up to 200 aircraft per month under sub-contract.

SOPWITH AVIATION COMPANY LTD./*UK*
T. O. M. Sopwith was pioneer sportsman/pilot. Rebuilt early aircraft before WW1, began development of own types and formed important associations with F. Sigrist (engineer and largely responsible for future success) and H. G. Hawker (pilot). Company registered March 1914. Became world-famous for fighter aircraft, built in great numbers by many companies, though Bat Boat of 1913 was notable flying-boat and Tabloid landplane of same year gained renown as floatplane by winning 1914 Schneider Trophy. Wartime developments were Schneider and Baby floatplanes. First landplane fighter built in great numbers was two-seat 1½-Strutter. Pup was smaller single-seater, and both types made major contributions to ship-flying. Triplane of 1916 resembled Pup, except for extra wing, and excelled in climb. Two-gun Camel, in service 1917 excelled in manoeuvrability; shipboard version had detachable rear fuselage. Cuckoo of 1917 was world's first deck-landing torpedo-bomber. Snipe was intended to succeed Camel late in war and remained in RAF service until 1926: Salamander was similar but armoured

Sopwith Camel single-seat biplane fighter

for ground attack. In 1920 the Sopwith Aviation Company was succeeded by the Hawker Engineering Company (*q.v.*).

The Sopwith fighters sacrificed stability for manoeuvrability, and became the most famous British aircraft of WWI.

Sopwith Triplane fighter

Sopwith Snipe fighter

Sopwith Pup fighter

SPAD XIII, extensively-built French fighter

SPAD 81, a post-WW1 fighter of the French AF

SOUTHERN AIRCRAFT CORPORATION/USA
At Garland, Texas, in 1940, built prototype biplane trainer. In new works made components for Consolidated B-24, Grumman Hellcat and Avenger.

SOUTHERN AIRCRAFT LTD./UK
Associated with Shoreham Aerodrome, Sussex, and F. G. Miles, who developed the Avro Baby into Martlet and Metal Martlet light aerobatic and sporting types. Last example flew 1931.

SPAD/France
Silk merchant Armand Deperdussin (1867–1924) was associated from 1910 with a series of notable monoplanes. Built Precursor in 1909 for show in a Paris store. By 1914 monoplanes bearing Deperdussin name were used not only privately but by several military authorities. Designed by Louis Béchereau, these aircraft were especially noted for speed performances in 1912–1913, and in some instances for monocoque construction. Deperdussin, a great promoter, became involved in financial difficulties and in 1915 the company as named above was declared bankrupt. The Deperdussin name had links with several companies, including the British Deperdussin Company with which John Porte (see Seaplane Experimental Station) was connected. Initials SPAD were also ascribed to Société Provisoire des Aéroplanes Deperdussin and Société Parisienne des Avions Deperdussin, as well as Société des Productions Armand Deperdussin.

After Deperdussin was arrested for embezzlement, the company was renamed Société Pour l'Aviation et ses Dérives in 1915, thus retaining these initials. Chief technician was at first Béchereau, later André Herbemont. Company became world-famous for SPAD single-seat fighters and fast reconnaissance adaptations. More than 2,000 fighters built at Suresnes factory alone; great numbers under licence in France and elsewhere. Classic tractor single-seat biplane flown late 1915 as SPAD

V: developed into SPAD VII of 1916, thus establishing company's name in aviation history. Characteristic design-feature was two-bay wing cellule with special form of bracing. Combination with Hispano-Suiza 8-cylinder vee-form engine was major factor in success. SPAD XII had a 37 mm engine-mounted gun. From May 1917 improved two machine-gun type XIII replaced VII. Large numbers ordered by US. SPAD XX of late 1918 was two-seat fighter to Herbemont design and precursor of new Blériot-SPAD line of single-strut monocoque-fuselage biplane fighters, built after Blériot (q.v.) took over SPAD company in 1921.

SPARMANN'S FLYGPLANVERKSTAD/Sweden
In 1936 built S-1 single-seat low-wing monoplane trainer. Several delivered to Swedish Air Force.

SPARTAN AIRCRAFT COMPANY/USA
Early in 1927 Spartan G-3 three-seat open-cockpit biplane was built by Mid-Continent Aircraft Company. Company as above established 1928 at Tulsa, Oklahoma. Built C-3 with Ryan-Siemens engine. Continued to build biplanes but by 1931 was producing series of 4/5-seat cabin monoplanes; also low-wing side-by-side 2-seaters, further developed as

Spartan Zeus light bomber

C2-60. Spartan Executive 4/5-seat all-metal monoplane of 1936 converted in 1938 to Zeus 2-seat military type; a few of which supplied to China and Mexico. In 1940 US Navy ordered 201 Spartan NP-1 biplane trainers for new Naval Reserve schools.

SPARTAN AIRCRAFT LTD./UK
Early in 1930 Simmonds Aircraft Ltd, who had made the Spartan biplane, was reconstituted under the above name. Made altered version of Simmonds Spartan called Spartan Arrow. Spartan Three Seater built at East Cowes, Isle of Wight, where company moved early 1931. Spartan Cruiser was development of Saro-Percival (later Spartan) Mailplane of 1931, and the refined Cruiser III ended production in May 1935.

SPCA/France
see Société Provençale de Constructions Aéronautiques

SPENCER-LARSEN AIRCRAFT CORPORATION/USA
Formed 1937 by P. H. Spencer (formerly of Amphibions Inc, q.v.) and V. A. Larsen (previously with Fokker, Standard and Sikorsky) to develop two-seat amphibian with remotely-driven pusher propeller.

Spartan Arrow floatplane

Spartan Cruiser II eight-seat light transport

Sportavia RF5 two-seat lightplane

Sperry experimental triplane amphibian

SPERRY, LAWRENCE, AIRCRAFT COMPANY/*USA*
Lawrence Sperry was son of Elmer Sperry (Sperry Gyroscope Co.) Worked on aeroplanes from 1911; company as named founded 1919. In 1920 made cantilever monoplane wing for Curtiss JN, and built experimental triplane amphibian. From 1921 tiny Messenger single-seat biplane (designed by Engineering Division, US Air Service, and called also Verville-Sperry) was in production. Also to official designs built Verville-Sperry Racers. A Messenger brought to England by Lawrence Sperry in 1923 came down in the Channel and Sperry lost his life, after which the company closed.

SPITFIRE HELICOPTER COMPANY/*USA*
Based at Media, Pennsylvania. In January 1975 began design of Spitfire Mark I light helicopter, developed from Enstrom F-28A but with turbine power plant. Other projects include helicopter with auxiliary propulsion engines at tips of stub wings.

SPORTAVIA-PUTZER GmbH u Co. KG/*Germany*
Formed 1966 to take over from Alpavia SA (*q.v.*) manufacture of Avion-Planeur series designed by René Fournier. By Spring 1969 had delivered 150 RF4D single-seaters. Two-seat RF5 flew 1968.

SRCM/*France*
see Société de Recherches et de Constructions Mécaniques

STAMPE ET RENARD SA/*Belgium*
Formed after WW2 by merger of Constructions Aéronautiques G. Renard and Stampe et Vertongen (both *q.v.*) Overhauled and modified highly successful S.V.4 series of trainer biplanes, as used by Belgian and French Air Forces. Developed modernised S.V.4D; also, as a collaborative venture with Farman (*q.v.*), new monoplane called Minitor using fuselage components of S.V.4. By 1970 had ceased aeronautical work.

STAMPE ET VERTONGEN/*Belgium*
Established 1922. Specialised in trainer aircraft. Early type designations signified that Alfred Renard was chief designer. In April 1923 flew RSV.32-90 and developed several biplane types and parasol monoplanes. Greatest success was S.V.4 series of two-seat trainer biplanes, built from 1933 and famed for manoeuvrability and strength. Type was also built by SNCAN (*q.v.*) in France. S.V.5 was military multi-purpose type; S.V.7 a bomber/reconnaissance biplane; S.V.10 a two-seat twin-engined military multi-purpose type for Belgian Government. Although the company's Antwerp factory was destroyed in WW2 the name lives on in aerobatic flying.

STANDARD AIRCRAFT CORPORATION/*USA*
Anticipating eventual entry of USA into WW1, was formed in 1916, with factories in New Jersey. Made to own designs SJ trainers; E-1 single-seat fighters, used for advanced training; H-3 landplane reconnaissance biplanes and H-4-H floatplanes. Also built 80 Curtiss HS single-engined flying-boats and began quantity production of Handley Page and Caproni large bombers. Also built about 140 de Havilland D.H.4s, and total wartime output was over 1,000 aircraft.

STANDARD MOTOR COMPANY LTD./*UK*
Established at Coventry, Warwickshire, built aircraft to government contracts during WW1 including RAF B.E.12 and R.E.8 and Sopwith Pups.

STAR AIRCRAFT COMPANY/*USA*
Formed in late 1920s, directors having connections with Phillips Petroleum Company. In early 1930s built Star Cavalier two-seat high-wing cabin monoplane.

STARK IBÉRICA SA/*Spain*
Successor to Stark Flugzeugbau AG of Minden/Westf, Germany. In late 1960s was continuing development and production of Stark version of Druine Turbulent and Stamo engine.

STARLING BURGESS COMPANY/*USA*
William Starling Burgess was yacht and boat builder. Made an aeroplane 1909/10. Built Wright biplanes under licence as Burgess-Wright. Also developed twin-engined type, tractor type and flying-boat. From 1913 under licence from Britain's J. W. Dunne, made Burgess-Dunne tailless floatplanes, Burgess

Standard Aircraft Mailplane

Standard E-1 fighter/trainer

Stampe aerobatic biplane

Steward-Davis Jet Packet, a jet-augmented version of the Fairchild C-82

developing the single main float. Two such seaplanes bought by US Navy 1916, and one used for gunnery trials. Navy also bought tractor floatplanes and UK bought 36 landplanes developed by the Burgess company.

STATE AIRCRAFT FACTORY/China
At Shenyang (formerly Mukden) built—after re-establishment of aircraft industry from 1949—several types under licence. These included An-2, Yak-12 and -18, Mi-4 helicopter and Czech Aero 45. First combat type was MiG-17, delivered to Chinese Air Force from 1956 of which well over 1,000 built, plus hundreds of MiG-15 trainers. These types were followed by versions of MiG-19 and -21, also Il-28 bomber. Aircraft have Chinese designations (MiG-19 = F-6) and fighters of type supplied to Pakistan are highly rated (especially when armed with Sidewinder missiles). Other types, some of Chinese origin, have been built in addition.

STATES AIRCRAFT CORPORATION/USA
In very early 1930s built, at Chicago Heights, Illinois, B-3 parasol monoplane, with two tandem seats.

STEARMAN/USA
Originally Stearman Aircraft Company, formed at Venice, California, by Lloyd Stearman in 1927. Stearman was already known in connection with Laird, Swallow and Travel Air; the new company was formed by consolidating Lyle-Hoyt Aircraft Corporation (formerly West Coast distributor of Travel Air)

and technical ability of Stearman. Factory soon moved to Wichita, Kansas, building private and commercial aircraft and becoming part of United Aircraft and Transport Corporation. Types built included three-seaters, trainers and mailplanes. On breaking-up of United combine in 1934, Stearman became a Boeing subsidiary and in 1939 the Wichita Division of Boeing. Nevertheless, biplane trainers built throughout WW2 were persistently called Stearman. Basic type was Model 75, dating from 1936 and having numerous service designations; production totalled about 10,000. Name Kaydet (originally Canadian) not favoured in USA, where Army models had PT and Navy models NS designations. Some versions had enclosed cockpits. After WW2 some 4,000 of Model 75 converted for crop-dusting. Stearmans are favoured collectors' pieces.

STEARMAN-HAMMOND AIRCRAFT CORPORATION/USA
Formed 1936, after Dean B. Hammond and Lloyd Stearman (see Hammond and Stearman entries) had spent two years developing the Hammond Model Y two-seat twin-boom pusher monoplane and the type had been granted an Approved Type Certificate. Aircraft had been redesigned for production as Y-1S and a few built before work was abandoned in 1938.

STEWARD-DAVIS INC./USA
Under name Steward-Davis/Jet-Packet made and promoted modernised commercial version of Fairchild C-82 with turbojet mounted above fuselage for augmented power. In 1961 adapted C-119 in similar manner as Jet-Pak.

STINSON AIRCRAFT DIVISION OF VULTEE AIRCRAFT INC./USA
In 1926 the Stinson Aeroplane Syndicate, West Detroit, Michigan, founded by E. A. Stinson, made Detroiter four-passenger biplane designed jointly by Stinson and F. Verville. Name Detroiter was confusingly retained for later monoplanes. Three Detroiter biplanes acquired in 1926 by Northwest Airways Inc. at which time manufacturing company renamed Stinson Airplane Corporation. Detroiters of several forms used widely by commercial and private operators; e.g. flew first regular air mail service in China. Detroiter monoplanes much developed, though general type was claimed as first US aircraft with sound proofed and heated cabin, engine starter and wheelbrakes. Detroiter Junior of 1928 was scaled-down version for private and executive work. Detroiters established several records, including 174 hrs airborne, July 1929. About 1933 new tapered wing form adopted for Reliant single-engined series, which succeeded Detroiter line. Reliant series was especially successful and built in great quantities, 500 being transferred to Royal Navy under Lend-Lease. Voyager was later two-seat high-wing monoplane. Sentinel liaison type very widely used under Vultee name, the Stinson company having undergone several corporate and nominal changes to become a Vultee division in 1940.

Stearman 75, a classic trainer

Stinson L-5B light ambulance

Stinson Reliant four/five-seat cabin monoplane

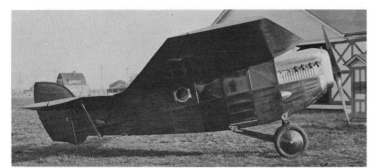
Stout Sedan commercial transport

Stout Air Pullman seven-passenger transport

STOUT METAL AIRPLANE COMPANY/USA

In 1919 W. B. Stout (former aeronautical writer and engineer) formed Stout Engineering Laboratories Inc. at Detroit, Michigan. Built Batwing cantilever monoplane hoping for US Navy and civil orders. In 1920/1922 built and flew large twin-engined coast-defence torpedo-carrier monoplane for Navy. In 1922 established Stout Metal Airplane Company with himself as chief designer and Edsel Ford as a director. Specialised in metal construction. Seven-passenger Stout Air Pullman of 1924 had corrugated metal skin. In August 1925 the company was bought by Henry Ford and joint publicity was gained when Stout Mail Plane marked 'Ford' operated on Detroit–Cleveland route. AT-4 of 1926 established famous Trimotor line, associated with name Ford. In 1931 Stout Engineering Laboratories exhibited Sky Car two-seat monoplane at Detroit.

STROUKOFF AIRCRAFT CORPORATION/USA

Formed at West Trenton, New Jersey, by Michael Stroukoff, responsible for design of Chase C-123 military transport, after controlling interest in the Chase Aircraft Company Inc.—of which Stroukoff was vice-president—had been acquired by the Kaiser-Frazer Corporation. New Stroukoff corporation developed design of C-123. Experimental model with boundary-layer control flown December 1954. Stroukoff also developed for amphibious aircraft of this class 'pantobase' landing gear (retractable land/water skis and wingtip floats).

STURTEVANT AEROPLANE COMPANY/USA

Formed 1915 at Boston, Massachusetts. Derived from B. F. Sturtevant Company which made steel products, including engines. From 1916 built steel-framed tractor seaplanes for US Navy and generally similar landplanes for US Army Signal Corps. Also built Curtiss JN and D.H.4 aircraft under sub-contract. No production of aircraft after WW1.

Stroukoff YC-134 transport prototype

SUD-AVIATION/France

Formed 1 March 1957 by amalgamation of Ouest-Aviation and Sud-Est Aviation, known until 1 September 1956 respectively as SN-CASO and SNCASE (both q.v.). Main responsibility was further development and marketing of highly successful S.E.210 Caravelle twin-jet airliner, first flown in 1955, and Alouette series of helicopters. Continued also development of S.E.5000 Baroudeur, S.O.9050 mixed-power interceptor and widely used S.O.4050 Vautour twin-jet multipurpose aircraft. Frelon series of large turbine-powered helicopters developed after first flight in February 1959, and Super Frelon flew December 1962, setting new world records. Design leadership in A300 European Airbus assumed and diversification into non-aeronautical fields undertaken. Jointly with Nord-Aviation (q.v.) made Corvette light rear-engined jet transport. In 1970 became major component of Aérospatiale (q.v.).

SUD-EST AVIATION/France

Until 1 September 1956 known as Société Nationale de Constructions Aéronautiques du Sud-Est (SNCASE) (q.v.). On 1 March 1957 amalgamated with Ouest-Aviation into Sud-Aviation (both q.v.).

Sud-Aviation Alouette helicopter

Sud-Aviation S.E.210 Caravelle jet transport

Sukhoi Su-7 close-support and ground-attack fighter

SUKHOI/*USSR*

P. O. Sukhoi was engaged in design long before WW2, and in 1932 was working with a team under A. N. Tupolev on ANT-25 long-range record-breaker. In WW2 Sukhoi's own name was especially associated with Su-2 light bomber and attack aircraft. He was responsible for the jet-propelled Su-7 seen in 1947. Current Su-7 of his second series is a swept-wing jet-propelled attack aircraft first seen 1956. Still used in large numbers, in several variants, by many air forces. Su-9, operational since 1959, and Su-11 are single-seat all-weather fighters with delta wing. Su-15 twin-jet delta-wing all-weather fighter now serves widely in many forms and was tested as STOL type in 1967. Su-17 is variable-geometry fighter developed from Su-7 and in service; has speed in excess of Mach 2 at optimum altitude. Su-19 is variable-geometry attack type, seating two side-by-side and in service since early 1975. Su-20 is export version Su-17. Sukhoi died in September 1975, but the Sukhoi design continues to honour his name.

SULLIVAN AIRCRAFT MANUFACTURING COMPANY/*USA*

In 1930 built a low-wing cabin monoplane which was developed as the K-3.

SUMMIT AERONAUTICAL CORPORATION/*USA*

In 1941 was testing and developing HM-5 two-seat cabin monoplane built by Vidal process (moulding under fluid pressure) for which company held licence from Aircraft Research Corporation. War production of other items then supervened.

SUNBEAM MOTOR CAR COMPANY LTD./*UK*

Famous for aero-engines to designs of Frenchman Louis Coatalen. Built aeroplanes in quantity under sub-contract during WW1, including Short types and Avro 504s. In 1917 the Sunbeam Bomber, a fairly large single-seat biplane with cockpit very far aft and machine-gun very far forward was evolved; probably one only built.

SUPERIOR AIRCRAFT COMPANY/*USA*

A division of the Priestly Hunt Aircraft Corporation was formed in mid-1956 at Culver City, California, to acquire the assets of Culver Aircraft Corporation (*q.v.*) which became bankrupt in 1946. Put into production the Superior Satellite, a two-seat low-wing cabin monoplane, derived from the Culver Model V.

SUPERMARINE AVIATION WORKS LTD./*UK*

Founded 1912 by Noel Pemberton-Billing (*see* Pemberton-Billing Ltd.). In 1915 designed Night Hawk anti-airship fighter with many ingenious features, including searchlight and recoilless gun. Other designs were a twin-float seaplane and Baby single-seat fighter flying-boat, the latter flying in February 1918. Company's post-war Schneider Trophy Sea Lion racing flying-boats were developed from Baby, but advanced S.4 racer of 1925 was a twin-float seaplane, though still of wooden construction. The S.5 and S.6 seaplanes, which followed, were renowned for race-winning and record-breaking, but especially as forerunners of WW2 Spitfire, designed by Reginald Mitchell (1895–1937) who had joined company in 1916. Well-known maritime aircraft included the Admiralty (AD) type built by Supermarine (and Pemberton-Billing) in WW1, and Seal/Seagull/Scarab/Sheldrake series developed during 1920s and 1930s. Company was absorbed by Vickers in 1928. Was then already famous for large multi-engined flying-boats, especially Southampton, distinguished in RAF service from 1925, especially for long cruises. Successors were much-refined Scapa of 1932 and Stranraer of 1935, and the Walrus and Sea Otter earned their place in FAA history during

Supermarine's historic Spitfire, designed by R. J. Mitchell

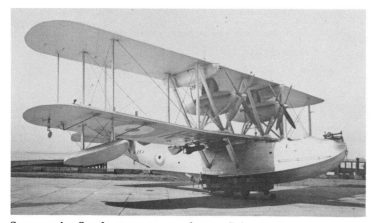

Supermarine Southampton reconnaissance flying-boat

Swearingen Merlin III 8/10-seat transport

WW2. The Supermarine Spitfire first flew 5 March 1936. Well over 20,000 were built by various makers. Basic change came when the Rolls-Royce was replaced by the Griffon engine. Seafire was naval development (over 2,500 built). Spiteful and Seafang were late piston-engined types with new wing, from which the jet-propelled Attacker was developed to enter service in 1951. Swept-wing Swift was unsuccessful as fighter, and twin-jet Scimitar of 1958 concluded fighter line.

SVENSKA AERO AKTIEBOLAGET/*Sweden*

From 1921 built aircraft at Lidingö to Heinkel design; sometimes called Svenska Aero Aktiebolaget (Heinkel). S.1 was typical Heinkel (Brandenburg) twin-float seaplane, variously powered; S.11 was development; H.D.14 was torpedo-bomber biplane; H.D.17 fighter-reconnaissance biplane. Of Swedish design were Pirat two-seat multi-purpose biplane, Falken trainer and Jaktfalk single-seat biplane fighter. In 1931 company liquidated and effects taken over by AB Svenska Järnvägsverkstädern (*q.v.*) which company brought Jaktfalk production to 18.

SVENSKA AEROPLAN AB/*Sweden*
    see SAAB

SVENSKA JÄRNVÄGSVERKSTÄDERNA, AB/*Sweden*

In early/mid-1930s, at Linköping, built Viking three-seat cabin monoplane with wheel or float landing gear, developed later into Viking II four-seater; also Type 2 light multi-purpose aircraft; and produced under licence Raab-Katzenstein Tigerschwalbe trainers for Swedish Air Force. In 1939 company's Aircraft Division amalgamated with Svenska Aeroplan AB, helping to form SAAB (*q.v.*).

SWALLOW AIRCRAFT COMPANY INC./*USA*

As Swallow Airplane Manufacturing Company of Wichita, Kansas, was successor to E. M. Laird Company (*q.v.*). First product was Model 1924 Swallow Commercial three-seater (a refined Laird Swallow). Type was successful, especially in Middle West, and improved progressively. On 6 April 1926 a Swallow biplane (modified New Swallow type, called Swallow Mail plane) made inaugural flight for Varney Air Lines (later part of United Air Lines) marking significant advance in US air transport. Swallow Commercial of 1928 offered with various engines; Swallow Special 3-seater had Axelson engine. In 1930s company developed Swallow Coupé light cabin monoplane. As Swallow Aircraft Company Inc. were developing two-seat low-wing types in 1941, but their production inhibited by WW2.

SWANSON AIRPLANE COMPANY INC./*USA*

S. S. Swanson was an amateur constructor, and in 1923 co-producer of Swanson-Freeman light biplane. Later worked with Lincoln-Standard Aircraft Corporation. Company named above incorporated 1930, and developed Swanson coupe two-seat high-wing cabin monoplane.

SWEARINGEN AIRCRAFT CORPORATION/*USA*

For some years before 1966, when its Merlin series of twin-turboprop executive aircraft reached production, this company had built prototypes for other makers, including Piper Twin Comanche. By late 1960s was building Merlin IIB eight-seater as successor to IIA (33 built) and 22-seat Metro commuter airliner. Also offered improved versions of Beechcraft types; Merlin III was 8/10-seat executive type; Merlin IV a corporate version of Metro. In 1971 the company became a subsidiary of Fairchild Industries. By February 1972 82 had been delivered of Merlin IIB alone. By January 1977 total of 165 Merlins and Metros of several models delivered to many countries.

SWISS-AMERICAN AVIATION CORPORATION/*Switzerland*

Formed 1960 by Mr. William P. Lear, former chairman of Lear Inc. of USA, to make fast executive aircraft known as Lear Jet (Lear Jet Model 23=SAAC 23). By 1964 all work had been transferred to USA.

SZEKELY CORPORATION/*USA*

In 1930, at Holland, Michigan, made small single-seat low-wing cantilever monoplane called Flying Dutchman.

Swearingen Metro commuter airliner

T

TACHIKAWA/*Japan*

New name from 1936 of Ishikawajima Aircraft Company Ltd. (*q.v.*). Built for Japanese Army Air Force the Ki-9 and Ki-17 two-seat biplane trainers from 1935–1942 and 1935–1944 respectively; Ki-36 Army co-operation monoplane and its trainer derivative, the Ki-55 (1938–1944 and 1939–1943); the twin-engined Ki-54 multi-purpose trainer-transport (1940–1945) and, under licence as the army Type LO, 64 examples of the Lockheed Model 14 twin-engined transport. Other ventures included the Ki-74 long-range pressurised twin-engined reconaissance-bomber of 1944–1945 and prototypes of the twin-engined reconaissance Ki-70, Ki-77 and Ki-94 high altitude 'heavy' fighter. Company reformed November 1949 as Shin Tachikawa Kokuki Kabushiki Kaisha. Built prototypes ·of the R-52 light-plane (first all-Japanese postwar aircraft) and R-53 in early/mid 1950s.

TALLERES GENERALES DE AERONÁUTICA MILITAR/*Mexico*
see next entry

TALLERES NACIONALES DE CONSTRUCCIONES AERONÁUTICAS/*Mexico*

National Aircraft Manufacturing Workshops, established November 1915 at Valbuena, near Mexico City. Began by building Blériot, Morane-Saulnier and other foreign types under licence. Own first products were the Microplane Veloz single-seat fighter biplane of 1918 and the Series A two-seat general-purpose biplane. Followed in late 1920s by the Azcarate-E training and reconnaissance sesquiplane. Aircraft design halted by Government 1930, but shortly afterwards built Chance Vought 02U Corsairs under licence. Later products included Teziutlan primary trainers in 1942, and in late 1940s the prototype TTS-5 six-seat twin-engined general-purpose transport.

TAMPIER, RENÉ/*France*

Exhibited a folding-wing roadable biplane at the 1921 Paris Salon. This had an auxiliary engine to drive the landing wheels, which could be used also as a self-starter for the main engine. When driven on the road it travelled tail first. He developed also for the French Army a two-seat reconnaissance aircraft designated T.4 which also featured a two-cylinder auxiliary engine. This was not only intended for main engine starting, but was used also to power a generator in flight to provide essential electrical services, and in particular to make possible the use of early air-to-ground communication equipment.

TARRANT, W. G./*UK*

Building contractors at Byfleet, near Brooklands, Surrey, who undertook aircraft component manufacture during WW1. Only aircraft produced was Tabor long-range bomber, designed with collaboration from Royal Aircraft Establishment; this six-engined triplane nosed-over and was wrecked in its first attempt to take off in May 1919.

TAYLOR AIRCRAFT COMPANY INC./*USA*

Formed 1929 by C. G. Taylor and brother as Taylor Brothers Aircraft Corporation to market the Chummy side-by-side two-seat lightplane. Became Taylor Aircraft Company Inc. founded in 1931 by C. G. Taylor to market the Cub, small tandem two-seat cabin monoplane, in Models E-2 and F-2. Company ran into financial difficulties; rights to Cub acquired by its secretary/treasurer, W. T. Piper, in 1935, who in 1937 formed Piper Aircraft Corporation (*q.v.*). Taylor formed the Taylorcraft Aviation Company (*q.v.*) in 1936.

Tarrant Tabor long-range bomber prototype

TAYLOR BROTHERS AIRCRAFT CORPORATION/*USA*

see Taylor Aircraft Company Inc.

TAYLORCRAFT AEROPLANES (ENGLAND) LTD./*UK*

Created November 1938 at Thurmaston, Leicester, to build US Taylorcraft cabin monoplanes in UK under name Auster. Eventually became Auster Aircraft Ltd. (*q.v.*) on 7 March 1946, by which time it had built more than 1,600 Taylorcraft C, Plus C, Plus D and Auster I, II, III, IV and V, as well as early Auster J-1 Autocrats and prototype of J-2 Arrow.

TAYLORCRAFT AVIATION CORPORATION/*USA*

Successor to Taylor Aircraft Company Inc. (*q.v.*) formed 1936 at Alliance, Ohio by C. G. Taylor as the Taylorcraft Aviation Company. Re-named Taylor-Young Airplane Company later that year, and Taylorcraft Aviation Corporation in 1940. Main pre-war lightplanes were Models B, C and D, of which C and D formed basis for formation of Taylorcraft Aeroplanes (England) Ltd. (*q.v.*). During WW2 built over 1,900 similar L-2 Grasshoppers for USAAF, TG-6 training gliders based on L-2, and components for Consolidated PBY, Curtiss C-46 and Douglas A-26. Built some 2,800 Model B-12Bs in 1945–1946; went bankrupt in 1946, but then reformed in 1947 as Taylorcraft Inc. producing models BC-12D, Ace, Traveler, Topper, Ranch, Wagon, Tourist, Sportsman and Special de Luxe. The factory moved to Pittsburgh in 1954 but then ceased manufacture four years later. It was reformed again in April 1968 as Taylorcraft Aviation Corporation, and from 1973 has resumed production of an updated two-seat Sportsman 100.

TEAL AIRCRAFT CORPORATION/*Canada/USA*

Since spring 1976 this company has held manufacturing and tooling rights for the Thurston (*q.v.*) Teal, which was previously owned by Schweizer Aircraft Corporation (*q.v.*). It was planned to restore the Teal to production in 1978, as the TSC-1A3 Marlin, from a factory at St. Augustine, Florida.

TECHNICAL CENTRE, CIVIL AVIATION DEPARTMENT/*India*

This is basically a research and development centre in Delhi. It has produced nine types of gliders since 1950, as well as the Revathi two/three seat trainer. Plans to manufacture a new version of the Revathi, the Mk II, were still pending in 1978.

Tellier TC6 cannon-armed bomber flying-boat

TELLIER/*France*

Motor-boat builder Alphonse Tellier (one of his craft towed Voisin's float glider in 1905) built his first aircraft, for Emile Dubonnet, in 1909–1910, but went into liquidation in 1911. Reformed upon outbreak of WW1, Tellier's company built floats and hulls for other marine aircraft before flying prototype of T2 flying-boat in June 1916. This soon crashed, but with new funds from Dubonnet, Tellier evolved the T3 two-seat bomber flying-boat of 1917 and its cannon-armed derivative, the TC6. Most were built by Nieuport and other manufacturers. Final products were the unsuccessful twin-engined T5 flying-boat and tri-motor T7. In August 1918 the company was absorbed by Nieuport (*q.v.*) with Tellier as its marine aircraft designer.

Taylorcraft Plus D two-seat light plane

Teal (formerly Thurston Teal) amphibian

Temco Swift two-seat cabin monoplane

Temco TT-1 Pinto jet primary trainer

TEMCO AIRCRAFT CORPORATION/*USA*

Title from about 1950 of Texas Engineering & Manufacturing Company Inc. (*q.v.*). Three TE-1A Buckaroo primary trainers (development of Globe Swift) evaluated by USAF 1951, leading in 1953 to civil Model 33 Plebe (no production) and military Model TE-1B. Temco also converted Navions to Twin Navions and Boeing C-97s into ambulance aircraft. Absorbed Luscombe (*q.v.*) in 1953, and in December that year acquired Riley Twin Navion programme. Major subcontractor in 1950s for Bell, Boeing, Convair, Douglas, Lockheed, Martin and McDonnell military aircraft. Last own product was TT-1 Pinto two-seat jet primary trainer, flown March 1956. The company became Temco Electronics about 1960, and reappeared in the aviation industry as part of Ling-Temco-Vought (*q.v.*).

Temco T-35 trainer prototype

TEXAS AIRCRAFT MANUFACTURING COMPANY/*USA*

Based at Stewart Airport, Tyler, Texas. Acquired in early 1950s from Johnson Aircraft Corporation (*q.v.*) the Bullet light aircraft, produced as Texas Bullet.

TEXAS AIRPLANE MANUFACTURING COMPANY INC./*USA*

Dallas-based company which in mid-1970s acquired assets of Carstedt Inc. (*q.v.*) and is continuing marketing of latter's Jetliner 600 lengthened-fuselage turboprop conversion of de Havilland Dove as the CJ600.

TEXAS ENGINEERING & MANUFACTURING COMPANY INC./*USA*

This company built 329 examples of the Globe Swift under licence before Globe (*q.v.*) went bankrupt in 1947, when it acquired rights in this aircraft. It was renamed Temco (*q.v.*) about 1950.

THK/*Turkey*

see Turk Hava Kurumu Ucak Fabrikasi

THOMAS BROTHERS AEROPLANE COMPANY/*USA*

Founded at Bath, New York, 1912 by William and Oliver Thomas, who built their first aircraft in Winter 1909–1910. Products included T-2 biplane (similar to Curtiss J) and D-5 two-seat observation biplane, of which two evaluated by US Army. Merged January 1917 with Morse Chain Company to form Thomas-Morse Aircraft Corporation (*q.v.*).

THOMAS-MORSE AIRCRAFT CORPORATION/*USA*

Formed January 1917 at Ithaca, New York, from merger of Thomas Brothers Aeroplane Company (*q.v.*) and Morse Chain Company. Principal products during and after WW1 were S-4 single-seat advanced training biplane and its S-5 seaplane version; MB-3 single-seat fighter; R-2 and R-5 Pulitzer Trophy racers of 1921–1922 and their unsuccessful MB-9 and

Thomas Brothers T-2 pre-WW1 biplane

Thomas-Morse MB-7 racing monoplane

MB-10 pursuit/training derivatives. Last aircraft produced were 0-19 two-seat observation biplane and 0-19-derived X0-932 sesquiplane of 1932. Development/production of these two continued after Thomas-Morse had been acquired in 1929 by Consolidated Aircraft Corporation (*q.v.*).

THOMPSON, NORMAN, FLIGHT COMPANY LTD./*UK*

Seaplane manufacturer of Bognor, Sussex, formed October 1915 to succeed White and Thompson Ltd. (*q.v.*). Products included N.1B two-seat flying-boat fighter, N.T.2B two-seat flying-boat trainer, which was also built by Supermarine and S.E. Saunders Ltd. (both *q.v.*) and N.T.4 and 4A four-seat antisubmarine and training flying-boats. One N.T.2B was shipped to Canada to make forestry patrols from Lake St. John, Quebec. The N.T.4s were similar to Curtiss H.4s and known as Americas, but there was no connection between these companies.

THORP AIRCRAFT COMPANY/*USA*

Formed about 1949–1950 at Pacoima, California by John W. Thorp to develop his Sky Skooter two-seat light aircraft, first flown August 1946, itself developed from Lockheed Little Dipper. Built three of T-111 model; introduced T-211 in 1953, production of which undertaken by Tubular Aircraft Products Company (*q.v.*). Currently Thorp Engineering markets plans for T-18 Tiger homebuilt.

THULINS, ENOCH, AB AEROPLANFABRIC/*Sweden*

Title from 1914 of the former AVIS (Aeroplanvarvet i Skane) company formed 1913 by Dr. Enoch Thulin and Oskar Ask. Models A, B, C and D were respectively Swedish versions of the Blériot monoplane, Morane-Saulnier monoplane, Albatross B.II and Morane-Saulnier parasol. Thulin designs included the Type E, FA, G, GA, H, K, L, LA, N and NA. Total factory output was 99 aircraft, of which 32 produced in 1918. Dr. Thulin died in flying accident in 1919. AB Thulinverken, a company which was formed a year later, is not connected with aviation.

THUNDERBIRD AIRCRAFT INC./*USA*

The Thunderbird Aircraft Company was established in November 1927 at Glendale, California, to build and develop the Thunderbird biplane, designed by Theodore A. Woolsey, and first flown in June 1926. The production W-14 was a three-seat open cockpit biplane powered by a Curtiss OX-5 engine.

THURSTON AIRCRAFT CORPORATION/*USA*

This company was organized in July 1966 by David B. Thurston to develop marine aircraft. It designed and manufactured the TSC-1A1 Teal two/three-seat light amphibian—since acquired by Teal Aircraft Corporation (*q.v.*).

TIMM AIRCRAFT CORPORATION/*USA*

Formed at Van Nuys, California; was inactive in aircraft manufacture for several years, but in late 1930s produced prototype T-840 twin-engined six-seat transport. Then it developed a plastic-bonded plywood Aeromold, applying this first to the S-160-K two-seat primary trainer of 1940, which was built in WW2 as N2T-1 trainers for US Navy. Timm was responsible also for building 434 Waco CG-4A cargo gliders, and other wartime subcontract work for Harlow, Lockheed, Vultee and other companies.

Transland Ag-2 agricultural aircraft

TIMMINS AVIATION LTD./*Canada*
Transport aircraft repair and overhaul works at Montreal International Airport which in early/mid-1960s produced a 'general aviation' conversion of the Catalina amphibian. Aircraft and Texaco Sky Service Divisions merged on 1 January 1967 with Atlantic Aviation of Wilmington, Delaware, USA.

TIPSY/*Belgium*
Formed in late 1930s together with Tipsy Aircraft Company Ltd. in UK (*q.v.*) to build ultralight aircraft designed by E. O. Tips and previously manufactured by Avions Fairey (*q.v.*). Pre-war products at Gosselies were single-seat S2 and two-seat B or B-2 (open cockpits) and BC (enclosed cabin). B-2 revived post-war as Tipsy Trainer, and BC as Belfair (from Belgian Fairey), together with new design of Junior in 1946 and Nipper in 1957. Production of Nipper taken over by Cobelavia in 1961, and by Nipper Aircraft Ltd. in 1966 (both *q.v.*)

TIPSY AIRCRAFT COMPANY LTD./*UK*
Formed 1937 at Hanworth Air Park, Middlesex, to licence-build Anglo-Belgian lightplanes of E. O. Tips. Continued production post-war but closed down in 1952.

TOWLE AIRCRAFT COMPANY INC./*USA*
Incorporated in 1928 at Detroit, Michigan, to build the Towle TA-3 eight-passenger amphibian flying-boat. A high-wing cantilever monoplane, it was powered by twin radial engines mounted on multi-strut pylons on the wing upper surface.

TRANSLAND AIRCRAFT/*USA*
A Division of Hi-Shear Rivet Tool Company, and manufacturer since early 1950s of equipment for agricultural aviation. Built Ag-1 agricultural research aircraft in about 1953, fol-lowed 1956 by Ag-2, utilising components from Vultee BT-13. Plans to build five Ag-2s in late 1950s thwarted. Revived in 1965, but still none produced.

TRAVEL AIR MANUFACTURING COMPANY/*USA*
Noted chiefly for its Model 2000/3000/4000/8000/9000 family of commercial and training biplanes of the mid/late 1920s, following its formation in 1924 by Walter H. Beech (later of Beechcraft, *q.v.*) and others. Travelair Model R 'Mystery Ships' came first in 1929 Thompson Trophy race and 2nd in 1930, easily beating best US Army and Navy entries. Company purchased by Curtiss-Wright Corporation (*q.v.*) in 1930.

TRECKER AIRCRAFT CORPORATION/*USA*
Division of Kearney & Trecker Corporation which in early/mid-1960s assembled at Milwaukee, Wisconsin, Italian Piaggio P.136L-1s and L-2s under names Trecker Gull and Super Gull.

TRELLA AIRCRAFT SYNDICATE/*USA*
Established in 1921 at Detroit, Michigan, to produce the Trella Speedster two-seat lightweight biplane, which was powered by a 48·5 kW (65 hp) Le Blond radial engine.

TRIDENT AIRCRAFT LTD./*Canada*
Established in early 1970s to develop Trigull-320 six-seat light amphibian, first flown August 1973, production scheduled to begin 1978.

TSENTRALNYI AERO-GIDRODINAMICHESKII INSTITUT/*USSR*
see ANT

Tupolev Tu-95 long-range bomber

TUBULAR AIRCRAFT PRODUCTS COMPANY INC./*USA*
Builder under licence from Thorp Aircraft Company (*q.v.*) the Model 211, a developed version of the Thorp Sky Skooter lightplane. Eight built by Spring 1965; suspended 1966.

TUGAN AIRCRAFT LTD./*Australia*
Built in 1936 six examples of the Gannet twin-engined, high-wing monoplane for cartographic survey/ambulance duties for the RAAF, designed by Wg. Cdr L. J. Wackett. Taken over 1936 by Commonwealth Aircraft Corporation (*q.v.*).

Tupolev ANT-4 (TB-1) heavy bomber

Tupolev Tu-16 twin-jet medium bomber

TUPOLEV/*USSR*

Doyen of Soviet aircraft designers, A. N. Tupolev (1888–1972) studied under great Soviet aviation pioneer N. E. Zhukovskii and during WW1 worked at Duks factory in Moscow. In 1918 assisted Zhukovskii to found ANT (*q.v.*) becoming head of design department 1920 and president of commission to design and build all-metal aircraft 1922. Initially followed Junkers formula, using corrugated metal skins; first to appear was ANT-2 (A. N. Tupolev) three-seat monoplane. During 1920–1936 most designs bore ANT designations although some emanated from his design team leaders—chief deputy A. A. Archangelskii, W. M. Petlyakov and P. O. Sukhoi (e.g. Sukhoi designed ANT-25 and 37). Tupolev's first major design was ANT-4 (TB-1) heavy bomber of 1925, forerunner of several very large machines including ANT-6 (TB-3) bomber; ANT-9 commercial passenger transport and huge ANT-20 *Maxim Gorkii* propaganda aircraft of 1934. Also designed ANT-40 (SB-2) twin-engined medium bomber.

In 1936 Tupolev was arrested during Stalin's purges for 'revolutionary activities' and condemned to death, but sentence commuted and after some five years' imprisonment was released and restored to favour—ostensibly in recognition of Tu-2 medium bomber, designed while in prison—and given his own design bureau. After WW2 continued to place emphasis on large aircraft—Tu-4 copy of Boeing B-29 Superfortress helped win him a Stalin Prize in 1948. Main post-war products include Tu-14 twin-jet naval medium bomber; Tu-16 twin-jet bomber; and trio of four-turboprop swept-wing giants—the Tu-95 long-range maritime patrol bomber, Tu-114 200-passenger transport and Tu-126 AWACS aircraft. Jet transport aircraft include twin-jet Tu-104 (based on Tu-16); Tu-124; Tu-134 and tri-jet Tu 154. Most recent military types are Tu-22 supersonic bomber, Tu-28P large all-weather fighter and Tu-26 variable geometry supersonic bomber. Tu-144 supersonic transport designed by his son A. A. Tupolev, believed to have succeeded his father as head of bureau.

Tupolev Tu-154 medium/long-range transport

TURBAY SA/*Argentina*

First design by Ing. Alfredo Turbay was the T-1 Tucan parasol-wing lightplane, first flown April 1943. Six Tucans ordered from Sfreddo & Paolini (*q.v.*) were halted when the latter firm was seized and nationalised by the government and plans to revive production in 1963 were also thwarted. The T-2 five-seat twin-engined monoplane was destroyed by fire in early 1949 before it had flown; thus the next

design to fly was the T-3A six-passenger light transport in December 1964. Turbay SA was formed in January 1961 to build the proposed T-3B production version and a lengthened fuselage development, the T-4, but no production was achieved.

Turbay T-3A light transport

TURK HAVA KURUMU UCAK FABRIKASI/*Turkey*

Aircraft factory of the Turkish Air League formed 1941 at Etimesgut, near Ankara. Built several gliders, including the THK-1 twelve-seat troop transport glider, and five types of light aircraft: the THK-2 single-seat aerobatic trainer; THK-5/5A twin-engined light transport/ambulance; THK-11 three-seat pusher-engined twin-boom light tourer; THK-15 tandem two-seat primary trainer; and THK-16 twin-jet trainer. Also built approx. 100 Miles M.14s under licence. Turkish Air League control ceased 1952; renamed Makina ve Kimya Endustrisi Kurumu (*see* MKEK).

UV

UAC/USA
see United Aircraft Corporation

UDET FLUGZEUGBAU GmbH/*Germany*
German air ace of WW1, Ernst Udet, lent his name to this company, established near Munich in 1921 by American, William Pohl. The Udet U-1 single-seat lightplane of 1922 was followed by a two-seat U-2; more powerful U-4; cabin monoplane U-5; another ultralight two-seat U-6; parasol-winged single-seat U-7 Kolibri; small airliner U-8; and an 11-seat high-wing transport U-11 Kondor. Udet left the company in 1925, after agreeing to production of a light training biplane, the Udet U-12 Flamingo, which was to become the company's best-known aircraft. A two-seat, open cockpit biplane of wooden construction, it was demonstrated throughout the world by Udet. Although the company went out of business in 1925, Flamingo production continued as Bayerische Flugzeugwerke AG (*q.v.*) in Germany, as well as in Austria, Hungary and Latvia. It served in many roles, notably as a trainer with the German civil flying clubs and at clandestine Luftwaffe pilot training centres.

UETZ FLUGZEUGBAU/*Switzerland*
This company developed an improved version of the French Jodel D119 two-seat light plane known as the Uetz U2V, first flown 1962. Series production began in 1964. In that year a redesigned four-seater—the U4M Pelikan —also went into production.

UKROVOZDUKHPUT/*USSR*
This company (The Ukranian Air Transport Co.) was one of the most important aviation companies in Russia in the 1920s. Besides operating several airlines, Ukrovozdukhput manufactured aircraft to the designs of K. A. Kalinin, who patented the elliptical wing planform in 1923. One of his best-known designs was the 1928 Kalinin K-4 single-engined cabin monoplane, which was produced as a transport or air ambulance.

UMBAUGH AIRCRAFT CORPORATION/*USA*
Developed the Umbaugh Model 18 two-seat, jump-start autogyro which first flew in 1959. Limited production followed, including five aircraft assembled and tested by the Fairchild Corporation (*q.v.*) in 1960. In 1965 production of the U-18 was taken over by Air & Space Manufacturing (*q.v.*) and the aircraft was redesignated Air & Space U-18A.

UMBRA SA/*Italy*
Founded in 1935 by Muzio Macchi, Umbra built Savoia-Marchetti S.M.79 torpedo-bombers under licence. Post-war production comprised aircraft and systems components until work was begun, in 1968, on the AUM-903 three-engined STOL light transport project. Current production is concentrated on licence manufacture of the Scheibe SF-25B Motorfalke motor glider for the Italian and North African markets.

UNGARISCHE FLUGZEUGBAU AG/*Hungary*
Founded by Baron Skoda, proprietor of the Skoda Gun Works, in association with a group of Hungarian banks, to build Loehner aircraft immediately after WW1.

UNION FLUGZEUGWERKE GmbH/*Germany*
Founded in 1956 by Ernst Heinkel Flugzeugbau and Messerschmitt AG (both *q.v.*) as a joint enterprise to manufacture under licence French Fouga-Potez Magister jet trainers for the Luftwaffe, production of 210 being completed in 1963. Current activities include the procurement of spares for German military aircraft and preparing technical manuals.

UNITED AIRCRAFT CORPORATION/*USA*
This conglomorate was founded in 1934 to group together the activities of Pratt & Whitney Aircraft and Engines, Hamilton-Standard (formerly Hamilton Metalplane), United Airports and Vought-Sikorsky, each company retaining its separate identity.

UNITED EASTERN AEROPLANE CORPORATION/*USA*
Established in New York; built three trainer biplanes for use in own Eastern School of Aviation. During WW2 built aircraft under contract.

Uetz U2V two-seat lightplane

Umbaugh Model 18 autogyro

United biplane trainer

UNITED HELICOPTER INC./USA

This company succeeded the Aircraft Division of Hiller Industries, established in 1942 to develop and produce helicopters with twin co-axial rotor blades. A two-seat C4 Commuter prototype was flown, together with the United J-5, which was the first US-built helicopter to employ jet torque conversion.

UNITED STATES ARMY ENGINEERING DIVISION/USA

Established at McCook Field, Ohio, the US Army Engineering Division was concerned with the design, development and manufacture of aircraft for the US Army. These included the FVL-8 and BVL-12, biplane fighter and bomber respectively, designed by Italian Ottorino Pomilio; USD-9 version of the British de Havilland D.H.9; XB-1 version of the Bristol F.2B fighter; M-1 and MAT communications aircraft designed by Alfred Verville and built by the Sperry Aircraft Company (q.v.); three R-3 low-wing monoplane racing aircraft, by the same Verville/Sperry combination; VCP-1 (Verville-Clark Pursuit) of 1918; NBL-1 'Barling' bomber designed by Britain's Walter Barling and built by Witteman-Lewis Aircraft Corporation (q.v.); and GA-1, or G.A.X. (Ground Attack Experimental), built by the Boeing Company (q.v.). With establishment of the United States Army Air Corps in 1926, the Engineering Division was replaced at McCook Field by the Matériel Division.

UNIVAIR AIRCRAFT CORPORATION/USA

Founded in 1946 to manufacture propellers and components for light aircraft. Acquired type certificates and production rights for a number of post-war American lightplanes, including the Globe Swift, Ercoupe and Mooney Mite. Builds to order updated version of the Stinson 108 Voyager.

UPPERCU-BURNELLI AIRCRAFT CORPORATION/USA

Formed 1930 to develop the theories of Vincent Burnelli on aerofoil-shaped fuselage structures, occupying the former Aeromarine Plane & Motor Company (q.v.) plant at New Jersey. First project was Model 101 high-speed twin-engined transport developed from earlier Remington-Burnelli Airliner projects—the 1920 RB-2, 1927 CU-16 and 1929 UB-20. Subsequently became the Burnelli Aircraft Corporation (q.v.).

URDANETA Y GALVEZ LTDA./Colombia

Established 1950. Since 1961 this company

Valmet Leko-70 Vinka light trainer

has been South American distributor for the products of the Cessna Aircraft Company (q.v.), assembling and part-manufacturing certain Cessna types such as the Model A188 AgWagon agricultural aircraft. It is planned that the company will eventually undertake licence manufacture of complete airframes from the Cessna range.

URMV-3/Romania

Before WW2 Regia Autonoma Industria Aeronautica Romana (q.v.) licence-manufactured Morane, Potez, Fleet and PZL aircraft under the IAR designation. After it was demilitarised by the Russians, the URMV-3 Factory, as the aircraft plant was known, produced a number of light aircraft including IAR 811 and IAR 813 two-seat low-wing trainers; the IAR 817 high-wing agricultural/ambulance aeroplane; the IAR 821 single-seat agricultural/utility aircraft, and the IAR 823 STOL utility transport.

UTVA, FABRICA AVIONA/Yugoslavia

Utva produces light utility aircraft, including the Utva 56 four-seater, first flown in 1956, and since developed through a number of U60 air-taxi/tourer/freight/agricultural/ambulance and floatplane versions. The Utva 65 was originally an agricultural aircraft, developed as the U66 to serve various utility roles, and series production of an armed U66V version began in 1974. The Utva 75 two-seat trainer/glider tug entered production in 1975.

VALMET OY KUOREVEDEN TEHDAS/Finland

Valmet Oy is shortened title since about 1958 of state-owned group (Valtion Metallitehtaat Lentokonetehdas, q.v.) consisting of several metal-working factories. Kuoreveden Tehdas (Kuorevesi Works) was formerly part of factory group Valmet Oy Tampere, from which it separated in 1974, and is now the largest aircraft factory in Finland. Foreign aircraft produced under licence have included Potez (Air Fouga) Magister jet trainers and Saab Draken fighters. Latest own-design is Leko-70 Vinka two-seat piston-engined trainer evolved by new design group created September 1970; Valmet will also assemble 50 Hawker Siddeley Hawk jet trainers for Finnish Air Force. Activities include overhaul and repair of military and civil aircraft and piston aero-engines. The other aviation member of group is Valmet Oy Linnavuoren Tehdas, at Siuro, concerned mainly with overhaul and repair of jet aero-engines.

VALSTS ELEKTROTECHNISKA FABRIKA/Latvia

(Government Electrotechnical Factory) at Riga. Aviation division established 1935 under Karlis Irbitis, pioneer aircraft designer/builder in Latvia since mid-1920s. First production was I-11 (Irbitis's 11th design), two-seat low-wing monoplane, built 1936. A year later came improved I-12. Single examples followed of small series of small, lightweight fighter/trainers and, in 1939, the 483 km/h (300 mph)

Utva 56 four-seat lightplane

Utva 65 agricultural aircraft

I-16 two/four-gun single-seat light fighter. VEF built I-17 two-seat primary trainer for Latvian Air Force in 1940, and two I-18 two-seaters developed from earlier Pulins/Irbitis I-8. When Latvia was invaded on 17 June 1940, VEF had 612-644 km/h (380-400 mph) I-19 fighter on drawing board.

VALTION LENTOKONETEHDAS/*Finland*

Finnish State Aircraft Factory, created February 1928 from former IVL (Ilmailuvoimien Lentokonetehdas = Aviation Force Aircraft Factory) which, from its formation near Helsinki in 1921, had built Hansa-Brandenburg W.33 seaplanes and Caudron C 60 trainers under licence for Finnish Air Force, plus the Finnish-designed Kotka maritime reconnaissance/bomber biplane. First VL product was the Sääski two-seat trainer, followed by licence production of de Havilland Moths and Blackburn Ripons. After producing the Vima light trainer and Tuisku advanced training/reconnaissance biplanes, the VL was reorganised in 1936 and moved to Tampere, where it produced Pyry monoplane trainers, Fokker C.X. biplanes, Fokker D.XXI fighters and Bristol Blenheim bombers under licence. Next native product was single-seat Myrsky fighter of 1942–1945. Became part of Valtin (next entry) after WW2.

VALTION METALLITEHTAAT LENTOKONETEHDAS/*Finland*

Soon after WW2 Valtion Lentokonetehdas (*q.v.*) was integrated into this larger group (State Metal Works, Aircraft Factory) with other nationally-owned metal-working factories. Works were at Tampere (main plant), Linnavuori (aero-engines) and Kuorevesi (aircraft repairs). First post-war product was the Vihuri two-seat advanced trainer, built for Finnish Air Force. Known from about 1958 by shortened title of Valmet Oy (*q.v.*).

VANCOUVER AIRCRAFT/*Canada*

The temporary name in 1938 of Boeing Aircraft of Canada Ltd. (*q.v.*). When it became wholly Canadian-owned, it soon reverted to the earlier title.

VARGA AIRCRAFT CORPORATION/*USA*

This company acquired from Shinn Engineering Inc. (*q.v.*) in 1965 full manufacturing rights, tooling and spares for Shinn Model 2150A. Put into production by Varga in 1977 as Model 2150A Kachina. Design originated from Morrisey Nifty of 1957, built by a former Douglas test pilot.

VECTO INSTRUMENT CORPORATION/*USA*

Since early 1960s has marketed Vecto Geronimo, an uprated-engine and refined airframe/equipment version of standard Piper Apache. About 31 conversions completed by Spring 1965; after death of Vecto's owner later that year, assets purchased by Geronimo (*q.v.*).

VEGA AIRCRAFT CORPORATION/*USA*

Title from 1941 of Vega Airplane Company (*q.v.*); continued production of Lockheed-Vega B-34 Ventura twin-engined medium bomber for USAAF/USN/RAF and Boeing B-17 Flying Fortress for USAAF between 1941 and 1944. Absorbed into Lockheed Aircraft Corporation (*q.v.*) 30 November 1943; name Vega abandoned; Vega plant became Lockheed's Factory A. Ventura B-34 production ended 1943; PV-1 naval version and Boeing B-17 manufacture continued until 1944 under responsibility of Lockheed.

VEGA AIRPLANE COMPANY/*USA*

Known formerly as Airover Company, formed at Burbank, California, as associated company of Lockheed Aircraft Corporation (*q.v.*) in 1937. Began research/development experiments with light aircraft, devising (with Menasco) a unit called Unitwin—two small engines coupled side-by-side to drive single propeller flight-tested in Lockheed Altair in 1938. Then designed five/six-seat Starliner twin-tailed low-wing cabin monoplane utilising similar power plant. Small batch of radio-controlled targets built in 1939. Factory expanded 1940, and mid-year received contract to build large numbers of Lockheed Ventura bombers for RAF. Then, in conjunction with Boeing and Douglas (*q.v.*), mass-produced Boeing B-17 Flying Fortress four-engined bombers; became wholly-owned subsidiary of Lockheed in 1941 as Vega Aircraft Corporation (*q.v.*).

VENDOME, RAOUL, & COMPANY/*France*

Designed or built several novel prototypes between 1906–1914, and after outbreak of WW1 produced small number of single-seat monoplanes for artillery spotting for French Army. Last known design was 1916 experimental military biplane with two Gnome engines mounted laterally.

VERCELLESE INDUSTRIE AERONÀUTICHE/*Italy*

Formed at Vercelli about 1940 to produce F.L.3 light tourer. Little known of company activities during WW2; possibly sub-

Vecto Geronimo version of the Piper Apache

contractor for military aircraft. In 1946–1947 was renamed AVIA (Azionaria Vercellese Industrie Aeronàutiche, *q.v.*), continuing to develop F.L.3.

VERTIDYNAMICS CORPORATION/*USA*

Founded March 1970 by Bruno Nagler to build Vertigiro VG-2, single-rotor combined autogyro/helicopter based on 1936 Nagler VG-1. VG-2P prototype and VG-2C production model were never manufactured, but in March 1971 Nagler formed Nagler Aircraft Corporation (*q.v.*), starting on completely new projects.

VERTOL AIRCRAFT COMPANY/*Canada*

A wholly-owned subsidiary of Vertol Aircraft Corporation (*q.v.*), the Canadian Company was operated as completely independent. It was formed in February 1954, on former RCAF airfield at Arnprior, Ontario, initially to service and overhaul helicopters. Entered production with the Model 42A, a modified version of the Piasecki (Vertol) H-21 helicopter. A tandem-rotor general purpose helicopter, it accommodated a crew of 1/2 and 18 passengers.

VERTOL AIRCRAFT CORPORATION/*USA*

Title from March 1956 of former Piasecki Helicopter Corporation of Morton, Pennsylvania (*q.v.*). Helicopter products included Model 107 (civil), and CH-46 Sea Knight for naval supply. The latter was being built by Kawasaki (*q.v.*) in Japan in 1978 as KV-107/II. Nearly 600 Vertol H-21 Work Horse military transport helicopters, Model 43 (military export version) and Model 44 (commercial transport based on H-21) were completed. Tilt-wing Model 76 VTOL research aircraft evaluated by USAF as VZ-2. Model 114/CH-47 Chinook heavy-lift military helicopter begun by Vertol, but primary development and production by Boeing Vertol. Company became Vertol Division of The Boeing Company (*q.v.*) on 31 March 1960; now known as Boeing Vertol Company (*q.v.*).

VEREINIGTE FLUGTECHNISCHE WERKE-FOKKER GmbH/*Germany*

Established late 1963, as Vereinigte Flugtechnische Werke GmbH (VFW), from merger of Focke-Wulf GmbH and Weser Flugzeugbau GmbH, joined in 1964 by Ernst Heinkel Flugzeugbau (all *q.v.*). During 1968–1969, acquired 65% holding in Rhein-Flugzeugbau GmbH (*q.v.*), later becoming 100% owner of RFB. From 1 January 1969 became joint partner with Fokker of the Netherlands (*q.v.*), mainly for marketing purposes. Programmes in late 1960s/early 1970s included VAK-191B V/STOL and VJ 101 tilt-engine research prototypes, H2 (autogyro) and H3 (compound helicopter) experimental rotorcraft. VFW was involved in major licence production of Lockheed F-104G Starfighters (with Fokker), Sikorsky CH-53Gs (with Dornier and MBB) and Bell UH-1D helicopters; and was overall programme manager for Transall C-160 heavy military transport (built with Nord/Aérospatiale and HFB/MBB). Was involved in design/construction of Dornier Do 31E VTOL transport; has built major components for Fokker Followship, Airbus A300B and Panavia Tornado; is major overhaul facility for several important military and civil aircraft; also member of European Spacelab consortium. Principal recent aircraft programme was VFW 614 twin-turbofan short-haul transport, but production of this halted early 1978; company may merge with MBB (*q.v.*).

VFW 614 twin-turbofan short-range transport

VFW VAK 191B V/STOL research aircraft

Vertol 76 tilt-wing research aircraft

Vertol HUP-1 Retriever tandem-rotor helicopter

VERVILLE AIRCRAFT COMPANY/*USA*

Alfred V. Verville was formerly a designer with Engineering Division of US Army Air Service, producing his first (unsuccessful) aeroplane in 1915. He is best known for his later Verville-Packard and Verville-Sperry racing aircraft of the early 1920s. In 1925–1927 he produced the Buhl-Verville Airster two-seat biplane, first civil aircraft to be certificated in US (March 1927).

VIBERTI/*Italy*

Formed shortly after WW2 by Dr. Angelo Viberti to build light aircraft. First product, Musca 1 two-seat tourer/trainer low-wing monoplane, first flown 1948; slightly modified Musca 1 *bis* appeared in 1949. There were designs for Musca 2 three-seat cabin monoplane and Musca 4 high-wing version of 1, and floatplane variant, but doubtful if they were built. Probably dissolved about 1950–1951.

VICKERS (AVIATION) LTD./UK

Famous shipbuilding/engineering/armaments group of Vickers Ltd. formed an Aviation Department on 28 March 1911, under Capt H. F. Wood. Production rights for Esnault-Pelterie REP tractor monoplane obtained in same year; several variants built before WW1. In 1912 Vickers produced Type 18 Destroyer for Admiralty—pusher-engined gun-carrying fighter from which evolved, via successive E.F.B. (Experimental Fighting Biplane) prototypes, the F.B.5 and F.B.9 'Gunbus' fighters of WW1. Later front-gunned tractor-engined F.19 was less successful. During war produced also B.E.2 series, B.E.8, F.E.8 and S.E.5a for Royal Aircraft Factory, and Sopwith 1½-Strutters. Vickers Vimy of 1917 remained standard RAF bomber throughout 1920s: one used by Alcock and Brown for first non-stop Atlantic crossing by aeroplane on 14/15 June 1919. Vimy Commercial was 11-passenger airliner with enlarged fuselage; Vernon troop transport developed from this. Vimy and Vernon succeeded respectively by Virginia and Victoria in mid-1920s, followed by Pegasus-engined development, the Valentia.

In July 1928 company renamed as Vickers (Aviation) Ltd, and four months later took over Supermarine Aviation Works (q.v.), specialists in marine aircraft. Vicker's own products continued in early 1930s with Vildebeest torpedo-bomber and Vincent general-purpose biplane. June 1935 saw first flight of Pegasus-engined long-range Wellesley bomber; this was first RAF aircraft to utilise then-revolutionary principle of geodetic construc-

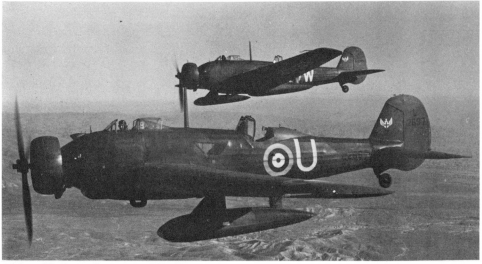

Vickers Wellesley long-range bomber

Vickers Vildebeest torpedo-bomber

Vickers (Supermarine) carrier-based Scimitar

VICTA LTD./Australia

Initially producer of 2-stroke engines and lawn mowers; Aviation Division established September 1959 to manufacture Airtourer, two-seat aerobatic lightplane designed by Henry Millicer, Chief Aerodynamicist of Government Aircraft Factories (q.v.). Prototype built by Air Tourer group of Australian Ultra Light Aircraft Association and first flew March 1959; production deliveries began mid-1962. Also that year produced prototype Victa 67A two-seat autogyro. Aviation Division closed 2 January 1967; manufacturing rights in Airtourer and later Aircruiser obtained by Aero Engine Services Ltd. (q.v.) of New Zealand.

Victa Airtourer lightplane

VICTOR AIRCRAFT CORPORATION/USA

This company built at Freeport, Long Island, New York, in 1917–1918, radial-engined scouting/advanced training biplanes designed by A. S. Heinrich.

VICTORY AIRCRAFT LTD./Canada

Originated 1942 at Malton, Ontario, under Canadian Ministry of Munitions and Supply, to takeover and manage Malton aircraft factory of National Steel Car Corporation to speed production of Avro Lancaster bombers. First Victory-built Lancaster delivered to RAF in August 1943. Total production 430, including seven unarmed mailplanes for transatlantic government service operated by Trans-Canada Air Lines; these were forerunners of the Lancastrian post-war transport version of the Lancaster. One Avro Lincoln Mk XV bomber built 1945. Company acquired from Canadian government in July 1945 by Hawker Siddeley Aircraft Company Ltd., becoming A. V. Roe (Canada) (q.v.) and subsequently designing first Canadian jet fighter.

VIKING FLYING BOAT COMPANY/USA

Built in 1936, at New Haven, Connecticut, five 00-1 single-pusher-engined flying-boats for US Coast Guard, based on French Schreck FBA 17HT-4.

VILLIERS/France

Founded late 1924 at Meudon. Products included Type 2 AMC2 fighter, and two prototypes of Type 4 HBA2 twin-float biplane for armed reconnaissance; Type 24 night fighters for Aéronautique Maritime; last design was Type 26 twin-float cabin monoplane. Company closed down in 1930; factory taken over following year by Potez (q.v.).

VINOT ET DEGUINAND/France

Long established as a manufacturer of motor cars, Vinot et Deguinand turned to the construction of aircraft after WW1, carrying out sub-contract work for the French government. The company was responsible for construction of the Pescara helicopter.

Vickers (Supermarine) Attacker carrier-based fighter

Vickers Viscount Srs 800 turboprop airliner

tion devised by Dr. B. N. (later Sir Barnes) Wallis, who remained as head of research until early 1970s. Subcontract production included Armstrong-Whitworth Siskin IIIAs (1929–1930), Hawker Harts (1932–1934) and Hart Trainers (1936). In March 1936 the prototype was flown of R. J. Mitchell's supreme design, the Supermarine Spitfire; and in June 1936 prototype of Vickers Wellington.

VICKERS-ARMSTRONGS LTD./*UK*

Vickers-Armstrongs Ltd. took over in October 1938 the former Vickers (Aviation) Ltd. and Supermarine Aviation Works (Vickers) Ltd.; each, however, retained the separate identity of its products, latter becoming Vickers-Armstrongs Ltd. (Supermarine Division). Vickers' main concern up to and during WW2 was production of Wellington bomber and Avro Lancaster; Wellington replaced at end of war and early post-war by its non-geodetic successor, the Warwick. In August 1946 came first flight of VC1 Viking, first post-war British transport to enter airline service. Subsequent products included four-jet Valiant (first British V-bomber); world's first turboprop airliner to enter production/service, the Viscount; and in 1959 the four-turboprop Vanguard airliner.

New subsidiary entitled Vickers-Armstrongs (Aircraft) Ltd. created from 1 January 1955, to continue all Vickers and Supermarine work under one management. In 1960 Vickers merged with Bristol Aeroplane Company and English Electric Company (*q.v.*) to form British Aircraft Corporation (*q.v.*).

VOISIN/*France*

First European commercial manufacturer of aircraft, formed by brothers Gabriel (1880–1973) and Charles (1888–1912) Voisin at Billancourt (Seine). Dominant partner was Gabriel, one of aviation's earliest pioneers who had built gliders—with varying success—for Archdeacon, Blériot and others from 1904. When Blériot formed his own company in February 1907, the AA Les Frères Voisin was formed in new premises at Lyons, and from spring 1907 began building series of boxkite biplanes (Hargrave-based) for Delagrange, Paulhan, Farman, Moore-Brabazon and others; by end of 1909 had built nearly 20, though by then this type had been separately much improved by Henry Farman. First, 'gunbus' biplane appeared 1910, a canard oddity in 1911, and the large Icare seaplane in 1913; but Voisin chiefly known for extensive series of successful military bombers of 1914–1918. Primitive but strong, these Voisin 'chicken-coops' appeared in many variants, principal being Types 3, 4, 5, 8, and 10 of which, collectively, nearly 3,400 were built. Although reliable, their design had progressed little by 1918, and in 1919 Gabriel Voisin left the aviation industry and subsequently entered the automobile industry.

Classic Voisin biplane of 1909

Voisin VIII LAP night bomber

VOJENSKA/*Czechoslavakia*
Created 1923, initially building the designs of
Alois Smolik. Major output was concerned
with S-1/S-2 reconnaissance/light bomber biplanes; S-4 fighter of 1922; S-6 bomber; S-10
trainer (licensed from Hansa-Brandenburg);
S-16 long-range reconnaissance biplane, built
late 1920s/early 1930s for Czechoslavakia,
Latvia and Turkey; S-18 trainer; S-19 four-
passenger civil transport; S-20 biplane fighter;
S-21 trainer version of S-20; S-32 five-
passenger high-wing tri-motor; and the S-
328/528 series of reconnaissance/light bomber
biplanes. Also undertook licence production of
Tupolev SB-2 twin-engined monoplane
bomber. Built Arado and Junkers types during
German occupation 1940–1945.

VOLAIRCRAFT INC./*USA*
Only product was Volaire Model 10, certified
1961. Limited production at Aliquippa, Pennsylvania, as Model 1050 four-seat high-wing
monoplane before, in mid-1965, becoming a
division of Aero Commander Inc. (*q.v.*), who
re-named it the Aero Commander 100.

VOLKSEIGENER BETRIEB/*Germany*
East German State aircraft factory; enjoyed
brief existence in 1950s, with plants at
Pirna/Elbe (Entwicklungsbau Pirna) and
Dresden/Klotzsche. Established 1954 to
licence-build Soviet Ilyushin Il-14 twin-
engined passenger transport and a variety of
gliders. In 1956 was selected to develop BB-
152 four-jet, swept-wing civil transport (Pirna
turbojets)—originally joint project from Prof.
Dipl. Ing. Brunolf Baade (deputy director of
VEB) and Soviet designer Dr. Bronin. Three
twin-jet prototypes developed as Type 150 at
Podberezje in USSR—themselves deriving
from Junkers Ju 287 bomber. Twenty-two BB-
152s laid down—only five prototypes completed; first flight in December 1960. Programme was closed down and state aircraft
manufacture in East Germany ended in 1961.

VOLPAR INC./*USA*
Formed in 1960, Volpar marketed tricycle
landing-gear kit for Beechcraft Model 18. Following merger with Volitan Aviation Inc, kits
produced to convert Model 18 to turboprop
power, designated Turbo 18. Lengthened-
fuselage versions followed—Turboliner and
Turboliner II; then came 'Packaged Power'
units for Beech 18, de Havilland Dove and
Beaver, Grumman Goose. Larger premises acquired February 1975 to increase production
of Turboliner II; since February 1976 has collaborated with Century Aircraft Corporation
(*q.v.*) in producing turboprop conversions for
Handley Page Jetstream.

Vought OS2U-1 Kingfisher observation aircraft

Volpar Turbo 18 turboprop conversion of the Beech 18

Vojenska S-16 reconnaissance biplane

Vojenska S-528 reconnaissance/bomber

VOUGHT CORPORATION/*USA*
Has operated under the above title since 1
January 1976; for previous history, see the
various entries under Lewis & Vought, Chance
Vought, Vought-Sikorsky, Ling-Temco-
Vought and LTV Aerospace Corporation.
Current programme is manufacture and pro-
duct support of the A-7 Corsair II tactical
fighter/attack aircraft.

VOUGHT-SIKORSKY/*USA*
Chance Vought and Sikorsky Aircraft Division
of United Aircraft Corporation formed as result of April 1939 reorganisation within UAC,
upon which Chance Vought moved headquarters to Stratford, Connectictut. From 1936

concentrated primarily upon manufacture for
the US Navy, major programmes including the
SB2U Vindicator scout-bomber, OS2U Kingfisher observation aircraft, and F4U Corsair
single-seat naval fighter. Of the massive production of the wartime Corsair, which continued until 1952, Vought alone built more
than 7,700 examples. Vought-Sikorsky products at this time included the Sikorsky-
designed VS-43 and VS-44 flying-boats, and
the historic VS-300, the world's first fully-
practical helicopter, from which the production R-4 and R-5 and later designs were developed. Vought and Sikorsky were reconstituted in January 1943 as separate manufacturing divisions of UAC, so that Sikorsky could
concentrate on helicopter development and

USMC version (AU-1) of the Vought Corsair

Vought on combat aircraft, primarily the F4U and OS2U. After the war, Chance Vought Aircraft Division moved to Dallas, Texas, in 1948–1949, and produced its first jet fighter for the US Navy, the F6U Pirate. On 1 July 1954 the company became independent of UAC, under the new name of Chance Vought Aircraft Inc. (*q.v.*)

VTI/CIAR/*International*
Single-seat ground attack fighter—Orao—being manufactured jointly by Vazduhoplovno-Tehnici Institut of Yugoslavia and Centrala Industriala Aeronautica Romana of Romania (*q.v.*). Believed first flown August 1974; two other prototypes and nine pre-production aircraft reported built. First production Orao was due to fly 1977; 200 or more to be produced for the two air forces.

VTOL AIRCRAFT COMPANY PTY. LTD./*Australia*
Formed in early 1970s by D. A. Phillips to develop Phillicopter Mk1 two-seat light helicopter. Design began 1962; prototype flown 1971; flight trials still in progress 1978.

VULCAN AIRCRAFT COMPANY/*USA*
Incorporated in 1928, the Vulcan Aircraft Company was established at Portsmouth, Ohio, to produce the American Moth two-seat lightweight sporting aircraft.

VULCAN/*UK*
Based at Crossens, Southport, Lancashire; built under sub-contract during WW1 Airco/de Havilland D.H.4; D.H.9; D.H.9A; and Royal Aircraft Factory B.E.2c/d/e.

VULTEE/*USA*
Vultee entered aircraft manufacturing in mid-1930s, having formed in 1932 the Airplane Development Corporation (*q.v.*), which two years later was acquired by the Aviation Manufacturing Corporation. A Vultee Aircraft Division of the latter company was formed in 1936, becoming Vultee Aircraft Inc. when it acquired the parent corporation's assets in 1939. First product was the V-1 eight-passenger monoplane, but became better known for its military aircraft, of which most notable were the V-11 two/three-seat attack monoplane, built for Brazil, China and Turkey, and a licence sold to the USSR; the improved V-12 for China; more than 11,000 BT-13/BT-15 and SNV Valiant two-seat basic trainers for the USAAF and Navy between 1940–1944; V-48 Vanguard single-seat fighters for China and USAAF: and V-72 Vengeance dive-bombers for the RAF, USAAF and Brazil between 1941–1942. Vultee purchased the Stinson Aircraft Division (*q.v.*) of the Aviation Manufacturing Corporation in 1940, producing Stinson Model 74s for the USAAF as L-1 Vigilant during WW2. In December 1941 Vultee bought a 34% controlling interest in another subsidiary of The Aviation Corporation, Consolidated Aircraft Inc. (*q.v.*), with which it merged in 1943 to form the Consolidated Vultee Aircraft Corporation (*q.v.*).

Vultee Vanguard single-seat fighter

Vultee Vengeance dive-bomber which served with USAAF and RAF

WYZ

WACO AIRCRAFT COMPANY/USA
Started by George 'Buck' Weaver in 1919 at Loraine, Ohio, as the Weaver Aircraft Company ('Waco' trademark), and built Cootie parasol-wing aircraft. Reorganised as Advance Aircraft Company in 1923 at Troy, Ohio. Waco became official name 1929. First really successful venture was three-seat Model 9 of 1924. Developed long and successful line of cabin biplanes, sporting, racing, and military aeroplanes. By 1936, largest constructors of commercial aircraft in USA. Wartime production of own design cargo and troop carrying assault glider, CG-4A Hadrian. After war developed, but abandoned in 1947, a new monoplane, the Airistocrat. Company went out of business, returned 1966 to build Savoia-Marchetti S.205 (Waco Vela II) and Socata Rallye Minerva (Waco Sirius). Became Waco Aircraft Division of Allied Aero Industries about 1972.

WAGENER, FLUGZEUGBAU/Germany
Hans Wagener of Hamburg produced his first aircraft, the HW4A, in 1933. Used as test-bed for experimental two-stroke engine.

WAGNER, HELICOPTER TECHNIK/Germany
Joseph Wagner of Friedrichshafen began developing a helicopter in 1960, as a basic, torque-free vehicle to which specialised equipment and accommodation could be added. Rotorcar III was roadable; main development vehicle was Sky-trac. Aerocar completed 1965; three Sky-trac 1 completed 1966.

WAITOMO AIRCRAFT LTD./New Zealand
Formerly Bennett Aviation Ltd. (q.v.) of Te Kuiti. Designed first commercial aircraft built in New Zealand, the Airtruk, which flew 1960. Small-scale production. Design based on Luigi Pellarini Transavia Airtruk.

WALLACE AIRCRAFT COMPANY/USA
Formed 1928 at Chicago, Illinois, to manufacture the B.330 Touroplane, shown at Detroit Aero Show. Stanley Wallace had been concerned with aircraft designs since 1915. Acquired 1929 by American Eagle Aircraft Corporation (q.v.), under E. E. Porterfield, who continued production of Touroplane B.

WALLIS AUTOGYROS LTD./UK
The first light autogyro developed by W/Cdr Ken Wallis flew in 1961. The original WA-116 appeared in various guises, including four Beagle-built military prototypes and a two-

Waco VKS-7 4-seat cabin biplane

seater. Holds Class E3/E3a records for height 4,639 m (15,220 ft) and speed 179 km/h (111·225 mph). Rolls-Royce powered WA-117 appeared 1965 and WA-118 Meteorite, WA-120 followed 1970. Current WA-121 is smallest and lightest of the range.

WALRAVEN/Netherlands
L. W. Walraven began designing and building light aircraft at Bandoeng, Java, in spare time as chief engineer to Netherlands East Indies Army Air Force, from 1922. Completed W.4 1938, which was ordered as trainer by Netherlands East Indies flying clubs.

Wallis WA-116 light autogyro

Waco CG-4A Hadrian troop carrying assault glider

Waitomo Airtruk light aircraft

WALTZ SA/*Mexico*
Franciso J. Waltz, Mexico City, was distributor for Aero Commander. Produced in 1959 a high-altitude conversion of de Havilland Heron with 291 kW (340 hp) Lycoming engine for Mexican use under name Super Heron.

WARING AND GILLOW LTD./*UK*
Undertook contract from government to build 500 de Havilland D.H.9s in WW1. Sub-contracted 50 to Wells Aviation Company Ltd. (*q.v.*). May have assembled some Handley-Page 0/400s in 1918, including some built in the US.

WASSMER/*France*
Founded 1905 by Benjamin Wassmer. Up to WW2 was repair and overhaul organisation. Started aircraft production at Issoire in 1945, building Jodel D.112 under licence. Opened own design department 1955. First production aircraft Jodel-Wassmer D.120 Paris-Nice. In 1959 built WA.40 Super Sancey, followed by Baladou and 1966 WA.52 Europa, one of the first aircraft extensively constructed from glassfibre. WA.54 Atlantic appeared 1973 and WA.80 Piranha in 1975. Formed in 1971 with Siren SA (*q.v.*) company named CERVA (*q.v.*) to develop an all-metal four/six-seat light aircraft.

Wassmer D.120 Paris-Nice lightplane

Wassmer WA.41 Baladou four-seat cabin monoplane

WATANABE TEKKOSHO KABUSHIKI KAISHA/*Japan*
The Watanabe Iron Works (K. K. Watanabe Tekkosho) began making aircraft parts during 1920s, building trainers from 1931. Ki-51 Army Type 99 still serving 1941, but obsolete. Developed seaplanes (E13A, E14Y) during WW2; fighters (A5M and J7W); K10W1 trainer, copied from North American NA-16, built in 1941; production after first 26 given to Nippon (*q.v.*). Built K11W1 bomber-crew trainer in 1940, and copy of Bücker Bü 131 Jungmann. In 1942 produced Q14 Tokai three-seat long-range naval patrol aircraft. Reorganised as Kyushu Hikoki K.K. in 1943 and products known retrospectively under that name.

WATERHOUSE AIRCRAFT INC./*USA*
Established at Glendale, California, incorporated 1926. Began by building a 3-seat monoplane known by the name Cruzair. Power plant comprised a 149 kW (200 hp) Wright radial engine.

WATERMAN AIRPLANE CORP./*USA*
Waldo D. Waterman of Santa Monica, California, produced in 1934 design for a two-seat tailless monoplane as a simple private aircraft. Corporation formed 1935 to develop roadable

Wassmer WA.52 Europa lightplane

aircraft with detachable wings and motor-car engine driving propeller by Vee belts. In 1967 produced the W-11 Chevvy Bird, his 11th design, as test bed for Chevrolet Corvair motor car engine.

WEATHERLEY AVIATION COMPANY INC./*USA*
John C. Weatherley operated the Weatherley Campbell Aircraft Company as a fixed base operator, at Dallas, Texas. Acquired plans of the Colt four seater from Luscombe Airplane Corporation (*q.v.*). Weatherley Aviation Company established at Hollister, California. Built WM 62C agricultural aircraft 1961–1965, a converted Fairchild 62. Developed W.201, a much-improved agricultural aircraft in 1967; followed by 201A in 1970 and 201C in 1975, the latter in production in 1978.

WEAVER AIRCRAFT COMPANY/*USA*
see Waco Aircraft Company

WEIR, G. & J. LTD./*UK*
An engineering firm of Cathcart, Glasgow, which built de Havilland D.H.9 and RAF B.E.2c, B.E.2e, and F.E.2b aircraft under sub-contract during WW1.

WEISER UND SOHN/*Austria*
During WW1 built Aviatik (*q.v.*) military types under sub-contract.

WEISS, MANFRED, FLUGZEUG UND MOTORENFABRIK AG/*Hungary*
One of the largest industrial organisations in Hungary; opened an aircraft department at Budapest 1928, beginning with licence-production of Fokker FVIII and CV and Bristol Jupiter engine. Built first of its own designs 1931 and produced two-seat biplane 1936.

WELCH AIRCRAFT INDUSTRIES/*USA*
Fixed-base operator Orin Welch built aircraft for his West Virginia Flying School in late 1920s. Introduced his aircraft Falcon OW-5 in 1931, of which about 65 built, at South Bend, Indiana, between 1935–1940.

Weatherley 201 agricultural aircraft

WELLS AVIATION LTD./UK

London company based at Whiteheads Grove, Chelsea. Built 50 de Havilland D.H.9s under contract to Waring and Gillow (*q.v.*). They built also 100 Sopwith 1½ strutters. In 1915 designed and built a small single-seat biplane. Went into liquidation 1917, but production continued under Sir Samuel Waring.

WENDT/USA

Formed in New York by George W. Constant in 1939 to build the W.2 two-seat monoplane.

WERFTE WARNEMÜNDE/Germany

Established in early 1917 as a subsidiary of Flugzeugbau Friedrichshafen; in 1933 Werfte Warnemünde became known as Arado Flugzeugwerke (*q.v.*).

WESER FLUGZEUGBAU AG/Germany

Formed, as Weser Flugzeugbau GmbH, aviation department of Deutsche Schiff- und Maschinenbau 'Weser' AG in 1934. Took over Rohrbach Metallflugzeugbau GmbH (*q.v.*). Undertook contract manufacture during WW1 for other manufacturers. Reconstituted in 1956 as the Finanz-und-Wervaltungs GmbH, reverting to Weser Flugzeugbau 1959. The company then built the Nord Noratlas under licence from 1960, with Hamburger Flugzeugbau and Siebelwerke-ATG (*q.v.*), under the name of Flugzeugbau Nord GmbH at Hamburg. In 1958, with Hamburger, Nord Aviation (*q.v.*), and Dipl. Ing. Prof. Walter Blume Leichtbau-und-Flugtechnik, it formed Arbeitsgemeinschaft Transall. Finally the company combined with Focke-Wulf Flugzeugbau (*q.v.*) in 1963, losing its individual identity entirely.

WEST AUSTRALIAN AIRWAYS LTD./Australia

Formed at Perth in 1921 to operate Geraldton–Derby airline and licensed to build the de Havilland D.H.50 in Australia. Produced first aircraft in 1926.

WESTERN AIRPLANE CORPORATION/USA

Formed at Chicago, Illinois, to build a three-seat biplane, powered by a 67 kW (90 hp) Curtiss OX-5 engine.

WEST VIRGINIA AIRCRAFT COMPANY/USA

This company was established at Wheeling, West Virginia, and produced a three-seat triplane during 1919–1920.

WESTLAND AIRCRAFT LTD./UK

Petters Ltd, an engineering company founded 1910, undertook government aircraft construction in 1915 at Westland Farm, Yeovil, Somerset. Produced Short 184, Short 166, Sopwith 1½-strutters, Airco/de Havilland D.H.4 and D.H.9; adapted the latter for Liberty engine as D.H.9A. Built also Vickers Vimy. First of their own designs were the single-seat N.1b scout and Wagtail and two-seat Weasel, but the war's end prevented production. First civil aircraft, the four-seat cabin Limousine, was followed by a D.H. 9A development, the Walrus, and the 1923 Dreadnought, a very advanced aircraft based on Woyevodsky's flying-wing theory. The Wood-pigeon and

Westland Lysander two-seat army co-operation aircraft

Westland Sea King all-weather anti-submarine helicopter

Widgeon I and II that followed were Westland's only attempt to enter light aircraft market. Apart from Westland IV/Wessex three-engined airliners of 1929–1931, the rest of the designs from Yeovil were military fighters or general purpose aircraft. Wapiti, built from 1927, was basically a modernisation of the D.H.9A and was followed in 1931 by an improved version, the Wallace. The Westland P.V.3 private prototype for the Wallace, was used on the Houston Everest expedition of 1933. From the P.V.7 monoplane, the last general purpose type, the Lysander was developed, the best-known and most numerous company design of WW2. Westland fighters have included the twin-engined Whirlwind

WEYMANN/France

Charles Weymann designed and built in 1916 an all-metal biplane with conventional fuselage. In 1929 joined with lePère, and Weymann-lePère was formed from the remains of a separate company called Avimeta (*q.v.*) which had closed in 1928. Weymann-lePère held a Cierva licence; when lePère left in 1930, Weymann reverted to original name.

WHITE AIRCRAFT COMPANY LTD./USA

Burd S. and Harold L. White, of Des Moines, Indiana, did general aircraft rebuilding work 1918–1926. Designed and produced their own private and commercial aircraft, Humming Bird, in 1926.

WHITE AIRCRAFT INC./USA

Donald G. White of Buffalo, New York, formed a company in 1939 to continue production, in modified form, of the Pirate amphibian designed and built previously by Argonaut Aircraft Inc. (*q.v.*).

WHITE AND THOMPSON LTD./UK

Based at Bognor, Sussex. Acquired UK rights to products of Curtiss Aeroplane Company (*q.v.*). Built Short S.38 trainers under subcontract in 1914. About 1910 had designed and built an unsuccessful aircraft with wings covered in sheet aluminium. Registered 1912 as private company; designed and built one- and two-engined flying-boats for the Admiralty in 1914.

Westland Wyvern single-seat carrier-based strike aircraft

which saw limited squadron service in WW2, followed by the high altitude Welkin, which did not enter service. Following the war, four naval strike squadrons were equipped with the turboprop Wyvern; this was the last fixed-wing aircraft built by the company. In the 1930s Westland built two autogiros for Juan de la Cierva and in 1946, with declining sales of fixed-wing aircraft, decided to concentrate on rotary-wing designs. Negotiated with Sikorsky (*q.v.*) a licence to build a modified version of the four-seat Sikorsky S-51. Re-engined and altered in detail, it was produced as the Dragonfly in 1948. Followed by the S-55 Whirlwind and in 1959 Westland's first turbine-powered helicopter, the Gnome-engined Whirlwind. In the reorganisation of Britain's aircraft industry Westland acquired the helicopter interest of Bristol Aircraft (1960), Fairey Aviation (1960), and Saunders-Roe (1959) (all *q.v.*). From this came production contracts for the army Belvedere and Scout and Royal Navy Wasp, while the Sikorsky designs, enhanced increasingly by Westland improvements, resulted in the S-58 Wessex. Beginning in 1966, the company was known as Westland Helicopters Ltd. (*See next entry*).

Westland Wapiti two-seat general purpose biplane

WESTLAND HELICOPTERS LTD./*UK*
Current activities include production of the Sea King, developed from the Sikorsky S-61 to Royal Navy requirements; Commando army version of Sea King; and Gazelle and Lynx, which are part of the Anglo-French helicopter co-operation programme with Aérospatiale (*q.v.*). Gazelle production started in 1971 and Lynx in 1975. Naval, military and civil versions are being constructed. Following the construction of 40 Aérospatiale/Westland Pumas for the RAF, the company continues to produce Puma component sets for Aérospatiale's production line.

Westland/Aérospatiale Lynx multi-purpose helicopter

WHITE, J. SAMUEL, & COMPANY LTD./*UK*
Boatbuilding company at Cowes, Isle of Wight, which in 1914 constructed to the design of Harris Booth of the Air Department, the largest aeroplane then built in Britain, the AD 1000 three-engined torpedo-bomber. Also built Short 184s under sub-contract and designed and built aircraft under name of Wight Aviation. (*q.v.*).

WHITEHEAD AIRCRAFT LTD./*UK*
Established at Richmond, Surrey, built under sub-contract during WW1 de Havilland D.H.9 and RAF B.E.2a and B.E.2b. Was a major supplier of Sopwith Pups. Built a prototype only of own-design single-seat scout.

WHITTLESEY MANUFACTURING COMPANY INC./*USA*
Formed 1929 at Bridgeport, Connecticut, by H. Newton Whittlesey, with exclusive US rights to manufacture the Avro Avian.

WIBAULT, MICHEL/*France*
Established in Paris. Wibault's first aircraft, a single-seat fighter, appeared too late to see service in WW1. Subsequently designed night bombers and fighters for the Armée de l'Air, as well as civil aircraft. Produced an all-metal aircraft in 1921 and changed from biplane to monoplane configuration 1923. In 1924 flew the prototype of a monoplane fighter, the Wibault 7, produced from 1925 and built under licence by PZL (*q.v.*) and Vickers (*q.v.*).

WIBAULT-PENHÖET/*France*
A new company formed in 1931 by a merger of Avions Michel Wibault with Chantiers de St. Nazaire Penhöet, which built a number of single- and multi-engined airliners in the 1930s. Taken over by Breguet (*q.v.*).

Wibault-Penhöet 282T-12 transport

WICKO/Australia

Wickner Aircraft of Australia, formed by Geoffrey Wickner in 1929 to build the high-wing Wizard monoplane and light single-seat Lion monoplane. Rebuilt several Avro Avians before helping to form Foster Wickner (q.v.).

WIDERÖES FLYVESELSKAP AS/Norway

The oldest flying company in Norway, established in 1933 a repair department for aircraft and engines. In 1945 built the C.5 Polar monoplane, a five-seat general purpose or ambulance aircraft which took part in the Norwegian-British-Swedish Antarctic expedition of 1951.

WIENER KARROSERIE FABRIK/Austria

Built an experimental fighter in 1918, but no details found of subsequent products.

WIENER-NEUSTADTER/Germany

Originally Wiener-Neustadter Flughafen Betriebs GmbH, after the Anschluss of 1938 was amalgamated with Hirtenberg, whose manufacturing department it absorbed under the name Wiener-Neustadter Flugzeugwerk GmbH. Light two-seat biplane in production 1937, later undertook sub-contracts on Bf 109. In 1943–1944 built the world's first tip-jet helicopter, designed by team under Friedrich von Doblhoff. Four built and tested. Conventional piston-engine provided compressed air which, mixed with fuel, was fed to tip-mounted combustion chambers through rotor blades. System adopted by other designers.

WIGHT AVIATION LTD./UK

Aviation department of J. Samuel White (q.v.) under Howard T. Wright, who joined company in 1912. Employed double-cambered aerofoils on early designs. Built training and operational seaplanes for Admiralty, a twin-engined torpedo bomber in 1915 and an experimental quadruplane.

WILDEN, HELMUT/Germany

Formed 1974 at Hennef-Sieg. Designed VoWi 8 two-seat lightweight sporting aircraft which first flew in 1974, followed by ultra-light single-seat, very simple VoWi 10, which was being built under sub-contract in 1977.

WILEY POST AIRCRAFT CORPORATION/USA

Founded in Oklahoma City in 1935 to build Model A, cheap two-seat aircraft. Powered by converted Model A Ford engine, the first example was built by Straughan Aircraft. Wiley Post acquired rights to Straughan assets 1935, and transferred production to Oklahoma City. Thirteen Model As built before company liquidated after Wiley Post's death.

WILLIAMS, GEO. AIRPLANE AND MANUFACTURING COMPANY/USA

George W. Williams designed and built his first aircraft, a light monoplane, about 1908 and started operations at Temple, Texas, as the Texas Aero Manufacturing Company. With George Carroll was credited with development of first full monocoque cantilever wing (not flown). Only production aircraft Texas-Temple of 1928–1929. On Williams's death in 1929 company reorganised as the Texas Aero Corporation.

WINDECKER RESEARCH INC./USA

Held licence from Dow Chemicals for a reinforced plastic aircraft developed by Dr. Leo Windecker, Midland, Texas. Flight tested 1967, production planned for 1968. First production Windecker Eagle I, mainly Fibraloy reinforced plastic, delivered 1970, and production continued on a limited basis.

WING AIRCRAFT COMPANY/USA

Subsidiary of Hi-Shear Corporation, Torrance, California. George S. Wing formed company 1960 to develop and market sporting twin-engined executive Wing Derringer. Company became independent 1966.

WITTEMAN-LEWIS AIRCRAFT CORPORATION/USA

Aeronautical construction engineers of Newark, New Jersey. Rebuilt Airco D.H.4s to D.H.4B standard for US Army. During 1922–1923 built the Barling six-engined triplane bomber to Walter Barling's design. Had produced own-design mail carrier in 1920, when firm moved to Teterboro. Built twin-engined Sundstedt-Hannevig seaplane 1923, for trans-Atlantic attempt by Capt. Sundstedt. Firm acquired by Fokker 1923–1924.

Wing Derringer high-performance lightplane

Witteman-Lewis floatplane

Witteman-Lewis-built Barling bomber of 1923

WKF/*Austria*
see Wiener Karroserie Fabrik

WNF/*Germany*
see Wiener Neustadter Flugzeugwerke

WOLSELEY MOTORS LTD./*UK*
Motor car manufacturers of Birmingham, Warwickshire, who produced under subcontract during WW1 RAF B.E.2c and S.E.5a aircraft. Also built improved Hispano-Suiza 149 kW (200 hp) engine as Wolseley Viper.

WOODSON AIRCRAFT CORPORATION/*USA*
Entered aviation at Bryan, Ohio, in 1926, producing a convertible cargo/passenger two-seat biplane, the 'Foto'.

WREN AIRCRAFT CORPORATION/*USA*
Fort Worth, Texas. Built James L. Robertson's Wren 460, STOL-configured Cessna 182, first flew 1963. Additions included foreplanes, wing spoilers and double-slotted flaps. Production in small numbers.

WRIGHT AERONAUTICAL COMPANY/*USA*
The Wright brothers built first successful aircraft in the world, 1903; first practical model 1905. Sold first military aircraft in world to US Army Signal Corps 1908. Continued producing same basic and outdated type though later, from Model I tractor biplane, aircraft were more conventional. Sold a few aircraft to US Navy 1914. Became Wright-Martin Aircraft Corporation (*q.v.*) 1916.

WRIGHT AERONAUTICAL CORPORATION/*USA*
Mainly an engine manufacturing company. After Wilbur's death, 1912, Orville continued at Dayton plant as independent experimenter. Built to official designs and produced Hispano-Suiza engines during the first World War. Giuseppe Bellanca joined 1924 and Wright-Bellanca monoplane and Apache shipboard fighter produced in 1925. Bellanca left 1927 to reform his own company (*see* Bellanca Aircraft Corporation). Wright became part of Curtiss-Wright (*q.v.*) 1929.

WRIGHT FLUGMASCHINE/*Germany*
Based at Adlershof, Berlin, built redesigned Wright models for military use during 1912–13. One was armoured.

Wren 460 STOL lightplane

Wright Model HS two-seat biplane

Wright-Martin Type V two-seat biplane

WRIGHT, HOWARD & WARWICK/*UK*
Howard and Warwick Wright set up small aircraft factory in Battersea and exhibited a monoplane at the 1910 Olympia show. Designed and built helicopters, ornithopter, biplanes, and series of monoplanes, including five *Avis*. In 1910 T. O. M. Sopwith achieved the longest all-British flight to date with a Howard Wright 1910 biplane, a distance of 272 km (169 miles).

WRIGHT-MARTIN AIRCRAFT CORPORATION/*USA*
Formed in 1916 at Los Angeles, California, by merger of Glenn L. Martin Company, Simplex Automobile Company, General Aeronautical Company and Wright Aeronautical Company. Current Martin designs of 1917 produced under Wright-Martin name; 1920 Pulitzer racer built to designs of Loening, but then reverted to Martin name.

WSK-MIELEC/*Poland*
The Transport Equipment Manufacturing Centre (WSK) was the largest Polish aircraft production factory post-war, building MiG-15 fighters under licence until 1959. Cut-back in military orders led to development of TS-8 Bies, An-2 (1958) and TS-11 Iskra Jet trainer (1960). By early 1977 more than 7,200 examples of the Russian Antonov-designed An-2 had been built, in several versions. Design office formed for M-15 agricultural and M-17 two/three-seat light aircraft which, together with the TS-11 Iskra, were in production in early 1978. Has built and flown prototypes in 1977 of M-18 Dromader agricultural aircraft, developed with Rockwell International (*q.v.*).

WSK-SWIDNIK/*Poland*
Produced jet fighters up to 1951, when defence cuts were made; then turned to Mi-1/SM-1 helicopter production and a helicopter design

WSK-Mielec example of the Antonov An-2

WSK MD-12F four-engined light commercial transport

WSK-built Mil Mi-2 helicopter

office was formed. Initially, Polish aircraft, licence-built or native, were produced under name of PZL: Polskie Zaklady Lotnicze (*q.v.*). In 1957 WSK renamed WSK im Zygmunta Pulawskiego. Production of SM-1 ended late 1960s and Mi-2 production began about 1970. In 1978 was producing civil and military versions of the Russian Mil Mi-2 helicopter.

YAKOVLEV/*USSR*

Aleksandir Sergievich Yakovlev won a design competition for lightplanes even before entering an engineering academy in 1927. His design bureau was established 1935, and first military design was the Yak-4 twin-engined fighter completed 1939. The Yak-1/3/9 series of single-seat fighters served the Soviet Union well in combat during WW2 and were built in larger numbers than any other Soviet wartime fighter. A Yak-3 airframe was modified to produce the Yak-15 jet fighter in 1945, developed subsequently as the Yak-17. The Yak-23 of 1947 was a complete redesign, resembling the earlier fighters only in fuselage configuration. Other Yakovlev designs have included the Yak-12 high-wing utility aircraft, produced also in Poland and China, and the Yak-11 and Yak-18 trainers. Yakovlev's later military contributions include the Yak-28 all-weather interceptor and Yak-36 VTOL combat aircraft. Civil aircraft include the Yak-40 and Yak-42 short-range transports, and Yak-50 single-seat aerobatic monoplane.

YEOMAN AIRCRAFT (PTY.) LTD./*Australia*

Formed 1958 as an associate of Kingsford-Smith Aviation Service to specialise in development of agricultural aircraft. First prototype Yeoman UA-1 conversion of Commonwealth CA.6 Wackett trainer flew in 1960 followed by production versions: KS.3 Cropmaster 250 and Fieldmaster 285.

YERMOLAEV/*USSR*

On Stalin's orders Vladimir Gregorovich Yermolaev began design work on a long-range bomber, the DB-240 prototype of which first flew in 1940. This twin diesel-engined low-

Yeoman Cropmaster agricultural aircraft

wing monoplane was based on the design of R. L. Bartini's Stal' 7 and had the same distinctive inverted gull wings. Designated Yer-2, more than 400 were built 1940–1944 and used principally as long-range night bombers. A Yer-20N special-purpose long-range transport version, which carried 18 passengers, was developed from the bomber.

YOKOSUKA NAVAL AIR DEPOT/*Japan*

Yokosuka's B3Y1 Navy Type 32 carrier biplane first flew in 1932. Some 200 B4Y1 attack aircraft followed, those remaining in service in WW2 known as 'Jean' to the Allies. The D4Y Suisei ('Judy') two-seat carrier dive-bomber,

Yakovlev Yak-40 three-turbofan transport aircraft

Yakovlev Yak-36 VTOL combat aircraft

Yokosuka B4Y1 carrier-based attack aircraft

Yokosuka MXY-7 Ohka piloted missile-bomb

was in service by the Battle of Midway in 1942 and appeared also in D4Y2-S night fighter and D4Y4 suicide attack variants. The P1Y1 Ginga ('Frances') twin-engined naval attack bomber/night fighter entered production in 1943 at Nakajima (*q.v.*) factories. Yokosuka developed also the MXY-7 Ohka (Cherry Blossom) kamikaze piloted missile-bomb, dubbed derisively *Baka*, which means 'fool' in Japanese, by the US Navy, and of which production by various manufacturers totalled about 800.

ZANDER & WEYL/*UK*
Established at Dunstable, Bedfordshire, was engaged in the design, manufacture and repair of sailplanes. Zander & Weyl built the Dart Flittermouse single-seat, ultra-light aeroplane in 1936. Built aircraft subsequently as Dart Aircraft Ltd. (*q.v.*).

ZAVODY/*Czechoslovkaia*
The Skoda company was the largest industrial organisation in Czechoslovakia in the 1920s, manufacturing engines of indigenous design alongside licence-built Hispano-Suiza and Lorraine Dietrich aero engines, Dewoitine aircraft and Curtiss Reed propellers. Skodovy Zavody had a controlling interest in the Czech Avia company (*q.v.*) and in Ceskoslovenska Letecka Spolecnost, the Czech airline. Parent company has also made cars, firearms, etc.

ZEEBRUGGE AERONAUTICAL CONSTRUCTION COMPANY/*Belgium*
This company designed and produced a two-seat light cabin monoplane and a two-seat fighter biplane in the mid-1920s.

ZENITH AIRCRAFT/*USA*
Formed in California in 1927 to specialise in the design and construction of high-performance commercial and military aircraft. A seven-seat passenger biplane designated Zenith Z6B was built.

ZENTRAL-AVIATIK UND AUTOMOBIL GmbH/*Austria*
This company produced the Aviatik B.1, one of the earliest purpose-designed combat aircraft, in 1914. The following year production on a large scale was initiated by Oesterreichische-Ungarische Flugzeugfabrik Aviatik (*q.v.*).

ZEPPELIN WERKE LINDAU GmbH/*Germany*
This company was established under the patronage of Graf von Zeppelin to design and construct aircraft with Claudius Dornier as chief designer. The company's first product, the Rs 1 multi-engined flying-boat, was wrecked before its first flight, but three differing examples were developed progressively, designated Rs II, Rs III and Rs IV. Other aircraft built by Zeppelin-Lindau included the C I, C II, D I and V I biplanes, and Cs I two-seat monoplane seaplane. Developed the Gs I commercial flying-boat after the Armistice, which was broken up on the instructions of the Allied Control Commission.

In 1922 the company was renamed Dornier GmbH (*q.v.*).

ZEPPELIN WERKE STAAKEN GmbH/*Germany*
This company, located formerly at Gotha, built the largest aircraft to see service in World War I—the *Riesenflugzeug* (giant aeroplane) 'R' series bombers. The Staaken design team evolved four, five and six-engined bombers, leading to the four-engined R. VI which was built by Automobil and Aviatik (*q.v.*), Ostdeutsche Albatros Werke and Luftfahrzeugbau Schütte-Lanz (*q.v.*) and carried out successful raids against Allied territory, dropping bombs as large as 1,000 kg. A floatplane version of the R. VI designated Staaken L was wrecked during trials in 1918. A post-war four-engined airliner derivative, the E.4/20, flew successfully in 1920 but was then destroyed by order of the Allied Control Commission under the terms of the Armistice.

Zlin 42 two-seat light trainer

ZLIN/*Czechoslovakia*
Zlinská Letecká Akciová Spolecnost formed 1935 as subsidiary of Bata Shoe Company. First aircraft produced was Zlin XII two-seat, low-wing cabin monoplane, followed by Zlin 381, a licence-built Bücker Bü 181 Bestmann. The Zlin 22 appeared in 1947 as a two-seat trainer and was produced also in three-seat Zlin 22M version. The Zlin 26 all-wood two-seat tandem trainer was superseded by the metal Zlin 126 Trener which went into production in 1953. The basic design has been developed subsequently through Z 226, Z 326, Z 526 and Z 726 models in both Trener (two-seat) and Akrobat (single-seat competition aircraft) variants with retractable landing gear and a variety of engines. As one of the world's foremost aerobatic aircraft, the Zlin has been widely exported outside the Eastern bloc. Production in early 1978 included Zlin 42 M two-seat light training and touring aircraft, Z 50 L aerobatic aircraft and Z 726 trainer.

ZMAJ/*Czechoslovakia*
Fabrica Aeroplana I Hydroplana *Zmaj* founded in 1927 by Jovan Petrovic to produce under licence the Hanriot H-41, Gourdou-Leseurre B-3 and Dewoitine D-27 fighters. Indigenous designs included a Wright-engined observation aircraft, an observation seaplane, and the two-seat Fizir AF-2 Amphibian.

ZODIAC/*France*
First established in 1896, this company produced the Zodiac S2 two-seat biplane in 1912.

GLOSSARY

ABSOLUTE CEILING: The maximum altitude above sea level at which a heavier-than-air craft can be maintained in level flight.

ACLS: (i) Air cushion landing system, or (ii) automatic carrier landing system.

ADF: Automatic Direction Finding; utilising an automated radio direction finding (*RDF*) technique.

AEROBATICS: Voluntary manoeuvres, initiated by a pilot, other than those for conventional flight.

AERODROME: An area set aside for the operation of aircraft.

AERODYNAMICS: The branch of fluid mechanics dealing with air (gaseous) motion, and the reactions of a body moving within that air.

AEROFOIL (AIRFOIL): A body or structure shaped to obtain an aerodynamic reaction when travelling through the air.

AERONAUTICS: Concerned with flight within the Earth's atmosphere.

AEROPLANE (AIRPLANE): Meaning in modern usage a heavier-than-air powered craft.

AEROSTAT: A lighter-than-air craft.

AEW: Airborne early warning; aircraft equipped to give maximum advance warning of approaching hostile aircraft.

AFCS: Automatic flight control system.

AFTERBURNER: Thrust augmentation feature of a gas turbine engine.

AI: Airborne interception; radar device carried by military aircraft to aid location and interception of hostile aircraft.

AILERONS: Movable control surfaces, usually mounted in the trailing-edge of a wing adjacent to the wingtips, to control an aircraft's rolling movements.

AIRBRAKE: A drag-inducing surface which can be deployed in flight, perhaps for speed reducing or limiting, but see also *spoilers*.

AIRFIELD: More modern term for aerodrome, and applying more particularly to one used by military aircraft.

AIRFLOW: The movement of air about a body (aircraft) in motion.

AIRFOIL (AEROFOIL): A structure shaped to obtain an aerodynamic reaction in the air, thus affecting the performance of the aircraft.

AIRFRAME: An aircraft's structure, without power plant and systems.

AIRPLANE (AEROPLANE): Meaning in modern usage a heavier-than-air powered craft, as opposed to a balloon or glider.

AIRPORT: More modern term for aerodrome, and applying more particularly to one used for civil transport operations.

AIRSCREW: Now little-used word for propeller; believed to have originated to provide distinction from ship's propeller.

AIRSHIP: A powered lighter-than-air craft.

AIRSPEED: The speed of an aircraft through the air, relative to the air mass in which it is moving.

AIRSTRIP: A natural surface used for the operation of aircraft, often in an unimproved state.

ALTIMETER: An instrument, most usually an aneroid barometer, calibrated in metres and/or feet, to indicate an aircraft's height.

ALTITUDE: Height.

AMPHIBIAN: An aircraft able to operate from both land and water surfaces.

ANGLE OF ATTACK: Angle at which the airstream meets an aerofoil surface.

ANGLE OF INCIDENCE: Angle at which an aerofoil surface is normally set in relation to the fore and aft axis of the airframe structure.

ANHEDRAL: Angle which the spanwise axis of an aerofoil makes to the fuselage when the wing or tailplane tip is lower than its root attachment point.

The Italian company Aeronàutica Ansaldo SA gained prestige during WW1 by being the first to produce a single-seat fighter of Italian design. The company's most successful post-war development was the 2/3-seat A.300, a multi-purpose aircraft built extensively and used widely.

APU: Auxiliary power unit. Usually small engine carried on board an aircraft to provide an independent power source for such services as electrics, hydraulics, pneumatics, ventilation and air conditioning, both on the ground and in the air if needed.

ASI: Air speed indicator.

ASPECT RATIO: Ratio of the span to the chord of an aerofoil. Hence, a high aspect ratio wing has great span and narrow chord, and *vice versa*.

ASTRODOME: Transparent dome, usually on dorsal surface of fuselage, to permit celestial navigation by traditional means.

ASW: Anti-submarine warfare.

ATC: Air traffic control.

AUTOGYRO: An aircraft with an unpowered rotary wing, which *autorotates* as the machine is propelled through the air by a conventional power plant. 'Autogiro' is the trade name for autogyros developed by Juan de la Cierva.

AUTOMATIC PILOT (AUTOPILOT): A gyroscopically-stabilised system maintaining an aircraft in level flight at predetermined heading and altitude.

AUTOROTATION: Automatic rotation of a rotary wing due to forward, or downward, movement of an autogyro.

AWACS: Airborne warning and control system; an advanced *AEW* aircraft, with additional facilities for deployment and control of defence, interception and counter-strike forces.

BALLISTIC MISSILE: A weapon which, in the terminal and unpowered stage of its flight, becomes a free-falling body subject to ballistic reactions.

BALLOON: An unpowered lighter-than-air craft, its direction of flight imposed by ambient airstreams.

BIPLANE: A fixed-wing aircraft with two sets of wings mounted, generally, one above the other.

BLEED AIR: Hot air, at high pressure, taken usually from the by-pass section of a gas turbine engine, for heating, de-icing and other useful work.

BLOWN FLAPS: Aerodynamic surface over which bleed air is discharged at high speed to prevent breakaway of the normal airflow.

BOUNDARY LAYER: Thin stratum of air nearest to an aircraft's external surface structure.

BOX KITE: Form of kite devised by Australian Lawrence Hargrave, used by many early constructors to provide rigid biplane structures.

BUFFET: Irregular, often violent, oscillations of an aircraft's structure, caused by turbulent airflow or conditions of compressibility.

CAA: Civil Aviation Administration (UK).

CAB: Civil Aeronautics Board (USA).

CABIN: Enclosed compartment for crew and/or passengers in an aircraft.

CAMBER: The curvature, convex or concave, of an aerofoil surface.

CANARD: Describes an aircraft which flies tail first, with its main lift surface at the aft end of its structure.

CANTILEVER: A beam, or other structure, supported at one end only, and without external bracing.

CATHEDRAL: Early word to describe *anhedral*, or negative dihedral.

CEILING: Normal maximum operating altitude of an aircraft.

CENTRE OF GRAVITY: (CG), the point on an aircraft's structure where the total combined weight forces act.

CENTRE-SECTION: The central panel, or section, of an aircraft's wing.

CHORD: The distance measured from the leading- to trailing-edge of an aerofoil.

COCKPIT: Compartment, originally open to the air, for accommodation of pilot and crew/passengers. Nowadays used informally by laymen to describe the forward part of the *cabin*, especially of an airliner, which is off-limits to passengers, and properly called *flight deck*.

COIN: Counter-insurgency aircraft.

COLLECTIVE PITCH CONTROL: Used to change simultaneously the pitch of all of a helicopter rotor's blades to permit ascent or descent.

CONSTANT-SPEED PROPELLER: One which governs an engine at its optimum speed, the blade pitch being increased or decreased automatically to achieve this result.

COWLING: The name of the fairing which, usually, encloses an engine.

CYCLIC PITCH CONTROL: Means of changing the pitch of a rotor's blades progressively, to provide a horizontal thrust component for flight in any horizontal direction.

DELTA WING: When viewed in plan has the shape of an isosceles triangle; the apex leads, the wing trailing-edge forming the base of the triangle.

DERATED: An engine which is restricted to a power output below its potential maximum.

DIHEDRAL: Angle which the spanwise axis of an aerofoil makes to the fuselage when the wing or tailplane tip is higher than its root attachment point (positive dihedral).

DIVE BRAKE: Drag-inducing surface deployed in a dive to maintain speed below structural limitations, or improve controllability (see *airbrake*).

DORSAL: Relating to the upper surface of an aircraft's fuselage.

DRAG: A force exerted on a moving body in a direction opposite to its direction of motion.

DRAG CHUTE: A heavy-duty parachute attached to an aircraft's structure which can be used to reduce its landing run.

DRONE: A pilotless aircraft, usually following a predetermined or programmed set of manoeuvres. See also *RPV*.

DROP TANK: An externally carried auxiliary tank, usually to contain fuel, which may be jettisoned if necessary.

ECM: Electronic counter-measures; airborne equipment to reduce the effectiveness of an enemy's radar or other devices which generate electromagnetic radiations.

ELEVATOR: Movable control surface, attached to the trailing-edge of an aircraft's tailplane (stabiliser) to control pitching movements.

ELEVONS: Movable control surfaces which act collectively as elevators, but differentially as ailerons.

ELT: Emergency locator transmitter; emits a homing signal from a crashed aircraft to simplify location for rescue services.

ENVELOPE: Container, usually flexible, or the lifting gas or hot air of an airship or balloon.

FAA: Federal Aviation Administration.

FAI: Fédération Aéronautique Internationale.

FAR: Federal Aviation Regulations.

FIN: A fixed vertical aerofoil surface, usually a dorsal component of the tail unit, to provide stability in yaw.

FIRING: An addition to an aircraft's basic structure which is intended primarily to reduce *drag*.

FLAP: Most usually a wing trailing-edge movable surface which can be deployed partially to increase lift, or completely to increase drag.

FLAT-FOUR: Characteristic description of a horizontally-opposed four-cylinder engine; hence flat-twin, flat-six.

FLIGHT DECK: (i) Separate crew compartment of a cabin aircraft, or (ii) the operational deck of an aircraft carrier.

FLIGHT SIMULATOR: A ground-based training device to permit the practice of flight operations; often specific to a particular aircraft for detailed training.

FLOATPLANE: Aircraft which is supported on the water by floats; more usually termed a seaplane.

FLUTTER: Unstable oscillation of an aerofoil surface.

FLYING-BOAT: A heavier-than-air craft which is supported on the water by its water-tight fuselage.

311

FLYING WIRES (LIFT WIRES): External bracing wires, usually of streamline section, which carry the weight of the fuselage in flight.

FULLY-FEATHERING PROPELLER: One in which the blades can be rotated so that the leading-edge of each faces the oncoming airstream. This reduces drag if an engine has to be stopped in flight.

FUSELAGE: The body structure of an aircraft.

GLIDER: A heavier-than-air, fixed wing, unpowered aircraft for gliding or soaring flight.

HARDPOINT: A strengthened section of the under-wing or fuselage, intended for the carriage of external weapons or stores, usually on pylons.

HELICOPTER: A heavier-than-air craft with a powered rotary wing.

HELIUM: A valuable non-inflammable lifting gas for use by lighter-than-air craft.

HIGH-WING MONOPLANE: An aircraft which has its single wing mounted high on the fuselage.

HULL: The water-tight fuselage or body of a flying-boat.

HYDRO-AEROPLANE: Early term for an aircraft which could operate from water.

HYDROGEN: The lightest known lifting gas, used to inflate balloons and airships, unfortunately highly inflammable.

IATA: International Air Transport Association.

ICAO: International Civil Aviation Organisation.

ICING: Condition arising when atmospheric moisture freezes on the external surfaces of an aircraft.

IFF: Identification, friend or foe; an electronic device to interrogate approaching aircraft.

IFR: Instrument Flight Rules; i.e. flight by reference to on-board instruments under conditions of poor visibility or darkness.

ILS: Instrument Landing System.

IN-LINE ENGINE: Engine in which the cylinders are one behind another, in straight lines.

INS: Inertial navigation system, in which highly sensitive accelerometers record, via a computer, the complex accelerations of an aircraft about its three axes, thus integrating its linear displacement from the beginning of a selected course and pinpointing the aircraft's position at all times.

ISA: Agreed International Standard Atmosphere (1013·2 millibars at 15°C) to permit accurate comparison of aircraft performance figures.

JASDF: Japan Air Self-Defence Force.

JATO: Jet-assisted take-off, utilising solid or liquid fuel rockets to augment the take-off power of an aircraft's engines. See also *RATO*.

JGSDF: Japan Ground Self-Defence Force.

JMSDF: Japan Maritime Self-Defence Force.

KINETIC HEATING: Heating of an aircraft's structure as a result of air friction.

KITE: Usually tethered heavier-than-air craft, sustained in the air by its aerofoil surfaces being inclined to the wind to generate lift.

LANDING WEIGHT: Normal maximum weight at which an aircraft is permitted to land.

LANDING WIRES: External bracing wires, usually of streamline section, which support the wings when the aircraft is on the ground.

LANDPLANE: A heavier-than-air craft which is equipped to operate from land surfaces only.

LBA: Luftfahrtbundesamt; the Federal German Civil Aviation Authority.

LEADING-EDGE: The edge of an aerofoil which first meets the airstream in normal flight.

LIFT: The force generated by an aerofoil section, acting at right angles to the airstream flowing past it.

LORAN: A long-range radio-based navigation aid.

LOW-WING MONOPLANE: An aircraft which has its single wing mounted low on the fuselage.

MAC: Military Airlift Command (USAF).

MACH NUMBER: Named after the Austrian physicist Ernst Mach, a means of recording the speed of a body as a ratio of the speed of sound in the same ambient conditions. The speed of sound in dry air at 0°C (32°F) is approximately 331 m (1087 ft)/sec; 1193 km/h (741 mph). Hence Mach 0·8 represents eight-tenths of the speed of sound.

MAD: Magnetic anomaly detector carried, for example, by maritime reconnaissance aircraft to locate a submarine beneath the surface of the sea.

MID-WING MONOPLANE: An aircraft which has its single wing mounted in a mid-position on the fuselage.

MONOCOQUE: Structure in which the outer skin carries the primary stresses, and is free of internal bracing.

MONOPLANE: A fixed-wing aircraft with a single set of wings, i.e. one wing on each side.

NACA: National Advisory Committee for Aeronautics. Now *NASA*.

NAF: Naval Aircraft Factory (US).

NASA: National Aeronautics and Space Administration.

NATO: North Atlantic Treaty Organisation.

ORNITHOPTER: Name for a flapping-wing aircraft. Only model ornithopters have flown to date.

PARACHUTE: Collapsible device which, when deployed, will retard the rate of descent of a body falling through the air. Used originally as a safety device, has been adopted for dropping troops, supplies, equipment, etc.

PARASOL MONOPLANE: A fixed-wing aircraft which has its single wing strut-mounted above the fuselage.

PAYLOAD: The useful load of an aircraft: cargo, passengers; in a military aircraft, its weapon load.

PITCH: The angle of incidence at which a propeller blade or rotor blade is set.

PORT: Left-hand side when facing forward.

PRESSURISATION: Artificially increased pressure in an aircraft to compensate for the reduced external pressure as the aircraft gains altitude.

PROPELLER: Rotating blades of aerofoil section, engine driven, each of which reacts as an aircraft's wing, generating low-pressure in front and higher behind, thus pulling the aircraft forward.

PROTOTYPE: The first airworthy example of a new aircraft design or variant.

PUSHER PROPELLER: Inaccurate but accepted description of propeller mounted behind an engine. It acts aerodynamically as described under *propeller*, and is thus a tractor in action.

PYLON: Structure attached to wing or airframe to carry load, e.g. engines or weapons.

RAAF: Royal Australian Air Force.

RADAR: Beamed and directed radio waves used for location and detection, as well as for navigational purposes.

RADIAL ENGINE: One in which the cylinders are mounted equidistant and circumferentially around a circular crankcase. Cylinders and crankcase are fixed, and the crankshaft rotates.

RAE: Royal Aircraft Establishment, formerly Royal Aircraft Factory.

RAF: (i) Royal Air Force, or (ii) Royal Aircraft Factory.

RAI: Registro Aeronàutico Italiano.

RAMJET ENGINE: An aerodynamic duct in which fuel is burned to produce a high-velocity propulsive jet. It needs to be accelerated to high speed before it can become operative.

RATO: Rocket-assisted take-off: virtually the same as *JATO*.

RCAF: Royal Canadian Air Force.

RDF: Radio direction finding; using the transmission from two or more stations to fix position of an aircraft by its bearing in relation to each.

RFC: Royal Flying Corps.

RNAS: Royal Naval Air Service.

RNZAF: Royal New Zealand Air Force.

ROCKET ENGINE: One burning liquid or solid fuel and carrying its own oxidiser, enabling combustion to continue outside of the earth's atmosphere.

ROLL: Movement of an aircraft about its longitudinal axis, representing a wing-over rolling action.

ROTARY ENGINE: Cylinders disposed as for *radial engine*, but in this case the crankshaft is fixed, and cylinders and crankcase rotate around it.

ROTOR: The rotating-wing assembly of an *autogyro* or helicopter, comprising the rotor hub and rotor blades.

RPV: Remotely piloted vehicles, directed usually by radio by a pilot in another aircraft or based on the ground.

RUDDER: Movable control surface, attached to trailing-edge of fin, to control aircraft movement in yaw.

SAAF: South African Air Force.

SAC: Strategic Air Command (USAF).

SAILPLANE: An unpowered heavier-than-air craft designed primarily for soaring flight.

SEAPLANE: A heavier-than-air craft which operates from water, and is supported on the surface of the water by floats.

SEMI-MONOCOQUE: An aircraft structure in which the outer skin is inadequate to carry the primary stresses, and is reinforced by frames, formers and longerons.

SERVICE CEILING: Normally height at which an aircraft can maintain a maximum rate of climb of 30 m (100 ft)/min.

SGAC: Secrétariat Générale à l'Aviation Civile.

SKIN: The external covering of an aircraft's basic inner structure.

SLAT: Auxiliary aerofoil surface, mounted forward of a main aerofoil, to maintain a smooth airflow over the main aerofoil at high angles of attack.

SLOT: The gap between the *slat* and leading-edge of the main aerofoil, which splits the airflow and maintains a smooth flow over the main aerofoil upper surface.

SPAN: The distance from tip to tip of the wing or tailplane.

SPAR: A primary structural member of an aerofoil surface, from which ribs or frames are mounted to form the desired aerofoil contours.

SPINNER: A streamlined fairing over a propeller hub.

SPOILERS: Drag-inducing surfaces which can be deployed differentially for lateral control, or simultaneously for lift dumping to improve the effectiveness of landing brakes.

STALL: Condition which arises when the smooth airflow over a wing's upper surface breaks down and its lift is destroyed.

STARBOARD: Right-hand side when facing forward.

STOL: Short take-off and landing capability.

STREAMLINE: To shape a structure so that it will cause the minimum aerodynamic drag.

STRUT: Solid or tubular member, usually streamlined, used for bracing, as, for example, between the two wings of a biplane. Can be required to carry tension or compression loads.

SUBSONIC: Flight at a speed below that of sound.

SUPERCHARGER: A form of compressor, often turbine-driven, to force more fuel/air mixture into the cylinders of a piston-engine than can be induced by the pistons at ambient atmospheric pressure.

SUPERSONIC: Speed in excess of that of sound.

SV-VS: Soviet Military Aviation Forces (*Sovietskaya Voenno-Vozdushnye Sily*).

SWEPT WING: Wing of which the angle between the wing leading-edge and the centre line of the rear fuselage is less than 90 degrees.

TABS: Small auxiliary control surfaces which can be adjusted to offset aerodynamic loads imposed on main control surfaces.

TAC: Tactical Air Command (USAF).

TAILPLANE (STABILISER): Primary horizontal aerofoil surface of tail unit. Can be fixed, or may have variable incidence, and its purpose is to provide longitudinal stability.

TAKE-OFF WEIGHT: Maximum allowable weight of an aircraft at the beginning of its take-off run.

THRUST: Force which propels an aircraft through the air; generated by conventional propeller or the jet efflux of a turbine engine.

TRACTOR PROPELLER: Propeller mounted forward of the engine. (See *propeller*.)

TRAILING-EDGE: The rear edge of an aerofoil.

TRIPLANE: Fixed-wing aircraft with three sets of wings, mounted one above another.

TURBOFAN: Gas turbine engine with large diameter forward fan. Air is ducted from the tips of these fan blades and by-passed around the engine, and added to the normal jet efflux to provide high propulsive efficiency.

TURBOJET: Gas turbine engine in its simplest form, producing a high velocity jet efflux.

TURBOPROP: Gas turbine engine in which maximum energy is taken from the turbine to drive a reduction gear and conventional propeller.

TURBOSHAFT: Gas turbine engine in which maximum energy is taken from the turbine to drive a high speed shaft. It can be used to drive a helicopter's rotor or any other form of machinery.

USAAC: United States Army Air Corps (predecessor of USAAF).

USAAF: United States Army Air Force (predecessor of USAF).

USAAS: United States Army Air Service (predecessor of USAAC).

USAF: United States Air Force.

USCG: United States Coast Guard.

USMC: United States Marine Corps.

USN: United States Navy.

VARIABLE-GEOMETRY WING: Wings which, fully extended, give the best low-speed performance for take-off and landing, and can be swept in flight to optimum positions for best cruising and high-speed flight performance.

VARIABLE-PITCH PROPELLER: Usually a propeller in which the blades can be set to two positions; a fine-pitch setting for take-off and landing, and a coarse-pitch setting for economic cruise performance.

VEE-ENGINE: One with two banks of in-line cylinders mounted with an angular separation on a common crankcase.

VENTRAL: Relating to the under-surface of an aircraft's fuselage.

VFR: Visual Flight Rules; i.e. flight under conditions of good external visibility, without dependence on aircraft instruments.

VSTOL: Vertical or short take-off and landing.

V/STOL: Vertical and/or short take-off and landing capability.

VTOL: Vertical take-off and landing capability.

WING-LOADING: The gross take-off weight of an aircraft divided by its wing area. A Boeing 747, for example, can have a maximum wing loading of 727·8 kg/m^2 (149 lb/sq ft); a high-performance sailplane, such as the Scheibe Bergfalke, can be as low as 29·4 kg/m^2 (6·02 lb/sq ft).

WING WARPING: Method of lateral control adopted by Wright brothers and many early builders/designers, in which a flexible wing is twisted (warped) to provide roll control as with ailerons.

YAW: Movement of an aircraft about its vertical axis, representing movement of its tail unit to port or starboard, to change the aircraft's heading.

Index

For reasons of space it has been necessary to limit as much as possible the number of entries in this index. It remains, however, a useful source of reference with more than 3,300 entries. An aircraft such as the Lockheed P-38 Lighting will not be included under a Lockheed heading, since companies are listed alphabetically in the main body of this work: it will, however, be entered in this index in the appropriate alphabetical positions under both Lightning and P-38. Aircraft which manufacturers identified only by a numerical designation, such as the Potez 25, are listed as Type 25, Potez. Aircraft which were allocated Model numbers, such as the Bell Model 47, can be found alphabetically in the M entries. The words *et seq* following an entry which has a numerical content to its designation, such as D-9, *et seq*, Jodel, implies that other similar and ensuing numerical designations are mentioned in the entry indicated, but these are not necessarily consecutive. The index does not include references to illustration captions.

A-1/-2, Etrich 155
A-1 Balilla, Ansaldo 80
A-2, *et seq*, Callair 112
A-2, Emigh Trojan 152
A-3, Aeronautical Products 68
A-3 Falcon, Curtiss 135
A-4, *et seq*, ANT 81
A4D Skyray, Douglas 148
A-5 Vigilante, North American 240
A5M, Watanabe 303
A5M4, Mitsubishi 230
A-6 Intruder, Grumman 180
A6M-2, Nakajima 234
A6M3, Mitsubishi 230
A7 Storch, Focke-Wulfe 166
A-7A, LTV 212
A-8, *et seq*, Curtiss-Wright 136
A-9, Call Air, IMCO 197
A-10A, Fairchild Republic 51
A 16, *et seq*, Focke-Wulf 166
A-17, Northrop 148
A-20, Douglas 148
A20, Flygindustri 164
A-22, Hansa 185
A-22, IVL 199
A-26, Douglas 148
A-37, Cessna 121
A-4S Skyhawk, LAS 216
A-80 Falcão, Avibras 89
A 109A, Agusta 72
A 129, Agusta 72
A300 Airbus Industrie 59, 70, 73, 117, 144
A.300, Ansaldo 80
AA.1 Góeland, Caudron 118
AA-1 Yankee, AAC 64
AAC-1 Toucan, Colombes 126
AAMSA Sparrow Commander 64
AAMSA Quail 64
A.B.20, Bordelaise 103
AC-1, *et seq*, Comper 128
AC-4, Comte 160
AC-12, Aerotécnica 71
AC-14, Aerotécnica 71
AC-35, Autogiro 86
AC-119, Fairchild 157
A-D 10, Arsenal-Delanne 142
AD 1000, White 305
Aé.C-1, *et seq*, FMA 165
AEG C IV 65
Aé.M-01, FMA 165
A.E.R.1, Aeronova 69
Aé.T-1, FMA 165
AF-4, Crusader 133
AG 01 Alouette, Gatard 175
AG 02 Poussin, Gatard 175
AG 03 Hirondelle, Gatard 174
Ag-1/-2, Transland 292
Ag.2, Agusta 72
AG-14, Anderson, Greenwood & Co. 80
AL-60, Lockheed-Kaiser 216
AM-1 Mauler, Martin 222
AM.3C, Macchi/Aerfer 219
A.M.6 *et seq*, Alaparma 76
AM-C 111, Air-Metal 74
An-2, Antonov 81
An-3, *et seq*, Antonov 81
ANT-44, ANT 81
AO-1, Atlantic 85
Ao 192 Kurier, Ago 71
Ao.C.1, FMA 82
AOP6, Auster 85
AOP9, Auster 85
A.P., Eagle-Lincoln 79
A.P.l, Caproni 116
AR 65, Arado 155
Ar 66, *et seq*, Arado 82, 168
Ar 68, Arado 155
Ar 196, Arado 144
Ar 199, Arado 144
Ar 396, Arado 144
ARK-3, Chetverikov 123
AS-1, Aeromarine 67
AS-2, Aeromarine 67
AS-202 Bravo, SIAI-Marchetti 161
AT-9 Jeep, Curtiss-Wright 136
AT-21, Aviolanda 89
AT-21 Gunner, Fairchild 149, 157
A.T.-35 Legers 210
AU-23 Peacemaker, Fairchild 157
AUM-903, Umbra 294
AVD-12, AISA 76
AVM-88, Avimeta 89
AZ-10, Agusta 72
AZ-101, *et seq*, Piasecki/Agusta 252
A series, Aero 71
A series, Cessna 121
Accountant, Aviation Traders 88
Ace, Series 1 CH-3, Chrislea 124
Active 1, Arrow 84
Aerial Mk II, Genair 174
Aeriel, SNCASO 280
Aeriel Mk II, Genair 149
Aero 145, Ceskoslovenské 120
Aerobatic 65-02, IABSA 196
Aerocar, Portsmouth Aviation 256
Aero Commander 520, Aero Design 67
Aero Commander 560, Aero Design 67
Aero Commander 680 Super, Aero Design 67
Aero Coupe, Aero-Craft 67
Aerodrome, aircraft 12
Aeronca 100, Aeronautical Corporation of Great Britain 68
Aeroscooter, Raab 258
Aerostar series, Ted Smith 275
Aero Subaru, FA-200, Fuji 171
Aerovan, Miles 230
Ag-Cat, Grumman 170
Agricola, Auster 85
Aigle, Druine 149
Aiglet, Auster 85
Airacobra, P-39, Bell 95
Airacomet, P-59, Bell 95
Air Baby, E.114, CKD-Praga 125, 191
Air-Boat, XIV, Benoist 96
Aircar, Gwinn 181
Air Coach, Kreutzer 206
Air Coach, F-18, International 198
Air Coupe, Alon 77
Aircoupe, F-1, Forney 169
Aircruiser, Victa 298
Air Fouga Magister, Potez 164
Air Horse, W.11, Cierva 125
Airistocrat, Waco 302
Air King, National 235
Airmaster, Cessna 121
Airphibian, FA-2/-3, Continental 131
Air Pullman, Stout 285
Air Scout, McCarthy 224
Airsedan, Buhl 109
Airster, Buhl 109
Airster, Security 270
Airtourer, AESL 71
Airtourer, Victa 298
AirTractor, L.101, Lamson 207
Airtrainer, AESL 71, 237
Air Trainer, Capital 115
Airtruk, Waitomo 302
Airtruk, P.L.11, Bennett 96
Airtruk, PL-12, Transavia 164
Air Yacht, Bach 90
Air Yacht, Keystone 205
Air Yacht, Loening 216
Ajeet, Hindustan 192
Akrobat, Zlin 309
Albatross, D.H.91, de Havilland 141
Albatross, Grumman 129
Albermarle, Armstrong Whitworth 83
Albessard monoplane, Peyret 250
Alcione, Z.1007, CANT 115
Alcor Duo-6, Alhambra 77
Alcotan, Type 202, CASA 117
Alcyon, Morane-Saulnier 232
Alfa 2, Meteor 228
Alfa 4, Meteor 228
Al Kahira, Helwan 189
Alouette, AG 01, Gatard 174
Alouette, III Aérospatiale 151
Alpha, Northrop 241
Alpha Jet, Dassault-Breguet/Dornier 139
Altair, Lockheed 214
Ambassadeur, DR 100, CEA 119
Ambassador, Airspeed 75
Ambassador, CA-1, Collier 126
American Trainer, AAC 64
American Traveler, AAC 64
Anbo 41, Karo 203
Anbo 51, Karo 203
Anson, Avro 114, 125, 126, 161
Antilope, SIPA 279
Apache, Piper 176, 254
Apollo, Armstrong Whitworth 83
Aqua I, Aquaflight 82
Aqua II, Aquaflight 82
Aquilon, SNCASE 280
Arado Ar 66, *et seq* 82
Arava, 101/102/201, IAI 199
Arctic Tern, S.1BE, Arctic 82
Argosy, Armstrong Whitworth 83
Argus, Fairchild 157
Argus, CL-28, Canadair 113
Aristocrat II, O'Neill 243
Aristocrat, 102A, GAC 172
Arrow, Aeronca 68
Arrow, Spartan 282
Arrow, Taylorcraft 289
Arrow biplane, Lohner-Daimler 216
Arrow, CF-105, Avro Canada 89
Artouste, Turboméca 226
Asro 4, Siemetzki 273
Atlanta, Armstrong Whitworth 83
Atlantic, Wassmer 303
Atlantic, Type 1150, Breguet 105
Atlantique, 1150, Dassault-Breguet 139
Atlas, Armstrong Whitworth 83
Attacker, Supermarine 287
Audax, Hawker 187
Aurora, CP-140, Lockheed 113
Auster, Taylorcraft 289
Autocar, Auster 85
Autocrat, Auster 85
Autocrat, Taylorcraft 289
Autogyro GN, AISA 76
Avenger, Grumman 150, 176
Avenger, TBM, Grumman 180
Avia 14, Ceskoslovenské 120
Aviastar, Lombardi 217
Aviastar, L.M.5, AVIA 86
Aviocar, C-212, CASA 117
Avion-Planeur RF3, Alpavia 78
Avis, Wright, Howard & Warwick 307
Avitruc, C-123, Chase 123
Avitruc, YC-122, Chase 123
Avrocar, Avro Canada 89
Ayr flying-boat, English Electric 154
Azcarate-E, TNCA 288
Aztec, Piper 124, 254

B series, DFW 144
B-1, Boeing 100
B-1/-2, Brantly 104
B.1, Luftverkehrs 218
B-1, Rockwell 241
B-1, Rockwell International 261
B.2, Flanders 163
B-2A/-2B, Brantly 104
B-2B, Brantly-Hynes 104
BII/III, Euler 156
B-2 Condor, Curtiss 135
B-3, Carden-Baynes 116
B-3, States 284
B-3 Custombuilt, Crown 133
B.3A, Emsco 153
B-3A/-4A/-5A/-6A, Keystone 205
B3Y1, Yokosuka 308
B-4, Miller 230
B4Y1, Yokosuka 308
B5N, Nakajima 234
B6N Tenzan, Nakajima 234
B7, Douglas 148
B.7, Emsco 153
B7A, Aichi 72
B-9, Boeing 101
B-10, Martin 220
B-12, Martin 222
B-17 Flying Fortress, Boeing 51, 101
B-18, Douglas 148
B-24 Liberator, Consolidated 45, 130, 169
B-26, Douglas 148
B-26 Marauder, Martin 222
B-29 Superfortress, Boeing 45, 46, 101, 136
B-32 Dominator, Consolidated Vultee 130
B-36, Consolidated Vultee 130
B45 Mentor, Beech 171
B-45 Tornado, North American 240
B-47 Stratojet, Boeing 101
B-52 Stratofortress, Boeing 51, 101
B-57, Martin 154
B-58 Hustler, Convair 131, 175
B-60 Mercurey, Boisavia 102
B-66 Destroyer, Douglas 148
B 71, Avia 87
B-85-C Bee, Funk 171
B-100, Mercury 226
B-121 Pup, Beagle 93
B.206, Beagle 93
B.330 Touroplane, Wallace 302
B-350-360 De Luxe Brigadier, Falcon 160
B 534, Avia 87
BA-4B, Andreasson 80, 133
BA-7, MFI 228
BA-7 Bölkow Junior Andreasson 80
Ba 27, Breda 104
BA-42, Burns 110
Ba 65, Breda 104
Ba 88 Lince, Breda 104
Ba 349 Natter, Bachem 91
BA400, BACC 90
BAX-3/-4 Sportsman, Bunyard 109
BB-152, VEB 300
BC-12D, Taylorcraft 289
B.E.1, RAF 141
Be-2, *et seq*, Beriev 97
B.E.2, RAF 20, 22, 83, 91, 108, 133, 138, 141, 143, 150, 200
B.E.12/12a, RAF 133
B.E.8, RAF 133
BF-1 Beija-Flor, CTA 133, 143
B.G.VI, Avis 89
BGA, CMASA 126
BH-1, *et seq*, Avia 87
BI, Aviatik 88
BK 117, MBB-Kawasaki 224
BM3, *et seq*, Maranda 220
BN-2 Islander, Britten-Norman 108, 196, 198
BN.1, Nieuport & General 238
BN-2a Trislander, Britten-Norman 108
BO 105, Bölkow 102
BO 105, MBB 102
BO 107, Bölkow 192
BO 207, Bölkow 102, 192
BO 208 C Junior, Bölkow 102, 192
BO 209, Bölkow 192
BS-12/-12D/-12D3S, Omega 243
B.T., Legers 210
BT-8, Seversky 271
BT-32 Condor, Curtiss-Wright 136
BT-120, Mercury 226
BU3, Breguet 105
Bü 131 Jungmann, Bücker 109, 117, 140
Bü 133 Jungmeister, Bücker 109, 115, 117
Bü 181 Bestmann, Bücker 109, 168, 189
BUC, Breguet-Michelin 105
BUM, Breguet-Michelin 105
Bv 138, Blohm und Voss 111
Bv 222 Viking, Blohm und Voss 111
Bv 238, Blohm und Voss 111
BVL-12, US Army 295
BW, Cessna 121
B & W Seaplane, Boeing 100
Baboon, F.K.24, BAT 92
Baby, Supermarine 286
Baby, F-2, Larson 208
Baby Biplane, Bristol 106
Baby Great Lakes, Great Lakes 180
Baby Bullet, Heath 188
Bachstelze, Fa 330, Focke-Achgelis 165
Baffin, Blackburn 98
Baladou, Wassmer 303
Balilla, A-1, Ansaldo 80
Balliol, P.108, Boulton Paul 103
Baltimore, Martin 222
Bamel, Gloucester 177
Bandeirante, EMBRAER 152
Banshee, McDonnell 224
Bantam, F.K.23, BAT 92
Barling Comber, Witteman-Lewis 306
Baroudeur, SNCASE 280
Barracuda, Fairey 159
Basant, HA-31, Hindustan 192
Basilisk, F.K.25, BAT 92
Basset, Beagle 93
Bat, F.K. 22, BAT 92
Bat Boat, Sopwith 281
Battle, Fairey 86
Bearcat, Grumman 180
Beaufighter, Bristol 42, 107, 143, 178
Beaufort, Bristol 143, 169, 178
Beaver, DHC-2, de Havilland Canada 142
Bébé, C.9, Jodel 199
Bede BD-1 64
Bee, Carden-Baynes 116
Bee, Scheutzow 269
Bee, B-85-C, Funk 171
Beija-Flor, BF-1, CTA 133, 143
Belfair, Tipsy 292
Belvedere, Westland 305
Belvedere, Type 192, Bristol 107
Berg-Scout, Oesterreichische 242
Bestmann, Bü 181, Bücker 109, 168, 189
Beta, General 174
Beta, Northrop 241
Bies, WSK-Mielec 307
Biplane, Bird 98
Bird Dog, L-19, Cessna 121
Bis, Meteor 228
Bizerte, Breguet 105
Blackburn, Blackburn 98
Black Widow, Northrop 241
Blenheim, Bristol 40, 42, 107, 169
Bluebird, Blackburn 83
Bolingbroke, Bristol 158
Bolkow Junior, BA-7, Andreasson 80
Bomber, Sunbeam 286
Bonanza, Model 35, Beech 59, 94
Boomerang, Commonwealth 127
Boston, Douglas 148
Bourges, P.7, Boulton Paul 103
Boxcar, Miles 230
Boxkite, Bristol 106
Brabazon 1, Bristol 53, 107, 155
Bravo, SIAI-Marchetti 273
Bravo, AS-202, SIAI-Marchetti 161
Bretagne, Ouest Aviation 244
Bretagne, SNCASO 280
Brigadier, Baumann 160
Brigadier, Model 250/290, Baumann 92
Brigadyr, L-60, Ceskoslovenské 120
Britannia, Bristol 107, 169
Bronco, Rockwell International 261
Broussard, Holste 193
Buccaneer, Blackburn 98
Buccaneer, LA-4-200, Lake 126, 129
Buccaneer, SB2A, Brewster 106
Buckaroo, Temco 290
Buckeye, Rockwell International 261
Buffalo, DHC-5, de Havilland Canada 142
Buffalo, F2A, Brewster 106
Bugle, Boulton Paul 103
Bulldog, Beagle 93
Bulldog, Bristol 107
Bulldog, Scottish Aviation 270
Bullet, Texas 290
Bullet 125, Johnson 200
Bullet Series, Alexander Aircraft 77
Bullfinch, Scottish Aviation 270
Bulte-Guldentops, Guldentops 181
Bumblebee, DJ-1, Driggs-Johnson 149
Bushmaster 15-AT, Hayden 188
Butterfly, LWF 218

C-class 'boat, Short 35
C Series, Aeronautical Corporation of America 68
C Series, Aeronca 68
C series, Ago 71
C Series, Aviatik 88, 184
C series, DFW 144
C series, Fokker 168
C series, Halberstadt 182
C Series, Hannover 184
C Series, Luftverkehrs 218
C series, Rumpler 266
C series, Schutte-Lanz 269
C-1/-2, Bergamaschi 97
C-1/-2, Crosley 133
C.1, Gourdou et Leseurre 178
C-1, Hoppi-Copter, Capital 115
C I/II, Zeppelin Werke Lindau 309
C-1 Skimmer, Colonial 126
C.1A, Rumpler 184
C II, AEG 65
C-2, Atlantic 85
C-2 Skimmer IV, Colonial 126
C2-60, Spartan 282
C-2A, Atlantic 85
CIII, Albatross 76
C.IV, AEG 167
C-4/-4S, Miller 230
C4 Commuter, United 295
C-4, Super, Carson 117
C4M, Atlas 85
C V, DFW 144
C5, Polar, Hönningstad 193
C.5 Polar, Wideröes 305
C-5A Galaxy, Lockheed 214
C.5/6, CANSA 115
C.6, *et seq*, Cierva 125
C.9 Bébé, Jodel 199

C. 10, Saiman 276
C. 19, Cierva 166
C 23, et seq, Caudron 118
C-35, EKW 151
C-36/-3603/-3604, Eidgenössische Flugzeugwerk 151
C-46 Commando, Curtiss 190
C-46 Commando, Curtiss-Wright 136
C-47, Douglas 87
C-54, Douglas 148
C-76 Caravan, Curtiss-Wright 136
C-82 Packet, Fairchild 157
C-87, Consolidated 130
C-101, CASA 117, 228
C-102 Jetliner, Avro Canada 89
C-119, Fairchild 157
C-119 Flying Boxcar, Fairchild 129
C-123 Avitruc, Chase 123
C-123 Provider, Fairchild 123, 157
C-124 Globemaster, Douglas 149
C-130 Hercules, Lockheed 214
C-133 Cargomaster, Douglas 149
C-141 Starlifter, Lockheed 214
C-160, Transall 297
C-212 Aviocar, CASA 117
Ca 1, et seq, Caproni 116
CA-1, et seq, Commonwealth 127
CA-1 Ambassador, Collier 126
CA-45D, Firestone 163
Ca 100, FNA/Caproni 157
Ca.405 Procellaria, Reggiane 258
Ca.602/.603, Predappio 257
CAP 10/20, CAARP 112
CBY-3, CCF 114, 115
CC-1, Caproni-Campini 116
CCW-5, Custer 137
CE biplane, Maryland 223
CE.43 Guépard, CERVA 120
CE.44 Cougar, CERVA 120
CE.45 Léopard, CERVA 120
C.F.2A, Central Aircraft 120
C.F.4, Central Aircraft 120
CF-100, Avro Canada 89
CF-105 Arrow, Avro Canada 89
CG-2, Sierra 121
CG-3A/-4A, Waco 128
CG-4A, Waco 169
CG-4A Hadrian, Waco 302
CG-18A, Chase 123
CH-1, Cessna 121
CH-3, Chrislea 124
CH-III, Cicaré 124
CH-46 Sea Knight, Vertol 296
CH-53E, Sikorsky 274
Che-2, Chetverikov 123
CJ600, Texas 290
C.K.1, Cicaré 124
CL-15, Colgate-Larsen 126
CL.20, Cierva 125
CL-28 Argus, Canadair 113
CL-41, Canadair 113
CL-44 Yukon, Canadair 113
CL-84, Canadair 113
CL-89, Canadair 113
CL-215, Canadair 113
CL-600 Challenger, Canadair 113
C.L.A.2, et seq, Comper 128
CM-1 Lone Eagle, Federal 161
CM.10, et seq, Fouga 170
CP.30 Emeraude, Piel 253
CP.80 Zef, Piel 253
C.P.100, CAARP 112
CP-140 Aurora, Lockheed 113
CP.301 Emeraude, Piel 160
CP 301 S Smaragd, Binder 98
CP.500, Piel 253
C.P.A.1, Provence-Aviation 257
CQ-1A, Fletcher 163
CR, Curtiss 135
C.R.32, Fiat 40, 192
CR 760/770, Caudron 118
CR.LTH-1, Cierva 125
C.S., CMASA 126
CS-102, Ceskoslovenské 120
CT4, AESL 237
CU-16, Uppercu-Burnelli 295
C.V-D/-E, Fokker 120, 206
C.V-E, Fokker 151
CV-139 Comet, Hockaday 192
CW-20, Curtiss-Wright 136
CW-21 Demon, Curtiss-Wright 136
Cabinaire, Paramount 247
Cadet, Avro 242
Cadet, Interstate 198
Calcutta, Short 105
Call Air A-9, IMCO 197
Camel, Sopwith 103, 108, 125, 193, 281
Campani, F.22, Fairey 91
Canary, Johnson Airplane 200
Canberra, General Electric 143
Canso, Canadian Vickers 114
Canuck, Model 80, Fleet 163, 210
Caravan, C-76, Curtiss Wright 136
Caravelle, Sud-Aviation 285
Cardinal, St. Louis 268
Cardinal Senior, St. Louis 268
Cargomaster, C-133, Douglas 149
Caribou, DHC-4, de Havilland Canada 142
Carioca, Type 5, CAP 115
Carrier Pigeon, Curtiss 135
Carvair, Aviation Traders 88
Casmuniz 52, Muniz 233
Castel C.255, et seq, Fouga 170
Catalina, OA-10, Consolidated 114
Catalina, P3Y/PBY, Consolidated 130
Cavalier, Star 283
Cayuse, OH-6A, Hughes 195
Centaur IIa, Central Aircraft 120
Centaur IV, Central Aircraft 120
Centaurus, Oakland 242
Ceres, Commonwealth 127

Challenger, Champion 122
Challenger, Emsco 153
Challenger, JC-1, Cook 132
Champion, Aeronca 68
Champion, Model 7, Aeronca 122
Chaparral, Aerostar 70
Cheetah, Grumman American 180
Cherokee, Piper 124
Chevvy Bird, Waterman 303
Cheyenne, Piper 124
Chiang Hung, Naval Air 235
Chief, Aeronca 68
Chief, Golden Eagle 177
Chincol trainer, FNA 157
Chinook, Boeing Vertol 72
Chinook, Vertol 296
Chipmunk, DHC-1, de Havilland Canada 142
Chirri, HA-132-1, Hispano 192
Chorlito, IMPA 197
Cigale, PA-201, Aubert 85
Cigale Major, PA-204, Aubert 85
Citabria, Champion 122
Citabria Pro, Model 8, Champion 122
Cloud, Saunders-Roe 268
Cloudster, Davis-Douglas 140
Cobra, Northrop 241
Cobra 400, Procaer 257
Coccinelle, SIPA 279
Codock, Codock 126
Colt, Piper 254
Comet, Ireland 198
Comet, D.H.88, de Havilland 141
Comet 1, de Havilland 55, 141, 169
Comet 4, de Havilland 55
Comet, CV-139, Hockaday 192
Commander 685, Rockwell 241
Commando, C-46, Curtiss 190
Commando, C-46, Curtiss-Wright 136
Commercial, Swallow 287
Commuter, Keystone 205
Commuter 110, Lanier 208
Commuter Jr H-1A, Helicom 188
Composite, Short-Mayo 34
Compostela, Aero-Difusión 67
Concorde, Concorde 58, 129
Concordia, Cunliffe-Owen 134
Condor, Druine 149
Condor, B-2, Curtiss 135
Condor, BT-32, Curtiss-Wright 136
Condor, Fw 200, Focke-Wulf 34, 166
Consul, Airspeed 75
Convair 580, Allison 77
Coot, Aerocar 66
Corisco, Nieva 236
Cornell, M-62, Fairchild 157
Coronado, PB2Y, Consolidated 130
Corsair, Mauboussin 223
Corsair, FG-1, Chance Vought 177
Corsair 02U/03U/SU, Chance Vought 122
Corsair II, LTV 212
Corsair 120, Mauboussin 223
Corsair Minor, Mauboussin 223
Corse, Ouest Aviation 244
Corvette, Aérospatiale 70
Corvette, Sud-Aviation 285
Cougar, Campbell 112
Cougar, Grumman American 180
Cougar CE.44, CERVA 120
Counter Invader, On Mark 243
Courier, Kinner 205
Coupé, CAC 112
Coupé, Swallow 287
Courier, Airspeed 75
Courier, Curtiss-Reid 135
Crane, Cessna 121
Cricket, Campbell 112
Cri-Cri, Salmson 122
Cri-Cri Major, D-7, CFA 122
Criquet, Morane-Saulnier 232
Cropmaster, Kingsford Smith 205
Cropmaster, Yeoman 308
Cruisemaster, Northern 241
Cruisemaster, Model 14-19-2, Downer 149
Cruiser, Spartan 282
Crusader, Gillis 176
Crusader, F-8, LTV 122
Cruzair, Waterhouse 303
Cuauhtemoc, Servicios Aereos 271
Cub, Piper 59, 133, 254
Cub, Taylor 288
Cuckoo, Sopwith 281
Curlew, Campbell 112
Custombuilt, B-3, Crown 133
Cutlass, F7U, Chance Vought 122
Cutty Sark, Saunders-Roe 268
Cygnet, Blackburn 98
Cygnet, C.W. Aircraft 137
Cygnet, General Aircraft 175
Cygnet, Shin Nihon 272

D, Orenco 135
D series, Halberstadt 182
D series, Phönix 251
D series, Schutte-Lanz 269
DI, et seq, Albatros 76
D.1, BAG 91
D-1, Davis 140
D.1, ei seq, Dewoitine 144
D1, Hansa 182
D-1/-7, Kondor 206
D.1, Larson 208
D-I, Siemens 273
D I, Zeppelin Werke 309
B.I. Berg-Scout, Oesterreichische 242
D1A, Aichi 72
D.II, Delanne 142
D3A, Aichi 72
D4Y Suisei, Yokosuka 308
D-7 Cri-Cri Major, CFA 122
D.VII/VIII, Fokker 167

D.9, et seq, Jodel 200
D-10B, Doman 116
D.11, Jodel 120
D.11, Luftfahrzeug 218
D.11, Roland 264
D.11a, BAG 91
D.XXI, Fokker 168
D.21C, Dewoitine 165
D21T-4 Super Phryganet, CFA 122
D-25, Jones 200
D-25, et seq, New Standard 137
D.37, et seq, SAF 277
D57 Phryganet, CFA 122
D.112, Jodel 67
D-117-A, Jodel 78
D.119, Jodel 67
D.120 Paris-Nice, Wassmer 303
D.140 Mousquetaire, SAN 277
D.150 Mascaret, SAN 277
D-158 Tipsy Nipper, Avions-Fairey 142
D.520, SNCAM 279
D-558-1 Skystreak, Douglas 149
D-558-2 Skyrocket, Douglas 149
D.750, SNCAM 279
D.1190S, Jodel 67
D2127, Bell 95
D-3803, FFA 161
DA-1, Davis 140
DB-7, Douglas 148
DB-10B, Dorman 145
DB-240, Yermolaev 308
DC-1, Douglas 148
DC-2, Douglas 33, 148
DC-3, Douglas 33, 113, 129, 148
DC-4, Douglas 88, 113, 148
DC-6/-6A/-6B, Cessna 55, 121, 149
DC-7/-7C, Douglas 55, 149
DC-8, McDonnell Douglas 55
DC-9, McDonnell Douglas 57, 149
DF-2, Douglas 148
DGA-1, et seq, Howard 193
DGA-15, et seq, Howard 194
D.H.1, et seq, Airco 73, 84, 97, 98, 133, 136, 137, 138, 205
DH-1, et seq, EKW 151
D.H.2, et seq, de Havilland 141
D.H.4, Airco 37, 67, 73, 84, 97, 140, 177, 200
D.H.51 Hummingbird, de Havilland 141
D.H.66 Hercules, de Havilland 141
D.H.84/89, Dragon Rapide, de Havilland 141, 142
D.H.88 Comet, de Havilland 141
D.H.91 Albatross, de Havilland 141
D.H.93 Don, de Havilland 141
D.H.94 Moth Minor, de Havilland 141
D.H.95 Flamingo, de Havilland 141
D.H.104 Dove, de Havilland 117
D.H.106 Comet 1, de Havilland 141
D.H.115 Vampire Trainer, Airspeed 75
D.H.121, Airco 73
D.H.121 Trident, de Havilland 141
D.H.125, de Havilland 141
DHA G2, de Havilland Aircraft 142
DHA 3 Drover, de Havilland Aircraft 142
DHC-1 Chipmunk, de Havilland Canada 142
DHC-2 Beaver, de Havilland Canada 142
DHC-3 Otter, de Havilland Canada 142
DHC-4 Caribou, de Havilland Canada 142
DHC-5 Buffalo, de Havilland Canada 142
DHC-6 Twin Otter, de Havilland Canada 142
DHC-7 QSTOL, de Havilland Canada 142
DJ-1 Bumblebee, Driggs-Johnson 149
Do 11, Dornier 146, 147
Do 17, Dornier 42, 178
Do 18, Dornier 34, 146
Do 23, Dornier 146
Do 24, Dornier 168
Do 25, Dornier 146
Do 26, Dornier 34
Do 27, Dornier 117, 146
Do 28 Skyservant, Dornier 146
Do 29, Dornier 146
Do 31, Dornier 146, 182
Do 217, Dornier 146
Do 335, Dornier 146
Do F, Dornier 147
Do N, Dornier 147
Do P, Dornier 147
Do X, Dornier 147
Do Y, Dornier 147
D.P.1, Dietrich 145
Dr 1, et seq, Euler 156
Dr.1, Fokker 167
DR.100, et seq, Robin 262
DR 100 Ambassadeur, CEA 119
DT, Douglas 148
DT-2, Douglas 218
D.W.1/.1A/.2, Chilton 123
DWC, Douglas 148
DST, Douglas 33
Dakota, Douglas 143
Danecock, Hawker 187
Dart, Blackburn 98
Dart I/II, Doyne 149
Dart II, Driggs 149
Dart Model 1, Driggs 149
Dart Flittermouse, Zander & Weyl 309
Darter, Rockwell Commander 241
Dauntless, SBD Douglas 149
Dauphin, Aérospatiale 70
Defender, Britten-Norman 108
Defender, FD-25, Fletcher 163
Defiant, P.82, Boulton Paul 103
Delta, Northrop 114
Delta 2, Fairey 159
Delphin, Aérospatiale 70
Delta Dagger, F-102, Convair 131
Delta Dart, F-106, Convair 131
De Luxe Brigadier, B-350/-360, Falcon 160
Demon, Hawker 187
Demon, McDonnell 224
Demon, CW-21, Curtiss-Wright 136

Desford, Reid & Sigrist 259
Destroyer, Vickers 298
Destroyer, B-66, Douglas 148
Detroiter, Stinson 284
Devastator, TBD, Douglas 148
Diplomate, SOCATA 277
Distributor Wing, Aerial Distributors 65
Djinn, Ouest Aviation 244
Djinn, SNCASO 280
Dolphin, Douglas 148
Dolphin, Sopwith 138, 193
Dominator, B-32, Consolidated Vultee 130
Don, D.H.93, de Havilland 141
Donryu, Nakajima 234
Douglas DC-3 81
Dove, D.H.104, de Havilland 117, 141
Drache, Fa223, Focke-Achgelis 165
Dragon/Dragon Rapide, D.H.84/89, de Havilland 141, 142
Dragonfly, Westland 305
Draken, SAAB 267
Dreadnought, Westland 304
Dromader, WSK-Mielec 307
Drover, DHA 3, de Havilland Aircraft 142
Duck, GA-2, Goodyear 177
Duck, J2F-6, Grumman 127
Duiker monoplane, Hawker 187
Dunstable Dart, Dart 138

E.1, BAG 91
E-1, Kellner-Béchereau 205
E-I, Siemens 273
E-1, Standard 283
E-2 Hawkeye, Grumman 180
E.4/20, Zeppelin Werke Staaken 309
E.5, SPCA 281
E7K, Kawanishi 203
E13A, Watanabe 303
E14Y, Watanabe 303
E16A, Aichi 72
E.28/39, Gloster/Whittle 53, 177
E.40, et seq, CKD-Praga 125
E.114 Air Baby, Praga 191
EC-1, Elias 152
E.F.100 Winglet, Eshelman 155
EM/EO, Elias 151
EMA 124, Meridionali 225
EMB-201A Ipanema, EMBRAER 152
EMB-710, et seq, Neiva 236
EP-1, Republic 259
ES53, Lualdi 217
Eagle, Curtiss 135
Eagle, Fisher 163
Eagle 1, B.K. 90
Eagle 1, Windecker 306
Eagle 2, B.A. 90
Eagle, F-15, McDonnell Douglas 51
Eaglerock, Alexander Aircraft 77
Eaglet, American Eagle 78
Eaglet, American Eaglecraft 79
Eaglet, Shin Nihon 272
Eastchurch Kitten,
RNAS Port Victoria 262
Ecureuil, Aérospatiale 70
El Boyero, FMA 165
El Boyero, Petrolini 250
Electra, Lockheed 92, 214
Elf, Parnall 248
Elster, Pützer 257
El TomCat III, et seq, Continental 131
Emeraude, Piel 98, 112, 160, 173, 174, 253
Ensign, Armstrong Whitworth 83
Envoy, Airspeed 75
Eon, Eliotts 152
Eon 2, Elliotts 152
Eon T.16/48, Elliotts 152
Epervier, Renard 259
Equator, Pöschel 256
Ercoupe, Engineering & Research 153
Espandon, SNCASO 280
Estafette, Mignet 228
Europa, Wassmer 303
Execta, Fornaire 169
Executive, Mooney 231
Executive, Seversky 271
Executive, Spartan 282
Expediter, Fornaire 169
Explorer, Abrams 64
Explorer, Fornaire 169
Explorer/Observer, Patchen 235

F series, Fokker 168
F.1, et seq, Felixstowe 270
F.1/.2, Flugzeugwerft Lübeck 164
F-1, Lockheed 214
F-1, Mitsubishi 230
F-1 Aircoupe, Forney 169
F1M2, Sasebo 268
F2, Dassault 139
F.2, Fairey 159
F.II, Fokker 167
F2A Buffalo, Brewster 106
F.2B, Bristol 165
F2H Banshee, McDonnell 224
F.3, Felixstowe 145
F.3, Martin & Handasyde 222
F3H Demon, McDonnell 224
F.4, et seq, Ambrosini 175
F.4, et seq, Caproni 116
F-4, McDonnell Douglas 157
F IV/IX, Avia 87
F.4 Buzzard, Martin & Handasyde 222
F4B-3, Boeing 101
F4U Corsair, Vought-Sikorsky 300
F.5, Felixstowe 114, 177
F-5, Northrop 241
F5E Tiger II, Northrop 73, 151, 152
F-5L, Aeromarine 67
F-5L, NAF 235
F-5L, Orenco 135
F6U Pirate, Vought 301

F.VII, Fokker 168
F7 Rondone, Ambrosini 78
F.VII/3m, Fokker 87, 168
F7U Cutlass, Chance Vought 122
F8C/0C Falcon, Curtiss 135
F8C/02C Helldiver, Curtiss 135
F8L, Falco 86
F-8 Crusader, LTV 122
F.8 Falco, Aviamilano 67
F.9/27, Vickers 133
F.9/27, Westland 133
F.9 Sparviero, Pasotti 248
F9C Sparrowhawk, Curtiss-Wright 136
F.10, Fokker 167
F-11 Husky, Fairchild 158
F11C/BFC Goshawk, Curtiss-Wright 136
F 13, Junkers 201
F.14 Nibbio, Aviamilano 86
F-14 Tomcat, Grumman 180
F-15, General Aviation 175
F-15 Eagle, McDonnell Douglas 51
F15 Picchio, Procaer 257
F-16, General Dynamics 159, 175, 176
F-17 Sportsman, International 198
F-18 Hornet, McDonnell/Northrop 241
F.19, Faucett 161
F.19, Vickers 298
F.20, et seq, Farman 160
F.20 Pegaso, General Avia 175
F.22 Campania, Fairey 91
F-23/-23A, Funk 171
F-23/-23A/-23B, Funk 171
F-27/FH-227, Fokker-VFW 157
F.28 Fellowship, Fokker 57, 182
F-28A, Enstrom 155
F.46A, Duramold 149
F.60 Goliath, Farman 160
F-84, Republic 260
F-86 Sabre, North American 113, 127, 162
F-89 Scorpion, Northrop 241
F-101 Voodoo, McDonnell 89
F-102 Delta Dagger, Convair 131, 175
F-104 Starfighter, Lockheed 89, 113, 168, 182
F-105 Thunderchief, Republic 157, 260
F-106 Delta Dart, Convair 131, 175
F-111, General Dynamics 175, 176
F-111/FB-111, Convair 131
F.250, Aviamilano 86
FA-2/-3 Airphibian, Continental 131
FA-200 Aero Subaru, Fuji 171
Fa 223 Drache, Focke-Achgelis 165
FA-300, Fuji 171
Fa 330 Bachstelze, Focke-Achgelis 165
F.B.5., Vickers 298
F.B.9., Vickers 298
FBA, Norman Thompson 177
FBA-1, et seq, Found 170
FBA-6, et seq, Schreck 269
FBT-2, Fletcher 163
FC-1/-2. Fairchild 157
F.C.12, CANSA 115
F.C.20, CANSA 115
FD-25 Defender, Fletcher 163
FDB-1, CCF 114
F.E.2, R.A.F. 103, 174, 177
F.E.4, R.A.F. 103, 174, 177
FF-1, Grumman 114, 180
FF 29, Friedrichshafen 171
FF 49, Friedrichshafen 171
FG-1 Corsair, Chance Vought 177
FH-1 Phantom 1, McDonnell 224
Fh 104, Siebelwerke 273
FH-1100, Hiller 191
Fi 2 Tiger, Fieseler 162
Fi 5R, Fieseler 162
Fi 97, Fieseler 162
Fi 156 Storch, Fieseler 162
Fi 167, Fieseler 162
FJ-Skytrac, HTM 189
F.K.1, et seq, Armstrong Whitworth 83
F.K. 22 Bat, BAT 92
F.K. 23 Bantam, BAT 92
F.K. 24 Baboon, BAT 92
F.K. 25 Basilisk, BAT 92
F.K. 26, et seq, BAT 92
F.K. 31, et seq, Koolhoven 143, 206
F.K. 41, Koolhoven 143
F.K. 43, SAFA 277
F.L.3, AVIA 86, 296
FL-3, Lombardi 217
Fl 184, et seq, Flettner 164
FM-1, General Motors 176
F.N.305, et seq, Nardi 235
Fo 108, Folland 169
Fo 139 Midge, Folland 169
Fo 141 Gnat, Folland 169
Fo 144 Gnat, Folland 169
FR-2, Raab 258
FU-1, Chance Vought 122
FU-24, Air Parts 74
FU-24, Fletcher 74
FU-24, Utility, Fletcher 163
FVL-8, US Army 295
F.W.1/.2/.3, Wicko 169
FW-5, Eshelman 155
FW44 Stieglitz, Focke-Wulf 120, 166, 173
FW 56 Stosser, Focke-Wulf 166
FW 58 Weihne, Focke-Wulf 166, 173
FW 61, Focke-Achgelis 165
FW 186, Focke-Achgelis 165
FW 189, Focke-Wulf 166
FW 190, Focke-Wulf 42, 166
FW 200 Condor, Focke-Wulf 34, 166
Fachiro, Partenavia 248
Falcão, A-80, Avibras 89
Falco 1, Reggiane 258
Falcon series, Dassault 139
Falcon, A-3, Curtiss 135
Falcon, F8C/0C, Curtiss 135
Falcon OW-5, Welch 303
Falcon 10, Dassault 117

Falke, Dornier 146
Falke, Slingsby 275
Fanliner, RFB/Grumman 260
Farfadet, SNCASO 280
Feiro I, Feigl e Rotter 161
Feiro Dongo, Feigle Rotter 161
Fellowship, F.28, Fokker 57
Fennec/Trojan, North American 240
Fieldmaster, Yeoman 308
Fighter, Bristol 177
Fighter, 18-T, Kirkham 205
Finnmark 5A, Hönningstad 193
Firebrand, Blackburn 98
Firefly, Fairey 125, 159
Firefly II, Fairey 159
Flamant, MD 315, Dassault 139
Flamingo, Udet 294
Flamingo, D.H.95, de Havilland 141
Fledgling, N2C, Curtiss 135
Fleet 10G, S.E.T. 157
Fleet Shadower, Airspeed 75
Flightsail VII, Flight Dynamics 164
Flittermouse, Dart 138
Fliver, Mattley 223
Fliver Plane, Mattley 223
Flyer, Wright 14
Flyer A, Wright 16
Flying Boxcar, C-119, Fairchild 129
Flying Dutchman, Szekeley 287
Flying Fortress, B-17, Boeing 51, 101
Flying Yacht, Eastman 150
Forwarder, UC-61, Fairchild 157
Fox, Fairey 159
Foxjet, Tony Team Industries 68
Fox Moth, de Havilland 142
Freedom Fighter, Northrop 241
Frégate, Aérospatiale 70
Freighter, Bristol 88
Freighter, Type 170, Bristol 107
Fulmar, Fairey 159
Fury, Felixstowe 270
Fury, Hawker 186, 187

G series, Caudron 118
G series, Daimler 138
G, Dart 138
G I, AEG 65
G.1, Fokker 168
G-1, Gashulyak 174
G2 Galeb, SOKO 281
G2H1, Hiro 192
G.IIR, Adlerwerke 65
G.IIR, Gerner 65, 176
G.3, Caudron 108
G III, Friedrichshafen 171
G.8, Dassault 139
G-20, Gyroplane 181
G-21C, McKinnon 226
G23/24, Flygindustri 164
G 24/31, Junkers 201
G 38, Junkers 201
G49, Fiat 162
G56, Schempp-Hirth 269
G80, Fiat 162
G91, Fiat 65, 162, 219
G91Y, Aeritalia 65
G91Y, Fiat 162
G.100, Martin & Handasyde 222
G.102, Martin & Handasyde 222
G222, Aeritalia 65
G222, Fiat 162
GA-1, Engineering Division/Boeing 100, 153, 295
GA-2 Duck, Goodyear 177
GA-21M, Cunningham-Hall 134
GA-36, Cunningham-Hall 134
GA.43, Clark 175
GA.43, General Aviation 175
GAL-GO Universal Freighter, General Aircraft 175
GA X, Engineering Division 153, 295
GC-1 Swift, Globe 176
G.C.A.2, Gyrodyne 181
GD-24, Gates-Day 237
GE-23, Grumman 114
GMG V, Muller 233
GN, Autogyro, AISA 76
Go 145, Gotha 178
Go 229 V3, Gotha 193
Go 242, Gotha 178
Go 244, Gotha 178
GP seaplane, Blackburn 98
GR.8, LACAB 84
Gs I, Zeppelin Werke Lindau 309
GV.38, Gotaverken 177
GV 103L, Gazuit-Valladeau 174
GY-80 Horizon, Gardan 173
GY90, et seq, SITAR 279
Gabbiano, Z.501, CANT 115
Gadfly, HSF.II, Glenny & Henderson 176
Galeb, SOKO 281
Gamecock, Gloucester 177
Gamma, Northrop 241
Gamma L, General 174
Gamma S, General 174
Gannet, Fairey 159
Gannet, Gloucestershire 116
Gannet, Tugan 292
Ganymede, Grahame-White 179
Gastambide-Levavasseur, Latham 209
Gauntlet, Gloster 177
Gawron, OKL 244
Gawron, PZL 246
Gazelle, Aérospatiale/Westland 70, 305
Gekko, Nakajima 234
Gelatik, LIPNUR 143
Gemini, Miles 230

Genairco, Genairco 174
Gentleman, Comte 128
Gerle 13, MSE 233
Geronimo, Seguin 270
Ghibli, Ca 309, Caproni 116
Giant, Kennedy 205
Giant Moth, de Havilland 142
Ginga, Yokosuka 309
Gladiator, Gloster 42
Globe Swift, Texas 290
Globemaster, C-124, Douglas 149
Gnat, Folland 192
Gnat, Fo 141, Folland 169
Gnat, Fo 144, Folland 169
Göeland, Caudron 118
Gol'duster, Model 202A, Gail 172
Goliath, F.60, Farman 160
Goose, Grumman 180
Goshawk, F11C/BFC, Curtiss-Wright 136
Gosport, Avro 82
Gossamer Condor, McReady 61
Graf Zeppelin, airship 29, 30, 34
Grain Griffin, RNAS Port Victoria 262
Grain Kitten, RNAS Port Victoria 262
Grebe, Gloucester 177
Greiff, He 177, Heinkel 188
Greyhound, Austin 86
Grifo, S1001, Ambrosini 78
Grognard, SNCASE 280
Guépard, CE.43, CERVA 120
Gulfstream II, Grumman America 180
Gull, Percival 250
Gunner, AT-21, Fairchild 149, 157
Guppy Conversions, Aero Resources 69
Gyro-Copter, Bensen 112
Gyrodyne, Fairey 159
Gyro-Glider, Bensen 112

H-1, Hughes 194
H.1/.2, Mann Egerton 220
H-1A, Commuter Jr. Helicom 188
H-2, Landgraf 207
H2/H3, VFW 297
H-3/-4, Standard 283
H-4 Small America, Curtiss 134
H6K, Kawanishi 203
H8K, Kawanishi 203
H.9, Huffer 194
H9A1, Aichi 72
H-10, Atlas 85
H-12/-16 Large America, Curtiss 134
H-16, Curtiss 235
H-21 Work Horse, Vertol 296
H-21B, Canadian Vertol 114
H-31, Doman 145
H43, Hanriot 185
H46 Styx, Hanriot 185
H-250, et seq, Helio 189
H-550A Stallion, Helio 189
H-1100, Hiller 191
HA-001 Libel, Hollandair 193
HA-31 Basant, Hindustan 192
HA-43D-1, Hispano 192
HA-100E1, Hispano 192
HA-132-1 Chirri, Hispano 192
Ha 138, HFB 111
Ha 138, Blohm und Voss 34
HA-200 Saeta, Hispano 189
HA-220 Super Saeta, Hispano 192
HA-300, Helwan 189
HA-1109/-111, Hispano 192
HA-1133, Hopfner 193
HAOP-27 Krishak, Hindustan 191
HB-2, Levy-Lepen 211
HB.28, Huffer 194
HD1, Hanriot 185
HD-10, et seq, Hurel-Dubois 195
H.D. 14, et seq, Svenska Aero 287
HD 193 Möwe, Dittmar 145
HD 156 Pater, Dittmar 145
H.D.M. 105, Miles 230
He 1, et seq, Heinkel 188
He 51, Heinkel 40, 155, 188
He 70, Heinkel 188
He 111, Heinkel 42, 117, 188
He 162, Heinkel 188
He 177 Greiff, Heinkel 188
He 178, Heinkel 53, 188
He 219 Uhu, Heinkel 188
H.F. XX-02, Maestranza Central 219
HF-24 Marut, Hindustan 192
HH-3F, Sikorsky 72
HH-43, Kaman 202
HJT-16 Kiran, Hindustan 191
HL-1, et seq, CNNA 126
H.M.1, et seq, AISA 76
HM-1, Hughes-Kaiser 202
HM-5, Summit 286
H.M.310 Estafette, Mignet 228
Ho V/VI, Horten 193
HOE-1, Hornet, Hiller 191
HOK-1, Kaman 202
H.P. 42/45, Handley Page 30, 183
H.P.137 Jetstream, Jetstream 199
HPR.3 Herald, Handley Page 184
HR.100, Robin 262
HS, Curtiss 134
HS-9, Hirtenberger 192
HS-21, Curtiss 218
Hs 123, Henschel 189
Hs 126, Henschel 189
Hs 132, Henschel 190
HS 748, Hawker Siddeley 74, 169
HS-1033, Hopfner 193
HSF.II Gadfly, Glenny & Henderson 176
HT-2, Hindustan 191
HTK-1, Kaman 202
HUL-26 Pushpak, Hindustan 191
Hadrian, Waco 302
Halcon, Type 202, CASA 117

Halifax, Handley Page 42, 45, 154, 184
Hamble Baby, Fairey 159
Hamilcar, General Aircraft 98
Hampden, Handley Page 42, 114, 154, 184
Hansa Jet, 320, HFB 182
Harpoon, Lockheed 214
Harrier, Hawker-Siddeley 52, 186
Harrow, Handley Page 35
Hart, Hawker 120, 177, 187
Harvard, North American 114
Hastings, Handley Page 184
Havoc, Douglas 148
Hawk, Curtiss 89
Hawk, Maranda 220
Hawk, Pacific 245
Hawk, Pilcher 11
Hawk I, et seq, Curtiss-Wright 136
Hawk 75, Curtiss 165
Hawk 75, Curtiss-Wright 136
Hawkeye, E-2, Grumman 180
Hayabusa, Mansu 220
Hayate, Nakajima 234
Heck, 3308, Hendy 189
Helicogyre, Isaaco 269
Helidyne, G.C.A.7, Gyrodyne 181
Hellcat, Grumman 180
Helldiver, Curtiss 114, 158
Helldiver, F8C/02C, Curtiss 135
Helvellyn, Hillson 191
Hendon, Fairey 159
Herald, HPR.3, Handley Page 184
Hercules, Hughes 194
Hercules, Lockheed 214
Hercules, D.H.66, de Havilland 141
Hereford, Handley Page 272
Hermes, Handley Page 184
Heron, de Havilland 141
Heyford, Handley Page 184
Hinaidi, Handley Page 184
Hindenburg, airship 29, 30
Hirondelle, AG 03, Gatard 174
Hobo, 281, Hendy 189
Honey Bee, Bee 94
Hoppi-Copter C-1, Capital 115
Horizon, SOCATA 277
Horizon, GY-80, Gardan 173
Hornet, de Havilland 46, 169
Hornet, Gyroflight 181
Hornet, McDonnell/Northrop 241
Hornet, HOE-1, Hiller 191
Horsley, Hawker 187
Hotspur, General Aircraft 98
Hudson, Lockheed 214
Huey Cobra, Bell 95
Hummel, Siebelwerke 273
Humming Bird, White 304
Hummingbird, D.H.51, de Havilland 141
Hunter, Hawker 83, 89, 151, 159, 168, 169, 186
Hurricane, Hawker 40, 114, 159, 177, 186, 191
Husky, F-11, Fairchild 158
Hustler, B-58, Convair 131
Hustler Model 400, AJI 76
Hyabusa, Nakajima 234
Hyderabad, Handley Page 184

I-11, AISA 76
I-11, Iberavia 196
I-11, et seq, VEF 295, 296
I-16 Rata, Polikarpov 256
I-22, Lavochkin 209
I-115, AISA 76
I-115, Iberavia 196
I.A.33 Pulgui II, Empresa 152
IA 35, et seq, DINFIA 145
I.A.35, Empress 152
IA.58 Pucará, FMA 165
IA-62, FMA 165
IAR.15, Regia 259
IAR 811, et seq, URMV-3 295
IAR-824, ICA 196
I-B, Phillips 251
Il-2, Ilyushin 43, 196
Il-4, Ilyushin 196
Il-12, Ilyushin 57, 196
Il-14, Ilyushin 57, 120, 196
Il-14M, Ilyushin 87
Il-18, Ilyushin 57, 196
Il-28, Ilyushin 120, 196
Il-38, Ilyushin 196
Il-62, Ilyushin 196
I.O., Ikarus 196
IP-2, Iberavia 196
IS-28/-29, ICA 196
Il'ya Murometz, Russo-Baltic 266
Impala, Atlas 85
Inflatable Aircraft, Goodyear 177
Intruder, A-6, Grumman 180
Invader, Douglas 148
Ipanema, EMB-210A, EMBRAER 152
Iroquois, Bell 72
Iskra, OKL 244
Iskra, WSK-Mielec 307
Islander, BN-2, Britten-Norman 59, 108, 196, 198

J, Jamieson 199
J.1, Durant-Standard 149
J1, Junkers 201
J-1, Standard 140
J-1 Autocrat, Taylorcraft 289
J-1 Jastreb, SOKO 281
J-1 Martin Fierro, Ronchetti, Razzetti 265
J1N1 Gekko, Nakajima 234
J II, AEG 65
J-2, Aero Resources 69
J-2, Jovair 200
J 2/4, Junkers 201
J-2 Arrow, Taylorcraft 289
J2F-6 Duck, Grumman 127
J-2-L1 Jupiter, Jamieson 199
J-3, Piper 175
J-6, Jona 220

J7W, Watanabe 303
J-22, FFVS 162
JC-1 Challenger, Cook 132
JF-1, Grumman 180
J.G.10, Guillemin 180
J.G.40, Guillemin 180
JN-3, Curtiss 114
JN-4, Curtiss 114, 134
JN-6, Curtiss 134
JOB 5, Oberlerchner 242
JOB 15, Oberlerchner 242
JOV-3, Jovair 200
J.P.2B, Pidek 253
J.S.54, CMASA 126
Ju 52/3m, Junkers 123, 126, 201
Ju 60/160, Junkers 201
Ju 86, Junkers 200
Ju 87, Junkers 39, 42, 104, 164, 201
Ju 88/188/388, Junkers 42, 201
Ju 90/290/390, Junkers 201
Ju 287, Junkers 201
Jaguar, SEPECAT 51, 139, 278
Jaktfalk, Svenska Aero 287
Jastreb, SOKO 281
Javelin, Gloster 83, 177
Jet Gyrodyne, Fairey 159
Jet Liner 600, Carstedt 117
Jetliner, C-102, Avro Canada 89
Jet-Pak, Steward-Davis 284
Jet Provost, P.84, Percival 195
Jet Ranger, Model 206, Agusta-Bell 72
Jet Ranger II, Bell 128
Jetstar II, Lockheed 215
Jetstream, Handley Page 120, 184
Jetstream, H.P.137, Jetstream 199
Jindivik, GAF 150, 178
Joigny, SRCM 278
Jungmann, Bü 131, Bücker 109, 117, 140
Jungmeister, Bü 133, Bücker 109, 115, 117
Junior, Rearwin 258
Junior, Tipsy 292
Junior, Bo 208 C, Bölkow 102
Junior Coupe, Alco 77
Jupiter, J-2-L1, Jamieson 199

K-1, et seq, Kalinin 202
K1-105/-107, Klemin 206
K-3/-4, Kellett 204
K-4, Kalinin 294
K10W1, Watanabe 303
K11W1, Watanabe 303
K-30C, Flygindustri 164
K-37, Flygindustri 164
K-47, Flygindustri 164
K-125A, Kaman 202
K 131, et seq, Klemm 206
K-190, Kaman 202
K-225, Kaman 202
Ka-1/-2, Kayaba 204
Ka-15, et seq, Kamov 202
KAL-1, Kawasaki 204
KB-3T, Continental 131
KB-6 Matajur, Letalski 211
KB-50J/K, Hayes 188
KC-135, LAS 216
KD-1, Kellett 204
KDW, Hansa 185
KE-14, Ramor 258
K.F.1, Kawanishi 203
KH-15, Kellett 204
Ki-3, et seq, Kawasaki 204
Ki-9, Tachikawa 288
Ki-17, Tachikawa 288
Ki-21, Mitsubishi 230
Ki-27, Nakajima 234
Ki-36, Tachikawa 288
Ki-43 Hyabusa, Nakajima 234
Ki-44 Shoki, Nakijima 234
Ki-46, Mitsubishi 230
Ki-49 Donryu, Nakajima 234
Ki-51, Watanabe 303
Ki-55, Tachikawa 288
Ki-67, Mitsubishi 230
Ki-70, Tachikawa 288
Ki-74, Tachikawa 288
Ki-77, Tachikawa 288
Ki-84 Hayate, Nakajima 234
Ki-86, Nippon 238
Ki-94, Tachikawa 288
KM-2/-2B, Fuji 171
KR Series, Kreider-Reisner 206
KS.3 Cropmaster, Yeoman 308
KV-107, Kawasaki 102
KZI, et seq, Skandinavisk 275
Kachina, Varga 296
Kanpur I/II, MMPL 231
Karhu, Karhumäki 203
Kaydet, Boeing/Stearman 78
Kestrel, Austin 86
Kestrel, P.1127, Hawker 186
Kfir, IAI 199
Kiebitz, Merckle 226
Kiebitz, S 24, Focke-Wulf 166
Kingbird, Curtiss-Robertson 135
KingCobra, P-63, Bell 95
Kingfisher, Vought-Sikorsky 300
Kingston flying-boat, English Electric 154
Kiran, HJT-16, Hindustan 191
Kite, Comper 128
Kite, Simplex 275
Kite, Sioux 275
Kitten, Dart 138
Kittiwake, Saunders 268
Knight, Deekay 140
Kolibir, Flettner 164
Kolibri, Udet 294
Kolibri, N.H.I., Aviolanda 89
Komet, Dornier 146
Komet, Me 163B 45, 46
Komta, ANT 81
Kondor, Udet 294

Krähe, Rock 261
Krishak, HAOP-27, Hindustan 191
Kruk, PZL 246, 247
Kurier, Ao 192, Ago 71

L.010-1, et seq, Leduc 210
L-1, Macchi 219
L II, Arado 82
L-2/-4, Lawson 209
L-4, Luscombe 218
L.8, et seq, Daimler 138
L-13, Consolidated Vultee 130
L-14 Super Electra, Lockheed 214
L.15, et seq, Daimler-Werke 138
L 15, et seq, Klemm 206
L-18 Lodestar, Lockheed 214
L-19 Bird Dog, Cessna 121
L.25, Klemm 90
L-26, Aero Design 67
L.28, et seq, Latécoère 209
L.32, Klemm 90
L-39, Aero 71
L-40 Meta-Sokol, Ceskoslovenské 120
L.55, et seq, Lualdi 217
L 58, et seq, Albatros 76
L-60 Brigadyr, Ceskoslovenské 120
L.101 Air Tractor, Lamson 207
L-200 Morava, Ceskoslovenské 120, 210
L-208, Ceskoslovenské 120
L450F, LTV 212
L.1049 Super Constellation, Lockheed 55
L.1649/L.1649A Starliner, Lockheed 55
LA-4-200 Buccaneer, Lake 126, 129
LA 4A, Lake 207
La-5, et seq, Lavochkin 209
LAGG-1, Lavochkin 209
LASA-60, Lockheed-Azcarate 216
LAT 4, Latécoère 209
LAT 6, Latécoère 209
LAZ-7, et seq, Lazarow 210
L.B.II Dankok, Orlogsvaerftet 244
LB-5A, Keystone 205
LB-10A, Keystone 205
LC, Laird 207
LC 13-A Zephyr 150, Bartlett 92
LCA, Culver 134
LC-DW Solution, Laird 207
LeO 45, Lioré et Olivier 213
LF-1, IMPA 197
Li-2, Lisunov 213
LM-1 Nikko, Fuji 171
L.M.5 Aviastar, AVIA 86
LM-5 Aviastar, Lombardi 217
LP-3, Lincoln-Page 212
LT-200, LIPNUR 143
LTR 14 Meteor, Laird 207
LUSAC-11, Packard-Le Père 245
LUSAC-21, Packard-Le Père 245
LZ-1a, et seq, Doman 145
La France, airship 10
Lancaster, Avro 42, 45, 55, 114, 134, 143, 161, 178, 184
Lancastrian, Avro 55
Lancer, Republic 259
Languedoc, SNCASE 280
Lansen, SAAB, 267
Large America, H-12/-16, Curtiss 134
Lark, Curtiss 135
Lark, Rockwell Commander 241
Lasconder, Larkin/Lasco 208
Lascoter, Larkin/Lasco 208
Lascowl, Larkin 80
Lascowl, Larkin/Lasco 208
Learjet, Gates Learjet 174
Learstar, Lear 210
Lebed' 12, Lebedev 210
Leko-70 Vinka, Valmet Oy 295
Leone, Z.1018, CANT 115
Léopard, CE.45, CERVA 120
Lerche, Dätwyler 140
Levriero, Marina 220
Libeccio, Ca 310/311/312, Caproni 116
Libel, HA-001, Hollandair 193
Libelle, Dornier 146
Libellula I/II/III, Manzolini 220
Liberator, B-24, Consolidated 130, 169
Liberty Tourist, Gallandet 173
Lictor 90, Gabardini 172
Lightning, English Electric 154
Lightning, P-38, Lockheed 45, 46
Lignel 20, SFCA 278
Lilienthal gliders 7
Limousine, Salmson 268
Limousine, Westland 304
Lince, Ba 88, Breda 104
Lincoln, Avro 83, 143, 178
Liner, Dumod 128
Linnet, Garland-Bianchi 160, 174
Lion, Wicko 169, 306
Little Liner, Hamilton 183
Loadmaster, Burnelli 115
Lodestar, Lockheed 193, 210, 214
Loire 46, et seq, SNCAO 279
London, Saunders-Roe 268
Lone Eagle, CM-1, Federal 161
Longhorn, MF-7, Farman 160
Long-range Monoplane, Fairey 159
Los, PZL 246
Lunar Rocket, Maule 223
Luscombe Silvaire, Alaska Int. 76
Lynx, Grumman American 180
Lynx, Westland 305
Lynx, Westland/Aérospatiale 70
Lysander, Westland 235, 304

M-1, Mahoney-Ryan 220
M.1, Mann & Grimmer 220
M-1, Moreland 232
M-1, et seq, Shchetinin 271
M-1, US Army 295
M-1 Cuauhtemoc, Servicios Aereas 271

M-2, McCandless 224
M-3, et seq, Macchi 219
M-4, Maule 223
M-4, McCandless 224
M.5, et seq, Miles 230
M-5-210C, Maule 223
M-5-220C Lunar Rocket, Maule 223
M-5-235, Maule 223
M6A, Aichi 72
M-7, et seq, Fábrica Brasiliera 157
M-7, et seq, Muniz 126
M-11, Muniz 126
M-15, et seq, PZL 247
M-15, et seq, WSK-Mielec 307
M-18, et seq, Messerschmitt 227
M-18, et seq, Mooney 231
M.19/.21, MSE 233
M-20, BFW 97
M20J, Mooney 231
M.33, et seq, Miles 230
M-52, Myasishchev 233
M-62 Cornell, Fairchild 157
M.129-48, Mauboussin 223
M-130, Martin 34
M-150 Schulmeister, Burgfalke 110
M1911-12, Oertz 242
M1912-13, Oertz 242
M.A.1/.2, Moss 233
MAC 125, Myers 228
MAC 145, Myers 228
MAT, US Army 295
MB, Moskovskiy 233
M.B.1, et seq, Martin-Baker 222, 223
MB-3, Thomas-Morse 290
MB-3A, Morse 232
MB-3A, Thomas-Morse 100
MB-0/-10, Thomas-Morse 291
M.B.35/36, Besson 97
M.B.70, et seq, Brochet 108
M.B.200, Aero 71
MB 200/210, Bloch 99
MB.308, et seq, Macchi 176, 219
MBR-2, Beriev 97
MC-4C, Jovair 200
MC-4E, McCulloch 224
MC.72, et seq, Macchi 40, 219
MD 315 Flamant, Dassault 139
MDR-6, Chetverikov 213
Me 108(Bf 108) Taifun, BFW 40, 42, 46, 87, 97, 109, 155, 162, 178
Me 108(Bf 108) Taifun, Messerschmitt 40, 42, 46, 87, 97, 109, 155, 162, 178
Me 109(Bf 109), BFW 40, 42, 46, 87, 97, 109, 155, 162, 178, 192
Me 109(Bf 109), Messerschmitt 40, 42, 46, 87, 97, 109, 155, 162, 178, 192
Me 110(Bf 110), Messerschmitt 227
Me 163B Komet, Messerschmitt 45, 46, 144
Me 210, Messerschmitt 227
Me 262, Messerschmitt 227
Me 321, Messerschmitt 192
Me 323, Messerschmitt 192
Me 410, Messerschmitt 227
MEM-165W, Meyers 228
MF, Curtiss 134
M.F.4, et seq, CMASA 126
MF-7 Longhorn, Farman 160
M.F.8, et seq, Marinens Flyvebatfabrikk 221
MF-11 Shorthorn, Farman 160
MFI-9, Malmö 102
MFI-9, et seq, MFI 228
MH.52, et seq, Holste 193
Mi-1, et seq, Mil 229
MiG-1, et seq, Mikoyan 229
MiG-15, Mikoyan 120
MiG-25, Mikoyan 51
ML-10, Millet-Lagarde 230
ML 250 Rubis, Scintex 270
MO-1, Martin 222
M.O.1, Rohr 264
MS-2, Solar 281
MS.3, Morane-Saulnier 232
MS.130, et seq, Morane-Saulnier 232
M-T, Irwin 198
M-T-2, Irwin 198
MTB-2, Ant 81
MU-2, Mitsubishi 230
MV-4, McCulloch 224
MXY-Y Okka, Yokosuka 309
Magister, Fouga 170
Maillet 20, SFCA 278
Mailplane, GAC 172
Mailplane, Swallow 287
Mallard, Grumman 170
Manchester, Avro 263
Mantis, Model 202, Gail 172
Marathon, Miles 184, 230
Marauder, Martin 222
Marendaz Trainer, March, Jones & Cribb 220
Mariner, Martin 222
Mark I, Spitfire 283
Marketeer, On Mark 243
Marksman, On Mark 243
Marlin, Martin 222
Marlin, Teal 289
Mars, Martin 159, 222
Mars biplane, DFW 144
Martin Fierro, Ronchetti, Razzetti 265
Martlet, Southern 282
Marut, HF-24, Hindustan 192
Maryland, Martin 222
Matajur, KB-6, Letalski 211
Mauboussin 123, Fouga 170
Mauler, Martin 222
Medina, Saunders 268
Menasco, Miller 230
Mentor, B45, Beech 171
Mentor, T-34A, Beech 114
Mercator, Martin 222
Merchantman, Miles 230

Mercure 200, Dassault 139
Mercurey, B-60, Boisavia 102
Mercury, Aerial Service 65
Merganser, Percival 250
Merkur, Dornier 146
Messenger, Dayton-Wright 140
Messenger, Miles 230
Messenger, Sperry 283
Metal Martlet, Southern 283
Metalplane, Hamilton 183
Meta-Sokol, L-40, Ceskoslovenské 120
Meteor, General Western 176
Meteor, Gloster 46, 53, 83, 89, 159, 177
Meteor, Monocoupe 231
Meteor, LTR 14, Laird 207
Météore 63, SPCA 281
Meteorite, Wallis 302
Metro, Swearingen 287
Metropolitan 240/340/440 series, Consolidated
  Vultee 130, 132
Mew Gull, Percival 250
Mewa, PZL 246
Microplane Veloz, TNCA 288
Midge, Fo 139, Folland 169
Milan, Dassault 139
Minicab, Gardan 173
Minicab GY-201, Béarn 93
Minijet, SIPA 279
Minuano, Nieva 236
Mirage series, Dassault 139
Mirage, Dassault-Breguet 139
Mirage III, Dassault 127
Mirage IV-A, Dassault 51
Mistel composite, DFS 144
Mistral, SNCASE 280
Mite, Mooney 231
Model I, Aerocar 66
Model I, Dumod 149
Model 1, et seq, MKEK 231
Model I-L, Morrow 232
Model II, Dumod 149
Model II, Fleet 163
Model II, General Airplane 175
Model 2-0-2, Martin 222
Model 4-0-4, Martin 222
Model 7 Champion, Aeronca 122
Model 8, Silvaire 274
Model 8 Citabria Pro, Champion 122
Model 8a, Luscombe 218
Model 10A, Electra, Lockheed 214
Model 10/11, Coventry Ordnance 133
Model 11, Thorp 292
Model 14, Bellanca 96, 149, 197
Model XIV Air-Boat, Benoist 96
Model 14-19-2 Cruisemaster, Downer 149
Model 14-19-3, Downer 149
Model 16 VZ-4Da, Doak 145
Model 16, Beech 149
Model 18, Umbaugh 294
Model 19-2S Skyrocket II, Bellanca 96
Model 23 Tandem, Fleetwing 163
Model 24C8, Kridner-Reisner 157
Model 25 Monoplane, Bonomi 103
Model 33, Fleetwings 163
Model 33, Plebe, Temco 290
Model 34-42 Niska, Fairchild 158
Model 35, Bonanza, Beech 59, 94
Model 39-A, Aeromarine 67
Model 39-B, Aeromarine 67
Model 40F, Aeromarine 67
Model 40, Boeing 100
Model 40F, Aeromarine 67
Model 42A, Vertol 114, 296
Model 43, Vertol 296
Model 44, Vertol 296
Model 45-80 Sikanis, Fairchild 158
Model 47, Bell 47, 72, 95, 117, 131, 206
Model 59K Sky-Car, Piasecki 252
Model 71, et seq, Fairchild 157, 158
Model 75, Stearman 78, 152, 284
Model 76, Vertol 296
Model 77, Hughes 195
Model 80/80A, Boeing 100
Model 80 Canuck, Fleet 163, 210
Model 101, Uppercu-Burnelli 295
Model 107, Boeing Vertol 102
Model 110, Consolidated Vultee 130
Model 112, Aero Commander 66
Model 114/CH-47 Chinook, Vertol 296
Model 140, Cessna 121
Model 150, Callair 112
Model 150, Cessna 59, 149
Model 150 Ag, Aero Boero 66
Model 150RV, Aero Boero 66
Model 167 Maryland, Martin 222
Model 170, Cessna 121, 149
Model 172, Cessna 121, 149
Model 175, Rearwin 128
Model 180, Aero Boero 66
Model 180, Cessna 121
Model 180 Ag, Aero Boero 66
Model 180RV, Aero Boero 66
Model 180RVR, Aero Boero 66
Model 182, Cessna 145
Model 185, Commonwealth 128
Model 187 Baltimore, Martin 222
Model 190T, Bernard 97
Model 200/221 Monomail, Boeing 101
Model 201, Mooney 231
Model 201 Picchiatelli, Breda 104
Model 202 Mantis, Gail 172
Model 202A Golduster, Gail 172
Model 204B, Agusta-Bell 72
Model 205, Brantly 104
Model 206 JetRanger, Agusta-Bell 72
Model 206B, JetRanger II, Bell 128
Model 212, Agusta-Bell 72
Model 247, Boeing 30, 101, 148
Model 250/290 Brigadier, Baumann 92
Model 260 Ag, Aero Boero 66
Model 269, Hughes 194

Model 305, ARDC 82
Model 305, Brantly-Hynes 104
Model 305, Cessna 121
Model 314, Boeing 35, 101
Model 367-80, Boeing 55
Model 377 Stratocruiser, Boeing 55, 101
Model 400, Hustler 76
Model 520, Aero Commander 66
Model 700, Rockwell Commander 66
Model 707, Boeing 55, 101, 149
Model 720/727/737, Boeing 55, 101, 149
Model 747, Boeing 58, 59, 101, 113, 136, 157
Model 880/990, Convair 131, 132, 175
Model 1050, Volaircraft 300
Model 2000/3000/4000/8000/9000, Travel Air 292
Model 2150-A, Shinn 272
Model 2150A Kachina, Varga 296
Model A, Call-Air 112
Model A, Wiley Post 306
Model A/AH/D/E/F, Curtiss 134
Model A/B/C, Cairns 112
Model A/B/C/D, Thulin 291
Model AKL-26, Klemm 67
Model B-2E, ARDC 82
Models B/C/D, Taylorcraft 289
Model C, Boeing 100
Model C, Ogden 242
Model C-1, Pacific 245
Model D, Orenco 244
Model D, Pander & Zonen 246
Model E, Pander & Zonen 246
Model F, Arrow 83
Model G, Dart 133
Model G, Lockheed 214
Model H, Navion 199
Model H Owl, LWF 218
Models H-250/350, BACC 90
Model J, Auster 85
Model J, Bendix 96
Model K, Bendix 96
Model L, Aeronautical Corporation of America 68
Model L, Wright 307
Model M-32W, Ong 243
Model PB, Ogden 242
Model PC, Ogden 242
Model R, Travel Air 292
Model T, LWF 218
Model V, Culver 134
Model W Winner O'Neill 243
Model Y, Hammond 183
Model Y, Stearman-Hammond 284
Monitor, Miles 230
Monitor I, et seq, Farman 160
Monocoupe, Central States 120
Monocoupe 70, Mono 231
Monocoupe 110, Mono 231
Monomail, Model 200/221, Boeing 101
Monoplane, Berliner 97
Monoplane, Humber-Blériot 195
Monoplane, Kronfeld 206
Monoplane, Ryan 29
Monoplane, Model 25, Bonomi 103
Monospar, Blackburn 98
Montgolfière balloon 10
Mosquito, de Havilland 42, 126, 141, 142, 152, 161, 169, 175
Mosquito, Gyroflight 181
Moth, de Havilland 30, 141
Moth Minor, D.H.94, de Havilland 141
Motor Tutor, Slingsby 275
Mountaineer, Ector 150
Mouse, Comper 128
Mousquetaire, Jodel 200
Möwe, HD 153, Dittmar 145
Musca 1, et seq, Viberti 297
Mustang, F-51, North American 119
Mustang II, Cavalier 119
Mya-4, Myasishchev 233
Myrsky, IVL 199
Mystère, Dassault 139

N.1B, Thompson 291
N.1B, Westland 304
N1K, Kawanishi 203
N2C Fledgling, Curtiss 135
N2T-1, Timm 291
N3N-1/3, NAF 235
N.4, Fairey 205
N-9, Curtiss 135
N52, Nihon 242
N-62 Eaglet, Shin Nihon 272
N-68 Cygnet, Shin Nihon 272
N-156 Freedom Fighter, Northrop 241
N262, Aérospatiale 70
NA-16 Yale, North American 132, 240
NA-35, Lockheed Brothers 216
NA-75, American Airmotive 78
NA-75, National 235
NB-4/-8, Nicholas-Beazley 237
NBL-1, US Army 295
NBS-1, Martin 287
NC-1/-2/-3/-4, Curtiss 135
NC.600, SNCAC 279
NC-853/856, Nord 239
N-D 481, et seq, Nieuport-Delage 238
NDN-1 Firecracker, NDN 236
N.H.I. Kolibrie, Aviolanda 89
NH-160, Nagler 234
NH-300C/-500C/-500D, Breda Nardi 105
NH-500M-D (TOW), Breda Nardi 105
NK, Keystone 205
NP-1, Spartan 282
N.T.2B, Thompson 291
N.T.4/.4A, Thompson 291
NY, Consolidated 130
Natter, Ba 349, Bachem 91
Navajo, Piper 124, 254
Navion, North American/Ryan 112
Neptune, Ireland 198

Neptune, Lockheed 214
Nibbio, F.14, Aviamilano 86
Nighthawk, Nieuport 177
Nighthawk, Nieuport & General 238
Nighthawk, Supermarine 286
Nikko, LM-1, Fuji 171
Nimbus, Martinsyde 65
Nimrod, Hawker-Siddeley 52
Nipper, Cobelavia 126
Nipper, Tipsy 292
Niska, 34-42, Fairchild 158
Nomad, GAF 178
Nomad, PacAero 245
Noralpha, Nord 239
Noratlas, Nord 182, 239
Noroit, Nord 239
Norseman, Norduyn 114, 239
Norvigie, Nord 239

0-1, et seq, Curtiss 135
02U Corsair, Chance Vought 122
03U Corsair, Chance Vought 122
0-17, Consolidated 130
0-19, Morse 232
0-19, Thomas-Morse 291
0-27, Fokker 167
0-52 Owl, Curtiss-Wright 136
0/100, Handley Page 26, 125
0/400, Handley Page 26, 98, 183
O.A.1/2, Cuncliffe-Owen 134
OA-10 Catalina, Consolidated 114
OH-6A Cayuse, Hughes 195
OH-23C/D Raven, Hiller 191
OKA-1, et seq, Antonov 81
OL-8, Keystone 205
OS2U Kingfisher, Vought-Sikorsky 300
OSGA-101, Chetverikov 123
OTW-160, Meyers 228
OV-10 Bronco, Rockwell International 261
Okka, Yokosuka 309
Olympic Duo-4, Lockheed Brothers 216
Omega II, Bratukhin 104
Omega, 2MG, Bratukhin 104
One-Eleven, BAC 57
Orao, VII/CIAR 120, 301
Oriole, Curtiss 135
Orion, P-3C, Lockheed 113, 214
Oscar, Partenavia 248
Osprey, Austin 86
Osprey, Hawker 187
Osprey, Ogden 242
Otter, DHC-3, de Havilland Canada 142
Ouragan, Dassault 139
Overstrand, Boulton Paul 103
Owl, LWF 218
Owl, 0-52, Curtiss-Wright 136
Owlet, Blackburn 98
Owlet, General Aircraft 175
Oxford, Airspeed 75, 152

P.1, Alliance 77
P-1, et seq, Curtiss 135
P-1, et seq, PZL 246
P1, et seq, Sablatnig 267
P1Y1 Ginga, Yokosuka 309
P-2/-3, Pilatus 253
P.2 Seabird, Alliance 77
P2Y, Consolidated 130
P.3, et seq, Boulton Paul 103
P-3, Pilatus 161
P-3C Orion, Lockheed 113
P3Y/PBY Catalina, Consolidated 130
P4M Mercator, Martin 222
P.5, Gabriel 172
P5M-2 Marlin, Martin 222
P-12E, Boeing 101
P-16, B/J Aircraft 98
P-16.04, FFA 161
P.19., Aviamilano 86
P-30, Consolidated 130
P.32, et seq, Piaggio 252
P-35/-44/-45 Lancer, Republic 259
P-35, Seversky 271
P-38 Lightning, Lockheed 45, 46
P-39 Airacobra, Bell 95
P-40, Curtiss-Wright 136
P-47 Thunderbolt, Republic 45, 136
P.50 Prince, Percival 195
P-51 Mustang, North American 45, 119, 127
P.56 Provost, Percival 195
P.57, et seq, Partenavia 248
P-59 Airacomet, Bell 95
P-61 Black Widow, Northrop 241
P-63 Kingcobra, Bell 95
P-75A, Fisher 163
P-80 Shooting Star, Lockheed 214
P.82 Defiant, Boulton Paul 103
P.84 Jet Provost, Percival 195
P.108 Balliol, Boulton Paul 103
P.110, CVV 137
P.111, Boulton Paul 103
P.120, Boulton Paul 103
P.300/.400, Pöschel 256
P.531, Saunders-Roe 269
P.1127 Kestrel, Hawker 186
PA-5, et seq, Pitcairn 255
PA-11, Piper 175
PA-12, Piper 175
PA-18 Cub, Piper 59
PA-20, Aubert 85
Pa.49, Payen 163, 249
PA-201 Cigale, Aubert 85
PA-204 Cigale Major, Aubert 85
PAA-1, Pitcairn 255
P.B.1, et seq, Pemberton-Billing 249
PB2Y Coronado, Consolidated 130
PB4Y, Consolidated 130
PC-6 Porter, Pilatus 253
PC-7 Turbo Trainer, Pilatus 253
PD-808 Vespa-jet, Douglas 149
PE-2, Petlyakov 250

PE-8, Petlyakov 250
PG-1, Aeromarine 67
PH-1, et seq, Hall 182
Pi 5, Aviatik 88
PIK-11, et seq, Polyteknikkojen 256
PJC-2, Harlow 133, 185
PK, Keystone 205
P.L.1, Grigorovich 180
PL-1/-2, Pazmany 73, 249
PL-1A, AIDC 73
PL-2, Pazmany 143
PL-7, Kingsford Smith 205
PL-8, Levasseur 211
P.L.11 Airtruck, Bennett 96
PL-12 Airtruk, Transavia 164
PM1, CNA 126
PM-1, et seq, Martin 222
PM-3-4 Vale, Magni 220
PM-4-1 Supervale, Magni 220
P.M.280 Tartuca, CVV 137
Po-2, Polikarpov 256
PQ-14, Culver 134
P.R.B. flying-boat, Pegna & Bonmartini 249
PS-1, Shin Meiwa 272
P.T., Eagle-Lincoln 79
PT-1, Consolidated 130
PT-1/2, NAF 235
PT-6, Cunningham-Hall 134
PT-6, Fleet 163
PT-19, Fairchild 173, 175
PT-19, Fairchild Cornell 163
P.V.1, RNAS Port Victoria 261
PV-1 Ventura, Lockheed 193, 214
P.V.3, Westland 304
P.V.7, Westland 304
PW-8, Curtiss 135
PW-9/FB, Boeing 100
PZL-101 Gawron, OKL 244
PZL-104 Wilga, OKL 244
PZV Harpoon, Lockheed 214
Pacer, Piper 254
Packet, C-82, Fairchild 157
Paladin, Paragon 199, 247
Paragon, Jackaroo 199
Parakeet, Maranseed 184
Paraplane I/II, Lanier 208
Parasol, Blériot 99
Parasol, Heath 188
Paris, Morane-Saulnier 232
Paris III, SEEMS 278
Pater, HD 156, Dittmar 145
Pathfinder, Keystone 205
Pathfinder II, Piasecki 252
Patrician, Keystone 205
Paulistinha, Type 4, CAP 115
Pawnee, Piper 124, 254
Peacemaker, AV-23, Fairchild 157
Pea Pod, O'Neill 243
Pegaso, F.20, General Avia 175
Pelican, Pilatus 253
Pelican, LZ-2a, Doman 145
Pelikan, Raab 258
Pembroke, Percival 195
Pennine, Hillson 191
Pete, Parnall 248
Phantom I, Luscombe 149, 218
Phantom I, McDonnell 224
Pheasant, Pheasant 251
Phillicopter Mk I, VTOL Aircraft 301
Phoenix, Heston 190
Phönix, Brandenburg 71
Phryganet, D56, CFA 122
Picchiatelli, Model 201, Breda 104
Pika, GAF 178
Pingouin, Nord 239
Pinto, Temco 290
Pinto, TT-1, Temco 76
Piranha, Wassmer 303
Pirat, Svenska Aero 287
Pirate, Argonaut 82
Pirate, Vought 301
Pirate, White 304
Planalto, Type 1, CAP 115
Playboy, Kinner 205
Playboy, Lincoln-Page 212
Plebe, Temco 290
Plover, Parnall 248
Polar, Widerões 306
Polar C5, Hönningstad 193
Popuplane, Aero-Difusión 67
Porte Baby, Felixstowe 270
Porter, Pilatus 253
Possum, Parnall 248
Potez 630, et seq, SNCAN 279
Poussin, AG 02, Gatard 174
Praga, Hillson 191
Premier 64-01, IABSA 196
Prentice, Percival 88, 250
Prestwick Pioneer, Scottish Aviation 270
Prince, Percival 250
Prince, P.50, Percival 195
Princess, Saunders-Roe 268
Privateer, Consolidated 130
Procellaria, Reggiane 258
Proctor, Percival 250
Prospector, Lancashire Aircraft 207
Provider, C-123, Fairchild 157
Provider, C-123B, Fairchild 123
Provost, Percival 250
Provost, P.56, Percival 195
Pucará, IA.58, FMA 165
Puffin, Parnall 248
Pulgni II., I.A.33, Empresa 152
Puma, Aérospatiale/Westland 70, 305
Pup, Dart 138
Pup, B.121, Beagle 93
Pup, Sopwith 25, 93, 281
Pushpak, HUL-26, Hindustan 191
Puss Moth, de Havilland 142

Q-6, Percival 250

Q14 Tokai, Watanabe 303
Q-Star, Lockheed Missiles 216
QR.14 Levriero, Marina 220
QSTOL, DHC-7, de Havilland Canada 142
QT-2, Lockheed Missiles 216
Quail, AAMSA 64
Quail, Rockwell 241
Quail Commander, AAMSA 64
Queen Air, Beech 156
Queenaire 800, Excalibur 156

R series, Zeppelin Werke Lindau 309
R type, Aviatik 88
R Series, Zeppelin Werke Staaken 309
R giant, Schutte-Lanz 269
R.I, DFW 144
R I et seq, Dornier 146
R.I/.II, Linke-Hofmann 213
R.I series, Siemens 273
R.II, DFW 144
R-2/-5, Thomas-Morse 290
R2C/R3C, Curtiss 135
R-3, et seq, Romano 264
R3Y Tradewind, Consolidated Vultee 130
R.4, Caudron 118
R-4/-5, Vought-Sikorsky 300
R.IV/23, Rieseler 260
R.6, et seq, Ricci 261
R-6/-8, Curtiss 135
R6H, Granville 179
R.22, Caudron 118
R-17, et seq, Renard 259
R22, Robinson 262
R.27, Raab 258
R.31, Renard 277
R42, Flygindustri 164
R.52/53, Tachikawa 288
R.100, airship 29
R.101, airship 29
R.A.14, et seq, Adam 64
RA-14, Maranda 220
RB Racer, Dayton-Wright 140
RB-2, Uppercu-Burnelli 295
R.E.7/8, RAF 133
Re.2000, et seq, Reggiane 116
Re.2000 Falco l, Reggiane 258
REP 1/2, Esnault-Pelterie 155
RF.01, Fournier 170
RF1, RFB 260
RF.2, et seq, Fournier 170
RF4D/5, Sportavia 283
RG-60/-75, SECAT 278
RH-1 Pinwheel, Rotor-Craft 265
Ro.1, et seq, Romeo 265
Ro-II, Rohrbach 264
Ro-IIIA, Rohrbach 264
Ro.37, et seq, Meridionali-Aerfer 226
RR-11, IMPA 197
R.S.3 Desford, Reid & Sigrist 259
R.S.14, CMASA 126
RSA 200, Afic 71
RSV.18-100, Stampe et Vertongen 174
RSV.26-100, Stampe et Vertongen 174
RSV.32-90, Stampe 283
R.T.1, Siddeley-Deasy 273
RW-3 Multoplane, RFB 260
RY, Consolidated 130
RAF B.E.2c 83
Rallye, Morane-Saulnier 232
Rallye 7, SOCATA 277
Rambler, Curtiss-Reid 135
Ranch, Taylorcraft 289
Rangemaster H, Navion 236
Ranger, Aerostar 70
Ranger, Mooney 231
Rata, Polikarpov 256
Raven, OH-23C/D, Hiller 191
Red Arrow, Simplex 275
Red Arrow, Sioux 275
Redskin, Mohawk 231
Redwing, Redwing 258
Reliant, Stinson 284
Revathi, Technical Centre 289
Ripon, Blackburn 98
Riviera, Nardi 235
Robin, Curtiss-Robertson 135
Roc, Blackburn 98
Rocket, Riley 261
Rocket 140, Johnson 200
Rocket 185, Johnson 200
Roitelet, JDM 199
Rondone, F7, Ambrosini 78
Rotorcar III, Wagner 302
Rotocycle, XRON-1, Gyrodyne 181
Rotodyne, Fairey 159
Rubis, Scintex 270

SI, Arado 82
S.1, Caspar 117
S.1, Hopfner 193
S-1, Lockheed 214
S-1/-2, Pitts 255
S.1, Martin & Handasyde 222
S-1, Sparmann 283
S.1, Svenska Aero 287
S-1, et seq, Vojenska 300
S.1A, Interstate 82
S1-B, American Aircraft 78
S.1BE Arctic Tern, Arctic 82
S.1, SABCA 277
S2/B-2/BC, Tipsy 292
S2, Zodiac 309
S-2B, Snow 75, 276
S2R-T Turbo Thrush, Marsh 221
S-3/-4A/-4B, Seibel 270
S.4/.5/.6, Supermarine 39, 286
S-4/-4B/-C, Morse 232
S-4/-5, Thomas-Morse 291
S.5, SECAT 278
S7, Super, Ambrosini 78

S.10, SIPA 279
S.11, *et seq*, Fokker 168
S-XI/XII, SABCA 277
S.11, Svenska Aero 287
S.12, 'De Schelde' 206
S-16, Messerschmitt 227
S-16, Russo-Baltic 266
S-16, *et seq*, SIAI 276
S.20 *Mercury*, Short-Mayo 34
S.21 *Maia*, Short-Mayo 34
S.23, Short 34
S 24 Kiebitz, Focke-Wulf 166
S-29, *et seq*, Sikorsky 274
S.47, *et seq*, SABCA 277
S-55, SIAI 78
S-55, Sikorsky 88, 189
S-55-T, Aviation Specialities 88
S-56, SIAI 78
S-61, Sikorsky 230
S-61R, Sikorsky 72
S-62, Sikorsky 230
S90, *et seq*, SIPA 279
S-103, Ceskoslovenské 120
S-1085, Univair 295
S-125, Jones 200
S-150, Jones 200
S-160-K, Timm 291
S 199, Avia 87
S.205/.208, SIAI-Marchetti 273
S 1001 Grifo, Ambrosini 78
SA.202 Bravo, SIAI-Marchetti 273
SAI 1, *et seq*, Ambrosini 78
SAN-101, SAN 277
SB-2 Pelican, Pilatus 253
SB-2, Tupolev 293
SB2A Buccaneer, Brewster 106
SB2C Helldiver, Curtiss-Wright 136
SB2U Vindicator, Vought-Sikorsky 300
SBA, Brewster 106
SBD Dauntless, Douglas 148
SBN, Brewster 106
SBU, Vought 122
SC Seahawk, Curtiss-Wright 136
SC.1, Short 272
SD II, *et seq*, Arado 82
S.E.1, RAF 141
S.E.2, RAF 141
S.E.5a, RAF 135
S.E.210 Caravelle, Sud-Aviation 285
SET 7K, *et seq*, SET 271
SF-1, Grumman 180
SF1, *et seq*, Sablatnig 267
SF-23A/-24A/-25, Scheibe 269
SF-25B, Scheibe 294
SF.260, SIAI-Marchetti 273
SG VI, Sznycer-Gottlieb 243
SG VI-D, Intercity 198
SGP-222, Simmering-Graz-Pauker 274
SH-3D, Sikorsky 72
SH-4, Silvercraft 274
SH-200, Silvercraft 274
Shch-2, Shcherbakov 271
Si 201, *et seq*, Siebelwerke 273
S.I.A.7/9, Società Italiano 277
SJ, Standard 283
Sk 257, Skoda 275
Sk-V4, Skoda 275
SL-15, Colgate-Larsen 126
S.M., Ikarus 196
SM-1, Salmson 268
SM-1, WSK-Swidnik 308
SM.30/.31, Merville 226
SM-67 Artouste, Turboméca 226
S.M.75, *et seq*, SIAI 276
S.M.79, Savoia-Marchetti 40
SM.1019 SIAI-Marchetti 273
SN3, Breguet 105
SNC, Curtiss-Wright 136
SO3C Seamew, Curtiss-Wright 136
SO.94, *et seq*, Ouest Aviation 244
SOC Seagull, Curtiss-Wright 136
SPL, Chetverikov 123
S.R.2 Siskin, Siddeley-Deasy 273
SR-71A/YF-12, Lockheed 215
SR.177, Saunders-Roe 269
SR/A1, Saunders-Roe 268
S.S.4, Ambrosini 78
ST-3, General Aircraft 175
ST-27/-28, Saunders 268
SU Corsair, Chance Vought 122
SU-7, *et seq*, Sukhoi 286
S.V.4, *et seq*, Stampe 160, 283
S.V.4, Stampe et Renard 283
SV-5 series, Martin Marietta 222
S.V.A.5, Ansaldo 80, 81
Saab-17, *et seq*, SAAB 267
Sääski, VL 296
Sabre, F-86, North American 113
Sabreliner, Rockwell International 261
Saeta, HA-200 Hispano 189
Saetta, Macchi 219
Safari, MFI 228
Safir, Saab 143, 267
SAIMAN 200, *et seq*, Saiman 276
Salamander, Sopwith 281
Sandringham, Short 272
Satellite, Planet 255
Satellite, Superior 286
Sausewind, Bäumer 92
Scandia, SAAB 267
Scapa, Supermarine 286
Scarab, Supermarine 286
Scarab, Supermarine 286
Scheldmeeuw, 'De Schelde' 206
Scheldmusche, 'De Schelde' 143, 206
Schulmeister, M-150, Burgfalke 110
Schwalbe, Raab 253, 258
Scimitar, Armstrong Whitworth 83
Scimitar, Supermarine 287
Scion, Short 255
Scion Senior, Short 255
Scorpion, Northrop 241
Scout, Aeronautical Corporation of America 68
Scout, Bristol 106
Scout, Nestler 237
Scout, Westland 305
Seabee, Republic 260
Seabird, Northern 241
Seabird, P.2, Alliance 77
Sea Cobra, Bell 95
Sea Dart, XF2Y, Consolidated Vultee 130
Seafang, Supermarine 287
Sea Fury, Hawker 125, 168, 186
Seagull, Curtiss 155
Seagull, Supermarine 286
Seagull, SOC, Curtiss-Wright 136
Sea Harrier, Hawker Siddeley 186
Sea Hawk, Hawker 83
Sea Hawk, Richmond 260
Seahawk, SC, Curtiss-Wright 136
Sea King, Westland 305
Sea Knight, Vertol 296
Seal, Supermarine 286
Sealand, Short 272
Sea Lion, Supermarine 286
Seamaster, Martin 222
Seamew, SO3C, Curtiss-Wright 136
Sea Otter, Saunders-Roe 268
Sea Otter, Supermarine 287
Sea Pirate, Eastman 150
Sea Prince, Percival 195
Sea Rover, Eastman 150
Seasprite, Kaman 202
Sea Venom, de Havilland 141
Sea Vixen, de Havilland 141
Sea Wolf, TBY, Consolidated 130
Security S1-B, American Aircraft 78
Sedan, 4E, Jovair 200
Sedan, 11A, Luscombe 78
Segrave Meteor 1, Aircraft Investment Corp. 74
Seneca, Piper 124, 254
Series A, TNCA 288
Series 1 CH.3 Ace, Chrislea 124
Series 2 CH.3 Super Ace, Chrislea 124
Series 4 CH.3 Skyjeep, Chrislea 124
Sertanejo, Nieva 236
Shark, Blackburn 98
Sheldrake, Supermarine 286
Shoki, Nakajima 234
Shooting Star, Lockheed 150, 214
Shorthorn, MF-11, Farman 160
Shrike, Curtiss-Wright 136
Shrike, Rockwell 241
Shrike Commander 500S, Aero Commander 67
Shrimp, Saunders-Roe 268
Sidestrand, Boulton Paul 103
Sikanis, 45-80, Fairchild 158
Silvaire, Luscombe 218
Silver Star, T-33, Lockheed 113
Simoun, Caudron 118
Sinsia, Siddeley-Deasy 273
Sipa 200/300, Gardan 173
Sirius, Lockheed 214
Sirius, Waco 302
Siskin, Armstrong Whitworth 83
Siskin, Siddeley-Deasy 273
Skeeter, W.14, Cierva 125
Skimmer, Lake 207
Skimmer, C-1, Colonial 126, 207
Skimmer, IV, C-2, Colonial 126, 207
Skua, Blackburn 98
Skybaby, Luscombe 218
Sky-Car, Piasecki 252
Sky Car, Stout 285
Skycrane, Sikorsky 274
Skyfarer, GAC 172
Skyjeep, Series 4 CH-3, Chrislea 124
Skylark, Pasped 248
Skylark III, Driggs 149
Skynight, Douglas 148
Skyraider, Douglas 148
Skyranger, Commonwealth 128
Skyray, A4D, Douglas 148
Skyrider, HTM 189
Skyrocket, D-558-2, Douglas 149
Skyrocket II, Model 19-25, Bellanca 96
Skyservant, Do 28, Dornier 146
Sky Skooter, Thorp 292
Skystreak, D-558-1, Douglas 149
Sky-Trac, Champion 122
Sky-trac, Wagner 302
Skytrader 800, Dominion 146
Skyvan, Short 272
Skywarrior, Douglas 148
Small America, H-4, Curtiss 134
Smaragd, CP 301 S, Binder 98
Snargasher, Reid & Sigrist 259
Snipe, Rockwell 241
Solent, Short 272
Solution, LC-DW, Laird 207
Sooper-Coot, Aerocar 66
Sopocaba, W-151, CONAL 128
Sopwith 1½-Strutter 103, 281
Southampton, Supermarine 286
SPAD V, *et seq*, SPAD 282
Sparrow Commander, AAMSA 64
Sparrow, Rockwell 241
Sparrowhawk, Miles 230
Sparrowhawk, Nieuport 177
Sparrowhawk, F9C, Curtiss-Wright 136
Spartan, Simmonds 274
Special, Cassutt 74
Special de Luxe, Taylorcraft 289
Speedster, Rearwin 258
Speedster, Ryan 183
Speedster, Trella 292
Speedwing, Laird 207
Spirit of St Louis, Ryan monoplane 29
Spiteful, Supermarine 287
Spitfire, Spitfire Helicopter 155
Spitfire, Supermarine 286
Sport, Arrow 83
Sport, Cain 112
Sport, Inland 197
Sport Lightweight, Lincoln-Page 212
Sport Pursuit, Arrow 83
Sportsman, Fournier 170
Sportsman, Taylorcraft 289
Sportsman, BAX-3/-4, Bunyard 109
Sportsman, F-17, International 198
Sports Monoplane, Wicko 169
Sportster, Kinner 205
Sport Trainer, Great Lakes 180
Sportwing, Kinner 205
Sprite, Essex Aero 155
Spurwing, Mohawk 231
Stallion, H-550A, Helio 189
Starfighter, F-104, Lockheed 89
Starfighter, Lockheed 214
Starliner, Lockheed Brothers 216
Starliner, Vega 296
Starliner, L.1649/L.1649A, Lockheed 55
Stealth Fighter, Lockheed 215
Stieglitz, Fw 44, Focke-Wulf 120, 166, 173
Stirling, Short 42, 45, 272
Stolifter, Conroy 129
Stomo 3, Möller 231
Storch, Fi 156, Fieseler 162
Stosser, Fw 56, Focke-Wulf 166
Stralsund, Luftfahrzeug 218
Stranraer, Supermarine 114, 286
Stratocruiser, Boeing 69, 101
Stratofortress, B-52, Boeing 51, 101
Stratojet, B-47, Boeing 101
Strato-Rocket, Maule 223
Streak, Aero-Flight 67
Streak, Comper 128
Strikemaster, BAC 195
Student, Miles 230
Stupar, Elias 152
Sturmer, Möller 231
Styx, H46, Hanriot 185
Suisei, Yokosuka 308
Sum, PZL 246
Sunderland, Short 169, 272
Super, Meteor 228
Super 4/21, Wassmer 120
Super 21, Mooney 70
Super 71, Fairchild 158
Super C-3, Carson 117
Super J-2, Aero Resources 69
Super S7, Ambrosini 78
Super T-6, Bacon 91
Super TM-1, Prudden 257
Super V, Oakland 242
Super VC10, Vickers 55
Super Ace, Series 2 CH-3, Chrislea 124
Super Aero, Ceskoslovenské 120
Super Agbat, Grumman American 180
Super Broussard, Holste 193
Supercab, Gardan 173
Super Cheetah, Cheetah 123
Super Chief, Aeronca 68
Super Constellation, L.1049, Lockheed 55
Super Courier, U-10, Helio 189
Super Cub, Piper 140
Super Drone, Kronfeld 206
Super Electra, Lockheed 214
Super Etendard, Dassault 139
Super Falco, Laverda 209
Superfortress, B-29, Boeing 45, 46, 101, 136
Super Frelon, Aérospatiale 70
Super Gull, Trecker 292
Super Heron, Waltz 303
Super Hummel, Siebelwerke 273
Super Husky, Husky 195
Super Mountaineer, Ector 150
Super Mystère, Dassault 139
Super Phryganet, D21T-4, CFA 122
Super Pinto, Aeronca 69
Super Pinto, AJI 76
Super Saeta, HA-220, Hispano 192
Super Sancey, Wassmer 303
Super Skymaster, Cessna 129
Super Soarer, Heath 188
Super Solution, Laird 207
Super Sport, Inland 197
Supervale, Magni 220
Super Widgeon, Gannet 173
Supporter, MFI 228
Supporter, SAAB 267
Surveyor, 101, GAC 172
Swallow, B.K 90
Swallow, Laird 207
Swift, Comper 128
Swift, Supermarine 287
Swift, GC-1, Globe 176
Swordfish, Fairey 42, 159
Sycamore, Bristol 107

T-1, Fuji 171
T.1, Moravko-Slezká 232
T-1, Rawdon 258
T.1, Ringhoffer-Tatra 261
T-1, *et seq*, Turbay 293
T.2, ACAZ 64
T-2, Hitachi 192
T-2, Mitsubishi 230
T2, *et seq*, Tellier 289
T-2, Thomas 290
T-2 Buckeye, Rockwell International 261
T2D, Douglas 148
T-3, Siemetzki 273
T3-BN.4, SPCA 281
T.4, Tampier 288
T-4, Thaden 255
T-6, Super, Bacon 91
T-6 Harvard/Texan, North American 91, 235, 239, 240
T.VII, Fokker 168
T.7, LACAB 84
T8P-1, Barkley-Grow 92
T-9, Guerchais 180
T-11, Thorp 291
T.16/48, Eon., Elliotts 152
T-23, Aerotec 70
T-28 Fennec/Trojan, North American 183, 240
T-33 Silver Star, Lockheed 113, 204
T-34A Mentor, Beech 114
T-38 Talon, Northrop 241
T-50, Cessna 121
T.126, Moravko-Slezká 232
T.131, Moravko-Slezká 232
T.131, Ringhoffer-Tatra 261
T320, Flight Engineers 164
TA-3, Towle 292
Ta 152, Focke-Wulf 166
TB-1, Tupolev 293
TB-3, Tupolev 293
TB 10, SOCATA 278
TB-25L/N, Hayes 188
TBD Devastator, Douglas 148
T-CH-1, AIDC 73
TBM Avenger, Grumman 180
TBM-1, General Motors 176
TBY Sea Wolf, Consolidated 130
TC6, Tellier 289
TE-1A Buckaroo, Temco 290
TG-1, Great Lakes 180
TG-6, Taylorcraft 289
THK-1, *et seq*, THK 293
TM-1, Prudden 257
TP-1, Engineering Division 153
TR-3, Dayton-Wright 140
TR-5, Dayton-Wright 140
TS-1/3, NAF 235
TS-8, *et seq*, WSK-Mielec 307
TS-11 Iskra, OKL 244
TsAGI-44, ANT 81
TSC-1A1 Teal, Thurston 291
TSC-1A3 Marlin, Teal 289
T.S.R.3, Airmark 74
TT-1 Pinto, Temco 76, 290
TTS-5, TNCA 288
Tu-2, *et seq*, Tupolev 293
Tu-104, Tupolev 57
Tu-114/-124/-134/-154, Tupolev 57
Tu-144, Tupolev 58
Tu-Sa, IMPA 197
TW-1, Engineering Division 153
TW-2, Cox-Klemen 133
Tabloid, Sopwith 281
Tabor, Tarrant 288
Taifun, Bf 108/Me 108, BFW 97
Taifun, Bf 108/Me 108, Messerschmitt 97
Take 1, Jamieson 199
Talon, Northrop 241
Tanager, Curtiss 135
Tandem, Model 23, Fleetwing 163
Tartuca, P.M.280, CW 137
Taube, Etrich 155
Tauro 300, Anahuac 79
Tauro 350, Anahuac 79
Taylorcraft C/D, Taylorcraft 289
T-cat, Grumman American 180
Tempest, Hawker 186
Tempo II, Smith 275
Tenzan, Nakajima 234
Texas Temple, Williams 306
Teziutlan, TNCA 288
Three Seater, Spartan 282
Thrush Commander, Aero Commander 67
Thrush Commander, Rockwell 241
Thruxton Jackaroo, Jackaroo 199
Thunderbolt, P-47, Republic 45, 136
Thunderchief, F-105, Republic 157
Thunderflash, Thunderjet, Thunderstreak, Republic 260
Tiger, Grumman American 180
Tiger II, F5E, Northrop 73
Tigercat, Grumman 180
Tiger Moth, de Havilland 141, 142
Tigerschwalbe, Raab 253, 258
Tipsy Nipper, D-158 Fairey Belge 142
Tokai, Watanabe 303
Tom-8, Ceskoslovenské 120
Tomahawk, Piper 254
Tomcat, F-14, Grumman 180
Topper, Taylorcraft 289
Tornado, North American 240
Tornado, Panavia 65, 246
Toucan, AAC-1, Colombes 126
Tourabout, Lincoln-Standard 212
Tourist, Taylorcraft 289
Touroplane, Wallace 302
Tradewind, Pacific Airmotive 245
Tradewind, R3Y, Consolidated Vultee 130
Trainer, Lincoln-Page 212
Trainer, Tipsy 292
Travelair, Beech 149
Traveler, Pheasant 251
Traveler, Taylorcraft 289
Traveler, 7EC, Champion 122
Trener, Zlin 120, 309
Trener-Master, Zlin 120
Tricolo-Experimental, Maestranza Central 219
Trident, Ouest Aviation 244
Trident, SNCASO 280
Trident, D.H.121, de Havilland 141
Trigull-320, Trident 292
Trimmer, Allied Aviation 77
Tri-Motor, Ford 110
Tri-Motor, 3-AT, Ford 169
Tri-Pacer, Piper 254
Triplane, Sopwith 125
Trislander, BN-2A, Britten-Norman 59, 108
TriStar, Lockheed 59
Tri-Traveler, 7FC, Champion 122
Tudor, Avro 55, 263
Tuisku, VL 296
Turbo 18, Volpar 300
Turbo Aztec, Piper 124
Turbo Equator, Pöschel 256
Turbo Goose, McKinnon 226

Turbo Hawk Commander, Rockwell 241
Turboliner, Volpar 300
Turbo Mustang III, Cavalier 119
Turbo-Porter, Pilatus 157
Turbo Star, Scenic Airlines 269
Turbo Three, Conroy 129
Turbo Thrush, Marsh 221
Turbo Trainer, Pilatus 253
Turbulent, Druine 149
Twin-60, Johnson Airplane 200
Twin-Bonanza, Beech 156
Twin Cadet, Slingsby/Osborne 275
Twin Comanche, Piper 254
Twin Hercules, Lockheed 215
Twin Navion, Riley 261
Twin Otter, DHC-6, de Havilland Canada 142
Twin Pioneer, Scottish Aviation 270
Type 00-1, Viking 298
Type 0.101, Arsenal 84
Type 1, ADC 65
Type I, et seq, ANEC 80
Type I, et seq, CAP 115
Type I, Dumond 128
Type 1, EAC 150
Type I/II, Cicaré 124
Type I, Voisin-Farman 16
Type 1-EA, et seq, ANT 81
Type II, et seq, Sage 268
Type 2, Salmson 268
Type 2/4, SFAN 278
Type 2/180, Avian 86
Type 2A2, Salmson 268
Type 2 AMC2, Villiers 298
Type 2-AT, Stout 169
Type 2MG Omega, Bratukhin 104
Type 2T-1A, Great Lakes 179
Type III series, Fairey 159
Type III, Farman 160
Type 3, et seq, Voisin 299
Type 3-AT Tri-Motor, Ford 169
Type 4, DAR 138
Type 4/7, SEA 278
Type 4-AT Tri-Motor, Ford 169
Type 4 HBA2, Villiers 298
Type 4E, Sedan, Jovair 200
Type 5, Auster 85
Type 5, Erla 155
Type 5, Heston 190
Type 5.501, Arsenal 84
Type 5A, Norsk 239
Type 5A, Finnmark, Hönningstad 193
Type 5-AT Tri-Motor, Ford 169
Type VI, Anatra 80
Type 6, et seq, CANT 115
Type 7, et seq, S.E.T. 157
Type 7, Wibault 305
Type 7EC Traveler, Champion 122
Type 7FC, Tri-Traveler, Champion 122
Type 10, Arsenal-Delanne 84
Type 10, et seq, Couzinet 133
Type 10, Mitsubishi 230
Type 10F, DAR 138
Type 11, Huntingdon 195
Type XI, et seq, Nieuport 237
Type XI, et seq, Nieuport-Macchi 238
Type XI monoplane, Blériot 19, 20, 99
Type 11A Sedan, Luscombe 78
Type 11D, Alpha 78
Type 12, Huntingdon 195
Type 12, et seq, SECM 278
Type 12C.1, SIMB 279
Type 12E, Hiller 191
Type 14, Avia 87
Type 14, Breguet 105
Type 14-bis, Santos-Dumont 15
Type 14C.1, SIMB 279
Type 15, et seq, Breda 104
Type 15, et seq, CNA 126
Type 15-AT, Bushmaster, Hayden 188
Type 16H-1C, Piasecki 252
Type 18 Destroyer, Vickers 298
Type 18-T Fighter, Kirkham 205
Type 19, Breguet 105, 180
Type 20, Bodiansky 99
Type 20, Delanne 142
Type 20/30, SCAN 277
Type 24, Villiers 298
Type 24T, PWS 255
Type 25, Potez 196
Type 26, Nieuport 237
Type 28, Nieuport 237
Type 30, et seq, Roche 262
Type 30-M-4, SPCA 281
Type 33, et seq, CAMS 113
Type 36, Avia 87
Type 36/38, NUD 242
Type 40T, SPCA 281
Type 45, Aero 210
Type 47-2, Latham 209
Type 51, et seq, Avia 87
Type 61 Falke, Slingsby 275
Type 62-C1, Nieuport-Delage 238
Type 64-01, Premier, IABSA 196
Type 65, Crawford 133
Type 65-02, Aerobatic, IABSA 196
Type 71, Couzinet 34
Type 82-C1, Nieuport-Delage 238
Type 88, Kawasaki 204
Type 90, Kari-Keen 203
Type 90-1, Hiro 192
Type 92, Kawasaki 204
Type 95, Earl 150
Type 100, GAC 172
Type 101, Amiot 79
Type 101, et seq, PZL 246
Type 101/102/201 Arava, IAI 199
Type 101 Surveyor, GAC 172
Type 102A Aristocrat, GAC 172
Type 104, PZL 143
Type 110/11000, Nieuport-Macchi 238
Type 110, Commuter, Lanier 208

Type 111M, Airmark 74
Type 115.R2, Mureaux 233
Type 122, Amiot 79
Type 125, Bullet, Johnson 200
T.126, Ringhoffer Tatra 261
Type 130/131, Bloch 99
Type 138A, Bristol 107
Type 140, Rocket, Johnson 200
Type 142, Bristol 107
Type 143, Amiot 79
Type 150, VEB 300
Type 151/152/155, Bloch 99
Type 153 Joigny, SRCM 278
Type 165, McKinnie 226
Type 170 Freighter, Bristol 107
Type 171, Bristol 107
Type 184, Short 109
Type 185, Rocket 261
Type 185, Rocket, Johnson 200
Type 190, Muniz 233
Type 190, SIMB 279
Type 192 Belvedere, Bristol 107
Type 200.A3, Muniz 233
Type 200, Myers 226
Type 201 Alcotan, CASA
Type 202 Halcon, CASA 117
Type 204, Aero 71
Type 204B, Bell 171
Type 205, Avi 89
Type 228, DFS 144
Type 230, DFS 144
Type 250/350/500, Howard 90, 193
Type 262, Nord 170, 239
Type 281 Hobo, Hendy 189
Type 285 Fieldmaster, Yeoman 308
Type 298, Mohawk 231
Type 300C/500C/500D/500M, Hughes 105
Type 302, Hendy 189
Type 304, Aero 71
Type 320, Hansa Jet, HFB 182
Type 346, DFS 144
Type 350, Amiot 79
Type 382, Parnall 248
Type 400, Interceptor 198
Type 460, Wren 307
Type 480, Camair 112
Type 504, et seq, Avro 262
Type 510, SPAD 204
Type 521, Latécoère 34
Type 614, VFW-Fokker 228
Type 800, Skytrader, Dominion 146
Type 830, Short 109
Type 941, Breguet 105
Type 941S, Dassault-Breguet 139
Type 1000, Clark 125
Type 1002, et seq, Nord 239
Type 1124 Westwind, IAI 199
Type 1150 Atlantic, Breguet 105
Type 2000, Bushmaster 110
Type 2000, SIMB 279
Type 2000, Cavalier 119
Type 2150, Morrisey 232
Type 3308 Heck, Hendy 189
Type 4500-300, Evangel 156
Type B, Mann Egerton 220
Type C, Euler 156
Type D, Anatra 80
Type DS, Anatra 80
Types E to N, Thulin 291
Type L, Morane-Saulnier 232
Type LO, Tachikawa 288
Type SI-A, Security 270
Typhon, Caudron 118
Typhoon, Hawker 42, 46, 177, 186

U.1/.2, Caspar 117
U-1, et seq, Udet 294
U-2, Lockheed 214
U2V, Uetz 294
U4M Pelikan, Uetz 294
U-10 Super Courier, Helio 189
UA-1, Yeoman 308
UB-14, Burnelli 134
UB-20, Uppercu-Burnelli 295
UC-61 Forwarder, Fairchild 157
UC-80, Harlow 185
UH-12, Hiller 117, 157
UH-12E, Hiller 191
UO-1, Chance Vought 122
US-1, Shin Meiwa 272
USB-1, Dayton-Wright 140
USD-9, US Army 295
USS Akron, airship 29
USS Los Angeles, airship 29
USS Macon, airship 29
Ugur, MKEK 231
Uhu, He 219, Heinkel 188
Uirapuru, Aerotec 70
Universal, Noorduyn 167
Universal, Zlin 309
Universal Freighter, GAL-GO, General Aircraft 175
Utility, FU-24, Fletcher 163
Utva 56, et seq, Utva 295

V-1, Airplane Development Corp 75
V-1, et seq, LWF 218
Vi, Zeppelin Werke, Lindau 309
V-1 flying-bomb 45
V2, SIMB 279
V-2 ballistic rocket 45
V-3, Davis 140
V-11, et seq, Vultee 301
V-19 Stralsund, Luftfahrzeug 218
V/1500, Handley Page 26, 183
VAK-191B, VFW 297
VB 10, Arsenal 84
VB-14B, Burnelli 110
VC10, Vickers 55
VCP-1, Engineering Division 153
VCP-1, US Army 295
VFW 614, VFW 297

VG-1/-2, Vertidynamics 296
VG-1 Vertigyro, Nagler 234
VG30, et seq, Arsenal 84
VG70, et seq, Arsenal 84
VJ101C, EWR 156
VoWi 8, Wilden 306
VoWi 10, Wilden 306
VS-43/-44, Vought-Sikorsky 300
VS-300, Sikorsky 274
VS-300, Vought-Sikorsky 300
VT-1 Weejet, Carma 117
VZ-7AP, Curtiss-Wright 136
Vlae, Magni 220
Valentia, Vickers 298
Valiant, Vickers-Armstrongs 299
Valiant, Vultee 301
Valkyrie, North American 240
Valkyrie, Saunders 268
Valkyrie series, Aeronautical Syndicate 68
Valparaiso, Vickers 242
Vampire, de Havilland 141, 142
Vampire Trainer, D.H.115, Airspeed 75
Vancouver, Canadian Vickers 114
Vanessa, Canadian Vickers 114
Vanguard, Vickers-Armstrongs 299
Vanguard, Vultee 301
Varivol, Gérin 176
Vautour, Ouest Aviation 244
Vautour, SNCASO 280
Vedette, Canadian Vickers 114
Vega, Lockheed 214
Vela II, Waco 302
Velos, Blackburn 180
Velos, Canadian Vickers 114
Veltro, Macchi 219
Venom, de Havilland 141
Ventura, PV-1, Lockheed 193
Vernon, Vickers 298
Vertigyro, Nagler 234
Varuna, Canadian Vickers 114
Vespa-jet, PD-808, Douglas 149
Victor, Handley-Page 184
Victoria, Vickers 298
Viggen, SAAB 267
Vigil, Canadian Vickers 114
Vigilante, North American 240
Vihuri, VLM 296
Viima, VL 296
Viking, AB Svenska 287
Viking, Lockheed 215
Viking, Vickers 55, 114
Viking, Vickers-Armstrongs 299
Viking series, Bellanca 96
Viking, Bv 222, Blohm und Voss 111
Vildbeest, Vickers 298
Vimy Commercial, Vickers 298
Vimy, Vickers 26, 28, 125, 298
Vincent, Vickers 298
Vindicator, Vought-Sikorsky 300
Vinka, Valmet Oy 295
Vipan, MFI 228
Virginia, Vickers 298
Viri, Karhumäki 203
Viscount, Vickers 55
Viscount, Vickers-Armstrongs 299
Vista, Canadian Vickers 114
Voodoo, F-101, McDonnell 89
Voyager, Stinson 284
Vulcan, Avro 263
Vultee, Stinson 284

W.2, Wendt 304
W.4, Walraven 302
W-6, Aquaflight 82
W8, Handley Page 183
W.9, Cierva 125
W.10, Cierva 134
W.11 Air Horse, Cierva 125
W-11 Chevvy Bird, Waterman 303
W.12, et seq, Hansa 185
W-14, Thunderbird 291
W.14 Skeeter, Cierva 125
W.33, Hansa-Brandenburg 199
W 33/34, Junkers 201
W-151 Sopocaba, CONAL 128
W.201, Weatherley 303
WA.40, et seq, Wassmer 303
WA-116, et seq, Wallis 302
W.B.III, Beardmore 93
WF.12, Farner 160
WF.21/C4, Farner 160
WGM22, Aerotechnik 71
WHE Airbuggy, Ekin 151
WM 62C, Weatherley 303
WN-16, Wiener-Neustadt 110
WNF 342, Doblhoff 145
Wackett, Commonwealth 127
Wagon, Taylorcraft 289
Wagtail, Westland 304
Wal, Dornier 89, 117, 126, 146, 204
Wallace, Westland 304
Walrus, Supermarine 286
Walrus, Westland 304
Wapiti, Westland 304
Warwick, Vickers-Armstrongs 299
Wasp, Westland 305
Waterhen, Northern 241
Weasel, Westland 304
Wee Bee, Bee 94
Weejet, VT-1, Carma 117
Wee Scotsman, Mooney 231
Weihe, Fw 58, Focke-Wulf 166
Welkin, Westland 305
Wellesley, Vickers 298
Wellington, Vickers 40, 42, 55, 299
Wessex, Westland 304, 305
Westward II/III/IV, Hamilton 183
Westwind, 1124, IAI 199
Wheelair IIIA, Puget 257

Whippet, Austin 86
Whippoorwill, Laird 207
Whirlwind, Westland 304, 305
Whitley, Armstrong Whitworth 83
Widgeon, Grumman 173, 180
Widgeon, Westland 304
Wildcat, Grumman 150, 176, 180
Wilga, OKL 244
Wilga, PZL 246
Winglet, E.F.100, Eshelman 155
Winjeel, Commonwealth 127
Winner, O'Neill 243
Wirraway, Commonwealth 127
Wizard, Wicko 306
Woik, PZL 246
Wood Pigeon, Westland 304
Work Horse, Vertol 276
Wren, English Electric 154
Wyvern, Westland 305

X-1, Bell 46, 95
X-1A, Bell 46, 95
X-3, Douglas 149
X-15, North American 240
X-24A, Martin Marietta 222
X-19A, Curtiss-Wright 136
X-90(N), Cunningham-Hall 134
XA-1, Cox-Klemen 133
XA-5, American Helicopter 79
XA-41, Consolidated Vultee 130
XB-1, US Army 295
XB-46, Consolidated Vultee 130
XB-70 Valkyrie, North American 240
XBT-1, Northrop 148
XBTK-1, Fleetwings 163
XC-2, AIDC 73
XC-109, Ford 169
XC-123A, Chase 123
XC-142A, LTV 212
XCG-14/-14A, Chase 123
XF2Y Sea Dart, Consolidated Vultee 130
XF-11, Hughes 194
XF-12, Republic 260
XF-92, Consolidated Vultee 130
XFG-1, Cornelius 132
XFG-1, Eberhart 150
XG-20, Chase 123
XH-16, Piasecki 253
XH-17, Hughes 194
XH-26, American Helicopter 79
XHJP-1, Piasecki 253
XHRP-1, Piasecki 252
XJL-1, Grumman 127
XLB-1, Huff-Daland 194
XLB-2, Atlantic 85
XLB-3, Huff-Daland 194
XN-1/XS2, Cox-Klemen 133
XNBS-2, LWF 218
XO-932, Thomas Morse 291
XOZ-1 Gyroplane, Pennsylvania 250
XP2H-1, Hall 182
XP6M-1 Seamaster, Martin 222
XP-41, Seversky 271
XP-56, Northrop 241
XP-67, McDonnell 224
XP-75, Fisher 163
XP-79, Northrop 89
XP-81, Consolidated Vultee 130
XPQ-15, Culver 134
XR-2, et seq, Kellett 204
XR-9B, Firestone 163
XR-11, Rotor-Craft 265
XRON-1 Rotocycle, Gyrodyne 181
XS2L, Loening 216
XSL-2, Loening 216
XSOE-1, Edo 151
XT-001, PAF 251
XV-15, Bell 95
XY, Silvercraft 274
Xavante, EMBRAER 152
Xingu, EMBRAER 152 152

Y-1S, Stearman-Hammond 183
YA-1, Cropmaster 133
YA-1, Yeoman 133
YA5 Fieldmaster, Cropmaster 133
YA-10A, Fairchild 158
YAH-64, Hughes 195
Yak-1, et seq, Yakovlev 308
Yak-11, Yakovlev 210
Yak-36, Yakovlev 52
YB-49, Northrop 241
YC-14, Boeing 81
YC-15, McDonnell Douglas 225
YC-122 Avitruc, Chase 123
Yer-2, Yermolayev 308
Yer-2ON, Yermolayev 308
YF-17 Cobra, Northrop 241
YG-1, Kellett 204
YH-22, Kaman 202
YO-3A, Lockheed Missiles 216
YS-11, NAMC 204, 238
Yale, North American 235, 240
Yankee, AAC AA-1 64
York, Avro 55
Yukon, CL-44, Canadair 113

Z-1, et seq, Miller 230
Z6, AEG 65
Z6B, Zenith 309
Z9, Aerauto 65
Z.226 Trener, Zlin 120
Z.326 Trener Master, Zlin 120
Z.501, et seq, CANT 115
Zef, Piel 259
Zephyr, Fouga 170
Zephyr 150, LC 13-A, Bartlett 92
Zeppelin airship 20, 22, 25, 26
Zeta, Miller 230
Zeus, Spartan 282
Zlin 22, et seq, Zlin 309